Lecture Notes in Computer Science 16475

The series Lecture Notes in Computer Science (LNCS), including its subseries Lecture Notes in Artificial Intelligence (LNAI) and Lecture Notes in Bioinformatics (LNBI), has established itself as a medium for the publication of new developments in computer science and information technology research, teaching, and education.

LNCS enjoys close cooperation with the computer science R & D community, the series counts many renowned academics among its volume editors and paper authors, and collaborates with prestigious societies. Its mission is to serve this international community by providing an invaluable service, mainly focused on the publication of conference and workshop proceedings and postproceedings. LNCS commenced publication in 1973.

Anni-Yasmin Turhan · Jonni Virtema
Editors

Foundations of Information and Knowledge Systems

14th International Symposium, FoIKS 2026
Hanover, Germany, March 23–26, 2026
Proceedings

Springer

Editors
Anni-Yasmin Turhan
Paderborn University
Paderborn, Germany

Jonni Virtema
University of Glasgow
Glasgow, UK

ISSN 0302-9743 ISSN 1611-3349 (electronic)
Lecture Notes in Computer Science
ISBN 978-3-032-21539-0 ISBN 978-3-032-21540-6 (eBook)
https://doi.org/10.1007/978-3-032-21540-6

This Springer imprint is published by the registered company Springer Nature Switzerland AG
The registered company address is: Gewerbestrasse 11, 6330 Cham, Switzerland

Preface

This volume contains the papers presented at the 14th International Symposium on Foundations of Information and Knowledge Systems, FoIKS 2026, held in Hanover, Germany, March 23–26, 2026.

The FoIKS symposia provide a biennial forum for presenting and discussing theoretical and applied research on information and knowledge systems. The goal is to bring together researchers interested in these topics, to share research experiences, to foster collaboration, and to identify new issues and directions for future research. Past FoIKS meetings have been held in Schloss Salzau (Germany, 2002), Vienna (Austria, 2004), Budapest (Hungary, 2006), Pisa (Italy, 2008), Sofia (Bulgaria, 2010), Kiel (Germany, 2012), Bordeaux (France, 2014), Linz (Austria, 2016), Budapest (Hungary, 2018), Dortmund (Germany, 2020), Helsinki (Finland, 2022), and Sheffield (UK, 2024).

The call for papers solicited original contributions that address any fundamental aspect of information and knowledge systems, including submissions that apply ideas, theories, or methods from specific disciplines to information and knowledge systems. Examples of such disciplines are discrete mathematics, logic and algebra, model theory, databases, information theory, complexity theory, algorithmics and computation, statistics, and optimization. FoIKS 2026 introduced, for the first time, a special track for poster contributions presenting fresh research ideas in the broad area of information and knowledge systems. This track targeted works describing early stages of work, starting points for discussions, or novel perspectives on known problems. The poster track was well received.

Traditionally, FoIKS symposia have been a forum for intensive discussion, with speakers given ample time to present their ideas and findings in the broader context of their research and to engage with researchers from other scientific subcommunities. In addition, participants were asked to prepare an initial response to another contributed talk to initiate the discussion.

FoIKS 2026 received 37 paper submissions and 9 poster submissions. Each paper submission, except 4 that were desk-rejected after deliberation by the PC chairs, received at least three single-blind reviews by the program committee members based on its significance, novelty, technical soundness, and appropriateness for the FoIKS audience. The poster submissions were lightly reviewed by two PC members. In the end, the committee decided to accept 18 papers (13 long and 5 short ones) and 7 poster papers for oral presentation at the symposium and publication in the archival proceedings.

The FoIKS Best Paper Award was inaugurated in 2024. For FoIKS 2026, it was decided to present a Best Paper Award and a Best Student Paper Award—the latter for the first time. The selection for the awards was made by a committee consisting of two members of the FoIKS Steering Committee and the PC co-chairs. We congratulate the winners of the awards:

- The Best Paper Award was awarded for the paper titled *"An Order-Theoretic View on Optimal Repairs and Complete Sets of Unifiers"* by Franz Baader. The award was accompanied with a prize of EUR 300 sponsored by Springer.
- The Best Student Paper Award was awarded for the paper titled *"Utilizing Binary Decision Diagrams for Compiling Argumentation Frameworks"* by Michael Baier and Johannes P. Wallner. The award was accompanied with a prize of EUR 200 sponsored by Springer.

We were delighted to have four outstanding keynote speakers covering the thematic breadth of FoIKS in their talks:

- Giuseppe De Giacomo (University of Oxford, UK):
  Reactive Program Synthesis in AI.
- Floris Geerts (University of Antwerp, Belgium):
  Relational Neural Networks.
- Wolfgang Nejdl (Leibniz Universität Hannover, Germany):
  Reasoning for LLM-based Agents.
- Ana Ozaki (University of Oslo, Norway):
  Semiring Provenance for Ontology-Based Data Access.

We thank all the people who contributed to making FoIKS 2026 a successful scientific event and meeting. In particular, we thank the invited speakers for their stimulating presentations, the authors for their high-quality submission, revision, and presentation of their work, and all the participants for their contributions to the symposium discussions. We thank the Program Committee and the external reviewers for their prompt and thorough reviews. We thank EasyChair for providing the online submission and proceedings system. Finally, we would like to thank Springer for their help in publishing the proceedings and for their generous sponsorship of the best paper awards. We would like to thank the Local Organizing Committee, chaired by Arne Meier, for being proactive and responsive throughout the non-trivial organizing process, and the members of the FoIKS Steering Committee for their trust and support.

January, 2026

Anni-Yasmin Turhan
Jonni Virtema

Organization

Program Committee Chairs

Anni-Yasmin Turhan	Paderborn University, Germany
Jonni Virtema	University of Glasgow, UK

Program Committee

Ringo Baumann	Leipzig University, Germany
Meghyn Bienvenu	CNRS, University of Bordeaux, France
Thomas Bolander	Technical University of Denmark, Denmark
Stefan Borgwardt	TU Dresden, Germany
Elena Botoeva	University of Kent, UK
Willem Conradie	University of the Witwatersrand, South Africa
Fabio Cozman	University of São Paulo, Brasil
Thomas Eiter	TU Wien, Austria
Flavio Ferrarotti	Software Competence Centre Hagenberg, Austria
Johannes K. Fichte	Linköping University, Sweden
Valentin Goranko	Stockholm University, Sweden
Guido Governatori	Central Queensland University, Australia
Marc Gyssens	Universiteit Hasselt, Belgium
Miika Hannula	University of Tartu, Estonia
Jelle Hellings	McMaster University, Canada
Andreas Herzig	CNRS, IRIT, University of Toulouse, France
Martin Homola	Comenius University in Bratislava, Slovakia
Tomi Janhunen	Tampere University, Finland
Matti Järvisalo	University of Helsinki, Finland
Gabriele Kern-Isberner	Technische Universität Dortmund, Germany
Sébastien Konieczny	CRIL — CNRS, University of Artois, France
Juha Kontinen	University of Helsinki, Finland
Mena Leemhuis	Free University of Bozen-Bolzano, Italy
Joao Leite	Universidade NOVA de Lisboa, Portugal
Sebastian Link	University of Auckland, New Zealand
Maria Vanina Martinez	Artificial Intelligence Research Institute (IIIA — CSIC)
Arne Meier	Leibniz Universität Hannover, Germany
Thomas Meyer	University of Cape Town and CAIR, South Africa

Daniel Neider	TU Dortmund University, Germany
Magdalena Ortiz	TU Wien, Austria
Nina Pardal	University of Edinburgh, UK
Elena Ravve	BRAUDE — College of Engineering, Israel
Sebastian Rudolph	TU Dresden, Germany
Katsuhiko Sano	Hokkaido University, Japan
Konstantin Schekotihin	Alpen-Adria Universität Klagenfurt, Austria
Klaus-Dieter Schewe	INPT-ENSEEIHT, France
Guillermo R. Simari	Universidad del Sur in Bahia Blanca, Argentina
Jan Van den Bussche	Hasselt University, Belgium
Stefan Woltran	TU Wien, Austria
Thomas Ågotnes	University of Bergen, Norway
Mantas Šimkus	TU Wien, Austria

Additional Reviewers

Aguilera Ventura, Carlos
Arndt, Dörthe
Bednarczyk, Bartosz
Buraglio, Giovanni
Corazza, Jan
De Giacomo, Giuseppe
Edmonds, Chelsea
Feyzbakhsh Rankooh, Masood
Heine, Anne-Marie
Ivanovska, Magdalena
Liang, Xiaolong
Sauerwald, Kai
Wang, Yunsong

Contents

Database Theory

Foundations

Explanations

Poster Papers

Team Semantics

Complexity Results in Team Semantics: Nonemptiness Is Not So Complex

Aleksi Anttila[1(✉)], Juha Kontinen[1], and Fan Yang[2]

[1] Department of Mathematics and Statistics, University of Helsinki, Helsinki, Finland
aleksi.ilari.anttila@gmail.com, juha.kontinen@helsinki.fi
[2] Department of Philosophy and Religious Studies, Utrecht University, Utrecht, The Netherlands
fan.yang.c@gmail.com

Abstract. We initiate the study of the complexity-theoretic properties of convex logics in team semantics. We focus on the extension of classical propositional logic with the nonemptiness atom NE, a logic known to be both convex and union closed. We show that the satisfiability problem for this logic is NP-complete, that its validity problem is coNP-complete, and that its model-checking problem is in P.

Keywords: Team semantics · Team logic · Complexity · Satisfiability problem · Validity Problem · Model-checking problem · Nonemptiness atom

1 Introduction

Team semantics is a mathematical framework for studying concepts and phenomena that arise in contexts involving a plurality of data, typically represented by sets of assignments or probability distributions. Logics employing team semantics have found application in many fields, including database theory [19,30], Bayesian networks and probabilistic dependencies [12,28], quantum foundations [1,2,14], as well as philosophical logic and formal semantics [3,8,10,21].

The core idea of team semantics is that formulas are interpreted over sets of evaluation points (called *teams*) rather than single evaluation points as in standard Tarskian semantics. Depending on the setting, teams can be, for instance, sets of assignments, propositional valuations, or possible worlds. The origins of team semantics can be traced back to Hodges' *trump semantics* [29] for Hintikka and Sandu's *independence-friendly logic* [26,27]; Väänänen developed team semantics on the basis of Hodges' work to interpret *dependence logic* [38], his refinement of independence-friendly logic. Dependence logic extends classical first-order logic with *dependence atoms* such as $=(x, y)$; informally, $=(x, y)$ expresses that the values of the variable x functionally determine the values of y within a team. Other team-based logics follow a similar pattern: a non-team-based logic is extended with connectives whose semantics make essential use of the fact the evaluation point is a team: a set, rather than a singleton. For

A.-Y. Turhan and J. Virtema (Eds.): FoIKS 2026, LNCS 16475, pp. 3–16, 2026.
https://doi.org/10.1007/978-3-032-21540-6_1

instance, *propositional inclusion logic* PL($\subseteq$) [24,41]—the propositional version of *inclusion logic* [18], another of the most prominent team-based logics—extends classical propositional logic PL with *inclusion atoms* such as $\alpha \subseteq \beta$, with $\alpha \subseteq \beta$ expressing that whatever truth values the PL-formula α is assigned by some valuation in a team must also be assigned to β by some valuation in the team.

Since the introduction of dependence logic, the expressivity and computational complexity of logics within the framework of team semantics have been extensively investigated (see, e.g., [15,16,20,33]). We contribute to this literature by characterizing the computational complexity of the satisfiability (SAT), validity (VAL), and model checking (MC) problems of the logic PL(NE) [39,43], which extends classical propositional logic PL with the *nonemptiness atom* NE, true in a team just in case the team is nonempty. Despite its simplicity, this logic has recently been attracting interest because it serves as the propositional basis for Aloni's *bilateral state-based modal logic* BSML [3,4], a modal team-based logic which can be used to account for free-choice inferences and related linguistic phenomena. We show that SAT[PL(NE)] is NP-complete; that VAL[PL(NE)] is coNP-complete; and that MC[PL(NE)] is in P.

The logic PL(NE) is also interesting due to its team-semantic *closure properties*. Unlike dependence logic, PL(NE) is not *downward closed* (where a logic is downward closed if for each of its formulas φ, the truth of φ in a team t implies truth in all subteams of t). Like inclusion logic, it is *union closed* (the truth of a formula in a nonempty collection of teams implies its truth in the union of the collection); however, PL(NE) differs from inclusion logic in that it does not have the *empty team property* (a logic has this property if all formulas are true in the empty team) and in that it is *convex* (the truth of a formula in two teams implies its truth in all teams between the two with respect to the subset relation). The convexity property has not been studied in the literature on team semantics until recently [6,9,25], and, to our knowledge, the literature does not contain any results on the complexity-theoretic properties of logics which are convex but not downward closed (convexity can be seen as a generalization of downward closure to a setting in which the empty team property fails).

Table 1. Complexity results for some propositional team-based logics (completeness results unless stated otherwise).

Logic	SAT	VAL	MC
PL	NP [11,32]	coNP [11,32]	NC^1 [7]
PL(NE)	NP [Corollary 3]	coNP [Prop. 6]	$\in$ P [Prop. 4]
PL($=(\cdot)$)	NP [33]	NEXP [37]	NP [17]
PL($\subseteq$)	EXP [23]	coNP [20]	P [22]
PL($\sim$)	ATIME-ALT(exp, poly) [20]	ATIME-ALT(exp, poly) [20]	PSPACE [35]

Table 1 lists our results alongside those for classical propositional logic PL, propositional dependence logic PL($=(\cdot)$) [42], propositional inclusion logic

PL($\subseteq$), and *propositional team logic* PL($\sim$) [34,35,38]. The logic PL($\sim$) is expressively complete for all propositional team properties [31] and many of the common team-semantic connectives are definable in PL($\sim$), so it provides a natural upper bound for the complexity of team-based extensions of PL. The proof in [33] that SAT[PL($=(\cdot)$)] is NP-complete—i.e., that adding dependence atoms to PL does not increase the complexity of the satisfiability problem—makes use of downward closure. Similarly, the proof in [20] that VAL[PL($\subseteq$)] is coNP-complete—i.e., that adding inclusion atoms to PL does not increase the complexity of the validity problem—makes use of union closure; as does the proof of the P-completeness of MC[PL($\subseteq$)] in [22]. The complexity results for the logic PL(NE) follow this pattern: being convex (downward closed up to a point), the complexity of its satisfiability problem is the same as that of PL; being union closed, the complexity of its validity problem is the same as that of PL, and its model-checking problem is tractable (our proofs of these results also make use of the relevant closure properties). As a result, we see that, at least with regard to the satisfiability and validity problems, adding the nonemptiness atom NE to PL does not increase complexity—in contrast, and as might be inferred from Table 1, many other team-based atoms and connectives *do* increase complexity, often quite considerably.

The paper is structured as follows. In Sect. 2, we define the syntax and semantics of PL(NE) and list some basic properties of this logic. In Sect. 3, we treat the model-checking problem; in Sect. 4, the satisfiability problem; and in Sect. 5, the validity problem. Section 6 concludes with some discussion of potential future work.

2 Preliminaries

In this section, we define the syntax and team semantics of classical propositional logic (PL) and its extension PL(NE) by the nonemptiness atom NE.

We fix a (countably infinite) set Prop of propositional variables.

Definition 1 (Syntax). *The set of formulas* α *of* classical propositional logic PL *is generated by:*

$$\alpha ::= p \mid \neg p \mid \bot \mid \top \mid \alpha \wedge \alpha \mid \alpha \vee \alpha$$

where $p \in \mathsf{Prop}$*. The language of* PL(NE) *extends that of* PL *with the* nonemptiness atom NE.[1]

We let $\bigvee \emptyset := \bot$, and $\bigwedge \emptyset := \top$. We also call formulas of PL *classical formulas.* The metavariable α ranges over classical formulas; and Λ, over sets of classical

[1] Some formulations of the syntax of PL(NE) in the literature feature a negation operator $\neg$ that can be applied to all PL-formulas, with the semantics $t \models \neg\alpha$ iff for all $v \in t$, $\{v\} \not\models \alpha$. Our results also hold for this variant of PL(NE)—this follows from the fact that formulas in this variant can be converted into negation normal form in polynomial time.

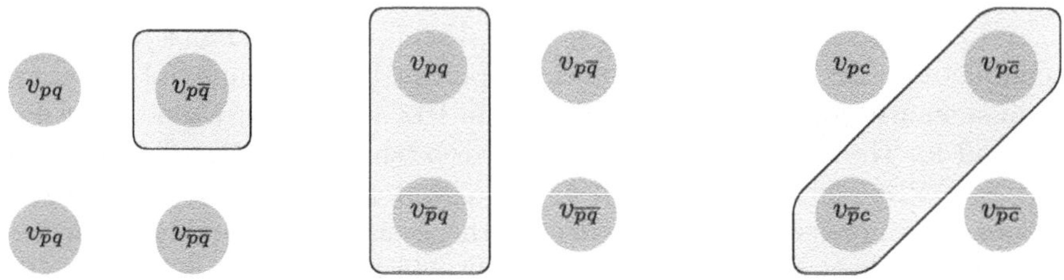

(a) $t \models p \vee \neg p$ (b) $s \models (p\wedge\text{NE})\vee(\neg p\wedge\text{NE})$ (c) $u \models ((p\wedge\text{NE})\vee(c\wedge\text{NE}))\wedge\text{NE}$ $u \models \Diamond p \wedge \Diamond c$

Fig. 1. Examples of the Semantics.

formulas; metavariables denoted by other Greek letters range over all (sets of) PL(NE)-formulas. We write $\mathsf{P}(\varphi)$ for the set of propositional variables appearing in φ. We write $\varphi(\psi/\chi)$ for the result of replacing all occurrences of χ in φ by ψ. We call formulas of the form p, $\neg p$, $\bot$, $\top$, or NE *literals*.

Let $\mathsf{X} \subseteq \mathsf{Prop}$. A *team with domain* X is a set $t \subseteq 2^{\mathsf{X}}$ of valuations over X.

Definition 2 (Semantics). *For any formula φ and any team t with domain containing $\mathsf{P}(\varphi)$, the satisfaction relation $t \models \varphi$ is defined inductively by:*

$t \models p$	*iff*	*for all $v \in t$, $v(p) = 1$;*
$t \models \neg p$	*iff*	*for all $v \in t$, $v(p) = 0$;*
$t \models \bot$	*iff*	$t = \emptyset$;
$t \models \top$		*always;*
$t \models \varphi \wedge \psi$	*iff*	$t \models \varphi$ *and* $t \models \psi$;
$t \models \varphi \vee \psi$	*iff*	*there exist $s, u \subseteq t$ such that $t = s \cup u$, $s \models \varphi$, and $u \models \psi$;*
$t \models \text{NE}$	*iff*	$t \neq \emptyset$.

For any set $\Gamma \cup \{\varphi\}$ of formulas, we write $t \models \Gamma$ if $t \models \psi$ for all $\psi \in \Gamma$, and we write $\Gamma \models \varphi$ if $t \models \Gamma$ implies $t \models \varphi$. We write $\varphi \models \psi$ for $\{\varphi\} \models \psi$. We write $\models \varphi$ if $t \models \varphi$ for all teams t with domain containing $\mathsf{P}(\varphi)$.

Figure 1 displays some examples of the semantics. Each node represents a valuation, and is labelled according to what is evaluated as true (1) by that valuation, e.g., $v_{p\overline{q}}(p) = 1$ and $v_{p\overline{q}}(q) = 0$. The encircled area is a team we wish to highlight. The team t in Fig. 1(a) satisfies the formula $p \vee \neg p$ because it can be split into two subteams, one ($\{v_{p\overline{q}}\}$) satisfying the disjunct p, the other (the empty team $\emptyset$) satisfying the other disjunct $\neg p$ (the connective $\vee$ is commonly known as the *split disjunction*). With the nonemptiness atom NE, we can enforce that teams be split into nonempty subteams: the team s in Fig. 1(b) satisfies the formula $(p\wedge\text{NE})\vee(\neg p\wedge\text{NE})$ because it can be split into a nonempty team ($\{v_{pq}\}$) satisfying p, and a nonempty team ($\{v_{\overline{p}q}\}$) satisfying $\neg p$.

Figure 1(c) relates to the applications of the atom NE in formal semantics and philosophical logic. On one possible interpretation of team semantics, teams represent *information states*: if the true information that one possesses is represented by a team t, one knows that the valuation that represents the way that things actually are (the actual world) is among the valuations in t, and hence whatever holds in all valuations in t must also be the case in the actual world.

Consider the defined operator $\Diamond\varphi := (\varphi \wedge \text{NE}) \vee \top$—observe that the formula $\Diamond\varphi$ is true in a team t just in case t contains a nonempty subteam in which φ is true. This operator is known as the *might-operator*: it, along with other similar connectives, has been used to model the meanings of epistemic possibility modalities such as the 'might' in "It might be raining" (see, e.g., [36,40]). For if one's information state contains a nonempty substate that supports the assertion that it is raining (if $t \models \Diamond r$), then the actual world might be one in which it is raining, and so, for all that one knows, it might be raining.

Now assume that Bob says, "Sue went to the park or to the cinema." One natural inference from this might be that Bob deems it possible both that Sue went to the park and that she went to the cinema. The atom NE has been used to model inferences such as this one by Aloni and her collaborators (see, e.g., [3,13]). On Aloni's account, humans have a cognitive tendency to disregard structures that verify sentences by virtue of some empty configuration (the *neglect-zero tendency*). In the setting of team semantics, these empty configurations are represented by the empty team, and the neglect-zero tendency is modelled by appending '$\wedge$NE' to all subformulas of any formula that formalises a sentence that is being interpreted under this tendency. Then, for instance, the inference discussed above may be accounted for by pointing to the entailment $((p\wedge\text{NE})\vee(c\wedge\text{NE}))\wedge\text{NE} \models \Diamond p\wedge\Diamond c$—Bob's utterance, when interpreted under the tendency (we append '$\wedge$NE' to all subformulas of the formula $p \vee c$, resulting in the formula $((p\wedge\text{NE})\vee(c\wedge\text{NE}))\wedge\text{NE}$) indicates that according to his information, Sue might have gone to the park and might have gone to the cinema ($\Diamond p \wedge \Diamond c$). See Fig. 1(c).[2]

We define standard *closure properties*. We say that φ has the

empty team property	iff $\emptyset \models \varphi$;
downward closure property	iff $[t \models \varphi \text{ and } s \subseteq t] \implies s \models \varphi$;
union closure property	iff $[t \models \varphi \text{ for all } t \in T \neq \emptyset] \implies \bigcup T \models \varphi$;
flatness property	iff $t \models \varphi \iff [\{v\} \models \varphi \text{ for all } v \in t]$;
convexity property	iff $[t \models \varphi, u \models \varphi, \text{ and } u \subseteq s \subseteq t] \implies s \models \varphi$.

It is easy to see that φ is flat iff it has the empty team, downward closure, and union closure properties.

Proposition 1 ([6]). *All formulas of* PL(NE) *satisfy the union closure and convexity properties. All formulas of* PL *additionally satisfy the empty team property, and hence also the downward closure and flatness properties.*

[2] We have simplified and modified this account due to space constraints and to make it function in the propositional setting. For more on the actual account, see [3,13].

Proposition 2. *For $\varphi \in \mathrm{PL}(\mathrm{NE})$, φ has the empty team property iff $\varphi \in \mathrm{PL}$.*

Proof. The right-to-left direction follows by Proposition 1. For the left-to-right direction, an easy induction on the complexity of φ shows that if NE occurs in φ, then φ does not have the empty team property. We only give the disjunction case here. If $\varphi = \psi \vee \chi$ and NE occurs in φ, then it must occur in ψ or χ. Without loss of generality, assume that NE occurs in ψ. Then, by the induction hypothesis, ψ does not have the empty team property, but then clearly neither does $\psi \vee \chi$.

We also have that the team semantics of formulas of PL on singletons coincide with their standard single-valuation semantics: $\{v\} \models \alpha \iff v \models \alpha$. Therefore:

Proposition 3. *For any $\alpha \in \mathrm{PL}$:*

$$t \models \alpha \iff \{v\} \models \alpha \text{ for all } v \in t \iff v \models \alpha \text{ for all } v \in t.$$

Corollary 1. *For any set $\Lambda \cup \{\alpha\}$ of classical formulas, $\Lambda \models^c \alpha \iff \Lambda \models \alpha$, where $\models^c$ stands for the usual (single-valuation) entailment relation.*

3 Model-Checking Problem

The model-checking problem MC[L] for a team-based logic L is defined as follows: given a formula φ of L and a team t, determine whether $t \models \varphi$. In this section, we show that $\mathrm{MC}[\mathrm{PL}(\mathrm{NE})] \in \mathrm{P}$. This is proved using an argument that is similar to that used for propositional inclusion logic $\mathrm{PL}(\subseteq)$ in [22], but we make some modifications to account for the fact that the empty team property fails in PL(NE) (whereas it holds in $\mathrm{PL}(\subseteq)$).

Let $\mathrm{maxsub}(t, \varphi)$ denote the maximum (with respect to the subset relation) subteam s of t such that $s \models \varphi$. Note that if φ is union closed and has the empty team property, such a maximum subteam always exists—this is the case in particular for $\varphi \in \mathrm{PL}(\subseteq)$. This is not the case, however, for formulas of PL(NE): the formula NE, for instance, is not satisfiable in any subteam of the empty team. We do, however, have the following property:

Lemma 1. *For union-closed φ, if φ is satisfiable in some subteam of t, then* $\mathrm{maxsub}(t, \varphi)$ *exists.*

Proof. Clearly $\mathrm{maxsub}(t, \varphi) = \bigcup\{s \subseteq t \mid s \models \varphi\}$.

Let $\mathrm{Maxsub}(t, \varphi) = \mathrm{maxsub}(t, \varphi)$ if $\mathrm{maxsub}(t, \varphi)$ exists, and $\mathrm{Maxsub}(t, \varphi) = \mathbf{0}$ otherwise, where $\mathbf{0}$ is a "null team" such that $\mathbf{0} \not\models \varphi$ for all φ. (Note that $\mathbf{0}$ is not an actual team, and in particular is not the empty team $\emptyset$—it is, rather, a notational shorthand we use to indicate that a formula φ is not satisfiable in any subteam of a team t.) Let $|t|$ denote the size of t, and $|\varphi|$ the number of symbols in φ.

Lemma 2. *If φ is a literal, then* $\mathrm{Maxsub}(t, \varphi)$ *can be computed in polynomial time with respect to $|t| + |\varphi|$.*

Proof. First check whether $\varphi = \text{NE}$. If yes, then if $t = \emptyset$, return $\mathbf{0}$, and otherwise return t. Clearly this can be done in polynomial time with respect to $|t| + |\varphi|$. If $\varphi \neq \text{NE}$, check $\text{maxsub}(t, \varphi)$; the result then follows by [22, Lemma 5.1].

Proposition 4. MC[PL(NE)] $\in$ P.

Proof. We want to check whether $t \models \varphi$ in polynomial time w.r.t. $|t| + |\varphi|$.

Let $\text{subOcc}(\varphi)$ denote the set of all occurrences of subformulas of φ. In the following, we denote occurrences as if they were formulas.

A function $f : \text{subOcc}(\varphi) \to 2^{2^{\mathsf{P}(\varphi)}} \cup \{\mathbf{0}\}$ is called a *labelling function*. We describe an algorithm for computing a sequence $f_0, f_1, \ldots$ of such labelling functions. In what follows, we let $\mathbf{0} \cap s := \mathbf{0}$ and $\mathbf{0} \cup s := \mathbf{0}$ for all teams s.

- $f_0(\psi) = t$ for all $\psi \in \text{subOcc}(\varphi)$.
- For odd $i \in \mathbb{N}$, define $f_i(\psi)$ bottom-up as follows:
  1. For literal ψ, define $f_i(\psi) := \begin{cases} \text{Maxsub}(f_{i-1}(\psi), \psi) & \text{if } f_{i-1} \neq \mathbf{0}; \\ \mathbf{0} & \text{if } f_{i-1} = \mathbf{0}. \end{cases}$
  2. $f_i(\psi \wedge \chi) := f_i(\psi) \cap f_i(\chi)$.
  3. $f_i(\psi \vee \chi) := f_i(\psi) \cup f_i(\chi)$.
- For even $i \in \mathbb{N}$ larger than 0, define $f_i(\psi)$ top-down as follows:
  1. $f_i(\varphi) := f_{i-1}(\varphi)$.
  2. If $\psi = \chi \wedge \theta$, define $f_i(\chi) := f_i(\theta) := f_i(\psi)$.
  3. If $\psi = \chi \vee \theta$, define $f_i(\chi) := f_{i-1}(\chi) \cap f_i(\chi \vee \theta)$ and $f_i(\theta) := f_{i-1}(\theta) \cap f_i(\chi \vee \theta)$.

For a given $i \in \mathbb{N}$, an easy induction on the complexity of formulas (with the induction going from more complex formulas to less complex for even $i \in \mathbb{N}$) shows that $f_{i+1}(\psi) \subseteq f_i(\psi)$, where we stipulate that $\mathbf{0} \subseteq s$ and $\mathbf{0} \subseteq \mathbf{0}$ (and $s \not\subseteq \mathbf{0}$) for all teams s. It follows that there is an integer $j \leq 2 \cdot (|t| + 1) \cdot |\varphi|$ such that $f_{j+2} = f_{j+1} = f_j$. We denote this fixed point of the sequence $f_0, f_1, \ldots$ by f_∞. By Lemma 2, the outcome of Maxsub is computable in polynomial time with respect to its input. Given this, f_{i+1} can be computed in polynomial time from f_i with respect to $|t| + |\varphi|$, so that f_∞ can also be computed in polynomial time with respect to $|t| + |\varphi|$.

Claim 1. For each $\psi \in \text{subOcc}(\varphi)$, $f_\infty(\psi) \models \psi$ iff $f_\infty(\psi) \neq \mathbf{0}$.

Proof of Claim 1. The left-to-right direction is immediate. We prove the right-to-left direction by induction on ψ. Fix an odd i and even j such that $f_\infty = f_i = f_j$.

- If ψ is a literal, the claim is true because $f_\infty = f_i$, and if $f_\infty(\psi) = f_i(\psi) \neq \mathbf{0}$, then $f_\infty(\psi) = f_i(\psi) = \text{maxsub}(f_{i-1}(\psi), \psi)$, where $f_{i-1}(\psi) \neq \mathbf{0}$.
- Assume $\psi = \chi \wedge \theta$, and that the claim is true for χ and θ. Since $f_\infty = f_j$, we have $f_\infty(\psi) = f_\infty(\chi) = f_\infty(\theta)$, so clearly by the induction hypothesis, $f_\infty(\psi) \neq \mathbf{0}$ implies $f_\infty(\psi) \models \chi \wedge \theta$.

- Assume $\psi = \chi \vee \theta$, and that the claim is true for χ and θ. Since $f_\infty = f_i$, we have $f_\infty(\psi) = f_\infty(\chi) \cup f_\infty(\theta)$. By the induction hypothesis, $f_\infty(\chi) \neq \mathbf{0}$ implies $f_\infty(\chi) \models \chi$, and $f_\infty(\theta) \neq \mathbf{0}$ implies $f_\infty(\theta) \models \chi$. We show that $f_\infty(\psi) \neq \mathbf{0}$ implies $f_\infty(\psi) \models \chi \vee \theta$. If $f_\infty(\psi) = f_\infty(\chi) \cup f_\infty(\theta) \not\models \chi \vee \theta$, then $f_\infty(\chi) \not\models \chi$ or $f_\infty(\theta) \not\models \theta$, whence $f_\infty(\chi) = \mathbf{0}$ or $f_\infty(\theta) = \mathbf{0}$, either of which imply $f_\infty(\psi) = \mathbf{0}$.

In particular, (1) if $f_\infty(\varphi) = s$ (for some actual non-null team s), then $s \models \varphi$. To finish the proof, it therefore suffices to prove that (2) if $t \models \varphi$, then $f_\infty(\varphi) = t$: for then, to check whether $t \models \varphi$, check whether $t = f_\infty(\varphi)$. If yes, then $f_\infty(\varphi) = t \neq \mathbf{0}$ so by (1), $f_\infty(\varphi) = t \models \varphi$; if no, then by (2), $t \not\models \varphi$.

To prove (2), suppose $t \models \varphi$. It is easy to see that then, for each $\psi \in \mathrm{subOcc}(\varphi)$, there is a team $t_\psi \subseteq t$ such that $t_\psi \models \psi$ and

- $t_\varphi = t$;
- $t_{\chi \wedge \theta} = t_\chi = t_\theta$;
- $t_{\chi \vee \theta} = t_\chi \cup t_\theta$.

Claim 2. $t_\psi \subseteq f_i(\psi)$ for all $\psi \in \mathrm{subOcc}(\varphi)$ and all $i \in \mathbb{N}$.

Proof of Claim 2. By induction on i. For $i = 0$ this is obvious since $f_0(\psi) = t$ for all ψ. Now assume $i+1$ is odd and that the claim is true for i. We prove the claim by a subinduction on ψ.

- If ψ is a literal, then since by the induction hypothesis $t_\psi \subseteq f_i(\psi)$, we have $f_i(\psi) \neq \mathbf{0}$, whence $f_{i+1}(\psi) = \mathrm{Maxsub}(f_i(\psi), \psi)$. Since $t_\psi \models \psi$ and $t_\psi \subseteq f_i(\psi)$, we have by Lemma 1 that $f_{i+1}(\psi) = \mathrm{Maxsub}(f_i(\psi), \psi) \neq \mathbf{0}$ so $f_{i+1}(\psi) = \mathrm{maxsub}(f_i(\psi), \psi)$; therefore $t_\psi \subseteq f_{i+1}(\psi)$.
- Assume that $\psi = \chi \wedge \theta$. By the subinduction hypothesis, $t_\psi = t_\chi \subseteq f_{i+1}(\chi)$ and $t_\psi = t_\theta \subseteq f_{i+1}(\theta)$, and so $t_\psi \subseteq f_{i+1}(\chi) \cap f_{i+1}(\theta) = f_{i+1}(\psi)$.
- Assume that $\psi = \chi \vee \theta$. By the subinduction hypothesis, $t_\chi \subseteq f_{i+1}(\chi)$ and $t_\theta \subseteq f_{i+1}(\theta)$. Then $t_\psi = t_\chi \cup t_\theta \subseteq f_{i+1}(\chi) \cup f_{i+1}(\theta) = f_{i+1}(\psi)$.

Now assume $i+1$ is even and that the claim is true for i. We prove the claim by a top-to-bottom subinduction on ψ.

- For $\psi = \varphi$, by the induction hypothesis, $t_\psi \subseteq f_i(\psi) = f_{i+1}(\psi)$.
- Assume that $\psi = \chi \wedge \theta$. By the subinduction hypothesis, $t_\chi = t_\theta = t_\psi \subseteq f_{i+1}(\psi) = f_{i+1}(\chi) = f_{i+1}(\theta)$.
- Assume that $\psi = \chi \vee \theta$. By the subinduction hypothesis, $t_\psi \subseteq f_{i+1}(\psi)$. By the induction hypothesis, $t_\chi \subseteq f_i(\chi)$. Then since $t_\chi \subseteq t_\psi$, we have $t_\chi \subseteq f_i(\chi) \cap t_\psi \subseteq f_i(\chi) \cap f_{i+1}(\psi) = f_{i+1}(\chi)$. Similarly $t_\theta \subseteq f_{i+1}(\theta)$.

Given Claim 2, $t = t_\varphi \subseteq f_\infty(\varphi)$. Since $f_\infty(\varphi) \subseteq f_0(\varphi) = t$, we have $f_\infty(\varphi) = t$.

In the proof of Proposition 4, we have followed the proof for $\mathrm{MC}[\mathrm{PL}(\subseteq)] \in \mathrm{P}$ in [22] in defining a sequence of labelling functions f_i for all $i \in \mathbb{N}$, and finding a fixed point f_∞ of this sequence. Presenting the proof in this way allows for an elegant way to prove the required facts about the relevant labelled subteams of the target team t, as well as for an easy comparison with the proof in [22]. It appears, though, that for PL(NE), the sequence of functions reaches its fixed point only a few elements into this sequence—seemingly by $i = 4$—whereas this need not be the case for PL($\subseteq$). We leave a detailed investigation into this matter, as well as any possible improvements to the algorithm, for future work.

4 Satisfiability Problem

We follow [20] in defining the satisfiability problem SAT[L] for a team-based logic L as follows: given a formula φ of L, determine whether there exists some nonempty team t such that $t \models \varphi$ (satisfaction in the empty team is easy to decide, both for PL(NE)—see Proposition 2—as well as for many other team-based logics—see [20]). In this section, we show that SAT[PL(NE)] is NP-complete. Hardness follows immediately by the NP-hardness of SAT[PL] together with Proposition 3, so we focus on showing SAT[PL(NE)] $\in$ NP.

Lemma 3. *For $\varphi \in$ PL(NE), if $t \models \varphi$, then there exists $s \subseteq t$ such that $s \models \varphi$ and $|s| \leq |\varphi|_{\mathrm{NE}}$, where $|\varphi|_{\mathrm{NE}}$ is the number of occurrences of* NE *in φ.*

Proof. By induction on the complexity of φ.

- φ is a classical literal. Immediate by the empty team property.
- $\varphi =$ NE. Take any singleton subteam of t.
- $\varphi = \psi \vee \chi$. If $t \models \psi \vee \chi$, we have $t = s \cup u$, where $s \models \psi$ and $u \models \chi$. By the induction hypothesis, there are $s' \subseteq s$ and $u' \subseteq u$ such that $s' \models \psi$, $u' \models \chi$, $|s'| \leq |\psi|_{\mathrm{NE}}$, and $|u'| \leq |\chi|_{\mathrm{NE}}$. Then $s' \cup u' \subseteq s \cup u \subseteq t$, $s' \cup u' \models \psi \vee \chi$, and $|s' \cup u'| \leq |s'| + |u'| \leq |\psi|_{\mathrm{NE}} + |\chi|_{\mathrm{NE}} = |\psi \vee \chi|_{\mathrm{NE}}$.
- $\varphi = \psi \wedge \chi$. If $t \models \psi \wedge \chi$, by the induction hypothesis there are $s, u \subseteq t$ such that $s \models \psi$ and $u \models \chi$. Then since $s, u \subseteq s \cup u \subseteq t$, we have by convexity that $s \cup u \models \psi \wedge \chi$. And we have $|s \cup u| \leq |s| + |u| \leq |\psi|_{\mathrm{NE}} + |\chi|_{\mathrm{NE}} = |\psi \wedge \chi|_{\mathrm{NE}}$

Corollary 2 (Small model property). *If $\varphi \in$ PL(NE) is satisfiable, it is satisfiable in a team of size $\leq |\varphi|_{\mathrm{NE}}$.*

Proposition 5. SAT[PL(NE)] $\in$ NP.

Proof. First check whether $\varphi \in$ PL. If yes, the result follows by Proposition 3 and SAT[PL] $\in$ NP. If no, note that we have $|\varphi|_{\mathrm{NE}} \geq 1$. The required algorithm guesses a nonempty team of size at most $|\varphi|_{\mathrm{NE}}$ and then runs the deterministic poly-time model-checking algorithm (Proposition 4). It is easy to see that the running time of this procedure is polynomial in $|\varphi|$, and hence containment in NP follows.

Corollary 3. SAT[PL(NE)] *is* NP*-complete.*

5 Validity Problem

We follow [20] in defining the validity problem VAL[L] for a team-based logic L as follows: given a formula φ of L, determine whether $t \models \varphi$ for all nonempty teams φ with domain $\supseteq \mathsf{P}(\varphi)$—i.e., whether $\textsc{ne} \models \varphi$ (note that due to Proposition 2 and Corollary 1, the validity problem of PL(NE) defined with respect to all teams—that is, including the empty team—is easily reducible to the validity problem of PL, and vice versa). In this section, we show that VAL[PL(NE)] is coNP-complete.

We make use of the following notion: the *flattening* $\varphi^f \in$ PL of $\varphi \in$ PL(NE) is defined by $\varphi^f := \varphi(\top/\textsc{ne})$ (see [5]; cf. [38]). It is easy to see that $\varphi \models \varphi^f$; observe also that by Proposition 2, $\varphi \in$ PL(NE) has the empty team property iff $\varphi = \varphi^f$.

Lemma 4. *For any $\varphi \in$ PL(NE) without the empty team property, the following are equivalent:*

1. $\textsc{ne} \models \varphi$;
2. *for all $\psi \in$ subOcc(φ) without the empty team property,* $\textsc{ne} \models \psi$;
3. *for all $\psi \in$ subOcc(φ) without the empty team property,* $\models \psi^f$.

Proof. 1 $\implies$ 2: Suppose $\textsc{ne} \models \varphi$. Fix some nonempty team t; we will show that for all $\psi \in$ subOcc(φ) without the empty team property, $t \models \psi$. We have that for any $v \in t$, $\{v\} \models \varphi$. Then for each $\psi \in$ subOcc(φ), there is a subteam $\{v\}_\psi \subseteq \{v\}$ as described in the proof of Proposition 4. For any $\psi \in$ subOcc(φ) without the empty team property, we must have $\{v\}_\psi \neq \emptyset$, so $\{v\}_\psi = \{v\}$, whence $\{v\} \models \psi$. Since v was arbitrary, by union closure we have $t \models \psi$.

2 $\implies$ 3: By $\psi \models \psi^f$ and the empty team property of ψ^f.

3 $\implies$ 2: Suppose that for all $\psi \in$ subOcc(φ) without the empty team property we have $\models \psi^f$. We show that for all $\psi \in$ subOcc(φ), either ψ has the empty team property or $\textsc{ne} \models \psi$ by induction on the structure of ψ.

- For ψ a classical literal, ψ has the empty team property by Proposition 1.
- For $\psi = \textsc{ne}$, the result is immediate.
- For $\psi = \chi \wedge \theta$, if both χ and θ have the empty team property, then so does ψ, and we are done. If neither has the empty team property, then neither does $\chi \wedge \theta$. Then by the induction hypothesis, $\textsc{ne} \models \chi$ and $\textsc{ne} \models \theta$, whence $\textsc{ne} \models \chi \wedge \theta$. If χ has the empty team property and θ does not, then $\chi \wedge \theta$ does not. Therefore, by assumption, $\models (\chi \wedge \theta)^f$, whence $\models \chi^f$ and $\models \theta^f$. Since χ has the empty team property, we have $\chi^f = \chi$, so $\models \chi$, whence also $\textsc{ne} \models \chi$. And since θ does not have the empty team property, we have $\textsc{ne} \models \theta$ by the induction hypothesis, so that $\textsc{ne} \models \chi \wedge \theta$. Similarly for the final case.
- For $\psi = \chi \vee \theta$, if both χ and θ have the empty team property, then so does $\chi \vee \theta$. If neither does, then neither does $\chi \vee \theta$; we have $\textsc{ne} \models \chi$ and $\textsc{ne} \models \theta$ by the induction hypothesis, and so $\textsc{ne} \models \chi \vee \theta$. If χ does and θ does not, then we have $\textsc{ne} \models \theta$ by the induction hypothesis. Then also $\textsc{ne} \models \chi \vee \theta$ since for any team t we have $t = \emptyset \cup t$. Similarly for the final case.

2 $\Longrightarrow$ 1: Immediate.

Proposition 6. VAL[PL(NE)] *is* coNP*-complete.*

Proof. Inclusion: First check whether $\varphi \in$ PL. If yes, then by Corollary 1 and the empty team property, we have NE $\models \varphi$ iff $\models \varphi$ iff $\models^c \varphi$, so it suffices to check whether $\models^c \varphi$—the result then follows by VAL[PL] $\in$ coNP. If no, then by Proposition 2, φ does not have the empty team property, so by Lemma 4 and Corollary 1, it suffices to check whether $\models^c \psi^f$ for all $\psi \in \text{subOcc}(\varphi)$. This problem can be shown to be in coNP by showing that its complement is in NP. For this, we non-deterministically guess a formula $\psi \in \text{subOcc}(\varphi)$ and then accept if the (classical) negation of ψ^f is satisfiable (given the standard Tarskian semantics). This is in NP given that SAT[PL] $\in$ NP, and so VAL[PL(NE)] $\in$ coNP.

Hardness: We reduce VAL[PL] to VAL[PL(NE)]. Fix $\varphi \in$ PL. Given Corollary 1 and the empty team property, $\models^c \varphi$ iff $\models \varphi$ iff NE $\models \varphi$.

6 Conclusion

In this article, we have studied the complexity aspects of the logic PL(NE). In particular, we proved that its model-checking problem is in P; that its satisfiability problem is NP-complete; and that its validity problem is coNP-complete. In addition, we proved that PL(NE) has certain semantic properties that are interesting in their own right (in Lemmas 3 and 4, and in Corollary 2).

We conclude by outlining some avenues for future research.

As we noted in Sect. 1, our results show that adding the nonemptiness atom NE to classical propositional logic does not increase the complexity of the satisfiability problem, or that of the validity problem. It would, then, be interesting to study the entailment problem of PL(NE), as well as to investigate whether our result concerning the model-checking problem can be improved upon (by either proving a stricter inclusion result, or a hardness result—cf. the P-hardness result for PL($\subseteq$) in [22]), in order to determine whether the same holds for these two problems.

We also mentioned that there are no other results on the complexity of convex but not downward closed logics in the literature. The next natural step, then, would be to study the complexity of other such logics. We conjecture that many of our results would extend naturally to other convex union-closed logics such as the modal extensions of PL(NE) (see [3,4,6]). Analogues of the results involving the use of convexity (such as Lemma 3) may also hold for logics which are convex but not union-closed (see [6]).

Acknowledgments. The first author received support from the Academy of Finland, decision number 368671, and from the European Research Council (ERC), grant 101020762. The authors would like to thank Maria Aloni for helpful discussions related to the content of this article; as well as the anonymous reviewers, for their valuable comments and suggestions.

Disclosure of Interests. The authors have no competing interests to declare that are relevant to the content of this article.

References

1. Abramsky, S., Puljujärvi, J., Väänänen, J.: Team semantics and independence notions in quantum physics. Bull. Symbolic Logic, 1–58 (2025). https://doi.org/10.1017/bsl.2025.10089
2. Albert, R., Grädel, E.: Unifying hidden-variable problems from quantum mechanics by logics of dependence and independence. Ann. Pure Appl. Logic **173**(10), Paper No. 103088 (2022). https://doi.org/10.1016/j.apal.2022.103088
3. Aloni, M.: Logic and conversation: the case of free choice. Semantics Pragmatics **15**(5) (2022). https://doi.org/10.3765/sp.15.5
4. Aloni, M., Anttila, A., Yang, F.: State-based modal logics for free choice. Notre Dame J. Form. Log. **65**(4), 367–413 (2024). https://doi.org/10.1215/00294527-2024-0027
5. Anttila, A.: Further remarks on the dual negation in team logics (2024). https://arxiv.org/abs/2410.07067
6. Anttila, A., Knudstorp, S.B.: Convex team logics (2025). https://arxiv.org/abs/2503.21850
7. Buss, S.R.: The Boolean formula value problem is in ALOGTIME. Proceedings of the nineteenth annual ACM symposium on Theory of computing (1987). https://api.semanticscholar.org/CorpusID:6489222
8. Ciardelli, I.: Inquisitive Logic—Consequence and Inference in the Realm of Questions, Trends in Logic—Studia Logica Library, vol. 60. Springer, Cham (2022). https://doi.org/10.1007/978-3-031-09706-5
9. Ciardelli, I.: Inquisitive neighborhood logic. J. Log. Lang. Inf. **34**(5), 419–461 (2025). https://doi.org/10.1007/s10849-025-09440-0
10. Ciardelli, I., Groenendijk, J., Roelofsen, F.: Inquisitive Semantics. Oxford University Press (2018). https://doi.org/10.1093/oso/9780198814788.001.0001
11. Cook, S.A.: The complexity of theorem proving procedures. In: Proceedings of the Third Annual ACM Symposium, pp. 151–158. ACM, New York (1971). https://doi.org/10.1145/800157.805047
12. Corander, J., Hyttinen, A., Kontinen, J., Pensar, J., Väänänen, J.: A logical approach to context-specific independence. Ann. Pure Appl. Logic **170**(9), 975–992 (2019). https://doi.org/10.1016/j.apal.2019.04.004
13. Degano, M., et al.: The ups and downs of ignorance. Natural Lang. Semantics **33**, 1–41 (2025). https://doi.org/10.1007/s11050-024-09226-3
14. Durand, A., Hannula, M., Kontinen, J., Meier, A., Virtema, J.: Probabilistic team semantics. In: Foundations of Information and Knowledge Systems. LNCS, pp. 186–206. Springer (2018). https://doi.org/10.1007/978-3-319-90050-6_11
15. Durand, A., Kontinen, J., de Rugy-Altherre, N., Väänänen, J.: Tractability frontier of data complexity in team semantics. ACM Trans. Comput. Logic **23**(1), 3:1–3:21 (2022). https://doi.org/10.1145/3471618
16. Durand, A., Kontinen, J., Väänänen, J.: Modular SAT-based techniques for reasoning tasks in team semantics. J. Comput. Syst. Sci. **146**, Paper No. 103575 (2024). https://doi.org/10.1016/j.jcss.2024.103575
17. Ebbing, J., Lohmann, P.: Complexity of model checking for modal dependence logic. In: Bieliková, M., Friedrich, G., Gottlob, G., Katzenbeisser, S., Turán, G. (eds.) SOFSEM 2012. LNCS, vol. 7147, pp. 226–237. Springer, Heidelberg (2012). https://doi.org/10.1007/978-3-642-27660-6_19
18. Galliani, P.: Inclusion and exclusion dependencies in team semantics — On some logics of imperfect information. Ann. Pure Appl. Logic **163**(1), 68–84 (2012). https://doi.org/10.1016/j.apal.2011.08.005

19. Hannula, M., Kontinen, J., Virtema, J.: Polyteam semantics. J. Log. Comput. **30**(8), 1541–1566 (2020). https://doi.org/10.1093/logcom/exaa048
20. Hannula, M., Kontinen, J., Virtema, J., Vollmer, H.: Complexity of propositional logics in team semantic. ACM Trans. Comput. Logic **19**(1), January 2018. https://doi.org/10.1145/3157054
21. Hawke, P., Steinert-Threlkeld, S.: Semantic expressivism for epistemic modals. Linguist. Philos. **44**(2), 475–511 (2020). https://doi.org/10.1007/s10988-020-09295-7
22. Hella, L., Kuusisto, A., Meier, A., Virtema, J.: Model checking and validity in propositional and modal inclusion logics. J. Log. Comput. **29**(5), 605–630 (2019). https://doi.org/10.1093/logcom/exz008
23. Hella, L., Kuusisto, A., Meier, A., Vollmer, H.: Satisfiability of modal inclusion logic: Lax and strict semantics. ACM Trans. Comput. Logic **21**(1) (2019). https://doi.org/10.1145/3356043
24. Hella, L., Luosto, K., Sano, K., Virtema, J.: The expressive power of modal dependence logic. In: Advances in Modal Logic, Vol. 10, pp. 294–312. Coll. Publ., London (2014). http://www.aiml.net/volumes/volume10/Hella-Luosto-Sano-Virtema.pdf
25. Hella, L., Luosto, K., Väänänen, J.: Dimension in team semantics. Math. Struct. Comput. Sci. **34**(5), 410–454 (2024). https://doi.org/10.1017/S0960129524000021
26. Hintikka, J.: The Principles of Mathematics Revisited. Cambridge University Press, Cambridge (1996). https://doi.org/10.1017/CBO9780511624919
27. Hintikka, J., Sandu, G.: Informational independence as a semantical phenomenon. In: Logic, methodology and philosophy of science, VIII (Moscow, 1987), Stud. Logic Found. Math., vol. 126, pp. 571–589. North-Holland, Amsterdam (1989). https://doi.org/10.1016/S0049-237X(08)70066-1
28. Hirvonen, M.: The implication problem for functional dependencies and variants of marginal distribution equivalences. ACM Trans. Comput. Log. **25**(4), 1–23 (2024). https://doi.org/10.1145/3677120
29. Hodges, W.: Compositional semantics for a language of imperfect information. Log. J. IGPL **5**(4), 539–563 (1997). https://doi.org/10.1093/jigpal/5.4.539
30. Kontinen, J., Link, S., Väänänen, J.: Independence in database relations. In: Logic, Language, Information, and Computation. Lecture Notes in Computer Science, vol. 8071, pp. 179–193. Springer Berlin Heidelberg (2013). https://doi.org/10.1007/978-3-642-39992-3_17
31. Kontinen, J., Müller, J.S., Schnoor, H., Vollmer, H.: A van Benthem theorem for modal team semantics. In: 24th EACSL Annual Conference on Computer Science Logic, LIPIcs. Leibniz Int. Proc. Inform., vol. 41, pp. 277–291. Schloss Dagstuhl. Leibniz-Zent. Inform., Wadern (2015). https://doi.org/10.4230/LIPIcs.CSL.2015.277
32. Levin, L.A.: Universal search problems [in Russian]. Probl. Inf. Transm. **9**, 115–116 (1973)
33. Lohmann, P., Vollmer, H.: Complexity results for modal dependence logic. Stud. Log. **101**(2), 343–366 (2013). https://doi.org/10.1007/s11225-013-9483-6
34. Lück, M.: Team Logic: Axioms, Expressiveness, Complexity. Ph.D. thesis, Leibniz University Hannover (2020). https://doi.org/10.15488/9376
35. Müller, J.S.: Satisfiability and Model Checking in Team Based Logics. Ph.D. thesis, Leibniz University Hannover (2014)
36. Veltman, F.: Defaults in update semantics. J. Philos. Logic **25**(3), 221–261 (1996). https://doi.org/10.1007/BF00248150
37. Virtema, J.: Complexity of validity for propositional dependence logics. Inf. Comput. **253**, 224–236 (2017). https://doi.org/10.1016/j.ic.2016.07.008

38. Väänänen, J.: Dependence Logic: A New Approach to Independence Friendly Logic, London Mathematical Society Student Texts, vol. 70. Cambridge University Press, Cambridge (2007). https://doi.org/10.1017/CBO9780511611193
39. Väänänen, J.: Multiverse set theory and absolutely undecidable propositions. In: Interpreting Gödel, pp. 180–208. Cambridge Univ. Press, Cambridge (2014). https://doi.org/10.1017/CBO9780511756306.013
40. Yalcin, S.: Epistemic modals. Mind 116(464), 983–1026 (2007). https://doi.org/10.1093/mind/fzm983
41. Yang, F.: Propositional union closed team logics. Ann. Pure Appl. Logic **173**(6), Paper No. 103102 (2022). https://doi.org/10.1016/j.apal.2022.103102
42. Yang, F., Väänänen, J.: Propositional logics of dependence. Ann. Pure Appl. Logic **167**(7), 557–589 (2016). https://doi.org/10.1016/j.apal.2016.03.003
43. Yang, F., Väänänen, J.: Propositional team logics. Ann. Pure Appl. Logic **168**(7), 1406–1441 (2017). https://doi.org/10.1016/j.apal.2017.01.007

Two Strong Undefinability Results in Inquisitive and Team Semantics

Fausto Barbero(✉)

University of Helsinki, Department of Philosophy, History and Art studies, Fabianinkatu 33, Helsinki, Finland
fausto.barbero@helsinki.fi

Abstract. We prove two (strong) undefinability results for logics based on inquisitive semantics (or its variant, team semantics). Namely: 1) we show that, in extended propositional inquisitive logic with tensor, intuitionistic implication is independent of the other connectives; 2) we show the undefinability of global disjunction in extended propositional dependence logic.

Keywords: Inquisitive logic · dependence logic · undefinability of connectives

Inquisitive semantics ([2,4,5]) and *team semantics* ([6,7,10,13,15,18]) were developed for two very different purposes, namely studying the logic of questions, and, respectively, the logic of dependencies among variables. However, it turns out that, in the propositional case, the two semantics are essentially equivalent; this observation allowed to unearth unexpected connections between questions and dependency (see e.g. [1]) and also lead to further technical developments in the two fields. A natural question it gave rise to is whether the logical operators used in one field are definable in the languages considered in the other field. The purpose of the present note is to make publicly available two undefinability results of this kind that were obtained during the final stages of preparation of the paper [3] and could not be included in the final manuscript. The results concern *extended propositional inquisitive logic with tensor* (the extension of propositional inquisitive logic with the tensor disjunction $\otimes$ and with the definable operators $\top, \neg$ and ?) and *extended propositional dependence logic* (whose syntax includes atoms expressing dependencies between arbitrary classical formulas).

Propositional inquisitive semantics evaluates formulas over *sets* of possible worlds and propositional team semantics does it over *sets* of finite Boolean valuations.[1] Evaluating formulas over sets of worlds or valuations leads to a more

The author was supported by the Research Council of Finland grants n. 316460 and 349803.

[1] Thus, the models considered in propositional team semantics are a special case of inquisitive models. However, for all the languages considered in this note, the two semantics frameworks produce the same logics.

A.-Y. Turhan and J. Virtema (Eds.): FoIKS 2026, LNCS 16475, pp. 17–28, 2026.
https://doi.org/10.1007/978-3-032-21540-6_2

complex theory of the (un)definability of connectives than what is attained with the usual notion of satisfaction at a single world (resp., a single assignment). It is well-known from the literature that the following two concepts do *not* coincide in inquisitive/team semantics (while they do in classical logic).

- A binary connective $\circ$ is *expressible*[2] in a language $\mathcal{L}$ if, for every $\psi, \chi \in \mathcal{L}$, there is a $\varphi \in \mathcal{L}$ that is equivalent to $\psi \circ \chi$.
- A binary connective $\circ$ is *definable*[3] in a language $\mathcal{L}$ if there is a template formula $\varphi(\ ,\ )$ such that, for every $\psi, \chi \in \mathcal{L}$, $\psi \circ \chi$ is equivalent to $\varphi(\psi, \chi)$.[4]

By a straightforward induction argument, definability implies expressibility. The converse goes through for logics that have the property of *uniform substitution*, i.e., when the equivalence of formulas $\psi(p_1, \ldots, p_n)$ and $\chi(p_1, \ldots, p_n)$ entails the equivalence of arbitrary substitution instances $\psi(\theta_1, \ldots, \theta_n), \chi(\theta_1, \ldots, \theta_n)$.[5] Many logics based on inquisitive/team semantics lack uniform substitution. For example, while atomic instances of the law of the excluded middle are valid (so that $p \vee \neg p \equiv \top$, where $\equiv$ denotes logical equivalence), that is not the case for arbitrary formulas (i.e., many languages feature formulas θ such that $\theta \vee \neg \theta \not\equiv \top$).

While (in)expressibility results usually follow as corollaries of characterizations of the expressive power of languages, an undefinability proof typically requires more sophisticate, and often *ad hoc*, techniques (see for example [3,6,16,17] for special results, and [2,8,12,14], [9,11] for more systematic approaches). We can make more explicit the meaning of *un*definability of a binary connective $\circ$ as follows:

> For every template formula $\varphi(\ ,\ )$, there are formulas $\psi_\varphi, \chi_\varphi$ such that $\varphi(\psi_\varphi, \chi_\varphi) \not\equiv \psi_\varphi \circ \chi_\varphi$.

However, the results in [3] and in the present note establish something more. Let us write $\psi \equiv_M \chi$ to say that ψ and χ have the same meaning in a certain model M.[6] Our results have the following form:

> There are ψ, χ and a model M such that, for every template formula $\varphi(\ ,\ )$, $\varphi(\psi', \chi') \not\equiv_{M'} \psi' \circ \chi'$, where ψ', χ' differ from ψ, χ only by renaming of atoms, and M' is isomorphic to M.

In other words, there is a single model (up to isomorphism) where all putative definitions of $\circ$ fail, and they all fail essentially because of the same substitution

[2] In the literature on team semantics the word "definable" is often used with this meaning.

[3] In the literature on team semantics the word "uniformly definable" is often used with this meaning.

[4] The template formula $\varphi(\ ,\ )$ can be seen as a formula containing some occurrences of "gap symbols" $[\ ]_L$ and $[\ ]_R$. In $\varphi(\psi, \chi)$, each occurrence of $[\ ]_L$ is replaced with ψ and each occurrence of $[\ ]_R$ is replaced with χ.

[5] See [3] for the fine details of this discussion.

[6] More exactly, ψ and χ express the same inquisitive proposition in M. This notion will receive a precise definition below.

instance.[7] We will refer to a result of this kind as a proof of *strong undefinability*. The proof method developed in [3] amounts to identifying an appropriate model M and substitution formulas ψ', χ' that ensure the failure of putative definitions of the connective; the latter is shown e.g. by identifying some invariant that is possessed by the (proposition expressed by) the formula $\psi' \circ \chi'$ but not by any substitution instance $\varphi(\psi', \chi')$. In this note we prove two results of this kind.

1. The paper [3] proved the independence of the connectives of propositional inquisitive logic plus the tensor operator. Here we consider a further extension of the logic with the operators $\top, \neg$ and ? that are commonly used in the literature on inquisitive logics. While these operators are definable in inquisitive logic (plus tensor), it is not trivial to see whether the other connectives remain independent in this context. The arguments from [3] can be reused to prove the independence of $\wedge$ and $\otimes$, but the independence of $\to$ (inquisitive implication) requires a new argument (Sect. 3).
2. In [17] it is proved, via a deep analysis of the properties of template formulas, that the global disjunction $\mathbin{\vee\mkern-7mu\vee}$ (typical of inquisitive logic) is not definable in propositional dependence logic. The result concerns propositional dependence logic in its most common presentation, which allows for dependence atoms of the form $=(p_1, \ldots, p_n; q)$. These say that the truth value of a propositional letter q is functionally determined by the truth values of $p_1, \ldots, p_n$. The argument used in [17] does not work if the logic is extended with atoms of the form $=(\alpha_1, \ldots, \alpha_n; \beta)$ (dependence among truth values of classical formulas) and, to the best of our knowledge, it is still an open problem whether $\mathbin{\vee\mkern-7mu\vee}$ is definable in this context. We prove that it is not (Sect. 4). Our argument also provides a new and much simpler proof for the case of propositional dependence logic.

Sections 1 and 2 present the syntax and the semantics of the languages considered in this note.

1 Syntax

We will consider 0-ary connectives $\bot, \top$, unary connectives $\neg$ and ?, and binary connectives $\wedge$, $\mathbin{\vee\mkern-7mu\vee}$, $\to$ and $\otimes$.

Given a list of connectives $\circ_1, \ldots, \circ_n$ we will denote by $\mathcal{L}[\circ_1, \ldots, \circ_n]$ the language having as atomic formulas a countable set of propositional letters $p, q, \ldots$ and closed under applications of the connectives (according to their arities). We will consider the following inquisitive languages:

- InqB (propositional inquisitive logic): $\mathcal{L}[\wedge, \mathbin{\vee\mkern-7mu\vee}, \to, \bot]$
- $\mathsf{InqB}^{\otimes}$ (propositional inquisitive logic with tensor): $\mathcal{L}[\wedge, \mathbin{\vee\mkern-7mu\vee}, \otimes, \to, \bot]$
- $\mathsf{EInqB}^{\otimes}$ (extended $\mathsf{InqB}^{\otimes}$): $\mathcal{L}[\wedge, \mathbin{\vee\mkern-7mu\vee}, \otimes, \to, \bot, \top, \neg, ?]$
- EInqB^{-} ($\mathsf{EInqB}^{\otimes}$ without $\to$): $\mathcal{L}[\wedge, \mathbin{\vee\mkern-7mu\vee}, \otimes, \bot, \top, \neg, ?]$.

[7] In all the results obtained so far, a small finite model sufficed.

The family of logics of dependence follows more unusual syntax rules, and thus we define the languages of interest in the more explicit BNF form. We consider the following:

- D (propositional dependence logic)

$$\varphi ::= p \mid \neg p \mid \bot \mid {=}(p_1, \ldots, p_n; q) \mid \varphi \wedge \varphi \mid \varphi \otimes \varphi$$

  where, $p, q, p_1, \ldots, p_n$ are propositional letters. Notice that $\neg$ is allowed to occur only in front of propositional letters. We will often write $=(\boldsymbol{p}; q)$ for the *dependence atom* $=(p_1, \ldots, p_n; q)$. If $\boldsymbol{p}$ is the empty list, we simply write $=(q)$ and call it a *constancy atom.*
- D^+ (extended propositional dependence logic)

$$\varphi ::= p \mid \neg p \mid \bot \mid {=}(\alpha_1, \ldots, \alpha_n; \beta) \mid \varphi \wedge \varphi \mid \varphi \otimes \varphi$$

  where $\alpha_1, \ldots, \alpha_n, \beta$ are *classical formulas*, i.e. D formulas without dependence atoms. The formula $=(\alpha_1, \ldots, \alpha_n; \beta)$ will be called a *generalized dependence atom.*

The syntax of D and D^+ does not allow us to write the formula $\neg\bot$; in the context of these languages, we will write $\top$ as an abbreviation for $p \otimes \neg p$.

We will also use the following abbreviation: if $\boldsymbol{\psi} = (\psi_1, \ldots, \psi_n)$ is a tuple of formulas, then $\bigwedge \boldsymbol{\psi}$ will denote their conjunction.[8] In case $\boldsymbol{\psi}$ is the empty tuple, we take $\bigwedge \boldsymbol{\psi}$ to stand for $\top$.

2 Semantics

We will work with inquisitive semantics, although in principle all the results in this note could be expressed and proved using team semantics. The models of inquisitive semantics are pairs $M = (W, V)$, where W is a set (of "possible worlds") and V is a valuation function that assigns to each world $w \in W$ a set of propositional letters (the set of letters "true at w"). Each formula is evaluated in a model $M = (W, V)$ at an *information state* (or simply *state*) $s \subseteq W$. We say that a formula φ is supported by state s in model M ($M, s \models \varphi$) if M, s and φ are in the ternary relation defined by the inductive clauses below. For the purposes of this paper, we can and will usually omit reference to the model M, writing just $s \models \varphi$.

- $s \models p \iff p \in V(w)$ for all $w \in s$
- $s \models \bot \iff s = \emptyset$
- $s \models \psi \wedge \chi \iff s \models \psi$ and $s \models \chi$
- $s \models \psi \mathbin{\mathbb{V}} \chi \iff s \models \psi$ or $s \models \chi$
- $s \models \psi \to \chi \iff \forall t \subseteq s : t \models \psi$ implies $t \models \chi$

[8] The operator $\wedge$, when given its semantics, will be associative; it is then irrelevant to specify how, exactly, parentheses are used in $\bigwedge \psi$.

- $s \models \psi \otimes \chi \iff \exists t_1, t_2$ s.t. $t_1 \models \psi, t_2 \models \chi$ and $s = t_1 \cup t_2$.
- $s \models \top$ unconditionally
- $s \models \neg\psi \iff s \models \psi \to \bot \iff t \not\models \psi$ for all $t \subseteq s$.
- $s \models ?\psi \iff s \models \psi \vee\!\!\!\vee \neg\psi \iff s \models \psi$ or $s \models \neg\psi$.
- $s \models =\!(\boldsymbol{\alpha}; \beta)$ iff for all $w, w' \in s$, if $\{w\} \models \bigwedge \boldsymbol{\alpha} \iff \{w'\} \models \bigwedge \boldsymbol{\alpha}$, then $\{w\} \models \beta \iff \{w'\} \models \beta$.

Notice in particular that, for a propositional letter p, $s \models \neg p$ iff $p \notin V(w)$ for each $w \in s$; and that a constancy atom $=\!(\beta)$ is just an alternative notation for $?\beta$.

We say that two formulas ψ, χ are *equivalent in* $M = (W, V)$ (and we write $\psi \equiv_M \chi$) in case $M, s \models \psi$ iff $M, s \models \chi$ for all $s \subseteq W$. We say that ψ, χ are *equivalent* ($\psi \equiv \chi$) iff $\psi \equiv_M \chi$ for all models M.

All the languages considered in this note have the property of *downwards closure*, that is: for any formula φ, if $s \models \varphi$ and $t \subseteq s$, then $t \models \varphi$. This can be shown by straightforward inductive arguments. Furthermore, the languages have the *empty set property*: the empty state $\emptyset$ supports all formulas.

For any formula φ and model $M = (W, V)$, we write

$$[\varphi]_M := \{s \subseteq W \mid s \models \varphi\};$$

this is the *inquisitive proposition* of φ in M, an element of $\wp(\wp(W))$ (i.e., a set of subsets of W). Notice that $\psi \equiv_M \chi$ iff $[\psi]_M = [\chi]_M$. We will omit the subscript M if the model is clear from the context or irrelevant. We remark that:

- $[\psi \wedge \chi] = [\psi] \cap [\chi]$.
- $[\psi \vee \chi] = [\psi] \cup [\chi]$.
- $[\psi \otimes \chi] = \{s \cup t \mid s, t \subseteq W$ and $s \in [\psi], t \in [\chi]\}$.

We will also write $[\psi] \otimes [\chi]$ for this latter set.

3 Independence of Inquisitive Implication in $\mathsf{EInqB}^{\otimes}$

In [3] it was shown that in $\mathsf{InqB}^{\otimes}$ the connectives $\wedge$ and $\otimes$ are independent, or more precisely strongly undefinable from the other connectives in the language. The exact same arguments show that these connectives are independent in $\mathsf{EInqB}^{\otimes}$, because the additional operators $\neg, \top$ and $?$ can simply be replaced, throughout the proofs, by equivalent formulas (e.g. $\neg\psi \equiv \psi \to \bot$, $\top \equiv (\psi \to \bot) \to \bot$, $?\psi \equiv \psi \vee\!\!\!\vee (\psi \to \bot)$) which do not involve either $\wedge$ or $\otimes$.

On the contrary, the argument given in [3] to show the independence of $\to$ in $\mathsf{InqB}^{\otimes}$ used a specific characteristic of language $\mathsf{InqB}^{\otimes}$: the fact that all of its connectives, except for $\to$, are increasing monotone in both arguments. This kind of argument is not suitable anymore for $\mathsf{EInqB}^{\otimes}$, where also the operators $\neg$ and $?$ lack monotonicity.[9] We provide instead a direct argument, showing that $\to$ is strongly undefinable in EInqB^{-}.

[9] The operator $?$ is definable in terms of $\vee\!\!\!\vee$ and $\neg$, so ultimately the cause of this technical difficulty is the negation operator $\neg$.

For each pair of (distinct) atoms p, q, we define a corresponding possible world model $M_{pq} = (W, V_{pq})$, where:

- $W = \{w_1, w_2, w_3\}$
- $V_{pq}(w_1) = \{p\}$
- $V_{pq}(w_2) = \{q\}$
- $V_{pq}(w_3) = \emptyset$.

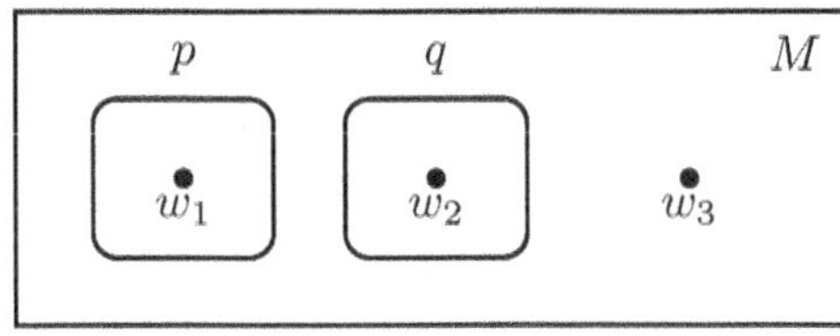

We will show that no EInqB^- formula $\varphi(a, b)$ without occurrences of p, q is such that $\varphi(?p, ?q) \equiv_{M_{pq}} ?p \rightarrow ?q$.

Lemma 1. *Let $\varphi(a, b)$ be an EInqB^- formula without occurrences of p, q. If $\varphi(?p, ?q) \not\equiv_{M_{pq}} \bot$, then $\{w_i\} \models \varphi(?p, ?q)$ for each $i = 1, 2, 3$.*

Proof. We first notice that, without loss of generality, we can assume the symbol ? not to occur in $\varphi(a, b)$ (just replace each subformula of the form $?\theta$ with $\theta \vee\!\!\!\vee \neg\theta$). We then proceed by induction on the syntax of $\varphi(a, b)$. Write φ^* for $\varphi(?p, ?q)$ and similarly for other formulas.

Base cases: the cases for $\varphi(a, b)$ being $\bot$ or $\top$ are straightforward. In case $\varphi(a, b)$ is a, then φ^* is $?p$, and each of the $\{w_i\}$ supports $?p$. The case for $\varphi(a, b)$ being b is analogous. Finally, suppose $\varphi(a, b)$ is an atom r distinct from a, b (and, by assumption, distinct from p and q). Since r is not true at any world in M_{pq}, by downward closure we have $\varphi^* \equiv_{M_{pq}} \bot$.

Inductive step: we have several cases.

- $\varphi(a, b)$ is of the form $\theta(a, b) \wedge \eta(a, b)$. If either θ^* or η^* is $\equiv_{M_{pq}} \bot$, then also φ^* is. Otherwise, by the inductive hypothesis $\{w_i\} \in [\theta^*] \cap [\eta^*] = [\theta^* \wedge \eta^*] = [\varphi^*]$ for each $i = 1, 2, 3$.
- $\varphi(a, b)$ is of the form $\theta(a, b) \vee\!\!\!\vee \eta(a, b)$. If $\theta^* \equiv_{M_{pq}} \bot$, then $\varphi^* \equiv_{M_{pq}} \eta^*$, so φ^* satisfies the statement by inductive hypothesis. Otherwise, by the inductive assumption $\{w_i\} \in [\theta^*]$; therefore, $\{w_i\} \in [\theta^*] \cup [\eta^*] = [\theta^* \vee\!\!\!\vee \eta^*] = [\varphi^*]$.
- $\varphi(a, b)$ is of the form $\theta(a, b) \otimes \eta(a, b)$. If both θ^* and η^* are $\equiv_{M_{pq}} \bot$, then φ^* is. Otherwise, wlog assume that $\theta^* \not\equiv_{M_{pq}} \bot$. Then, by the inductive assumption on θ^*, we have $\{w_i\} \models \theta^* \models \theta^* \otimes \eta^*$, where the last step is justified by the empty set property.
- $\varphi(a, b)$ is of the form $\neg\theta(a, b)$. If $\theta^* \equiv_{M_{pq}} \bot$, then $\varphi^* \equiv_{M_{pq}} \top$, so the $\{w_i\}$ satisfy this formula. Otherwise, by the inductive assumption each $\{w_i\}$ satisfies θ^*; but then by downward closure $\varphi^* \equiv_{M_{pq}} \bot$.

Given any $S \in \wp(\wp(W))$, we write $S^\downarrow := \{t \in \wp(W) \mid t \subseteq s \text{ for some } s \in S\}$ (the *downward closure* of S). It is an easy exercise, left to the reader, to verify that in M_{pq} we have:

- $[?p \vee\!\!\!\vee ?q] = \{\{w_1, w_3\}, \{w_2, w_3\}\}^\downarrow$.
- $A := [?p \rightarrow ?q] = \{\{w_1, w_2\}, \{w_1, w_3\}\}^\downarrow$.

- $B := [?q \to ?p] = \{\{w_1, w_2\}, \{w_2, w_3\}\}^{\downarrow}$.
- $C := [?p \to ?q] \cap [?q \to ?p] = \{\{w_1, w_2\}, \{w_3\}\}^{\downarrow}$.

We want to show that no EInqB^- formula of the form $\varphi(?p, ?q)$ can be equivalent to $?p \to ?q$ in M_{pq} (in case $\varphi(a, b)$ has no occurrences of p, q). In order to have a stronger inductive assumption, we prove more generally that the inquisitive proposition of $\varphi(?p, ?q)$ cannot be A, B or C.

Lemma 2. *Let $\varphi(a, b)$ be an EInqB^- formula without occurrences of p, q. Then $[\varphi(?p, ?q)] \neq A, B, C$.*

Proof. By induction on the syntax of $\varphi(a, b)$. As before, we can assume that this formula contains no occurrences of ?, and we write φ^* for $\varphi(?p, ?q)$.

The base cases are easy.

Inductive step: we have several cases.

- $\varphi(a, b)$ is of the form $\theta(a, b) \wedge \eta(a, b)$.
  - Observe that there is only one proper subfamily of $\wp(W)$ which extends A (namely, $\wp(W) \setminus \{W\} = \{\{w_1, w_2\}, \{w_2, w_3\}, \{w_1, w_3\}\}^{\downarrow}$). Therefore, A cannot be obtained as intersection of two subsets of $\wp(W)$ which are both distinct from A. Since, by the inductive hypothesis, we also have that $[\theta^*] \neq A \neq [\eta^*]$, we can then conclude that $[\varphi^*] = [\theta^*] \cap [\eta^*] \neq A$. By a similar argument we conclude $[\varphi^*] \neq B$.
  - The fact that $[\varphi^*] \neq C$ is proved similarly, observing first that the only way of writing C as an intersection of subsets of $\wp(W)$ which strictly include C is $A \cap B$.
- $\varphi(a, b)$ is of the form $\theta(a, b) \vee\!\!\!\vee \eta(a, b)$.
  - If $\theta^* \equiv_{M_{pq}} \bot$, then $\varphi^* \equiv_{M_{pq}} \eta^*$; and $[\eta^*] \neq A, B, C$ by the inductive hypothesis. In case instead $\eta^* \equiv_{M_{pq}} \bot$, we have a similar proof.
  - Suppose neither θ^* nor η^* is $\equiv_{M_{pq}} \bot$. We need to check a few subcases.
    - Suppose for the sake of contradiction that $[\varphi^*] = C$. Then, either $[\theta^*]$ or $[\eta^*]$ contains $\{w_1, w_2\}$; say, $\{w_1, w_2\} \in [\theta^*]$. By lemma 1 we have $\{w_3\} \in [\theta^*]$. So, $C \subseteq [\theta^*]$. Since furthermore $[\theta^*] \subseteq [\varphi^*] = C$, we must conclude that $[\theta^*] = C$, which contradicts the inductive hypothesis.
    - Suppose for the sake of contradiction that $[\varphi^*] = A$. As before, we have, say, that $\{w_1, w_2\} \in [\theta^*]$. By lemma 1 we have $\{w_3\} \in [\theta^*]$. Since furthermore $[\theta^*] \subseteq [\varphi^*] = A$, we must conclude that $[\theta^*]$ is either C or A, which contradicts the inductive hypothesis.
    - The case for $[\varphi^*] = B$ is similar.
- $\varphi(a, b)$ is of the form $\theta(a, b) \otimes \eta(a, b)$. The subcase in which either $\theta^* \equiv_{M_{pq}} \bot$ or $\eta^* \equiv_{M_{pq}} \bot$ is treated as in the $\vee\!\!\!\vee$ case. If instead neither of these holds, by lemma 1 both θ^* and η^* are satisfied by each of the $\{w_i\}$. But then $\{w_i, w_j\} \in [\theta^* \otimes \eta^*]$ for each $i, j = 1, 2, 3$, in particular when $i \neq j$; so, $[\theta^* \otimes \eta^*] \neq A, B, C$.
- $\varphi(a, b)$ is of the form $\neg\theta(a, b)$. If $\theta^* \equiv_{M_{pq}} \bot$, then $\varphi^* \equiv_{M_{pq}} \top$; and $[\top] \neq A, B, C$. Otherwise, by lemma 1, $\{w_i\} \models \theta^*$ for each $i = 1, 2, 3$. But then, by downward closure, $[\varphi^*] = \{\emptyset\} \neq A, B, C$.

Theorem 1. *The connective* $\to$ *is strongly undefinable in* EInqB^-.

Proof. Suppose for the sake of contradiction that there is a formula $\varphi(a,b) \in \mathsf{EInqB}^-$ such that, for all formulas $\eta, \theta \in \mathsf{EInqB}^-$, $\varphi(\eta,\theta) \equiv \eta \to \theta$. Let p, q be two distinct atoms which do not occur in $\varphi(a,b)$. Then, as a special case of lemma 2, we obtain that $[\varphi(?p,?q)]_{M_{pq}} \neq [?p \to ?q]_{M_{pq}}$, i.e. $\varphi(?p,?q) \not\equiv_{M_{pq}} ?p \to ?q$. Thus $\varphi(?p,?q) \not\equiv ?p \to ?q$, contradicting our initial assumption.

4 Strong Undefinability of $\mathbin{\rotatebox[origin=c]{-90}{$\vee$}}$ in (Extended) Propositional Dependence Logic

In this section we will prove that the global disjunction[10] $\vee\!\!\!\vee$ is strongly undefinable in propositional dependence logic D, and later show how this proof can be adapted to extended propositional dependence logic D^+. Undefinability simpliciter was shown for D in [17] by a more informative but quite complicated method, which does not straightforwardly extend to D^+.

For any distinct propositional letters p, q we consider a model $M_{pq} = (W, V_{pq})$ where:

- $W = \{w_1, w_2, w_3\}$
- $[p] = \{w_1, w_2\}^{\downarrow}$
- $[q] = \{w_2, w_3\}^{\downarrow}$
- $[r] = \{\emptyset\}$ for each $r \neq p, q$

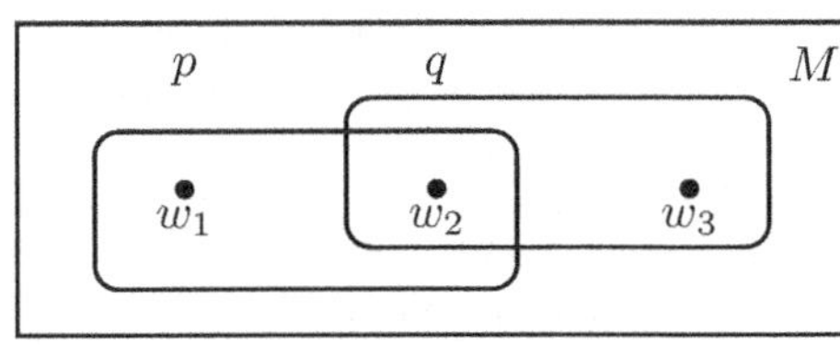

Differently from the case of inquisitive logic, not every D formula can be accepted as a definition of a connective; we must ensure that substitution instances are still well-formed D formulas (remember that expressions such as $\neg{=}(p)$ and ${=}({=}(p);q)$ are not well-formed D formulas). Towards this goal, we call $\varphi(a,b)$ a *context* if it is a D formula in which a and b do not occur negated nor in a dependence atom.[11]

We want to show that, for every context $\varphi(a,b)$ without occurrences of p, q, $\varphi({=}(p), {=}(q)) \not\equiv_{M_{pq}} {=}(p) \vee\!\!\!\vee {=}(q)$.

Lemma 3. *Let* δ *be a dependence atom without occurrences of* p, q. *Then* $\delta \equiv_{M_{pq}} \top$.

Lemma 4. *Let* $\varphi(a,b)$ *be a context without occurrences of* p, q. *Then the formula* $\varphi({=}(p), {=}(q))$ *is equivalent in* M_{pq} *to one of the following:*

- $\top$
- $({=}(p) \wedge {=}(q)) \otimes ({=}(p) \wedge {=}(q))$
- ${=}(p)$
- ${=}(q)$

[10] Also variously known as *inquisitive*, *Boolean* or *intuitionistic* disjunction.
[11] The terminology is from [17].

- $=(p)\wedge =(q)$
- $\bot$

Proof. By induction on φ. Write φ^* for $\varphi(=(p),=(q))$, and similarly for other formulas.

- Base cases.
  - If $\varphi(a,b)$ is a, then φ^* is $=(p)$, and we are done. Similarly if $\varphi(a,b)$ is b.
  - If $\varphi(a,b)$ is r for some $r \neq a,b,p,q$, then φ^* is r, so $\varphi^* \equiv_{M_{pq}} \bot$.
  - If $\varphi(a,b)$ is $\neg r$ for some $r \neq a,b,p,q$, then φ^* is $\neg r$, so $\varphi^* \equiv_{M_{pq}} \top$.
  - If $\varphi(a,b)$ is a dependence atom, then, by the definition of context, a and b do not occur in $\varphi(a,b)$, and $\varphi^* = \varphi(a,b)$. Thus, by lemma 3, $\varphi^* \equiv_{M_{pq}} \top$.
- Case $\varphi(a,b) = \eta(a,b) \wedge \theta(a,b)$. By induction hypothesis, η^* and θ^* are equivalent in M_{pq} to one out of $\top, =(p), =(q), =(p)\wedge =(q), (=(p)\wedge =(q)) \otimes (=(p)\wedge =(q)), \bot$. We verify that the set of the inquisitive propositions of these six formulas is closed under intersection.
  Clearly no set gets modified by intersection with $[\top]$, and intersecting anything with $[\bot]$ gives $[\bot]$. For the rest, observe that
  - $[=(p)] \cap [=(q)] = [=(p)] \cap [=(p)\wedge =(q)] = [=(q)] \cap [=(p)\wedge =(q)] = [=(p)\wedge =(q)]$, where the first two equalities follow from the associativity, commutativity and idempotence of $\wedge$.
  - Note that, in M_{pq}, $[(=(p)\wedge =(q)) \otimes (=(p)\wedge =(q))] = \{\{w_1,w_2\},\{w_2,w_3\},\{w_1,w_3\}\}^{\downarrow}$, while $[=(p)] = \{\{w_1,w_2\},\{w_3\}\}^{\downarrow}$, $[=(q)] = \{\{w_1\},\{w_2,w_3\}\}^{\downarrow}$ and $[=(p)\wedge =(q)] = \{\{w_1\},\{w_2\},\{w_3\}\}^{\downarrow}$. Thus, $[=(p)], [=(q)], [=(p)\wedge =(q)] \subset [(=(p)\wedge =(q)) \otimes (=(p)\wedge =(q))]$. So, if η^* is either $=(p), =(q)$ or $=(p)\wedge =(q)$, then $[\eta^*] \cap [(=(p)\wedge =(q)) \otimes (=(p)\wedge =(q))] = [\eta^*]$.
- Case $\varphi(a,b) = \eta(a,b) \otimes \theta(a,b)$. By induction hypothesis, each of η^* and θ^* is equivalent in M_{pq} to one out of $\top, =(p), =(q), =(p)\wedge =(q), (=(p)\wedge =(q)) \otimes (=(p)\wedge =(q)), \bot$. We verify that the set of the inquisitive propositions of these six formulas is closed under the set-theoretical operator $\otimes$. Again, this is trivial if $\top$ or $\bot$ are involved.
  - $[=(p)] \otimes [=(p)] = \wp(s) = [\top]$, because, first, $W = \{w_1,w_2\} \cup \{w_3\}$; secondly, $\{w_1,w_2\},\{w_3\} \in [=(p)]$, so that $W \in [=(p) \otimes =(p)]$; and lastly, the language is downward closed. Similarly for $=(q)$.
  - $[=(p)] \otimes [=(q)] = \wp(s) = [\top]$, because $W = \{w_1,w_2\} \cup \{w_2,w_3\}$ where $\{w_1,w_2\} \in [=(p)], \{w_2,w_3\} \in [=(q)]$, and the language is downward closed.
  - Let η^* be either $=(p), =(q)$ or $(=(p)\wedge =(q)) \otimes (=(p)\wedge =(q))$. Then either $\{w_1,w_2\}$ or $\{w_2,w_3\}$ is in $[\eta^*]$. Now, since both $\{w_3\}$ and $\{w_1\}$ are in $[=(p)\wedge =(q)]$, and $W = \{w_1,w_2\} \cup \{w_3\} = \{w_1\} \cup \{w_2,w_3\}$, in each of these cases $[\eta^*] \otimes [=(p)\wedge =(q)] = \wp(s) = [\top]$. For similar reasons, $[\eta^*] \otimes [(=(p)\wedge =(q)) \otimes (=(p)\wedge =(q))] = [\top]$.
  - The only remaining case is η^*, θ^* being both equal to $=(p)\wedge =(q)$. But in this case $\eta^* \otimes \theta^*$ is just $(=(p)\wedge =(q)) \otimes (=(p)\wedge =(q))$.

Theorem 2. *The connective* $\mathbin{\mathbb{V}}$ *is strongly undefinable in* D.

Proof. Let $\varphi(a,b)$ be a context. Let p,q be two atoms which do not occur in $\varphi(a,b)$. We show that $\varphi(=(p),=(q)) \not\equiv =(p) \mathbin{\mathbb{V}} =(q)$. Consider the model M_{pq} corresponding to p,q. In it, $[=(p) \mathbin{\mathbb{V}} =(q)] = \{\{w_1,w_2\},\{w_2,w_3\}\}^{\downarrow}$. By lemma 4, $[\varphi(=(p),=(q))]$ is either $[\top],[=(p)],[=(q)],[=(p)\wedge =(q)],[(=(p)\wedge =(q)) \otimes (=(p)\wedge =(q))],[\bot]$. It is easily checked that none of these sets is $[=(p) \mathbin{\mathbb{V}} =(q)]$; so, $\varphi(=(p),=(q)) \not\equiv_{M_{pq}} =(p) \mathbin{\mathbb{V}} =(q)$; and thus $\varphi(=(p),=(q)) \not\equiv =(p) \mathbin{\mathbb{V}} =(q)$.

We briefly show that the result above easily extends to a proof of strong undefinability of $\mathbin{\mathbb{V}}$ in D^+, the language that differs from D only in that it allows dependence atoms of the form $=(\boldsymbol{\alpha};\beta)$, where $\boldsymbol{\alpha},\beta$ are D formulas without occurrences of dependence atoms.

First of all, the analogue of lemma 3 can be proved by pointing out that any (generalized) dependence atom without occurrences of p,q is of the form $=(\boldsymbol{\alpha};\beta)$, where β is a formula without occurrences of p,q. Since in M_{pq} all worlds agree on the truth value of propositional letters different from p,q, it can be shown by a straightforward induction that all worlds in M_{pq} agree about the truth value of β. Therefore, $=(\boldsymbol{\alpha};\beta)$ is trivially satisfied by all substates of W, i.e. $=(\boldsymbol{\alpha};\beta) \equiv_{M_{pq}} \top$.

Secondly, observe that, in the analogue of lemma 4, the generalized dependence atoms play a role only in the base case for dependence atoms. But this case is taken care by the analogue of lemma 3 exactly in the same way as in the original proof.

Thirdly, the generalized dependence atoms play no role in the rest of the proof of theorem 2. Thus we have:

Theorem 3. *The connective* $\mathbin{\mathbb{V}}$ *is strongly undefinable in* D^+.

This result can be slightly strengthened. It is not uncommon, in some presentations of dependence logics, to allow applying negation in front of arbitrary *classical* formulas; this is well-known not to increase the expressivity of propositional dependence logic, but it might in principle affect the issue of the definability of $\mathbin{\mathbb{V}}$. Let us call $\mathsf{D}^+_\neg$ the extension of D^+ that allows for formulas of the form $\neg\alpha$, where α is a $\mathsf{D}^+_\neg$ formula without occurrences of dependence atoms. We can prove that global disjunction is not definable in this language, either. To see this, we make a simple observation:

Lemma 5. *Let* α *be a* $\mathsf{D}^+_\neg$ *formula without occurrences of dependence atoms, and without occurrences of the distinct propositional letters* p,q. *Then, in* M_{pq}, $[\alpha]=[\top]$ *or* $[\alpha]=[\bot]$.

Proof. First observe that we can assume, without loss of generality, that such an α is in disjunctive normal form. By definition of M_{pq}, if r is any propositional letter different from p and q, $[r]=[\bot]$, and $[\neg r]=[\top]$. Thus, any conjunction of literals has proposition $[\top]$ if all conjuncts are negated formulas, and $[\bot]$ otherwise. Therefore α, which is a (tensor) disjunction of such formulas, has itself proposition $[\top]$ or $[\bot]$.

We can then prove an analogue of lemma 4 by adding the following inductive clause to the proof:

- Case $\varphi(a,b)$ is $\neg\alpha(a,b)$. By definition of context, the letters a, b do not occur in $\alpha(a,b)$, therefore $\alpha^* = \alpha(a,b)$ is a $\mathsf{D}^+_\neg$ formula without occurrences of dependence atoms, nor occurrences of p, q. By lemma 5, then, $[\alpha^*] = [\top]$ or $[\alpha^*] = [\bot]$. But then, $[\varphi^*] = [\bot]$ or $[\varphi^*] = [\top]$.

Thus, the strong undefinability proof still works as before.

Theorem 4. *The connective* $\mathbin{\rotatebox[origin=c]{90}{$\geq$}}$ *is strongly undefinable in* $\mathsf{D}^+_\neg$.

Acknowledgments. This research was supported by the Research Council of Finland grants n. 316460 and 349803.

The author expresses gratitude to Ivano Ciardelli and Fan Yang for being made aware of the two open problems addressed in this work.

References

1. Ciardelli, I.: Dependency as question entailment. In: Dependence Logic: Theory and Applications, pp. 129–181. Springer (2016)
2. Ciardelli, I.: Questions in logic. PhD thesis, Institute for Logic, Language and Computation, University of Amsterdam (2016)
3. Ciardelli, I., Barbero, F.: Undefinability in inquisitive logic with tensor. In: Blackburn, P., Lorini, E., Guo, M. (eds.) Logic, Rationality, and Interaction, pp. 29–42, Berlin, Heidelberg (2019). Springer Berlin Heidelberg
4. Ciardelli, I., Groenendijk, J., Roelofsen, F.: Inquisitive semantics. Oxford University Press (2018)
5. Ciardelli, I., Roelofsen, F.: Inquisitive logic. J. Philos. Log. **40**(1), 55–94 (2011)
6. Galliani, P.: Epistemic operators in dependence logic. Stud. Logica. **101**, 367–397 (2013)
7. Grädel, E., Väänänen, J.: Dependence and independence. Stud. Logica. **101**, 399–410 (2013)
8. Hella, L., Luosto, K., Sano, K., Virtema, J.: The expressive power of modal dependence logic. Adv. Modal Logic **10**, 294–312 (2014)
9. Hella, L., Luosto, K., Väänänen, J.: Dimension in team semantics. Math. Struct. Comput. Sci. 1–45 (2024)
10. Hodges, W.: Compositional semantics for a language of imperfect information. Logic J. IGPL **5**, 539–563 (1997)
11. Häggblom, M., Hirvonen, M., Väänänen, J.: Expressibility and inexpressibility in propositional team logics (2025). arXiv: 2512.15680
12. Lück, M., Vilander, M.: On the succinctness of atoms of dependency. Logical Methods Comput. Sci. **15** (2019)
13. Mann, A.L., Sandu, G., Sevenster, M.: Independence-Friendly Logic — a Game-Theoretic Approach, volume 386 of London Mathematical Society lecture note series. Cambridge University Press (2011)
14. Rönnholm, R.: Arity Fralments of Logics with Team Semantics. PhD thesis, University of Tampere (2018)

15. Väänänen, J.: Dependence Logic: A New Approach to Independence Friendly Logic, volume 70 of London Mathematical Society Student Texts. Cambridge University Press (2007)
16. Wang, H., Wang, Y., Wang, Y.: An epistemic interpretation of tensor disjunction. In: Advances in Modal Logic (2022)
17. Yang, F.: Uniform definability in propositional dependence logic. Rev. Symbolic Logic **10**(1), 65–79 (2017)
18. Yang, F., Väänänen, J.: Propositional logics of dependence. Ann. Pure Appl. Logic **167**(7), 557–589 (2016)

Implication Problems Over Positive Semirings

Minna Hirvonen(✉)

Institut für Theoretische Informatik, Leibniz Universität Hannover, Hanover, Germany
minna.hirvonen@thi.uni-hannover.de

Abstract. We study various notions of dependency in semiring team semantics. Semiring teams are essentially database relations, where each tuple is annotated with some element from a positive semiring. We consider semiring generalizations of several dependency notions from database theory and probability theory, including functional and inclusion dependencies, marginal identity, and (probabilistic) independence. We examine axiomatizations of implication problems, which are rule-based characterizations for the logical implication and inference of new dependencies from a given set of dependencies. Semiring team semantics provides a general framework, where different implication problems can be studied simultaneously for various semirings. The choice of the semiring leads to a specific semantic interpretation of the dependencies, and hence different semirings offer a way to study different semantics (e.g., relational, bag, and probabilistic semantics) in a unified framework.

Keywords: Dependency · Semiring · Team semantics · Relational database · Probability distribution · Axiomatization

1 Introduction

Various notions of dependency appear in many research areas, such as mathematics, statistics, and computer science. For example, the notions of functional and inclusion dependencies are applied in relational databases as primary and foreign key constraints to maintain data integrity, and the notions of independence and marginal identity of random variables (IID variables) are used in probability theory and statistics to simplify the underlying mathematics. Many of these dependency notions share analogous properties across different domains of application. For example, the complete axiomatizations for inclusion dependencies over relational databases [4] and for marginal identities over probability distributions [18] are very similar, and the semigraphoid axioms [22] are sound for both embedded multivalued dependency and conditional independence.

It would therefore be useful to study these notions in a general framework that could help explain how the characteristics of different application domains affect the interpretation and properties of the notions. One possible way to

A.-Y. Turhan and J. Virtema (Eds.): FoIKS 2026, LNCS 16475, pp. 29–47, 2026.
https://doi.org/10.1007/978-3-032-21540-6_3

do this is to consider *semirings*, which is a generalization of rings without the requirement that every element must have an additive inverse. The K-relations, introduced in [14], are relations such that each of their tuples is annotated by some element from a semiring K. In [14], K-relations over commutative semirings were used for *data provenance* that refers to meta-information obtained about the origin and processing history of data based on propagation of tuple annotations through queries, but K-relations have also been studied in relation to dependencies. For example, conditional independence, functional dependency, marginal identity, and multivalued dependency over semirings have been studied in [15,16][1] and join operations over K- relations in [2].

In [3], semirings were introduced into the framework of *team semantics*, which is a semantical system for logics that can express different dependencies using new kinds of atomic formulas. This is possible because in team semantics, the satisfaction of logical formulas is determined on a set of assignments, instead of just a single assignment, as, e.g., in the case of the usual semantics of first-order logic. These sets of assignments are called teams, and they are essentially database relations. The most well-known logic based on team semantics is the *dependence logic* [23] that extends first-order logic with dependency atoms that correspond to the notion of functional dependency. Other well-known variants include the inclusion logic [12] and the independence logic [13]. The framework of team semantics has been generalized to multi-team (bag) semantics [8] and probabilistic team semantics [9], and also extended to various logics, including propositional [25], modal [24], and inquisitive logic [6].

The goal of this paper is to define and study axiomatizations over general K-teams for various classes of atoms that have previously been studied separately in different variants of team semantics. We use the terminology of K-teams, as defined in [3], but since K-teams are essentially annotated relations, the results also apply to K-relations. In particular, we study the logical inference of atoms in the form of *implication problems*. The implication problem for a class of atoms $\mathcal{C}$ over a semiring K is the problem of deciding whether, for a given finite set $\Sigma \cup \{\tau\}$ of $\mathcal{C}$ atoms, any K-team that satisfies every atom of Σ also satisfies τ.

One of the main results of this paper is that the axiomatization of the implication problem for functional dependencies and the unary variants of marginal identity and marginal distribution equivalence over probabilistic teams introduced in [20] is sound and complete more generally for any additively cancellative positive semiring. Another main contribution is analyzing a concept of weighted inclusion dependency that on suitable semirings coincides with the notions of inclusion dependency and marginal identity; we show that the weighted inclusion dependency has a certain symmetry property exactly on additively cancellative positive semirings, and the well-known axioms for the usual inclusion dependencies form a sound and complete axiomatization for the implication problem of weighted inclusion dependencies over a certain class of non-additively cancellative semirings. The unary variant of weighted inclusion dependencies can also

[1] Note that [15] is the full version of the paper [16]; both versions are cited in this paper as some results that are referenced here are only in the full version.

be considered together with functional dependencies or with both unary functional dependencies and independence atoms. In both cases, we obtain a sound and complete axiomatization over certain classes of non-additively cancellative semirings. We also introduce a notion of marginal distribution inclusion, which is a non-symmetric variant of marginal distribution equivalence, and present a sound and complete axiomatization for its unary variant over a certain class of non-additively cancellative semirings. Tables 3 and 2 summarize our results.

2 Preliminaries

In this section, we give the basic definitions for semirings, K-teams, and the dependencies considered in this paper.

2.1 Semirings

Semirings are structures that correspond to rings without the requirement that every element must have an additive inverse.

Definition 1. *A* semiring K *is a tuple* $(K, +, \times, 0, 1)$ *such that*

(i) $+$ *and* $\times$ *are binary operations on* K*,*
(ii) $(K, +, 0)$ *is a commutative monoid with identity element 0,*
(iii) $(K, \times, 1)$ *is a monoid with identity element 1,*
(iv) $a \times (b + c) = a \times b + a \times c$ *and* $(a + b) \times c = a \times c + b \times c$ *for all* $a, b, c \in K$*,*
(v) $0 \times a = a \times 0 = 0$ *for all* $a \in K$*.*

A semiring K is *commutative* if $(K, \times, 1)$ is a commutative monoid. A semiring K is *positive* if $a + b = 0$ implies $a = b = 0$ and $a \times b = 0$ implies $a = 0$ or $b = 0$. A semiring K is *additively cancellative* if $a + b = a + c$ implies $b = c$, and *multiplicatively cancellative* if $a \times b = a \times c$ implies $b = c$, and $b \times a = c \times a$ implies $b = c$ for all $a \neq 0$. We say that an element $a \in K$ is *(additively) idempotent* if $a + a = a$. Note that if K is additively cancellative, then 0 is the only idempotent element of K.

A semiring is *ordered* if there exists a reflexive, transitive, and antisymmetric relation $\leq$ (i.e., a partial order) such that for all $a, b, c \in K$ $a \leq b$ implies $a + c \leq b + c$ and ($a \leq b$ and $0 \leq c$) implies ($a \times c \leq b \times c$ and $c \times a \leq c \times b$). We write $a < b$ if $a \leq b$ and $a \neq b$. An order $\leq$ is *total* if for all $a, b \in K$ $a \leq b$ or $b \leq a$. We say that an order on K is *zero-min order* if $a \leq 0$ implies $a = 0$ for all $a \in K$.

Example 1. The following structures are examples of semirings[2].

[2] Note that the minimum and the maximum in (iv)–(v) are taken with respect to the usual total order of (the extended) reals. The (possibly partial) order of the semiring in general does not need to be the same as this, as long as it respects these operations defined via the usual order of reals, as required in the definition of ordered semiring.

(i) The *Boolean semiring* $\mathbb{B} = (\mathbb{B}, \vee, \wedge, 0, 1)$ is the two-element Boolean algebra that models logical truth.
(ii) The *semiring of natural numbers* $\mathbb{N} = (\mathbb{N}, +, \times, 0, 1)$ consists of the natural numbers with standard addition and multiplication.
(iii) The *probability semiring* $\mathbb{R}_{\geq 0} = (\mathbb{R}_{\geq 0}, +, \times, 0, 1)$ consists of the non-negative reals with standard addition and multiplication.
(iv) The *tropical semiring* $\mathbb{T} = (\mathbb{R} \cup \{\infty\}, \min, +, \infty, 0)$ consists of the expanded reals with minimum and standard addition as addition and multiplication, respectively.
(v) The *Viterbi semiring* $\mathbb{V} = ([0,1], \max, \times, 0, 1)$ consists of the unit interval with maximum and standard multiplication as addition and multiplication, respectively.
(vi) The *Lukasiewicz semiring* $\mathbb{L} = ([0,1], \max, \times, 0, 1)$ consists of the unit interval with maximum and multiplication $a \times b := \max\{0, a+b-1\}$ as addition and multiplication, respectively.

The Boolean semiring, the tropical semiring, and the Viterbi semiring are commutative, positive, and multiplicatively cancellative, but not additively cancellative. The semiring of natural numbers and the probability semiring are commutative, positive, and additively and multiplicatively cancellative. Lukasiewicz semiring is commutative, but not positive or additively or multiplicatively cancellative. The Boolean semiring, the tropical semiring, the Viterbi semiring, and the Lukasiewicz semiring are idempotent, i.e., all of their elements are idempotent. Note that the tropical semiring with the usual order of the extendend reals is not zero-min ordered, because its zero element is ∞.

In this paper, we only consider positive nontrivial semirings, i.e., $0 \neq 1$, so our results do not cover the Lukasiewicz semiring that is not positive. Since the positiveness of the semiring is assumed throughout this paper, we do not mention it for each theorem statement separately. Additional assumptions are necessary for some of the results, but these will be specified later in the relevant sections of the paper. The following lemma will also be useful later.

Lemma 1. *If K is additively cancellative, then $a < b$ and $c \leq d$ imply $a + c < b + d$.*

2.2 K-Teams and Dependencies

Let K be a positive (and commutative, totally zero-min ordered, multiplicatively cancellative[3]) semiring, D a finite set of variables, and A a finite set of values. An *assignment* s is a function $s\colon D \to A$. A *team* X of A over D is a finite set of assignments $s\colon D \to A$. We may assume that the set D is totally ordered, e.g., $D = \{x_1, \ldots, x_n\}$ and hence an assignment $s \in X$ can also be viewed as the tuple $(s(x_1), \ldots, s(x_n))$. A K-team is a function $\mathbb{X}\colon X \to K$. The value $\mathbb{X}(s)$ is called the *weight* of the assignment s.

[3] See Remark 1.

The *support* of a K-team $\mathbb{X}$ is the set of those assignments that have non-zero weight, i.e., $\mathrm{Supp}(\mathbb{X}) := \{s \in X : \mathbb{X}(s) \neq 0\}$. Let $\bar{x}$ and $\bar{a}$ be a tuple of variables and a tuple of values, respectively. The *marginal* of $\mathbb{X}$ over $\bar{x} = \bar{a}$ is defined as $|\mathbb{X}_{\bar{x}=\bar{a}}| := \sum_{\substack{s \in X,\\ s(\bar{x})=\bar{a}}} \mathbb{X}(s)$, where the empty sum is interpreted as 0. We denote by $|\mathbb{X}|$ the weight of the whole K-team, i.e., $|\mathbb{X}| := \sum_{s \in X} \mathbb{X}(s)$. Define also $X(\bar{x}) := \{\bar{a} \in A^{|\bar{x}|} : |\mathbb{X}_{\bar{x}=\bar{a}}| \neq 0\}$.

A multiset (B, m) is a set equipped with a multiplicity function $m\colon B \to \{1, 2, \dots\}$ such that $m(b)$ is the number of copies of the element $b \in B$ in the multiset. We write $b \in (B, m)$ if $b \in B$, and $(B', m') \subseteq (B, m)$ if $B' \subseteq B$ and $m'(b) \leq m(b)$ for all $b \in B'$. For simplicity, we often write multisets with double wave brackets, e.g., $(\{a, b\}, m)$ such that $m(a) = 1$ and $m(b) = 2$ can be represented as $\{\{a, b, b\}\}$. A tuple $\bar{x} = (x_1, \dots, x_n)$ is said to be *repetition-free*, if $x_i = x_j$ implies $i = j$ for all $i, j \in \{1, \dots, n\}$. Let $\mathrm{Var}(\bar{x})$ denote the set of variables that appear in the tuple $\bar{x}$. We say that the tuples $\bar{x}$ and $\bar{y}$ are *disjoint*, if $\mathrm{Var}(\bar{x}) \cap \mathrm{Var}(\bar{y}) = \emptyset$. The length of the tuple $\bar{x}$ is denoted by $|\bar{x}|$.

Let $\bar{x}$ and $\bar{y}$ be tuples of variables. Then $=(\bar{x}, \bar{y})$ is the (functional) dependency (FD) atom. If the tuple $\bar{x}$ is empty, we write $=(\bar{y})$ instead of $=(\emptyset, \bar{y})$ and say that $=(\bar{y})$ is a constancy atom (CA). If the tuples $\bar{x}$ and $\bar{y}$ are repetition-free, then $\bar{x} \subseteq^* \bar{y}$ and $\bar{x} \approx^* \bar{y}$ are the marginal distribution inclusion (IND*), and the marginal distribution equivalence (MDE) atoms, respectively. If the tuples $\bar{x}$ and $\bar{y}$ are repetition-free and of the same length, then $\bar{x} \leq \bar{y}$ and $\bar{x} \approx \bar{y}$ are the (weighted) inclusion dependency (IND) and the marginal identity (MI) atom, respectively. If $\bar{x}$ and $\bar{y}$ are disjoint[4] tuples (not necessarily of the same length), then $\bar{x} \perp \bar{y}$ is the independence atom (IA). If $|\bar{x}| = |\bar{y}| = 1$, then the corresponding atom is called *unary*, and the letter "U" is added in front of the abbreviation of the atom name, e.g., UFD, UIND, UMDE etc. A constancy atom $=(\bar{y})$ is unary if $|\bar{y}| = 1$, and UCAs are considered UFDs in this work. We extend the notation $\mathrm{Var}(\bar{x})$ to atoms and sets of atoms in the obvious way.

Let σ be an atom and $\mathbb{X}$ a K-team of X over D such that $\mathrm{Var}(\sigma) \subseteq D$. The satisfaction relation $\mathbb{X} \models \sigma$ is defined as follows.

- $\mathbb{X} \models =(\bar{x}, \bar{y})$ iff for all $s, s' \in \mathrm{Supp}(\mathbb{X})$, $s(\bar{x}) = s'(\bar{x})$ implies $s(\bar{y}) = s'(\bar{y})$,
- $\mathbb{X} \models \bar{x} \leq \bar{y}$ iff $|\mathbb{X}_{\bar{x}=\bar{a}}| \leq |\mathbb{X}_{\bar{y}=\bar{a}}|$ for all $\bar{a} \in A^{|\bar{x}|}$,
- $\mathbb{X} \models \bar{x} \subseteq^* \bar{y}$ iff $\{\{|\mathbb{X}_{\bar{x}=\bar{a}}| : \bar{a} \in X(\bar{x})\}\} \subseteq \{\{|\mathbb{X}_{\bar{y}=\bar{a}}| : \bar{a} \in X(\bar{y})\}\}$,
- $\mathbb{X} \models \bar{x} \approx \bar{y}$ iff $|\mathbb{X}_{\bar{x}=\bar{a}}| = |\mathbb{X}_{\bar{y}=\bar{a}}|$ for all $\bar{a} \in A^{|\bar{x}|}$,
- $\mathbb{X} \models \bar{x} \approx^* \bar{y}$ iff $\{\{|\mathbb{X}_{\bar{x}=\bar{a}}| : \bar{a} \in X(\bar{x})\}\} = \{\{|\mathbb{X}_{\bar{y}=\bar{a}}| : \bar{a} \in X(\bar{y})\}\}$,
- $\mathbb{X} \models \bar{x} \perp \bar{y}$ iff $|\mathbb{X}_{\bar{x}\bar{y}=s(\bar{x}\bar{y})}| \times |\mathbb{X}| = |\mathbb{X}_{\bar{x}=s(\bar{x})}| \times |\mathbb{X}_{\bar{y}=s(\bar{y})}|$ for all $s\colon \mathrm{Var}(\bar{x}\bar{y}) \to A$.

In the semantics of $\bar{x} \perp \bar{y}$, the multiplication with $|\mathbb{X}|$ comes from the fact that the atom is a special case of conditional independence $\bar{x} \perp_{\bar{z}} \bar{y}$ where the tuple $\bar{z}$ is empty. The equation in the semantic clause of $\bar{x} \perp_{\bar{z}} \bar{y}$ is of the form

[4] In the usual team semantics setting, it is common to also allow non-disjoint tuples in the definition of IAs, but here we assume disjointness. In this paper, we occasionally use the terms *disjoint* and *non-disjoint* for these different types of IAs when the distinction is necessary to avoid confusion.

$|\mathbb{X}_{\bar{x}\bar{y}\bar{z}=s(\bar{x}\bar{y}\bar{z})}| \times |\mathbb{X}_{\bar{z}=s(\bar{z})}| = |\mathbb{X}_{\bar{x}\bar{z}=s(\bar{x}\bar{z})}| \times |\mathbb{X}_{\bar{y}\bar{z}=s(\bar{y}\bar{z})}|$, where $|\mathbb{X}_{\bar{z}=s(\bar{z})}| = |\mathbb{X}|$ if $\bar{z}$ is empty. In the case of the Boolean semiring or a probability distribution, the value of $|\mathbb{X}|$ can be disregarded as it is always 1, but for arbitrary semirings this is not the case.

If $\mathbb{X} \models \tau$, we say that $\mathbb{X}$ *satisfies* τ. If Σ is a set of atoms, we write $\mathbb{X} \models \Sigma$ iff $\mathbb{X} \models \sigma$ for all $\sigma \in \Sigma$.

Table 1. The K-team $\mathbb{X}$ of Example 2 that is also used in the proof of Proposition 1.

x	y	z	v	w	$\mathbb{X}$
0	0	1	0	0	a
0	1	1	0	0	b
1	0	0	1	0	c

Example 2. Consider the K-team $\mathbb{X}$ of $A = \{0,1\}$ over $D = \{x, y, z, v, w\}$ depicted in Table 1, and let a, b, c be nonzero elements of K such that $a + b < c$. First note that since a, b, c are nonzero, the support of $\mathbb{X}$ consists of all of the three rows in the table. We have $\mathbb{X} \models =\!(x, z)$ because the values of z agree on those rows where the values of x agree. However, $\mathbb{X} \not\models =\!(x, y)$ because on the first two rows x has the same value, 0, but the values for y are different, namely 0 and 1. We also have $\mathbb{X} \models =\!(w)$ and $\mathbb{X} \not\models =\!(z)$ because the value of w is constant, but the value of z is not.

We have $\mathbb{X} \models x \leq v$ and $\mathbb{X} \models x \approx v$ because $|\mathbb{X}_{x=0}| = a + b = |\mathbb{X}_{v=0}|$ and $|\mathbb{X}_{x=1}| = c = |\mathbb{X}_{v=1}|$, but $\mathbb{X} \not\models x \leq z$ and $\mathbb{X} \not\models x \approx z$ because $|\mathbb{X}_{x=1}| = c > a + b = |\mathbb{X}_{z=1}|$. We also have $\mathbb{X} \models x \subseteq^* z$ and $\mathbb{X} \models x \approx^* z$ because $|\mathbb{X}_{x=0}| = a + b = |\mathbb{X}_{z=1}|$ and $|\mathbb{X}_{x=1}| = c = |\mathbb{X}_{z=0}|$, so $\{|\mathbb{X}_{x=i}| : i \in \{0,1\}\} = \{\{a + b, c\}\} = \{|\mathbb{X}_{z=i}| : i \in \{0,1\}\}$. However, $\mathbb{X} \not\models x \subseteq^* w$ and $\mathbb{X} \not\models x \approx^* w$ because $|\mathbb{X}_{x=0}| = a + b$, $|\mathbb{X}_{x=1}| = c$, $|\mathbb{X}_{w=0}| = a + b + c$, and $|\mathbb{X}_{w=1}| = 0$, and hence $\{|\mathbb{X}_{x=i}| : i \in \{0,1\}\} = \{\{a + b, c\}\} \not\subseteq \{\{a + b + c\}\} = \{|\mathbb{X}_{w=i}| : i \in \{0\}\}$.

We have $\mathbb{X} \models x \perp w$ and $\mathbb{X} \not\models x \perp y$. The former holds since $|\mathbb{X}_{xw=ij}| \times |\mathbb{X}| = |\mathbb{X}_{xw=ij}| \times (a + b + c) = |\mathbb{X}_{x=i}| \times (a + b + c) = |\mathbb{X}_{x=i}| \times |\mathbb{X}_{w=j}|$ if $j = 0$ and $|\mathbb{X}_{xw=ij}| \times |\mathbb{X}| = 0 \times (a+b+c) = |\mathbb{X}_{x=i}| \times 0 = |\mathbb{X}_{x=i}| \times |\mathbb{X}_{w=j}|$ if $j = 1$, implying that $|\mathbb{X}_{xw=ij}| \times |\mathbb{X}| = |\mathbb{X}_{x=i}| \times |\mathbb{X}_{w=j}|$ for all $i, j \in \{0,1\}$. The latter holds since $|\mathbb{X}_{xy=11}| \times |\mathbb{X}| = 0 \neq c \times b = |\mathbb{X}_{x=1}| \times |\mathbb{X}_{y=1}|$.

Remark 1. Recall that we only consider positive semirings K. In the beginning of this section we also assumed that K is commutative, totally zero-min ordered, and multiplicatively cancellative. A total zero-min order is needed for the atoms $\bar{x} \leq \bar{y}$, to ensure that the values that do not appear for x in the support of $\mathbb{X}$ cannot prevent the satisfaction of the atom. Commutativity and multiplicative cancellativity is needed for the atoms $\bar{x} \perp \bar{y}$ to ensure the soundness of the usual axioms for independence.[5]

[5] For the atoms whose satisfaction condition does not refer to the multiplication of the semiring, it would also suffice to consider commutative monoids $(K, +, 0)$. Since we

Example 3. If $K = \mathbb{B}$ with the usual order, i.e., $0 < 1$, then $=(\bar{x}, \bar{y})$, $\bar{x} \leq \bar{y}$, and $\bar{x} \perp \bar{y}$ correspond to functional dependency $\mathrm{Var}(\bar{x}) \rightarrow \mathrm{Var}(\bar{y})$, inclusion dependency $\bar{x} \subseteq \bar{y}$, and embedded multivalued dependency $\emptyset \twoheadrightarrow \mathrm{Var}(\bar{x})|\mathrm{Var}(\bar{y})$ over (uni)relational databases. For any $\mathbb{B}$-team $\mathbb{X}$, the corresponding database relation is $\mathrm{Supp}(\mathbb{X})$. If $K = \mathbb{R}_{\geq 0}$, then $\bar{x} \approx \bar{y}$, $\bar{x} \approx^* \bar{y}$, and $\bar{x} \perp \bar{y}$ correspond to marginal identity, marginal distribution equivalence, and independence over probability distributions. Note that each $\mathbb{R}_{\geq 0}$-team $\mathbb{X}$ can be viewed as the probability distribution $p_{\mathbb{X}}$ obtained by normalizing $\mathbb{X}$, i.e., $p_{\mathbb{X}} \colon X \rightarrow [0, 1]$ such that $p_{\mathbb{X}}(s) = \mathbb{X}(s)/|\mathbb{X}|$ for any $s \in X$; this is also why $\mathbb{R}_{\geq 0}$ is called the probability semiring.

As seen in the above example, the atoms other than the marginal distribution inclusion atom $\bar{x} \subseteq^* \bar{y}$ already appear in the literature at least for some semirings. The idea of $\bar{x} \subseteq^* \bar{y}$ is to introduce a non-symmetric variant of the marginal distribution equivalence atom $\bar{x} \approx^* \bar{y}$ analogously to the way that $\bar{x} \leq \bar{y}$ relates to $\bar{x} \approx \bar{y}$. For example, in the case of the Boolean semiring, $\bar{x} \subseteq^* \bar{y}$ states that $|X(\bar{x})| \leq |X(\bar{y})|$, i.e., in the support of the team, the number of different values for $\bar{x}$ is at most the number of different values for $\bar{y}$. For the tropical semiring, $\bar{x} \subseteq^* \bar{y}$ states that the minimal weight of any value in $X(\bar{x})$ must also appear in $X(\bar{y})$ for some value. In the next section, we will see that $\bar{x} \leq \bar{y}$ and $\bar{x} \subseteq^* \bar{y}$ are symmetric over additively cancellative semirings, so it does not make sense to consider these variants, e.g., in the case of semirings $\mathbb{N}$ or $\mathbb{R}_{\geq 0}$.

3 Implication Problems and Axiomatizations Under Semiring Semantics

In this section, we define implication problems and axiomatizations in the general framework of semiring semantics, and show that certain axiomatizations completely characterize implication problems over suitable classes of semirings.

3.1 Implication Problems

For a finite set of atoms $\Sigma \cup \{\tau\}$ such that $\mathrm{Var}(\Sigma \cup \{\tau\}) \subseteq D$, we write $\Sigma \models_K \tau$ if $\mathbb{X} \models \Sigma$ implies $\mathbb{X} \models \tau$ for all K-teams $\mathbb{X}$ of X over D. If $\Sigma \models_K \tau$, we say that Σ *logically implies* τ over K. The implication problem for a class of atoms $\mathcal{C}$ over K is defined as follows: given a finite set $\Sigma \cup \{\tau\}$ of atoms from class $\mathcal{C}$, decide whether $\Sigma \models_K \tau$. If the semiring K is clear from the context, we write $\Sigma \models \tau$ instead of $\Sigma \models_K \tau$.

Before we define axiomatizations to characterize the implication problems for different classes of atoms, we present some results concerning logical implication that depend on certain properties of the semiring.

Proposition 1. *(i)* $\{\bar{x} \leq \bar{y}\} \models_K \{\bar{y} \leq \bar{x}\}$ *iff* K *is additively cancellative,*

---

consider these atoms together with independence atoms that concern multiplication, we have decided to stay in the semiring framework.

(ii) $\{\bar{x} \subseteq^* \bar{y}\} \models_K \{\bar{y} \subseteq^* \bar{x}\}$ *iff for all* $a, b \in K$, $a + b = a$ *implies* $b = 0$.

Proof. We first show the right-to-left directions of the claims. For item (i), we show that if K is additively cancellative, then $|\mathbb{X}_{\bar{x}=\bar{a}}| \leq |\mathbb{X}_{\bar{y}=\bar{a}}|$ for all $\bar{a} \in A^{|\bar{x}|}$ implies $|\mathbb{X}_{\bar{x}=\bar{a}}| = |\mathbb{X}_{\bar{y}=\bar{a}}|$ for all $\bar{a} \in A^{|\bar{x}|}$, which means that $\{\bar{x} \leq \bar{y}\} \models_K \{\bar{y} \leq \bar{x}\}$. Suppose for a contradiction that $|\mathbb{X}_{\bar{x}=\bar{a}}| < |\mathbb{X}_{\bar{y}=\bar{a}}|$ for some $\bar{a} \in A^{|\bar{x}|}$. Then by Lemma 1, $\sum_{\bar{a} \in A^{|\bar{x}|}} |\mathbb{X}_{\bar{x}=\bar{a}}| < \sum_{\bar{a} \in A^{|\bar{x}|}} |\mathbb{X}_{\bar{y}=\bar{a}}|$. This is a contradiction, as $\sum_{\bar{a} \in A^n} |\mathbb{X}_{\bar{x}=\bar{a}}| = |\mathbb{X}| = \sum_{\bar{a} \in A^n} |\mathbb{X}_{\bar{y}=\bar{a}}|$. For item (ii), we show that if for all $a, b \in K$, $a + b = a$ implies $b = 0$, then $\{\{|\mathbb{X}_{\bar{x}=\bar{a}}| : \bar{a} \in X(\bar{x})\}\} \subseteq \{\{|\mathbb{X}_{\bar{y}=\bar{a}}| : \bar{a} \in X(\bar{y})\}\}$ implies $\{\{|\mathbb{X}_{\bar{x}=\bar{a}}| : \bar{a} \in X(\bar{x})\}\} = \{\{|\mathbb{X}_{\bar{y}=\bar{a}}| : \bar{a} \in X(\bar{y})\}\}$, which means that $\{\bar{x} \subseteq^* \bar{y}\} \models_K \{\bar{y} \subseteq^* \bar{x}\}$. From $\bar{x} \subseteq^* \bar{y}$, it follows that there exists an injective function $f \colon X(\bar{x}) \to X(\bar{y})$ such that $|\mathbb{X}_{\bar{x}=\bar{a}}| = |\mathbb{X}_{\bar{y}=f(\bar{a})}|$ for all $\bar{a} \in X(\bar{x})$. It suffices to show that f is surjective. If this is not the case, let $B = X(\bar{y}) \setminus f(X(\bar{x}))$. Now we have $|\mathbb{X}| = \sum_{\bar{a} \in X(\bar{x})} |\mathbb{X}_{\bar{x}=\bar{a}}| = \sum_{\bar{a} \in X(\bar{x})} |\mathbb{X}_{\bar{y}=f(\bar{a})}| \neq \sum_{\bar{a} \in X(\bar{x})} |\mathbb{X}_{\bar{y}=f(\bar{a})}| + \sum_{\bar{b} \in B} |\mathbb{X}_{\bar{y}=\bar{b}}| = \sum_{\bar{a} \in X(\bar{y})} |\mathbb{X}_{\bar{y}=\bar{a}}| = |\mathbb{X}|$, where the inequality follows from $0 \neq \sum_{\bar{b} \in B} |\mathbb{X}_{\bar{y}=\bar{b}}|$ by the assumption. Since $|\mathbb{X}| \neq |\mathbb{X}|$ is clearly a contradiction, the claim follows.

We now show the left-to-right directions by contraposition. Without loss of generality, we show the claims for unary atoms. For item (i), suppose that K is not additively cancellative. Then there exists $a, b, c \in K$ such that $a + b = a + c$, but $b < c$. Let $\mathbb{X}$ be as in Table 1 of Example 2, and assume that the elements $a, b, c \in K$ of the table are such that $a+b = a+c$ and $b < c$. Then $|\mathbb{X}_{x=0}| = a+b = a + c = |\mathbb{X}_{y=0}|$ and $|\mathbb{X}_{x=1}| = b < c = |\mathbb{X}_{y=1}|$, so $\mathbb{X} \models x \leq y$, but $\mathbb{X} \not\models y \leq x$, meaning that $\{\bar{x} \leq \bar{y}\} \not\models_K \{\bar{y} \leq \bar{x}\}$. For item (ii), let again $\mathbb{X}$ be as in Table 1, but this time assume that $a, b, c \in K$ are such that $a + b = a$, $b \neq 0$, and $c = 0$. Then $|\mathbb{X}_{x=0}| = a + b = a + c = a = |\mathbb{X}_{y=0}|$, but $|\mathbb{X}_{x=1}| = c = 0 \neq b = |\mathbb{X}_{y=1}|$. Hence, $\{\{|\mathbb{X}_{x=a}| : a \in X(x)\}\} = \{\{a\}\} \subsetneq \{\{a, b\}\} = \{\{|\mathbb{X}_{y=a}| : a \in X(y)\}\}$, so $\mathbb{X} \models x \subseteq^* y$, but $\mathbb{X} \not\models y \subseteq^* x$, meaning that $\{\bar{x} \subseteq^* \bar{y}\} \not\models_K \{\bar{y} \subseteq^* \bar{x}\}$.

Note that if K is additively cancellative, then in particular, $a+b = a$ implies $b = 0$ for all $a, b \in K$. As a consequence of Proposition 1, $\mathbb{X} \models \bar{x} \leq \bar{y}$ iff $\mathbb{X} \models \bar{x} \approx \bar{y}$ and $\mathbb{X} \models \bar{x} \subseteq^* \bar{y}$ iff $\mathbb{X} \models \bar{x} \approx^* \bar{y}$ for any K-team $\mathbb{X}$, where K is additively cancellative. Hence, for additively cancellative semirings, we consider the atoms $\bar{x} \approx \bar{y}$ and $\bar{x} \approx^* \bar{y}$ instead of $\bar{x} \leq \bar{y}$, and $\bar{x} \subseteq^* \bar{y}$.

3.2 Sound Axiomatizations

An axiom is an expression of the form $\Lambda \vdash \tau$, where Λ is a set of atoms and τ is a single atom. For a set of axioms $\mathcal{A}$, we define the deduction relation $\vdash_{\mathcal{A}}$ such that $\Sigma \vdash_{\mathcal{A}} \sigma$ if and only if there is a finite sequence $(\tau_1, \ldots, \tau_n)$ of atoms such that $\tau_n = \sigma$, and for each τ_i, $i \in \{1, \ldots, n\}$, either $\tau_i \in \Sigma$ or $\Lambda \vdash \tau_i \in \mathcal{A}$ for some $\Lambda \subseteq \Sigma \cup \{\tau_1, \ldots, \tau_{i-1}\}$. If $\Sigma \vdash_{\mathcal{A}} \sigma$, we say that there is an $\mathcal{A}$-deduction of σ from Σ. Note that if $\Lambda \vdash \tau \in \mathcal{A}$, then also $\Lambda \vdash_{\mathcal{A}} \tau$. We sometimes write $\Sigma \vdash \sigma$ instead of $\Sigma \vdash_{\mathcal{A}} \sigma$, if the set of axioms $\mathcal{A}$ is clear from the context. We say that the set of axioms $\mathcal{A}$ is *sound* for a class of semirings $\mathcal{C}$, if $\Sigma \vdash_{\mathcal{A}} \tau$ implies $\Sigma \models_K \tau$ for all $\Sigma \cup \{\tau\}$ and all $K \in \mathcal{C}$.

We denote by $\mathcal{A}_{FD}$ the *Armstrong axiomatization* [1] consisting of the following three axioms on the left; reflexivity, transitivity, and augmentation. When restricted to unary FDs, we use the notation $\mathcal{A}_{UFD}$ for the set of the following axioms on the right.

FD1 $\emptyset \vdash =(\bar{x}, \bar{x}'),\ \mathrm{Var}(\bar{x}') \subseteq \mathrm{Var}(\bar{x})$	UFD1 $\emptyset \vdash =(x, x)$
FD2 $\{=(\bar{x}, \bar{y}), =(\bar{y}, \bar{z})\} \vdash =(\bar{x}, \bar{z})$	UFD2 $\{=(x, y), =(y, z)\} \vdash =(x, z)$
FD3 $\{=(\bar{x}, \bar{y})\} \vdash =(\bar{x}\bar{z}, \bar{y}\bar{z})$	UFD3 $\{=(y)\} \vdash =(x, y)$

Let $1 \leq k \leq n$, and denote by ρ_k any function $\rho_k\colon D^n \to D^k$ such that $\rho_k(x_1, \ldots, x_n) = (x_{i_1}, \ldots, x_{i_k})$ for all $(x_1, \ldots, x_n) \in D^n$, where $i_1, \ldots, i_k$ is a sequence of distinct elements from $\{1, \ldots, n\}$. Let P^n_k be the set of these functions ρ_k, and define $P^n = \bigcup_{1 \leq k \leq n} P^n_k$. We define the axiomatizations $\mathcal{A}_{IND}$ and $\mathcal{A}_{MI}$, consisting of the following axioms for INDs [4] and MIs [18], respectively.

IND1 $\emptyset \vdash \bar{x} \leq \bar{x}$	MI1 $\emptyset \vdash \bar{x} \approx \bar{x}$
	MI2 $\{\bar{x} \approx \bar{y}\} \vdash \bar{y} \approx \bar{x}$
IND2 $\{\bar{x} \leq \bar{y}, \bar{y} \leq \bar{z}\} \vdash \bar{x} \leq \bar{z}$	MI3 $\{\bar{x} \approx \bar{y}, \bar{y} \approx \bar{z}\} \vdash \bar{x} \approx \bar{z}$
IND3 $\{\bar{x} \leq \bar{y}\} \vdash \rho(\bar{x}) \leq \rho(\bar{y}),\ \rho \in P^{\lvert\bar{x}\rvert}$	MI4 $\{\bar{x} \approx \bar{y}\} \vdash \rho(\bar{x}) \approx \rho(\bar{y}),\ \rho \in P^{\lvert\bar{x}\rvert}$

For IND*s and MDEs, we define the sets $\mathcal{A}_{IND^*}$ and $\mathcal{A}_{MDE}$, consisting of the corresponding axioms below.

IND*1 $\emptyset \vdash \bar{x} \subseteq^* \bar{x}$
IND*2 $\{\bar{x} \subseteq^* \bar{y}, \bar{y} \subseteq^* \bar{z}\} \vdash \bar{x} \subseteq^* \bar{z}$
IND*3 $\{\bar{x} \subseteq^* \bar{y}\} \vdash \rho(\bar{x}) \subseteq^* \rho'(\bar{y}),\ \rho \in P^{\lvert\bar{x}\rvert}_{\lvert\bar{x}\rvert}, \rho' \in P^{\lvert\bar{y}\rvert}_{\lvert\bar{y}\rvert}$.

MDE1 $\emptyset \vdash \bar{x} \approx^* \bar{x}$
MDE2 $\{\bar{x} \approx^* \bar{y}\} \vdash \bar{y} \approx^* \bar{x}$
MDE3 $\{\bar{x} \approx^* \bar{y}, \bar{y} \approx^* \bar{z}\} \vdash \bar{x} \approx^* \bar{z}$
MDE4 $\{\bar{x} \approx^* \bar{y}\} \vdash \rho(\bar{x}) \approx^* \rho'(\bar{y}),\ \rho \in P^{\lvert\bar{x}\rvert}_{\lvert\bar{x}\rvert}, \rho' \in P^{\lvert\bar{y}\rvert}_{\lvert\bar{y}\rvert}$.

For UINDs, UIND*s, UMIs, and UMDEs, we define the axiomatizations $\mathcal{A}_{UIND}$, $\mathcal{A}_{UIND^*}$, $\mathcal{A}_{UMI}$, and $\mathcal{A}_{UMDE}$, consisting of the unary variants of the axioms IND1-2, IND*1-2, MI1-3, and MDE1-3, respectively. For IAs, we define the axiomatization $\mathcal{A}_{IA}$, consisting of the axioms listed below.

IA1 $\emptyset \vdash \emptyset \perp \bar{x}$
IA2 $\{\bar{x} \perp \bar{y}\} \vdash \bar{y} \perp \bar{x}$
IA3 $\{\bar{x} \perp \bar{y}\} \vdash \bar{x}' \perp \bar{y}',\ \mathrm{Var}(\bar{x}') \subseteq \mathrm{Var}(\bar{x}), \mathrm{Var}(\bar{y}') \subseteq \mathrm{Var}(\bar{y})$
IA4 $\{\bar{x} \perp \bar{y}, \bar{x}\bar{y} \perp \bar{z}\} \vdash \bar{x} \perp \bar{y}\bar{z}$

For the interaction of MIs and MDEs, CAs and MDEs, and IAs and FDs, respectively, we define the following axioms.

MI & MDE $\{\bar{x} \approx \bar{y}\} \vdash \bar{x} \approx^* \bar{y}$

CA & MDE 1 $\{\bar{x} \approx^* \bar{y}, =(\bar{y})\} \vdash =(\bar{x})$ IA & FD 1 $\{\bar{x} \perp \bar{y}, =(\bar{z})\} \vdash \bar{x} \perp \bar{y}\bar{z}$
CA & MDE 2 $\{=(\bar{x}), =(\bar{y})\} \vdash \bar{x} \approx^* \bar{y}$ IA & FD 2 $\{\bar{x} \perp \bar{y}, =(\bar{x}, \bar{y})\} \vdash =(\bar{y})$

We also define the following notations for the sets of axioms for MIs and MDEs: $\mathcal{A}_{MI\&MDE} := \{MI\ \&\ MDE\}$, for CAs and MDEs: $\mathcal{A}_{CA\&MDE} := \{CA\ \&\ MDE\ 1, CA\ \&\ MDE\ 2\}$, and for IAs and FDs: $\mathcal{A}_{IA\&FD} := \{IA\ \&\ FD\ 1, IA\ \&\ FD\ 2\}$. We also use analogous notations for the unary variants of the axioms and sets defined above.

Let $k \in \{1, 3, 5, \dots\}$ and define $S_k\colon \{0, 1, \dots, k\} \to \{0, 1, \dots, k\}$ such that $S_k(i) = i+1 \mod k+1$. We then define the following axioms for the interaction of UFDs and UINDs, and UFDs and UMDEs, respectively.

k-CYCLE-UIND
$\{=(x_i, x_{S_k(i)}) : 0 \leq i \leq k-1, i \text{ even}\} \cup \{x_{S_k(i)} \leq x_i : 1 \leq i \leq k, i \text{ odd}\} \vdash$
$=(x_{S_k(i)}, x_i),\ 0 \leq i \leq k-1, i$ even, and $x_i \leq x_{S_k(i)},\ 1 \leq i \leq k, i$ odd

k-CYCLE-UMDE
$\{=(x_i, x_{S_k(i)}) : 0 \leq i \leq k-1, i \text{ even}\} \cup \{x_i \approx^* x_{S_k(i)} : 1 \leq i \leq k, i \text{ odd}\} \vdash$
$=(x_{S_k(i)}, x_i),\ 0 \leq i \leq k-1, i$ even, and $x_i \approx^* x_{S_k(i)},\ 0 \leq i \leq k-1, i$ even

Since the cycle rules are defined for each odd k, we define the following infinite sets of axioms to cover all k-cycle rules $\mathcal{A}_{CYCLE-UIND} := \{k\text{-CYCLE-UIND} : k \in \mathbb{N}, k \text{ is odd}\}$ and $\mathcal{A}_{CYCLE-UMDE} := \{k\text{-CYCLE-UMDE} : k \in \mathbb{N}, k \text{ is odd}\}$.

We now show that these axioms are sound for suitable classes of semirings.

Proposition 2. *The axioms $\mathcal{A}_{FD}$, $\mathcal{A}_{IND}$, $\mathcal{A}_{IND^*}$, $\mathcal{A}_{MI}$, $\mathcal{A}_{MDE}$, $\mathcal{A}_{MI\&MDE}$, $\mathcal{A}_{CA\&MDE}$, $\mathcal{A}_{CYCLE-UIND}$, and $\mathcal{A}_{CYCLE-UMDE}$ are sound for any semiring K.*

Proof. The axioms and the satisfaction relation for FDs are the same as in the case of relational databases [1], so it is easy to see that the axioms are sound. Excluding the cycle rules, the soundness of the other axioms follows straightforwardly from the definitions of the marginal and the satisfaction relation for the relevant atoms.

For the cycle rules, the soundness proofs are similar to the Boolean and the probability semiring cases of [7,20], except that for k-cycle-UIND the situation is slightly more complicated in the case of general K. For a team $\mathbb{X}\colon X \to K$, we have that $=(x, y)$ implies $|X(y)| \leq |X(x)|$, $x \leq y$ implies $X(x) \subseteq X(y)$, and $x \approx^* y$ implies $|X(x)| = |X(y)|$. Hence, the existence of the alternating FD/IND (or FD/UMDE) cycle $x_0, x_1 \dots, x_k, x_0$ implies that $|X(x_i)| = |X(x_j)|$ for all $i, j \in \{0, 1, \dots, k\}$. By the finiteness of X, this means that each surjective function associated with $=(x_i, x_{S_k(i)})$, where i even, is also injective, implying that $=(x_{S_k(i)}, x_i)$.

For UMDEs, note that the existence of the bijective function f associated with $=(x_i, x_{S_k(i)})$ and $=(x_{S_k(i)}, x_i)$ implies that $|\mathbb{X}_{x_i=a}| = |\mathbb{X}_{x_{S_k(i)}=f(a)}|$ for all $a \in X(x_i)$ and $|\mathbb{X}_{x_i=f^{-1}(b)}| = |\mathbb{X}_{x_{S_k(i)}=b}|$ for all $b \in X(x_{S_k(i)})$, so we have $x_i \approx^* x_{S_k(i)}$.

For the case of UINDs, first define an equivalence relation $\sim$ on A such that $a \sim b$ iff $|\mathbb{X}_{x_0=a}| = |\mathbb{X}_{x_0=b}|$. Denote by $[a]$ the equivalence class of a under $\sim$. The total zero-min order on K induces an order on the equivalence classes such that $[a] \leq [b]$ iff $|\mathbb{X}_{x_0=a}| \leq |\mathbb{X}_{x_0=b}|$. Let $a_0 \in A$ be such that its equivalence class is the smallest in this order. Then

$$\begin{aligned}|\mathbb{X}_{x_0=a_0}| &= |\mathbb{X}_{x_1=f_1(a_0)}| \geq |\mathbb{X}_{x_2=f_1(a_0)}| \\ &= |\mathbb{X}_{x_3=(f_3\circ f_1)(a_0)}| \geq |\mathbb{X}_{x_4=(f_3\circ f_1)(a_0)}| \cdots \\ &= |\mathbb{X}_{x_k=(f_k\circ\cdots\circ f_1)(a_0)}| \geq |\mathbb{X}_{x_0=(f_k\circ\cdots\circ f_1)(a_0)}|,\end{aligned}$$

where each $f_i \colon A \to A$ is some bijective extension of the bijective function from $X(x_{S_k^{-1}(i)})$ to $X(x_i)$ associated with $=(x_{S_k^{-1}(i)}, x_i)$ for an odd i. If any of the inequalities is strict, then $|\mathbb{X}_{x_0=a_0}| > |\mathbb{X}_{x_0=(f_k\circ\cdots\circ f_1)(a_0)}|$. This is a contradiction as $|\mathbb{X}_{x_0=a_0}|$ is the smallest marginal of x_0. This means that all of the inequalities above are actually equalities, i.e., $|\mathbb{X}_{x_i=(f_i\circ\cdots\circ f_1)(a_0)}| = |\mathbb{X}_{x_{S_k(i)}=(f_i\circ\cdots\circ f_1)(a_0)}|$ for all odd i. Moreover, since each f_i is injective, the composite function $f_k \circ \cdots \circ f_1$ is also injective, and $(f_k \circ \cdots \circ f_1) \upharpoonright [a_0]$ must be a permutation on $[a_0]$.

Suppose then that $|\mathbb{X}_{x_i=(f_i\circ\cdots\circ f_1)(a_n)}| = |\mathbb{X}_{x_{S_k(i)}=(f_i\circ\cdots\circ f_1)(a_n)}|$ for all odd i and the function $(f_k \circ \cdots \circ f_1) \upharpoonright [a_n]$ is a permutation on $[a_n]$. Let then $a_{n+1} \in A$ be such that its equivalence class is minimal in $(A/\sim) \setminus \{[a_0], \ldots, [a_n]\}$. Now $(f_k \circ \cdots \circ f_1)(a_{n+1}) \notin \bigcup_{j=0}^{n}[a_j]$, and we can repeat an argument analogous to the case of a_0 to obtain that $|\mathbb{X}_{x_i=(f_i\circ\cdots\circ f_1)(a_{n+1})}| = |\mathbb{X}_{x_{S_k(i)}=(f_i\circ\cdots\circ f_1)(a_{n+1})}|$ for all odd i and the function $(f_k \circ \cdots \circ f_1) \upharpoonright [a_{n+1}]$ is a permutation on $[a_{n+1}]$. Hence, we have $|\mathbb{X}_{x_i=(f_i\circ\cdots\circ f_1)(a)}| = |\mathbb{X}_{x_{S_k(i)}=(f_i\circ\cdots\circ f_1)(a)}|$ for all $a \in A$ and odd i. Since $(f_i \circ \cdots \circ f_1)(A) = A$, we have $|\mathbb{X}_{x_i=a}| = |\mathbb{X}_{x_{S_k(i)}=a}|$ for all $a \in A$, and $x_i \leq x_{S_k(i)}$ for all odd i.

The following claim is straightforward to check (and was partly proven in [15]).

Proposition 3. *The axioms $\mathcal{A}_{IA}$ and $\mathcal{A}_{IA\&FD}$ are sound for any commutative and multiplicatively cancellative semiring K.*

3.3 Complete Axiomatizations over Classes of Positive Semirings with and Without Additive Cancellativity

In this section, we show that some of the axiomatizations from the previous section completely characterize certain implication problems, i.e., they are complete for the corresponding class of atoms over a suitable class of semirings. We say that axiomatization $\mathcal{A}$ is *complete* for a class of atoms $\mathcal{C}$ over a class of semirings $\mathcal{C}'$, if $\Sigma \models_K \tau$ implies $\Sigma \vdash_{\mathcal{A}} \tau$ for all sets $\Sigma \cup \{\tau\}$ of atoms from the class $\mathcal{C}$ and all semirings K from $\mathcal{C}'$.

The separate considerations for semirings with and without additive cancellativity are important for our results because additive cancellativity affects the symmetry properties of some atoms. Recall that if K is additively cancellative, the atoms $\bar{x} \leq \bar{y}$ and $\bar{x} \approx \bar{y}$, and the atoms $\bar{x} \subseteq^* \bar{y}$ and $\bar{x} \approx^* \bar{y}$ are equivalent.

If K is not additively cancellative, we can consider the non-symmetric variants $\bar{x} \leq \bar{y}$ and $\bar{x} \subseteq^* \bar{y}$ instead.

We begin by noting that it is known that the axiomatization for MIs over probability distributions introduced in [18] is known to be complete for any positive semiring.

Theorem 1 ([15]). *The axiomatization $\mathcal{A}_{MI}$ is sound and complete for the implication problem for MIs over any semiring K.*

We now show that many axiomatizations originally introduced in the relational or the probabilistic setting, i.e., $K = \mathbb{B}$ or $K = \mathbb{R}_{\geq 0}$, are complete more generally over some classes of semirings. Recall that throughout this paper we assume that the semiring K is positive. Since the soundness of the axiomatizations follows from Propositions 2 and 3, it suffices to prove the completeness for each theorem.

We first present some results for additively cancellative semirings. We begin by showing that the axiomatization $\mathcal{A}_{FD+UMI+UMDE} := \mathcal{A}_{FD} \cup \mathcal{A}_{UMI} \cup \mathcal{A}_{UMDE} \cup \mathcal{A}_{UMI\&UMDE} \cup \mathcal{A}_{CYCLE-UMDE}$ is sound and complete for the implication problem for FDs+UMIs+UMDEs over any additively cancellative semiring K. The proof is a simple modification of the proof for the analogous completeness result in the more restricted case of probability distributions [20].

Let $\mathcal{A}$ be an axiomatization and D a set of variables such that $\mathrm{Var}(\Sigma) \subseteq D$. Define the closure of Σ under $\mathcal{A}$ and D as $\mathrm{Cl}_{\mathcal{A},D}(\Sigma) := \{\sigma : \Sigma \vdash_{\mathcal{A}} \sigma, \mathrm{Var}(\sigma) \subseteq D\}$. If $\mathcal{A}$ and D are clear from the context we just write $\mathrm{Cl}(\Sigma)$.

Lemma 2 ([20]). *Let Σ be a set of FDs, UMIs, and UMDEs such that $\mathrm{Var}(\Sigma) \subseteq D$. Then there exists $A = \{0, \ldots, n\}$, and a set X of assignments $s\colon D \to A$ that satisfies the following properties, where $(A_u, m_u) := \{\{s(u) \in A : s \in X\}\}$ for all $u \in D$.*

(i) for $\sigma :== (\bar{x}, \bar{y})$, $\sigma \in \mathrm{Cl}(\Sigma)$ iff for all $s, s' \in X$, $s(\bar{x}) = s'(\bar{x})$ implies $s(\bar{y}) = s'(\bar{y})$,
(ii) for $\sigma := x \approx y$, $\sigma \in \mathrm{Cl}(\Sigma)$ iff $(A_x, m_x) = (A_y, m_y)$,
(iii) for $\sigma := x \approx^* y$, $\sigma \in \mathrm{Cl}(\Sigma)$ iff $\{\{m_x(i) : i \in A_x\}\} = \{\{m_y(i) : i \in A_y\}\}$.

Theorem 2. *The axiomatization $\mathcal{A}_{FD+UMI+UMDE}$ is sound and complete for the implication problem for FDs+UMIs+UMDEs over any additively cancellative semiring K.*

Proof. Construct the set X as in Lemma 2, and define $\mathbb{X}\colon X \to K$ as $\mathbb{X}(s) = 1$ for all $s \in X$. We show that $\mathbb{X} \models \sigma$ iff $\sigma \in \mathrm{Cl}(\Sigma)$, which implies the completeness by contraposition, since it provides a K-team witnessing $\Sigma \not\models \sigma$ for any $\sigma \notin \mathrm{Cl}(\Sigma)$. Assume first that $\sigma :==(\bar{x}, \bar{y})$. Note that $\mathrm{Supp}(\mathbb{X}) = X$, so by Lemma 2, item (i), we have $\mathbb{X} \models \sigma$ iff $\sigma \in \mathrm{Cl}(\Sigma)$. Assume then that $\sigma := x \approx y$. Extend the functions $m_u : A_u \to \{1, 2, \ldots\}$ to A by defining $m_u(i) = 0$ for any $i \in A \setminus A_u$. Note that by positivity and additive cancellativity of K, $\sum_{1 \leq j \leq m_x(i)} 1 \neq \sum_{1 \leq j \leq m_y(i)} 1$ for any $i \in A$ such that $m_x(i) \neq m_y(i)$. By Lemma 2, item (ii), we have $\sigma \in \mathrm{Cl}(\Sigma)$ iff $(A_x, m_x) = (A_y, m_y)$. By the definition of $\mathbb{X}$, we then have $(A_x, m_x) = (A_y, m_y)$

iff $|\mathbb{X}_{x=i}| = \sum_{1\leq j\leq m_x(i)} 1 = \sum_{1\leq j\leq m_y(i)} 1 = |\mathbb{X}_{y=i}|$ for all $i \in A$. Hence, $\mathbb{X} \models \sigma$ iff $\sigma \in \mathrm{Cl}(\Sigma)$. Assume finally that $\sigma := x \approx^* y$. Then by Lemma 2, item (iii), $\sigma \in \mathrm{Cl}(\Sigma)$ iff $\{\{m_x(i) : i \in A_x\}\} = \{\{m_y(i) : i \in A_y\}\}$ iff $\{\{|\mathbb{X}_{x=i}| : i \in X(x)\}\} = \{\{|\mathbb{X}_{y=i}| : i \in X(y)\}\}$ iff $\mathbb{X} \models \sigma$.

Note that the proof of Theorem 2 also entails the existence of the so-called *Armstrong relations* for the class FD+UMI+UMDE.

Definition 2. *Let Σ be a set of atoms of class $\mathcal{C}$. We say that a K-team $\mathbb{X}$ is an* Armstrong relation *for Σ over K if $\mathbb{X} \models \sigma$ iff $\Sigma \models \sigma$. We say that class $\mathcal{C}$* enjoys Armstrong relations *over K if every finite set of atoms of class $\mathcal{C}$ has an Armstrong relation over K.*

Corollary 1. *The class FD+UMI+UMDE enjoys Armstrong relations over any positive and additively cancellative semiring K.*

It is known that for probability distributions (i.e., $K = \mathbb{R}_{\geq 0}$), the only interaction between non-disjoint IAs and UMIs or UMDEs is via constancy atoms expressed as $x \perp x$, so non-disjoint IAs can be considered separately as disjoint IAs and UCAs [19]. Since IAs are required to be disjoint in our setting, we can consider disjoint IAs, UCAs (expressed as $=\!(x)$), UMIs, and UMDEs instead of non-disjoint IAs, UMIs, and UMDEs. We define $\mathcal{A}_{IA+UCA+UMI+UMDE} := \mathcal{A}_{IA} \cup \{IA\ \&\ FD\ 1\} \cup \mathcal{A}_{UCA\&UMDE} \cup \mathcal{A}_{UMI} \cup \mathcal{A}_{UMDE} \cup \mathcal{A}_{UMI\&UMDE}$. The below lemma essentially follows from [19], as the the proof can be adapted for UCAs.

Lemma 3 ([19]). *Let $\Sigma \cup \{\tau\}$ be a set of (disjoint) IAs, UCAs, UMIs, and UMDEs such that* $\mathrm{Var}(\Sigma \cup \{\tau\}) \subseteq D$ *and $\tau \notin \mathrm{Cl}(\Sigma)$. Then there exists a $\mathbb{R}_{\geq 0}$-team $\mathbb{X} : X \to \mathbb{R}_{\geq 0}$ over D such that $\mathbb{X}(s) = 1/|X|$ for all $s \in X$, and $\mathbb{X} \models \Sigma$, but $\mathbb{X} \not\models \tau$.*

Now we obtain the following theorem by using the above lemma.

Theorem 3. *The axiomatization $\mathcal{A}_{IA+UCA+UMI+UMDE}$ is sound and complete for the implication problem for IAs+UCAs+UMIs+UMDEs over any additively and multiplicatively cancellative commutative semiring K.*

Proof. Suppose that $\Sigma \not\vdash \tau$. We show that $\Sigma \not\models \tau$ by constructing a K-team $\mathbb{X}$ such that $\mathbb{X} \models \Sigma$, but $\mathbb{X} \not\models \tau$. Construct the set X as in Lemma 3, and define $\mathbb{X}\colon X \to K$ as $\mathbb{X}(s) = 1$ for all $s \in X$. Let $\mathbb{X}'$ be the $\mathbb{R}_{\geq 0}$-team of Lemma 3. We show that for all $\sigma \in \Sigma \cup \{\tau\}$, $\mathbb{X} \models \sigma$ iff $\mathbb{X}' \models \sigma$. Now $\mathbb{X}' \models \bar{x} \perp \bar{y}$ iff $|\mathbb{X}'_{\bar{x}\bar{y}=\bar{a}\bar{b}}| \times |\mathbb{X}'| = |\mathbb{X}'_{\bar{x}=\bar{a}}| \times |\mathbb{X}'_{\bar{y}=\bar{b}}|$ for all $\bar{a}\bar{b} \in A^{|\bar{x}\bar{y}|}$. Note that by the definition of $\mathbb{X}$, we have $|\mathbb{X}_{\bar{z}=\bar{c}}| = \sum_{1\leq i\leq |X|\times|\mathbb{X}'_{\bar{z}=\bar{c}}|} 1$ for all $\bar{z} \in D^{|\bar{z}|}$ and $\bar{c} \in A^{|\bar{z}|}$. Then $|\mathbb{X}'_{\bar{x}\bar{y}=\bar{a}\bar{b}}| \times |\mathbb{X}'| = |\mathbb{X}'_{\bar{x}=\bar{a}}| \times |\mathbb{X}'_{\bar{y}=\bar{b}}|$ iff $|X| \times |\mathbb{X}'_{\bar{x}\bar{y}=\bar{a}\bar{b}}| \times |X| \times |\mathbb{X}'| = |X| \times |\mathbb{X}'_{\bar{x}=\bar{a}}| \times |X| \times |\mathbb{X}'_{\bar{y}=\bar{b}}|$ iff $|\mathbb{X}_{\bar{x}\bar{y}=\bar{a}\bar{b}}| \times |\mathbb{X}| = |\mathbb{X}_{\bar{x}=\bar{a}}| \times |\mathbb{X}_{\bar{y}=\bar{b}}|$. Therefore $\mathbb{X}' \models \bar{x} \perp \bar{y}$ iff $\mathbb{X} \models \bar{x} \perp \bar{y}$. The claim for UMIs and UMDEs follows analogously from the observation that $|\mathbb{X}_{\bar{z}=\bar{c}}| = \sum_{1\leq i\leq |X|\times|\mathbb{X}'_{\bar{z}=\bar{c}}|} 1$ for all $\bar{z} \in D^{|\bar{z}|}$ and $\bar{c} \in A^{|\bar{z}|}$. Since $\mathrm{Supp}(\mathbb{X}') = \mathrm{Supp}(\mathbb{X})$, the claim also clearly holds for all UCAs.

We now move to the results for classes of semirings without additive cancellativity. For unary marginal distribution inclusion, the axiomatization $\mathcal{A}_{UIND^*}$ is complete for the semirings that lack the property of Proposition 1 (ii) that characterizes when the atom is symmetric.

Theorem 4. *The axiomatization $\mathcal{A}_{UIND^*}$ is sound and complete for the implication problem for UIND*s over any semiring K containing two non-zero elements a and b such that $a + b = a$.*

Proof. Suppose that $\Sigma \nvdash \tau$. We show that $\Sigma \not\models \tau$ by constructing a very simple K-team $\mathbb{X}$ such that $\mathbb{X} \models \Sigma$, but $\mathbb{X} \not\models \tau$. Let $\tau := x \subseteq^* y$, and define $Z := \{z \in D : \Sigma \vdash x \subseteq^* z\}$. Let $X := \{s, s'\}$, where $s, s' \colon D \to \{0, 1\}$ are such that $s(u) = 0$ for all $u \in D$, and $s'(u) = 1$ if $u \in Z$ and $s'(u) = 0$ if $u \in D \setminus Z$. Define then $\mathbb{X} \colon X \to K$ such that $\mathbb{X}(s) = a$ and $\mathbb{X}(s') = b$, where a and b are as in the statement of the theorem. Note that if $u \in Z$ and $u' \in D \setminus Z$, then $|\mathbb{X}_{u=0}| = a$, $|\mathbb{X}_{u=1}| = b$, $|\mathbb{X}_{u'=0}| = a + b = a$, and $|\mathbb{X}_{u'=1}| = 0$. Therefore, $\mathbb{X} \not\models u \subseteq^* u'$ iff $u \in Z$ and $u' \in D \setminus Z$. Now clearly $\mathbb{X} \not\models \tau$, because $x \in Z$ and $y \in D \setminus Z$. Let $v \subseteq^* w \in \Sigma$. Then either $\Sigma \vdash x \subseteq^* v$ or $\Sigma \nvdash x \subseteq^* v$. In the first case, by UIND*2, we have $\Sigma \vdash x \subseteq^* w$, so $v, w \in Z$, and $\mathbb{X} \models v \subseteq^* w$. In the latter case, $v \in D \setminus Z$, and thus also $\mathbb{X} \models v \subseteq^* w$.

Remark 2. The class of UIND*s does not enjoy Armstrong relations over $\mathbb{B}$: by the definition of UIND*, for all $\mathbb{B}$-teams $\mathbb{X}$ over $D = \{x, y\}$, we have $\mathbb{X} \models x \subseteq^* y$ or $\mathbb{X} \models y \subseteq^* x$, but $\{x \subseteq^* x, y \subseteq^* y\} \nvdash x \subseteq^* y$ and $\{x \subseteq^* x, y \subseteq^* y\} \nvdash y \subseteq^* x$.

Next, we show that the axiomatizations $\mathcal{A}_{IND}$, $\mathcal{A}_{FD+UIND} := \mathcal{A}_{FD} \cup \mathcal{A}_{UIND} \cup \mathcal{A}_{CYCLE-UIND}$, and $\mathcal{A}_{UFD+UIND+IA} := \mathcal{A}_{UFD} \cup \mathcal{A}_{UIND} \cup \mathcal{A}_{IA} \cup \mathcal{A}_{IA\&FD} \cup \mathcal{A}_{CYCLE-UIND}$ are sound and complete for the respective implication problems for INDs, FDs+UINDs, and UFDs+UINDs+IAs over any totally zero-min ordered (commutative) semiring K containing an idempotent non-zero element. Note that the examples of non-additively cancellative semirings given in the preliminaries section all contain idempotent non-zero elements, so this class of semirings covers, e.g., the Boolean, the tropical, and the Viterbi semirings.

In the case of the Boolean semiring, the axiomatizations $\mathcal{A}_{IND}$, $\mathcal{A}_{FD+UIND}$, and $\mathcal{A}_{UFD+UIND+IA}$ correspond to the sound and complete axiomatizations for the finite implication problems for inclusion dependencies [4], for functional dependencies and unary inclusion dependencies [7], and for unary functional dependencies, unary inclusion dependencies, and independence atoms [17] over (uni)relational databases. This means that we can utilize these results in the form of the following lemma to prove the completeness in the more general case of semirings. Note that in the lemma, we assume that the Boolean semiring has the usual order, i.e., $0 < 1$.

Lemma 4 ([4,7,10,17]).

(i) Let $\Sigma \cup \{\tau\}$ be a set of FDs and UINDs such that $\mathrm{Var}(\Sigma \cup \{\tau\}) \subseteq D$ *and $\tau \notin \mathrm{Cl}(\Sigma)$. Then there exists a Boolean team $\mathbb{X} : X \to \{0, 1\}$ over D such that $\mathbb{X}(s) = 1$ for all $s \in X$, and $\mathbb{X} \models \Sigma$, but $\mathbb{X} \not\models \tau$.*

(ii) *Let Σ be a set of INDs or a set of UFDs, UINDs, and IAs such that* $\mathrm{Var}(\Sigma) \subseteq D$. *Then there exists a Boolean team* $\mathbb{X} : X \to \{0,1\}$ *over* D *such that* $\mathbb{X}(s) = 1$ *for all* $s \in X$, *and* $\mathbb{X} \models \sigma$ *iff* $\sigma \in \mathrm{Cl}(\Sigma)$ *for all* σ.

Remark 3. For any Boolean team $\mathbb{X} : X \to \{0,1\}$, we have $\mathbb{X} \models \bar{x} \leq \bar{y}$ iff $X(\bar{x}) \subseteq X(\bar{y})$, and $\mathbb{X} \models \bar{x} \perp \bar{y}$ iff for all $s, s' \in X$, there is $s'' \in X$ such that $s''(\bar{x}) = s(\bar{x})$ and $s''(\bar{y}) = s'(\bar{y})$.

Theorem 5. *The axiomatization $\mathcal{A}_{IND}$ is sound and complete for the implication problem for INDs over any totally zero-min ordered semiring K containing an idempotent non-zero element.*

Proof. We show that there is a K-team $\mathbb{X}$ such that $\mathbb{X} \models \sigma$ iff $\sigma \in \mathrm{Cl}(\Sigma)$. Let the set X of assignments $s\colon D \to A$ be as in Lemma 4 (ii). Let $k \in K$ be an idempotent non-zero element, and define $\mathbb{X}\colon X \to K$ as $\mathbb{X}(s) = k$ for all $s \in X$. If $\sigma := \bar{x} \leq \bar{y} \in \mathrm{Cl}(\Sigma)$, then by Lemma 4 (ii) and Remark 3, we have $X(\bar{x}) \subseteq X(\bar{y})$. By the definition of $\mathbb{X}$, we then have $|\mathbb{X}_{\bar{x}=\bar{a}}| = 0 \leq |\mathbb{X}_{\bar{y}=\bar{a}}|$ or $|\mathbb{X}_{\bar{x}=\bar{a}}| = k = |\mathbb{X}_{\bar{y}=\bar{a}}|$ for all $\bar{a} \in A^{|\bar{x}|}$. Suppose then that $\sigma := \bar{x} \leq \bar{y} \notin \mathrm{Cl}(\Sigma)$. By Lemma 4 (i) and Remark 3, there is $\bar{a} \in X(\bar{x})$ such that $\bar{a} \notin X(\bar{y})$. This means that $|\mathbb{X}_{\bar{x}=\bar{a}}| = k > 0 = |\mathbb{X}_{\bar{y}=\bar{a}}|$, so $\mathbb{X} \not\models \sigma$.

The following theorem is a straightforward consequence of Lemma 4 (i) and the proof of Theorem 5.

Theorem 6. *The axiomatization $\mathcal{A}_{FD+UIND}$ is sound and complete for the implication problem for FDs+UINDs over any totally zero-min ordered semiring K containing an idempotent non-zero element.*

Finally, when IAs are also included, we obtain the following.

Theorem 7. *The axiomatization $\mathcal{A}_{UFD+UIND+IA}$ is sound and complete for the implication problem for UFDs+UINDs+IAs over any totally zero-min ordered multiplicatively cancellative and commutative semiring K containing an idempotent non-zero element.*

Proof. We show that there is a K-team $\mathbb{X}$ such that $\mathbb{X} \models \sigma$ iff $\sigma \in \mathrm{Cl}(\Sigma)$. Define $\mathbb{X}$ analogously to the proof of Theorem 5. For $\sigma :== (x, y)$ or $\sigma := x \leq y$, the claim clearly holds or can be shown as in the proof of Theorem 5. Let $\sigma := \bar{x} \perp \bar{y}$. Then by Lemma 4 (ii) and Remark 3, we have $\sigma \in \mathrm{Cl}(\Sigma)$ iff for all $s, s' \in X$, there is $s'' \in X$ such that $s''(\bar{x}) = s(\bar{x})$ and $s''(\bar{y}) = s'(\bar{y})$ iff $|\mathbb{X}_{\bar{x}\bar{y}=s(\bar{x}\bar{y})}| \times |\mathbb{X}| = |\mathbb{X}_{\bar{x}=s(\bar{x})}| \times |\mathbb{X}_{\bar{y}=s(\bar{y})}|$ for all $s\colon \mathrm{Var}(\bar{x}\bar{y}) \to A$ iff $\mathbb{X} \models \sigma$.

The proofs of Theorems 5 and 7 also entail the existence of Armstrong relations.

Corollary 2. *The class IND (UFD+UIND+IA) enjoys Armstrong relations over any totally zero-min ordered (multiplicatively cancellative and commutative) semiring K containing an idempotent non-zero element.*

In the literature, there exist polynomial time algorithms for the implication problems for FDs+UINDs [7], for UFDs+UINDs+IAs [17], for FDs+UMIs+UMDEs [20], and for IAs+UMIs+UMDEs [19] over either relational databases or probability distributions. Since we showed that the same axioms are sound and complete more generally for certain classes of semirings, we obtain the following corollary.

Corollary 3. *The implication problem is in polynomial time for*

(i) FDs+UINDs, over totally zero-min ordered semirings containing an idempotent non-zero element,
(ii) UFDs+UINDs+IAs, over totally zero-min ordered multiplicatively cancellative and commutative semirings containing an idempotent non-zero element,
(iii) FDs+UMIs+UMDEs, over additively cancellative semirings,
(iv) IAs+UCAs+UMIs+UMDEs, over additively and multiplicatively cancellative semirings.

Table 2. The table summarizes results for different implication problems. A "yes" or inclusion in a complexity class refers to the result over the class of semirings described in Table 3. In contrast, a "no" or a hardness result holds for the semiring in parentheses. The question mark symbol " ? " means that the problem is open. (For the (non)existence of Armstrong relations for FD+IND, cf. [11] for multirelational databases.) The results marked with ($\star$) are from this paper.

Implication problem	Complete ax.	Armstrong rel.	Complexity
IND	yes ($\star$)	yes ($\star$)	PSPACE-compl. ($\mathbb{B}$) [4]
IND*	?	no ($\mathbb{B}$) ($\star$)	?
MI	yes [15]	?	?
MDE	?	?	?
UIND*	yes ($\star$)	no ($\mathbb{B}$) ($\star$)	?
FD+IND	no ($\mathbb{B}$) [5]	?	undecidable ($\mathbb{B}$) [5]
FD+IA	no ($\mathbb{R}_{\geq 0}$) [21]	?	undecidable ($\mathbb{R}_{\geq 0}$) [21]
FD+UIND	yes ($\star$)	?	in polynomial time ($\star$)
FD+UMI+UMDE	yes ($\star$)	yes ($\star$)	in polynomial time ($\star$)
UFD+UIND+IA	yes ($\star$)	yes ($\star$)	in polynomial time ($\star$)
IA+UCA+UMI+UMDE	yes ($\star$)	?	in polynomial time ($\star$)
UFD+IA+UMI+UMDE	?	?	?

Table 3. The table describes for each implication problem the semiring class for which the existence of a sound and complete axiomatization is shown. The "zero-min" means that the semiring is zero-min ordered, $+$ and $\times$ refer to the additive and multiplicative cancellativity, "$a + a = a$" and "$a + b = a$" refer to the existence of an idempotent non-zero element, and two non-zero elements a and b such that $a + b = a$. A "yes"/"no" in a column means that the property is required/not allowed, and the hyphen symbol " – " means that either option is possible. Column values implied by another column are in parentheses.

Implication problem	zero-min	$+$	$\times$	$a+a=a$	$a+b=a$
IND	yes	(no)	–	yes	(yes)
UIND*	–	(no)	–	–	yes
MI [15]	–	–	–	–	–
FD+UIND	yes	(no)	–	yes	(yes)
UFD+UIND+IA	yes	(no)	yes	yes	(yes)
FD+UMI+UMDE	–	yes	–	(no)	(no)
IA+UCA+UMI+UMDE	–	yes	yes	(no)	(no)

4 Conclusion and Open Questions

In this paper, we have studied implication problems for various classes of atoms in semiring team semantics, and have shown that many known axiomatizations generalize to suitable classes of semirings. The properties of the semiring impact which atoms are sensible to consider; in particular, additive cancellativity seems to be relevant for a symmetry property of certain atoms. We list some questions that are left open in this paper.

(i) Can the completeness results for some classes of non-additively cancellative semirings be improved to require less specific assumptions?
(ii) Can the complete axiomatizations for FDs+UINDs or UFDs+UINDs+IAs be extended to cover UIND*s?
(iii) Are the axioms IND*1–IND*3 (MDE1–MDE4) complete for marginal distribution inclusion (equivalence) atoms over some classes of semirings?
(iv) Are the axioms $\mathcal{A}_{UFD} \cup \mathcal{A}_{UMI} \cup \mathcal{A}_{UMDE} \cup \mathcal{A}_{IA} \cup \mathcal{A}_{UMI\&UMDE} \cup \mathcal{A}_{IA\&FD} \cup \mathcal{A}_{CYCLE-UMDE}$ complete for UFDs+UMIs+UMDEs+IAs over some classes of semirings?

The examples of non-additively cancellative semirings given in the preliminaries section all contain idempotent non-zero elements, so the results with the assumptions used in this paper cover some well-known semirings. On the other hand, the requirement of zero-min order for weighted marginal inclusion dependencies might not be desirable for some applications that use tropical semirings for optimization, because we might actually want that the nonexistence of some value in the support prohibits the satisfaction of a weighted marginal inclusion dependency. Note that the results cannot be extended to obtain complete axiomatizations for any classes of atoms containing FDs+INDs or FDs+IAs over all positive semirings. In the first case, the reason is that the implication problem for FDs+INDs is undecidable[6] over the Boolean semiring [5]. In the latter case, this follows from the fact that the implication problem for FDs+IAs is an undecidable fragment of the implication problem for (non-disjoint) conditional independence [21].

Acknowledgments. The author thanks the anonymous referees for their valuable comments. The author received funding from the Magnus Ehrnrooth foundation.

Disclosure of Interests. The author has no competing interests to declare that are relevant to the content of this article.

References

1. Armstrong, W.W.: Dependency structures of data base relationships. In: Proceedings of IFIP World Computer Congress, pp. 580–583 (1974)
2. Atserias, A., Kolaitis, P.G.: Consistency, acyclicity, and positive semirings (2020). https://arxiv.org/abs/2009.09488
3. Barlag, T., Hannula, M., Kontinen, J., Pardal, N., Virtema, J.: Unified foundations of team semantics via semirings. In: Proceedings of the 20th International Conference on Principles of Knowledge Representation and Reasoning, KR '23 (2023). https://doi.org/10.24963/kr.2023/8
4. Casanova, M.A., Fagin, R., Papadimitriou, C.H.: Inclusion dependencies and their interaction with functional dependencies. In: Proceedings of the 1st ACM SIGACT-SIGMOD Symposium on Principles of Database Systems, PODS '82, pp. 171–176. ACM, New York (1982). https://doi.org/10.1145/588111.588141
5. Chandra, A.K., Vardi, M.Y.: The implication problem for functional and inclusion dependencies is undecidable. SIAM J. Comput. **14**(3), 671–677 (1985). https://doi.org/10.1137/0214049
6. Ciardelli, I., Roelofsen, F.: Inquisitive logic. J. Philosophical Logic **40**(1), 55–94 (2011). http://www.jstor.org/stable/41487503
7. Cosmadakis, S.S., Kanellakis, P.C., Vardi, M.Y.: Polynomial-time implication problems for unary inclusion dependencies. J. ACM **37**(1), 15–46 (1990)
8. Durand, A., Hannula, M., Kontinen, J., Meier, A., Virtema, J.: Approximation and dependence via multiteam semantics. Ann. Math. Artif. Intell. **83**(3-4), 297–320 (2018). https://doi.org/10.1007/s10472-017-9568-4
9. Durand, A., Hannula, M., Kontinen, J., Meier, A., Virtema, J.: Probabilistic team semantics. In: Ferrarotti, F., Woltran, S. (eds.) Foundations of Information and Knowledge Systems, pp. 186–206. Springer, Cham (2018)
10. Fagin, R.: Horn clauses and database dependencies. J. ACM **29**, 952–985 (1982)

[6] If an implication problem is undecidable, there cannot be a variable bounded axiomatization for it. (An axiomatization $\mathcal{A}$ is variable bounded if every deduction $\Sigma \vdash_{\mathcal{A}} \tau$ can be witnessed by a sequence $(\tau_1, \ldots, \tau_n)$ such that $Var(\{\tau_1, \ldots, \tau_n\}) \subseteq \mathrm{Var}(\Sigma \cup \{\tau\})$.) If there was a variable bounded axiomatization, then given a finite set of atoms $\Sigma \cup \{\tau\}$, such that $\mathrm{Var}(\Sigma \cup \{\tau\}) = D$, there are only finitely many possible deductions for $\Sigma \vdash \tau$ using the variables in D. An algorithm checking these deductions would determine $\Sigma \models \tau$, making the implication problem decidable.

11. Fagin, R., Vardi, M.Y.: Armstrong databases for functional and inclusion dependencies. Inform. Process. Lett. **16**(1), 13–19 (1983). https://doi.org/10.1016/0020-0190(83)90005-4. https://www.sciencedirect.com/science/article/pii/0020019083900054
12. Galliani, P.: Inclusion and exclusion dependencies in team semantics: on some logics of imperfect information. Ann. Pure Appl. Logic **163**(1), 68–84 (2012)
13. Grädel, E., Väänänen, J.: Dependence and independence. Stud. Logica. **101**(2), 399–410 (2013). https://doi.org/10.1007/s11225-013-9479-2
14. Green, T.J., Karvounarakis, G., Tannen, V.: Provenance semirings. In: Proceedings of the Twenty-Sixth ACM SIGMOD-SIGACT-SIGART Symposium on Principles of Database Systems, PODS '07, pp. 31–40. Association for Computing Machinery, New York (2007). https://doi.org/10.1145/1265530.1265535
15. Hannula, M.: Conditional independence on semiring relations (2023). https://arxiv.org/abs/2310.01910
16. Hannula, M.: Conditional independence on semiring relations. In: Cormode, G., Shekelyan, M. (eds.) 27th International Conference on Database Theory (ICDT 2024). Leibniz International Proceedings in Informatics (LIPIcs), vol. 290, pp. 20:1–20:20. Schloss Dagstuhl – Leibniz-Zentrum für Informatik, Dagstuhl, Germany (2024). https://doi.org/10.4230/LIPIcs.ICDT.2024.20, https://drops.dagstuhl.de/entities/document/10.4230/LIPIcs.ICDT.2024.20
17. Hannula, M., Kontinen, J., Link, S.: On the interaction of functional and inclusion dependencies with independence atoms (2021). https://arxiv.org/abs/2101.02466
18. Hannula, M., Virtema, J.: Tractability frontiers in probabilistic team semantics and existential second-order logic over the reals. Annal. Pure Appl. Logic **173**(10), 103108 (2022). https://doi.org/10.1016/j.apal.2022.103108, https://www.sciencedirect.com/science/article/pii/S0168007222000239, logics of Dependence and Independence
19. Hirvonen, M.: Axiomatization of implication for probabilistic independence and unary variants of marginal identity and marginal distribution equivalence. In: Meier, A., Ortiz, M. (eds.) Found. Inf. Knowl. Syst., pp. 222–234. Springer Nature Switzerland, Cham (2024)
20. Hirvonen, M.: The implication problem for functional dependencies and variants of marginal distribution equivalences. ACM Trans. Comput. Logic **25**(4) (2024). https://doi.org/10.1145/3677120
21. Li, C.T.: Undecidability of network coding, conditional information inequalities, and conditional independence implication. IEEE Trans. Inf. Theory **69**(6), 3493–3510 (2023). https://doi.org/10.1109/TIT.2023.3247570
22. Pearl, J.: Probabilistic Reasoning in Intelligent Systems: Networks of Plausible Inference. Morgan Kaufmann Publishers Inc., San Francisco, CA, USA (1988)
23. Väänänen, J.: Dependence Logic. Cambridge University Press (2007)
24. Väänänen, J., et al.: Modal dependence logic. N. Perspect. Games Interact. **4**, 237–254 (2008)
25. Yang, F., Väänänen, J.: Propositional logics of dependence. Ann. Pure Appl. Logic **167**(7), 557–589 (2016). https://doi.org/10.1016/j.apal.2016.03.003

Structures for Argumentation and Modal Logics

Simplifying Argumentation Frameworks by Clustering Structural Patterns

Iosif Apostolakis and Johannes P. Wallner(✉)

Graz University of Technology, Graz, Austria
{iosif.apostolakis,johannes.p.wallner}@tugraz.at

Abstract. Argumentation frameworks (AFs) provide a central formalism for abstract argumentation, representing arguments and their interactions as attack graphs and serving as reasoning engines across diverse domains. One of their main strengths lies in their ability to support explanations. However, their usefulness can be limited by size and structural complexity, which can hinder understanding. To address this challenge, we investigate simplification techniques for AFs, with particular emphasis on clustering-based abstraction. By grouping arguments into clusters and interpreting attacks accordingly, clustered AFs provide reduced representations that preserve essential argumentative properties while hiding redundant details. We study formal underpinnings for clustering on AFs in particular combined with other simplification techniques, and analyze their effects on main argumentation semantics, and explore conditions under which simplifications remain faithful and avoid spurious results. Our approach positions clustering as a principled method of abstraction and highlights its potential for enhancing explainability in argumentation.

1 Introduction

Computational argumentation is a prominent research direction within Artificial Intelligence (AI) studying representational and computational aspects [6,16] arising when modeling real-world debates, arguments, discourses, and dialogues, with heterogeneous applications, e.g., in legal and medical reasoning [2].

Automated argumentative reasoning relies on formal approaches defining how to represent arguments and how to reason on such arguments. In particular, many formal approaches to computational argumentation [9,10,17–20] utilize abstract argumentation frameworks (AFs) [12] as their reasoning engine.

AFs have an appealing quality for reasoning: they represent arguments as abstract entities and relations between arguments, namely attacks or a counter-argument relation between arguments, as directed edges between the abstract arguments. This simplicity on the one side and their ability to capture many forms of non-monotonic reasoning [6,12] on the other side lead AFs to being a prominent approach to define argumentative reasoning.

To enable argumentative reasoning, argumentation semantics drive the reasoning process in AFs. Semantics define jointly acceptable subsets of arguments

A.-Y. Turhan and J. Virtema (Eds.): FoIKS 2026, LNCS 16475, pp. 51–67, 2026.
https://doi.org/10.1007/978-3-032-21540-6_4

in AFs, according to certain criteria, which vary from very cautious semantics to more brave forms of reasoning.

A key property of many such semantics is the concept of admissibility. A set of arguments is deemed admissible, in a given AF, if there are no attacks between any arguments in the set, and the set defends itself against attacks from outside, by countering all such attacks with attacks from the set.

Example 1. Let us consider the AF shown in Fig. 1(a). This AF represents a way of interpreting a legal case, called the Simonshaven case [21]. We spare the reader with concrete details, unless necessary, due to the gruesome details of the case. Concretely, consider argument a, which can be interpreted as an argument deeming a person as guilty. That is, if one finds an admissible set containing a, this set of arguments argues in "favour" of guilt of the person, or can be seen as a coherent way of arguing in this direction. We remark that in this paper we take no stance on the actual case and use the case as a real-world example.

There are, in fact, several admissible sets containing a, and also some that argue in a different direction (admissible sets attacking a). For instance $\{a, c, d, h, i, k, l, 1\}$ is a reason to accept a and $\{b, f, f', h, i, j, 2\}$ is an admissible set attacking a (countering it).

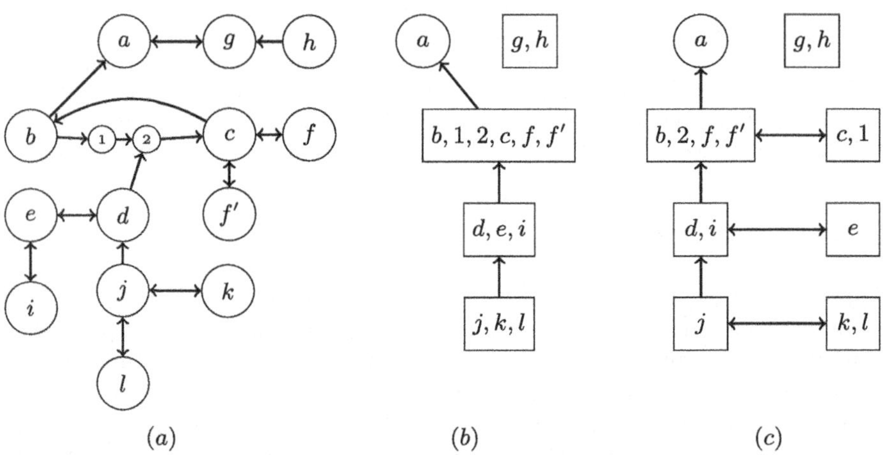

Fig. 1. An AF from a legal reasoning case by Prakken [21] (left). In its original formalization an extended argumentation framework (EAF) [20], here represented as a direct adaptation to an AF (arguments 1 and 2 replace an attack from d to the attack (b, c)). SCCs of this AF (middle) except g and h. SCCs divided into two partitions (right).

Inspecting the AF in Fig. 1, while this AF is not overly large, it is not immediate how to "digest" this argumentative scenario. A usual human behavior when faced with (somewhat) complicated situations is to approach them in a step-by-step manner, looking at parts of the whole.

Looking at the AF, with some background in computational argumentation, one can come to the conclusion that the argument a is influenced by its two attackers b and g. These two, in turn, are behaving quite differently. Let us first consider argument g. Since argument h is unattacked, i.e., has no reason not to accept it, major semantics of AFs accept h. But then g is defeated (again in prominent semantics of AFs). Then the attack (g, a) is countered.

Argument b is different, as it relies on many other arguments. Here, classical concepts from graph theory can assist in dividing (and conquering) the AF. Concretely, it is known that cycles in AFs affect reasoning drastically: even-length cycles can introduce "choices" [7] and odd-length cycles can prevent to accept anything [13]. See also a recent work using SCCs for explanations [1].

In the example AF, there is no odd-length cycle, but several even-length cycles. In its simplest form, a cycle (x, y) and (y, x) means that one can choose to accept either x or y (assuming no other attacks). In the example, e.g., one can choose l together with k or, otherwise j.

These "choices" follow a certain order: when considering the strongly connected components (SCCs) of the example we see (except for g and h that are already handled) three such SCCs: $\{j, k, l\}$, $\{d, e, i\}$, $\{b, c, f, f', 1, 2\}$, and $\{a\}$. The condensation graph (nodes compacted to their SCCs), see Fig. 1 middle, suggests that one can go through the SCCs in a standard topological order.

One can view each such SCC as a "sub-argumentation". And the outcome of each might affect the next SCC. In the example AF, each such SCCs has an argument what can be called a "decision argument": the only argument with an attack going out of the SCC. Moreover, since there are no odd-cycles, each SCC is also free of odd-cycles, and, in turn, each SCC can be further divided into two partitions, as odd-cycles freeness implies bipartiteness in SCCs (Fig. 1 right). Taking the admissible set $\{a, c, d, h, i, k, l, 1\}$ from above, this can be interpreted as choosing k and l from the first SCC, i from the second SCC, and c and 1 from the third SCC. Alternatively, one can choose, among the bipartitions, the whole partitions on the right. Then all "decision arguments" are rejected.

In this work we look at simplifications, as illustrated in the real-world example, by considering a combination of approaches supporting explanations, in particular including clustering of arguments aligned with the SCC structure.

Our main contributions are as follows.

- We utilize AF patterns that can be used for simplification together with clustering, e.g., using the grounded semantics and following path structures.
- We then show that while abstracting an AF into its SCC structure is useful, it still does not reflect reasoning in AFs sufficiently, by considering abstraction by clusterings on the SCCs.
- We show that subdividing the SCC clustering further, when assuming both odd-cycle-freeness and "decision arguments", utilizing bipartiteness of SCCs leads to a more faithful approach of clusterings. One can find (part of) a stable extension in favour of a topical argument in polynomial time.

2 Preliminaries

In this section, we first recall background on argumentation frameworks [12] and then clustering of AFs [24].

Argumentation Frameworks. Argumentation frameworks were first introduced by Dung [12] and provide a formal basis for representing argumentation in AI. In an AF arguments are modeled as vertices in a graph and directed edges capture the attack relation between them.

Definition 1. *An argumentation framework (AF) is a pair $F = (A, R)$, where A is a finite non-empty set of arguments and $R \subseteq A \times A$ denotes an attack relation. If $(a, b) \in R$ then argument a attacks argument b.*

Within this setting, a set of arguments $S \subseteq A$ is said to attack an argument $a \in A$ if there exists some $b \in S$ such that $(b, a) \in R$. Furthermore, an argument a is considered defended by S if, for every b that attacks a, there exists some $c \in S$ such that $(c, b) \in R$. Assuming S to be a set of arguments, we define the characteristic function $\mathcal{F}_F$ as $\mathcal{F}_F(S) = \{x \in A \mid x \text{ is defended by } S\}$.

The semantics of AFs [5] specify how to determine acceptable sets of arguments, commonly called extensions. We recall prominent semantics.

Definition 2. *Let $F = (A, R)$ be an AF and $S \subseteq A$.*

- *S is conflict-free in F iff there are no $a, b \in S$ such that $(a, b) \in R$.*
- *S is admissible in F iff S is conflict-free in F and $S \subseteq \mathcal{F}_F(S)$.*
- *S is complete in F iff S $S = \mathcal{F}_F(S)$.*
- *S is the grounded extension in F iff S is the least fixed point of $\mathcal{F}_F$.*
- *S is stable in F iff S is conflict-free and for every $a \in A \setminus S$, there exists $b \in S$ with $(b, a) \in R$.*
- *S is preferred in F iff S is a $\subseteq$-maximal admissible set in F.*

We will sometimes also use the labeling-based versions of the semantics [11]. An extension defines whether an argument is in the extension or not. A labeling uses three values: *in*, *out*, and *undec*, standing in for accepted (in the extension), defeated or out (attacked by the extension), and undecided, respectively.

Given an extension $E \subseteq 2^A$, then the corresponding labeling can be defined using E, $E_R^+ = \{a \mid (b, a), b \in E\}$, and the remaining arguments in A: $L_E = (E, E_R^+, A \setminus (E \cup E_R^+))$, denoting the arguments that are *in*, *out*, and *undec*, respectively. Conversely, given a labeling $L = (I, O, U)$, its corresponding extension is I. All semantics considered here have labeling-based counterparts [11].

These semantics allow us to reason about the acceptance of arguments. We sometimes abbreviate the conflict-free, admissible, complete, grounded, stable, and preferred semantics via *cf*, *adm*, ,, *grd*, *stb*, *prf*, respectively. An argument $a \in A$ is said to be credulously accepted under a semantics $\sigma \in \{cf, adm, , , grd, stb, prf\}$ if there exists some $E \in \sigma(F)$ with $a \in E$. In contrast, a is skeptically accepted under σ if $a \in E$ for all $E \in \sigma(F)$.

Definition 3. *Let $F = (A, R)$ be an argumentation framework and $S \subseteq A$ a set of arguments. The* restriction *of F to S, denoted $F|_S$, is defined as*

$$F|_S = (S, R|_S),$$

where $R|_S = R \cap (S \times S)$ is the set of attacks in R whose source and target both belong to S.

Abstraction via Clustering. We now formally introduce clustered argumentation frameworks (cAFs) [24], which provide the basis for our approach to abstraction. The idea is to group arguments into clusters by means of a mapping, so that reasoning can be carried out on a simplified representation while preserving essential properties of the original AF.

The main component of clustering is a mapping on arguments.

Definition 4. *Let A be a set of arguments. Given a partition $\hat{A}$ of A, a clustering is a surjective mapping $m : A \to \hat{A}$.*

We extend m to sets of arguments and to sets of such sets as follows: for $S \subseteq A$, let $m(S) = \{m(a) \mid a \in S\}$, and for $E \subseteq 2^A$, let $m(E) = \{m(S) \mid S \in E\}$.

Intuitively, this surjective mapping, creates groups of arguments that are now treated as one entity. Whenever convenient, and when m is clear from the context, we identify a clustered argument $\hat{a} \in \hat{A}$ with its preimage $m^{-1}(\hat{a}) = \{a \in A \mid m(a) = \hat{a}\}$. The notion of preimage is extended to sets of clusters, signaling a set of arguments that consist a hitting set of the set of clusters.

A clustered AF is formally an AF whose set of arguments consist of clusters that are created according a clustering m.

Definition 5. *A clustered AF (cAF) $\hat{F}$ is a triple $(\hat{A}, \hat{R}, m)$, where $\hat{A}$ is the image of m through the set of arguments A and $\hat{\mathcal{R}}$ is the set of attacks among clusters.*

An attack $(\hat{a}, \hat{b}) \in \hat{\mathcal{R}}$ signals that in each original framework that maps to $\hat{F}$, there are arguments $a \in \hat{a}$ and $b \in \hat{b}$ so that a attacks b. When the contents of clusters are clear we may refer to a cAF as a pair $(\hat{A}, \hat{R})$, omitting the clustering mapping m.

Thus, arguments in F are grouped into clusters, and attacks between arguments are mapped to attacks between the corresponding clusters. In the definition above, we assume the existence of an original set of arguments A. The interactions between arguments in A is unknown, however an AF $F = (A, R)$ that maps to a clustered AF $\hat{F}$ via m, must be such, so that the interaction of arguments in F aligns with the interaction of their corresponding clusters in $\hat{F}$. Note that multiple attacks in F may map to the same attack in $\hat{F}$. An original framework F that maps to the cAF $\hat{F}$, is called a preimage of $\hat{F}$.

A clustered argument $\hat{a}$ is a singleton if $|m^{-1}(\hat{a})| = 1$. We denote the set of singleton clusters by $single(\hat{A})$. For convenience, we assume that singletons are always mapped to themselves, i.e., if $x \in single(\hat{A})$, then $x \in A$ and $m(x) = x$.

Example 2. In the introduction we explicated how one can draw conclusions using simplified versions of a given framework, basically by proposing a way of clustering. Considering Fig. 1 (middle), formally we use the following clustering: $m(a) = a$, $m(g) = m(h) = \hat{g}$, $m(b) = m(c) = m(f) = m(f') = m(1) = m(2) = \hat{b}$, $m(d) = m(e) = m(i) = \hat{d}$, $m(j) = m(k) = m(l) = \hat{j}$. Here a remains a singleton while all other arguments are grouped into clusters.

Syntactically, clustered AFs resemble classical AFs. However, applying classical semantics directly is not appropriate in the context of cAFs. As an example, consider g and h from Fig. 1 left and middle, i.e., a cluster $\{g, h\}$ consisting of two arguments that attack each other. Applying conflict-free semantics directly, the cluster would be considered self-attacking and therefore rejected. Yet at the level of the original AF, one argument is in fact acceptable.

Therefore, we require semantics that are specifically defined for clustered AFs. To avoid confusion, we will refer to semantics on cAFs as "abstract semantics" and on AFs as "classical semantics" whenever there is a risk of ambiguity. Abstract semantics must respect the abstracted information while retaining their connection with the classical case. In particular, the desired property is to ensure that if a clustered AF is obtained from some classical AF, then the extensions of the classical AF are consistently mapped to abstract extensions of the clustered AF. An abstract semantics that satisfies the property above with respect to a classical semantics is said to over-approximate it.

Definition 6. *Let σ be a classical semantics and $\hat{\sigma}$ an abstract semantics. We say that $\hat{\sigma}$* over-approximates *σ if for every argumentation framework F and every mapping m, it holds that $m(\sigma(F)) \subseteq \hat{\sigma}(m(F))$.*

That is, every extension of the classical semantics, when mapped to the abstract level, is also an extension under the abstract semantics. In the following, we recall definitions of over-approximating conflict-free, admissible and stable semantics for clustered AFs.

Definition 7. *Let $\hat{F} = (\hat{A}, \hat{R})$ be a clustered AF according to m and $\hat{E} \subseteq \hat{A}$. We define the following semantics on clustered AFs:*

- *$\hat{E} \in \hat{cf}(\hat{F})$ iff for each $\hat{a}, \hat{b} \in single(\hat{E})$ we have $(\hat{a}, \hat{b}) \notin \hat{R}$,*
- *$\hat{E} \in \hat{adm}(\hat{F})$ iff $\hat{E} \in \hat{cf}(\hat{F})$ and if $\hat{a} \in \hat{E}$ with $(\hat{b}, \hat{a}) \in \hat{R}$ s.t. $|\hat{a}| = 1$, then there is a $\hat{c} \in \hat{E}$ with $(\hat{c}, \hat{b}) \in \hat{R}$,*
- *$\hat{E} \in \hat{stb}$ iff $\hat{E} \in \hat{cf}(\hat{F})$, $\hat{b} \notin \hat{E}$ implies that there is an $\hat{a} \in \hat{E}$ with $(\hat{a}, \hat{b}) \in \hat{R}$, and if $\hat{E}$ does not attack an $\hat{a} \in \hat{E}$ then $\hat{b} \notin \hat{E}$ whenever $(\hat{a}, \hat{b}) \in \hat{R}$ and $|\hat{b}| = 1$.*

Since abstraction is intertwined with information loss, it is often that reasoning over clustered frameworks gives results that do not hold in the original scenario. In our case, an abstract extension that does not correspond to an original one, is called spurious. Then, a clustered framework with no spurious sets under a semantics $\hat{\sigma}$ is called faithful with respect to $\hat{\sigma}$.

3 Simplification Patterns for Clustering

In this section we consider several graph theoretic patterns on AFs. We utilize simplification strategies that entail meaningful abstractions when used together with clusterings, ensuring that the simplified frameworks preserve the essential argumentative properties of the originals.

The simplifications in this section can be summarized as modifications of an AF (partly to a cAF) such that the arguments modified have a fixed semantical status or the status is direct-to-obtain from the simplification.

In particular, given an AF F, the modifications modify F to obtain a cAF $\hat{F}$, yet, in contrast to applying a clustering m to F to obtain $\hat{F}$, we apply certain modifications. Importantly, while $\hat{F}$ may contain clusters, we treat them as singletons. The reason is that such a cluster $\hat{a}$, while formally a group of possibly several arguments, the acceptance status of $x \in \hat{a}$ is either fixed or direct to obtain. Thus, the simplifications in this section modify F with new clusters $\hat{a}$, while considering the outcome as singletons only (i.e., $\hat{a}$ is then a singleton).

In order to simplify a given AF, it is useful to deal with arguments whose acceptance status is deterministically fixed by the structure of the graph itself. Such arguments do not require further evaluation under the semantics, as their acceptance or rejection can be inferred directly.

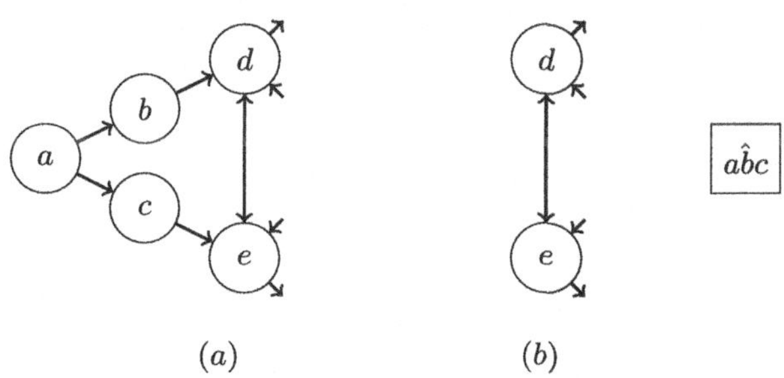

Fig. 2. Grounded clusters.

The following definition addresses simplifying parts of an AF that are determined by grounded semantics.

Definition 8. *Let $F = (A, R)$ be an AF and (I, O, U) be the grounded labeling of F. The grounded simplification clusters $\hat{g} = I \cup O$ into one cluster disconnected from the rest of the framework $F|_U$, which remains the unaltered. Moreover $\hat{g}$ is considered a singleton.*

The grounded cluster is a cluster that contains parts of a framework whose acceptance is determined by unattacked arguments and iteratively defended arguments. All considered semantics in this work, except for admissible sets, label arguments in if they are in the grounded extension, and label an argument out if the argument is out in the grounded extension (undecided arguments are evaluated differently).

The grounded simplification is strictly speaking not a clustering as defined above, since the attacks outgoing from arguments that are in or out are not considered. Nevertheless, a grounded cluster captures the effect of the grounded semantics directly: one can accept the cluster (an argument inside) and the attacks outgoing are attacks from arguments labeled out, which have no further effect on semantics considered in this work.

Example 3. In Fig. 2(a) the arguments a, b, c have fixed statuses, since a is unattacked and determines the acceptance status of b and c. A grounded cluster is shown on the right of this figure. Also in Fig. 1 the argument h is unattacked. Then, we can cluster arguments g, h into a cluster $\{g, h\}$, signaling that this cluster does not influence reasoning over the rest of the framework.

Proposition 1. *Let F be an AF and $\hat{F}$ is the clustered framework that occurs after applying grounded simplification. Then $\hat{F}$ is faithful w.r.t. stable semantics.*

Proof. Let $\hat{E}$ be in $\hat{stb}(\hat{F})$. Then $\hat{E}$ contains singletons that lie in $\mathcal{A} \setminus grd(F)$ as well as the grounded cluster. Then E consisting of these singletons together with the set $grd(F)$ is a stable extension in F and is a preimage of $\hat{E}$ ($m(E) = \hat{E}$).

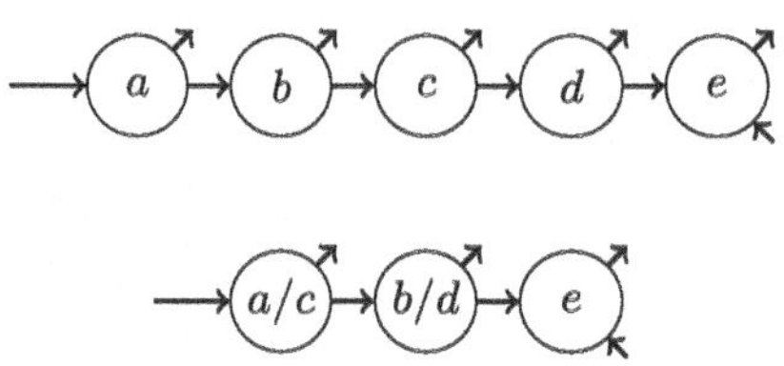

Fig. 3. Path-length preserving clustering.

Even in cases where no argument is unattacked, there may exist arguments whose acceptance is inherently interconnected. It can be the case that certain sets of arguments consistently appear together across all extensions, indicating that their acceptance or rejection is always jointly determined. Such sets can therefore be regarded as forming clusters whose acceptance status is universal within the framework.

As such clusters we refer to arguments that lie in a path that receives no external attacks. Then, the acceptance of one of the propagates naturally to the next arguments.

Definition 9 (Path-length preserving clusters). *Let F be an AF and let $p = (a_0, a_1, \dots, a_n)$ be a directed path such that $\forall i, 1 \leq i \leq n-1$, $\nexists b \in A \setminus \{a_{i-1}\}$ s.t. $(b, a_i) \in R$. The clusters $\{a_0, a_2, \dots\}$ (even arguments in the path) and $\{a_1, a_3, \dots\}$ (odd arguments in the path) are called the pair of path-length preserving clusters of p. Both clusters are considered singletons.*

This simplification aims to shorten paths, since the acceptance status of the arguments within them is interconnected.

Example 4. Consider Fig. 3, which depicts a chain a, b, c, and d of arguments with only outgoing attacks, except for those from the previous argument in the path. Argument e stops the path. Clustering these as shown in the bottom of the figure preserves the main interconnections required for semantics on AFs. While certain admissible sets may be lost when utilizing this simplification, for instance those in which a is accepted and consequently c is defended, yet c remains undecided, this form of simplification still yields faithful results under stable semantics, where such intermediate undecided cases do not arise.

Proposition 2. *Let F be an AF and $\hat{F}$ be the clustered framework after applying path preserving clustering. Then $\hat{F}$ is faithful w.r.t. stable semantics.*

Proof. Let $\hat{E} \in \hat{stb}(\hat{F})$. If $\hat{E}$ just contains unabstracted elements, then $E = \hat{E}$ is trivially a stable preimage. If $\hat{E}$ contains a path-length preserving cluster, then simply define E to be the union of the elements of $\hat{E}$. Then clearly this is a preimage of E. Additionally E is stable as it attacks all arguments that map not in $\hat{E}$ in $\hat{F}$ which is the same as all the arguments not in E in F.

Additionally, in some cases there exist arguments that are guaranteed never to appear in a stable extension.

Definition 10. *Let F be an AF. An argument a_0 is defeated if in all stable extensions E there is $a \in E$, such that $(a, a_0) \in R$. We simplify F by removing a_0, restricting to graph $F|_{A\setminus\{a_0\}}$.*

A particularly interesting case of defeated arguments arises in the presence of an even cycle containing two arguments that exclude each other from stable sets. An example of this situation is illustrated in Fig. 4, where arguments g and h mutually attack each other, ensuring that they can never appear together in the same stable extension. However, any stable extension that accepts either g or h cannot include argument d, as both g and h attack it. This structure illustrates how mutual exclusion within even cycles can indirectly determine the rejection of other arguments in the framework.

As an example of a defeated cluster, in Fig. 4, argument b can never be part of a stable extension, since either g or h will always be included in the extension, thereby defeating b. Consequently, argument e must always appear in a stable extension, as it is consistently defended by either g or h.

Proposition 3. *Let F be an AF and $\hat{F}$ be the clustered framework that occurs after applying a defeated simplification. Then $\hat{F}$ is faithful w.r.t. stable semantics.*

Proof. Let $\hat{A}$ be a stable set in $\hat{F}$. Then, $\hat{A}$ is a set of singletons, i.e. arguments that lie in F. Hence $A = \hat{A}$ is a preimage of itself. Additionally, this set is also stable, as it attacks all arguments that are attacked by $\hat{A}$ and defeats the rest by definition.

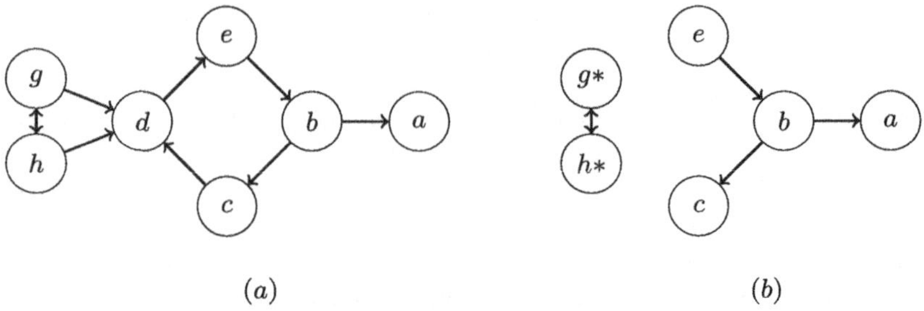

Fig. 4. Defeated simplification.

Since each type of clustering is faithful under stable semantics, applying them in any sequence still produces faithful results.

Proposition 4. *Let F be an AF and $\hat{F}$ is the clustered framework that occurs after simplifying multiple times. Then $\hat{F}$ is faithful w.r.t. stable semantics.*

Proof. Proof by induction on the number of clustering applications, say n. For $n = 0$ no clustering is applied and thus the abstract semantics coincide with the originals [24]. Then, assuming the framework $\hat{F^i}$ that occurs after applying clusterings i times is faithful to F, then by applying any clustering on $\hat{F^i}$ we need to prove that $\hat{F}^{i+1}$ is faithful to F. However, it suffices to show that $\hat{F}^{i+1}$ is just faithful to $\hat{F^i}$, which is just an AF since each of its nodes works as a singleton. This holds by propositions 1, 2, and 3. Thus, $\hat{F}^{i+1}$ is faithful to $\hat{F}$

4 SCC Clusterings

In previous work on abstraction on argumentation frameworks [24], it has been proposed that, in order to find a faithful clustering, one can start with some "naive" clustering, and then refine until faithfulness is achieved. One such clustering suggests grouping all arguments into a single large cluster, and then iteratively remove arguments while checking whether the resulting clustering is faithful.

Definition 11 (Coarse clustering). *Let $F = (A, R)$ be an AF. We call m the coarse clustering over F if m maps A into one cluster.*

The coarse clustering is guaranteed to be faithful w.r.t. stable semantics, given there is a non-empty stable set.

Proposition 5. *Let $\hat{F}$ be the coarse clustering over F. If $\hat{stb}(\hat{F}) \neq \emptyset$ we get that $\hat{F}$ is faithful wrt F under stb.*

Proof. Given any non empty stable set in F trivially maps to the only cluster, the it only remains to show that the cluster is abstract stable. The only way such a cluster would not be stable, is if it was a self-attacking singleton. But then, this would mean that the original framework would consist only of a single self-attacking argument, and therefore $stb(F)$ would be the empty set, which is a contradiction.

Example 5. In the framework shown in Fig. 1(a), the coarse cluster would be faithful under stable semantics, as there are non-empty original sets that are deemed acceptable under *stb*. To reason over argument a, we would then have to break this cluster down step by step by removing arguments. First by removing a and continuing removing until we reach a clustering where we could draw conclusions safely. For example, just by refining a, we would get that the set $\{a\}$ is stable, which is not the case in the original framework. This means that this clustered stable set would be spurious w.r.t. to our original framework.

Formally, for a given AF $F = (A, R)$ and a cAF $\hat{F} = (\hat{A}, \hat{R})$ with F a preimage, a refinement of $\hat{F}$, w.r.t. F, is $\hat{F}' = (\hat{A}', \hat{R}')$ such that F is a preimage of $\hat{F}'$ and for each $\hat{a}' \in \hat{A}'$ it holds that there is an $\hat{a} \in \hat{A}$ with $\hat{a}' \subseteq \hat{a}$. If one follows a refinement process (breaking up clusters) for sufficiently many steps, one reaches at some point the original AF (all arguments again singletons). Thus, in the worst case it will terminate after refining all clusters back into singletons, yielding the original framework. In this case, the abstract semantics coincide with the classical semantics. With more sophisticated strategies one can find faithful clusterings in this way.

Proposition 6 ([24]). *If $m = id$, i.e. $\hat{F} = F$, then $\hat{stb}(\hat{F}) = stb(F)$.*

Although the coarse clustering is faithful under the assumptions stated in proposition 5, starting the refinement process from such a clustering may be unnecessary. In our view, abstraction should serve as a tool to reduce the complexity of an argumentation framework by forming meaningful clusters. While abstracting all information of the framework may technically lead to a faithful result, such an abstraction is essentially meaningless, as it fails to provide any useful simplification or insight.

To address this, we propose starting from a less coarse clustering. While such a clustering might not guarantee faithfulness in the first place, it retains intuitive meaning and provides a more informative abstraction of the framework. In particular, we propose using the condensation graph of an AF as the basis for clustering, that is, mapping each strongly connected component (SCC) of the AF to a clustered argument.

We will now briefly recall some standard definitions from graph theory. SCCs provide a natural structural decomposition of directed graphs. They capture groups of arguments that are mutually reachable through attack relations and thus cannot be evaluated independently.

Definition 12. *Let $F = (A, R)$ be an argumentation framework. A non-empty subset $S \subseteq A$ is called a strongly connected component (SCC) of F if, for every pair of arguments $a, b \in S$, there exists a directed path from a to b and from b to a in F, and S is maximal with respect to this property.*

The SCCs of an AF form a partition of its argument set A. That is, every argument belongs to exactly one SCC, and no two SCCs overlap. By contracting each SCC into a single node and preserving the direction of attacks between components, we obtain the condensation graph of F.

Definition 13. *Let $\mathcal{S} = \{S_1, S_2, \ldots, S_k\}$ be the set of SCCs of an AF $F = (A, R)$. The condensation graph of F is the directed graph $cond(F) = (\mathcal{S}, B)$, where*

$$B = \{(S_i, S_j) \mid \exists a \in S_i,\, b \in S_j \text{ such that } (a, b) \in R,\, i \neq j\}.$$

We may occasionally refer to elements of B as bridges between the SCCs.

A well-known property of the condensation graph is that it is always acyclic. This means that attacks between SCCs induce a partial order among them, while cycles, if any, are contained entirely within the components themselves. This acyclic structure allows reasoning procedures to evaluate arguments incrementally. Once the acceptance status of arguments in one SCC is determined, it can influence, but cannot be influenced by, arguments in subsequent components.

Definition 14 (SCC clustering). *Let $F = (A, R)$ be an AF and m be the following mapping:*

$$\forall a, b \in A, m(a) = m(b) \text{ iff } a, b \text{ are path equivalent.}$$

Then, $\hat{F}$ is the SCC clustering of F.

Clustering arguments according to their strongly connected components is particularly intuitive since SCCs already represent natural substructures within an AF. By definition, every argument inside an SCC is mutually reachable via attacks, which means that their acceptance can be interdependent. For instance, an argument cannot be evaluated in isolation if it is part of a cycle of attacks, and SCCs provide a principled way of identifying and grouping together such sets of arguments.

Next, we focus on refining the SCC clustering further, with the goal of guiding the search process toward more meaningful and informative results.

As mentioned already, SCC clustering is intended to provide a more intuitive starting point than the coarse clustering. However, clustering into SCCs inevitably abstracts away some critical structural information, which can in turn hinder detailed reasoning about the acceptance of individual arguments.

Restricting our attention to specific classes of graphs, such as odd-cycle free graphs, imposes well-defined structural properties on the SCCs of an argumentation framework. In particular, the absence of odd cycles constrains the internal organization of each SCC, resulting in a bipartite structure.

Proposition 7 ([3]). *An odd-cycle free graph with more than two vertices which is strongly connected, is also bipartite.*

Reasoning over an argument requires zooming in its SCC. Consider first an "initial" SCC, i.e., one without incoming edges in the condensation graph. If this SCC is a bipartite graph, there is a stable extension within the SCC that contains it. In general, preferred semantics and stable semantics coincide on odd-cycle free AFs [12,13]. Clearly a bipartite graph can naturally be partitioned into two mutually attacking sets that do not self-attack themselves. Accepting all arguments in either set, yields a stable extension within the SCC. In case this SCC is a singleton, we still have two options: accepting the argument or rejecting it.

The above hints an intuitive refinement, that is, breaking SCCs down to two sets forming their bipartition. In general, refinement refers to the process of subdividing existing clusters in a cAF into smaller ones, thereby producing a more detailed and informative abstraction. Consequently, such a refinement exhibit a choice-like behavior, where acceptance of one part entails rejection in the other.

Definition 15. *Let F be an AF without odd-cycles and let $SCC(F)$ be its SCC clustering. We call the choice clustering to be the refinement of the SCC clustering where each non-singleton node in $SCC(F)$ is represented by two clusters corresponding to its bipartition.*

In general, the interconnections of SCCs can lead to complex argumentative behavior (statuses). One way to make sure that the choice propagates properly to the SCC S is require that there is a unique path connecting each initial SCC with S.

Let F be an AF and $\hat{F}$ be the choice clustering of F. If each non-singleton bipartition has a unique path to the initial SCCs, we call the choice clustering a well-formed clustering.

Note that well-formedness is satisfied in the example legal case from the introduction (Fig. 1).

We call a well-formed clustering a grounded well-formed clustering if the grounded simplification is applied before bipartitioning the SCCs.

Then, with this clustering we aim to show that by choosing a part of the bipartition of the predecessor SCC, one can always find clusters that support any stable extension that lies in an SCC.

Theorem 1. *Let F be an AF without odd-cycles with $\hat{F} = (\hat{A}, \hat{R})$ a grounded well-formed clustering of F, and $\hat{a}$ a cluster in $\hat{F}$. It holds that one can compute in polynomial time sets $I, O \subseteq \hat{A}$ with $\hat{a} \in I$ and $I \cup O$ are all predecessors of $\hat{a}$ in $\hat{F}$ such that there is a non-spurious abstract stable extension $\hat{E} \supseteq I$ with $\hat{E} \cap O = \emptyset$.*

In words, we can compute a "partial" in and out labeling of the predecessors of a queried cluster $\hat{a}$ such that we are certain these can be extended to a full abstract stable extension in $\hat{F}$ such that all clusters in I are included and O are excluded. Moreover this abstract stable extension is not spurious, meaning there is a classical stable extension mapping to it in the original AF F. Further, by construction, cluster $\hat{a}$ is fully accepted in this classical stable extension.

The AF in Fig. 1 (AF on the left, grounded well-formed clustering on the right) is one case that falls under the preceding theorem.

Proof (Proof of Theorem 1). Let $S \in SCC(F)$ such that $\hat{a}$ is part of its bipartition. Then, since $\hat{F}$ is grounded well-formed there is a unique path connecting it to its predecessor initial cluster. Assuming (X_p, Y_p) is one of its direct predecessor bipartition, then there is either an attack from X_p or from Y_p towards $\hat{a}$ or towards the other part of the bipartition of S. W.l.o.g. let X_p attack $\hat{a}$. Then we may choose to label Y_p as "in" (in set of clusters I) and reject X_p (put it in O). We then repeat the same process with X_p and Y_p instead of $\hat{a}$ up until we exhaust the path to the initial cluster. The result is a labeling on all clusters that are predecessors of $\hat{a}$ in $\hat{F}$. By construction, taking the preimage in F as all in I, we find that this preimage is admissible in F. Since F is odd-cycle free, it holds that F is coherent and preferred and stable semantics coincide. Since for each admissible set there is a superset that is a preferred extension, there is a superset that is a stable extension. By construction, all of O are attacked by this stable extension. Finally, the above algorithm can be carried out in polynomial time.

With the choice clustering, we obtain that for any cluster, there exists a corresponding selection of predecessor clusters that can be entirely accepted, such that the union of these chosen clusters together with the chosen cluster, constitutes a stable extension in the original framework. In other words, such a combination of clusters cannot be spurious. An immediate consequence of this result is that if we refined an SCC, then any locally selected stable set can be extended to a globally stable one by appropriately selecting the corresponding clusters. Hence, the choices made outside of a given SCC are independent with respect to the stable sets within it, and thus the information lying within them is redundant in this case.

Example 6. Consider the example of Fig. 1, where we argued over argument a, consider also having applied the grounded clustering to cluster arguments h and g. Then the choice clustering would be the one shown in Fig. 1(c). Now a stable set that includes a, could be the one that accepts $\widehat{c,1}, \widehat{d,i}$ and $\widehat{k,l}$ entirely. Then it is up to ones need for details to refine these cluster and get all the information on why such a set is stable indeed.

As a by-product, Theorem 1 also indicates a class of cAFs where one can find parts of a non-spurious abstract stable extension (containing a queried argument) in polynomial time. In general, verifying whether a given set of clusters is spurious is a coNP-completeness problem [24].

5 Discussion

The simplifications we study in this paper on the one hand allow for faithful abstractions, such as the simplification patterns studied in Sect. 3 and on the other hand provide means for simplification or abstraction via clustering alongside the SCC structure of AFs. In case the AF satisfies graph-theoretical properties, the abstraction via SCCs allows for direct generation of non-spurious stable extensions in favour or against a topical argument.

For instance, for argument a in the example from the introduction, which can be seen as an argument of interest, we can directly infer from the choice clustering (Fig. 1 on the right) a way to argue in favour and argue against a: by using Theorem 1. These can be computed in polynomial time. Importantly, these are direct to be shown in the choice clustering: in each bipartition a "winning" and "losing" side can be seen.

There are, however, other potential stable extensions that do not fall into the generation procedure. For example, instead of treating choice clusters as entities that must be either fully accepted or fully rejected, there can be stable extensions that accept only part of them. Reflecting on this in the abstraction seems to require a further refinement of the clustering to better capture the internal dynamics of each SCC and to examine in greater detail the interactions arising from the even cycles contained within.

Taking a closer look at clusters composed of a small number of arguments, one observes that a cluster consisting of two arguments must be mutually attacking, and can therefore be regarded as self-attacking. Similarly, if an SCC cluster contains three arguments, the arguments must be arranged in a linear connection with two mutual attacks, otherwise, the component would form an odd cycle. These observations illustrate the structural regularities imposed by restricting attention to even-cycle frameworks. However, no clear structural pattern emerges in clusters containing more than four arguments, as the possible interactions among a larger number of arguments grow combinatorially.

Related Works. Our work extends a previous clustering approach [24] by in particular focusing on applying clustering on structures from the real-world and utilizing structural constraints satisfied in the example. Additionally, we extended clustering by the simplification patterns.

Connected to our work are other works aimed at simplification, such as Input/Output frameworks [4], replacement patterns [14], and works e.g., focusing on sub parts of AFs [15,25,26]. In contrast to these works, we focus on clusterings and combine several techniques with clusterings under an existentially interpreted semantics of clusterings.

While abstraction approaches similar to argumentation have been investigated in ASP [22,23], our work distinguishes itself by specifically exploiting the graph-theoretic patterns of AFs.

In the literature the concept of the E-reduct has been investigated in various works for simplifying argumentation frameworks by utilizing the grounded extension [8]. In contrast to these, our approach aggregates the grounded extension and its range into a single cluster rather than removing them, thereby retaining their presence within the simplified framework. This aligns with our clustering formalism, where structural patterns are condensed rather than eliminated. Additionally, our concept of defeated simplification aligns with the dynamic analysis of works who investigate the impact of removing arguments. However, our approach considers a specific notion of faithfulness and therefore we employ a specific notion of a defeated arguments.

Future Works. We think that simplifications or abstractions of (the reasoning in) AFs is a necessary step for wider deployment of approaches to formal argumentation. While AFs offer strong capabilities of following the reasoning process, medium-sized or larger AFs already face the risk of being difficult to grasp. Simplifying parts, showing only parts, abstracting parts, or step-by-step explication of the reasoning can allow for clear understanding of what is going on in such AFs in terms of argumentative reasoning.

Our work is a step towards simplification procedures. Ultimately, we think that combinations of several such approaches, together with adequate visualization, have high potential for broader application of formal argumentation machinery, with our approach constituting one basis for such approaches.

Extending our clustering approach to other semantics, by finding specific graph structures where more involved semantics can be over-approximated, is an appealing direction.

Acknowledgement. This research was funded in whole or in part by the Austrian Science Fund (FWF) P35632. For open access purposes, the authors have applied a CC BY public copyright license to any author accepted manuscript version arising from this submission.

References

1. Alfano, G., Calautti, M., Greco, S., Parisi, F., Trubitsyna, I.: Explainable acceptance in probabilistic and incomplete abstract argumentation frameworks. Artif. Intell. **323**, 103967 (2023)
2. Atkinson, K., et al.: Towards artificial argumentation. AI Mag. **38**(3), 25–36 (2017)
3. Bang-Jensen, J., Gutin, G.Z.: Digraphs - Theory, Algorithms and Applications, Second Edition. Springer Monographs in Mathematics, Springer (2009)
4. Baroni, P., Boella, G., Cerutti, F., Giacomin, M., van der Torre, L.W.N., Villata, S.: On the input/output behavior of argumentation frameworks. Artif. Intell. **217**, 144–197 (2014)
5. Baroni, P., Caminada, M., Giacomin, M.: An introduction to argumentation semantics. Knowl. Eng. Rev. **26**(4), 365–410 (2011)
6. Baroni, P., Gabbay, D., Giacomin, M., van der Torre, L. (eds.): Handbook of Formal Argumentation. College Publications (2018)
7. Baumann, R., Ulbricht, M.: Choices and their consequences - explaining acceptable sets in abstract argumentation frameworks. In: Bienvenu, M., Lakemeyer, G., Erdem, E. (eds.) Proceedings of KR, pp. 110–119 (2021)
8. Baumann, R., Ulbricht, M.: On cycles, attackers and supporters - a contribution to the investigation of dynamics in abstract argumentation. In: Zhou, Z. (ed.) Proceedings of IJCAI, pp. 1780–1786. ijcai.org (2021)
9. Besnard, P., Hunter, A.: Elements of Argumentation. MIT Press (2008)
10. Bondarenko, A., Dung, P.M., Kowalski, R.A., Toni, F.: An abstract, argumentation-theoretic approach to default reasoning. Artif. Intell. **93**, 63–101 (1997)
11. Caminada, M.W.A., Gabbay, D.M.: A logical account of formal argumentation. Stud. Logica. **93**(2–3), 109–145 (2009)

12. Dung, P.M.: On the acceptability of arguments and its fundamental role in non-monotonic reasoning, logic programming and n-person games. Artif. Intell. **77**(2), 321–358 (1995)
13. Dunne, P.E.: Computational properties of argument systems satisfying graph-theoretic constraints. Artif. Intell. **171**(10–15), 701–729 (2007)
14. Dvořák, W., Järvisalo, M., Linsbichler, T., Niskanen, A., Woltran, S.: Preprocessing argumentation frameworks via replacement patterns. In: Calimeri, F., Leone, N., Manna, M. (eds.) JELIA 2019. LNCS (LNAI), vol. 11468, pp. 116–132. Springer, Cham (2019). https://doi.org/10.1007/978-3-030-19570-0_8
15. Fan, X., Toni, F.: On computing explanations in argumentation. In: Bonet, B., Koenig, S. (eds.) Proceedings of AAAI, pp. 1496–1502. AAAI Press (2015)
16. Gabbay, D., Giacomin, M., Simari, G.R., Thimm, M. (eds.): Handbook of Formal Argumentation, vol. 2. College Publications (2021)
17. García, A.J., Simari, G.R.: Defeasible logic programming: an argumentative approach. Theory Pract. Log. Program. **4**(1–2), 95–138 (2004)
18. Gordon, T.F., Prakken, H., Walton, D.: The Carneades model of argument and burden of proof. Artif. Intell. **171**(10–15), 875–896 (2007)
19. Kakas, A.C., Moraitis, P., Spanoudakis, N.I.: GORGIAS: applying argumentation. Argument Comput. **10**(1), 55–81 (2019)
20. Modgil, S.: Reasoning about preferences in argumentation frameworks. Artif. Intell. **173**(9–10), 901–934 (2009)
21. Prakken, H.: An argumentation-based analysis of the Simonshaven case. Top. Cogn. Sci. **12**(4), 1068–1091 (2020)
22. Saribatur, Z.G., Eiter, T.: Omission-based abstraction for answer set programs. Theory Pract. Log. Program. **21**(2), 145–195 (2021)
23. Saribatur, Z.G., Knorr, M., Gonçalves, R., Leite, J.: On abstracting over the irrelevant in answer set programming. In: Marquis, P., Ortiz, M., Pagnucco, M. (eds.) Proceedings of KR (2024)
24. Saribatur, Z.G., Wallner, J.P.: Existential abstraction on argumentation frameworks via clustering. In: Bienvenu, M., Lakemeyer, G., Erdem, E. (eds.) Proceedings of KR, pp. 549–559. ijcai.org (2021)
25. Saribatur, Z.G., Wallner, J.P., Woltran, S.: Explaining non-acceptability in abstract argumentation. In: Giacomo, G.D., Catalá, A., Dilkina, B., Milano, M., Barro, S., Bugarín, A., Lang, J. (eds.) Proc. ECAI. Frontiers in Artificial Intelligence and Applications, vol. 325, pp. 881–888. IOS Press (2020)
26. Ulbricht, M., Wallner, J.P.: Strong explanations in abstract argumentation. In: Proceedings of AAAI, pp. 6496–6504. AAAI Press (2021)

Utilizing Binary Decision Diagrams for Compiling Argumentation Frameworks

Michael Baier and Johannes P. Wallner(✉)

Graz University of Technology, Graz, Austria
johannes.p.wallner@tugraz.at

Abstract. Central reasoning tasks arising in computational argumentation are NP-hard. The field of knowledge compilation studies formal representations that permit efficient reasoning, which, however, have so far not found their way into mainstream research in computational argumentation. We study how to compile parts of argumentation frameworks (AFs)—a central representation for argumentative reasoning—to binary decision diagrams (BDDs) in search-based algorithms. We show promise of compilation in an experimental evaluation of the resulting algorithms, which incorporate multiple heuristics.

1 Introduction

Computational argumentation is a branch in Artificial Intelligence (AI) studying non-monotonic argumentative reasoning both from a representational and a computational perspective [5,17], with heterogeneous application areas, e.g., in medical reasoning and legal reasoning [2].

Core principles of argumentative reasoning are represented by formalizations in so-called structured argumentation approaches [7,10,19,21,23,27]. A common core to many of these is to base reasoning on argumentation frameworks (AFs) [14], which view arguments as abstract nodes in a directed graph, with the directed edges being interpreted as attacks between arguments. In these structured approaches AFs are instantiated from knowledge bases to perform argumentative reasoning.

Argumentation semantics drive the reasoning process by finding acceptable sets of arguments in an AF. Prominently, admissible sets constitute an essential concept for many such semantics: conflict-free sets of arguments (no attacks between them) that defend themselves (countering attacks from outside). An admissible set can be seen as a coherent way of arguing for arguments in the set.

For the aim of automated reasoning such argumentation semantics are central. However, it was shown that almost all forms of argumentative reasoning are NP-hard, see, e.g., an overview by Dvořák and Dunne [15]. For instance, checking whether there exists an admissible set containing a queried argument, dubbed credulous acceptance under admissibility, is NP-hard.

As highlighted in previous works [26], there is in fact not only one barrier to computation: also instantiating an AF in the first place can be computationally

A.-Y. Turhan and J. Virtema (Eds.): FoIKS 2026, LNCS 16475, pp. 68–85, 2026.
https://doi.org/10.1007/978-3-032-21540-6_5

intensive, e.g., because of the number of arguments to be generated or due to the complexity of finding arguments. One can view the instantiation process as a rational instantiation of arguments (and attacks) of the given knowledge base, to perform informed argumentative reasoning. However, this process is not necessarily aimed at computational efficacy.

Knowledge compilation (KC) [12] is an area dedicated to finding representations that permit efficient reasoning, with binary decision diagrams (BDDs) [1,9] likely being among the most prominent approaches in KC.

Utilization of approaches studied in KC have not yet found their way into mainstream computational argumentation, we are aware of only few works [16, 28] in this direction.

We take up this opportunity and study ways of utilizing KC for argumentative reasoning. We focus on first steps towards this research agenda: investigating ways of representing AFs utilizing insights from KC. This step is vital for understanding (i) how to utilize KC for complex reasoning on AFs and (ii) what needs to be instantiated in the arguably more general structured argumentation approaches. For the latter, an instantiation (compilation) not directly to AFs but to other formalisms that permit more efficient reasoning can pay off computationally. Nevertheless, first insights are needed how to apply, e.g., KC to AFs (to then have a target representation suited for structured approaches). In contrast to the related works mentioned above [16,28] that apply KC on generalizations of AFs, we utilize KC on AFs directly.

In particular we focus on how to utilize BDDs for AF reasoning. In preliminary experiments we looked at a direct usage of BDDs and the related sentential decision diagrams (SDDs) [11] for AFs: rewriting Boolean formulas representing AF semantics [6] into BDDs or SDDs. However, the resulting size of the BDDs or SDDs was a barrier, and we follow a different route for this work.

When looking at current successful approaches to reasoning in AFs as, e.g., witnessed by the biannual International Competition on Computational Models of Argumentation (ICCMA) [8,18,22,25,29], we find that many are based on modern search algorithms, such as those used in Boolean Satisfiability (SAT) [3] or answer set programming [20]. In this work we aim to combine aspects of compilation to BDDs and aspects of search algorithms. We view our work as steps towards the aim of finding suitable computational representations of argument structures. Our main contributions are as follows.

- We represent core concepts of AFs and semantics in BDDs, such as argument defense.
- We develop algorithms for credulous and skeptical acceptance in AFs under admissibility, and under complete and stable semantics.
- We present several heuristics for improving, e.g., size of BDDs.
- In an experimental evaluation, we show promise of our approach when compared to the state-of-the-art AF solver `crustabri` [24].

2 Preliminaries

We recall background of argumentation frameworks (AFs) [14] and binary decision diagrams (BDDs) [1,9].

Argumentation Frameworks. AFs are composed of abstract arguments and an attack relation (counter-argument relation) between arguments.

Definition 1. *An argumentation framework (AF) is a pair $F = (A, R)$, where A is a finite non-empty set of arguments and $R \subseteq A \times A$ is an attack relation. The pair $(a, b) \in R$ indicates that a attacks b.*

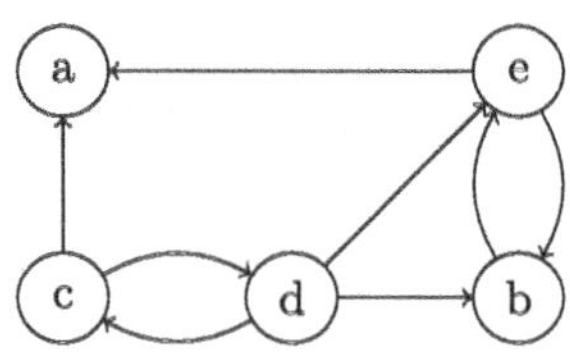

Fig. 1. An example AF

Towards argumentation semantics on AFs [4], we recall the concept of defense of arguments.

Definition 2. *Let $F = (A, R)$ be an AF. An argument $a \in A$ is defended (in F) by a set $S \subseteq A$ if for each $b \in A$ such that $(b, a) \in R$ there is a $c \in S$ such that $(c, b) \in R$.*

For a set of arguments $S \subseteq A$ we say that S attacks an $a \in A$ if there is a $b \in S$ such that $(b, a) \in R$.

The semantics considered in this work can be defined via functions $\sigma(F) \subseteq 2^A$ for a given AF $F = (A, R)$, as follows.

Definition 3. *Let $F = (A, R)$ be an AF. A set $S \subseteq A$ is conflict-free (in F) if there are no $a, b \in S$ such that $(a, b) \in R$. We denote the collection of conflict-free sets of F by $cf(F)$. For a conflict-free set $S \in cf(F)$, it holds that*

- *S is a stable extension in F ($S \in stb(F)$) iff S attacks each $a \in A \setminus S$;*
- *S is an admissible set in F ($S \in adm(F)$) iff S defends each $a \in S$; and*
- *S is a complete extension in F ($S \in com(F)$) iff $S \in adm(F)$ and if $a \in A$ is defended by S then $a \in S$.*

If $S \in \sigma(F)$, then S is called a σ-extension.

We say that an argument $a \in A$ is credulously accepted in F under a semantics σ if there is a σ-extension E in F with $a \in E$. Conversely, a is said to be skeptically accepted in F under σ if $a \in E$ holds for all σ-extensions E in F.

Example 1. Consider an example AF $F = (A, R)$ with $A = \{a, b, c, d, e\}$, and $R = \{(b, e), (c, a), (c, d), (d, b), (d, c), (d, e), (e, a), (e, b)\}$. Figure 1 shows this AF as a directed graph. In this AF we find that $adm(F) = \{\emptyset, \{c\}, \{d\}, \{a, d\}, \{b, c\}, \{c, e\}\}$, $com(F) = \{\emptyset, \{c\}, \{a, d\}, \{b, c\}, \{c, e\}\}$, and $stb(F) = \{\{a, d\}, \{b, c\}, \{c, e\}\}$. For instance, a is credulously accepted under admissibility, and under complete and stable semantics. No argument is skeptically accepted under admissible, complete, or stable semantics in F.

It was shown [13–15] that credulous acceptance under admissibility, and under complete and stable semantics is NP-complete, that skeptical acceptance under admissibility is trivial (due to the empty set being always admissible), that skeptical acceptance under complete semantics is in P, and that skeptical acceptance under stable semantics is coNP-complete.

Binary Decision Diagrams. An established target language for knowledge compilation are *binary decision diagrams* (BDDs) [1,9]. BDDs are acyclic, rooted, directed graphs, consisting of internal (decision) nodes and two terminal nodes representing true and false. A path from the root node to a terminal node describes a (partial) variable assignment.

Definition 4. *A binary decision diagram B over variables X is a rooted directed acyclic graph with two terminal nodes labeled with $\top$ or $\bot$ and internal nodes u with two outgoing edges given by $low(u)$ and $high(u)$. Each internal node u is associated with a variable $x \in X$.*

Paths from the root to $\top$ correspond to partial assignments on X (variables assigned to true for high and false for low), and their completions (assigning remaining variables in X) to models of B that satisfy an underlying Boolean formula represented by the given BDD.

Example 2. Figure 2a shows a BDD representing the Boolean formula $a \wedge \neg e \wedge \neg c \wedge (b \vee d) \wedge d$. The clause $(b \vee d)$ is redundant due to the unit clause d in this example. In subsequent constructions redundant parts may be constructed, yet we apply several heuristics in our algorithms. High edges are represented via solid edges and low ones via dashed edges. For instance, a is the root node, a path from root to terminal node $\top$ is (a, e, b, c, d), and using high edges for a, b, and d, and low for e and c, standing in for the truth value assignment $\{a \mapsto \top, b \mapsto \top, c \mapsto \bot, d \mapsto \top, e \mapsto \bot\}$, satisfying the Boolean formula.

3 Representing AFs as BDDs

In this section we look at a way of utilizing BDDs to represent parts of AFs and AF semantics.

Due to the specifics of AFs, we will use a different representation of BDDs. For a set of variables X, we use its set of negated literals $\neg X = \{\neg x \mid x \in X\}$ as nodes, as well. Then a "positive" node represents the choice of assigning this variable to true (positive literal) and the "negative" one represents assigning the variable to false (negative literal). See, e.g., Fig. 2b for an example that corresponds to the BDD in Fig. 2a. Then a path from the root to (one of the) terminal nodes is a set of literals, representing a particular truth value assignment. Note that we do not need to distinguish edge types (high or low) in this case.

Note that we in general will not require prominent properties of BDDs such as being reduced or ordered. That is, on a path a variable might occur multiple times, for instance. We discuss optimizations and heuristics at a later point and first introduce the general definitions.

Let us consider, for illustration, a basic ingredient of many argumentation semantics: defense of arguments. To defend an argument a from its attackers $b_i, \dots, b_n$ we require a defender for each such attacker. In standard encodings [6] in Boolean logic, this amounts to $a \rightarrow (\bigwedge_{(b,a)\in R} \bigvee_{(c,b)\in R} c)$, which we can state slightly differently as

$$a \rightarrow (\bigwedge_{(b,a)\in R} (\neg b \wedge \bigvee_{(c,b)\in R} c)).$$

That is, if we want a accepted (in an admissible set, say), then each attacker must be "rejected" (assigned false) and at least one defender per attacker accepted, as well. Considering one such attacker b, with $(b, a) \in R$, and possible defenders $D = \{c \mid (c, b) \in R\}$, we arrive at what we call an attack-defend pair $(\neg b, D)$ for a in F. The reason for "b" being negated in the pair is that attackers need to be "out" (as opposed to defenders).

One such attack-defend pair can be straightforwardly represented as a BDD: have $\neg b$ as the root and then have outgoing edges to all defenders, i.e., elements in D. We use shorthand $\texttt{BDD}(\neg b, D)$ to represent this BDD.

A basic operation we will utilize several times is combining BDDs, particularly ones such as BDDs representing attack-defend pairs. Given two BDDs B and B' with roots r_b and r'_b, and terminal nodes T and T', respectively, we combine them, symbolically $B \mid\mid B'$ by defining a new BDD B'' that has the root r_b of B and the terminal nodes T' of B' as its terminal nodes. The terminal nodes T of the first BDD are then connected uniformly to the root r'_b of the second BDD. That is, the set of nodes of B'' is the union of nodes from B and B', and the set of directed edges is the union of both B and B' with additionally (t, r'_b) for each $t \in T$ and T' are the terminal nodes of B''. See Fig 2b for an example. Note that we tacitly assume, for the sake of a simpler illustration, that we can distinguish the nodes from B and B'. In particular, two nodes representing the same variable assignment (e.g., two nodes for variable d) are viewed as different nodes. In implementations this can be achieved, e.g., via unique identifiers for each node.

Definition 5. *Let $F = (A, R)$ be an AF and $a \in A$ an argument. Define the attack-defense diagram (ADD) for a in F as the BDD*

$$B = B_a \mid\mid \texttt{BDD}(\neg b_1, D_1) \mid\mid \cdots \mid\mid \texttt{BDD}(\neg b_n, D_n)$$

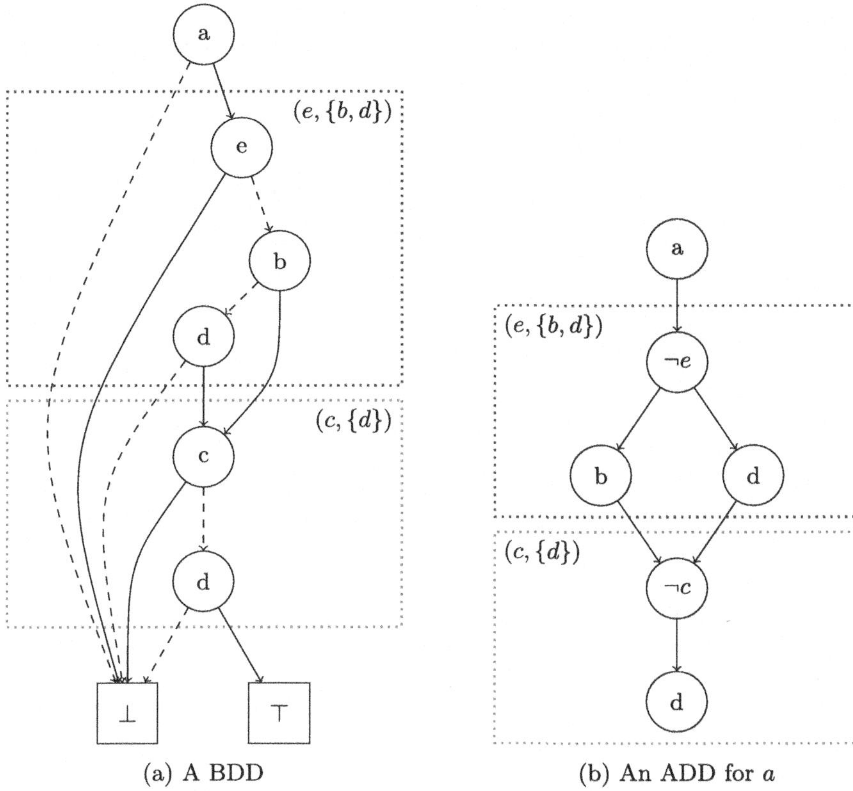

Fig. 2. A BDD (left) and a different representation for this BDD (right). Parts of the BDDs representing attack-defend pairs are inside the dashed boxes.

with B_a being the BDD representing a single node for a, and $b_1, \ldots, b_n$ the attackers of a, and $(\neg b_i, D_i)$ the attack-defend pairs of a.

That is, an ADD for an argument a is a BDD that has a as its root node, and then combined with all attack-defend pairs $(\neg b_i, D_i)$.

Example 3. Consider again the AF from Example 1. The ADD for a is shown in Fig 2b. Any path from the root to a terminal node goes through a, $\neg e$, $\neg c$, and d, indicating that a is selected, e and c must be "false" (they are the attackers of a), and d is required as a defender. For defending against e either b or d is possible, for defending against c one requires argument d.

Intuitively, a path through an ADD for an argument a consists of assigning a to true, all attackers b_i of a to false, and one choice of defenders for each attacker to true.

We extend the notion of an ADD to be associated with a set of arguments S: given ADDs $B_1, \ldots, B_n$ for $a_1, \ldots, a_n$, respectively, then BDD $B_1 \mid\mid \cdots \mid\mid B_n$ is an ADD for $S = \{a_1, \ldots, a_n\}$.

Example 4. Consider again the AF from Example 1. Consider $S = \{a, d\}$. The ADD B_{ad} for S, with considering a first and then d, consists of the ADD as shown in Fig. 3.

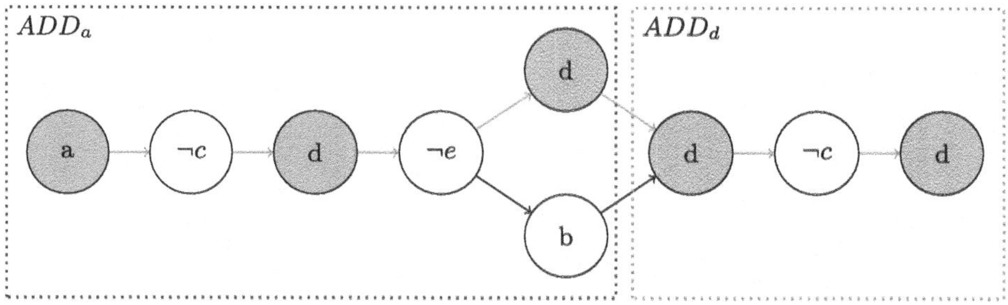

Fig. 3. ADD B_{ad}, to show that a is part of an admissible set. The conflict-free path (positive literals) is marked in green. (Color figure online)

Naturally, in general a path from root a to a terminal node in an ADD for a will not constitute a set of interest directly (like an admissible set containing a). We define properties of interest. For the sake of a simpler illustration, we apply certain set operations also on paths (on tuples) such as intersection, with the associated natural definition.

Definition 6. *Let $F = (A, R)$ be an AF, and $a \in A$ an argument. Moreover, let B be an ADD for $S \subseteq A$ in F. A path P (from root to a terminal node) in B is called*

- *conflict-free if there is no $x \in A$ such that $\{x, \neg x\} \subseteq P$,*
- *self-defending if $P \cap A$ defends each $x \in P \cap A$ in F, and*
- *admissible if P is conflict-free and self-defending.*

Note that $P \cap A$ means to collect all positive variables in the path (intuitively excluding attackers). From now on we will simply say path (in a BDD) if we mean a path from the root node to a terminal node.

Proposition 1. *Let $F = (A, R)$ be an AF, $S \subseteq A$, and B an ADD for S in F with a path P such that $P \cap A = S$. It holds that S is admissible in F iff P is admissible in B.*

Proof. By construction, a path contains all arguments in S, all attackers of S are occurring negatively in a path, as well. Moreover, by construction, a path contains at least one defender per attacker. Since the positive nodes in P, by assumption, equal S, it holds that S is defending itself. Moreover, S is conflict-free if and only if P is conflict-free. The preceding points imply that S is admissible in F if and only if P is admissible in B.

As witnessed in the preceding proof, to find admissible sets we can combine ADDs for each member in a candidate for an admissible set and check conflict-freeness of paths (self-defense is due to construction of ADDs).

Example 5. Revisiting Example 1 and the ADD in Fig. 3, we can see that there is a path $(a, \neg c, d, \neg e, d, d, \neg c, d)$ in this ADD. This means that a is defended by $\{d\}$ and $\{b, d\}$, and d defends itself.

To compute complete extensions and stable extensions, we utilize a different form which we call inverse attacks: for an argument $a \in A$, we assign $\neg a$ as the root of a specific BDD, with the root having edges towards the set of attackers $T = \{b \mid (b, a) \in R)\}$. See Fig. 4b for an example. For stable semantics, if a is outside a current candidate set, at least one attacker must be selected. For complete extensions, one can then check whether all attackers are attacked, then a is defended. The latter check is somewhat outside the BDDs we defined. While one could transform the Boolean formula that models an implication of an argument being defended to be assigned true, we opted to utilize the inverse attack-defense diagrams for this purpose.

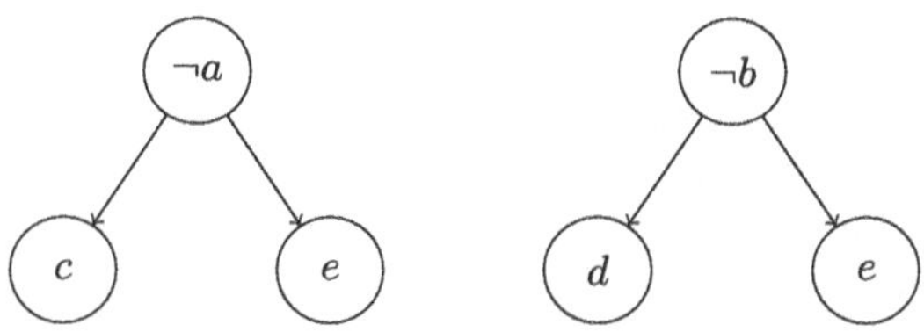

Fig. 4. Inverse attack-defense diagrams for $\neg a$ and $\neg b$

4 Algorithmic Approach Using BDDs

Our approach to utilize strengths of BDDs for reasoning in AFs is based on partially compiling AFs and AF semantics, in the form of ADDs, and utilizing them in search-based algorithms.

Let us focus on credulous reasoning under admissibility, a central computational reasoning task on AFs.

We will first describe the basic Algorithm 1 for credulous reasoning, skeptical reasoning then below, and in Sect. 5 we propose several heuristics.

The algorithm is initialized with a set of arguments S. The aim is to check if there is an admissible set $S' \supseteq S$. For instance, $S = \{a\}$ and we check credulous acceptance, under admissibility, of a in the AF F. Moreover, an ADD B for S is given.

In Line 1 we check whether the given set S, viewed here as a path in B, is already admissible. By going through the ADD using S as a path (in fact the negated nodes directly follow, one only needs to specify the positive nodes where there is a choice), we check conflict-freeness. If the given ADD is for S, we can directly check self-defendedness: if by using S to go through B we end up in a terminal node and not use any positive node other than those in S, it holds that S is self-defended.

If, on the other hand, S is not admissible, we check whether there is a conflict-free path in B. This check is direct, since we can remove all positive occurrences of nodes if they are also negatively in the BDD (since we have to "go through" all negative nodes). In case no such path exists, we cannot find an admissible set containing S, and return *fail*).

In the main for loop in Line 3 we go over each path, fetch the first argument *next* occurring in P that is not already in S, and recursively check admissibility of $S \cup \{next\}$. Note that B is an ADD for an $X \subseteq S$ and not necessarily for S.

Example 6. Considering again the AF from Example 1 and the ADD in Fig. 2b. It holds that $S = \{a\}$ is not admissible (does not reach a terminal node using only a as a positive node). Therefore, the two conflict-free paths in the ADD (a, d) and (a, b, d) are checked, and d is picked first. As shown in Fig. 3 the set $S = \{a, d\}$ is conflict- free and self-defending, and therefore an admissible set is found, showing that a is part of an admissible set.

For complete semantics, inverse attack-defense diagrams can be used. First we check if a set of arguments S is admissible in a given AF $F = (A, R)$ (Algorithm 1). To check additionally completeness, for each argument x within distance two of S not attacked by S (arguments that are possibly defended) we combine all inverse attack diagrams of their attackers. Then a path using only S indicates that all attackers are attacked by S and the argument in question defended.

For stable semantics, a similar procedure applies. Starting from an admissible set, or complete extension as in our implementation, check whether all arguments $A \setminus S$ are attacked by S, using again the combination of inverse attack-defense diagrams for $A \setminus S$. If using S as a path goes from root to a terminal node, we can infer that S is a stable extension.

Algorithm 1. $\texttt{Cred}_{adm}(F, B, S)$

Require: An AF $F = (A, R)$, a set $S \subseteq A$, and an ADD B (for some $X \subseteq S$).
Ensure: An admissible set containing all arguments of S.
1: **if** S is admissible in B **then return** S
2: **if** there is no conflict-free path in B **then return** *fail*
3: **for** conflict-free path P in B **do**
4:     $next = \texttt{first}(P \setminus S)$
5:     $B' = B \mid\mid \texttt{ADD}(next)$
6:     $S' = \texttt{Cred}_{adm}(F, B', S \cup \{next\})$
7:     **if** $S' \neq fail$ **return** S'
8: **return** *fail*

For skeptical acceptance, following current state-of-the-art algorithms, we aim to construct a witness for the "no" case, i.e., when the queried argument is not skeptically accepted. Then a σ-extension not containing the query exists, which we aim to find. This can be achieved by including the query argument negated as a root node, and applying otherwise the semantics discussed above.

5 Heuristics

Our search-based algorithms utilize BDDs for compilation of parts of an AF. As usual for search-based algorithms, heuristics are useful for improving performance. In this section we go over several heuristics we applied and experimented on, see Sect. 6.

Duplicates in ADDs. In an ADD B for an argument $a \in A$, given an AF $F = (A, R)$, we can find duplicated arguments. Say there is a path P in B with b occurring multiple times in P, that is, there are two nodes v and u in P with either positive b or negative literals $\neg b$. We now look at ways of simplifying B.

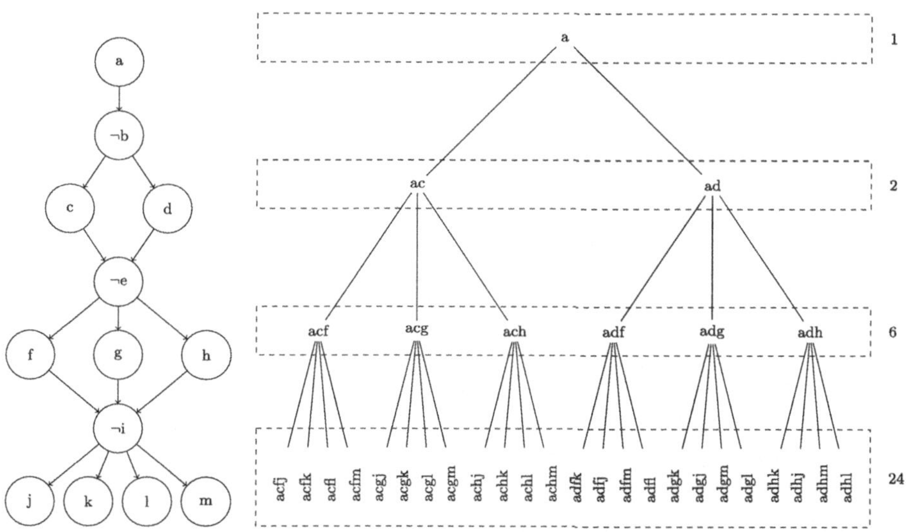

(a) Example BDD (b) All possible 32 merge operations of the BDD on the left. The numbers next to the dashed boxes show the number of possible merge operations per level in the binary decision diagram.

Fig. 5. Sorting order and number of merge operations

The way of resolving duplicates from the ADD is dependent on them being attackers or defenders. The duplicates v and u cannot be both negated, because an argument cannot be attacked by the same argument twice. If the duplicates are both positive (both represent b), the following reductions can be applied. The duplicate v can be removed if u is the only possible defender of an argument in the ADD (all edges from the preceding attacker go to u). If a duplicate v is removed, also all the other possible defenders get removed, as it is already defended by the other duplicate. That is, if (x, v) and (x, v') are edges in the ADD, then v' can be removed, as well. Formally, for E the edges in the ADD, $V_r = \{v\} \cup \{v' \mid (x, v), (x, v') \subseteq E\}$ can be removed if v is the duplicate to be removed. Afterwards, one can in a straightforward fashion "re-connect" the disconnected parts of the ADD. For instance, if (x, v) (and (x, v')) were removed and y is the successor of v, then (x, y) can be added.

Testing Possible Argument Pairings. This optimization checks for incompatibilities in the AF before combining ADDs. Concretely, for two ADDs B_1 and B_2, they are said to be compatible if there is no argument that occurs positively in one and negatively in the other.

Never In Set Arguments. In the compilation step of AFs to ADDs it is possible that an argument can never be in any resulting σ-extension. An argument can never be "in" if the argument is self-attacking or if the ADD for this argument has no conflict-free paths.

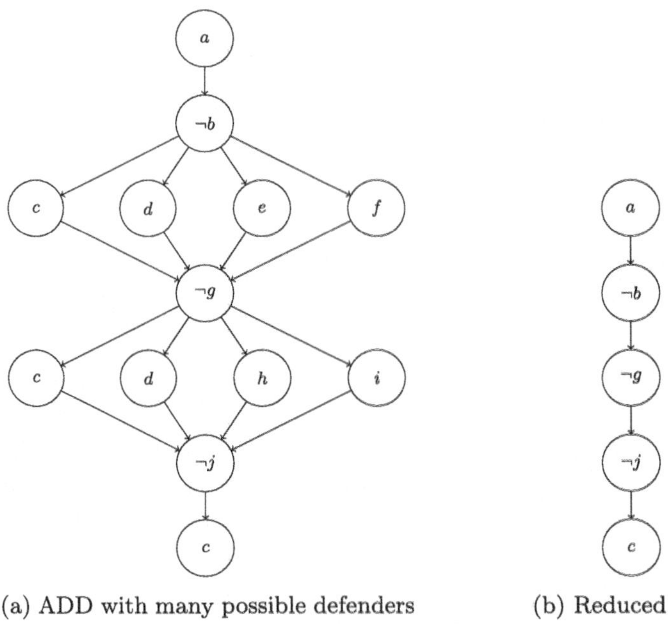

(a) ADD with many possible defenders (b) Reduced ADD

Fig. 6. Subsumed defenders in an ADD

Sorting of Attack Defense Diagrams. In this heuristic, we apply a certain ordering to the attackers in an ADD for an argument a (or a set of arguments). That is, when combining the attack-defend pairs of a, we can liberally choose the order of the attackers. We sort the attack-defend pairs to be sorted by the in-degree of the attackers, from lowest to highest.

Since in our algorithms we oftentimes combine ADDs, lowering the number of such combinations can lead to increased performance. Consider, e.g., Fig 5. We might need to combine this ADD (on the left in the figure) with ADDs for all positive arguments (except the root) in the ADD (see right of the figure). If one would first consider the attack-defense pair for attacker i and its four possible defenders and then the others, more combinations would be possibly performed.

Subsumed Defender Sets. Say an argument a is attacked by both b and c. Moreover, let (d, b), (d, c), and (e, c) be further attacks. To defend argument a against the attack from b, argument d can be utilized. Defender d also defends against c, and the potential defender e is not required anymore. More concretely, if for two attack-defend pairs $(\neg b, D_b)$ and $(\neg c, D_c)$ we find that $D_b \subseteq D_c$ then in an ADD where both occur, we can remove D_c, since choosing a defender from D_b suffices for D_c, as well. An example can be seen in Fig. 6: there c defends a against b, g, and j.

Heuristically Choosing Paths. Finally, we consider finding "good" paths in an ADD. When possible, this heuristics chooses a defending argument over another if the former attacks more arguments (defends against more arguments). See Fig. 7 for an example.

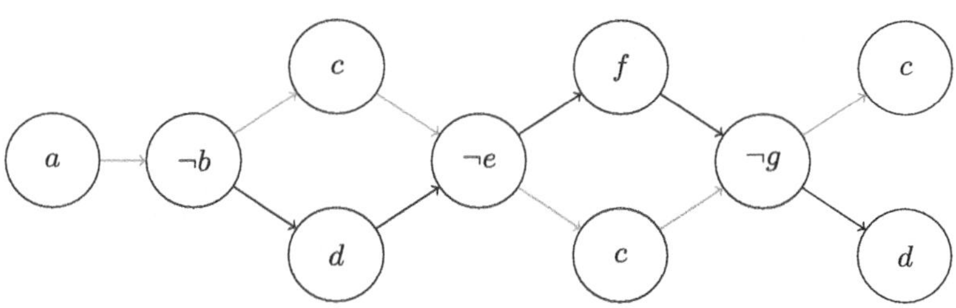

Fig. 7. Choosing defenders based on how many arguments they attack.

6 Experimental Evaluation

We report on an experimental evaluation we conducted on a Rust-based prototype[1], which we provide under an open license.

[1] https://gitlab.tugraz.at/6A1AB4D383C7E26F/attack-defend-compiler.

Instances. We considered all instances from the International Competition on Computational Models of Argumentation (ICCMA) in 2023 [22].

Reasoning Tasks. We considered the NP-complete or coNP-complete reasoning tasks of checking credulous acceptance under admissibility, complete semantics, and stable semantics, as well as skeptical acceptance under stable semantics.

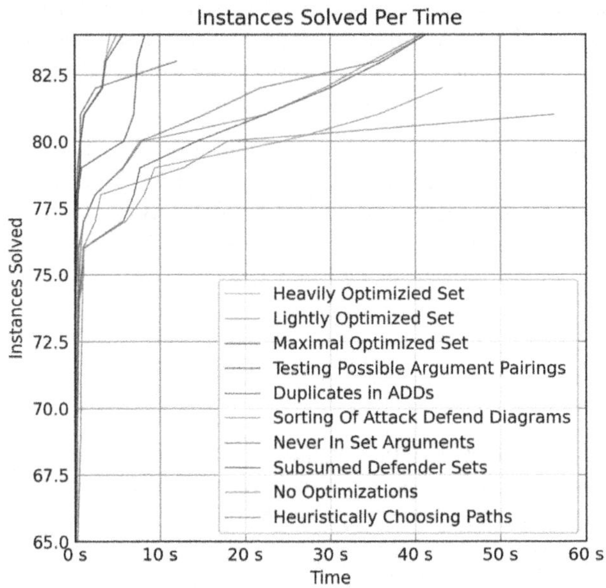

Fig. 8. Comparing number of instances solved using different heuristics.

Experimental Setup. We executed all tasks on an AMD Ryzen 9 3900X (12 Core, 24 Thread, 4.6 GHz), 32 GB (3600 MHz), Samsung SSD 980 PRO 1 TB, under Arch Linux x86_64.

As a competitor system, we compared our prototype to `crustabri` [24], a state-of-the-art solver for AF reasoning tasks, which also scored first place in several tracks in the last ICCMA 2023 competition.

Results. We present empirical results (i) evaluating the heuristics, (ii) comparing to `crustabri`, and (iii) evaluating the compilation time. For the first two, we evaluated runtimes without compilation times of the given AF to ADDs for each argument, and in the last part we look at the compilation time needed. For the solving time, all runs were restricted to one minute runtime.

Evaluating Heuristics. We first consider the effect of the heuristics on twelve instances from ICCMA'23 from the instance families taking part of this competition. We grouped the heuristics in the following way.

- The first set of optimizations, dubbed the "maximal optimized set", contains all heuristics presented in this work.
- The second set of optimizations, dubbed the "heavily optimized set", contains all heuristics except heuristically choosing paths to verify the usefulness of these heuristics.
- The third set of optimizations, dubbed the "lightly optimized set", is a set of heuristics including the pairing optimization, the never in set optimization, and the duplicate removal.

Figure 8 shows how many instances were solved (individually) within a certain time. The figure shows that all three groups of heuristics improved the runtimes compared to the compiler without or with only one heuristic. Furthermore, the heavily optimized set finds the most solutions in the least amount of time.

Comparing Against State of the Art. To show the potential of ADDs we compared our implementation to the state-of-the-art solver `crustabri`, results summarized in Fig. 9, using here the heavily optimized set of heuristics. We first compiled the ADDs for each argument, and then compare the runtime afterwards, with a one-minute timeout per instance. We considered all instances from ICCMA'23.

As shown in the figure, our implementation is outperformed on skeptical reasoning under stable semantics, while our implementation shows promise for credulous reasoning under admissible and complete semantics. Note these are in fact the same reasoning tasks, but we utilized the algorithms for admissibility and complete semantics, respectively.

To compare the compilation and reasoning times of our solution Fig. 10 shows the times grouped by different reasoning tasks. Here the compilation time refers to the time the compiler took, the loading time refers to the time the solver took to load the compiled structures from disk, and the reasoning time shows the time needed to solve an instance. This figure contains only the times where the solver could solve the instance in a one minute limit.

The compilation time of our solver are high compared to the reasoning times it takes to solve instances, which is also due to the fact that most heuristics are on a compile time basis.

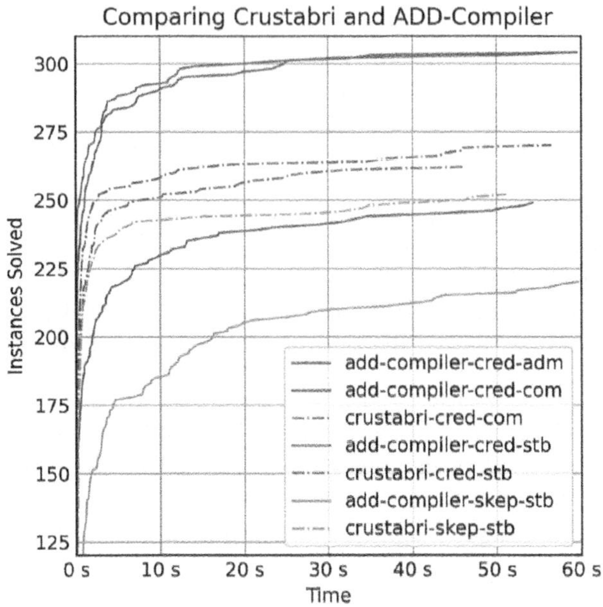

Fig. 9. Number of instances solved within a certain amount of time. Comparing solving times of our approach and `crustabri`.

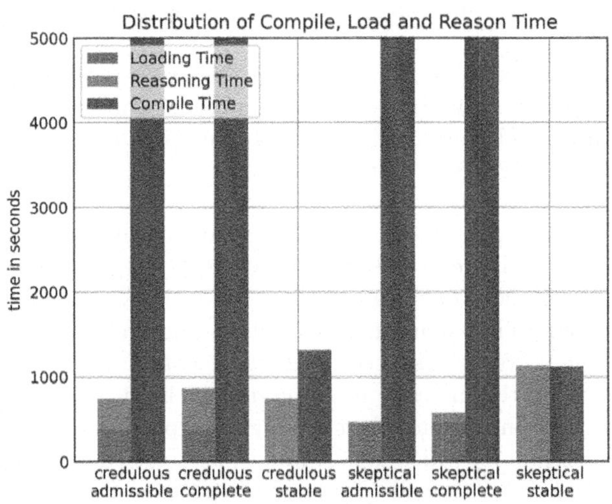

Fig. 10. Bar plot showing loading, reason, and compilation time of our approach for different problems and semantics.

7 Conclusions

In this work, we considered ways of utilizing BDDs for computationally complex reasoning in AFs. We combined compilation of BDDs with search-based algorithms. Our prototype implementation in Rust shows promise when compared to the state-of-the-art solver `crustabri`.

While solvers based on SAT solvers remain the state of the art for reasoning in AFs, in particular due to higher compilation time, our approach can be a basis for future investigations of compiling AFs and reasoning tasks. Moreover, after compilation, our solver shows interesting running times even compared to the state of the art.

In future works we aim to extend our approach of compilation in particular to forms of structured argumentation. For instance, we aim to answer research questions on how to compile structured argumentation frameworks into computationally efficient structures. Since defense is a main driver for reasoning also in structured argumentation, a question is whether one should compile structured approaches similarly in a defense-oriented way or utilize different directions. On the other hand, compilation of structured formalisms might not only take into account solving times for reasoning tasks but also how to compute argument-based explanations or explications of the reasoning process, indicating that compilation on structured argumentation is a challenging research endeavour.

Acknowledgments. This research was funded in whole or in part by the Austrian Science Fund (FWF) P35632. For open access purposes, the authors have applied a CC BY public copyright license to any author accepted manuscript version arising from this submission.

References

1. Akers, S.B.: Binary decision diagrams. IEEE Trans. Comput. **27**(6), 509–516 (1978)
2. Atkinson, K., et al.: Towards artificial argumentation. AI Mag. **38**(3), 25–36 (2017)
3. Bacchus, F., Järvisalo, M., Martins, R.: Maximum satisfiabiliy. In: Biere, A., Heule, M., van Maaren, H., Walsh, T. (eds.) Handbook of Satisfiability, 2nd edn. Frontiers in Artificial Intelligence and Applications, vol. 336, pp. 929–991. IOS Press (2021)
4. Baroni, P., Caminada, M., Giacomin, M.: An introduction to argumentation semantics. Knowl. Eng. Rev. **26**(4), 365–410 (2011)
5. Baroni, P., Gabbay, D., Giacomin, M., van der Torre, L. (eds.): Handbook of Formal Argumentation. College Publications (2018)
6. Besnard, P., Doutre, S.: Checking the acceptability of a set of arguments. In: Delgrande, J.P., Schaub, T. (eds.) Proceedings of the NMR, pp. 59–64 (2004)
7. Besnard, P., Hunter, A.: A review of argumentation based on deductive arguments, chap. 9. In: Baroni, P., Gabbay, D., Giacomin, M., van der Torre, L. (eds.) Handbook of Formal Argumentation, pp. 437–484. College Publications (2018)
8. Bistarelli, S., Kotthoff, L., Santini, F., Taticchi, C.: Summary report for the third international competition on computational models of argumentation. AI Mag. **42**(3), 70–73 (2021)

9. Bryant, R.E.: Graph-based algorithms for Boolean function manipulation. IEEE Trans. Comput. **35**(8), 677–691 (1986)
10. Čyras, K., Fan, X., Schulz, C., Toni, F.: Assumption-based argumentation: disputes, explanations, preferences, chap. 7. In: Baroni, P., Gabbay, D., Giacomin, M., van der Torre, L. (eds.) Handbook of Formal Argumentation, pp. 365–408. College Publications (2018)
11. Darwiche, A.: SDD: a new canonical representation of propositional knowledge bases. In: Walsh, T. (ed.) Proceedings of the IJCAI, pp. 819–826. IJCAI/AAAI (2011)
12. Darwiche, A., Marquis, P.: A knowledge compilation map. J. Artif. Intell. Res. **17**, 229–264 (2002)
13. Dimopoulos, Y., Torres, A.: Graph theoretical structures in logic programs and default theories. Theor. Comput. Sci. **170**(1–2), 209–244 (1996)
14. Dung, P.M.: On the acceptability of arguments and its fundamental role in nonmonotonic reasoning, logic programming and n-person games. Artif. Intell. **77**(2), 321–358 (1995)
15. Dvořák, W., Dunne, P.E.: Computational problems in formal argumentation and their complexity, chap. 13. In: Baroni, P., Gabbay, D., Giacomin, M., van der Torre, L. (eds.) Handbook of Formal Argumentation, pp. 631–688. College Publications (2018)
16. Ellmauthaler, S., Gaggl, S.A., Rusovac, D., Wallner, J.P.: Representing abstract dialectical frameworks with binary decision diagrams. In: Gottlob, G., Inclezan, D., Maratea, M. (eds.) Proceedings of the LPNMR. LNCS, vol. 13416, pp. 177–189. Springer, Heidelberg (2022). https://doi.org/10.1007/978-3-031-15707-3_14
17. Gabbay, D., Giacomin, M., Simari, G.R., Thimm, M. (eds.): Handbook of Formal Argumentation, vol. 2. College Publications (2021)
18. Gaggl, S.A., Linsbichler, T., Maratea, M., Woltran, S.: Design and results of the second international competition on computational models of argumentation. Artif. Intell. **279** (2020)
19. García, A.J., Simari, G.R.: Argumentation based on logic programming, chap. 8. In: Baroni, P., Gabbay, D., Giacomin, M., van der Torre, L. (eds.) Handbook of Formal Argumentation, pp. 409–435. College Publications (2018)
20. Gelfond, M., Lifschitz, V.: The stable model semantics for logic programming. In: Proceedings of the ICLP/SLP, pp. 1070–1080. MIT Press (1988)
21. Gordon, T.F., Prakken, H., Walton, D.: The Carneades model of argument and burden of proof. Artif. Intell. **171**(10–15), 875–896 (2007)
22. Järvisalo, M., Lehtonen, T., Niskanen, A.: ICCMA 2023: 5th international competition on computational models of argumentation. Artif. Intell. **342**, 104311 (2025)
23. Kakas, A.C., Moraitis, P., Spanoudakis, N.I.: GORGIAS: applying argumentation. Argument Comput. **10**(1), 55–81 (2019)
24. Lagniez, J., Lonca, E., Mailly, J.: A SAT-based approach for argumentation dynamics. In: Dastani, M., Sichman, J.S., Alechina, N., Dignum, V. (eds.) Proceedings of the AAMAS, pp. 2351–2353. International Foundation for Autonomous Agents and Multiagent Systems/ACM (2024)
25. Lagniez, J., Lonca, E., Mailly, J., Rossit, J.: Introducing the fourth international competition on computational models of argumentation. In: Gaggl, S.A., Thimm, M., Vallati, M. (eds.) Proceedings of the SAFA. CEUR Workshop Proceedings, vol. 2672, pp. 80–85. CEUR-WS.org (2020)
26. Lehtonen, T., Rapberger, A., Ulbricht, M., Wallner, J.P.: Argumentation frameworks induced by assumption-based argumentation: relating size and complexity.

In: Marquis, P., Son, T.C., Kern-Isberner, G. (eds.) Proceedings of the KR, pp. 440–450 (2023)

27. Modgil, S., Prakken, H.: Abstract rule-based argumentation, chap. 6. In: Baroni, P., Gabbay, D., Giacomin, M., van der Torre, L. (eds.) Handbook of Formal Argumentation, pp. 287–364. College Publications (2018)
28. Tang, Y., Norman, T.J., Parsons, S.: Computing argumentation in polynomial number of BDD operations: a preliminary report. In: McBurney, P., Rahwan, I., Parsons, S. (eds.) ArgMAS 2010. LNCS (LNAI), vol. 6614, pp. 268–285. Springer, Heidelberg (2011). https://doi.org/10.1007/978-3-642-21940-5_16
29. Thimm, M., Villata, S.: The first international competition on computational models of argumentation: results and analysis. Artif. Intell. **252**, 267–294 (2017)

A Modal Logic for Possibilistic Reasoning with Fuzzy Formal Contexts

Prosenjit Howlader and Churn-Jung Liau(✉)

Institute of Information Science, Academia Sinica, 115 Taipei, Taiwan
{prosen,liaucj}@iis.sinica.edu.tw

Abstract. We introduce a *two-sort weighted modal logic* for possibilistic reasoning with fuzzy formal contexts. The syntax of the logic includes two types of weighted modal operators corresponding to classical *necessity* (□) and *sufficiency* (⊟) modalities and its formulas are interpreted in *fuzzy formal contexts* based on possibility theory. We present its axiomatization that is *sound* with respect to the class of all fuzzy context models. In addition, both the necessity and sufficiency fragments of the logic are also individually *complete* with respect to the class of all fuzzy context models. We highlight the expressive power of the logic with some illustrative examples. As a formal context is the basic construct of formal concept analysis (FCA), we generalize three main notions in FCA, i.e., *formal concepts*, *object oriented concepts*, and *property oriented concepts*, to their corresponding *c*-cut concepts in fuzzy formal contexts. Then, we show that our logical language can represent all three of these generalized notions. Finally, we demonstrate the possibility of extending our logic to reasoning with multi-relational fuzzy contexts, in which the Boolean combinations of different fuzzy relations are allowed.

Keywords: weighted modal logic · possibilistic reasoning · formal concept analysis · rough set theory

1 Introduction

Formal concept analysis (FCA) is a mathematical theory for studying structures of concepts [33]. In FCA, a *formal context* (or simply context), aka *polarity*, is a triple (G, M, I), where G and M are sets of objects and attributes, respectively, and $I \subseteq G \times M$ is a binary incidence relation connecting them. Given a context, a *formal concept* is a pair of subsets of objects and attributes (A, B) such that A is the set of objects possessing all attributes in B and B is the set of attributes shared by all objects in A. For the formal concept, A and B are called its extent and intent, respectively. Furthermore, inspired by rough set theory [32], notions of rough concepts including object and property oriented concepts, have been also defined [14,34,35].

The theoretical framework of FCA has evolved into an indispensable tool for knowledge discovery from complex datasets which are usually presented as formal contexts. Traditionally, most data mining methods represent the discovered

A.-Y. Turhan and J. Virtema (Eds.): FoIKS 2026, LNCS 16475, pp. 86–105, 2026.
https://doi.org/10.1007/978-3-032-21540-6_6

knowledge as simple if-then rules. However, this is not expressive enough for the representation of more complicated knowledge. Moreover, when applying to decision-making, simple rules can facilitate only shallow reasoning by matching their antecedents with the decision situation and taking consequents of matched rules. By employing a logical approach, we can address the expressivity of knowledge representation formalisms for data mining from formal contexts.

For the knowledge representation and reasoning with formal contexts, several logical formalisms have received much attention [5,9,10,19–22]. In a recent work, it is shown that two-sorted Boolean modal logic can serve as a reliable base for the representation of both formal and rough concepts [24]. The logic is a synergy of two-sorted modal logic and Boolean modal logic.

On one hand, two-sorted modal logic is an instance of many-sorted polyadic modal logic, which was studied in [25] and then extended to a many-sorted hybrid logic in [26]. Because a formal context has two domains and an incidence relation, it is an appropriate semantic model for two-sorted modal logic. On the other hand, Boolean modal logic combines two dual branches of modal logic: one with the box modality ($\Box$) representing necessity, and the other with the window modality ($\boxminus$) representing sufficiency [17]. These two kinds of modalities correspond to basic operators in rough approximations and FCA, and thus facilitate the representation of different notions of concepts in formal contexts.

While FCA has been an effective tool for data analysis, because of the pervasive uncertainty and vagueness of information in complex datasets, the binary relation in formal contexts may be not two-valued in many applications. In particular, to deal with vague information in formal contexts, various fuzzy FCA methods have been proposed [1–4,6], in which a formal context is extended to a fuzzy context by replacing the crisp incidence relation with a fuzzy one. The derivation operators map fuzzy sets on G to fuzzy sets on M and vice versa, forming a Galois connection. Consequently, fuzzy concepts are pairs of fuzzy sets mutually determined by these operators. Typically, membership functions of these fuzzy sets measure the degree to which an attribute (object) connects with all objects (attributes). However, unlike the existing approaches, we further define the derivation operators using (strict) c-cuts for $c \in [0, 1]$ on these fuzzy sets, mapping a set of objects to the attributes whose degree of connecting with all these objects meets or exceeds c, and vice versa.

As logics for fuzzy formal contexts are under-explored yet, there exist only a few works on this topic. Among them, two approaches to connecting logic with fuzzy formal contexts have been proposed in [7]. One is to follow an idea in [8] by interpreting fuzzy logic formulas as formal concepts, and the other is to consider semantic evaluations and formulas of a fuzzy logic as objects and attributes of a fuzzy context, respectively, and use the fuzzy relation between them to denote the satisfaction degree of a formula in an evaluation.

In this paper, we present yet another approach based on the weighted extension of the above-mentioned two-sorted Boolean modal logic. By considering the fuzzy incidence relation as a class of possibility distributions, we use weighted modalities to represent uncertainty measures corresponding to different operators in FCA as explicated in [13]. In addition, as these weighted modalities correspond to our cut-based derivation operators, we define c-cut concepts as the generalization of formal and rough concepts in fuzzy contexts and show that our logic can represent and reason with these generalized concepts.

The remainder of the paper is organized as follows. The next section contains background knowledge on FCA, fuzzy sets, and possibility theory. In Sect. 3, we introduce basic operators for constructing generalized concepts in fuzzy formal contexts. In addition, we define the cut-based notions of formal and rough concepts. In Sect. 4, we present the two-sorted weighted modal logic and show its application to the representation of different c-cut concepts. While the completeness of the proposed logic remains an open issue, we prove that its necessity and sufficiency fragments are individually complete in Sect. 5. In Sect. 6, we discuss the possible extension of the logic to reasoning with multi-relational fuzzy contexts. We conclude the paper with some directions of future work in Sect. 7.

2 Preliminaries

In this section, we introduce some preliminary notions about FCA and possibility theory.

2.1 Formal Concept Analysis

Let us recall the definition of a context (G, M, I) introduced in the previous section. A given context induces two derivation operators $+ : (\mathcal{P}(G), \subseteq) \to (\mathcal{P}(M), \supseteq)$ and $- : (\mathcal{P}(M), \supseteq) \to (\mathcal{P}(G), \subseteq)$, where for all $A \in \mathcal{P}(G)$ and $B \in \mathcal{P}(M)$:

$$A^+ = \{m \in M \mid \forall g(g \in A \Rightarrow gIm)\}, \quad B^- = \{g \in G \mid \forall m(m \in B \Rightarrow gIm)\}.$$

It can be shown that the pair of maps forms a Galois connection. Moreover, every Galois connection is associated with some formal context, and this correspondence is bijective. For details, we refer the reader to [16].

A *(formal) concept* is a pair of sets (A, B) such that $A^+ = B$ and $A = B^-$, where A and B are called its *extent* and *intent*, respectively. We denote the set of all concepts by $\mathbf{B}(\mathbb{K})$. It forms a complete lattice and is denoted by $\underline{\mathbf{B}}(\mathbb{K})$.

Düntsch and Gediga [14] defined sufficiency, dual sufficiency, possibility and necessity operators based on a context. In particular, for a context $\mathbb{K} := (G, M, I)$, $A \subseteq G$, and $B \subseteq M$, the pairs of possibility and necessity operators are defined as follows:

$$A^\diamond := \{m \in M \mid \exists g(gIm \wedge g \in A)\}, \quad A^\Box := \{m \in M \mid \forall g(gIm \Rightarrow g \in A)\}$$

.

$$B^{\Diamond} := \{g \in G \mid \exists m(gIm \wedge m \in B)\}, \quad B^{\Box} := \{g \in G \mid \forall m(gIm \Rightarrow m \in B)\}$$

.

These operators correspond to approximation operators in rough set theory (RST) [31]. Based on them, Düntsch and Gediga [14] and Yao [35] introduced property oriented concepts and object oriented concepts, respectively. A pair (A, B) is a *property oriented concept* of $\mathbb{K}$ iff $A^{\Diamond} = B$ and $B^{\Box} = A$, and it is an *object oriented concept* of $\mathbb{K}$ iff $A^{\Box} = B$ and $B^{\Diamond} = A$. These two kinds of concepts are also called rough concepts.

In addition to formal concept lattices mentioned above, the set $\mathbf{O}(\mathbb{K})$ of all object oriented concepts and the set $\mathbf{P}(\mathbb{K})$ of all property oriented concepts also form complete lattices, which are called *object oriented concept lattices* and *property oriented concept lattices*, respectively. The relationship among the three kinds of concept lattices are investigated in [34].

Regarding the motivation of the paper, we use the following example to show how a formal context can represent a dataset in practical applications.

Example 1 Let us consider a formal context (G, M, I), where G is the set of readers (users) of an on-line document repository M containing books, articles, and so on. In such a scenario, for $g \in G$ and $m \in M$, gIm means that the reader g has downloaded the document m. Assume that A is a particular group of users and B is a special class of documents. Then, the above-mentioned operators of FCA may contain the following information:

- $g \in B^{\Box}$: the reader g only downloaded documents in B
- $m \in A^{\Box}$: only readers in A downloaded the document m
- $g \in B^{-}$: the reader g downloaded all documents in B
- $m \in A^{+}$: all readers in A downloaded the document m

2.2 Fuzzy Set, Possibility Theory, and Possibilistic Reasoning

Fuzzy set theory is invented by Zadeh [36] to model vagueness in set membership. A fuzzy set is a set without a precise boundary between its elements and non-elements. Given a universe W, a fuzzy set $\tilde{A}$ over W is defined as a membership function $\tilde{A} : W \to [0, 1]$. We denote the class of all fuzzy subsets of a universe W by $\tilde{\mathcal{P}}(W)$. A fuzzy binary relation between two domains U and V is simply a fuzzy subset of its Cartesian product $U \times V$. Let $\tilde{A}$ be a fuzzy set over W and $c \in [0, 1]$. Then, the c-cut and strict c-cut of $\tilde{A}$ are defined as $\tilde{A}_c = \{w \in W \mid \tilde{A}(w) \geq c\}$ and $\tilde{A}_{>c} = \{w \in W \mid \tilde{A}(w) > c\}$, respectively.

When the universe W is a set of possible worlds (or states), we can interpret a fuzzy set as a *possibility distribution* . This leads to the development of possibility theory [37].

Definition 1. [13] Let W be a set. Then, we define

- a possibility distribution over W as a function $\pi : W \to [0,1]$,
- the possibility measure $\Pi : \mathcal{P}(W) \to [0,1]$ by $\Pi(X) := \sup_{x\in X} \pi(x)$,
- the necessity measure $N : \mathcal{P}(W) \to [0,1]$ by $N(X) := \inf_{x\notin X}(1-\pi(x))$,
- the guaranteed possibility measure Δ: $\mathcal{P}(W) \to [0,1]$ by $\Delta(X) := \inf_{x\in X} \pi(x)$,
- the potential certainty measure $\nabla : \mathcal{P}(W) \to [0,1]$ by $\nabla(X) := \sup_{x\notin X}(1-\pi(x))$.

By mathematical convention, $\sup\emptyset = 0$ and $\inf\emptyset = 1$. Hence, by the definition, we have $\Pi(\emptyset) = \nabla(W) = 0$ and $N(W) = \Delta(\emptyset) = 1$.

Possibilistic logic has been proposed for reasoning about possibility distributions [11,12]. By the analogy between necessity (resp. possibility) measure and the modal operator $\Box$ (resp. $\Diamond$) indicated in [12], more expressive modal formulations of possibilistic reasoning have been also investigated in [15,27–29]. The necessity fragment of the logic to be introduced below will be the two-sorted version of the QML proposed in [27].

3 Fuzzy Formal Context and Cut-Based Concepts

Let us recall the scenario in Example 1. Sometimes, the data may contain vague or more fine-grained information. For example, it may be known that how strongly a reader is interested in a document. To model such situations, we introduce the fuzzy formal context, which is a special instance of formal **L**-contexts defined in [2], where **L** is any residuated lattice.

Definition 2. A *fuzzy formal context* is defined as $(G, M, \tilde{I})$, where G and M are the same as above, but $\tilde{I} : G \times M \to [0,1]$ is now a fuzzy binary relation.

Intuitively, $\tilde{I}(g,m)$ specifies the strength or intensity of the connection between g and m.

Given a fuzzy formal context $(G, M, \tilde{I})$, we can define possibility distributions $\pi_g : M \to [0,1]$ for each $g \in G$ and $\pi_m : G \to [0,1]$ for each $m \in M$ in the following way:

$$\pi_g(m) = \tilde{I}(g,m),\ m \in M$$

$$\pi_m(g) = \tilde{I}(g,m),\ g \in G.$$

The definitions of $(\cdot)^+$, $(\cdot)^-$, and approximation operators in fuzzy formal context are similar to those for formal context except that the incidence relation I is replaced by $\tilde{I}$ and logical connectives and quantifiers are replaced by those for fuzzy logic. Formally, we can use the residuum of Łukasiewicz t-norm [18] to define these operators. As the Łukasiewicz t-norm $* : [0,1]^2 \to [0,1]$ is simply $a * b = \max(a+b-1, 0)$, its residuum $\Rightarrow$: $[0,1]^2 \to [0,1]$ is defined as $a \Rightarrow b = \sup\{c \mid a * c \leq b\}$. By the definition, we have $a \Rightarrow b = 1$ if $a \leq b$ and $a \Rightarrow b = 1 - a + b$ if $a > b$. Then, we can define corresponding operators in fuzzy formal contexts as follows.

Definition 3. Let $(G, M, \tilde{I})$ be a fuzzy formal context and let $A \in \mathcal{P}(G)$ and $B \in \mathcal{P}(M)$. Then, we define membership functions of fuzzy sets $A^+, A^\Box, A^\Diamond, B^-, B^\Box$, and $B^\Diamond$ by the following equations.

$$A^+(m) := \inf_{g \in G}(\chi_A(g) \Rightarrow \tilde{I}(g, m)) \tag{1}$$

$$B^-(g) := \inf_{m \in M}(\chi_B(m) \Rightarrow \tilde{I}(g, m)) \tag{2}$$

$$A^\Box(m) := \inf_{g \in G}(\tilde{I}(g, m) \Rightarrow \chi_A(g)) \tag{3}$$

$$B^\Box(g) := \inf_{m \in M}(\tilde{I}(g, m) \Rightarrow \chi_B(m)) \tag{4}$$

$$A^\Diamond(m) := \sup_{g \in G} \min(\tilde{I}(g, m), \chi_A(g)) \tag{5}$$

$$B^\Diamond(g) := \sup_{m \in M} \min(\tilde{I}(g, m), \chi_B(m)) \tag{6}$$

where χ_A and χ_B are the characteristic functions of A and B, respectively.

Intuitively, $A^+(m)$ denotes the degree of m being an attribute of all objects in A, whereas $B^-(g)$ means the degree of g being an object with all properties in B. On the other hand, $A^\Box(m)$ is the degree that all objects with attribute m belong to A and $B^\Box(g)$ denotes the degree that all attributes of g are in B. In terms of rough set theory, $A^\Box(m)$ (resp. $B^\Box(g)$) denotes the membership degree of m (resp. g) in the lower approximation of A (resp. B). Analogously, $A^\Diamond$ and $B^\Diamond$ correspond to upper approximations of A and B in fuzzy contexts, respectively.

Note that the operators above are defined with respect to a fuzzy context. Hence, they are also implicitly indexed by its fuzzy incidence relation. Sometimes, in particular when we are working with more than one contexts at the same time, we may need to make the index explicit to indicate the context in which the operators are defined. For example, we may have to write the more cumbersome $A^\Box_{\tilde{I}}$ instead of simply $A^\Box$ in such case.

Given the definition above, we can establish the connection between measures in possibility theory and operators in fuzzy formal context [13].

Proposition 1. 1. $A^+(m) = \inf_{g \in A} \pi_m(g) = \Delta_m(A)$
2. $B^-(g) = \inf_{m \in B} \pi_g(m) = \Delta_g(B)$
3. $A^\Box(m) = \inf_{g \notin A} 1 - \pi_m(g) = N_m(A)$
4. $B^\Box(g) = \inf_{m \notin B} 1 - \pi_g(m) = N_g(B)$
5. $A^\Diamond(m) = \sup_{g \in A} \pi_m(g) = \Pi_m(A)$
6. $B^\Diamond(g) = \sup_{m \in B} \pi_g(m) = \Pi_g(B)$

As operators in Definition 3 map subsets of a domain to fuzzy subsets of its codomain, we can use (strict) c-cut to transform them into subsets of the codomain again. Hence, we obtain the following pairs of operators for any $c \in [0, 1]$:

$$(\cdot)^+_c : (\mathcal{P}(G), \subseteq) \longleftrightarrow (\mathcal{P}(M), \supseteq) : (\cdot)^-_c \tag{7}$$

$$(\cdot)^{\Diamond}_{>1-c} : (\mathcal{P}(G), \subseteq) \longleftrightarrow (\mathcal{P}(M), \subseteq) : (\cdot)^{\Box}_{c} \tag{8}$$

Theorem 1. The two pairs of operators in (7) and (8) form Galois connections.

PROOF. Because of the limitation on space, we cannot include the proof here. For the details, see [23].⊣

This motivates the following definition of cut-based generalizations of concepts.

Definition 4. For a fuzzy formal context $(G, M, \tilde{I})$, $A \subseteq G$ and $B \subseteq M$ and $c \in [0, 1]$,

- (A, B) is called a c-formal concept if $(A)^{+}_{c} = B$ and $(B)^{-}_{c} = A$
- (A, B) is called a c-object oriented concept if $A^{\Box}_{c} = B$ and $B^{\Diamond}_{>1-c} = A$.
- (A, B) is called a c-property oriented concept if $A^{\Diamond}_{>1-c} = B$ and $B^{\Box}_{c} = A$.

For a fuzzy context $\tilde{\mathbb{K}}$, we denote the set of all c-formal concepts, the set of all c-object oriented concepts, and the set of all c-property oriented concepts by $\mathbf{B}_c(\tilde{\mathbb{K}})$, $\mathbf{O}_c(\tilde{\mathbb{K}})$, and $\mathbf{P}_c(\tilde{\mathbb{K}})$, respectively.

Each classical formal context (G, M, I) naturally induces a fuzzy one $(G, M, \tilde{I})$, where the fuzzy relation $\tilde{I}(g, m) := 1$ if $(g, m) \in I$ and 0 if $(g, m) \notin I$. Then, the pairs of maps $((\cdot)^{+}_{1}, (\cdot)^{-}_{1})$, $((\cdot)^{\Diamond}_{>0}, (\cdot)^{\Box}_{1})$, and $((\cdot)^{\Box}_{1}, (\cdot)^{\Diamond}_{>0})$ are equivalent to the classical pair $(^{+}, ^{-})$, $(\Diamond, \Box)$, and $(\Box, \Diamond)$, respectively. As a consequence, classical concepts coincide with the 1-cut concepts if we consider a classical context as a special kind of fuzzy context. In fact, cut-based concepts enjoy many basic properties of classical ones. Further details regarding this can be found in [23].

4 Two-Sorted Weighted Modal Logic

To represent and reason with information about fuzzy formal context, we present the two-sorted weighted modal logic **2WML**. The signature of **2WML** consists of two sorts $\{s_1, s_2\}$ and two sets of modalities $\Sigma_{s_1 s_2}$ and $\Sigma_{s_2 s_1}$ with arities $s_1 \to s_2$ and $s_2 \to s_1$, respectively:

$$\Sigma_{s_1 s_2} = \{[c]_{\mathbf{o}}, [c^{+}]_{\mathbf{o}}, [\![c]\!]_{\mathbf{o}}, [\![c^{+}]\!]_{\mathbf{o}} \mid c \in [0, 1]\},$$

$$\Sigma_{s_2 s_1} = \{[c]_{\mathbf{p}}, [c^{+}]_{\mathbf{p}}, [\![c]\!]_{\mathbf{p}}, [\![c^{+}]\!]_{\mathbf{p}} \mid c \in [0, 1]\}.$$

Let P_{s_1} and P_{s_2} be sets of propositional symbols. Then, the formulas of **2WML** are defined by the following grammars, where φ and ψ denote formulas of sorts s_1 and s_2, respectively:

$$\varphi ::= p_{s_1} \mid \neg\varphi \mid \varphi \wedge \varphi \mid [c]_{\mathbf{p}}\psi \mid [c^{+}]_{\mathbf{p}}\psi \mid [\![c]\!]_{\mathbf{p}}\psi \mid [\![c^{+}]\!]_{\mathbf{p}}\psi,$$

$$\psi ::= p_{s_2} \mid \neg\psi \mid \psi \wedge \psi \mid [c]_{\mathbf{o}}\varphi \mid [c^{+}]_{\mathbf{o}}\varphi \mid [\![c]\!]_{\mathbf{o}}\varphi \mid [\![c^{+}]\!]_{\mathbf{o}}\varphi,$$

where $p_{s_i} \in P_{s_i}$ and $c \in [0,1]$. The formulas of sorts s_1 and s_2 are usually called object and property formulas, respectively. We use $\mathcal{L}^{[\cdot],[\![\cdot]\!]} = (\mathcal{L}_{s_1}^{[\cdot],[\![\cdot]\!]}, \mathcal{L}_{s_2}^{[\cdot],[\![\cdot]\!]})$ to denote the set of **2WML** formulas. As usual, we define abbreviations of some common logical connectives and dual modalities as follows (we omit the subscript as the definition applies to both sorts of formulas): $\alpha \vee \beta := \neg(\neg\alpha \wedge \neg\beta)$, $\alpha \to \beta := \neg\alpha \vee \beta$, $\alpha \equiv \beta := (\alpha \to \beta) \wedge (\beta \to \alpha)$, $\langle c\rangle\alpha := \neg[(1-c)^+]\neg\alpha$, $\langle c^+\rangle\alpha := \neg[1-c]\neg\alpha$, $\langle\!\langle c\rangle\!\rangle\alpha := \neg[\![(1-c)^+]\!]\neg\alpha$, and $\langle\!\langle c^+\rangle\!\rangle\alpha := \neg[\![1-c]\!]\neg\alpha$.

Intuitively, a formula describes a set of objects or attributes in a fuzzy formal context and modal operators correspond to necessity and guaranteed possibility measures. More specifically, propositional symbols are atomic formulas describing basic sets of objects and properties, whereas logical negation and conjunction correspond to set complement and intersection, respectively. On the other hand, modal operators transform formulas of one sort to the other one. They correspond to c-cut and strict c-cut of operators defined in Definition 3. Based on the connection established in Proposition 1, they also express (strict) lower bounds on necessity and guaranteed possibility measures of a set. The semantics below reflects the intuition precisely.

Formally, we define a *fuzzy context model* as $\mathfrak{M} := (G, M, \tilde{I}, v)$, where $(G, M, \tilde{I})$ is a fuzzy formal context and $v = (v_1, v_2)$ is a truth valuation function such that $v_1 : P_{s_1} \to \mathcal{P}(G)$ and $v_2 : P_{s_2} \to \mathcal{P}(M)$. In the model, G and M are called its s_1-sorted and s_2-sorted domains, respectively. Below, we define the satisfaction of formulas in the domains G and M. For atomic, negated, and conjunctive formulas, the definition is standard. The following lists the definition for the satisfaction of modal formulas in $g \in G$ and $m \in M$.

- $\mathfrak{M}, g \models_{s_1} [c]_{\mathbf{p}}\psi$ iff $N_g(|\psi|) \geq c$
- $\mathfrak{M}, g \models_{s_1} [c^+]_{\mathbf{p}}\psi$ iff $N_g(|\psi|) > c$
- $\mathfrak{M}, g \models_{s_1} [\![c]\!]_{\mathbf{p}}\psi$ iff $\Delta_g(|\psi|) \geq c$
- $\mathfrak{M}, g \models_{s_1} [\![c^+]\!]_{\mathbf{p}}\psi$ iff $\Delta_g(|\psi|) > c$
- $\mathfrak{M}, m \models_{s_2} [c]_{\mathbf{o}}\varphi$ iff $N_m(|\varphi|) \geq c$
- $\mathfrak{M}, m \models_{s_2} [c^+]_{\mathbf{o}}\varphi$ iff $N_m(|\varphi|) > c$,
- $\mathfrak{M}, m \models_{s_2} [\![c]\!]_{\mathbf{o}}\varphi$ iff $\Delta_m(|\varphi|) \geq c$
- $\mathfrak{M}, m \models_{s_2} [\![c^+]\!]_{\mathbf{o}}\varphi$ iff $\Delta_m(|\varphi|) > c$.

where $|\psi| = \{m \in M \mid \mathfrak{M}, m \models \psi\}$ and $|\varphi| = \{g \in G \mid \mathfrak{M}, g \models \varphi\}$ are truth sets of ψ and φ, respectively and the necessity and guaranteed possibility measures are induced from respective possibility distributions π_g for $g \in G$ and π_m for $m \in M$.

To further see the intuition behind the semantics of modal formulas in **2WML**, let us consider the case of $[c]_{\mathbf{p}}\psi$. Expanding the definition of the necessity measure based on the possibility distribution π_g, we have $N_g(|\psi|) = \bigwedge_{m\in M}(\tilde{I}(g,m) \to \psi(m))$, where $\psi(m) = 1$ if $\mathfrak{M}, m \models_{s_1} \psi$ and $\psi(m) = 0$ elsewhere. Hence, $N_g(|\psi|)$ specifies the degree that for any attribute m related to g, m satisfies ψ. Thus, $\mathfrak{M}, g \models_{s_2} [c]_{\mathbf{p}}\psi$ means that such a degree is at least c. Analogously, because $\Delta_g(|\psi|) = \bigwedge_{m\in M}(\psi(m) \to \tilde{I}(g,m))$ specifies the degree that for any attribute m satisfying ψ, m is related to g, $\mathfrak{M}, g \models_{s_2} [\![c^+]\!]_{\mathbf{p}}\psi$ means that such a degree is greater than c.

Example 2. Returning to Example 1, let us slightly modify the context. Assume that G and M remain the same, and based on the users' download history, we can infer whether a user is interested in a document. However, such inference cannot be precise by its nature. Hence, there is some kind of uncertainty about a user's real interest in a document, and we can use $\tilde{I}$ to denote such uncertain information. More specifically, $\tilde{I}(g, m)$ denotes the degree of possibility of g being interested in m. Let φ and ψ be formulas describing the sets A and B, respectively. Then, for a fuzzy context model $\mathfrak{M}$ in which $|\varphi| = A$ and $|\psi| = B$, we have the following interpretation of formulas:

- $\mathfrak{M}, g \models [0.9]_{\mathbf{p}}\psi$: it is highly certain that g is only interested in documents in B
- $\mathfrak{M}, m \models [0.9]_{\mathbf{o}}\varphi$: it is highly certain that only readers in A are interested in the document m
- $\mathfrak{M}, g \models [\![0.9]\!]_{\mathbf{p}}\psi$: it is highly certain that the reader g is interested in all documents in B
- $\mathfrak{M}, m \models [\![0.9]\!]_{\mathbf{o}}\varphi$: it is highly certain that all readers in A are interested in the document m

Example 3. Continuing with Example 2, let us consider an alternative interpretation of the fuzzy binary relation. Assume that, through users' feedback, we have information about users' real interests. Hence, $\tilde{I}$ can denote how strongly a reader is interested in a document. In other words, $\tilde{I}(g, m)$ is the degree of strength of g being interested in m. Then, in the fuzzy context model $\mathfrak{M}$, the interpretation of formulas in the previous example becomes

- $\mathfrak{M}, g \models [0.9]_{\mathbf{p}}\psi$: g is hardly interested in documents outside B
- $\mathfrak{M}, m \models [0.9]_{\mathbf{o}}\varphi$: readers outside A are hardly interested in the document m
- $\mathfrak{M}, g \models [\![0.9]\!]_{\mathbf{p}}\psi$: g is highly interested in all documents in B
- $\mathfrak{M}, m \models [\![0.9]\!]_{\mathbf{o}}\varphi$: all readers in A are highly interested in the document m

Given the satisfaction of modal formulas and Proposition 1, we can establish the connection between the semantics of **2WML** and operators in fuzzy formal contexts.

Proposition 2. For any object formula φ and property formula ψ, we have

1. $|\varphi|^{+}_{>c} = |[\![c^{+}]\!]_{\mathbf{o}}\varphi|$, 2. $|\varphi|^{+}_{c} = |[\![c]\!]_{\mathbf{o}}\varphi|$, 3. $|\varphi|^{\square}_{\geq c} = |[c^{+}]_{\mathbf{o}}\varphi|$, 4. $|\varphi|^{\square}_{c} = |[c]_{\mathbf{o}}\varphi|$,
5. $|\psi|^{-}_{>c} = |[\![c^{+}]\!]_{\mathbf{p}}\psi|$, 6. $|\psi|^{-}_{c} = |[\![c]\!]_{\mathbf{p}}\psi|$, 7. $|\psi|^{\square}_{>c} = |[c^{+}]_{\mathbf{p}}\psi|$, 8. $|\psi|^{\square}_{c} = |[c]_{\mathbf{p}}\psi|$.

As a corollary, we also have the connection between the derived modalities $\langle c\rangle$ and $\langle c^{+}\rangle$ and upper approximation operators as follows.

Corollary 1. For any object formula φ and property formula ψ, we have
1. $|\varphi|^{\Diamond}_{>c} = |\langle c^{+}\rangle_{\mathbf{o}}\varphi|$, 2. $|\varphi|^{\Diamond}_{c} = |\langle c\rangle_{\mathbf{o}}\varphi|$, 3. $|\psi|^{\Diamond}_{>c} = |\langle c^{+}\rangle_{\mathbf{p}}\psi|$, 4. $|\psi|^{\Diamond}_{c} = |\langle c\rangle_{\mathbf{p}}\psi|$.

Next, we define some basic notions in the semantics of **2WML**.

Definition 5. Let Γ be a set of s-sorted formulas and let $\mathfrak{M}$ be a model. Then, for any element w in its s-sorted domain, $\mathfrak{M}, w \models_s \Gamma$ if $\mathfrak{M}, w \models_s \phi$ for all $\phi \in \Gamma$. In addition, Γ is *satisfiable* if there exist a model $\mathfrak{M}$ and a w in its s-sorted domain such that $\mathfrak{M}, w \models_s \Gamma$. We say that Γ is *finitely satisfiable* if every finite subset of Γ is satisfiable.

Let $\mathbf{C}$ be a class of models. Then, for a set $\Gamma \cup \{\phi\}$ of s-sorted formulas, ϕ is a *local semantic consequence* of Γ over $\mathbf{C}$ and denoted as $\Gamma \models_s^{\mathbf{C}} \phi$ if $\mathfrak{M}, w \models_s \Gamma$ implies $\mathfrak{M}, w \models_s \phi$ for all models $\mathfrak{M} \in \mathbf{C}$ and w in its s-sorted domain. If $\mathbf{C}$ is the class of all models, we omit the superscript and denote it by $\Gamma \models_s \phi$. When $\Gamma = \emptyset$, we say that ϕ is valid and simply write $\models_s^{\mathbf{C}} \phi$ or $\models_s \phi$. Note that, for a finite set of formulas Γ, $\Gamma \models_s \phi$ is equivalent to the validity of $\bigwedge \Gamma \to \phi$.

To axiomatize the local semantic consequence in **2WML**, we present a Hilbert-style axiomatic system in Fig. 1. In the system, we omit the subscript **o** or **p** in modal operators as the axioms and rules hold for both sorts of formulas, and we use ϕ, ϕ_1, and ϕ_2 to denote formulas when we do not specify their sorts particularly. By contrast, in axioms (d), (e), (h), and (i), φ and ψ are formulas of sorts s_1 and s_2, respectively.

The axioms ($K_{[c]}$) and ($K_{[c^+]}$) are the weighted analogue of the standard (K) axiom in normal modal logic systems. The axioms ($B_{[c]}$) and ($B_{[c^+]}$) stipulates that the two possibility distributions π_g and π_m are mutually symmetric in the sense that $\pi_g(m) = \pi_m(g)$ for any $g \in G$ and $m \in M$. They are also the weighted analogue of the (B) axiom in normal modal logic for symmetric Kripke frames and converse axiom in temporal logic. Axioms ($K_{[\![c]\!]}$),($K_{[\![c^+]\!]}$), ($B_{[\![c]\!]}$), and ($B_{[\![c^+]\!]}$) correspond to the translation of necessity modalities to sufficiency ones in a complemented context, which will be detailed in the next section. The (CON_1) and (CON_2) axioms describe the connection between necessity and guaranteed possibility measures. They rely on the fact that $\Pi(X) \geq \Delta(X)$ for any nonempty subset X of a domain. The antecedent of these two axioms $\neg([1]\neg\phi \wedge [\![1]\!]\phi)$ simply excludes the exceptional case when $\Pi(\emptyset) = 0$ and $\Delta(\emptyset) = 1$. Finally, the (Bookkeeping) axioms specify the boundaries of the weights and their ordereding. The inference rules include the standard necessitation rule and its translation for sufficiency modalities.

Definition 6. In the axiomatic system **2WML**, a sequence of formulas $\phi_1, \phi_2, \ldots \phi_n$ is called a *proof* for the formula ϕ if $\phi_n = \phi$ and ϕ_i is an instance of its axioms or inferred from $\phi_1, \ldots, \phi_{i-1}$ using modus pones (MP) or universal generalization (UG) rules. If an s-sorted formula ϕ has a proof in **2WML**, we say that ϕ is a *theorem* and write $\vdash_s \phi$. Let $\Gamma \cup \{\phi\}$ be a set of s-sorted formulas. Then, we say that ϕ is *provable* (or derivable) form Γ, denoted by $\Gamma \vdash_s \phi$, if there exist $\phi_1, \ldots, \phi_n \in \Gamma$ such that $\vdash_s (\phi_1 \wedge \ldots \wedge \phi_n) \to \phi$. In addition, the set Γ is inconsistent if $\bot$ is provable from the set, otherwise it is consistent.

Lemma 1. The following are derivable in the system **2WML**

1. $\neg([1]\neg\phi \wedge [\![1]\!]\phi) \to (\neg\langle c^+\rangle\phi \to \langle\!\langle 1-c\rangle\!\rangle\neg\phi)$.
2. $\neg([1]\neg\phi \wedge [\![1]\!]\phi) \to (\neg\langle c\rangle\phi \to \langle\!\langle (1-c)^+\rangle\!\rangle\neg\phi)$.

1. Axioms
   (a) (PL): All propositional tautologies.
   (b) ($K_{[c]}$): $[c](\phi_1 \to \phi_2) \to ([c]\phi_1 \to [c]\phi_2)$
   (c) ($K_{[c^+]}$): $[c^+](\phi_1 \to \phi_2) \to ([c^+]\phi_1 \to [c^+]\phi_2)$
   (d) ($B_{[c]}$): $\varphi \to [c]_{\mathbf{p}}\langle(1-c)^+\rangle_{\mathbf{o}}\varphi$; $\psi \to [c]_{\mathbf{o}}\langle(1-c)^+\rangle_{\mathbf{p}}\psi$
   (e) ($B_{[c^+]}$): $\varphi \to [c^+]_{\mathbf{p}}\langle 1-c\rangle_{\mathbf{o}}\varphi$; $\psi \to [c^+]_{\mathbf{o}}\langle 1-c\rangle_{\mathbf{p}}\psi$
   (f) ($K_{[\![c]\!]}$): $[\![c]\!](\phi_1 \wedge \neg\phi_2) \to ([\![c]\!]\neg\phi_1 \to [\![c]\!]\neg\phi_2)$
   (g) ($K_{[\![c^+]\!]}$): $[\![c^+]\!](\phi_1 \wedge \neg\phi_2) \to ([\![c^+]\!]\neg\phi_1 \to [\![c^+]\!]\neg\phi_2)$
   (h) ($B_{[\![c]\!]}$): $\varphi \to [\![c]\!]_{\mathbf{p}}[\![c]\!]_{\mathbf{o}}\varphi$; $\psi \to [\![c]\!]_{\mathbf{o}}[\![c]\!]_{\mathbf{p}}\psi$
   (i) ($B_{[\![c^+]\!]}$): $\varphi \to [\![c^+]\!]_{\mathbf{p}}[\![c^+]\!]_{\mathbf{o}}\varphi$; $\psi \to [\![c^+]\!]_{\mathbf{o}}[\![c^+]\!]_{\mathbf{p}}\psi$
   (j) (CON_1): $\neg([1]\neg\phi \wedge [\![1]\!]\phi) \to ([1-c]\neg\phi \to \neg[\![c^+]\!]\phi)$
   (k) (CON_2): $\neg([1]\neg\phi \wedge [\![1]\!]\phi) \to ([(1-c)^+]\neg\phi \to \neg[\![c]\!]\phi)$
   (l) (Bookkeeping):
      i. $[c]\phi \to [d^+]\phi$ if $c > d$
      ii. $[\![c]\!]\phi \to [\![d^+]\!]\phi$ if $c > d$
      iii. $[c^+]\phi \to [c]\phi$
      iv. $[\![c^+]\!]\phi \to [\![c]\!]\phi$
      v. $\neg[1^+]\phi$, $[0]\phi$
      vi. $\neg[\![1^+]\!]\phi$, $[\![0]\!]\phi$
2. Inference rules:
   (a) (MP):
   $$\frac{\phi_1, \phi_1 \to \phi_2}{\phi_2}$$
   (b) ($UG_{[1]}$):
   $$\frac{\phi}{[1]\phi}$$
   (c) ($UG_{[\![1]\!]}$):
   $$\frac{\neg\phi}{[\![1]\!]\phi}$$

Fig. 1. The axiomatic system **2WML**

PROOF. It follows from axioms CON_1 and CON_2 directly. ⊣

Theorem 2. The system **2WML** is sound with respect to the class of all fuzzy context models. That is, for any $s \in \{s_1, s_2\}$, $\Gamma \vdash_s \phi$ implies that $\Gamma \models_s \phi$ for any set of s-sorted formulas $\Gamma \cup \{\phi\}$.

4.1 Application

As an application of our logic, we show that it can represent different notions of c-cut concepts in fuzzy formal contexts.

Definition 7. Let $\mathbf{C}$ denote the class of all fuzzy context models based on a fuzzy context $\mathbb{K}$. Then, for $c \in [0,1]$, we define $Fm^c_{PC}, Fm^c_{OC} \subseteq \mathcal{L}^{[\cdot]}_{s_1} \times \mathcal{L}^{[\cdot]}_{s_2}$ by

(a) $Fm^c_{PC} := \{(\varphi, \psi) \mid \models^{\mathbf{C}}_{s_1} \varphi \equiv [c]_{\mathbf{P}}\psi, \models^{\mathbf{C}}_{s_2} \langle(1-c)^+\rangle_{\mathbf{O}}\varphi \equiv \psi\}$
(b) $Fm^c_{OC} := \{(\varphi, \psi) \mid \models^{\mathbf{C}}_{s_1} \varphi \equiv \langle(1-c)^+\rangle_{\mathbf{P}}\psi, \models^{\mathbf{C}}_{s_2} [c]_{\mathbf{O}}\varphi \equiv \psi\}$
(c) $Fm^c_{PC_{ext}} := \pi_1(Fm^c_{PC})$ and $Fm^c_{PC_{int}} := \pi_2(Fm^c_{PC})$
(d) $Fm^c_{OC_{ext}} := \pi_1(Fm^c_{OC})$ and $Fm^c_{OC_{int}} := \pi_2(Fm^c_{OC})$

where π_1 and π_2 are projection operators[1].

By the definition, we have $Fm^c_{PC_{ext}} = \{\varphi \in \mathcal{L}^{[\cdot]}_{s_1} \mid \models^{\mathbf{C}}_{s_1} [c]_{\mathbf{P}}\langle(1-c)^+\rangle_{\mathbf{O}}\varphi \equiv \varphi\}$, $Fm^c_{PC_{int}} = \{\varphi \in \mathcal{L}^{[\cdot]}_{s_2} \mid \models^{\mathbf{C}}_{s_2} \langle(1-c)^+\rangle_{\mathbf{O}}[c]_{\mathbf{P}}\varphi \equiv \varphi\}$, $Fm^c_{OC_{ext}} = \{\varphi \in \mathcal{L}^{[\cdot]}_{s_1} \mid \models^{\mathbf{C}}_{s_1} \langle(1-c)^+\rangle_{\mathbf{P}}[c]_{\mathbf{O}}\varphi \equiv \varphi\}$, and $Fm^c_{OC_{int}} = \{\varphi \in \mathcal{L}^{[\cdot]}_{s_2} \mid \models^{\mathbf{C}}_{s_2} [c]_{\mathbf{O}}\langle(1-c)^+\rangle_{\mathbf{P}}\varphi \equiv \varphi\}$.

Note that these sets are implicitly parameterized by the underlying fuzzy context and should be indexed with $\mathbb{K}$. However, for simplicity, we omit the index. Obviously, when $(\varphi, \psi) \in Fm^c_{PC}$, we have $(|\varphi|, |\psi|) \in \mathbf{P}_c(\tilde{\mathbb{K}})$ for any $\tilde{\mathbb{K}}$-based models. Hence, Fm^c_{PC} consists of pairs of formulas representing c-property oriented concepts. Analogously, Fm^c_{OC} provides the representation of c-object oriented concepts.

Definition 8. Let $\tilde{\mathbb{K}} = (G, M, \tilde{I})$ be a fuzzy formal context and let $\mathbf{C}$ be the class of all $\tilde{\mathbb{K}}$=based models. Then, we define $Fm^c_{FC} \subseteq \mathcal{L}^{[\![\cdot]\!]}_{s_1} \times \mathcal{L}^{[\![\cdot]\!]}_{s_2}$ by

(a) $Fm^c_{FC} := \{(\varphi, \psi) \mid \models^{\mathbf{C}}_{s_1} \varphi \equiv [\![c]\!]_{\mathbf{P}}\psi, \models^{\mathbf{C}}_{s_2} [\![c]\!]_{\mathbf{O}}\varphi \equiv \psi\}$
(b) $Fm^c_{FC_{ext}} := \pi_1(Fm^c_{FC})$ and $Fm^c_{FC_{int}} := \pi_2(Fm^c_{FC})$

From the definition, we can derive $Fm^c_{FC_{ext}} = \{\varphi \in \mathcal{L}^{[\![\cdot]\!]}_{s_1} \mid \models^{\mathbf{C}}_{s_1} [\![c]\!]_{\mathbf{P}}[\![c]\!]_{\mathbf{O}}\varphi \equiv \varphi\}$ and $Fm^c_{FC_{int}} = \{\varphi \in \mathcal{L}^{[\![\cdot]\!]}_{s_2} \mid \models^{\mathbf{C}}_{s_2} [\![c]\!]_{\mathbf{O}}[\![c]\!]_{\mathbf{P}}\varphi \equiv \varphi\}$. Hence, the set Fm^c_{FC} provides a logical representation of c-formal concepts induced from the fuzzy context $(G, M, \tilde{I})$.

Example 4 Continuing with Example 3, if $(\varphi, \psi) \in Fm^{0.9}_{FC}$, then according to the interpretation given in that example, $|\varphi|$ is the set of users who are highly interested in all documents in $|\psi|$, and $|\psi|$ is the set of documents that strongly attract common interest of all users in $|\varphi|$. This means that φ and ψ describe a group of users and a type of documents that have strong connection. For instance, φ and ψ may denote a reading club for a particular author and all books written by the author, respectively.

5 Necessity and Sufficiency Fragments of 2WML

While we have established the soundness of **2WML** with respect to fuzzy context models, it remains an open question whether the logic is also complete. However, we can show that the necessity and sufficiency fragments of **2WML** are both sound and complete with respect to fuzzy context models. The language of the necessity fragment includes all propositional connectives along with the modal operators $[c]$ and $[c^+]$, whereas the language of the sufficiency fragment is formed using the modalities $[\![c]\!]$ and $[\![c^+]\!]$.

[1] That is, for a subset $S \subseteq A \times B$, $\pi_1(S) = \{a \in A \mid \exists b \in B, (a.b) \in S\}$ and $\pi_2(S) = \{b \in B \mid \exists a \in A, (a.b) \in S\}$.

5.1 The System 2WKB

In this section, we discuss the necessity fragment of **2WML**. The logic is called **2WKB**. Its signature is derived from that of **2WML** omitting sufficiency modalities $[\![c]\!]$ and $[\![c^+]\!]$. Syntax and semantics, particularly the definition of formulas and their satisfaction, are inherited from **2WML** without modification. We use $\mathcal{L}^{[\cdot]} = (\mathcal{L}^{[\cdot]}_{s_1}, \mathcal{L}^{[\cdot]}_{s_2})$ to denote the set of **2WKB** formulas. The corresponding axiomatic system for **2WKB** consists of axioms (a)–(e), (1)(i,iii,v), and inference rules (a) and (b) of **2WML**. Also, we still use $\models$ and $\vdash$ to denote the semantic consequence and provability relations in **2WKB**, respectively. Essentially, **2WKB** is a weighted extension of the two-sorted modal logic **KB** introduced in [22,24] and a two-sorted variant of the quantitative modal logic (QML) introduced in [27]. Hence, we can prove the completeness of **2WKB** employing a synergy of the canonical model construction techniques used in **KB** and QML.

As in QML, **2WKB** lacks the compactness theorem in its semantics. That is, a finitely satisfiable set of formulas is not necessarily satisfiable in **2WKB**. However, since the derivation in an axiomatic system is always finitary, we can not have the completeness without any restriction. Hence, we restrict our consideration to the case that only finite number of weights is allowed in the set of formulas. For this, we define the set of degrees occurring (explicitly or implicitly) in a formula ϕ as

$$deg(\phi) = \{0,1\} \cup \{c \mid [c]_i, [1-c]_i, [c^+]_i, \text{ or } [(1-c)^+]_i \text{ appears in } \phi \text{ for some } i = \mathbf{o}, \mathbf{p}\},$$

and for a set of formulas Φ, let $deg(\Phi) := \bigcup_{\phi \in \Phi} deg(\phi)$. Moreover, for any subset $D \subseteq [0,1]$, we use $\mathcal{L}(D) = (\mathcal{L}_{s_1}(D), \mathcal{L}_{s_2}(D))$ to denote the set of **2WKB** formulas in which only degrees in D occur (for simplicity, we omit the superscript $[\cdot]$ here).

We can now state the main theorem of this section.

Theorem 3. **2WKB** *is sound and complete with respect to the class of all fuzzy context models. That is for any $s \in \{s_1, s_2\}$, $\Gamma \vdash_s \phi$ iff $\Gamma \models_s \phi$ where $\Gamma \cup \{\phi\}$ is a set of s-sorted formulas such that $deg(\Gamma \cup \{\phi\})$ is finite.*

Proof. The soundness follows from that of **2WML**. Here, we simply sketch the proof of the completeness and its details are included in [23]. Suppose that $\Gamma \nvdash_s \phi$. Hence, $\Gamma \cup \{\neg\phi\}$ is consistent. By the standard Lindenbaum lemma, $\Gamma \cup \{\neg\phi\}$ can be extended to a maximally consistent subset Φ_s of s-sorted formulas. Then, by the canonical model construction, we construct a model whose domains are the sets of all maximally consistent subsets. The model satisfies the truth lemma, that is, a formula is true in an element of the domains iff it belongs to that element. Thus, we have a model and its domain element Φ_s in which all formulas in Γ is true but ϕ is false, i.e. $\Gamma \not\models_s \phi$.⊣

To construct the canonical model, let us consider the set of two-sorted formulas $\mathcal{L}(D) = (\mathcal{L}_{s_1}(D), \mathcal{L}_{s_2}(D))$, where $D = deg(\Gamma \cup \{\phi\})$. For any $\Sigma_g \subseteq \mathcal{L}_{s_1}(D)$, $\Sigma_m \subseteq \mathcal{L}_{s_2}(D)$, and $c \in D$, we define the following notations.

$$\Sigma_g/[c]_\mathbf{p} = \{\psi \mid d \geq c, [d]_\mathbf{p}\psi \in \Sigma_g \text{ or } [d^+]_\mathbf{p}\psi \in \Sigma_g\}$$

$$\Sigma_m/[c]_{\mathbf{o}} = \{\varphi \mid d \geq c, [d]_{\mathbf{o}}\varphi \in \Sigma_m \text{ or } [d^+]_{\mathbf{o}}\varphi \in \Sigma_m\}$$

$$\Sigma_g/[c^+]_{\mathbf{p}} = \{\psi \mid d > c, [d]_{\mathbf{p}}\psi \in \Sigma_g\} \cup \{\psi \mid d \geq c, [d^+]_{\mathbf{p}}\psi \in \Sigma_g\}.$$

$$\Sigma_m/[c^+]_{\mathbf{o}} = \{\varphi \mid d > c, [d]_{\mathbf{o}}\varphi \in \Sigma_g\} \cup \{\varphi \mid d \geq c, [d^+]_{\mathbf{o}}\varphi \in \Sigma_g\}.$$

Based on these notations, we have the following lemma.

Lemma 2 Let Σ_g and Σ_m be maximally consistent subsets of $\mathcal{L}_{s_1}(D)$ and $\mathcal{L}_{s_2}(D)$, respectively. Then, we have

1. $\Sigma_g/[c]_{\mathbf{p}} \subseteq \Sigma_m$ iff $\Sigma_m/[c]_{\mathbf{o}} \subseteq \Sigma_g$,
2. $\Sigma_g/[c^+]_{\mathbf{p}} \subseteq \Sigma_m$ iff $\Sigma_m/[c^+]_{\mathbf{o}} \subseteq \Sigma_g$.

With this lemma, we can now define the notion of canonical models.

Definition 9. A fuzzy context model $\mathfrak{M} = (G, M, \tilde{I}, v)$ is called a $\mathcal{L}(D)$-canonical model if

- G is the set of all maximally consistent subsets of $\mathcal{L}_{s_1}(D)$
- M is the set of all maximally consistent subsets of $\mathcal{L}_{s_2}(D)$
- $\tilde{I}$ satisfies the following two conditions for all $\Sigma_g \in G$ and $\Sigma_m \in M$:
  - if $c > 0$, then $\Sigma_g/[c]_{\mathbf{p}} \subseteq \Sigma_m$ (or equivalently $\Sigma_m/[c]_{\mathbf{o}} \subseteq \Sigma_g$) iff $\tilde{I}(\Sigma_g, \Sigma_m) > 1 - c$
  - $\Sigma_g/[c^+]_{\mathbf{p}} \subseteq \Sigma_m$ (or equivalently $\Sigma_m/[c^+]_{\mathbf{o}} \subseteq \Sigma_g$) iff $\tilde{I}(\Sigma_g, \Sigma_m) \geq 1 - c$
- the valuation $v = (v_1, v_2)$ is defined by $v_1(p_{s_1}) = \{\Sigma_g \mid p_{s_1} \in \Sigma_g\}$ and $v_2(p_{s_2}) = \{\Sigma_m \mid p_{s_2} \in \Sigma_m\}$.

The conditions on the fuzzy incidence relation above only specify a range of possible values between elements of G and M but do not give us a unique canonical model constructively. The following lemma shows that canonical models indeed exist.

Lemma 3. [Model Existence Lemma] There exists a fuzzy binary relation $\tilde{I}$: $G \times M \to [0,1]$ satisfying the two conditions for the definition of canonical models.

Finally, we finish the proof of the completeness by providing the truth lemma.

Lemma 4. [Truth Lemma] Let $\mathfrak{M} = (G, M, \tilde{I}, v)$ be a $\mathcal{L}(D)$-canonical model and let $\varphi \in \mathcal{L}_{s_1}(D)$ and $\psi \in \mathcal{L}_{s_2}(D)$. Then, for any $\Sigma_g \in G$ and $\Sigma_m \in M$, we have

1. $\mathfrak{M}, \Sigma_g \models_{s_1} \varphi$ iff $\varphi \in \Sigma_g$ and
2. $\mathfrak{M}, \Sigma_m \models_{s_2} \psi$ iff $\psi \in \Sigma_m$.

5.2 The System 2WKF

This section is devoted to the sufficiency fragment of **2WML**, called **2WKF**. Its signature is obtained by removing the modalities $[c]$ and $[c^+]$ from the full language of **2WML**. Despite this reduction, its syntax and semantics, particularly the notions of formula formation and satisfaction remain the same with those defined for **2WML**. We use $\mathcal{L}^{[\![\cdot]\!]} = (\mathcal{L}^{[\![\cdot]\!]}_{s_1}, \mathcal{L}^{[\![\cdot]\!]}_{s_2})$ to denote the set of **2WKF** formulas. The axiomatization for **2WKF** consists of axioms (a), (f)–(i), and (l) (ii, iv, vi), and rules (a) and (c) in the axiomatic system of **2WML**. Also, **2WKF** is the weighted extension of the two-sorted modal logic **KF** introduced in [22,24]. Hence, as in the case of **KF**, we prove the completeness of **2WKF** by a translation mapping between **2WKF** and **2WKB**. As the completeness of **2WKF** depends on that of **2WKB**, they have the same restriction. For this, we define $deg(\phi)$ for a **2WKF** formula ϕ and extend it to a set of formulas as in the case of **2WKB** except that necessity modalities are replaced with sufficiency ones.

Theorem 4. **2WKF** is sound and complete with respect to the class of all fuzzy context models. That is, for any $s \in \{s_1, s_2\}$, $\Gamma \vdash_s \phi$ iff $\Gamma \models_s \phi$ where $\Gamma \cup \{\phi\}$ is a set of s-sorted formulas such that $deg(\Gamma \cup \{\phi\})$ is finite.

To establish this result, we first define a translation mapping $\rho = (\rho_1, \rho_2)$ that maps each formula in **2WKF** to one of the same sort in **2WKB** as follows:

1. $\rho_i(p) := p$ for all $p \in P_{s_i}$ where $i = 1, 2$,
2. $\rho_i(\phi_1 \wedge \phi_2) := \rho_i(\phi_1) \wedge \rho_i(\phi_2)$,
3. $\rho_i(\neg\phi) := \neg\rho_i(\phi)$,
4. $\rho_1([\![x]\!]_{\mathbf{p}}\psi) := [x]_{\mathbf{p}}\neg\rho_2(\psi)$ for s_2-sorted formula ψ and $x \in \{c, c^+\}$,
5. $\rho_2([\![x]\!]_{\mathbf{o}}\varphi) := [x]_{\mathbf{o}}\neg\rho_1(\varphi)$ for s_1-sorted formula φ and $x \in \{c, c^+\}$,

where ϕ, ϕ_1, ϕ_2 are s_i-sorted formulas for $i = 1, 2$. Also, for a set Γ of **2WKF** formulas, we write $\rho(\Gamma) := \{\rho(\phi) \mid \phi \in \Gamma\}$.

An inverse translation mapping ρ^{-1} can also be similarly defined. The only difference is that we exchange the position of $[\![x]\!]$ and $[x]$ in items 4 and 5 above. By induction on the complexity of formulas, we can derive $\vdash_s \phi \equiv \rho^{-1}(\rho(\phi))$ and $\vdash_s \phi \equiv \rho(\rho^{-1}(\phi))$ in **2WKF** and **2WKB**, respectively.

Using these two mapping, we can prove the following correspondence theorem. For simplicity, we use the same notations $\vdash$ and $\models$ for both logics without confusion, as the formulas to which the relations are applied can disambiguate them.

Theorem 5. Let $\Gamma \cup \{\phi\}$ be a set of s-sorted **2WKF** formulas. Then,

1. $\Gamma \vdash_s \phi$ iff $\rho(\Gamma) \vdash_s \rho(\phi)$
2. Let $\mathfrak{M} := (G, M, \tilde{I}, v)$ be a fuzzy context model and let $\overline{\mathfrak{M}} := (G, M, \tilde{J}, v)$ be its complemented model defined by $\tilde{J}(g, m) = 1 - \tilde{I}(g, m)$ for any $g \in G$ and $m \in M$. Then, for any $g \in G, \mathfrak{M}, g \models_{s_1} \phi$ iff $\overline{\mathfrak{M}}, g \models_{s_1} \rho_1(\phi)$, and for any $m \in M, \mathfrak{M}, m \models_{s_2} \phi$ iff $\overline{\mathfrak{M}}, m \models_{s_2} \rho_2(\phi)$

3. $\Gamma \models_s \phi$ iff $\rho(\Gamma) \models_s \rho(\phi)$.

PROOF.

1. By the definition of provability relation, we only need to prove $\vdash_s \phi$ iff $\vdash_s \rho(\phi)$. For the forward direction, if $\phi_1, \phi_2, \cdots, \phi_k = \phi$ is a proof of ϕ in **2WKF**, then $\rho(\phi_1), \rho(\phi_2), \cdots, \rho(\phi_k) = \rho(\phi)$ is a proof of $\rho(\phi)$ in **2WKB** since ρ transforms each instance of axioms or rules in **2WKF** to one in **2WKB**. For the backward direction, analogously, if $\rho(\phi_1), \rho(\phi_2), \cdots, \rho(\phi_k) = \rho(\phi)$ is a proof of $\rho(\phi)$ in **2WKB**, then $\rho^{-1}(\rho(\phi_1)), \rho^{-1}(\rho(\phi_2)), \cdots, \rho^{-1}(\rho(\phi_k)) = \rho^{-1}(\rho(\phi))$ is a proof of $\rho^{-1}(\rho(\phi))$ in **2WKF**. As $\phi \equiv \rho^{-1}(\rho(\phi))$ is provable in **2WKF**, ϕ is also provable.
2. By induction on the complexity of formulas, the only nontrivial case is the modal formulas. For example, let $\phi = [\![c]\!]_{\mathbf{p}}\psi$. Then, $\mathfrak{M}, g \models_{s_1} \phi$ iff $\Delta_g(|\psi|) \geq c$ iff $\inf_{m\in|\psi|} \tilde{I}(g, m) \geq c$ iff $\inf_{m\notin|\neg\rho_2(\psi)|}(1 - \tilde{J}(g, m)) \geq c$ (by the inductive hypothesis and the definition of $\tilde{J}$) iff $\overline{\mathfrak{M}}, g \models_{s_1} [c]_{\mathbf{p}}\neg\rho_2(\psi)$, i.e., $\overline{\mathfrak{M}}, g \models_{s_1} \rho_1(\phi)$.
3. It follows from 2 immediately because the mapping of fuzzy context models to their complements is bijective. $\dashv$

The completeness of **2WKF** then follows from that of **2WKB** by the correspondence theorem (1) and (3).

6 Extension to Multi-relational Fuzzy Contexts

In this section, we demonstrate the possibility of extending the logic to reasoning with Boolean combinations of relations in multi-relational fuzzy contexts.

In classical modal logic, when both necessity and sufficiency modalities are available in a logical language, it can be extended to express all Boolean combinations of multiple modalities. This leads to Boolean modal logic in [17]. Semantically, each primitive modality in Boolean modal logic is interpreted with respect to a binary accessibility relation in Kripke models and Boolean combinations of modalities correspond to the set-theoretic Boolean algebra of multiple relations. In particular, sufficiency modalities correspond to complements of binary relations.

Analogously, we can also extend **2WML** to a kind of two-sorted weighted Boolean modal logic (**2WBML**). Let Π_0 be a set of primitive modality indices and let $cl(\Pi_0)$ be its inductive closure over union, intersection, and complement. Formally, an index in $cl(\Pi_0)$ is defined by

$$\mathsf{i} ::= 0 \mid \mathsf{a} \mid \mathsf{i} \cap \mathsf{i} \mid \mathsf{i} \cup \mathsf{i} \mid \bar{\mathsf{i}},$$

where $\mathsf{a} \in \Pi_0$. Then, we modify the signature of **2WML** by attaching to each modality an index from $cl(\Pi_0)$. Thus, for example, we have a **2WBML** formula of the form $[c]_{\mathbf{o}}^{\mathsf{i}\cap\mathsf{j}}\varphi$. Semantically, these formulas are interpreted in multi-relational fuzzy context models $\mathfrak{M} = (G, M, (\tilde{I}_{\mathsf{i}})_{\mathsf{i}\in cl(\Pi_0)}, v)$, where G, M, and v are defined as in fuzzy context models, and each $\tilde{I}_{\mathsf{i}} : G \times M \to [0, 1]$ is a fuzzy binary relation such that for any $g \in G$ and $m \in M$

1. $\tilde{I}_{\mathsf{0}}(g, m) = 0$
2. $\tilde{I}_{\mathsf{i} \cap \mathsf{j}}(g, m) = \min(\tilde{I}_{\mathsf{i}}(g, m), \tilde{I}_{\mathsf{j}}(g, m))$
3. $\tilde{I}_{\mathsf{i} \cup \mathsf{j}}(g, m) = \max(\tilde{I}_{\mathsf{i}}(g, m), \tilde{I}_{\mathsf{j}}(g, m))$
4. $\tilde{I}_{\bar{\mathsf{i}}}(g, m) = 1 - \tilde{I}_{\mathsf{i}}(g, m)$.

To obtain axiomatization of **2WBML**, we simply replace modalities in the **2WML** system with indexed ones and add the extra axioms and rule as follows:

1. Axioms
   (a) (DefU): $[x]^{\mathsf{i} \cup \mathsf{j}}\phi \equiv ([x]^{\mathsf{i}}\phi \wedge [x]^{\mathsf{j}}\phi)$
   (b) (DefI): $[\![x]\!]^{\mathsf{i} \cap \mathsf{j}}\phi \equiv ([\![x]\!]^{\mathsf{i}}\phi \wedge [\![x]\!]^{\mathsf{j}}\phi)$
   (c) (DefC): $[x]^{\bar{\mathsf{i}}}\phi \equiv [\![x]\!]^{\mathsf{i}}\neg\phi$
   (d) (Def0): $[1]^{\mathsf{0}}\phi$
2. Rule (EQ): $\vdash [x]^{\mathsf{i}}\phi \equiv [x]^{\mathsf{j}}\phi$ if $\vdash_{ZA} \mathsf{i} = \mathsf{j}$

for $x \in \{c, c^+\}$, where ZA is the set of axioms for Zadeh algebra. That is, if BA is the set of Boolean algebra axioms, then $ZA = BA - \{\mathsf{i} \cup \bar{\mathsf{i}} = \bar{\mathsf{0}}, \mathsf{i} \cap \bar{\mathsf{i}} = \mathsf{0}\} \cup \{\bar{\bar{\mathsf{i}}} = \mathsf{i}\}$. We denote these axioms and rule as **BM**.

Note that axioms (DefU) and (DefI) are mutually derivable given axiom (DefC) and the rule (EQ). In fact, (DefC) and(EQ) are powerful enough to eliminate one of the necessity or sufficiency fragments in the **2WML** system. The axioms for necessity and sufficiency modalities in **2WML** also become mutually derivable via the connection of (DefC) and (EQ). Hence, we can remove one of them if the independence of axioms is an objective of the axiomatization. More specifically, let us still use the same naming conventions to denote the indexed versions of the axiomatic system **2WML** and its fragments, axioms and rules. Then, we can define

1. **2WBML**=**2WML**+**BM**,
2. **2WBML**^{N}=**2WKB**+**BM**+{(CON$_1$),(CON$_2$)}-{(DefI)}, and
3. **2WBML**$^\Delta$=**2WKF**+**BM**+{(CON$_1$),(CON$_2$)}-{(DefU)},

and prove the following result.

Proposition 3. **2WBML**, **2WBML**^{N}, and **2WBML**$^\Delta$ are equivalent.

Finally, we note that (EQ) is an unorthodox rule since its premises relies on an external reasoning mechanism, i.e., the equational reasoning on a set of axioms for an algebra.

7 Concluding Remarks

We have introduced a 2-sorted weighted modal logic for reasoning with fuzzy formal contexts. Our illustrative examples demonstrate its potential applicability to the representation of knowledge discovered from fuzzy databases. As the logic is at the early stage of development yet, there are a lot of open issues to be addressed. First, the most pressing issue is the completeness of the axiomatization for **2WML** and **2WBML**. Second, while **2WML** is still a two-valued logic, more generally, we may also study genuine many-valued modal logic following the mathematical fuzzy logic paradigm initiated by Hájek [18]. In addition, considering the frequency of connections between objects and attributes, we can also study probabilistic reasoning [30] about formal contexts. Last, to apply the formalism to practical data mining problem, we will need to implement its automated reasoning system and test it on some real datasets.

Acknowledgments. This work is partially supported by the National Science and Technology Council of Taiwan under Grants: NSTC 113-2221-E-001-018-MY3 and NSTC 113-2221-E-001-021-MY3. We are very grateful to three anonymous referees for their insightful comments and valuable suggestions.

References

1. Antoni, L., Krajči, S., Krídlo, O.: On fuzzy generalizations of concept lattices. In: Kóczy, L.T., Medina, J. (eds.) Interactions Between Computational Intelligence and Mathematics. SCI, vol. 758, pp. 79–103. Springer, Cham (2018). https://doi.org/10.1007/978-3-319-74681-4_6
2. Belohlávek, R.: Concept lattices and order in fuzzy logic. Ann. Pure Appl. Logic **128**(1–3), 277–298 (2004)
3. Belohlavek, R.: What is a fuzzy concept lattice? II. In: Kuznetsov, S.O., Ślęzak, D., Hepting, D.H., Mirkin, B.G. (eds.) RSFDGrC 2011. LNCS (LNAI), vol. 6743, pp. 19–26. Springer, Heidelberg (2011). https://doi.org/10.1007/978-3-642-21881-1_4
4. Belohlávek, R., Vychodil, V.: What is a fuzzy concept lattice? In: Belohlávek, R., Snásel, V. (eds.) Proceedings of the International Workshop on Concept Lattices and their Applications (CLA). CEUR Workshop Proceedings, vol. 162. CEUR-WS.org (2005)
5. Bimbó, K., Dunn, M.: Four-valued logic. Notre Dame J. Formal Logic **42**(3), 171–192 (2001)
6. Brito, A., Barros, L., Laureano, E., Bertato, F., Coniglio, M.: Fuzzy formal concept analysis. In: Barreto, G.A., Coelho, R. (eds.) NAFIPS 2018. CCIS, vol. 831, pp. 192–205. Springer, Cham (2018). https://doi.org/10.1007/978-3-319-95312-0_17
7. Codara, P., Esteva, F., Godo, L., Valota, D.: Connecting systems of mathematical fuzzy logic with fuzzy concept lattices. In: Medina, J., et al. (eds.) IPMU 2018. CCIS, vol. 854, pp. 275–286. Springer, Cham (2018). https://doi.org/10.1007/978-3-319-91476-3_23
8. Codara, P., Valota, D.: On Gödel algebras of concepts. In: Hansen, H., Murray, S., Sadrzadeh, M., Zeevat, H. (eds.) 11th International Tbilisi Symposium on Logic, Language, and Computation, TbiLLC 2015, Revised Selected Papers. LNCS, vol. 10148, pp. 251–262. Springer, Heidelberg (2015)
9. Conradie, W., Frittella, S., Palmigiano, A., Piazzai, M., Tzimoulis, A., Wijnberg, N.M.: Categories: how i learned to stop worrying and love two sorts. In: Väänänen, J., Hirvonen, Å., de Queiroz, R. (eds.) WoLLIC 2016. LNCS, vol. 9803, pp. 145–164. Springer, Heidelberg (2016). https://doi.org/10.1007/978-3-662-52921-8_10

10. Conradie, W., Frittella, S., Palmigiano, A., Piazzai, M., Tzimoulis, A., Wijnberg, N.: Toward an epistemic-logical theory of categorization. Electron. Proc. Theoret. Comput. Sci. (EPTCS) **251**, 167–186 (2017)
11. Dubois, D., Lang, J., Prade, H.: Possibilistic logic. In: Gabbay, D., Hogger, C., Robinson, J. (eds.) Handbook of Logic in Artificial Intelligence and Logic Programming, Vol 3 : Nonmonotonic Reasoning and Uncertain Reasoning, pp. 439–513. Clarendon Press, Oxford (1994)
12. Dubois, D., Prade, H.: An introduction to possibilistic and fuzzy logics. In: Smets, P., Mamdani, A., Dubois, D., Prade, H. (eds.) Non-Standard Logics for Automated Reasoning, pp. 253–286. Academic Press (1988)
13. Dubois, D., de Saint-Cyr, F.D., Prade, H.: A possibility-theoretic view of formal concept analysis. Fund. Inform. **75**(1–4), 195–213 (2007)
14. Düntsch, I., Gediga, G.: Modal-style operators in qualitative data analysis. In: Kumar, V., et al. (eds.) Proceedings of the 2002 IEEE International Conference on Data Mining, pp. 155–162. IEEE Computer Society (2002)
15. del Cerro, L.F., Herzig, A.: A modal analysis of possibility theory. In: Kruse, R., Siegel, P. (eds.) ECSQARU 1991. LNCS, vol. 548, pp. 58–62. Springer, Heidelberg (1991). https://doi.org/10.1007/3-540-54659-6_66
16. Ganter, B., Wille, R., Franzke, C.: Formal Concept Analysis: Mathematical Foundations, 1st edn. Springer-Verlag (1997)
17. Gargov, G., Passy, S., Tinchev, T.: Modal environment for Boolean speculations. In: Skordev, D. (ed.) Mathematical Logic and Its Applications, pp. 253–263. Springer, Boston (1987). https://doi.org/10.1007/978-1-4613-0897-3_17
18. Hájek, P.: Metamathematics of Fuzzy Logic. Kluwer Academic Publisher (1998)
19. Hartonas, C.: Game-theoretic semantics for non-distributive logics. Logic J. IGPL **27**(5), 718–742 (2019)
20. Hartonas, C.: Lattice logic as a fragment of (2-sorted) residuated modal logic. J. Appl. Non-Class. Logics **29**(2), 152–170 (2019)
21. Howlader, P., Banerjee, M.: A non-distributive logic for semiconcepts and its modal extension with semantics based on Kripke contexts. Int. J. Approximate Reasoning **153**, 115–143 (2023)
22. Howlader, P., Liau, C.: Two-sorted modal logics for formal and rough concepts. In: Campagner, A., et al. (eds.) Rough Sets. LNCS, vol. 14481, pp. 154–169. Springer, Cham (2023). https://doi.org/10.1007/978-3-031-50959-9_11
23. Howlader, P., Liau, C.: A modal logic for possibilistic reasoning with fuzzy formal contexts (2025). https://arxiv.org/abs/2512.24980
24. Howlader, P., Liau, C.: On the logical and algebraic aspects of reasoning with formal contexts. ACM Trans. Comput. Logic **26**(3) (2025)
25. Leuştean, I., Moangă, N., Şerbănuţă, T.: A many-sorted polyadic modal logic. Fund. Inform. **173**(2–3), 191–215 (2020)
26. Leuştean, I., Moangă, N., Şerbănuţă, T.: Many-sorted hybrid modal languages. J. Logical Algebraic Meth. Program. **120**, 100644 (2021)
27. Liau, C., Lin, I.: Quantitative modal logic and possibilistic reasoning. In: Neumann, B. (ed.) Proceedings of the 10th ECAI, pp. 43–47. Wiley (1992)
28. Liau, C., Lin, I.: Proof methods for reasoning about possibility and necessity. Int. J. Approximate Reason. **9**(4), 327–364 (1993)
29. Liau, C., Lin, I.: Possibilistic reasoning - a mini-survey and uniform semantics. Artif. Intell. **88**(1–2), 163–193 (1996)
30. Ognjanovic, Z., Raskovic, M., Markovic, Z.: Probability Logics: Probability-Based Formalization of Uncertain Reasoning. Springer, Cham (2016). https://doi.org/10.1007/978-3-319-47012-2

31. Pawlak, Z.: Rough sets. Int. J. Comput. Inform. Sci. **11**(5), 341–356 (1982)
32. Pawlak, Z.: Rough Sets: Theoretical Aspects of Reasoning about Data. Kluwer Academic Publishers, Dordrecht (1991)
33. Wille, R.: Restructuring lattice theory: an approach based on hierarchies of concepts. In: Ordered Sets, vol. 83, pp. 445–470. Reidel, Dordrecht-Boston, Mass (1982)
34. Yao, Y.: A comparative study of formal concept analysis and rough set theory in data analysis. In: Tsumoto, S., Słowiński, R., Komorowski, J., Grzymała-Busse, J.W. (eds.) RSCTC 2004. LNCS (LNAI), vol. 3066, pp. 59–68. Springer, Heidelberg (2004). https://doi.org/10.1007/978-3-540-25929-9_6
35. Yao, Y.Y.: Concept lattices in rough set theory. In: IEEE Annual Meeting of the Fuzzy Information Processing Society-NAFIPS, vol. 2, pp. 796–801. IEEE (2004)
36. Zadeh, L.: Fuzzy sets. Inf. Control **8**(3), 338–353 (1965)
37. Zadeh, L.: Fuzzy sets as a basis for a theory of possibility. Fuzzy Sets Syst. **1**(1), 3–28 (1978)

Belief Bases and Revision

Abductive Expansion for Belief Bases

Moritz Bayerkuhnlein[1(✉)], Özgür Lütfü Özçep[2], and Diedrich Wolter[1]

[1] University of Lübeck, Lübeck, Germany
{moritz.bayerkuhnlein,diedrich.wolter}@uni-luebeck.de
[2] University of Hamburg, Hamburg, Germany
oezguer.oezcep@uni-hamburg.de

Abstract. Belief expansion is the operation of incorporating new information into a belief base or theory. If a belief state can draw on a set of fundamental beliefs, new pieces of information are often not simply added, but explicitly tied to fundamental beliefs by means of explanations. Abductive expansion is an AGM-style belief change operation that augments a theory with an underlying explanation by means of abduction. AGM-style belief change presupposes deductively closed theories and thus makes no distinction between the explanation and the explained. In this paper, we extend abductive expansion to belief bases, which do not presuppose deductive closure. Within bases, abduced information is introduced in response to unexplained input and can therefore be explicitly identified as a newly formed belief. We provide an axiomatic characterization along with constructive methods.

Keywords: Belief Bases · Abduction · Hypotheses

1 Introduction

The model of the world held by an inquiring agent becomes less ambiguous whenever new information is incorporated into the beliefs of the agent. Well-known models of belief change, such as AGM-style frameworks [1] or Hansson's belief base change [13] employ an expansion operation that incorporates all the information presented as is. However, most information, such as observations of natural phenomena, can be justified by appealing to hypotheses drawn from fundamental beliefs that explain the new information.

In an effort to formalize a more natural expansion operation that accounts for these aspects of inquiry, *abductive expansion* was introduced into the AGM framework [2,5,20]. Intuitively, abductive expansion supplements the incoming information with abductive inferences to explain it. Depending on the agent's predisposition, these explanations may be bold, committing to a single specific hypothesis and thus eliminating alternatives, or cautious, incorporating disjunctions to avoid jumping to conclusions that are not fully justified. The abductive expansion operator has been studied in the context of symbolic machine learning [21], philosophy of science [3,24] and in the integration of default reasoning within belief revision [20].

A.-Y. Turhan and J. Virtema (Eds.): FoIKS 2026, LNCS 16475, pp. 109–120, 2026.
https://doi.org/10.1007/978-3-032-21540-6_7

When operating on deductively closed belief sets, abductive expansion does not make the explanatory step explicit; rather, the abduction(s) responsible for the change in an agent's epistemic state are, in a sense, obscured, since the entire expansion is internalized within the belief set itself.

In deductively closed theories, the abductions that drive changes in epistemic states are hidden, since the entire expansion is absorbed into the belief set. By contrast, using belief bases instead of belief sets allows us to separate explicit beliefs from implicit ones [13]. This makes abductions easier to trace, by comparing the belief base before and after an abductive expansion. A further advantage of employing belief bases lies in the fact that syntactic features can be used to identify possible abductions.

To our knowledge, no formal account of abductive expansion for belief bases has yet been developed. The development is challenged by the problems identified by Pagnucco [20], which make ad-hoc approaches infeasible. One major challenge is that a single observation can often be explained by several different abductions. This makes it necessary to preserve the distinction between facts, and hypotheses, as well as their abductive consequences, which is something that cannot be achieved simply by adding abductions and epistemic inputs to a belief base.

In this paper, we provide a formalization of abductive expansion for belief bases that addresses these challenges. We offer an axiomatic characterization of abductive expansion by adapting the postulates of AGM-style abductive expansion (Sect. 3). We then present constructions of the operation (Sect. 4). Finally, we establish the associated representation theorems, which are formalized and mechanically verified in an interactive proof assistant building on an existing formalization of AGM belief revision [7].

2 Notation and Background

Beliefs are formulated in an object language $\mathcal{L}$ which we assume to be closed under the usual connectives: negation ($\neg$), conjunction ($\wedge$), disjunction ($\vee$), implication ($\rightarrow$), equivalence ($\leftrightarrow$), and the zero-ary connective for contradiction ($\bot$). We define a *consequence operator* $\mathrm{Cn} : 2^{\mathcal{L}} \rightarrow 2^{\mathcal{L}}$ that derives the logical consequences of a set of sentences. The operator Cn satisfies the Tarskian properties: inclusion, $K \subseteq \mathrm{Cn}(K)$; monotonicity, $K \subseteq K' \Rightarrow \mathrm{Cn}(K) \subseteq \mathrm{Cn}(K')$; and iteration, $\mathrm{Cn}(\mathrm{Cn}(K)) = \mathrm{Cn}(K)$ [25].
We further assume that Cn is *supraclassical* and *compact*.

For notation, we write $K \vdash \phi$ whenever $\phi \in \mathrm{Cn}(B)$. We also write $K \vdash \Gamma$ for a set of formulae Γ to mean that $K \vdash \gamma$ for all $\gamma \in \Gamma$. Lowercase Greek letters are used as metavariables for formulae of $\mathcal{L}$.

The semantics of a logic $\langle \mathcal{L}, \mathrm{Cn} \rangle$ are given by an interpretation domain $\mathcal{I}$, a collection of models M, where each $M \in \mathcal{I}$ assigns meaning to the formulae of $\mathcal{L}$. In propositional logic, $\mathcal{I}$ is the powerset of the set of propositional symbols of the language. A satisfaction relation $\models \subseteq \mathcal{I} \times \mathcal{L}$ specifies which models satisfy which formulae: a model M is a model of α whenever $M \models \alpha$. The set of all models of α is written as $[\![\alpha]\!]$. More generally, for a set of formulae K, we define $[\![K]\!]$ as the set of models that satisfy every formula in K. Dually, we define $\mathrm{th}(A) = \{\varphi \in \mathcal{L} \mid M \models \varphi \text{ for all } M \in A\}$ as the set of all formulae in $\mathcal{L}$ that are satisfied by every model in A.

2.1 Belief Change

The AGM framework [1] characterises belief change operations on *theories* guided by general rationality postulates. A theory, or belief set, is a set of formulae $K \subseteq \mathcal{L}$ such that $K = \mathrm{Cn}(K)$, and thus is *deductively closed.* The framework defines three core operations: expansion $(+)$, contraction $(-)$, and revision $(*)$, each mapping a theory and a formula to an updated theory. Their behaviour is specified by rationality postulates and constructive definitions.

In the AGM framework, every belief in a theory is treated alike, including those that follow from logical closure. When it is useful to distinguish explicit from implicit beliefs, one can instead use Hansson's notion of a *belief base*[1], which is not deductively closed [13]. As in the AGM framework, Hansson proposes rationality postulates for operations on belief bases.

Contraction operators can be constructed syntactically using remainder sets and selection functions for theories as well as bases, resulting in the class of *partial meet contraction* operators. A remainder set, denoted $K \perp \alpha$, is the set of all maximal consistent subsets of K that do not imply α. A selection function $\gamma : (2^{\mathcal{L}} \times \mathcal{L}) \rightarrow 2^{2^{\mathcal{L}}}$ picks some subset of the remainder set, where $\gamma(K \perp \alpha)$ is a non-empty subset of $K \perp \alpha$, except if $K \perp \alpha$ is empty: in that case $\gamma(K \perp \alpha) = \{K\}$. The partial meet contraction generated by γ yields the operation defined as $B -_{\gamma} \alpha = \bigcap \gamma(B \perp \alpha)$.

Expansion is defined in terms of adding epistemic inputs to the beliefs, i.e. $K + \alpha = \mathrm{Cn}(K \cup \{\alpha\})$. A semantic characterization of AGM expansion is $[\![K + \alpha]\!] = [\![K]\!] \cap [\![\alpha]\!]$, which means that by accepting α as a belief we eliminate all models not satisfying α.

Revision operations are obtained by combining contraction and expansion via the so-called Levi identity[2] i.e. $K * \alpha = (K - \neg\alpha) + \alpha$. Well-known semantic constructions for operators on theories are given by Grove's system of spheres [9] and faithful pre-orders [14]. Recently, Ribeiro [22] has offered a systematic treatment of semantic constructions for bases.

2.2 Logic-Based Abduction

Informally speaking, abduction is the generation of explanations for a given fact φ. Formally, it is studied as a *propositional abduction problem* (P-ABD), where $\mathcal{P}$ is a finite set of variables, $H \subseteq \mathcal{P}$ is the set of hypotheses, $OBS \subseteq \mathcal{P}$ is the

[1] Additionally, belief bases are naturally more compact, which lends itself to computational approaches.

[2] Belief Bases distinguish here between *internal* and *external* revisions based on the order of contraction and expansion due to syntax dependence [10].

set of manifestations (observations), and $T \subseteq \mathcal{L}(\mathcal{P})$ is a consistent theory. A set $S \subseteq H$ is a solution (or explanation) if $T \cup S$ is consistent and $T \cup S \vdash OBS$. This framework usually restricts hypotheses to positive atoms, but this is no loss of generality since an arbitrary formula Ψ can be encoded by fresh variables x_Ψ together with equivalences $x_\Psi \leftrightarrow \Psi$ in T [15]. The set of all explanations is denoted by $Sol((\mathcal{P}, T, H, OBS))$.

In general, P-ABD is Σ_2^{P}-complete [4,16]. Therefore, any exact algorithm must in the worst case perform an exhaustive search over candidate hypothesis sets.

2.3 Abductive Expansion

Expansion (+) in the AGM framework, as well as in Hansson's approach, simply incorporates new information as is—in a case of AGM expansion, additionally, by closing the outcome w.r.t. the consequence operator. Rather than adding new information alone, we incorporate an explanation for it into the current beliefs by abducing an underlying cause. The resulting ($\oplus$) operation is called abductive expansion.

Example 1. On a walk, you observe a dog (d) passing by. Your belief is represented as a theory K. You belief, $K = \{$*if there is a dog there are no cats around* ($d \rightarrow \neg c$), *a wild dog is a dog* ($w \rightarrow d$), *a wild dog is dangerous* ($w \rightarrow g$), and *a dog owner has a dog* ($o \rightarrow d$) finally, *dogs either have owners or not* $\}$.
Modelling the dog encounter using an AGM-expansion $K+d$, you now also know that *there are no cats around* $\neg c \in \mathrm{Cn}(K \cup \{d\})$.
With an abductive expansion $K \oplus d$ you may also hypothesize that *there has to be an owner* (o) *somewhere*, or *you are in danger* (g) and this dog is *a wild dog* (w), or you consider both options and suspend judgment.

Abductive expansion ($\oplus$) in the context of theories (i.e. assuming deductive closure), is characterized by the following set of rationality postulates:

(K$\oplus$1) $K \oplus \alpha = \mathrm{Cn}(K \oplus \alpha)$ (closure)
(K$\oplus$2) If $\neg\alpha \notin K$, then $\alpha \in (K \oplus \alpha)$ (limited success)
(K$\oplus$3) $K \subseteq K \oplus \alpha$ (inclusion)
(K$\oplus$4) If $\neg\alpha \in K$, then $(K \oplus \alpha) = K$ (failure)
(K$\oplus$5) If $\neg\alpha \notin K$, then $\neg\alpha \notin (K \oplus \alpha)$ (consistency)
(K$\oplus$6) If $K \vdash \alpha \leftrightarrow \beta$, then $(K \oplus \alpha) = (K \oplus \beta)$ (extentionality)

The *supplementary postulates* below formalize how explanations that assume as little as possible should behave within the belief expansion process. Specifically, they express the logical relationship between abductions of different strengths, such as between a disjunctive (weaker) explanation and a more specific (stronger) one.

(K$\oplus$7) $K \oplus \alpha \subseteq K \oplus (\alpha \vee \beta) + \alpha$ (supp 1)
(K$\oplus$8) If $\neg\alpha \notin K \oplus (\alpha \vee \beta)$, then $K \oplus (\alpha \vee \beta) \subseteq K \oplus \alpha$ (supp 2)

Intuitively, these postulates ensure that expanding a belief set with a weaker abduction (e.g. for $\alpha \vee \beta$) yields results that are correspondingly weaker or more general than those obtained by expanding with an abduction for a stronger epistemic input (e.g. α). Together, they imply the disjunctive factoring condition where $K \oplus (\alpha \vee \beta)$ is either $K \oplus \alpha$, or $K \oplus \beta$, or $(K \oplus \alpha) \cap (K \oplus \beta)$ [5,20].

Pagnucco additionally defines a class of expansion operators based on *logic-based abduction*:

Definition 1 ([20]). *For a theory K and formula α, $\oplus$ is called an* abductive expansion operator *iff it has the following form:*

$$K \oplus \alpha = \begin{cases} \mathrm{Cn}(K \cup \{\beta\}) & \exists \beta \in \mathcal{L} : (K \cup \{\beta\} \vdash \alpha \;\wedge\; K \cup \{\beta\} \nvdash \bot), \\ K & \textit{otherwise.} \end{cases}$$

This class of operators can be shown to be equal to those satisfying the postulates stated above.

Constructions. An *syntactic construction* similar to that of AGM contraction can be formulated by means of selection functions and replacing remainder sets with sets of maximal consistent supersets of K that imply α, denoted $K \top \alpha$. The *partial meet abductive expansion* generated by γ yields the operation: $K \oplus_\gamma \alpha = \bigcap \gamma(K \top \alpha)$ if $B \top \alpha \neq \emptyset$, otherwise K. A fully rational version (additionally satisfying (K$\oplus$7) and (K$\oplus$8)) is obtained by imposing a transitive ordering over the elements of $K \top \alpha$, a *transitive relational partial meet abductive expansion*, then selects only from the set of best elements w.r.t. the imposed ordering.

Similar to the partial meet contraction in the AGM framework, two extreme cases are considered in abductive expansion. A maxichoice abductive expansion chooses a single *best* element of $K \top \alpha$, thereby committing entirely to a single hypothesis, a bold and risky strategy. The other extreme is full meet abductive expansion, where the whole of $K \top \alpha$ is selected. By believing in every possibility, no information is accepted beyond the epistemic input. As such, an AGM expansion can also be considered a kind of full meet abductive expansion. An agent following this strategy could be considered hypochondriacal, fearing any commitment to errors.

A fully rational *semantic construction* of abductive expansion is given by Grove's system of spheres [9,20]. An alternative construction using an *abductive entrenchment ordering*, analogous to epistemic entrenchment, was given by Pagnucco and Rajaratnam [21]. For both syntactic and semantic constructions, representation theorems have been obtained [20].

3 Abductive Expansion for Belief Bases

A belief base distinguishes between *explicit* beliefs, which are directly contained in the base, and *implicit* beliefs, which are merely logical consequences [6,17,18].

However, any hypothesis formed by abduction may compete with other possible alternatives and is therefore uncertain.

An agent can choose to actively commit to a specific hypothesis or be cautious in its inference and consider multiple potentially conflicting hypotheses. In his seminal work on abductive expansion, Pagnucco [20] concludes by highlighting Ghose's approach [8], which employs a richer representation of epistemic states to distinguish between facts and defeasible defaults, encoding limitations using constraints.

The operator we propose here follows a similar intention by drawing a distinction between the firm beliefs within the belief base and the set of (competing) hypotheses, which remain tentative. This way any syntactic restrictions on hypotheses can be parametrised, for example to rule out the trivial or the universal disjunctive explanation. A successful application therefore depends on choosing an appropriate hypothesis space.

Recalling P-Abd, we treat the belief base as a background theory. In P-Abd, hypotheses are (typically positive) literals, whereas here we allow sets of arbitrary formulae as hypotheses. Such an approach is equivalent to constraining (i.e., excluding) certain combinations of hypothesis literals in the encoded instance.

The Isabelle/HOL formalization of the following development is available in our companion repository[3].

Definition 2. *The set of* candidate abductions *from a set of hypotheses* $H \subseteq 2^{2^{\mathcal{L}}}$ *for an observation* $\varphi \in \mathcal{L}$ *relative to a background theory* $T \subseteq \mathcal{L}$ *is defined as*

$$Sol\big((T, H, \varphi)\big) = \big\{\Delta \in H \;\big|\; T \cup \Delta \vdash \varphi \;\wedge\; T \cup \Delta \nvdash \bot\big\}$$

Observation 1. *If* $H = 2^{2^{\mathcal{L}}}$ *and* $T \cup \{\varphi\}$ *is consistent, then* $Sol\big((T, H, \varphi)\big) \neq \emptyset$.

3.1 Postulates

On belief bases, we define an operation $\oplus : 2^{\mathcal{L}} \times 2^{2^{\mathcal{L}}} \times \mathcal{L} \to 2^{\mathcal{L}}$, where $B \oplus_{\mathrm{H}} \alpha$ denotes the *abductive expansion of* B *for* α *relative to a set of hypotheses* H. Additionally, the operation $\oplus^{\uparrow} : 2^{\mathcal{L}} \times 2^{2^{\mathcal{L}}} \times \mathcal{L} \Rightarrow 2^{2^{\mathcal{L}}}$ yields the set of post-expansion hypotheses conditioned on the epistemic input. For a finite belief base B, a set of hypotheses H, and an epistemic input α these operators are characterized by the following postulates:

(B$\oplus$1) $B \oplus^{\mathrm{H}}_{\uparrow} \alpha \subseteq Sol\big((B, H, \alpha)\big)$ (inclusionA)
(B$\oplus$2) $B \subseteq B \oplus_{\mathrm{H}} \alpha$ (inclusionB)
(B$\oplus$3) $(B \oplus_{\mathrm{H}} \alpha) \cup \Delta \vdash \alpha$ forall $\Delta \in B \oplus^{\mathrm{H}}_{\uparrow} \alpha$ (limited success)
(B$\oplus$4) If $B \oplus^{\mathrm{H}}_{\uparrow} \alpha = \emptyset$, then $B \oplus_{\mathrm{H}} \alpha = B$ (failure)
(B$\oplus$5) If $(B \cup \{\alpha\}) \nvdash \bot$, then $B \oplus_{\mathrm{H}} \alpha \nvdash \bot$ (consistency)
(B$\oplus$6) If $B \oplus^{\mathrm{H}}_{\uparrow} \alpha \neq \emptyset$, then $B \oplus_{\mathrm{H}} \alpha = B \cup \bigcap B \oplus^{\mathrm{H}}_{\uparrow} \alpha$ (solidify)
($B\oplus$0) If $Sol\big((B, H, \alpha)\big) \neq \emptyset$, then $B \oplus^{\mathrm{H}}_{\uparrow} \alpha \neq \emptyset$ (nonempty)

[3] Companion repository: https://github.com/mob00/abductive-base-expansion.

Here, $B \oplus_{\uparrow}^{\mathrm{H}} \alpha$ denotes the subset of candidate hypotheses (inclusionA) that the agent actually conditions on. As with abductive expansion on belief sets, the operation on bases may fail when no candidate hypothesis is available (failure). Since $B \oplus_{\mathrm{H}} \alpha$ captures only the agent's certain beliefs, the abductive consequence is tied to the conditioned hypothesis space (limited success). When the set of hypotheses converges on a formula that formula stabilizes as a concrete belief (solidify). Finally, $B \oplus_{\uparrow}^{\mathrm{H}} \alpha$ must be assumed non-empty, such that an agent cannot reject all hypotheses outright and conditions on at least one available candidate hypothesis (nonempty).

Proposition 1. *An abductive expansion operation for a belief base B satisfying* inclusionA, failure, *and* solidify *also satisfies* consistency *and* inclusionB.

An immediate advantage of abductive expansion on belief bases rather than belief sets is that the hypotheses remain explicit and are not immediately internalized under deductive closure.

Extracting the abduced hypotheses from a belief set typically requires a set-difference of pre- and post-expansion belief states, followed by a finite axiomatization of the residue, i.e. reconstructing the expansion on an equivalent belief base, of which there are many to choose from [11,20]. For belief bases, the abduction can be simply obtained by $B \oplus_{\mathrm{H}} \alpha \setminus B$, and checking the hypotheses in $B \oplus_{\uparrow}^{\mathrm{H}} \alpha$. This opens up the option to examine the underlying explicit beliefs, and in particular to inspect *why* something is believed.

Following belief change tradition, we refer to an abductive expansion validating the above postulates as *rational*.

4 Construction

Belief change operations on belief bases are most commonly studied under syntactic constructions, particularly for belief contraction; these include partial meet contraction and kernel contraction [12]. A contraction operator based on kernels removes at least one formula from each such minimal set, picked using an incision function to ensure that the target sentence is no longer entailed. Partial meet constructions of contraction identify and intersect maximal consistent subsets of a base that avoid an epistemic input, whereas kernel contraction instead relies on minimal entailment sets which are the smallest subsets that imply the epistemic input.

Using such selection functions, we select among the possible hypotheses, and define a partial meet construction for abductive expansion.

Definition 3. *Let γ be a function satisfying the following conditions for all belief bases B and epistemic inputs α:*

1. $\gamma(Sol((B,H,\alpha))) \neq \emptyset$ *if* $Sol((B,H,\alpha)) \neq \emptyset$ *(non-emptiness)*
2. $\gamma(Sol((B,H,\alpha))) \subseteq Sol((B,H,\alpha))$ *if* $Sol((B,H,\alpha)) \neq \emptyset$ *(selection)*
3. $\gamma(Sol((B,H,\alpha))) = H$ *if* $Sol((B,H,\alpha)) = \emptyset$ *(failure)*

Intuitively, we use the selection among all the potential hypotheses to model an agent's preference for which hypotheses are regarded as plausible or can be ignored. This selection is maintained in the belief base as a grounded set of beliefs, as well as in the tentative conditioned hypothesis space.

This notion parallels the hypothesis space and version space frameworks in concept learning [19]. In contrast to concept learning, selection of hypotheses as described in this paper is determined by γ, which picks hypotheses along the *preference* of an agent. Similar to the number of models after expansion, the size of the hypothesis set decreases as it is conditioned on new information, generally $B \oplus_{\uparrow}^{\mathrm{H}} \alpha \subseteq H$.

Definition 4. *Given a selection function γ as specified in Definition 3, for a belief base B, a set of hypotheses H, and a formula α, a* partial meet abductive expansion *is defined as $B \oplus_{\gamma\mathrm{H}} \alpha = B \cup \bigcap \gamma(Sol((B, H, \alpha)))$ if $B \oplus_{\widehat{\gamma}}^{\mathrm{H}} \alpha \neq \emptyset$ otherwise B and its associated conditioning operation as $B \oplus_{\widehat{\gamma}}^{\mathrm{H}} \alpha = \gamma(Sol((B, H, \alpha)))$ if $Sol((B, H, \alpha)) \neq \emptyset$ otherwise $\emptyset$.*

Theorem 1. *Let $\oplus_{\gamma\mathrm{H}}$ be an abductive expansion operator on belief bases with hypotheses H, and let $\oplus_{\widehat{\gamma}}^{\mathrm{H}}$ be its associated conditioning operator. For every belief base B, the operator $B \oplus_{\gamma\mathrm{H}} \alpha$ is a partial meet abductive base expansion iff it satisfies postulates* $(\mathrm{B} \oplus 0)$–$(\mathrm{B} \oplus 6)$.

Special instances of partial meet abductive expansion are the maxichoice and full meet variants. Their construction and interpretive implications mirror those of their counterparts in belief set change.

Under a maxichoice variant, a single hypothesis is immediately solidified in the belief base, yielding a bold strategy. By contrast, a full meet abductive expansion incorporates only those abductions that are necessary for explaining the observation, leaving all other potential hypotheses tentative within the hypothesis set.

Observation 2. *Let $\oplus_{\gamma}$ be a maxichoice abductive expansion operation. Any formula $\varphi \in \mathcal{L}$ is a consequence of abductively expanding a belief base by φ, i.e., $\varphi \in \mathrm{Cn}(B \oplus_{\mathrm{H}} \varphi)$, provided that $Sol((B, H, \varphi)) \neq \emptyset$.*

Belief base contraction can alternatively be represented by *kernel-based* constructions, particularly for operators satisfying Hansson's postulates of relative closure and core-retainment, i.e., removing only beliefs essential to deriving a sentence while retaining all consequences of the remainder. A formulation for abductive expansion using an analog to kernel sets has not yet been developed. Since explanatory sets are already captured through the notion of consistent candidates for an abduction, a kernel approach would offer limited additional insight within the present framework. Nevertheless, such a formulation may provide a finer syntactic characterization of minimal abductions, which we revisit in Sect. 5.

5 Supplementary Postulates

Explanations that assume as little as possible are a common goal in abduction and go hand in hand with the minimality principles of belief change. With belief bases in abductive expansion, our goal is to keep the distinction between hypotheses and firm beliefs; whenever a base is logically closed, the difference between a weaker explanation and its strong counterpart is lost. The supplementary postulates introduced in this section aim to recreate their belief-set counterparts, keeping the goal of separation in mind.

Since belief bases are not deductively closed and the abductive consequences are uncertain, we define a *sceptical* consequence operator Cn^s.

Definition 5. *The sceptical consequence of a belief base B under the set of hypotheses H is defined:*

$$\mathrm{Cn}^s_{\mathrm{H}}(B) \;=\; \bigcap_{\Delta \in \mathrm{H}} \mathrm{Cn}(B \cup \Delta)$$

As a shorthand, we denote $\mathrm{Cn}^s_{B \oplus^{\mathrm{H}}_{\uparrow} \alpha}(B \oplus_{\mathrm{H}} \alpha)$ with $\mathrm{Cn}^s(B \oplus_{\mathrm{H}} \alpha)$, dropping the index. Intuitively, since an agent may not be able to commit to a single hypothesis, the sceptical consequence operation only gives consequences of B that are true regardless of what hypothesis is chosen. This has two advantages, first, the distinction between hypotheses and their abductive consequences remains intact, and, second, the collapse of the effects of more general hypotheses upon closure is avoided, since the operation remains lifted.

Proposition 2. *For a belief base B and a set of hypotheses H, the* sceptical consequence Cn^s *as defined in Definition 5 is* monotonic *w.r.t. B,* antitone *w.r.t. H, and* deductively closed *w.r.t.* Cn.

Furthermore, the sceptical consequence coincides with a successful abductive expansion. We can now revisit Observation 2 and create its sceptical counterpart, showing that the set of hypotheses are conditioned on the epistemic input in case of full and partial meet abductive expansion.

Observation 3. *Let $\oplus$ be a rational abductive expansion operation. Any formula $\varphi \in \mathcal{L}$ is a sceptical consequence of the result of abductively expanding a belief base with that formula*[4], *i.e., $\varphi \in \mathrm{Cn}^s(B \oplus_{\mathrm{H}} \varphi)$.*

For the definitions of the supplementary postulates in the belief base context, we use sceptical consequence. A rational abductive expansion additionally satisfying the following supplementary postulates is dubbed *fully rational*:

(B $\oplus$ 7*a*) $(B \oplus_{\mathrm{H}} \alpha) \cap (B \oplus_{\mathrm{H}} \beta) \subseteq B \oplus_{\mathrm{H}} (\alpha \vee \beta)$
(B $\oplus$ 7*b*) $\left(B \oplus^{\mathrm{H}}_{\uparrow} (\alpha \vee \beta)\right) \subseteq \left(B \oplus^{\mathrm{H}}_{\uparrow} \alpha\right) \cup \left(B \oplus^{\mathrm{H}}_{\uparrow} \beta\right)$

[4] this includes the case where $B \oplus^{\mathrm{H}}_{\uparrow} \varphi = \emptyset$.

The supplementary postulate (B$\oplus$7a) is analogous to a consequence of (K$\oplus$7) in the context of theories and states in the following sense: an adopted explanation, i.e., one that is certain to explain both α and β in isolation, will also be adopted when explaining $\alpha \vee \beta$. Clearly, this postulate requires some form of minimality, which we will explore in the construction.

The same applies to (B $\oplus$ 8a) which is a translation of (K $\oplus$ 8):

(B $\oplus$ 8a) If $\neg\alpha \notin \mathrm{Cn}^s(B \oplus_{\mathrm{H}} (\alpha \vee \beta))$, then $\mathrm{Cn}^s(B \oplus_{\mathrm{H}} (\alpha \vee \beta)) \subseteq \mathrm{Cn}^s(B \oplus_{\mathrm{H}} \alpha)$
(B $\oplus$ 8b) If $\neg\alpha \notin \mathrm{Cn}^s(B \oplus_{\mathrm{H}} (\alpha \vee \beta))$, then $(B \oplus^{\mathrm{H}}_{\uparrow} \alpha) \subseteq (B \oplus^{\mathrm{H}}_{\uparrow} (\alpha \vee \beta))$

Here, if any explanation of α would also explain $\alpha \vee \beta$, as formalized by $\neg\alpha$ not being a sceptical consequence of $B \oplus^{\mathrm{H}}_{\uparrow} (\alpha \vee \beta)$, then any explanation chosen for the more general $\alpha \vee \beta$ is also chosen for α. Note the similarity of the supplementary postulates for abducitve expansion for belief sets on the one hand and for belief bases (contraction) on the other hand.

As defined in the previous section, the partial meet abductive expansion is not *fully* rational. According to the selection function (Definition 3), a selection can potentially choose only one branch of possible explanations on a disjunction.

Example 2. Assume a belief base $B = \emptyset$, $\alpha = p$ and $\beta = q$ and a finite $H = \{\Delta_1, \Delta_2, \Delta_3 \dots\}$ where $\Delta_1 = \{t, t \rightarrow p\}$, $\Delta_2 = \{t, t \rightarrow q\}$, $\Delta_3 = \{q\}$. Let $\oplus_\gamma$ be a partial meet abductive expansion operation, such that, based on a selection function γ, we get $B \oplus_{\gamma\mathrm{H}} \alpha = B \oplus^{\mathrm{H}}_{\hat{\gamma}} \alpha = \{\Delta_1\}$, $B \oplus_{\gamma\mathrm{H}} \beta = B \oplus^{\mathrm{H}}_{\hat{\gamma}} \beta = \{\Delta_2\}$ and $B \oplus^{\mathrm{H}}_{\hat{\gamma}} (\alpha \vee \beta) = \{\Delta_2, \Delta_3\}$, thus $B \oplus_{\gamma\mathrm{H}} (\alpha \vee \beta) = \bigcap\{\Delta_2, \Delta_3\} = \emptyset$.
This expansion operation violates (B$\oplus$7), since $\{t, t \rightarrow p\} \cap \{t, t \rightarrow q\} = \{t\} \nsubseteq \emptyset$.

And it also violates (B$\oplus$8), since $\mathrm{Cn}^s(B \oplus_{\mathrm{H}} \alpha \vee \beta) = \mathrm{Cn}(\{t, t \rightarrow q\}) \cap \mathrm{Cn}(\{q\})$ and $q \in \mathrm{Cn}^s(B \oplus_{\mathrm{H}} \alpha \vee \beta)$ but $q \notin \mathrm{Cn}^s(B \oplus_{\mathrm{H}} \alpha)$ despite the antecedent $\neg p \notin \mathrm{Cn}(\{q\})$.

Interestingly, Rott's construction [23] can be used in the disjunctive case to obtain these properties. We need to impose the following conditions on the selection function to obtain a fully rational operation with disjunctive factoring:

S1 $\gamma(Sol((B, H, (\alpha \vee \beta)))) \subseteq \gamma(Sol((B, H, \alpha))) \cup \gamma(Sol((B, H, \beta)))$
S2 $\gamma(Sol((B, H, \alpha))) \subseteq \gamma(Sol((B, H, (\alpha \vee \beta))))$, if $\neg\alpha$ is not a sceptical consequences of belief state obtained through γ

Theorem 2. *Let* $\oplus_{\gamma\mathrm{H}}$ *be a fully rational abductive expansion operator on belief bases with* γ *satisfying* S1 *and* S2, *and let* $\oplus^{\mathrm{H}}_{\hat{\gamma}}$ *be its associated conditioning operator. For every belief base* B, *the operator* $\oplus_{\gamma\mathrm{H}}$ *is fully rational abductive base expansion iff it satisfies postulates* (B $\oplus$ 0)–(B $\oplus$ 8).

6 Conclusion and Future Work

We advance abductive expansion from belief sets to belief bases, treating explanations and hypotheses as first-class, foundational elements that drive belief change. By keeping hypotheses explicit, our framework preserves separation between firm beliefs and tentative explanations, thereby clarifying why beliefs hold.

Several open challenges remain besides expansion. Beyond the operation addressed in this paper, there are further interesting operations, for example revision. A full characterization of abductive revision remains largely open. Since belief bases admit multiple types of contraction, a possible approach could be to combine different contraction operators with an abductive expansion to obtain an appropriate revision operation. A fully rational semantic construction may be achievable. Such a semantic account would also pave the way for iterated versions of the operation, which have been largely unexplored even in the seminal work on belief sets.

References

1. Alchourrón, C.E., Gärdenfors, P., Makinson, D.: On the logic of theory change: partial meet contraction and revision functions. J. Symbol. Logic **50**(2), 510–530 (1985)
2. Aliseda, A.: Abductive Reasoning, vol. 330. Springer, Dordrecht (2006). https://doi.org/10.1007/1-4020-3907-7
3. Cevolani, G.: Truth approximation via abductive belief change. Log. J. IGPL **21**(6), 999–1016 (2013)
4. Eiter, T., Gottlob, G.: The complexity of logic-based abduction. J. ACM (JACM) **42**(1), 3–42 (1995)
5. Fermé, E., Hansson, S.O.: Belief Change: Introduction and Overview. Springer, Cham (2018). https://doi.org/10.1007/978-3-319-60535-7
6. Fermé, E.L., Herzig, A., Martinez, M.V.: On the logic of theory base change: reformulation of belief bases. In: Proceedings of the AAAI Conference on Artificial Intelligence, vol. 39, pp. 14922–14929 (2025)
7. Fouillard, V., Taha, S., Boulanger, F., Sabouret, N.: Belief revision theory. Archive of Formal Proofs, October 2021. Formal proof development, https://isa-afp.org/entries/Belief_Revision.html
8. Ghose, A.K.: Practical Belief Change. Ph.D. thesis, University of Alberta (1995)
9. Grove, A.: Two modellings for theory change. J. Philos. Log. **17**(2), 157–170 (1988). https://doi.org/10.1007/BF00247909
10. Hansson, S.O.: Reversing the Levi identity. J. Philos. Log. **22**(6), 637–669 (1993)
11. Hansson, S.O.: Theory contraction and base contraction unified. J. Symbolic Logic **58**(2), 602–625 (1993)
12. Hansson, S.O.: Kernel contraction. J. Symbolic Logic **59**(3), 845–859 (1994)
13. Hansson, S.O.: A Textbook of Belief Dynamics: Theory Change and Database Updating. Kluwer Academic Publishers, Dordrecht (1999)
14. Katsuno, H., Mendelzon, A.O.: Propositional knowledge base revision and minimal change. Artif. Intell. **52**(3), 263–294 (1991)
15. Konolige, K.: Abduction versus closure in causal theories. Artif. Intell. **53**(2–3), 255–272 (1992)
16. Lagerkvist, V., Maizia, M., Schmidt, J.: A fine-grained complexity view on propositional abduction - algorithms and lower bounds. In: Kwok, J. (ed.) Proceedings of the Thirty-Fourth International Joint Conference on Artificial Intelligence, IJCAI-25, pp. 4562–4569 (2025). Main Track, https://doi.org/10.24963/ijcai.2025/508

17. Levesque, H.J.: A logic of implicit and explicit belief. In: Proceedings of the AAAI Conference on Artificial Intelligence (AAAI-84), pp. 198–202 (1984). https://cdn.aaai.org/AAAI/1984/AAAI84-038.pdf
18. Lorini, E.: Rethinking epistemic logic with belief bases. Artif. Intell. **282**, 103233 (2020). https://doi.org/10.1016/j.artint.2020.103233, https://www.sciencedirect.com/science/article/pii/S0004370219300293
19. Mitchell, T.M.: Machine Learning. McGraw-Hill, New York (1997)
20. Pagnucco, M.: The role of abductive reasoning within the process of belief revision. Ph.D. thesis, University of Sydney (1996)
21. Pagnucco, M., Rajaratnam, D.: Inverse resolution as belief change. In: Proceedings of the 19th International Joint Conference on Artificial Intelligence (IJCAI-05), pp. 540–545 (2005). https://www.ijcai.org/Proceedings/05/Papers/0765.pdf
22. Ribeiro, J.S.: Semantic constructions for belief base contraction: partial meet vs smooth kernel. In: Proceedings of the 21st International Conference on Principles of Knowledge Representation and Reasoning, KR 2024, pp. 620–630 (2024). https://doi.org/10.24963/kr.2024/58, https://proceedings.kr.org/2024/58/
23. Rott, H.: Belief contraction in the context of the general theory of rational choice. J. Symbolic Logic **58**(4), 1426–1450 (1993)
24. Schurz, G.: Abductive belief revision in science. In: Belief Revision Meets Philosophy of Science, pp. 77–104. Springer, Dordrecht (2010). https://doi.org/10.1007/978-90-481-9609-8_4
25. Tarski, A.: Logic, Semantics, Metamathematics: Papers from 1923 to 1938, 2nd edn. Hackett Publishing Company, Indianapolis (1983)

Mutual Irreducibility of Revision and Multiple Revision

Sebastian Rudolph[1] and Kai Sauerwald[2](✉)

[1] Computational Logic Group, Technische Universität Dresden, Germany
[2] Faculty of Mathematics and Computer Science, FernUniversität in Hagen, Germany
kai.sauerwald@fernuni-hagen.de

Abstract. We show that revision by single sentences and multiple revision are, in general, mutually irreducible processes. The result is given for revision in base logics, a framework for studying revision in arbitrary classical logics for various notions of bases. Within this framework, we demonstrate that revision by single sentences can not be represented as multiple revision. The result employs general relational semantics for base revision. In combination with the well-known result that multiple revision cannot be reduced to sentence revision, we obtain that sentence revision and multiple revision are mutually irreducible.

1 Introduction

Adaptation of an agent's beliefs according to new information is a central issue of artificial intelligence. One of the premier change processes is

> *revision*: the integration of new information,
> while resolving inconsistencies, whenever possible.

Revision is studied in several different flavours [8]; notably one distinguishes between the task of integrating one piece of information—which is here called *sentence revision*—and *multiple revision*, which is the task of revision by multiple pieces of information at the same time, such that all pieces are integrated.

It is known that, in general, multiple revision cannot be reduced to sentence revision [16]. Our main contribution is to complement this observation by showing that sentence revision cannot be reduced to multiple revision, which might seem counterintuitive at first sight. This shows that sentence revision and multiple revision are mutually different kinds of operations. Our example employs recent results on the semantics of revision within base logics[3] [5–7], a framework generalizing work on the semantics of revision [4] to arbitrary Tarskian logics, a broad class of logics including propositional logic and first-order predicate logic.

In the following sections, we consider the preliminaries of this paper, introduce base logics and change operators within this framework. We consider revision within base logics and the semantics of base revision. Finally, we show that sentence revision cannot be reduced to multiple revision.

[3] Disclaimer: Some texts here are from joint work with Faiq Miftakhul Falakh [7].

A.-Y. Turhan and J. Virtema (Eds.): FoIKS 2026, LNCS 16475, pp. 121–133, 2026.
https://doi.org/10.1007/978-3-032-21540-6_8

2 Preliminaries

In order to study (sentence and multiple) revision formally, one uses logics, which is convenient, as logics provide an intrinsic notion of consistency and consequence, which describes interrelations between beliefs. We will employ a generic view on logics with a classical model-theoretic semantics represented by satisfaction systems [20]. A logic's satisfaction system is a triple $(\mathcal{L}, \Omega, \models)$, consisting of a (possibly infinite) set of *sentences* $\mathcal{L}$, a (potentially infinite) class Ω of *interpretations* (also referred to as *worlds*) and a binary relation $\models$ between Ω and $\mathcal{L}$ where $\omega \models \varphi$ indicates that ω is a *model* of φ. For some $\varphi \in \mathcal{L}$, we use the shortcut $[\![\varphi]\!]$ to denote the set $\{\omega \mid \omega \models \varphi\}$ of models of φ. Logical entailment is defined as usual via models: for two sentences φ and ψ we say φ *entails* ψ (written $\varphi \models \psi$) if $[\![\varphi]\!] \subseteq [\![\psi]\!]$. Note that this means we overload the symbol "$\models$" in the usual way.

The notions of modelhood and entailment can be easily lifted from single sentences to sets. We obtain the models of a set $\mathcal{K} \subseteq \mathcal{L}$ of sentences via $[\![\mathcal{K}]\!] = \bigcap_{\varphi \in \mathcal{K}} [\![\varphi]\!]$. For $\mathcal{K} \subseteq \mathcal{L}$ and $\mathcal{K}' \subseteq \mathcal{L}$ we say $\mathcal{K}$ *entails* $\mathcal{K}'$ (written $\mathcal{K} \models \mathcal{K}'$) if $[\![\mathcal{K}]\!] \subseteq [\![\mathcal{K}']\!]$. We write $\mathcal{K} \equiv \mathcal{K}'$ to express $[\![\mathcal{K}]\!] = [\![\mathcal{K}']\!]$. A sentence, respectively, a set of sentences, is called *consistent* if it has models. A set of sentences is called *consistent with* another set of sentences if the two have models in common.

The existence of a classical model-theoretic semantics as above is equivalent to the logic being *Tarskian* [21], i.e., the following is satisfied[4]:

$$\text{If } \varphi \in \mathcal{K} \text{ then } \mathcal{K} \models \varphi. \qquad \text{(extensivity)}$$
$$\text{If } \mathcal{K} \models \varphi \text{ and } \mathcal{K} \subseteq \mathcal{K}', \text{ then } \mathcal{K}' \models \varphi. \qquad \text{(monotonicity)}$$
$$\text{If } \mathcal{K} \models \mathcal{K}' \text{ and } \mathcal{K}' \models \varphi, \text{ then } \mathcal{K} \models \varphi. \qquad \text{(idempotence)}$$

The notion of Tarskian logic captures many well-known classical logical formalisms, including propositional logic, first- and second-order predicate logic, and well-known fragments as Horn fragments and description logics. A great variety of formalisms can be conceived as Tarskian logics, even if they're typically not considered as logics in the stricter sense [7].

In knowledge representation and its applications, one often works with (knowledge) bases which are sets of formulas of some underlying logic. In the belief revision community, the term of *base* commonly denotes an arbitrary (possibly infinite) set of sentences. However, in certain scenarios, other assumptions might be more appropriate. Hence, for the sake of generality, we decided to define the notion of a base on an abstract level with minimal requirements (just as we introduced our notion of *logic*), allowing for its instantiation in many ways.

Definition 1 ([7]). *A* base logic *is a tuple* $\mathbb{B} = (\mathcal{L}, \Omega, \models, \mathfrak{B}, \Cup)$, *where*

- $(\mathcal{L}, \Omega, \models)$ *is a logic (specified by a satisfaction system),*
- $\mathfrak{B} \subseteq \mathcal{P}(\mathcal{L})$ *is a family of sets of sentences, called* bases, *and*
- $\Cup : \mathfrak{B} \times \mathfrak{B} \to \mathfrak{B}$ *is a binary operator over bases, called the* abstract union, *satisfying* $[\![\mathcal{B}_1 \Cup \mathcal{B}_2]\!] = [\![\mathcal{B}_1]\!] \cap [\![\mathcal{B}_2]\!]$.

[4] See [7] for a proof of equivalence via the closure $\mathrm{Cn}(K) = \{\varphi \mid \mathcal{K} \models \varphi\}$.

Given a logic, typical choices of which kind of sets to pick as bases are *arbitrary sets* (as in the setting of base revision à la Hansson), *finite sets* which are a natural representation in the context of computation, e.g. when computational properties or implementations are to be investigated. Another common scenario are *belief sets*, i.e., the bases are deductively closed sets of sentences. One might also consider the setting where the bases are all *singleton sets*, which comes close to the setting investigated by Katsuno and Mendelzon [12].

3 AGM Revision and Multiple Revision in Base Logics

The work by Alchourrón, Gärdenfors, and Makinson [1] (AGM) answers the question of how to conduct sentence revision for many settings that satisfy the principle of minimal change. In AGM theory, an agent's beliefs are represented as set of sentences $\mathcal{K}$ and then, one formalizes revision of $\mathcal{K}$ by a sentence φ as the application of a binary operation $*$, resulting in $\mathcal{K} * \varphi$.

As one observe by inspecting Definition 1, in the setting of base logics, sentences are not first-level citizens of the formalism. To accommodate the setting of AGM theory with the the setting of base logics, we identify sentences with singleton bases and focus on base logics that contain such bases.

Definition 2. *A base logic* $\mathbb{B} = (\mathcal{L}, \Omega, \models, \mathfrak{B}, \uplus)$ *is called* sentential *if*

- $\{\ \{\psi\}\ \mid \psi \in \mathcal{L}\} \subseteq \mathfrak{B}$ *holds and*
- *for all* $\psi_1, \psi_2 \in \mathcal{L}$ *there is* $\psi_1 \owedge \psi_2 \in \mathcal{L}$ *with* $[\![\psi_1 \owedge \psi_2]\!] = [\![\psi_1]\!] \cap [\![\psi_2]\!]$.

Here, by $\psi_1 \owedge \psi_2$ we refer to a formula that behaves semantically like the conjunction of ψ_1 and ψ_2. The logic $(\mathcal{L}, \Omega, \models)$ does not necessarily need to feature conjunction $\wedge$ as a syntactic construct. However, if this is the case, then we can just set $\psi_1 \owedge \psi_2 = \psi_1 \wedge \psi_2$. For a sentential base logic we write $\mathbb{B} = (\mathcal{L}, \Omega, \models, \mathfrak{B}, \uplus, \owedge)$ to explicitly expose $\owedge$ (which formally is a function of type $\mathcal{L} \times \mathcal{L} \to \mathcal{L}$).

Belief change operators for single sentences are called *sentential base change operators* in our setting.

Definition 3. *Let* $\mathbb{B} = (\mathcal{L}, \Omega, \models, \mathfrak{B}, \uplus, \owedge)$ *be a sentential base logic. A* sentential base change operator *for* $\mathbb{B}$ *is a function* $* : \mathfrak{B} \times \mathcal{L} \to \mathfrak{B}$.

Most famously, AGM provide an axiomatization of those revision operators that satisfy minimal change [1]. In the following, we use $\mathcal{K} + \psi$ as a shortcut for $\mathcal{K} \uplus \{\psi\}$. The AGM postulates for sentence revision are present in the following, accommodated to the setting of a sentential base logic $\mathbb{B} = (\mathcal{L}, \Omega, \models, \mathfrak{B}, \uplus, \owedge)$:

(S1) $\mathcal{K} * \psi \models \psi$
(S2) If $[\![\mathcal{K} + \psi]\!] \neq \emptyset$ then $\mathcal{K} * \psi \equiv \mathcal{K} + \psi$
(S3) If $[\![\psi]\!] \neq \emptyset$ then $[\![\mathcal{K} * \psi]\!] \neq \emptyset$
(S4) If $\mathcal{K}_1 \equiv \mathcal{K}_2$ and $\psi_1 \equiv \psi_2$ then $\mathcal{K}_1 * \psi_1 \equiv \mathcal{K}_2 * \psi_2$
(S5) $(\mathcal{K} * \psi_1) + \psi_2 \models \mathcal{K} * (\psi_1 \owedge \psi_2)$
(S6) If $[\![(\mathcal{K} * \psi_1) + \psi_2]\!] \neq \emptyset$ then $\mathcal{K} * (\psi_1 \owedge \psi_2) \models (\mathcal{K} * \psi_1) + \psi_2$

For an explanation of these postulates, we recommend considering one of the books on the topic [8,9,11].

In the context of base logics, the default setting is to change a base based on information that is provided as a base. This corresponds to what is often called multiple revision, i.e., when multiple pieces of information are given at the same time to revise with. Formally, base change operators take two bases as inputs and output a base.

Definition 4. *Let* $\mathbb{B} = (\mathcal{L}, \Omega, \models, \mathfrak{B}, \Cup)$ *be a base logic. A* base change operator *for* $\mathbb{B}$ *is a function* $\circ : \mathfrak{B} \times \mathfrak{B} \to \mathfrak{B}$.

Analogously, multiple revision of prior beliefs $\mathcal{K}$ by a set of sentences Γ is formalized as the application of a binary operation $\circ$, resulting in $\mathcal{K} \circ \Gamma$. The postulates (S1)–(S6) for revision were extended to sets of sentences [15, 16]. In the following, such postulates are given in the notation of this paper:

(G1) $\mathcal{K} \circ \Gamma \models \Gamma$
(G2) If $[\![\mathcal{K} \Cup \Gamma]\!] \neq \emptyset$ then $\mathcal{K} \circ \Gamma \equiv \mathcal{K} \Cup \Gamma$
(G3) If $[\![\Gamma]\!] \neq \emptyset$ then $[\![\mathcal{K} \circ \Gamma]\!] \neq \emptyset$
(G4) If $\mathcal{K}_1 \equiv \mathcal{K}_2$ and $\Gamma_1 \equiv \Gamma_2$ then $\mathcal{K}_1 \circ \Gamma_1 \equiv \mathcal{K}_2 \circ \Gamma_2$
(G5) $(\mathcal{K} \circ \Gamma_1) \Cup \Gamma_2 \models \mathcal{K} \circ (\Gamma_1 \Cup \Gamma_2)$
(G6) If $[\![(\mathcal{K} \circ \Gamma_1) \Cup \Gamma_2]\!] \neq \emptyset$ then $\mathcal{K} \circ (\Gamma_1 \Cup \Gamma_2) \models (\mathcal{K} \circ \Gamma_1) \Cup \Gamma_2$

Clearly, the postulates (G1)–(G6) follow the same intuition as (S1)–(S6).

As discussed, we consider "revision by bases", also referred to as *multiple revision* [8]. Thereby, we focus on *package semantics*, meaning that all given sentences have to be incorporated, that is, given a base $\mathcal{K}$ and new information Γ (also a base here), we demand – as per (G1) – success of revision for all elements from Γ, i.e., $\mathcal{K} \circ \Gamma \models \varphi$ for every $\varphi \in \Gamma$.

4 Multiple Revision to Sentence Revision

Pavlos Peppas studied the interrelation of sentence revision and multiple revision [16]. First, he observed that in logics, where everything can be represented with finite sets, e.g., propositional logic, sentence revision and multiple revision are interdefinable. One can mutually reduce sentence revision and multiple revision in the following way:

[S⇒M] For each sentence revision operator $*$, there is a multiple revision operator $\circ$ such that $\mathcal{K} * \varphi \equiv \mathcal{K} \circ \{\varphi\}$ for all $\mathcal{K}$ and φ.
[M⇒S] For each multiple revision operator $\circ$, there is a sentence revision operator $*$ such that $\mathcal{K} \circ \Gamma \equiv \mathcal{K} * \bigwedge_{\varphi \in \Gamma} \varphi$ for all $\mathcal{K}$ and finite Γ.

In a setting where infinite sets are permitted, one cannot employ the construction from [M⇒S], as in many logics conjunction is limited to finite conjunctions.

Observation 5 ([16]). *In general, multiple revision cannot be reduced to sentence revision.*

Interestingly, Peppas showed that, even in infinite settings, one can reduce multiple revision to sentence revision in some interesting cases by employing constructions different from [M⇒S] [16]. We do not consider this direction further, and will focus on whether sentence revision can be reduced to multiple revision.

5 Relational Semantics of Base Revision

Recently, the general relational semantics of AGM-style revision in the sense of (G1)–(G6) in base logics was studied [7]. In the following, we present the main definitions and representation result.

For describing belief revision on the semantic level, it is expedient to endow the interpretation space Ω with some structure [10, 12]. We will employ binary relations $\preceq$ over Ω (formally: $\preceq \subseteq \Omega \times \Omega$), where the intuitive meaning of $\omega_1 \preceq \omega_2$ is that ω_1 is "equally good or better" than ω_2 when it comes to serving as a model. We call $\preceq$ *total* if $\omega_1 \preceq \omega_2$ or $\omega_2 \preceq \omega_1$ for any $\omega_1, \omega_2 \in \Omega$ holds. We write $\omega_1 \prec \omega_2$ as a shorthand, whenever $\omega_1 \preceq \omega_2$ and $\omega_2 \not\preceq \omega_1$ (the intuition being that ω_1 is "strictly better" than ω_2). For a selection $\Omega' \subseteq \Omega$ of interpretations, an $\omega \in \Omega'$ is called *$\preceq$-minimal in Ω'* if $\omega \preceq \omega'$ for all $\omega' \in \Omega'$.[5] We let $\min(\Omega', \preceq)$ denote the set of $\preceq$-minimal interpretations in Ω'. We call $\preceq$ a *preorder* if it is transitive and reflexive. While in many classical logics (most notably propositional logic), revision operators are known to be representable by total-preorders over the interpretations [10, 12], generalizing the representation theorems to arbitrary Tarskian logics requires adjusting the formal properties of the preference relation.

Definition 6 (min-complete, min-retractive, min-friendly). *Given a base logic $\mathbb{B} = (\mathcal{L}, \Omega, \models, \mathfrak{B}, \uplus)$, a binary relation $\preceq$ over Ω is called*

- min-complete *(for $\mathbb{B}$) if* $\min(\llbracket \Gamma \rrbracket, \preceq) \neq \emptyset$ *holds for every $\Gamma \in \mathfrak{B}$ with $\llbracket \Gamma \rrbracket \neq \emptyset$,*
- min-retractive *(for $\mathbb{B}$) if, for every $\Gamma \in \mathfrak{B}$ and $\omega', \omega \in \llbracket \Gamma \rrbracket$ with $\omega' \preceq \omega$, $\omega \in \min(\llbracket \Gamma \rrbracket, \preceq)$ implies $\omega' \in \min(\llbracket \Gamma \rrbracket, \preceq)$,*
- min-friendly *(for $\mathbb{B}$) if it is both min-retractive and min-complete.*

Min-completeness is close to the limit assumption by Lewis [14] or smoothness by Kraus, Lehmann and Magidor [13]. Specific for the general setting of base logics is min-retractivity, that guarantees that minimality of models with respect to a base carries over to equal elements. Note that every total preorder (over interpretations) is a min-retractive relation.

Definition 7 (assignment, faithful). *Let $\mathbb{B} = (\mathcal{L}, \Omega, \models, \mathfrak{B}, \uplus)$ be a base logic. An* assignment *for $\mathbb{B}$ is a function $\preceq_{(.)} : \mathfrak{B} \to \mathcal{P}(\Omega \times \Omega)$ that assigns to each belief base $\mathcal{K} \in \mathfrak{B}$ a total binary relation $\preceq_{\mathcal{K}}$ over Ω. An assignment $\preceq_{(.)}$ for $\mathbb{B}$ is called* faithful *if it satisfies for all $\omega, \omega' \in \Omega$ and all $\mathcal{K}, \mathcal{K}' \in \mathfrak{B}$:*

(F1) If $\omega, \omega' \models \mathcal{K}$, then $\omega \prec_{\mathcal{K}} \omega'$ does not hold.
(F2) If $\omega \models \mathcal{K}$ and $\omega' \not\models \mathcal{K}$, then $\omega \prec_{\mathcal{K}} \omega'$.
(F3) If $\mathcal{K} \equiv \mathcal{K}'$, then $\preceq_{\mathcal{K}} = \preceq_{\mathcal{K}'}$.

An assignment $\preceq_{(.)} : \mathfrak{B} \to \mathcal{P}(\Omega \times \Omega)$ is called min-friendly if $\preceq_{\mathcal{K}}$ is min-friendly for all $\mathcal{K} \in \mathfrak{B}$.

Intuitively, faithful assignments provide information about which of the two interpretations is "closer to $\mathcal{K}$-modelhood". Consequently, the actual $\mathcal{K}$-models

[5] If $\preceq$ is total, this definition is equivalent to the *absence* of any $\omega'' \in \Omega'$ with $\omega'' \prec \omega$.

are $\preceq_{\mathcal{K}}$-minimal. The next definition captures the idea of an assignment adequately representing the behaviour of a revision operator.

Definition 8 (compatible). *A base change operator* $\circ$ *for a base logic* $\mathbb{B}$ *is called* compatible *with some assignment* $\preceq_{(.)}$ *for* $\mathbb{B}$ *if it satisfies*

$$[\![\mathcal{K} \circ \Gamma]\!] = \min\left([\![\Gamma]\!], \preceq_{\mathcal{K}}\right)$$

for all bases $\mathcal{K}$ *and* Γ *from* $\mathfrak{B}$.

Compatibility will be treated as a symmetric notion, so saying $\circ$ is compatible with $\preceq_{(.)}$ means the same as saying $\preceq_{(.)}$ is compatible with $\circ$ or simply saying that $\preceq_{(.)}$ and $\circ$ are compatible.

Theorem 9 ([7]). *A base change operator* $\circ$ *for a base logic* $\mathbb{B}$ *satisfies (G1)–(G6) if and only if* $\circ$ *is compatible with a min-friendly faithful assignment for* $\mathbb{B}$.

Example 10 ([7]). Let $\mathbb{B} = (\mathcal{L}, \Omega, \models, \mathfrak{B}, \Cup)$ be an arbitrary base logic. We define the *trivial revision operator* $\circ^{\text{fm}}$ for $\mathbb{B}$ by

$$\mathcal{K} \circ^{\text{fm}} \Gamma = \begin{cases} \mathcal{K} \Cup \Gamma & \text{if } [\![\mathcal{K} \Cup \Gamma]\!] \text{ is consistent;} \\ \Gamma & \text{otherwise.} \end{cases}$$

To show satisfaction of (G1)–(G6), we construct a min-friendly faithful assignment $\preceq^{\text{fm}}_{(.)}$ compatible with $\circ^{\text{fm}}$. For each $\mathcal{K} \in \mathfrak{B}$ let $\omega_1 \preceq^{\text{fm}}_{\mathcal{K}} \omega_2$ if $\omega_1 \models \mathcal{K}$ or $\omega_2 \not\models \mathcal{K}$. Obviously, the relation $\preceq^{\text{fm}}_{\mathcal{K}}$ is a total preorder where ω_1, ω_2 are $\preceq^{\text{fm}}_{\mathcal{K}}$-equivalent, if either $\omega_1, \omega_2 \models \mathcal{K}$ or $\omega_1, \omega_2 \not\models \mathcal{K}$ holds. One can show that the relation $\preceq^{\text{fm}}_{\mathcal{K}}$ is min-complete and min-retractive. By construction of $\preceq^{\text{fm}}_{(.)}$, we obtain that $\min([\![\Gamma]\!], \preceq^{\text{fm}}_{\mathcal{K}}) = [\![\Gamma]\!]$ if $\mathcal{K} \Cup \Gamma$ is inconsistent. If $\mathcal{K} \Cup \Gamma$ is consistent, we obtain $\min([\![\Gamma]\!], \preceq^{\text{fm}}_{\mathcal{K}}) = [\![\mathcal{K}]\!] \cap [\![\Gamma]\!] = [\![\mathcal{K} \Cup \Gamma]\!]$. In summary, the assignment $\preceq^{\text{fm}}_{(.)}$ is min-friendly, and the base change operator $\circ^{\text{fm}}$ is compatible with it.

6 Sentence Revision to Multiple Revision

In this section we consider the reducibility of sentence revision to multiple revision. First, we define the reduction of sentential base change operators to base change operators.

Definition 11 (Reducible). *Let* $\mathbb{B} = (\mathcal{L}, \Omega, \models, \mathfrak{B}, \Cup)$ *be a sentential base logic and let* $*$ *be a sentential base change operator for* $\mathbb{B}$. *We say* $*$ *is* reducible to a base change operator $\circ$ for $\mathbb{B}$ *if for all* $\mathcal{K} \in \mathfrak{B}$ *and* $\psi \in \mathcal{L}$ *holds:*

$$K * \psi = K \circ \{\psi\}$$

Our main contribution is the insight that sentence revision is not reducible to multiple revision in the sense of Definition 11.

Theorem 12. *There is a sentential base logic $\mathbb{B}$ and a sentential base change operator for $\mathbb{B}$ that satisfies (S1)–(S6) which is **not** reducible to any base change operator for $\mathbb{B}$ that satisfies (G1)–(G6).*

In what remains, we will consider two proofs for Theorem 12. For that we construct a base logic and sentential base change operator that witness the result. We consider two such witnesses; one employs a cyclic situation and one employs an infinite descending chain (and no cyclic situation).

6.1 Proof of Theorem 12 via a Cyclic Situation

In the first proof of Theorem 12 we construct a sentential belief revision operator $*_c$ for which we will show that any base change operator $\circ_c$ to which $*_c$ is reducible is only compatible with assignments that contain a cycle. Non-reducibility follows then by a contradiction, because, as we will show, the setting is constituted in a way that any base change operator $\circ_c$ to which $*_c$ is reducible cannot contain the specified cycle and satisfy (G1)–(G6) at the same time. The feature that permits this contradiction is that base change operators have a higher expressiveness that allows performing revision by all bases (instead of just the singleton bases). Because of that, the mathematical object $\circ_c$ is more constrained (for fulfilling (G1)–(G6)) than $*_c$ (to fulfil (S1)–(S6)). More concretely, in the construction below, there are bases ψ_{AB}, ψ_{BC}, ψ_{CA} and $*_c$ chosen such that $\mathcal{K} *_c \psi_{\mathrm{XY}} = \{X\}$ holds. Now recall that a corresponding assignment for $\circ_c$ encodes the behaviour of $\circ_c$ via an order and selection of minimal elements, i.e., "$[\![\mathcal{K} \circ_c \{\psi_{\mathrm{XY}}\}]\!] = \min([\![\Gamma]\!], <)$" (see Definition 8). The above sketched behaviour of $*_c$ forces that a corresponding assignment for $\circ_c$ contains a cycle $A < B < C < A$. As we will see below, because of that cycle, there is a non-singleton base Γ with $[\![\mathcal{K} \circ_c \Gamma]\!] = \emptyset$, while at the same time (G1)–(G6) postulate $[\![\mathcal{K} \circ_c \Gamma]\!] \neq \emptyset$. Note that the situation above do not provide any conflict between the behaviour of $*_c$ and (S1)–(S6), especially, because Γ is a non-singleton base and hence, is Γ not in the domain of $*_c$.

The logic we are considering here has as interpretations Ω the natural numbers $\mathbb{N} = \{1, 2, 3, \ldots\}$ and four distinct elements $\square, A, B, C$. Formulas of the logic are the falsum $\bot$ (without any models), formulas of type ψ_x which have x as the one and only model, formulas of type ψ_{xy} which have $x, y \in \{A, B, C\}$ exactly as the one two models, and formulas of $\psi_{\mathbb{N}\setminus N}$ for finite sets $N \subsetneq \mathbb{N}$ that have $\{A, B, C, 1, 2, \ldots,\} \setminus N$ as models. As we will see, the formulas ψ_{AB}, ψ_{BC}, ψ_{CA} will later permit a circle situation between A, B and C. More formally, we're defining a logic $(\mathcal{L}, \Omega, \models)$ with:

$$\begin{aligned}\mathcal{L} &= \{\bot,\ \psi_{\square},\ \psi_{\mathrm{A}},\ \psi_{\mathrm{B}},\ \psi_{\mathrm{C}},\ \psi_{\mathrm{AB}},\ \psi_{\mathrm{BC}},\ \psi_{\mathrm{CA}}\ \} \\ &\quad \cup \{\psi_i \mid i \in \mathbb{N}\} \cup \{\ \psi_{\mathbb{N}\setminus N} \mid N \subseteq \mathbb{N} \text{ is finite}\} \\ \Omega &= \{\square, A, B, C, 1, 2, 3, \ldots\}\end{aligned}$$

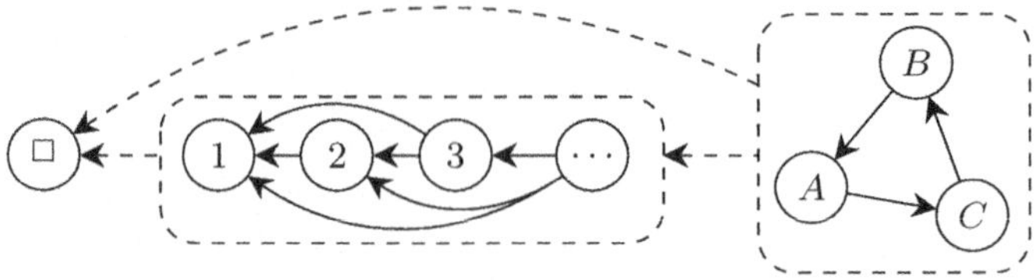

Fig. 1. Relation $\preceq_\square$ imposed by $*_c$ in the proof of Lemma 15.

The model-relation $\models$ is given by the following, where N ranges over all finite subsets of $\mathbb{N}$ and i ranges over the natural numbers:

$$\begin{aligned} [\![\bot]\!] &= \emptyset & [\![\psi_A]\!] &= \{A\} & [\![\psi_{AB}]\!] &= \{A,B\} \\ [\![\psi_\square]\!] &= \{\square\} & [\![\psi_B]\!] &= \{B\} & [\![\psi_{BC}]\!] &= \{B,C\} \\ [\![\psi_i]\!] &= \{i\} & [\![\psi_C]\!] &= \{C\} & [\![\psi_{CA}]\!] &= \{C,A\} \\ [\![\psi_{\mathbb{N}\setminus N}]\!] &= \{A,B,C,1,2,\ldots,\}\setminus N \end{aligned}$$

Note that for every two formulas $\psi,\varphi \in \mathcal{L}$ there is a unique formula $\chi \in \mathcal{L}$ with $[\![\chi]\!] = [\![\psi]\!] \cap [\![\varphi]\!]$. For every two formulas $\psi,\varphi \in \mathcal{L}$ we denote with $\psi \owedge \varphi$ the respective "conjunction", e.g., we let $\psi_{AB} \owedge \psi_{BC} = \psi_B$ or $\psi_{\mathbb{N}\setminus\{1,2\}} \owedge \psi_{BC} = \psi_{BC}$. The existence of $\owedge$ will allow us to extend the logic to a sentential base logic below. Furthermore, note that every formula $\psi_{\mathbb{N}\setminus N}$ has infinitely many models from $\mathbb{N}$, yet $[\![\psi_{\mathbb{N}\setminus N}]\!]$ has always a minimal element[6] from $\mathbb{N}$ as model. Moreover, every conjunction $\psi_{\mathbb{N}\setminus N} \owedge \psi_{\mathbb{N}\setminus M}$ is the formula $\psi_{\mathbb{N}\setminus(N\cup M)}$.

We now extend the logic $(\mathcal{L},\Omega,\models)$ to a base logic $\mathbb{B}_c = (\mathcal{L},\Omega,\models,\mathfrak{B},\Cup)$. The set $\mathfrak{B}$ is defined by

$$\mathfrak{B} = \{\ \{\psi\}\ \mid \psi \in \mathcal{L}\} \cup \{\ \Gamma_{ABC}\ \}\ ,$$

whereby $\Gamma_{ABC} = \{\ \psi_{\mathbb{N}\setminus N} \mid N \subseteq \mathbb{N} \text{ is finite}\}$. Note that the models of Γ_{ABC} are $[\![\Gamma_{ABC}]\!] = \{A,B,C\}$. The abstract union $\Cup$ is defined by setting $\{\psi\} \Cup \{\varphi\} = \{\psi \owedge \varphi\}$ and for all other bases:

$$\Gamma_{ABC} \Cup \Gamma = \Gamma \Cup \Gamma_{ABC} = \begin{cases} \Gamma & \text{if } \Gamma \in \{\{\psi_A\},\{\psi_B\},\{\psi_C\},\{\psi_{AB}\},\{\psi_{BC}\},\{\psi_{CA}\}\}; \\ \{\bot\} & \text{if } \Gamma \in \{\{\bot\},\{\psi_\square\},\{\psi_1\},\{\psi_2\},\ldots\}; \\ \Gamma_{ABC} & \text{otherwise.} \end{cases}$$

One can verify that $[\![\Gamma_1 \Cup \Gamma_2]\!] = [\![\Gamma_1]\!] \cap [\![\Gamma_2]\!]$ holds, and thus, together with the existence of $\owedge$, this renders $\mathbb{B}_c$ as a sentential base logic.

Lemma 13. *$\mathbb{B}_c$ is a sentential base logic.*

We are now ready to define the sentential base change operator $*_c$ for $\mathbb{B}_c$. For $K_\square = \{\psi_\square\}$ and for all $K \neq \{\psi_\square\}$, we let $*_c$ be as follows (whereby one selects

[6] With respect to the usual order on $\mathbb{N}$

the uppermost matching case in the case distinctions):

$$K_{\Box} *_{\mathrm{c}} \psi = \begin{cases} \{\psi_{\min(\mathbb{N}\setminus N)}\} & \text{if } \psi = \psi_{\mathbb{N}\setminus N}; \\ \{\psi_{\mathrm{A}}\} & \text{if } \psi = \psi_{\mathrm{AB}}; \\ \{\psi_{\mathrm{B}}\} & \text{if } \psi = \psi_{\mathrm{BC}}; \\ \{\psi_{\mathrm{C}}\} & \text{if } \psi = \psi_{\mathrm{CA}}; \\ \{\psi\} & \text{otherwise.} \end{cases} \quad \mathcal{K} *_{\mathrm{c}} \psi = \begin{cases} \mathcal{K} \Cup \{\psi\} & \text{if } [\![\mathcal{K} \Cup \{\psi\}]\!] \neq \emptyset; \\ \{\psi\} & \text{otherwise} \end{cases}$$

One can check case by case that (S1)–(S6) are satisfied.

Lemma 14. *$*_{\mathrm{c}}$ is a sentential base change operator for $\mathbb{B}_{\mathrm{c}}$ satisfying (S1)–(S6).*

We show that $*_{\mathrm{c}}$ cannot be reduced to any base change operator that satisfies (G1)–(G6). For that, we employ Theorem 9, and show that any candidate $\circ$ is not compatible with a min-friendly faithful assignment for $\mathbb{B}_{\mathrm{c}}$.

Lemma 15. *$*_{\mathrm{c}}$ is not reducible to any base change operator for $\mathbb{B}_{\mathrm{c}}$ that satisfies (G1)–(G6).*

Proof. Towards a contradiction, let $\circ_{\mathrm{c}}$ be a base change operator for $\mathbb{B}_{\mathrm{c}}$ that satisfies (G1)–(G6) and $*_{\mathrm{c}}$ is reducible to $\circ_{\mathrm{c}}$. Due to Theorem 9, there is a min-friendly faithful assignment $\preceq_{(.)}$ for $\mathbb{B}_{\mathrm{c}}$ that is compatible with $\circ_{\mathrm{c}}$. In the following, we write $\preceq_{\Box}$ for $\preceq_{\{\psi_{\Box}\}}$. Because $*_{\mathrm{c}}$ is reducible to $\circ_{\mathrm{c}}$, we have:

$$[\![\{\psi_{\Box}\} \circ_{\mathrm{c}} \{\psi_{\mathrm{AB}}\}]\!] = \{A\} = \min([\![\{\psi_{\mathrm{AB}}\}]\!], \preceq_{\Box})$$
$$[\![\{\psi_{\Box}\} \circ_{\mathrm{c}} \{\psi_{\mathrm{BC}}\}]\!] = \{B\} = \min([\![\{\psi_{\mathrm{BC}}\}]\!], \preceq_{\Box})$$
$$[\![\{\psi_{\Box}\} \circ_{\mathrm{c}} \{\psi_{\mathrm{CA}}\}]\!] = \{C\} = \min([\![\{\psi_{\mathrm{CA}}\}]\!], \preceq_{\Box})$$

Recall that $[\![\{\psi_{\mathrm{AB}}\}]\!] = \{A, B\}$, $[\![\{\psi_{\mathrm{BC}}\}]\!] = \{B, C\}$, and $[\![\{\psi_{\mathrm{CA}}\}]\!] = \{C, A\}$ holds. Consequently, we have:

$$A \preceq_{\Box} B \qquad B \not\preceq_{\Box} A \qquad B \preceq_{\Box} C \qquad C \not\preceq_{\Box} B \qquad C \preceq_{\Box} A \qquad C \not\preceq_{\Box} A$$

This yields that $\preceq_{\Box}$ has the strict cycle $A \prec_{\Box} B \prec_{\Box} C \prec_{\Box} A$. Next, observe that $[\![\Gamma_{\mathrm{ABC}}]\!] = \{A, B, C\}$. Yet, because of the strict cycle above, we obtain that $\min([\![\Gamma_{\mathrm{ABC}}]\!], \preceq_{\Box}) = \emptyset$. The latter is impossible in $\preceq_{\Box}$, as $\preceq_{\Box}$ is min-friendly (and thus, min-complete). □

6.2 Proof of Theorem 12 via an Infinite Descending Chain

In the second proof of Theorem 12 we construct a sentential belief revision operator $*_d$ for which we will show that any base change operator $\circ_d$ to which $*_d$ is reducible is only compatible with assignments that contain an infinite descending chain. The proof strategy is similar as in Section 6.1, and works by showing that there is a non-singleton base Γ such that $[\![\mathcal{K} \circ_d \Gamma]\!] = \emptyset$ holds, when $*_d$ is reducible to $\circ_d$, yet (G1)–(G6) postulate $[\![\mathcal{K} \circ_d \Gamma]\!] \neq \emptyset$. Despite the structural similarity, we are required to construct a completely different logical setting to permit the required behaviour of $*_d$ and $\circ_d$.

We start, again, by defining a logic $(\mathcal{L}, \Omega, \models)$ by letting:

$$\mathcal{L} = \{\bot\} \cup \{ [=1/i],\ [\geq 1/i] \mid i \in \mathbb{Z} \setminus \{0\} \} \qquad \Omega = \{ 1/i \mid i \in \mathbb{Z} \setminus \{0\}\}$$

The model-relation $\models$ is given by the following (where i ranges over $\mathbb{Z} \setminus \{0\}$):

$$[\![\bot]\!] = \emptyset \qquad [\![[=1/i]]\!] = \{1/i\} \qquad [\![[\geq 1/i]]\!] = \{1/n \in \Omega \mid 1/n \geq 1/i\}$$

That is the formulas of the logic $(\mathcal{L}, \Omega, \models)$ express either a fraction of the form $\pm 1/i$ or an interval of all fractions of the form $\pm 1/n$ between $\pm 1/i$ and 1 (or nothing via the formula $\bot$). For every two formulas $\psi, \varphi \in \mathcal{L}$ we denote with $\psi \oslash \varphi$ the respective "conjunction" defined by:

$$\varphi \oslash \psi = \begin{cases} \varphi & \text{if } [\![\varphi]\!] \subseteq [\![\psi]\!]; \\ \psi & \text{if } [\![\psi]\!] \subsetneq [\![\varphi]\!]; \\ \bot & \text{otherwise.} \end{cases}$$

We extend $(\mathcal{L}, \Omega, \models)$ to a sentential base logic $\mathbb{B}_\mathrm{d} = (\mathcal{L}, \Omega, \models, \mathfrak{B}, \Cup, \oslash)$. The set $\mathfrak{B}$ is defined by

$$\mathfrak{B} = \{ \ \{\psi\} \ \mid \psi \in \mathcal{L}\} \cup \{ \ \Gamma^\infty \ \} \ ,$$

whereby $\Gamma^\infty = \{ [\geq -1/i] \mid i \in \mathbb{N}\}$. The sets of models of Γ^∞ consists of all positive fractions $[\![\Gamma^\infty]\!] = \{1/i \mid i \in \mathbb{N}\}$ from Ω. The abstract union $\Cup$ is defined by setting $\{\psi\} \Cup \{\varphi\} = \{\psi \oslash \varphi\}$ and for all other cases we have:

$$\Gamma^\infty \Cup \Gamma = \Gamma \Cup \Gamma^\infty = \begin{cases} \Gamma & \text{if } \Gamma = \{[=1/i]\} \text{ or } \Gamma = \{[\geq 1/i]\} \text{ for } i \in \mathbb{N}; \\ \Gamma^\infty & \text{if } \Gamma = \Gamma^\infty \text{ or } \Gamma = \{[\geq 1/{-i}]\} \text{ for } i \in \mathbb{N}; \\ \{\bot\} & \text{otherwise.} \end{cases}$$

Again, one easily verifies that $[\![\Gamma_1 \Cup \Gamma_2]\!] = [\![\Gamma_1]\!] \cap [\![\Gamma_2]\!]$ holds, and thus, together with the existence of $\oslash$, we obtain the following.

Lemma 16. $\mathbb{B}_\mathrm{d}$ *is a sentential base logic.*

We define a sentential base change operator $*_\mathrm{d}$ for $\mathbb{B}_\mathrm{d}$. For $\mathcal{K}_\bot = \{\bot\}$ and all $K \neq \{\bot\}$, we let $*_\mathrm{d}$ be as follows:

$$\mathcal{K}_\bot *_\mathrm{d} \psi = \begin{cases} \{[=1/i]\} & \text{if } \psi = [\geq 1/i]; \\ \{\psi\} & \text{otherwise.} \end{cases} \qquad \mathcal{K} *_\mathrm{d} \psi = \begin{cases} \mathcal{K} \Cup \{\psi\} & \text{if } [\![\mathcal{K} \Cup \{\psi\}]\!] \neq \emptyset; \\ \{\psi\} & \text{otherwise} \end{cases}$$

One can check case by case that (S1)–(S6) are satisfied.

Lemma 17. $*_\mathrm{d}$ *is a sentential base change operator for* $\mathbb{B}_\mathrm{d}$ *satisfies (S1)–(S6).*

To proof non-reducibility of $*_\mathrm{d}$, we show that any base change operator that embeds $*_\mathrm{d}$ does not satisfy (G1)–(G6).

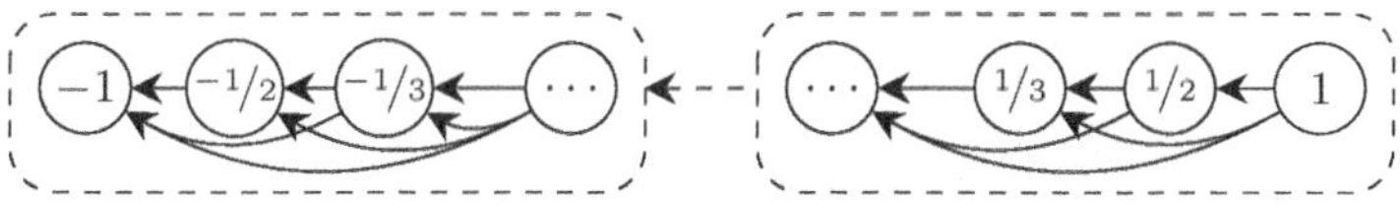

Fig. 2. Relation $\preceq_\bot$ imposed by $*_\mathrm{d}$ in the proof of Lemma 18.

Lemma 18. *$*_\mathrm{d}$ is not reducible to any base change operator for $\mathbb{B}_\mathrm{d}$ that satisfies (G1)–(G6).*

Proof. Towards a contradiction, let $\circ_\mathrm{d}$ be a base change operator for $\mathbb{B}_\mathrm{d}$ that satisfies (G1)–(G6) and $*_\mathrm{d}$ is reducible to $\circ_\mathrm{d}$. Due to Theorem 9, there is a min-friendly faithful assignment $\preceq_{(.)}$ for $\mathbb{B}_\mathrm{d}$ that is compatible with $\circ_\mathrm{d}$. The latter means especially, that $[\![\mathcal{K} \circ_\mathrm{d} \Gamma]\!] = \min\big([\![\Gamma]\!], \preceq_\mathcal{K}\big)$ holds for all $\mathcal{K}, \Gamma \in \mathfrak{B}$. In the following, we write $\preceq_\bot$ for $\preceq_{\mathcal{K}_\bot}$. Because $*_\mathrm{d}$ is reducible to $\circ_\mathrm{d}$, we obtain the following for all $i \in \mathbb{N}$:

$$[\![\mathcal{K}_\bot \circ_\mathrm{d} \{ [\geq{}^1\!/\!_i] \}]\!] = \{{}^1\!/\!_i\} \qquad (\#)$$

Now suppose that there is some $i, j \in \mathbb{N}$ such that ${}^1\!/\!_i < {}^1\!/\!_j$ and ${}^1\!/\!_j \preceq_\bot {}^1\!/\!_i$. Because of the latter and ${}^1\!/\!_j \in [\![[\geq{}^1\!/\!_i]]\!]$, we have ${}^1\!/\!_j \in \min([\![[\geq{}^1\!/\!_i]]\!], \preceq_\bot)$. From compatibility of $\preceq_{(.)}$ with $\circ_\mathrm{d}$ we obtain ${}^1\!/\!_j \in [\![\mathcal{K}_\bot \circ_\mathrm{d} \{[\geq{}^1\!/\!_i]\}]\!]$. Thus, we obtain a contradiction of the latter with (#). This shows that${}^1\!/\!_j \preceq_\bot {}^1\!/\!_i$ does not hold and consequently, $\preceq_\bot$ contains an infinite descending chain $\ldots \prec_\bot {}^1\!/\!_3 \prec_\bot {}^1\!/\!_2 \prec_\bot 1$. From this chain and $[\![\Gamma^\infty]\!] = \{1, {}^1\!/\!_2, {}^1\!/\!_3, \ldots\}$, we obtain that $\min([\![\Gamma^\infty]\!], \preceq_\bot) = \emptyset$ holds. The latter is impossible in $\preceq_\bot$, as $\preceq_\bot$ is min-friendly (and thus, $\min([\![\Gamma^\infty]\!], \preceq_\bot) \neq \emptyset$ holds due to min-completeness). □

7 Summary and Conclusion

In this paper, we demonstrated that sentence revision cannot be reduced to multiple revision. Together with Observation 5, this means that sentence revision and multiple revision are mutually different kinds of operations. We considered two examples that witness our observation: one example with a cyclic situation and one example without a cyclic situation. Having both examples is very important, as there is a debate whether belief revision with cyclic situations is appropriate or not [4]. Because we consider both cases, our result is independent of this debate. In summary, the main contribution is the following.

Observation 19. *Sentence revision and multiple revision are mutually irreducible, even in the presence or absence of cyclic situations.*

One might remark that the examples we discovered require "unnatural" logical settings and that sentence revision might be reducible to multiple revision. However, even for many natural settings, it is not immediately clear wether this is the case. Furthermore, the general lesson is that when one leaves safe grounds, one must be very careful in assuming intuitive results. This is in line with many other observations made in the area of belief change in recent years, e.g., representability [2, 3, 17–19] and semantics [4, 7].

References

1. Alchourrón, C.E., Gärdenfors, P., Makinson, D.: On the logic of theory change: Partial meet contraction and revision functions. Journal of Symbolic Logic **50**(22), 510–530 (1985). https://doi.org/10.2307/2274239
2. Baader, F., Wassermann, R.: Contractions based on optimal repairs. In: Marquis, P., Ortiz, M., Pagnucco, M. (eds.) Proceedings of the 21st International Conference on Principles of Knowledge Representation and Reasoning, KR 2024, Hanoi, Vietnam. November 2-8, 2024 (2024). https://doi.org/10.24963/KR.2024/9
3. Baader, F., Wassermann, R.: Gärdenfors's supplementary postulates for partial product contractions. In: Sauerwald, K., Thimm, M. (eds.) Proceedings of the 18th European Conference on Symbolic and Quantitative Approaches to Reasoning with Uncertainty (ECSQARU 2025). Lecture Notes in Computer Science, vol. 16099, pp. 269–284. Springer (2025). https://doi.org/10.1007/978-3-032-05134-9_19
4. Delgrande, J.P., Peppas, P., Woltran, S.: General belief revision. Journal of the ACM **65**(5), 29:1–29:34 (2018). https://doi.org/10.1145/3203409
5. Falakh, F.M., Rudolph, S.: AGM revision in description logics under fixed-domain semantics. In: Arieli, O., Homola, M., Jung, J.C., Mugnier, M. (eds.) Proceedings of the 35th International Workshop on Description Logics (DL 2022) co-located with Federated Logic Conference (FLoC 2022). CEUR Workshop Proceedings, vol. 3263. CEUR-WS.org (2022), https://ceur-ws.org/Vol-3263/paper-8.pdf
6. Falakh, F.M., Rudolph, S., Sauerwald, K.: Semantic characterizations of AGM revision for Tarskian logics. In: Governatori, G., Turhan, A. (eds.) Proceedings of the 6th International Joint Conference on Rules and Reasoning (RuleML+RR 2022). Lecture Notes in Computer Science, vol. 13752, pp. 95–110. Springer (2022). https://doi.org/10.1007/978-3-031-21541-4_7
7. Falakh, F.M., Rudolph, S., Sauerwald, K.: AGM belief revision, semantically. ACM Trans. Comput. Log. **26**(4), 23:1–23:54 (2025). https://doi.org/10.1145/3763234
8. Fermé, E.L., Hansson, S.O.: Belief Change – Introduction and Overview. Springer Briefs in Intelligent Systems, Springer (2018). https://doi.org/10.1007/978-3-319-60535-7
9. Gärdenfors, P.: Knowledge in flux : modeling the dynamics of epistemic states. MIT Press Cambridge (1988)
10. Grove, A.: Two modellings for theory change. Journal of Philosophical Logic **17**(2), 157–170 (1988). https://doi.org/10.1007/BF00247909
11. Hansson, S.O.: A Textbook of Belief Dynamics: Theory Change and Database Updating. Springer (1999)
12. Katsuno, H., Mendelzon, A.O.: Propositional knowledge base revision and minimal change. Artificial Intelligence **52**(3), 263 – 294 (1991). https://doi.org/10.1016/0004-3702(91)90069-V
13. Kraus, S., Lehmann, D., Magidor, M.: Nonmonotonic reasoning, preferential models and cumulative logics. Artificial Intelligence **44**(1-2), 167–207 (1990). https://doi.org/10.1016/0004-3702(90)90101-5
14. Lewis, D.K.: Counterfactuals. Harvard University Press, Cambridge, Massachusetts (1973). https://doi.org/10.2307/2273738
15. Lindström, S.: A semantic approach to nonmonotonic reasoning: Inference operations and choice. Theoria **88**(3), 494–528 (2022). https://doi.org/https://doi.org/10.1111/theo.12405
16. Peppas, P.: The limit assumption and multiple revision. Journal of Logic and Computation **14**(3), 355–371 (2004). https://doi.org/10.1093/logcom/14.3.355

17. Ribeiro, M.M.: Belief Revision in Non-Classical Logics. Springer Briefs in Computer Science, Springer (2013). https://doi.org/10.1007/978-1-4471-4186-0
18. Ribeiro, M.M., Wassermann, R., Flouris, G., Antoniou, G.: Minimal change: Relevance and recovery revisited. Artificial Intelligence **201**, 59–80 (2013). https://doi.org/10.1016/j.artint.2013.06.001
19. Sauerwald, K.: Credibility-limited revision for epistemic spaces. In: Destercke, S., Martinez, M.V., Sanfilippo, G. (eds.) Proceedings of the 16th International Conference on Scalable Uncertainty Management (SUM 2024). pp. 429–444. Springer, Cambridge (2024). https://doi.org/10.1007/978-3-031-76235-2_32
20. Sernadas, A., Sernadas, C., Caleiro, C.: Synchronization of logics. Studia Logica **59**(1), 217–247 (1997). https://doi.org/10.1023/A:1004904401346
21. Tarski, A.: Logic Semantics, Metamathematics Papers From 1923 to 1938. Translated by J.H. Woodger. Clarendon Press (1956)

Conditional Constraint and Solution Splittings of Belief Bases in the Context of c-Representations

Lars-Phillip Spiegel[1](✉), Christoph Beierle[1], Gabriele Kern-Isberner[2], and Alexander Hahn[2]

[1] FernUniversität in Hagen, Hagen, Germany
{lars-phillip.spiegel,christoph.beierle}@fernuni-hagen.de
[2] TU Dortmund University, Dortmund, Germany
{gabriele.kern-isberner,alexander.hahn}@tu-dortmund.de

Abstract. In this paper we investigate splitting notions for conditional belief bases that allow us to localize reasoning and computations to only the relevant parts of a belief base. The focus of our investigations lies on splitting notions for c-representations, which are special kinds of Spohn's ranking models for belief bases and which can be specified via a constraint satisfaction problem. We extend the notion of constraint splittings for c-representations to conditional constraint splittings, covering also cases where the subbases may share conditionals. Inspired by conditional syntax splittings, we identify the subclass of safe conditional constraint splittings, allowing us to solve the constraint systems of the subbases independently from each other. We elaborate the relationships of constraint and safe conditional constraint splittings to safe and generalized safe conditional syntax splittings and also to safe covers, which have been proposed for localized computation of c-representations. Additionally, we generalize solution splittings for c-representations to safe conditional c-solution splittings and show how they relate to conditional constraint splittings.

1 Introduction

In the area of knowledge representation and reasoning conditionals provide a means to portrait defeasible rules. A conditional $(B|A)$ is meant to represent plausible but not certain statements and read "If A then usually, plausibly, typically etc. B". For inductive inference with sets of conditionals, called belief bases, the syntax splitting principle [15] provides a way to localize reasoning to only the relevant conditionals. The core idea of syntax splitting goes back to Parikh [17] where it is introduced in the context of belief revision, stating that only syntactically relevant parts of a belief base should influence the revision result. This idea was applied to inductive inference under the motto "syntax splitting = relevance + independence" in [15]. Because syntax splitting requires the signature to split into disjoint parts, the notion of conditional syntax splitting was

A.-Y. Turhan and J. Virtema (Eds.): FoIKS 2026, LNCS 16475, pp. 134–153, 2026.
https://doi.org/10.1007/978-3-032-21540-6_9

introduced [12], allowing also for an overlap of the signatures. The idea of focusing only on the relevant parts of a belief base has also been investigated in other works, e.g., [2,19–21,23,25]. Splitting techniques provide a variety of benefits for inductive inference. They allow for localized reasoning, significantly simplifying inference tasks. Furthermore, they also uncover structural information about the belief base, making it easier to spot (in)dependencies and understand the reasoning process. In order to reason with belief bases a semantics must be provided; a popular one being ordinal conditional functions (OCFs), also called ranking functions [22]. In this paper we investigate a special class of ranking functions called c-representations [13,14]. They can be specified via a constraint satisfaction problem (CSP) [1,13] and have been shown to comply with a variety of splitting properties [2,6,15,21,25]. In particular, splittings specifically for c-representations have been investigated in the form of constraint and solution splittings [2,25]. We extend this line of research by employing the idea underlying conditional syntax splitting. We introduce the notions of conditional constraint and solution splittings for c-representations, allowing the subbases that a belief base splits into to also share conditionals, thus making localized computation of c-representations possible in many more cases. We embed the different splitting techniques in a hierarchy representing the interrelationships among them, and we also investigate connections of our work to safe covers [24] which are motivated similarly through localized computation of c-representations. In summary, the main contributions of this paper are:

- We generalize constraint splittings to conditional constraint splittings, allowing subbases to share conditionals.
- We identify the subclass of safe conditional constraint splittings, allowing us to solve the underlying constraint satisfaction problems independently.
- We generalize c-solution splittings to safe conditional c-solution splittings, allowing subbases to also share conditionals.
- We investigate how syntax splitting notions and also safe covers relate to our newly introduced splitting notions.
- We embed our new notions into a splitting hierarchy, showcasing the relationships among different splitting techniques.

In Sect. 2, we recall required basics and present conditional syntax splitting in Sect. 3. In Sect. 4, we address c-representations and constraint splittings and generalize the latter to conditional constraint splittings in Sect. 5. In Sect. 6, we lift conditional splittings for c-representations to the semantical level and in Sect. 7 we compare our approach to related work before concluding in Sect. 8.

2 Formal Basics

Let $\mathcal{L}$ be a finitely generated propositional language over a signature Σ with atoms $a, b, c, \ldots$ and with formulas $A, B, C, \ldots$ We may write AB instead of $A \wedge B$, and overline formulas to indicate negation, i.e., $\overline{A}$ means $\neg A$. Let Ω denote the set of *possible worlds* over $\mathcal{L}$, taken here simply as the set of all propositional interpretations over $\mathcal{L}$. $\omega \models A$ means that the propositional formula $A \in \mathcal{L}$ holds in $\omega \in \Omega$; in this case ω is called a *model* of A, and the set of all models of A is denoted by $Mod\,(A)$. For propositions $A, B \in \mathcal{L}$, $A \models B$ holds iff $Mod\,(A) \subseteq Mod\,(B)$, as usual. We will use ω both for the model and the corresponding complete conjunction of all positive or negated atoms, allowing us to use ω both as an interpretation and a proposition.

For $\Theta \subseteq \Sigma$, let $\mathcal{L}(\Theta)$ or short $\mathcal{L}_\Theta$ denote the propositional language defined by Θ, with associated set of interpretations $\Omega(\Theta)$ or short Ω_Θ. Note that while each formula of $\mathcal{L}(\Theta)$ can also be considered as a formula of $\mathcal{L}$, the interpretations $\omega^\Theta \in \Omega(\Theta)$ are not elements of $\Omega(\Sigma)$ if $\Theta \neq \Sigma$. But each interpretation $\omega \in \Omega$ can be written uniquely in the form $\omega = \omega^\Theta \omega^{\overline{\Theta}}$ with concatenated $\omega^\Theta \in \Omega(\Theta)$ and $\omega^{\overline{\Theta}} \in \Omega(\overline{\Theta})$, where $\overline{\Theta} = \Sigma \backslash \Theta$. The world ω^Θ is called the *reduct* of ω to Θ [8]. If $\Omega' \subseteq \Omega$ is a subset of models, then $|\Omega'\Theta = \{\omega^\Theta | \omega \in \Omega'\} \subseteq \Omega(\Theta)$ restricts Ω' to a subset of $\Omega(\Theta)$. In the following, we will sometimes denote subsignatures of Σ by $\Sigma_1, \Sigma_2, \ldots$ and write ω^i instead of ω^{Σ_i} to ease notation.

By making use of a conditional operator $|$, we introduce the language $(\mathcal{L}|\mathcal{L}) = \{(B|A) \mid A, B \in \mathcal{L}\}$ of *conditionals* over $\mathcal{L}$. Conditionals $(B|A)$ are meant to express plausible, defeasible rules "If A then plausibly (usually, possibly, probably, typically etc.) B". For a world ω a conditional $(B|A)$ is either *verified* by ω if $\omega \models AB$, *falsified* by ω if $\omega \models A\overline{B}$, or *not applicable* to ω if $\omega \models \overline{A}$. A conditional $(F|E)$ is called *self-fulfilling*, if $E \models F$, i.e., there is no world that can falsify it. Belief bases $\Delta = ((B_1|A_1), \ldots, (B_n|A_n))$ (over Σ) consist of finitely many conditionals from $(\mathcal{L} \mid \mathcal{L})$. For a conditional $\delta_i = (B_i|A_i)$

$$ver(\delta_i) = \{\omega \in \Omega(\Sigma) \mid \omega \models A_i B_i\}$$
$$fal(\delta_i) = \{\omega \in \Omega(\Sigma) \mid \omega \models A_i \overline{B_i}\}$$

denote the sets of verifying respectively falsifying worlds.

A popular semantic framework for interpreting conditionals are ordinal conditional functions (OCFs) $\kappa : \Omega \to \mathbb{N} \cup \{\infty\}$ with $\kappa^{-1}(0) \neq \emptyset$. OCFs, also called *ranking functions*, introduced, in a more general form, by [22]. Intuitively, less plausible worlds are assigned higher numbers, where at least one world ω must be entirely plausible, i.e., $\kappa(\omega) = 0$. Formulas are assigned the rank of their most plausible models, i.e., $\kappa(A) := \min\{\kappa(\omega) \mid \omega \models A\}$. A conditional $(B|A)$ is *accepted* by κ, written as $\kappa \models (B|A)$, iff $\kappa(AB) < \kappa(A\overline{B})$, i.e., iff AB is strictly more plausible than $A\overline{B}$. This is lifted to belief bases via $\kappa \models \Delta$ if $\kappa \models (B|A)$ for all $(B|A) \in \Delta$. Consistency of such a belief base Δ can be defined in terms of OCFs [18]: Δ is (strongly) consistent iff there is an OCF κ such that $\kappa \models \Delta$ and $\kappa(\omega) < \infty$ for all $\omega \in \Omega$. We focus on (strongly) consistent belief bases in the sense of [9,18] in order to elaborate our approach without having to deal with distracting technical particularities.

3 Conditional Syntax Splitting

Syntax splittings describe that a belief base contains completely independent information about different parts of the signature. According to [15], a belief base Δ *splits* into subbases Δ_1, Δ_2 if $\{\Sigma_1, \Sigma_2\}$ is a partition of Σ such that $\Delta = \Delta_1 \cup \Delta_2$, $\Delta_i \subset (\mathcal{L}_i|\mathcal{L}_i)$, $\mathcal{L}_i = \mathcal{L}(\Sigma_i)$ for $i \in \{1,2\}$, $\Sigma_1 \cap \Sigma_2 = \emptyset$, and $\Sigma_1 \cup \Sigma_2 = \Sigma$, denoted as

$$\Delta = \Delta_1 \bigcup_{\Sigma_1,\Sigma_2} \Delta_2. \tag{1}$$

Syntax splittings are very useful for formalizing the idea that independent information about different topics should not affect each other in reasoning [15]. Syntax splittings were generalized to *conditional* syntax splittings [12], which allow subbases to share some atoms in a given subsignature Σ_3.

Definition 1 (conditional syntax splitting [12]). *A belief base* Δ splits into subbases Δ_1, Δ_2 conditional on Σ_3 *if there are* $\Sigma_1, \Sigma_2 \subseteq \Sigma$ *such that* $\Delta_i = \Delta \cap (\mathcal{L}(\Sigma_i \cup \Sigma_3) \mid \mathcal{L}(\Sigma_i \cup \Sigma_3))$ *for* $i \in \{1,2\}$, *and* $\{\Sigma_1, \Sigma_2, \Sigma_3\}$ *is a partition of* Σ. *This is denoted as*

$$\Delta = \Delta_1 \bigcup_{\Sigma_1,\Sigma_2} \Delta_2 \mid \Sigma_3. \tag{2}$$

Unlike syntax splitting, conditional syntax splitting does not require Δ_1 and Δ_2 to be disjoint. For the rest of this paper we will use, for $i \in \{1,2\}$,

$$\Delta_3 = \Delta_1 \cap \Delta_2$$
$$\Delta_{i\setminus 3} = \Delta_i \setminus \Delta_3$$

for ease of reading. Given a complete conjunction over Σ_3, i.e., a world in $\Omega(\Sigma_3)$, conditional syntax splittings in general do not ensure complete independence of Δ_1 and Δ_2; for details see [12, Ex.6]. Therefore, *safe* conditional syntax splittings were introduced.

Definition 2 (safe conditional syntax splitting [12]). *A conditional syntax splitting* $\Delta = \Delta_1 \bigcup_{\Sigma_1,\Sigma_2} \Delta_2 \mid \Sigma_3$ *is called* safe, *denoted as*

$$\Delta = \Delta_1 \overset{s}{\bigcup_{\Sigma_1,\Sigma_2}} \Delta_2 \mid \Sigma_3 \tag{3}$$

if the following safety property *holds for* $i, i' \in \{1,2\}$, $i \neq i'$:

$$\begin{aligned} &\textit{for every } \omega^i\omega^3 \in \Omega(\Sigma_i \cup \Sigma_3), \ \textit{there is } \omega^{i'} \in \Omega(\Sigma_{i'}) \\ &\quad s.t.\ \omega^i\omega^3\omega^{i'} \not\models \bigvee_{(F|E)\in\Delta_{i'}} E \wedge \neg F. \end{aligned} \tag{4}$$

Intuitively, the safety condition (4) guarantees proper independence with respect to falsification between the subbases Δ_1 and Δ_2; for a more detailed analysis we refer to [12,21]. In the following proposition, we show that the safety condition (4) demands, in essence, that no complete conjunction over Σ_3 may force the falsification of a conditional in Δ when considering Σ as a whole.

Proposition 1. *Let $\Delta = \Delta_1 \bigcup_{\Sigma_1,\Sigma_2} \Delta_2 \mid \Sigma_3$. Then the safety property is equivalent to the following: For every $\omega^3 \in \Omega(\Sigma_3)$ there is $\omega^1\omega^2 \in \Omega(\Sigma \setminus \Sigma_3)$ s.t. $\omega = \omega^1\omega^2\omega^3 \in \Omega(\Sigma)$ does not falsify any conditional in Δ.*

Proof. Direction "$\Rightarrow$": Let $\omega^3 \in \Omega(\Sigma_3)$. Now choose some $\widehat{\omega}^1 \in \Omega(\Sigma_1)$. According to the safety property, there is $\omega_2 \in \Omega(\Sigma_2)$ such that $\widehat{\omega}^1\omega^2\omega^3$ does not falsify any conditionals in Δ_2. Therefore, also $\omega^2\omega^3$ does not falsify any conditional in Δ_2. By applying the safety property again, we can obtain a new $\omega^1 \in \Omega(\Sigma_1)$ such that $\omega^1\omega^2\omega^3$ does not falsify any conditional in Δ_1. Since the conditionals in Δ_2 do not contain any symbols from Σ_1, appending ω_1 to $\omega^2\omega^3$ does not lead to new conditionals from Δ_2 being falsified. Therefore, $\omega^1\omega^2\omega^3$ does not falsify any conditionals from $\Delta_1 \cup \Delta_2 = \Delta$.

Direction "$\Leftarrow$": We show this by contraposition. Let $i, j \in \{1, 2\}, i \neq j$. Let $\omega^i\omega^3 \in \Omega(\Sigma_i \cup \Sigma_3)$. Assume the safety property does not hold, i.e., (*) there is some $\omega^i\omega^3 \in \Omega(\Sigma_i \cup \Sigma_3)$ such that there is no ω^j such that $\omega^i\omega^j\omega^3$ falsifies no conditional in Δ_j. Because $\Delta_j \subseteq (\mathcal{L}(\Sigma_j \cup \Sigma_3)|\mathcal{L}(\Sigma_j \cup \Sigma_3))$ we have for any conditional $(B_l|A_l) \in \Delta_j$ that $\omega^i\omega^j\omega^3 \models A_l\overline{B_l}$ iff $\omega^j\omega^3 \models A_l\overline{B_l}$. Thus, (*) implies that there is ω^3 such that there is no ω^j such that $\omega^3\omega^j$ falsifies no conditional in Δ_j. Reversing the roles of i and j we obtain the corresponding result for $\omega^3\omega^i$. Thus, it follows that there cannot be a $\omega^3\omega^i\omega^j$ falsifying no conditional in Δ. Then, by setting $i = 1$, $j = 2$, it follows that there cannot be $\omega^1\omega^2 \in \Omega(\Sigma \setminus \Sigma_3)$ s.t. $\omega^1\omega^2\omega^3$ does not falsify any conditional in Δ. □

Safe conditional syntax splitting provides similar benefits for inductive inference as syntax splitting [12]. Reasoning in the language of Δ_1 is independent of the conditionals in Δ_2 and vice versa, given we have full knowledge over the *conditional pivot* Σ_3, i.e., we know the valuation assigned to all elements in Σ_3. The conditional pivot thereby represents the elements shared between the subbases. The safety condition was generalized, leading to so-called generalized safe conditional syntax splittings [21], which allow for more splittings of a belief base and more belief bases with relevant splittings.

Definition 3 (generalized safe conditional syntax splitting [21]). *A conditional syntax splitting $\Delta = \Delta_1 \bigcup_{\Sigma_1,\Sigma_2} \Delta_2 \mid \Sigma_3$ is* generalized safe, *denoted as*

$$\Delta = \Delta_1 \overset{\mathbf{gs}}{\underset{\Sigma_1,\Sigma_2}{\bigcup}} \Delta_2 \mid \Sigma_3 \tag{5}$$

if the following generalized safety property *holds for $i, i' \in \{1, 2\}, i \neq i'$:*

$$\begin{aligned} &\textit{for every } \omega^i\omega^3 \in \Omega(\Sigma_i \cup \Sigma_3), \textit{ there is } \omega^{i'} \in \Omega(\Sigma_{i'}) \\ &\textit{s.t. } \omega^i\omega^3\omega^{i'} \not\models \bigvee_{(F|E)\in\Delta_{i'\setminus 3}} E \wedge \neg F. \end{aligned} \tag{6}$$

The decisive difference in (6) compared to (4) is that only conditionals in $\Delta_{i'\setminus 3}$ are considered for the generalized safety property as opposed to all conditionals in $\Delta_{i'}$ for the safety property.

4 c-Representations and Constraint Splitting

c-Representations [13,14] are special ranking functions that are obtained by assigning integer impacts $\vec{\eta} = (\eta_1, \ldots, \eta_n)$ to conditionals of a belief base $\Delta = \{(B_1|A_1), \ldots, (B_n|A_n)\}$ and are the given by

$$\kappa_{\vec{\eta}}(\omega) = \sum_{\substack{1 \leqslant i \leqslant n \\ \omega \models A_i \overline{B}_i}} \eta_i \tag{7}$$

where the η_i are chosen such that $\kappa_{\vec{\eta}} \models \Delta$. This condition can be characterized by a constraint satisfaction problem (*CSP*) [1,13]. The constraints in this CSP can be expressed using, for each conditional $\delta_i \in \Delta$, the following sets of sets of verified and falsified conditionals [5]:

$$V_\Delta(\delta_i) = \{\{(B_j|A_j) \in \Delta \setminus \{\delta_i\} \mid \omega \models A_j\overline{B_j}\} \mid \omega \in ver(B_i|A_i)\} \tag{8}$$
$$F_\Delta(\delta_i) = \{\{(B_j|A_j) \in \Delta \setminus \{\delta_i\} \mid \omega \models A_j\overline{B_j}\} \mid \omega \in fal(B_i|A_i)\} \tag{9}$$

Employing these *constraint-inducing sets* (8), (9), the constraint satisfaction problem $CSP(\Delta) = \{C_\Delta(\delta_1), \ldots, C_\Delta(\delta_n)\}$ is specified as follows for all $\delta_i \in \Delta$:

$$C_\Delta(\delta_i) : \eta_i > \min\{\sum_{\delta_j \in S} \eta_j \mid S \in V_\Delta(\delta_i)\} - \min\{\sum_{\delta_j \in S} \eta_j \mid S \in F_\Delta(\delta_i)\}. \tag{10}$$

We denote with $Sol(CSP(\Delta))$ the set of all solutions of $CSP(\Delta)$. For $\vec{\eta} \in Sol(CSP(\Delta))$ and $\Delta' \subseteq \Delta$ we denote with $\vec{\eta}|_{\Delta'}$ the projection of $\vec{\eta}$ to the conditionals of Δ'. With $(\vec{\eta}^1, \vec{\eta}^2)$ we denote the concatenation of $\vec{\eta}^1$ and $\vec{\eta}^2$.

Example 1. Let $\Delta^b = \{(f|b), (\overline{f}|p), (b|p), (w|b)\}$. Then $CSP(\Delta^b)$ is given by:

$$C_{\Delta^b}(\delta_1) : \eta_1 > \min\{0, \eta_2, \eta_2 + \eta_4, \eta_4\} - \min\{0, \eta_4\}$$
$$C_{\Delta^b}(\delta_2) : \eta_2 > \min\{\eta_1, \eta_3, \eta_1 + \eta_4\} - \min\{0, \eta_3, \eta_4\}$$
$$C_{\Delta^b}(\delta_3) : \eta_3 > \min\{\eta_1, \eta_2, \eta_1 + \eta_4, \eta_2 + \eta_4\} - \min\{0, \eta_2\}$$
$$C_{\Delta^b}(\delta_4) : \eta_4 > \min\{0, \eta_1, \eta_2\} - \min\{0, \eta_1, \eta_2\}$$

The verification and falsification behaviour of worlds w.r.t. Δ^b can be seen in Table 1. A possible solution for $CSP(\Delta^b)$ is $\vec{\eta} \in Sol(CSP(\Delta))$ with $\vec{\eta} = (1, 2, 2, 1)$. The projection of $\vec{\eta}$ to $\Delta' = \{(\overline{f}|p), (w|b)\}$ is $\vec{\eta}|_{\Delta'} = (2, 1)$.

Definition 4 (solution-preserving constraint reduction, spcr [25]). *Let Δ be a conditional belief base. Furthermore, let $\psi : (V, F) \mapsto (\psi(V), \psi(F))$ be defined such that $\psi(V) \sqsubseteq V$ and $\psi(F) \sqsubseteq F$, with $X' \sqsubseteq X$ meaning that (a) for every $x' \in X'$, there is $x \in X$ such that $x' \subseteq x$, and (b) for every $x \in X$,*

Table 1. Verification and falsification behaviour of worlds w.r.t. Δ^b in Example 1. The letters v and f indicate which conditionals are verified (v) or falsified (f).

ω	$(f\|b)$	$(\overline{f}\|p)$	$(b\|p)$	$(w\|b)$	ω	$(f\|b)$	$(\overline{f}\|p)$	$(b\|p)$	$(w\|b)$
$\overline{p}\,\overline{b}\,\overline{f}\,w$					$\overline{p}\,\overline{b}\,\overline{f}\,\overline{w}$				
$\overline{p}\,\overline{b}\,f\,w$					$\overline{p}\,\overline{b}\,f\,\overline{w}$				
$\overline{p}\,b\,\overline{f}\,w$	f			v	$\overline{p}\,b\,\overline{f}\,\overline{w}$	f			f
$\overline{p}\,b\,f\,w$	v			v	$\overline{p}\,b\,f\,\overline{w}$	v			f
$p\,\overline{b}\,\overline{f}\,w$		v	f		$p\,\overline{b}\,\overline{f}\,\overline{w}$		v	f	
$p\,\overline{b}\,f\,w$		f	f		$p\,\overline{b}\,f\,\overline{w}$		f	f	
$p\,b\,\overline{f}\,w$	f	v	v	v	$p\,b\,\overline{f}\,\overline{w}$	f	v	v	f
$p\,b\,f\,w$	v	f	v	v	$p\,b\,f\,\overline{w}$	v	f	v	f

there is $x' \in X'$ such that $x' \subseteq x$. The mapping $CSP(\Delta) \mapsto CSP^{\psi}(\Delta)$ with $CSP^{\psi}(\Delta) = \{C^{\psi}_{\Delta}(\delta_i) \mid C_{\Delta}(\delta_i) \in CSP(\Delta)\}$ such that

$$C^{\psi}_{\Delta}(\delta_i) : \eta_i > \min\{\sum_{\delta_j \in S} \eta_j \mid S \in \psi(V_{\Delta}(\delta_i))\} - \min\{\sum_{\delta_j \in S} \eta_j \mid S \in \psi(F_{\Delta}(\delta_i))\}. \tag{11}$$

is a solution-preserving constraint reduction (spcr) *w.r.t. ψ if $Sol(CSP^{\psi}(\Delta)) = Sol(CSP(\Delta))$ for all consistent belief bases Δ.*

In the following, we will use ψ to refer both to the mapping between constraint inducing sets, as well as to the corresponding spcr w.r.t. ψ, i.e., the mapping between CSPs. Note that choosing ψ as the identity function yields a (trivial) spcr. A convenient way to implement solution-preserving constraint reductions is through the use of rewriting systems. Figure 1 shows the set $\rho = \{R1, \ldots, R6\}$ of rewriting rules for simplifying $CSP(\Delta)$. These rules were first given in [5] for speeding up the computation of c-representations and of c-inference [1] and then extended in [2,25]. Since they only make use of general arithmetic properties of the minimum, they do not change the set of solutions $Sol(CSP(\Delta))$. Furthermore, ρ is terminating and confluent; thus, exhaustive application of ρ yields a uniquely determined CSP.

Proposition 2 (spcr ρ [25]). *Let $\rho = \{R1, \ldots, R6\}$ be the set of transformation rules on constraint-inducing sets from Fig. 1, and let ρ also denote the mapping obtained by exhaustive application of these rules. Then $\rho : CSP(\Delta) \mapsto CSP^{\rho}(\Delta)$ is an spcr.*

For the rest of this paper, ρ refers to the specific spcr defined in Proposition 2, while ψ will be used when referring to any spcr in general.

R1 *subset-V*: $\dfrac{\langle V_\Delta \cup \{S, S'\},\ F_\Delta\rangle_i}{\langle V_\Delta \cup \{S\},\ F_\Delta\rangle_i}$ $\quad S \subsetneq S'$

R2 *subset-F*: $\dfrac{\langle V_\Delta,\ F_\Delta \cup \{S, S'\}\rangle_i}{\langle V_\Delta,\ F_\Delta \cup \{S\}\rangle_i}$ $\quad S \subsetneq S'$

R3 *element*: $\dfrac{\langle \{V_1 \cup \{\delta\}, \ldots, V_p \cup \{\delta\}\},\ \{F_1 \cup \{\delta\}, \ldots, F_q \cup \{\delta\}\}\rangle_i}{\langle \{V_1, \ldots, V_p\},\ \{F_1, \ldots, F_q\}\rangle_i}$

R4 *trivial*: $\dfrac{\langle V_\Delta,\ F_\Delta\rangle_i}{\langle \{\varnothing\},\ \{\varnothing\}\rangle_i}$ $\quad V_\Delta = F_\Delta$

R5 *subsets*: $\dfrac{\langle \{S_1 \dot\cup T, \ldots, S_p \dot\cup T\},\ \{S_1 \dot\cup T', \ldots, S_p \dot\cup T'\}\rangle_i}{\langle \{T\},\ \{T'\}\rangle_i}$

R6 *circle*: $\dfrac{\langle \mathcal{D} \dot\cup \{\{\delta_j\}\},\ \{\varnothing\}\rangle_i \quad \langle \mathcal{D} \dot\cup \{\{\delta_i\}\},\ \{\varnothing\}\rangle_j}{\langle \mathcal{D},\ \{\varnothing\}\rangle_i \quad \langle \mathcal{D},\ \{\varnothing\}\rangle_j}$ $\quad i \neq j$

Fig. 1. Transformation rules $\rho = \{R1, \ldots, R6\}$ for simplifying (the constraint-inducing sets of) $CSP(\Delta)$. A pair $\langle \mathcal{V},\ \mathcal{F}\rangle_i$ represents the sets of constraint variables in the minimum expressions associated to the verification and the falsification, respectively, of the i-th conditional $\delta_i \in \Delta$ in the constraint $C_i \in CSP(\Delta)$ modeling the acceptance condition of δ_i.

Example 2. Applying ρ to $CSP(\Delta^b)$ from Example 1 yields $CSP^\rho(\Delta^b)$ given by

$$C^\rho_{\Delta^b}(\delta_1) : \eta_1 > \min\{0\} - \min\{0\}$$
$$C^\rho_{\Delta^b}(\delta_2) : \eta_2 > \min\{\eta_1\} - \min\{0\}$$
$$C^\rho_{\Delta^b}(\delta_3) : \eta_3 > \min\{\eta_1\} - \min\{0\}$$
$$C^\rho_{\Delta^b}(\delta_4) : \eta_4 > \min\{0\} - \min\{0\}.$$

The rules R_1 and R_2 eliminate the supersets in all constraints, and rule R_6 removes the cyclic dependency between $C_{\Delta^b}(\delta_2)$ and $C_{\Delta^b}(\delta_3)$.

For a conditional $\delta_i \in \Delta$ we denote with $scope^\psi_\Delta(\delta_i)$ the set of constraints whose corresponding constraint variables occur in C^ψ_i. More precisely, the scope of a conditional can be defined in terms of the sets V_Δ and F_Δ:

$$scope^\psi_\Delta(\delta) = \left(\bigcup \psi(V_\Delta(\delta))\right) \cup \left(\bigcup \psi(F_\Delta(\delta))\right).$$

Note that application of ρ may reduce the scope of constraints significantly. For instance, in Example 1, we have $scope^{\mathrm{id}}_\Delta(\delta_2) = \{\delta_1, \delta_3, \delta_4\}$, while after applying ρ in Example 2, we have just $scope^\rho_\Delta(\delta_2) = \{\delta_1\}$. In this way, the spcr ρ helps with reducing dependencies among the impact factors to relevant dependencies. It should be emphasized that relevance here is not based on numerical (sometimes accidental) relationships among the impact factors but on algebraic properties of arithmetics.

In [2] notions of constraint-based dependence and independence between conditionals and sets thereof were defined.

Definition 5 ($\rightsquigarrow^{dp}, \rightsquigarrow^{*}$, $\perp\!\!\!\perp$ [2]). *Let $\Delta = \{\delta_1, \ldots, \delta_m\}$ be a belief base and ψ an spcr. We say that δ_i directly depends on δ_j in Δ w.r.t. ψ, written $\delta_i \rightsquigarrow^{dp}_{\Delta,\psi} \delta_j$, if $\delta_j \in scope^{\psi}_{\Delta}(\delta_i)$. Then $\rightsquigarrow^{*}_{\Delta,\psi}$ is the reflexive and transitive closure of $\rightsquigarrow^{dp}_{\Delta,\psi}$. We lift $\rightsquigarrow^{*}_{\Delta,\psi}$ to belief bases $\Delta_1, \Delta_2 \subseteq \Delta$ via $\Delta_1 \rightsquigarrow^{*}_{\Delta,\psi} \Delta_2$ if there is $\delta_1 \in \Delta_1$ such that there is $\delta_2 \in \Delta_2$ with $\delta_1 \rightsquigarrow^{*}_{\Delta,\psi} \delta_2$.*

We call Δ_1 and Δ_2 constraint-wise independent in Δ w.r.t. ψ if $\Delta_1 \not\rightsquigarrow^{*}_{\Delta,\psi} \Delta_2$ and $\Delta_2 \not\rightsquigarrow^{*}_{\Delta,\psi} \Delta_1$, written $\Delta_1 \perp\!\!\!\perp^{\psi}_{\Delta} \Delta_2$.

Note that $\Delta_1 \not\rightsquigarrow^{*}_{\Delta,\psi} \Delta_2$ means that for all $\delta_1 \in \Delta_1, \delta_2 \in \Delta_2$ we have $\delta_1 \not\rightsquigarrow^{*}_{\Delta,\psi} \delta_2$. Utilizing these notions of constraint (in)dependence, the notion of constraint splittings was introduced in [2].

Definition 6 (constraint splitting [2]**).** *A partition $\{\Delta_1, \ldots, \Delta_m\}$ of Δ is a constraint splitting w.r.t. ψ, written $\Delta = \Delta_1 \cup^{\mathsf{cs}}_{\psi} \ldots \cup^{\mathsf{cs}}_{\psi} \Delta_m$, if, for all $i, j \in \{1, \ldots, m\}$ with $i \neq j$: $\Delta_i \perp\!\!\!\perp^{\psi}_{\Delta} \Delta_j$.*

(Unconditional) constraint splittings in the sense of Definition 6 imply that the constraint systems can be computed and solved independently on the subbases after applying ψ and that each solution for Δ can be built from solutions from the subbases [2].

Example 3. Consider again Δ^b from Example 1 and $CSP(\Delta^b)$. This CSP admits no constraint splitting at all. However, after applying ρ from Fig. 1 we set $CSP^{\rho}(\Delta^b)$ given in Example 2 having the constraint splitting

$$\{(\overline{f}|p), (b|p), (f|b)\} \cup^{\mathsf{cs}}_{\rho} \{(w|b)\}$$

This is also a safe conditional syntax splitting with $\Sigma_1 = \{f, p\}, \Sigma_2 = \{w\}$ and $\Sigma_3 = \{b\}$. Observe that $(\overline{f}|p) \not\rightsquigarrow^{*}_{\Delta^b,\rho} (w|b)$, $(b|p) \not\rightsquigarrow^{*}_{\Delta^b,\rho} (w|b)$ and $(f|b) \not\rightsquigarrow^{*}_{\Delta^b,\rho} (w|b)$. Therefore $\{(\overline{f}|p), (b|p), (f|b)\} \not\rightsquigarrow^{*}_{\Delta^b,\rho} \{(w|b)\}$. Since $\{(w|b)\} \not\rightsquigarrow^{*}_{\Delta^b,\rho} \{(\overline{f}|p), (b|p), (f|b)\}$ holds as well, we have $\{(\overline{f}|p), (b|p), (f|b)\} \perp\!\!\!\perp^{\rho}_{\Delta^b} \{(w|b)\}$.

Safe conditional syntax splittings yield a constraint splitting for the case $\Delta_3 = \emptyset$ [25]. The following proposition extends this result to the case $\Delta_3 \neq \emptyset$.

Proposition 3. *$\Delta = \Delta_1 \bigcup^{\mathsf{s}}_{\Sigma_1,\Sigma_2} \Delta_2 \mid \Sigma_3$ implies $\Delta = \Delta_{1\setminus 3} \cup^{\mathsf{cs}}_{\rho} \Delta_{2\setminus 3} \cup^{\mathsf{cs}}_{\rho} \Delta_3$.*

Proof. We refer to the proof for the already established result in [25] and extend this for the case where $\Delta_3 = \Delta_1 \cap \Delta_2 \neq \emptyset$. That means we only need to show that $\Delta = \Delta_1 \bigcup^{\mathsf{s}}_{\Sigma_1,\Sigma_2} \Delta_2 \mid \Sigma_3$ implies $\Delta_3 \perp\!\!\!\perp^{\rho}_{\Delta} (\Delta_i \setminus \Delta_3)$ for $i \in \{1, 2\}$. We know that Δ_3 contains only conditionals which cannot be falsified [6, cf. Lemma 19]. Therefore, these conditionals cannot appear in any constraints induced by the other conditionals. Let $\delta \in \Delta_3$ be such a conditional. Then clearly $F_{\Delta}(\delta) = \emptyset$. Additionally, due to Proposition 1, we have $\emptyset \in V_{\Delta}(\delta)$. Then by applying R2 we obtain $\rho(V_{\Delta}(\delta)) = \emptyset$ and thus, for $i \in \{1, 2\}$, $\Delta_3 \perp\!\!\!\perp^{\rho}_{\Delta} (\Delta_i \setminus \Delta_3)$. □

A result analogous to Proposition 3 does not hold for generalized safe splittings.

Proposition 4. *There is some* $\Delta = \Delta_1 \bigcup^{gs}_{\Sigma_1,\Sigma_2} \Delta_2 \mid \Sigma_3$ *such that* $\Delta = \Delta_{1\setminus 3} \cup^{cs}_{\rho} \Delta_{2\setminus 3} \cup^{cs}_{\rho} \Delta_3$ *is not a constraint splitting of* Δ *w.r.t.* ρ.

Proof. Let $\Delta^c = \{(c|a), (c|b), (\overline{c}|\top)\}$ be a belief base. Then $\Delta^c = \{(c|a), (\overline{c}|\top)\} \bigcup^{gs}_{\{a\},\{b\}} \{(c|b), (\overline{c}|\top)\} \mid \{c\}$ is a generalized safe conditional syntax splitting of Δ^c but not a constraint splitting of Δ^c w.r.t. ρ because the reduced $CSP^{\rho}(\Delta^c)$ is given by:

$$C^{\rho}_{\Delta^c}(\delta_1) : \eta_1 > \min\{\eta_3\} - \min\{0\}$$
$$C^{\rho}_{\Delta^c}(\delta_2) : \eta_2 > \min\{\eta_3\} - \min\{0\}$$
$$C^{\rho}_{\Delta^c}(\delta_3) : \eta_3 > \min\{0\} - \min\{0\}$$

□

As Proposition 4 shows, constraint splittings are not able to capture generalized safe conditional syntax splittings. Guided by the generalization from syntax splitting to conditional syntax splitting, we will therefore generalize constraint splittings to conditional constraint splittings in the next section.

5 Extending Constraint Splitting

In this section we introduce the notion of conditional constraint splitting as a generalization of constraint splittings and in analogy to conditional syntax splitting, we further refine this notion via safe conditional constraint splittings.

5.1 Conditional Constraint Splitting

Conditional constraint splittings allow the subbases of a constraint splitting to also share conditionals. First, we define the notion of conditional constraint (in)dependence.

Definition 7 (conditional constraint independence). *Let* Δ *be a belief base. Subbases* $\Delta_i, \Delta_j \subseteq \Delta$ *are* constraint-wise independent in Δ *w.r.t.* ψ given $\Delta_0 \subseteq \Delta$, *written* $\Delta_i \perp\!\!\!\perp^{\psi}_{\Delta} \Delta_j \mid \Delta_0$, *if* $(\Delta_i \setminus \Delta_0) \perp\!\!\!\perp^{\psi}_{\Delta\setminus\Delta_0} (\Delta_j \setminus \Delta_0)$.

The expression $\Delta_i \perp\!\!\!\perp^{\psi}_{\Delta} \Delta_j \mid \Delta_0$ describes a conditional constraint independence of Δ_i and Δ_j given Δ_0. That means that the conditionals of Δ_0 are ignored when checking for constraint independence between Δ_i and Δ_j. This is meant to simulate that the "conditional pivot" Δ_0 is already known or fixed, for example if the constraint variables of Δ_0 have already been assigned a fixed value. Utilizing this notion yields the following generalization of constraint splittings.

Definition 8 (conditional constraint splitting). *A set* $\{\Delta_1, \ldots, \Delta_m\}$ *is a conditional constraint splitting of* Δ *w.r.t.* ψ *given* $\Delta_0 \subseteq \Delta$*, written* $\Delta = \Delta_1 \cup_{\psi}^{\mathsf{cs}} \ldots \cup_{\psi}^{\mathsf{cs}} \Delta_m \mid \Delta_0$*, if* $\bigcup_{k=1}^{m} \Delta_k = \Delta$ *and for all* $i, j \in \{1, \ldots, m\}$ *with* $i \neq j$*:* $\Delta_i \perp\!\!\!\perp_{\Delta}^{\psi} \Delta_j \mid \Delta_0$.

We illustrate conditional constraint splittings with an example.

Example 4. Consider again $\Delta^b = \{(f|b), (\overline{f}|p), (b|p), (w|b)\}$ from Example 3. Δ^b has a conditional constraint splitting w.r.t. ρ given $\Delta_0^b = \{(f|b)\}$:

$$\Delta^b = \{(\overline{f}|p), (f|b)\} \cup_{\rho}^{\mathsf{cs}} \{(b|p), (f|b)\} \cup_{\rho}^{\mathsf{cs}} \{(w|b)\} \mid \{(f|b)\}.$$

This can be verified by checking the constraints of the subbases $\Delta_i^b \setminus \Delta_0^b$ with regard to the belief base $\Delta^b \setminus \Delta_0^b$, resulting in a *CSP* ignoring Δ_0^b.

$$C^{\rho}_{\Delta^b \setminus \Delta_0^b}(\delta_2) : \eta_2 > \min\{0\} - \min\{0\}$$
$$C^{\rho}_{\Delta^b \setminus \Delta_0^b}(\delta_3) : \eta_3 > \min\{0\} - \min\{0\}$$
$$C^{\rho}_{\Delta^b \setminus \Delta_0^b}(\delta_4) : \eta_4 > \min\{0\} - \min\{0\}$$

Because these constraints and thus the subbases are independent of one another, the subbases are constraint independent given $\{(f|b)\}$. For example, $\{(\overline{f}|p), (f|b)\} \perp\!\!\!\perp_{\Delta^b}^{\psi} \{(b|p), (f|b)\} \mid \Delta_0^b$ because $\{(\overline{f}|p)\} \perp\!\!\!\perp_{\Delta^b \setminus \Delta_0^b}^{\psi} \{(b|p)\}$ but $\{(\overline{f}|p), (f|b)\} \not\perp\!\!\!\perp_{\Delta^b}^{\psi} \{(b|p), (f|b)\}$ because the transitivity of $\rightsquigarrow^*_{\Delta^b,\psi}$ yields $(f|b) \rightsquigarrow^*_{\Delta^b,\psi} (f|b)$.

Consider next $\Delta^c = \{(c|a), (c|b), (\overline{c}|\top)\}$ from the proof of Proposition 4. Then $\Delta^c = \{(c|a), (\overline{c}|\top)\} \cup_{\rho}^{\mathsf{cs}} \{(c|b), (\overline{c}|\top)\} \mid \{(\overline{c}|\top)\}$.

As seen in Example 4, conditional constraint splittings allow us to find more splittings for a belief base Δ and also to find constraint splittings for belief bases which previously did not admit one at all. Next we state a basic fact regarding the conditional pivot Δ_0.

Proposition 5. *Let* $\Delta = \Delta_1 \cup_{\psi}^{\mathsf{cs}} \ldots \cup_{\psi}^{\mathsf{cs}} \Delta_m \mid \Delta_0$*. For any* Δ_i, Δ_j *with* $i, j \in \{1, \ldots, m\}, i \neq j$ *we have* $\Delta_i \cap \Delta_j \subseteq \Delta_0$

Proof. Towards a contradiction, assume that there was some $\delta \in \Delta_i \cap \Delta_j$ with $\delta \notin \Delta_0$. Note that $\delta \rightsquigarrow^*_{\Delta \setminus \Delta_0,\psi} \delta$ holds because $\rightsquigarrow^*_{\Delta \setminus \Delta_0,\psi}$ is reflexive by definition. Therefore, $\Delta_i \perp\!\!\!\perp_{\Delta}^{\psi} \Delta_j \mid \Delta_0$ would not hold, which means that $\Delta = \Delta_1 \cup_{\psi}^{\mathsf{cs}} \ldots \cup_{\psi}^{\mathsf{cs}} \Delta_m \mid \Delta_0$ would not be a conditional constraint splitting. □

Just like conditional syntax splittings coincide with syntax splittings when $\Sigma_3 = \emptyset$ [6], conditional constraint splittings coincide with constraint splittings whenever $\Delta_0 = \emptyset$.

Proposition 6. $\Delta = \Delta_1 \cup_{\psi}^{\mathsf{cs}} \ldots \cup_{\psi}^{\mathsf{cs}} \Delta_m$ *iff* $\Delta = \Delta_1 \cup_{\psi}^{\mathsf{cs}} \ldots \cup_{\psi}^{\mathsf{cs}} \Delta_m \mid \emptyset$.

In another similarity to purely syntactical conditional syntax splittings (see [12, Ex. 6]), conditional constraint splittings do not guarantee complete independence of the constraints in the subbases as the following example shows.

Example 5. Let $\Delta^a = \{(c|a \vee b), (c|a), (c|b)\}$. $CSP^\rho(\Delta^a)$ is given by:

$$C^\rho_{\Delta^a}(\delta_1) : \eta_1 > \min\{0\} - \min\{\eta_2, \eta_3\}$$
$$C^\rho_{\Delta^a}(\delta_2) : \eta_2 > \min\{0\} - \min\{\eta_1\}$$
$$C^\rho_{\Delta^a}(\delta_3) : \eta_3 > \min\{0\} - \min\{\eta_1\}.$$

Thus $\Delta^a = \{(c|a), (c|a \vee b)\} \cup^{cs}_\rho \{(c|b), (c|a \vee b)\} \mid \{(c|a \vee b)\}$.

In Example 5 we obtain a constraint splitting $\Delta^a = \{(c|a), (c|a \vee b)\} \cup^{cs}_\rho \{(c|b), (c|a \vee b)\} \mid \{(c|a \vee b)\}$, but η_2 and η_3 appear together in the constraint for δ_1 and are thus connected via δ_1. As a consequence we cannot guarantee that independently computed solutions of the constraint systems for the subbases yield a solution for the constraint system of the entire belief base. For example, selecting $\eta_1 = 0, \eta_2 = 1$ in the first subbase and $\eta_1 = 1, \eta_3 = 0$ in the other yields solutions disagreeing on η_1. We will therefore refine the notion of constraint splittings in the next section.

5.2 Safe Conditional Constraint Splitting

In analogy to (generalized) safe conditional syntax splittings, we introduce the notion of safe conditional constraint splittings.

Definition 9 (safe conditional constraint splitting). *A constraint splitting $\Delta = \Delta_1 \cup^{cs}_\psi \ldots \cup^{cs}_\psi \Delta_m$ is safe, written $\Delta = \Delta_1 \cup^{cs}_\psi \ldots \cup^{cs}_\psi \Delta_m \mid^s \Delta_0$, if additionally, for all $i \in \{1, \ldots, m\}$: $\Delta_0 \not\rightharpoonup^*_{\Delta,\psi} (\Delta_i \setminus \Delta_0)$.*

Safe conditional constraint splittings guarantee that constraints of the conditional pivot Δ_0 may only depend on conditionals in Δ_0 itself. Thus they can guarantee independence of the constraints in the subbases. Thus, given Δ_0, they let us iteratively solve $CSP(\Delta)$ by first computing solutions for $CSP(\Delta_0)$ and feeding the results into the constraints of the subbases which can then be solved independently from one another.

Example 6. $\Delta^b = \{(\overline{f}|p), (f|b)\} \cup^{cs}_\rho \{(b|p), (f|b)\} \cup^{cs}_\rho \{(w|b)\} \mid^s \{(f|b)\}$ from Example 4 is a safe conditional constraint splitting of Δ^b. For this splitting it is possible to solve $C^\rho_{\Delta^b}(\delta_1)$, the only constraint in $CSP^\rho(\Delta^b_0)$, first, e.g. by setting $\eta_1 = 1$, as this constraint is not dependent on any other constraints. Utilizing $\eta_1 = 1$ we can then solve $C^\rho_{\Delta^b}(\delta_2)$, $C^\rho_{\Delta^b}(\delta_3)$ and $C^\rho_{\Delta^b}(\delta_4)$

$$C^\rho_{\Delta^b}(\delta_2) : \eta_2 > \min\{1\} - \min\{0\}$$
$$C^\rho_{\Delta^b}(\delta_3) : \eta_3 > \min\{1\} - \min\{0\}$$
$$C^\rho_{\Delta^b}(\delta_4) : \eta_4 > \min\{0\} - \min\{0\}$$

independently from one another because they do not mention any of the other constraint variables. Thus we can obtain a solution $\vec{\eta} \in Sol(CSP(\Delta))$ with, e.g., $\vec{\eta} = (1,2,2,1)$ by solving $C^{\rho}_{\Delta^b}(\delta_2)$, $C^{\rho}_{\Delta^b}(\delta_3)$ and $C^{\rho}_{\Delta^b}(\delta_4)$ independently. Note that it would also be possible to choose $\Delta^b_0 = \{(f|b),(w|b)\}$ because $C^{\rho}_{\Delta^b}(\delta_4)$ also does not mention any other constraint variable.

The following proposition presents an important characterization of safe conditional constraint splittings in terms of independence of subbases excluding Δ_0.

Proposition 7. $\Delta = \Delta_1 \cup^{\mathsf{cs}}_{\psi} \dots \cup^{\mathsf{cs}}_{\psi} \Delta_m \mid^{\mathsf{s}} \Delta_0$ *iff for* $i,j \in \{0,\dots,m\}, i \neq j$*:* $\Delta_i \not\rightsquigarrow^*_{\Delta,\psi} (\Delta_j \setminus \Delta_0)$.

Now we show that every generalized safe conditional syntax splitting yields a safe conditional constraint splitting, closing the gap put forth by Proposition 4.

Proposition 8. $\Delta = \Delta_1 \bigcup^{\mathsf{gs}}_{\Sigma_1,\Sigma_2} \Delta_2 \mid \Sigma_3$ *implies* $\Delta = \Delta_1 \cup^{\mathsf{cs}}_{\rho} \Delta_2 \mid^{\mathsf{s}} (\Delta_1 \cap \Delta_2)$.

Proof. Let $\Delta = \Delta_1 \bigcup^{\mathsf{gs}}_{\Sigma_1,\Sigma_2} \Delta_2 \mid \Sigma_3$ and let $\Delta_0 = \Delta_1 \cap \Delta_2$. First we show that $\Delta = \Delta_1 \cup^{\mathsf{cs}}_{\rho} \Delta_2 \mid^{\mathsf{s}} \Delta_0$ is a conditional constraint splitting w.r.t. ρ, i.e., $\Delta_1 \perp\!\!\!\perp^{\psi}_{\Delta} \Delta_2 \mid \Delta_0$. Towards a contradiction, assume $\Delta_1 \perp\!\!\!\perp^{\psi}_{\Delta} \Delta_2 \mid \Delta_0$ were not the case. Then either $(\Delta_1 \setminus \Delta_0) \rightsquigarrow^*_{\Delta\setminus\Delta_0,\rho} (\Delta_2 \setminus \Delta_0)$ or $(\Delta_2 \setminus \Delta_0) \rightsquigarrow^*_{\Delta\setminus\Delta_0,\rho} (\Delta_1 \setminus \Delta_0)$. We consider the first case here, the second case is symmetrical. This means there must be some $\delta_1 \in \Delta_1 \setminus \Delta_0$ such that there is a $\delta_2 \in \Delta_2 \setminus \Delta_0$ with $\delta_1 \rightsquigarrow^*_{\Delta\setminus\Delta_0,\rho} \delta_2$. Note that $\delta_2 \notin \Delta_0$ implies with Corollary 5 that $\delta_2 \notin \Delta_1$. This means there is some set S with $\delta_2 \in S$ and either $S \in V_{\Delta}(\delta_1)$ or $S \in F_{\Delta}(\delta_1)$. Again we assume the first case as the second is analogous. Because $\delta_2 \in \Delta_2 \setminus \Delta_0$, the generalized safety property implies that there must be a set S' with $S' \subset S$ and $\delta_2 \notin S'$. Thus R1 (or R2 in the second case) from ρ would remove this set S from $V_{\Delta}(\delta_1)$. In this way δ_2 is eliminated from $V_{\Delta}(\delta_1)$ and therefore $\delta_1 \not\rightsquigarrow^*_{\Delta\setminus\Delta_0,\rho} \delta_2$, contradiction. To show that $\Delta_1 \cup^{\mathsf{cs}}_{\rho} \Delta_2 \mid^{\mathsf{s}} \Delta_0$ is safe we can apply the same arguments as above, as the generalized safety condition demands that the minimal constraint inducing sets for conditionals in Δ_0 can only include conditionals in Δ_0 itself. □

6 Safe Conditional c-Solution Splitting

In this section, we lift the notion of constraint splittings to the semantical level by introducing the notion of safe conditional c-solution splitting. To keep notation concise and to avoid being distracted by technical particularities we investigate only binary splittings in this section. Splittings at the semantical level have been investigated in the literature utilizing the notion of model combinations [2] as a means to combine ranking functions via the operators $\oplus$ and $\ominus$.

$$M_1 \oplus M_2 = \{\kappa \mid \kappa(\omega) = \kappa_1(\omega) + \kappa_2(\omega), \kappa_1 \in M_1, \kappa_2 \in M_2\}$$
$$M_1 \ominus M_2 = \{\kappa \mid \kappa(\omega) = \kappa_1(\omega) - \kappa_2(\omega), \kappa_1 \in M_1, \kappa_2 \in M_2\}$$

These combinations were employed to define the notion of semantic splitting [2]. If a belief base Δ semantically splits into a partition $\{\Delta_1, \Delta_2\}$ w.r.t. a semantics Sem, then the models of Δ can be obtained by combining the models of the subbases Δ_1, Δ_2 as stated in the following equation.

$$Mod_{\Sigma}^{Sem}(\Delta) = Mod_{\Sigma}^{Sem}(\Delta_1) \oplus Mod_{\Sigma}^{Sem}(\Delta_2) \tag{12}$$

This notion was extended to conditional semantic splitting [6,7] where the subbases Δ_1 and Δ_2 may overlap. This overlap means that the intersection of the subbases is "counted" twice and must be subtracted again to obtain models of Δ as stated in the next equation.

$$Mod_{\Sigma}^{Sem}(\Delta) = Mod_{\Sigma}^{Sem}(\Delta_1) \oplus Mod_{\Sigma}^{Sem}(\Delta_2) \ominus Mod_{\Sigma}^{Sem}(\Delta_1 \cap \Delta_2) \tag{13}$$

Semantic splitting is quite general and defined for any ranking semantics. As before, we will focus on c-representations as a special ranking semantics here. Non-conditional semantic splittings for c-representations were characterized by the notion of c-solution splittings [2] where a partition $\{\Delta_1, \Delta_2\}$ is a solution splitting for Δ if the following equation holds.

$$Sol(CSP(\Delta)) = \{(\vec{\eta}^1, \vec{\eta}^2) \mid \vec{\eta}^1 \in Sol(CSP(\Delta_1)), \vec{\eta}^2 \in Sol(CSP(\Delta_2))\} \tag{14}$$

This means that the solutions of $CSP(\Delta)$ are exactly the concatenations of the solutions of $CSP(\Delta_1)$ and $CSP(\Delta_2)$. A straightforward adaptation of c-solution splitting to the conditional case in the sense of (13) fails however, because the solutions of the subbases might not match on their intersection.

Example 7. Recall $\Delta^b = \{(f|b), (\overline{f}|p), (b|p), (w|b)\}$ from Example 2 with its associated simplified constraints. Observe that $\Delta^b = \{(f|b), (\overline{f}|p), (b|p)\} \cup_{\rho}^{\mathsf{cs}} \{(f|b), (w|b)\} \mid^{\mathsf{s}} \{(f|b)\}$. Then we have $(1,2,2) \in Sol(CSP(\Delta_1^b))$, $(3,1) \in Sol(CSP(\Delta_2^b))$ and $(1) \in Sol(CSP(\Delta_1^b \cap \Delta_2^b))$. But these can not be combined into a solution for $CSP^{\rho}(\Delta^b)$; for example $(3,2,2,1) \notin Sol(CSP(\Delta^b))$ as both $C^{\rho}_{\Delta^b}(\delta_2)$ and $C^{\rho}_{\Delta^b}(\delta_3)$ are violated by this solution.

Note that Example 7 exploits the freedom of choosing arbitrarily high impacts for conditionals. Indeed, there is no real reason to select $(3,1) \in Sol(CSP(\Delta_2))$ as opposed to the smaller vector $(1,1) \in Sol(CSP(\Delta_2))$ which also matches the other impacts. The crucial point here is that the constraints induced by the intersection of the subbases may be solved differently in the respective *CSPs*. It is therefore reasonable to presuppose that this intersection should be "treated the same" in all subbases. This assumption then implies that the intersection $\Delta_1 \cap \Delta_2$ plays the role of the conditional pivot for the solution splitting. This is in analogy to inference with conditional syntax splitting where it is presupposed that full information on the conditional pivot Σ_3 is available (cf. [12,21]); this is lifted to the semantic level here by demanding that the solutions of $CSP(\Delta_1 \cap \Delta_2)$ are available and can be matched with. By setting $\Delta_0 = \Delta_1 \cap \Delta_2$ this is also in line with the other notions of conditional splittings, leading to the notion of safe conditional c-solution splittings.

Definition 10 (safe conditional c-solution splitting). *A set* $\{\Delta_1, \Delta_2\}$ *yields a* safe conditional c-solution splitting *of* Δ *if* $\Delta = \Delta_1 \cup \Delta_2$ *and*

$$Sol(CSP(\Delta)) = \{\vec{\eta} \mid \vec{\eta}|_{\Delta_1} \in Sol(CSP(\Delta_1)), \vec{\eta}|_{\Delta_2} \in Sol(CSP(\Delta_2))\} \tag{15}$$

Safe conditional c-solution splittings generalize solutions splittings by no longer requiring a partition of Δ, but only subbases of Δ that yield Δ when combined; while $\vec{\eta}^1$ and $\vec{\eta}^2$ in (14) are defined over disjoint subbases, an implication of (15) is that $\vec{\eta}^1$ and $\vec{\eta}^2$must coincide on the intersection of Δ_1 and Δ_2, i.e., $\vec{\eta}^1|_{\Delta_1 \cap \Delta_2} = \vec{\eta}^2|_{\Delta_1 \cap \Delta_2}$. Thus, safe conditional c-solution splittings still demand that any solution for $CSP(\Delta)$ can be derived by a combination of solutions of Δ_1 and Δ_2, but with the additional stipulation that the solutions match with respect to the intersection $CSP(\Delta_1 \cap \Delta_2)$. Conversely, if there are solutions for $CSP(\Delta_1)$ and $CSP(\Delta_2)$ that match on the intersection, then the combination of these vectors must yield a solution for $CSP(\Delta)$.

Example 8. For Δ^b from Example 7, $\{\Delta_1^b = \{(f|b), (\overline{f}|p), (b|p)\}, \Delta_2^b = \{(f|b), (w|b)\}\}$ is a safe conditional solution splitting of Δ^b. For example, $(1, 2, 2, 1) \in Sol(\Delta^b)$ implies $(1, 2, 2) \in Sol(CSP(\Delta_1^b))$ and $(1, 1) \in Sol(CSP(\Delta_2^b))$. Conversely, $(2, 3, 3) \in Sol(CSP(\Delta_1^b))$ and $(2, 1) \in Sol(CSP(\Delta_2^b))$ implies $(2, 3, 3, 1) \in Sol(CSP(\Delta^b))$ because the two vectors match on $\Delta_1^b \cap \Delta_2^b = \{(f|b)\}$. But $(1, 2, 2) \in Sol(CSP(\Delta_1^b))$ and $(3, 1) \in Sol(CSP(\Delta_2^b))$ does not imply $(3, 2, 2, 1) \in Sol(CSP(\Delta^b))$ because the solutions don't match on $\Delta_1^b \cap \Delta_2^b$.

We now compare safe conditional c-solution splittings to other splitting notions. First we state the following straightforward result.

Proposition 9. *Every c-solution splitting is a safe conditional c-solution splitting.*

Proof. Let $\{\Delta_1, \Delta_2\}$ be a c-solution splitting of a belief base Δ. Then (14) holds. Since $\{\Delta_1, \Delta_2\}$ is a partition, (14) implies (15) and thus $\{\Delta_1, \Delta_2\}$ is also a safe conditional c-solution splitting. □

Somewhat surprisingly, safe conditional constraint splittings in general are not safe conditional solution splittings.

Proposition 10. *There is an spcr* ψ *such that there is a* $\Delta = \Delta_1 \cup_{\psi}^{\mathsf{cs}} \Delta_2 \mid^{\mathsf{s}} \Delta_0$ *such that* $\{\Delta_1, \Delta_2\}$ *is no safe conditional c-solution splitting of* Δ.

However, there is an spcr such that the following implication holds.

Proposition 11. *Let* ψ *be given by the identity function. If* $\Delta = \Delta_1 \cup_{\psi}^{\mathsf{cs}} \Delta_2 \mid^{\mathsf{s}} \Delta_0$, *then* $\{\Delta_1, \Delta_2\}$ *is a safe conditional c-solution splitting of* Δ.

Proposition 10 reveals an important distinction to be made between solution and constraint splittings. Safe conditional constraint splittings regard the constraint system built upon the entire belief base and delegate only the solving process to the subbases. Safe conditional c-solution splittings demand that the constraint systems themselves can be built and solved directly on the subbases, without taking the other subbases into account at all. Thus, the deciding difference between the two splittings is the level at which the constraint system can be computed. From an application perspective, this means that any spcr that satisfies the implication in Proposition 11 allows not only for localized solving but also for localized computation of the constraint systems. Thus, while there are safe conditional constraint splittings that are not safe conditional solution splittings, the latter are computationally more advantageous.

7 Related Work: Comparison to Safe Covers

There are several works on splitting techniques in the literature, e.g., [12,15–17,19,25]. Some papers [2,6,15,21] investigate reasoning with c-representations in the context of syntax splitting postulates for inductive inference. Next to the works on constraint splitting [2,25] which are the starting point of this paper, there is only one other paper concerned itself chiefly with splittings for c-representations based on their constraints [24]. Following a similar line of thought to ours, the notion of *safe covers* [24] aims at breaking down belief bases into smaller subbases to compute c-representations locally.

Definition 11 (safe cover [24]). *Let Δ be a belief base. A set $\{\Delta_1, \dots, \Delta_m\}$ is a* safe cover *of Δ if there is an spcr ψ such that $\bigcup_{k=1}^{m} \Delta_k = \Delta$ and Δ_i is closed under $\rightsquigarrow^*_{\Delta,\psi}$ for all $i \in \{1, \dots, m\}$.*

Constraint splittings are also safe covers [24]. The following example shows that conditional constraint splittings are more general than safe covers.

Example 9. Consider again $\Delta^a = \{(c|a \vee b), (c|a), (c|b)\}$ from Example 5 with the constraints

$$C^{\rho}_{\Delta^a}(\delta_1) : \eta_1 > \min\{0\} - \min\{\eta_2, \eta_3\} \tag{16}$$
$$C^{\rho}_{\Delta^a}(\delta_2) : \eta_2 > \min\{0\} - \min\{\eta_1\} \tag{17}$$
$$C^{\rho}_{\Delta^a}(\delta_3) : \eta_3 > \min\{0\} - \min\{\eta_1\}. \tag{18}$$

Then $\Delta^a = \{(c|a \vee b), (c|a)\} \cup^{\mathsf{cs}}_{\rho} \{(c|a \vee b), (c|b)\} \mid \{(c|a \vee b)\}$, cf. Example 5. However, the only safe cover of Δ^a is the trivial cover $\{\Delta^a\}$.

On the other hand, safe conditional constraint splittings are as expressive as safe covers as shown in the following two propositions. In order to construct a safe cover from a safe conditional constraint splitting, the conditionals in Δ_0 must be taken into account in all subbases.

Proposition 12. *If $\Delta_1 \cup^{\mathsf{cs}}_{\psi} \dots \cup^{\mathsf{cs}}_{\psi} \Delta_m \mid^{\mathsf{s}} \Delta_0$ then $\{\Delta_0, (\Delta_1 \cup \Delta_0), \dots, (\Delta_m \cup \Delta_0)\}$ is a safe cover of Δ w.r.t. ψ.*

To construct a safe conditional constraint splitting from a safe cover, the conditional pivot Δ_0 needs to be constructed by taking into account the overlap between any two subbases of the safe cover.

Proposition 13. *If* $\{\Delta_1, \ldots, \Delta_m\}$ *is a safe cover of* Δ *w.r.t.* ψ*, then* $\Delta = \Delta_1 \cup^{\mathsf{cs}}_{\psi} \ldots \cup^{\mathsf{cs}}_{\psi} \Delta_m \mid^{\mathsf{s}} \Delta_0$ *with*

$$\Delta_0 = \bigcup_{\substack{i,j \in \{1,\ldots,n\} \\ i \neq j}} (\Delta_i \cap \Delta_j).$$

Propositions 12 and 13 confirm that our approach to conditional constraint splittings can be utilized to compute c-representations locally. On the other hand, our comparison underlines the concept of safe covers by showing that they can be understood as a conditional splitting of constraints derived in analogy to notions of conditional syntax splitting.

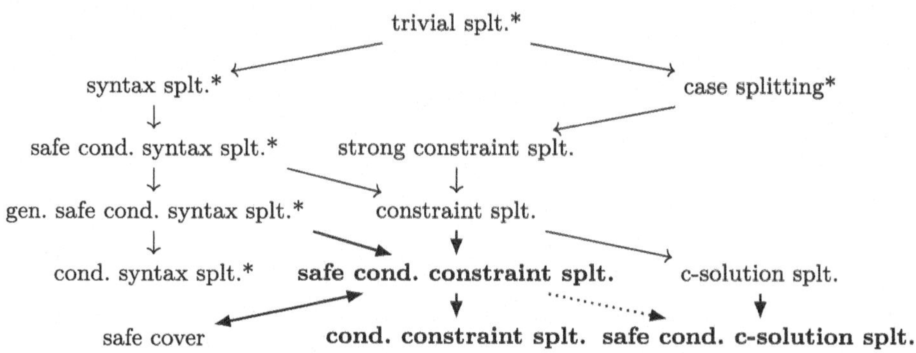

Fig. 2. Hierarchy of splittings of belief bases. Splitting techniques marked with $*$ are independent of the semantics of c-representations. A solid arrow from S_1 to S_2 indicates that each splitting of type S_1 yields also a splitting of type S_2 while dotted arrows indicate that this only holds in special cases (cf. Proposition 11). The splitting notions in bold and the bold arrows are introduced and shown in this paper; for the other splitting notions see [2,12,15,17,21,24,25].

8 Conclusion and Future Work

In this paper we applied generalizations from syntax splitting to the notion of constraint splitting for c-representations by introducing conditional constraint splittings, allowing the subbases to also share conditionals. We identified the subclass of safe conditional constraint splittings, allowing the constraint systems of the subbases to be solved independently provided the constraint system of the conditional pivot is solved first. Furthermore, we applied these techniques to c-solution splittings, leading to the definition of safe conditional c-solution splittings and generalizing c-solutions splittings to the case where subbases may share conditionals. Additionally, we compared our approaches to syntax splitting notions and also safe covers, embedding them in a hierarchy shown in Fig. 2.

For future work we plan to exploit these new concepts for the computation and implementation of inference with c-representations in the online reasoning platform InfOCF-Web[1] and its underlying library [3,4]. In particular, we want to investigate the difference in computational gain between safe conditional constraint and conditional solution splittings. Furthermore we plan to investigate for which other spcrs the implication in Proposition 11 holds, starting with subsets of the rules R1-R6. We will also extend the investigations presented here by considering not only strongly consistent belief bases but also belief bases that are only weakly consistent [10,11].

Acknowledgments. We thank the reviewers for their helpful feedback and comments. This work was supported by the Deutsche Forschungsgemeinschaft (DFG, German Research Foundation), project number 512363537, grant BE 1700/12-1 awarded to Christoph Beierle, and grant KE 1413/15-1 awarded to Gabriele Kern-Isberner. Lars-Phillip Spiegel was supported by grant BE 1700/12-1, and Alexander Hahn was supported by grant KE 1413/15-1.

References

1. Beierle, C., Eichhorn, C., Kern-Isberner, G., Kutsch, S.: Properties of skeptical c-inference for conditional knowledge bases and its realization as a constraint satisfaction problem. Ann. Math. Artif. Intell. **83**(3-4), 247–275 (2018). https://doi.org/10.1007/s10472-017-9571-9
2. Beierle, C., Haldimann, J., Kern-Isberner, G.: Semantic splitting of conditional belief bases. In: Raschke, A., Riccobene, E., Schewe, K. (eds.) Logic, Computation and Rigorous Methods - Essays Dedicated to Egon Börger on the Occasion of His 75th Birthday. LNCS, vol. 12750, pp. 82–95. Springer, Cham (2021). https://doi.org/10.1007/978-3-030-76020-5_5
3. Beierle, C., et al.: Scaling up reasoning from conditional belief bases. In: Destercke, S., Martinez, M.V., Sanfilippo, G. (eds.) Scalable Uncertainty Management - 16th International Conference, SUM 2024, Palermo, Italy, 27–29 November 2024, Proceedings. LNCS, vol. 15350, pp. 29–44. Springer, Cham (2024). https://doi.org/10.1007/978-3-031-76235-2_3
4. Beierle, C., Haldimann, J., Sanin, A., Spang, A., Spiegel, L., von Berg, M.: The InfOCF library for reasoning with conditional belief bases. In: Casini, G., Dundua, B., Kutsia, T. (eds.) Logics in Artificial Intelligence, 19th European Conference (JELIA 2026), Proceedings, Part II. LNAI, vol. 16094, pp. 19–27. Springer, Cham (2025). https://doi.org/10.1007/978-3-032-04590-4_2
5. Beierle, C., Kutsch, S., Sauerwald, K.: Compilation of static and evolving conditional knowledge bases for computing induced nonmonotonic inference relations. Ann. Math. Artif. Intell. **87**(1-2), 5–41 (2019). https://doi.org/10.1007/s10472-019-09653-7
6. Beierle, C., Spiegel, L.P., Haldimann, J., Wilhelm, M., Heyninck, J., Kern-Isberner, G.: Conditional splittings of belief bases and nonmonotonic inference with c-representations. In: Marquis, P., Ortiz, M., Pagnucco, M. (eds.) Principles of Knowledge Representation and Reasoning: Proceedings of the 21st International Conference, KR 2024, pp. 106–116 (2024). https://doi.org/10.24963/kr.2024/10

[1] https://www.fernuni-hagen.de/wbs/research/infocf-web/index.html.

7. Beierle, C., Spiegel, L.P., Haldimann, J., Wilhelm, M., Heyninck, J., Kern-Isberner, G.: Conditional syntax and semantic splittings of strongly and weakly consistent belief bases. Eur. J. Artif. Intell. (2025, to appear). https://doi.org/10.1177/30504554251410836
8. Delgrande, J.P.: A knowledge level account of forgetting. J. Artif. Intell. Res. **60**, 1165–1213 (2017). https://doi.org/10.1613/jair.5530
9. Goldszmidt, M., Pearl, J.: Qualitative probabilities for default reasoning, belief revision, and causal modeling. Artif. Intell. **84**, 57–112 (1996)
10. Haldimann, J., Beierle, C., Kern-Isberner, G.: Syntax splitting and reasoning from weakly consistent conditional belief bases with c-inference. In: Meier, A., Ortiz, M. (eds.) Foundations of Information and Knowledge Systems - 13th International Symposium, FoIKS 2024. LNCS, vol. 14589, pp. 85–103. Springer, Cham (2024). https://doi.org/10.1007/978-3-031-56940-1_5
11. Haldimann, J., Beierle, C., Kern-Isberner, G.: Inductive inference from weakly consistent belief bases. Knowl. Eng. Rev. **40**(e8), 1–32 (2025). https://doi.org/10.1017/S0269888925100088
12. Heyninck, J., Kern-Isberner, G., Meyer, T., Haldimann, J.P., Beierle, C.: Conditional syntax splitting for non-monotonic inference operators. In: Williams, B., Chen, Y., Neville, J. (eds.) Proceedings of the 37th AAAI Conference on Artificial Intelligence, vol. 37, pp. 6416–6424 (2023). https://doi.org/10.1609/aaai.v37i5.25789
13. Kern-Isberner, G.: Conditionals in Nonmonotonic Reasoning and Belief Revision, LNAI, vol. 2087. Springer (2001)
14. Kern-Isberner, G.: A thorough axiomatization of a principle of conditional preservation in belief revision. Ann. Math. Artif. Intell. **40**(1–2), 127–164 (2004)
15. Kern-Isberner, G., Beierle, C., Brewka, G.: Syntax splitting = relevance + independence: new postulates for nonmonotonic reasoning from conditional belief bases. In: Calvanese, D., Erdem, E., Thielscher, M. (eds.) Principles of Knowledge Representation and Reasoning: Proceedings of the 17th International Conference, KR 2020, pp. 560–571. IJCAI Organization (2020). https://doi.org/10.24963/kr.2020/56
16. Kern-Isberner, G., Brewka, G.: Strong syntax splitting for iterated belief revision. In: Sierra, C. (ed.) Proceedings International Joint Conference on Artificial Intelligence, IJCAI 2017, pp. 1131–1137. ijcai.org (2017)
17. Parikh, R.: Beliefs, belief revision, and splitting languages. Log. Lang. Comput. **2**, 266–278 (1999)
18. Pearl, J.: System Z: A natural ordering of defaults with tractable applications to nonmonotonic reasoning. In: Proceedings of the 3rd Conference on Theoretical Aspects of Reasoning About Knowledge (TARK 1990), pp. 121–135. Morgan Kaufmann Publishers Inc., San Francisco, CA, USA (1990)
19. Peppas, P., Williams, M.A., Chopra, S., Foo, N.Y.: Relevance in belief revision. Artif. Intell. **229**(1–2), 126–138 (2015)
20. Dupin de Saint-Cyr, F., Bisquert, P.: The form and the content: non-monotonic reasoning with syntactic contextual filtering. In: ECAI 2024, pp. 1309–1316. IOS Press (2024)
21. Spiegel, L.P., Haldimann, J., Heyninck, J., Kern-Isberner, G., Beierle, C.: Generalized safe conditional syntax splitting of belief bases. In: Kwok, J. (ed.) Proceedings of the 34th International Joint Conference on Artificial Intelligence, IJCAI-25, pp. 4678–4686. IJCAI Organization (2025). https://doi.org/10.24963/ijcai.2025/521

22. Spohn, W.: Ordinal conditional functions: a dynamic theory of epistemic states. In: Harper, W., Skyrms, B. (eds.) Causation in Decision, Belief Change, and Statistics, II, pp. 105–134. Kluwer Academic Publishers (1988)
23. Weydert, E.: System JZ - how to build a canonical ranking model of a default knowledge base. In: Cohn, A., Schubert, L., Shapiro, S. (eds.) Proceedings of the Sixth International Conference on Principles of Knowledge Representation and Reasoning (KR 1998), pp. 190–201. Morgan Kaufmann (1998)
24. Wilhelm, M., Kern-Isberner, G.: Decomposing constraint networks for calculating c-representations. In: Wooldridge, M.J., Dy, J.G., Natarajan, S. (eds.) Thirty-Eighth AAAI Conference on Artificial Intelligence, AAAI 2024, Thirty-Sixth Conference on Innovative Applications of Artificial Intelligence, IAAI 2024, Fourteenth Symposium on Educational Advances in Artificial Intelligence, EAAI 2014, 20–27 February 2024, Vancouver, Canada, pp. 10740–10747. AAAI Press (2024). https://doi.org/10.1609/AAAI.V38I9.28946
25. Wilhelm, M., Sezgin, M., Kern-Isberner, G., Haldimann, J., Beierle, C., Heyninck, J.: Splitting techniques for conditional belief bases in the context of c-representations. In: Gaggl, S.A., Martinez, M.V., Ortiz, M. (eds.) Logics in Artificial Intelligence - 18th European Conference, JELIA 2023, Dresden, Germany, 20–22 September 2023, Proceedings. LNCS, vol. 14281, pp. 462–477. Springer, Cham (2023). https://doi.org/10.1007/978-3-031-43619-2_32

Database Theory

Independence Under Incomplete Information

Miika Hannula[1,2], Minna Hirvonen[3](✉), Juha Kontinen[2], and Sebastian Link[4]

[1] Institute of Computer Science, University of Tartu, Tartu, Estonia
miika.hannula@ut.ee
[2] Department of Mathematics and Statistics, University of Helsinki, Helsinki, Finland
juha.kontinen@helsinki.fi
[3] Institut für Theoretische Informatik, Leibniz Universität Hannover, Hanover, Germany
minna.hirvonen@thi.uni-hannover.de
[4] Department of Computer Science, The University of Auckland, Auckland, New Zealand
s.link@auckland.ac.nz

Abstract. We initiate an investigation how the fundamental concept of independence can be represented effectively in the presence of incomplete information in relational databases. The concepts of possible and certain independence are proposed, and first results regarding the axiomatisability and computational complexity of implication problems associated with these concepts are established. In addition, several results for the data and the combined complexity of model checking are presented. The findings help reduce computational overheads associated with the processing of updates and answering of queries.

Keywords: Axiomatisation · Implication problem · Independence · Incomplete information · Null value · Relational database

1 Introduction

The concept of independence is appealing to many fields. In databases, it describes when a relation is the cross product for some of its projections [20]. Indeed, the cross product is one of the most fundamental operations, important to designing and querying databases [5,21]. Informally, a relation satisfies the independence atom (IA) $X \perp Y$ whenever for two tuples there is a third that has values matching with the first on all attributes in X and values matching with the second on all attributes in Y [20]. In other words, values on X are independent of values on Y. For example, the relation in Table 1 satisfies the IA *status* $\perp$ *gender*. IAs form a decidable fragment [20] of embedded multivalued dependencies whose implication problem is undecidable [10]. Similarly, probabilistic independence statements form a decidable fragment [7] for the undecidable class of probabilistic conditional independence statements, fundamental in statistics and distributed computing [15].

A.-Y. Turhan and J. Virtema (Eds.): FoIKS 2026, LNCS 16475, pp. 157–175, 2026.
https://doi.org/10.1007/978-3-032-21540-6_10

Table 1. Example relation r

a(ge)	*e(ducation)*	*s(tatus)*	*r(ace)*	*g(ender)*
25	bachelor	not-in-family	white	male
25	*	in-family	white	male
27	*	not-in-family	white	female
*	graduate	in-family	*	female

Table 2. Possible world w_1 of relation r from Table 1

a	e	s	r	g
25	bachelor	not-in-fml	white	m
25	bachelor	in-fml	white	m
27	graduate	not-in-fml	white	f
27	graduate	in-fml	white	f

Table 3. Possible world w_2 of relation r from Table 1

a	e	s	r	g
25	bachelor	not-in-fml	white	m
25	graduate	in-fml	white	m
27	bachelor	not-in-fml	white	f
25	graduate	in-fml	black	f

However, database relations are naturally incomplete, where missing values are denoted by null markers (denoted by $*$ in this work). Nulls are common since they are used whenever an actual value is unknown at the time of data acquisition [2], a value simply does not exist [3], or no information about the value is known [12,18,23]. Indeed, nulls accommodate flexibility within the rigid structure that relational databases enforce. If nulls are disallowed in any column, one may specify these columns as `NOT NULL` in SQL [4,8], the de-facto language for defining and querying data. Similar situations occur in statistical models where zeros are often used to denote missing values [19].

In this work we ask the following fundamental question: *How can independence be represented when data is missing?* In fact, nulls have led to a broad and deep study of query answering in the presence of incomplete information [11,17], and no single best solution has been proposed [22]. A promising direction is the approach where nulls are universally interpreted as values that exist but are currently unknown [2]. This leads naturally to a possible world semantics of database relations, where a possible world is obtained by replacing the occurrence of every null marker by some actual domain value. Query answers are then certain or possible. The former are answers in every possible world, while the latter are answers in some possible world [16]. In the context of our running example, the universal query *Which levels of education are associated with all statuses?* has no certain but possible answers `bachelor` and `graduate`, see world w_1 in Table 2.

Interestingly, the worlds w_1 in Table 2 and w_2 in Table 3 demonstrate that the IA $e \perp s$ is possible but not certain. In contrast, since neither column *status* nor *gender* contain nulls, IA $s \perp g$ holds necessarily in every possible world, so it is certain. Consider the universal query that asks for each status associated with every gender. Since r satisfies the certain IA $s \perp g$, its certain answers are simply all values in column *status*. Generally, the certain (possible) answers to universal queries become certain (possible) answers to simple selection queries whenever the corresponding certain (possible) IA holds. For example, the possible answers to the universal query that returns levels of education associated with all values of status can be obtained by selecting simply all values of education, given the IA $e \perp s$ holds possibly.

IAs are important for the most fundamental database operations, which are updates and queries. Firstly, IAs may express important semantic constraints that every database instance ought to comply with. As a consequence, updates can only be considered compliant when the instance resulting from the update satisfies every semantic constraint that has been specified on the database schema. This motivates the study of two computational problems associated with IAs: model checking and implication. While model checking refers directly to validating updates, efficient solutions to the implication problem enable us to minimise the overhead for validation, in other words we can reduce validation to non-redundant sets of IAs. Secondly, we have seen how IAs can lead to significant optimisations of expensive queries. For example, expensive universal queries [14] reduce to simple selection queries whenever the underlying relation satisfies a corresponding IA. While checking independence may be as expensive as evaluating the query itself, the optimisation could already be applied if the IA is implied by the given set of constraints. For example, the possible answers to the universal query that returns all combinations of *status* and *gender* affiliated with all levels of *education* cannot be returned as projection on these combinations since the possible IA $e \perp sg$ is not implied by the two possible IAs $e \perp s$ and $es \perp g$, as shown by the relation r in Table 1. Indeed, as we will uncover later, the exchange rule, known from classical IAs over complete relations [7,20], does not hold for possible IAs, but it does hold for combinations of possible and certain IAs. This illustrates the challenge and motivates a rigorous study of the underlying model checking and implication problems for possible and certain IAs, and their combination.

Informally, our contributions can be summarised as follows. (1) We propose the concepts of possible and certain IAs, (2) we establish several results regarding the axiomatisability and computational complexity of the implication problem associated with the individual and combined classes for possible and certain IAs, and (3) we establish several results for the data and the combined complexity of model checking for possible and certain IAs. In the realistic setting of database instances with missing data, we can assign a possible and certain semantics to the classical concept of independence. Similarly to how database queries then have possible and certain answers, update operations may have possible and certain updates. This distinction comes at the prize of an overhead for computing such answers, checking possible and certain models, and deciding possible and certain implication.

2 Preliminaries

We begin the section by defining the underlying data model that accommodates incomplete information. We then introduce the syntax and semantics of possible and certain IAs, and define the implication problems that we will study in the latter sections of this paper.

2.1 Relations with Incomplete Information

The natural numbers $\mathbb{N}$ are taken to start from 1 in this work. Given a natural number n, we write $[n]$ for the set $\{1, \dots, n\}$. Let Att and Val be disjoint infinite sets of symbols called *attributes* and *values*. For attribute sets X and Y, we often write XY for their set union $X \cup Y$. A *relation schema* is a finite set $R = \{A_1, \dots, A_n\}$ of attributes from Att. Each attribute A of a relation schema is associated with a domain $\text{Dom}(A) \subseteq \text{Val}$ which is the set of values that can occur in the column A. In order to allow the data to contain incomplete information about the values of the attributes, we use a special null symbol $*$, which represents an unknown attribute value. We always assume that $* \in \text{Dom}(A)$ and $|\text{Dom}(A) \setminus \{*\}| \geq 2$. The latter assumption is made because an attribute with a domain that has only one non-null value, cannot contain incomplete information, because the unknown value could only be the one non-null value.

A *tuple* over R is a function $t : R \to \bigcup_{A \in R} \text{Dom}(A)$ with $t(A) \in \text{Dom}(A)$ for all $A \in R$. The tuple t is called *complete* if does not contain any nulls; that is, $t(A) \neq *$ for all $A \in R$—otherwise it is called *incomplete*. The tuple t is called a null tuple if $t(A) = *$ for all $A \in R$. A non-null tuple is a tuple that is not a null tuple. For $X \subseteq R$, let $t(X)$ denote the restriction of the tuple t over R on X, and $\text{Dom}(X) = \prod_{A \in X} \text{Dom}(A)$ the Cartesian product of the domains of attributes in X. For example, the first tuple of relation r in Table 1 is complete but all remaining tuples are incomplete. However, the restrictions of all tuples onto *status* and *gender* are complete.

A multiset is a pair $M = (B, f)$ consisting of a set B and a multiplicity function $f\colon B \to \mathbb{N}$. The function f determines for each $b \in B$ how many copies of b the multiset (B, f) contains. We sometimes say that M *contains* an element b, written $b \in M$, if $b \in B$. If f is a constant function for some $n \in \mathbb{N}$, i.e., $f(i) = n$ for all $i \in B$, we denote it by n. For example, $(B, 1)$ corresponds to the set B in the usual sense. A multiset (B, f) is finite if the set B is finite, and it is a *included* in a multiset (A, g) if $B \subseteq A$ and $f(a) \leq g(a)$ for all $a \in B$.

A *relation* over R is a finite multiset $r = (r', f)$, where r' is a set of tuples over R. The relation r is *complete* if it contains only complete tuples, and otherwise incomplete. The *projection* of r on $X \subseteq R$ is defined as $r(X) = (r'(X), f')$, where $r'(X) = \{t(X) \mid t \in r'\}$ and $f'\colon r'(X) \to \mathbb{N}$ is such that $f'(t) = \sum_{s(X)=t} f(s)$. For example, the projection of relation r from Table 1 onto *status* and *race* consists of ((not-in-family, white), 2), ((in-family, white), 1) and ((in-family, *), 1). We define relations as multisets instead of the more common choice, sets, because we want to allow relations to have more than one copy of tuples that have null symbols. This is because two unknown values that are marked with the null symbol could have two different values if they were known. Our definition also allows multiple copies of tuples without null symbols, but the number of copies for those rows does not affect the satisfaction of the atoms that we will consider.

2.2 Possible and Certain IAs and Implication Problems

We introduce possible and certain variants of the IAs. These variants are based on groundings of incomplete relations, each representing a possible world obtained by replacing all null symbols by actual domain values.

Definition 1 (Grounding). *For a tuple t and a relation r over a schema R,*

(i) a grounding *of t is any complete tuple t' over R obtained from t by replacing its null symbols with non-null values (from their respective domains), and*
(ii) a grounding *of r is any relation r' over R that is obtained from r by replacing its null symbols with non-null values (from their respective domains) for each copy of a tuple independently.*

For example, projections of all the groundings of the relation r from Table 1 onto *status* and *gender* are the same, while they can be different on *education* and *gender*. In analogy to query answers [16], an IA is possible (certain) whenever it is satisfied by some (all) grounding(s).

Definition 2 (Independence, possible and certain independence). *For a relation schema R, and $X, Y \subseteq R$, the expressions $X \perp Y$, $X \perp_p Y$, and $X \perp_c Y$ are called* independence atom (IA), possible independence atom (PIA), *and* certain independence atom (CIA) *over R, respectively. For any of these atoms σ, we write $r \models \sigma$ to mean that a relation r over R satisfies σ, which is defined as follows:*

(i) $r \models X \perp Y$ iff $r(XY)$ is complete, and for all $t_1, t_2 \in r$ there is some $t \in r$ such that $t(X) = t_1(X)$ and $t(Y) = t_2(Y)$,
(ii) $r \models X \perp_p Y$ iff there is a grounding r' of r such that $r' \models X \perp Y$,
(iii) $r \models X \perp_c Y$ iff every grounding r' of r satisfies $r' \models X \perp Y$.

An IA $X \perp Y$ is called *disjoint* if X and Y do not intersect. *Disjoint* PIAs and CIAs are defined analogously. Of course, if a relation satisfies an IA, then the IA is certain; and if an IA is certain, then it is also possible. For example, the relation r from Table 1 satisfies $s \perp g$, $s \perp_c g$, and $s \perp_p g$. Furthermore, r satisfies neither $e \perp_c s$ nor $r \perp_c r$, but it satisfies $e \perp_p s$ and $r \perp_p r$.

Understanding the interaction between constraints provides us with means to control them in applications. The Introduction has already indicated that a deep understanding of the implication problem for independence statements has direct applications for the most fundamental tasks in data processing: update and query operations. For a set of atoms Σ, we write $r \models \Sigma$ if and only if $r \models \sigma$ for all $\sigma \in \Sigma$. Let $\Sigma \cup \{\sigma\}$ be a set of atoms over R. We say that a set of atoms Σ *logically implies* the atom σ, written as $\Sigma \models \sigma$, if and only if for all relations r over R,

$r \models \Sigma$ implies $r \models \sigma$. For our running example, $\{e \perp_c s, es \perp_c g\}$ implies $e \perp_c sg$, $\{e \perp_p s, es \perp_p g\}$ does not imply $e \perp_p sg$, and $\{e \perp_c s, es \perp_p g\}$ implies $e \perp_p sg$. For two subclasses[1] of IAs $\mathcal{P}$, $\mathcal{Q}$, the $(\mathcal{P}, \mathcal{Q})$*-implication problem* is to decide whether $\Sigma \models \sigma$, for any finite set of atoms Σ from $\mathcal{P}$ and any atom σ from $\mathcal{Q}$. If $\mathcal{P} = \mathcal{Q}$, we refer to the $(\mathcal{P}, \mathcal{Q})$-implication problem as the *implication problem for* $\mathcal{P}$.

3 Axiomatisations

Due to the central role of implication problems, our first goal is to establish axiomatic characterisations for combinations of PIAs and CIAs. Throughout, we will observe interesting differences to what is known from the idealised and well-known special case of having complete information.

3.1 Inference Rules

We define possible and certain variants of inference rules known from the special case [7,13,20], and also recall its major results. Let $\mathcal{T}, \mathcal{S}, \mathcal{C}, \mathcal{D}, \mathcal{E}$ be the inference rules for IAs depicted in Table 4. We use the subscript c or p for the rule that is obtained from the corresponding rule for IAs by replacing each $\perp$ symbol by the certain independence symbol $\perp_c$ or possible independence symbol $\perp_p$, respectively. The rules with subscript $p\&c$ are given in Table 5. We define the following sets of inference rules. Independence: $\mathfrak{I} = \{\mathcal{T}, \mathcal{S}, \mathcal{C}, \mathcal{D}, \mathcal{E}\}$, certain independence: $\mathfrak{I}_c = \{\mathcal{T}_c, \mathcal{S}_c, \mathcal{C}_c, \mathcal{D}_c, \mathcal{E}_c\}$, possible independence: $\mathfrak{I}_p = \{\mathcal{T}_p, \mathcal{S}_p, \mathcal{C}_p, \mathcal{D}_p\}$, and mixed exchange rules: $\mathfrak{I}_{p\&c} = \{\mathcal{E}_{p\&c}, \mathcal{E}_{c\&p}\}$. Note that the set $\mathfrak{I}_p$ is similar to the sets $\mathfrak{I}$ and $\mathfrak{I}_c$, except that the exchange rule is missing. This is a necessary omission, as Example 1 demonstrates that the exchange fails for possible independence. The implication of $X \perp_p Y$ by $X \perp_c Y$ follows from mixed exchange $\mathcal{E}_{c\&p}$ and trivial independence $\mathcal{T}_p$.

Let $\mathfrak{A}$ be a set of axioms. We say that there is an $\mathfrak{A}$-deduction for an atom σ from the set of atoms Σ, written as $\Sigma \vdash_{\mathfrak{A}} \sigma$, if and only if there is a finite sequence $(\tau_1, \ldots, \tau_n)$ of atoms such that $\tau_n = \sigma$, and each τ_i, $i \in \{1, \ldots, n\}$, is either an element of Σ or is obtained by applying a rule from $\mathfrak{A}$ to some atoms of $\Sigma \cup \{\tau_1, \ldots, \tau_{i-1}\}$. We sometimes write $\Sigma \vdash \sigma$ instead of $\Sigma \vdash_{\mathfrak{A}} \sigma$, if the set of axioms $\mathfrak{A}$ is clear from the context.

Let $\mathfrak{A}$ be an axiomatisation, and $\mathcal{P}$ and $\mathcal{Q}$ classes of atoms. We say that an axiomatisation $\mathfrak{A}$ is (i) *sound* for the $(\mathcal{P}, \mathcal{Q})$-implication problem iff for all sets of atoms Σ of the class $\mathcal{P}$ and all atoms σ of the class $\mathcal{Q}$, $\Sigma \vdash_{\mathfrak{A}} \sigma$ implies $\Sigma \models \sigma$, and (ii) *complete* for the $(\mathcal{P}, \mathcal{Q})$-implication problem iff for all sets of atoms Σ of the class $\mathcal{P}$ and all atoms σ of the class $\mathcal{Q}$, $\Sigma \models \sigma$ implies $\Sigma \vdash_{\mathfrak{A}} \sigma$. We write $\mathrm{Cl}_{\mathfrak{A}}(\Sigma)$ for the closure of Σ with respect to the axiomatisation $\mathfrak{A}$ consisting of axioms, i.e., $\mathrm{Cl}_{\mathfrak{A}}(\Sigma) = \{\sigma \mid \Sigma \vdash_{\mathfrak{A}} \sigma\}$. For example, if Σ consists of

[1] That is, a class of certain, possible or usual IAs such that some restrictions are imposed. Examples of subclasses considered in this paper include CIAs, PIAs, PIAs with arity restrictions, and disjoint CIAs and PIAs.

Table 4. Rules $\mathfrak{I}$ for independence

$$\frac{}{X \perp \emptyset} \text{ (trivial ind., } \mathcal{T}) \qquad \frac{X \perp Y}{Y \perp X} \text{ (symmetry, } \mathcal{S})$$

$$\frac{X \perp X \quad Y \perp Z}{XY \perp Z} \text{ (constancy, } \mathcal{C}) \qquad \frac{X \perp YZ}{X \perp Y} \text{ (decomposition, } \mathcal{D})$$

$$\frac{X \perp Y \quad XY \perp Z}{X \perp YZ} \text{ (exchange, } \mathcal{E})$$

Table 5. Rules $\mathfrak{I}_{p\&c}$ for possible and certain independence

$$\frac{X \perp_p Y \quad XY \perp_c Z}{X \perp_p YZ} \text{ (mixed exchange, } \mathcal{E}_{p\&c})$$

$$\frac{X \perp_c Y \quad XY \perp_p Z}{X \perp_p YZ} \text{ (mixed exchange, } \mathcal{E}_{c\&p})$$

$e \perp_c s$, $es \perp_p g$ and $r \perp_p r$, then $rsg \perp_p e \in \text{Cl}_{\{\mathcal{E}_{c\&p}, \mathcal{S}_p, \mathcal{C}_p\}}(\Sigma)$ due to the following $\{\mathcal{E}_{c\&p}, \mathcal{S}_p, \mathcal{C}_p\}$-deduction:

$$\cfrac{r \perp_p r \quad \cfrac{\cfrac{e \perp_c s \quad es \perp_p g}{\mathcal{E}_{c\&p} : \; e \perp_p sg}}{\mathcal{S}_p : \; sg \perp_p e}}{\mathcal{C}_p : \; rsg \perp_p e}$$

For a CIA or PIA σ define $ind(\sigma)$ as the corresponding IA, i.e., $ind(X \perp_c Y) = X \perp Y$ and $ind(X \perp_p Y) = X \perp Y$. We extend the definition of ind to sets of CIAs and PIAs in the obvious way, i.e., $ind(\Sigma) = \{ind(\sigma) \mid \sigma \in \Sigma\}$.

The following result about the idealised special case of complete relations is well-known from the research literature [7,13,20].

Theorem 1. *The set $\mathfrak{I}$ forms a sound and complete axiomatisation for the implication problem for IAs.*

Indeed, a stronger result is known [6,7,13] that allows us to construct a single complete relation, known as an Armstrong relation, that satisfies an IA if and only if it is implied by a given set of IAs. Hence, the implication problem reduces to a model checking problem on such a relation. This is known to be useful for acquiring those constraints perceived to encode business rules of the underlying application [6]. Let Σ be a set of atoms of class $\mathcal{P}$ over a schema R. A relation r over R is called an *Armstrong relation* for a set Σ of atoms of class $\mathcal{P}$ if for all atoms σ of class $\mathcal{P}$ over R, $r \models \sigma$ if and only if $\Sigma \models \sigma$. We say that a class $\mathcal{P}$ of atoms enjoys Armstrong relations, if every set of atoms Σ of class $\mathcal{P}$ has an Armstrong relation.

Theorem 2. *The class of IAs enjoys Armstrong relations.*

3.2 Results for Certain and Possible IAs Separately

As our first major result we establish the completeness of the axiomatisation $\mathfrak{I}_c$ for CIAs. This follows from the completeness of $\mathfrak{I}$ for IAs, by showing that if $\Sigma \not\vdash_{\mathfrak{I}_c} \sigma$, then $ind(\Sigma) \not\vdash_{\mathfrak{I}} ind(\sigma)$, and the relation that witnesses $ind(\Sigma) \not\models ind(\sigma)$ also witnesses $\Sigma \not\models \sigma$.

Theorem 3. *The set $\mathfrak{I}_c$ forms a sound and complete axiomatisation for the implication problem for CIAs.*

Proof. The soundness of the axiomatisation is clear, as it is easy to check that all of the inference rules in $\mathfrak{I}_c$ are sound. We show that the axiomatisation is also complete. Let $\Sigma \cup \{\sigma\}$ be a set of CIAs. Suppose that $\Sigma \not\vdash_{\mathfrak{I}_c} \sigma$. We show that $\Sigma \not\models \sigma$. It is clear that $\Sigma \vdash_{\mathfrak{I}_c} \sigma$ if and only if $ind(\Sigma) \vdash_{\mathfrak{I}} ind(\sigma)$, because rules of $\mathfrak{I}_c$ and $\mathfrak{I}$ are the same, except that in $\mathfrak{I}_c$, we have CIAs instead of IAs. Thus, $ind(\Sigma) \not\vdash_{\mathfrak{I}} ind(\sigma)$, and by the completeness of the axiomatisation $\mathfrak{I}$, we have $ind(\Sigma) \not\models ind(\sigma)$. This means that there is a relation r over the relation schema $R = \{A \in \text{Att} \mid A$ appears in some atom of $\Sigma \cup \{\sigma\}\}$ such that $r \models ind(\Sigma)$, but $r \not\models ind(\sigma)$. Moreover, since $ind(\Sigma \cup \{\sigma\})$ is a set of IAs, the relation r must be complete. This means that there are no null symbols in r, and therefore $r \models ind(\Sigma)$ implies $r \models \Sigma$, and $r \not\models ind(\sigma)$ implies $r \not\models \sigma$. Hence, the relation r witnesses that $\Sigma \not\models \sigma$, and the axiomatisation $\mathfrak{I}_c$ is complete. □

From Theorems 1 and 3, we now obtain that the implication problems for IAs and CIAs are equivalent in the following sense.

Theorem 4. *Let $\Sigma \cup \{\sigma\}$ be a set of CIAs. Then $\Sigma \models \sigma \iff ind(\Sigma) \models ind(\sigma)$.*

It follows that IAs in the idealised special case of having complete information correspond exactly to CIAs in the general case of permitting incomplete information. Intuitively, our finding assures us that known results from an idealised case hold in a more general and realistic context in the principled sense of certainty. This view extends further to Armstrong relations.

Theorem 5. *The class of CIAs enjoys Armstrong relations.*

Proof. Let R be a relation schema and Σ a set of CIAs over R. Then there exists a complete relation r such that for all CIAs σ over R, we have

$$\Sigma \models \sigma \iff \sigma \in \text{Cl}_{\mathfrak{I}_c}(\Sigma) \iff ind(\sigma) \in \text{Cl}_{\mathfrak{I}}(ind(\Sigma))$$
$$\iff ind(\Sigma) \models ind(\sigma) \iff r \models ind(\sigma) \iff r \models \sigma.$$

The first equivalence follows from Theorem 3, and the second one from the fact that $\Sigma \vdash_{\mathfrak{I}_c} \sigma$ iff $ind(\Sigma) \vdash_{\mathfrak{I}} ind(\sigma)$. The third equivalence follows from Theorem 1, and the fourth one from the definition of Armstrong relations for independence atoms. The Armstrong relation r for $ind(\Sigma)$ exists by Theorem 2. The last equivalence follows from the completeness of r.

Apart from positioning known results in the broader framework of incomplete information, we also need to consider the case where IAs may possibly hold. Here, things are different. Indeed, Theorem 4 does not hold if we consider PIAs instead of CIAs, because the exchange rule is not sound in the possible case. This is demonstrated by the following example.

Example 1. There exists a set $\Sigma \cup \{\sigma\}$ of PIAs such that $ind(\Sigma) \models ind(\sigma)$, but $\Sigma \not\models \sigma$. Let $\Sigma = \{A \perp_p B, AB \perp_p C\}$ and $\sigma = A \perp_p BC$. Then $ind(\Sigma) = \{A \perp B, AB \perp C\}$ and $ind(\sigma) = A \perp BC$, and by the soundness of exchange $\mathcal{E}$, $ind(\Sigma) \models ind(\sigma)$. Consider then the relation r depicted in Table 6. We have $r \models \Sigma$, because r has groundings r' and r'' such that $r' \models A \perp B$ and $r'' \models AB \perp C$. But $r \not\models A \perp_p BC$, since there is no way to replace all null symbols in the column A such that $A \perp BC$ would hold. This is because r has two different values for A and four different values for BC, making it impossible to fit all of the eight different values for ABC in just four rows.

Table 6. The relations r, r', and r''.

ABC	ABC	ABC
0 0 0	0 0 0	0 0 0
$*$ 1 0	0 1 0	1 1 0
$*$ 0 1	1 0 1	0 0 1
1 1 1	1 1 1	1 1 1

Table 7. The relation r from the proof of Theorem 6 in the case $k = 3$, $m = 2$.

X_1	X_2	X_3	Y_1	Y_2	$Z_1 \ldots Z_n$	#
0	0	0	0	0	0 ... 0	1
0	0	1	0	1	0 ... 0	1
0	1	0	1	0	0 ... 0	1
0	1	1	$*$	$*$	0 ... 0	1
1	0	0	$*$	$*$	0 ... 0	1
1	0	1	$*$	$*$	0 ... 0	1
1	1	0	$*$	$*$	0 ... 0	1
1	1	1	$*$	$*$	0 ... 0	1
$*$	$*$	$*$	$*$	$*$	0 ... 0	15

The invalidity of the exchange rule for PIAs also means that the completeness proof for the axiomatisation of IAs does not work for PIAs. However, the set $\mathfrak{I}_p$ forms a complete axiomatisation for a restricted version of the implication problem for PIAs.

Theorem 6. *The set $\mathfrak{I}_p$ forms a sound and complete axiomatisation for the* (PIA, PIA*)*-implication problem, where* PIA* *is the class of* PIAs $X \perp_p Y$ *such that at least one of the following conditions hold:*
(i) $|X| = 1$ *or* $|Y| = 1$, *or* *(ii)* $||X| - |Y|| \in \{0, 1\}$.

Proof. The soundness of the axiomatisation is again easy to show by checking that all of the inference rules are sound. We show that the axiomatisation is complete. Let Σ be a set of PIAs and $X \perp_p Y$ a PIA. Suppose that $\Sigma \nvdash X \perp_p Y$. We show that $\Sigma \not\models X \perp_p Y$. Note that if $\Sigma \vdash A \perp_c A$, we can use constancy $\mathcal{C}_p$ and symmetry $\mathcal{S}_p$ to obtain $\Sigma \nvdash X \setminus \{A\} \perp_p Y \setminus \{A\}$, and it suffices to show the claim for this atom. Hence, we may assume that there are no $A \in XY$ such that $\Sigma \vdash A \perp_p A$. The case that $X \perp_p Y$ is non-disjoint is considered in the full version of the proof in [9]. The case that $X \perp_p Y$ is disjoint can be handled in two parts. The first case that $|X| - |Y| \leq 1$ and $|Y| \geq 2$. The second case is that $|Y| = 1$. Note that by symmetry we may assume that $|X| \geq |Y|$, so it suffices to consider these two cases. We consider the first case only. The proof of the second case can be found in the full version of the proof in [9].

For the first case, let $|X| = k \geq m = |Y|$, and assume that $m \geq 2$. Let $\mathrm{Dom}(A) = \{0, 1, *\}$ for all $A \in R$. Construct then a relation r over R as follows. The relation r consists of $2^k(2^m - 1) - 1$ rows. On the first 2^k rows, let the values of X be the tuples from $\{0, 1\}^k$. For the first $2^m - 1$ rows of these 2^k rows, let the values of Y be the tuples from $\{0, 1\}^m \setminus \{(1, 1, \ldots, 1)\}$ and for the rest of the $2^k - (2^m - 1)$ rows, let the values of Y be null symbols. Then add rows with only null symbols such that you obtain $2^k(2^m - 1) - 1$ rows in total. Let all the values for the attributes $A \in R \setminus XY$ be constant 0.

We show that $r \models \Sigma$, but $r \not\models X \perp_p Y$. First note that $r(X)$ has 2^k different complete tuples, and $r(Y)$ has $2^m - 1$ different complete tuples. Therefore, it is impossible for $X \perp_p Y$ to hold in the relation r, because r has only $2^k(2^m - 1) - 1$ tuples. Suppose then that $V \perp_p W \in \Sigma$. We will show that $r \models V \perp_p W$. Since every attribute $A \in R \setminus XY$ is constant, we may assume that $VW \subseteq XY$, and therefore also $V \cap W = \emptyset$. (For the latter, recall that there are no $A \in XY$ such that $\Sigma \vdash A \perp_p A$.) Moreover, we may assume that $VW = XY$, because by decomposition $\mathcal{D}_p$, $r \models V \perp_p W$ implies $r \models V' \perp_p W'$ for every $V' \subseteq V$ and $W' \subseteq W$. We may assume that $|V| \geq |W|$.

Suppose first that $|V| \geq k + 1$. Since r has 2^k different non-null tuples, this means that $r(V)$ has at most 2^k different non-null tuples and $r(W)$ has at most $2^{k+m-|V|} \leq 2^{m-1}$ different non-null tuples. Then in order to $V \perp_p W$ hold, we need to fit at most $2^k \cdot 2^{m-1}$ values of XY in the relation. Since we have $2^k(2^m - 1) - 1 (> 2^k \cdot 2^{m-1})$ rows in r, and no non-null tuple is repeated in r, we have enough room to contain all the needed rows. This can be done by a grounding r' of $r(XY)$ that replaces all the null symbols on the first 2^k rows with 0 s, and replaces the null symbol rows with tuples from the Cartesian product of the projections of these first 2^k rows on V and W. Since replacing all the null symbols on the first 2^k rows with 0 s preserves the amounts of different non-null tuples, the cardinality approximations above hold for r'. Thus $r \models V \perp_p W$.

Suppose then that $|V| = k$. Since $|V| + |W| = |VW| = |XY| = |X| + |Y| = k + m$, we have $|W| = m$. Since $V \neq X$ and $W \neq X$, there are $A \in V$ and $B \in W$ such that $A, B \in Y$. As the relation r does not contain the tuple where every attribute of Y has value 1, it must be that by picking suitable values for the null symbols on the first 2^k row, we obtain at most $2^k - 1$ different values for V and $r(W)$ has at most $2^m - 1$ different values for W. Since no non-null tuple is repeated in r, we have enough room to contain all the needed rows. This can be done by a grounding r' of $r(XY)$ that replaces the null symbols on the first 2^k rows such that we obtain at most $2^k - 1$ and $2^m - 1$ different values for V and W, respectively. The grounding r' replaces the null symbol rows with tuples from the Cartesian product of the projections of these first 2^k rows on V and W, as before. Thus $r \models V \perp_p W$. Note that it cannot be that $|V| \leq k - 1$. Otherwise, from $|X| - |Y| \leq 1$ and $|X| = k$, it follows that $k + (k-1) \leq |X| + |Y| = |XY| = |VW| = |V| + |W| \leq k - 1 + |W|$, i.e., $|W| \geq k$, which is impossible because $|W| \leq |V| \leq k - 1$. This finishes the proof in the case that $m \geq 2$. Table 7 depicts the relation r in the case $k = 3$, $m = 2$, where $X = \{X_1, X_2, X_3\}$, $Y = \{Y_1, Y_2\}$, and $R \setminus XY = \{Z_1, \ldots, Z_n\}$. □

For our running example, the incomplete relation r of Table 1 shows that $\sigma = e \perp_p sg$ is not implied by the set Σ consisting of $e \perp_p s$ and $es \perp_p g$. Indeed, while grounding w_1 of r in Table 2 satisfies $e \perp s$ and grounding w_2 of r in Table 3 satisfies $es \perp g$, there cannot be any grounding of r that satisfies both. Theorem 6 shows that there is no $\mathfrak{I}_p$-deduction of σ from Σ. It is future work to investigate the axiomatisability for other fragments of PIAs.

3.3 Combining Certain and Possible IAs

The most general implication problem combines the classes of CIAs and PIAs. In this context, the following theorem shows that, when restricted to disjoint atoms, we may add PIAs to the set Σ, and still obtain a complete axiomatisation.

Theorem 7. *The set* $(\mathfrak{I}_c \cup \mathfrak{I}_p \cup \mathfrak{I}_{p\&c}) \setminus \{\mathcal{C}_c, \mathcal{C}_p\}$ *forms a sound and complete axiomatisation for the restriction of the* (CIA ∪ PIA, CIA)*-implication problem to disjoint atoms.*

Proof. The soundness of the axiomatisation again follows from the soundness of the inference rules. We show that the axiomatisation is complete. Let Σ be a set of disjoint CIAs and PIAs, and $X \perp_c Y$ a disjoint CIA. Suppose that $\Sigma \nvdash X \perp_c Y$. We show that $\Sigma \not\models X \perp_c Y$. We may assume that $X \perp_c Y$ is minimal in the sense that for all nonempty $X' \subseteq X$ and $Y' \subseteq Y$ such that $X'Y' \neq XY$, we have $\Sigma \vdash X' \perp_c Y'$. If $X \perp_c Y$ is not minimal, we can remove attributes from X and Y until we obtain a minimal atom. It suffices to show the claim for the minimal atom as decomposition $\mathcal{D}_c$ ensures that the claim must hold also for the original atom. Note that by trivial independence $\mathcal{T}_c$ and symmetry $\mathcal{S}_c$, neither X nor Y is empty.

Let $Z = R \setminus XY$ and $\text{Dom}(A) = \{0, 1, *\}$ for all $A \in R$. Define then $\text{Dom}^*(A) = \text{Dom}(A)$ for all $A \in XY$ and $\text{Dom}^*(A) = \{0, *\}$ for all $A \in Z$. Let

$A_1 \in X$, and define $r_1 = \{t \in \prod_{A \in R}(\mathrm{Dom}^*(A) \setminus \{*\}) \mid t(A_1) = \sum_{A \in R \setminus A_1} t(A) \bmod 2\}$ and $r_2 = \{t(*/A_1) \mid t \in r_1\}$, where $t(*/A_1)$ is the tuple obtained from t by replacing the value of attribute A_1 by $*$. Let then $r = (r_1 \cup r_2, 1)$. Now $r \not\models X \perp_c Y$, because the null values can be filled in such a way that the resulting relation is just $r' = (r_1, 2)$ and hence, there are tuples $t_1, t_2 \in r'$ such $t_1(A_1) = 1$, $t_1(A) = 0$ for $A \in X \setminus A_1$, and $t_2(A) = 0$ for $A \in Y$, but there is no $t \in r'$ such that $t(X) = t_1(X)$ and $t(Y) = t_2(Y)$ because for all $t \in r'$, $t(A_1) = \sum_{A \in R \setminus A_1} t(A) \bmod 2$. Now we show that $r \models \Sigma$. First note that it is possible to fill the null values in r such that the resulting relation is $(\prod_{A \in R}(\mathrm{Dom}^*(A) \setminus \{*\}), 1)$, and therefore all of the disjoint PIAs in Σ hold.

Note then that any way of filling the null values in r (with 0 and 1) results in a relation such that for any $U \subseteq R$, if $U \subseteq Z$, then every attribute in U is constant, and if $U \cap Z = \emptyset$ and $XY \not\subseteq U$, then $r(U) = (\prod_{A \in U})(\mathrm{Dom}(A) \setminus \{*\}, f)$ for some f. This means that showing that all of the disjoint CIAs in Σ hold can be done as in the proof of Theorem 1 in [7]. We include the proof for the sake of comprehensiveness. Suppose that $V \perp_c W \in \Sigma$. Assume first that $VW \cap XY = \emptyset$. Then $VW \subseteq Z$, so by the definition of r, every attribute in VW is constant. Thus clearly, $r \models V \perp_c W$.

Assume then that $VW \cap XY \neq \emptyset$ and $XY \not\subseteq VW$. We show that $r \models V \perp_c W$. Because every attribute in Z is constant, it suffices to check that $r \models V \setminus Z \perp_c W \setminus Z$. But since $r((VW) \setminus Z) = (\prod_{A \in (VW) \setminus Z}(\mathrm{Dom}(A) \setminus \{*\}), f)$ for the function f such that $f(t) = \sum_{s((VW) \setminus Z) = t} 1(s)$, clearly $r \models V \setminus Z \perp_c W \setminus Z$.

Assume finally that $XY \subseteq VW$. We show that this results in a contradiction. Denote $V = X'Y'Z'$ and $W = X''Y''Z''$, where $X = X'X''$, $Y = Y'Y''$, and $Z'Z'' \subseteq Z$. By the minimality of $X \perp_c Y$ and symmetry $\mathcal{S}_c$, we have $\Sigma \vdash X' \perp_c Y'$ and $\Sigma \vdash Y \perp_c X''$. From $\Sigma \vdash X'Y'Z' \perp_c X''Y''Z''$, we obtain $\Sigma \vdash X'Y' \perp_c X''Y''$ by using decomposition $\mathcal{D}_c$. Then by applying exchange $\mathcal{E}_c$ to $\Sigma \vdash X' \perp_c Y'$ and $\Sigma \vdash X'Y' \perp_c X''Y''$, we obtain $\Sigma \vdash X' \perp_c X''Y'Y''$. Then by symmetry $\mathcal{S}_c$, we obtain $\Sigma \vdash YX'' \perp_c X'$. Then by applying exchange $\mathcal{E}_c$ to $\Sigma \vdash Y \perp_c X''$ and $\Sigma \vdash YX'' \perp_c X'$, we obtain $\Sigma \vdash Y \perp_c X''X'$. Then by applying symmetry $\mathcal{S}_c$, we have $\Sigma \vdash X \perp_c Y$. □

Note that in the above, the constancy rules $\mathcal{C}_c$ and $\mathcal{C}_p$ are removed from the axiomatisation since we only consider disjoint atoms, and therefore we do not have any constancy atoms of the form $X \perp_c X$ or $X \perp_p X$, making these rules redundant. Moreover, in the disjoint case, the PIAs in Σ do not affect whether a CIA is logically implied or not, as described in the following theorem.

Theorem 8. *Let Σ be a set of disjoint CIAs and PIAs, and σ a disjoint CIA. Then $\Sigma \models \sigma$ if and only if $\Sigma \setminus \{\tau \in \Sigma \mid \tau$ is a PIA$\} \models \sigma$.*

Proof. By Theorem 7, $\Sigma \models \sigma$ if and only if $\Sigma \vdash_{(\mathfrak{I}_c \cup \mathfrak{I}_p \cup \mathfrak{I}_{p\&c}) \setminus \{\mathcal{C}_c, \mathcal{C}_p\}} \sigma$. Since no rule in $(\mathfrak{I}_c \cup \mathfrak{I}_p \cup \mathfrak{I}_{p\&c}) \setminus \{\mathcal{C}_c, \mathcal{C}_p\}$ is such that it has a PIA in the antecedent and a CIA in the consequent, we have $\Sigma \vdash_{(\mathfrak{I}_c \cup \mathfrak{I}_p \cup \mathfrak{I}_{p\&c}) \setminus \{\mathcal{C}_c, \mathcal{C}_p\}} \sigma$ if and only if $\Sigma \vdash_{\mathfrak{I}_c \setminus \{\mathcal{C}_c\}} \sigma$. The latter is clearly equivalent with $\Sigma \setminus \{\tau \in \Sigma \mid \tau$ is a PIA$\} \vdash_{\mathfrak{I}_c \setminus \{\mathcal{C}_c\}} \sigma$. Since all the atoms considered are disjoint, it does not matter whether we consider the set $\mathfrak{I}_c \setminus \{\mathcal{C}_c\}$ or $\mathfrak{I}_c$. Then by Theorem 3, $\Sigma \setminus \{\tau \in \Sigma \mid \tau \text{ is a PIA}\} \vdash_{\mathfrak{I}_c} \sigma$ if and only if $\Sigma \setminus \{\tau \in \Sigma \mid \tau \text{ is a PIA}\} \models \sigma$.

The following example demonstrates that the disjointness assumption in the previous two theorems is crucial.

Example 2. Let $\Sigma = \{A \perp_p A, B \perp_p B, C \perp_p C, A \perp_c C, B \perp_c C\}$. Then we have $\Sigma \nvdash_{\mathfrak{I}_c \cup \mathfrak{I}_p \cup \mathfrak{I}_{p\&c}} AB \perp_c C$, but $\Sigma \models AB \perp_c C$. For the first part, note that no rule in $\mathfrak{I}_c \cup \mathfrak{I}_p \cup \mathfrak{I}_{p\&c}$ with a PIA in the antecedent has a CIA in the consequent. Therefore it suffices to show that $\{A \perp_c C, B \perp_c C\} \nvdash_{\mathfrak{I}_c} AB \perp_c C$. By Theorem 3, this follows from the fact that $\{A \perp_c C, B \perp_c C\} \not\models AB \perp_c C$, which is witnessed by the relation r' of Table 6.

To see that $\Sigma \models AB \perp_c C$, note that each of A, B, and C is either constant or contains at most one non-null value. Without loss of generality, assume this value is 0. Since the domain of each attribute contains at least two non-null values, any nulls can be filled so that each column has zeros except at one position, which we set to 1. If there are no nulls, the column consists entirely of zeros. If $\Sigma \models C \perp_c C$, we clearly have $\Sigma \models AB \perp_c C$. Now assume, that $\Sigma \not\models C \perp_c C$. Then $\Sigma \models A \perp_c C$ and $\Sigma \not\models C \perp_c C$ imply that the column A is all zeros at the beginning, i.e., $\Sigma \models A \perp_c A$. (If both $\Sigma \not\models A \perp_c A$ and $\Sigma \not\models C \perp_c C$ hold, then the corresponding columns can be filled such that they have zeros in every position except one position in each column where the value is one, as described above. Then $\Sigma \models A \perp_c C$ cannot hold.) Similarly, $\Sigma \models B \perp_c C$ and $\Sigma \not\models C \perp_c C$ imply that the column B is all zeros at the beginning, i.e., $\Sigma \models B \perp_c B$. But this means that $\Sigma \models AB \perp_c AB$, and hence $\Sigma \models AB \perp_c C$.

Corollary 1. *The set $\mathfrak{I}_c \cup \mathfrak{I}_p \cup \mathfrak{I}_{p\&c}$ does not form a complete axiomatisation for the* (CIA $\cup$ PIA, CIA)*-implication problem.*

4 Computational Complexity

This section covers the computational complexity of PIAs and CIAs with respect to some key problems. We start our analysis with the combined complexity and the data complexity of model checking and conclude by considering the implication problem. In this section we assume that the domains of attributes are finite. The results do not depend on how the multiplicities of the tuples are encoded; that is, they can be written either in unary or in binary.

Let $\mathcal{P}$ be a class of independencies. The *combined complexity problem for* $\mathcal{P}$ is to decide, given a relation r over attributes $A_1, \ldots, A_n$, the associated (finite) domains $\mathrm{Dom}(A_1), \ldots, \mathrm{Dom}(A_n)$, and an independency σ from $\mathcal{P}$ as the input, whether r satisfies σ. If the input independency σ is fixed, the problem is called the *data complexity problem of* σ. Given a complexity class $\mathbf{C}$, we say that the *data complexity problem for* $\mathcal{P}$ is

- in $\mathbf{C}$ if for any $\sigma \in \mathcal{P}$, the data complexity problem of σ is in $\mathbf{C}$;
- $\mathbf{C}$-hard if for some $\sigma \in \mathcal{P}$, the data complexity problem of σ is $\mathbf{C}$-hard; and

– **C**-complete when it is both in **C** and **C**-hard.

First we show that for PIAs already data complexity is NP-complete.

Theorem 9. *The combined complexity and data complexity problems for possible independence are both* NP*-complete. The* NP*-hardness holds for any subclass of PIAs that contains an IA of the form* $A \perp_p BC$*, where* A, B, C *are distinct attributes.*

Proof. The membership in NP is straightforward for combined complexity (and therefore also for data complexity). For the NP-hardness, it suffices to consider only data complexity. Letting $\sigma := VP \perp_p C$, we construct a reduction from the satisfiability problem (SAT) to the data complexity of σ. The input of SAT is a Boolean formula in conjunctive normal form: $\phi = C_1 \wedge \cdots \wedge C_m$, where $C_i = l_{i,1} \vee \cdots \vee l_{i,n}$, $i \in [m]$, are such that each $l_{i,j}$, $j \in [n]$, is a propositional variable p or a negated propositional variable $\overline{p}$. We construct a relation r from ϕ in the following way. Assuming that W is the set of variables appearing in ϕ, and representing each tuple $t : (V, P, C) \mapsto (a, b, c)$ simply as (a, b, c), we construct the relation r as follows:

1. For each $p \in W$, add $(*, +, p)$ and $(*, -, p)$ to r. Furthermore, for all $q \in W \setminus \{p\}$, add $(q, *, p)$ and $(\overline{q}, *, p)$ to r.
2. For each clause $C_i = l_{i,1} \vee \cdots \vee l_{i,n}$, add $(\overline{l_{i,1}}, *, i), \ldots, (\overline{l_{i,n}}, *, i)$ to r. Add also $(*, *, i)$ with multiplicity $n - 1$, and $(*, +, i)$ with multiplicity 1 to r. Furthermore, assuming $l_{i,1}, \ldots, l_{i,n}$ are literals over variables of some set W', add $(v, *, i)$ and $(\overline{v}, *, i)$ for all $v \in W \setminus W'$.

Above it is to be understood that the doubly-nested negation $\overline{\overline{p}}$ of a variable p is p itself. Also the multiplicity of each tuple is assumed to be 1 unless otherwise stated. The construction of r is illustrated in Table 8. It suffices to show that ϕ is satisfiable if and only if $r \models VP \perp_p C$.

Suppose first ϕ is satisfiable by some variable assignment s. We construct a grounding r' of the relation r in the following way. We ensure that each tuple has the form $(l, +, *)$ when $s(l) = 1$, and $(l, -, *)$ when $s(l) = 0$, where $*$ represents an arbitrary value of the variable C. It is easy to see that this is possible whenever s satisfies ϕ. Moreover, this way the obtained grounding r' satisfies the IA $VP \perp C$.

For the converse direction, suppose r satisfies $VP \perp_p C$, and let r' be the grounding of r satisfying $VP \perp C$. Let us first consider how the tuples introduced in Item 1 are grounded. For each variable p there are only two possibilities: either the pair $(p, +, v)$ and $(\overline{p}, -, v)$, or the pair $(p, -, v)$ and $(\overline{p}, +, v)$ must appear in the grounding r' consistently for all values v of C. Thus the grounding of Item 1 represents an assignment s of the variables in ϕ. Before considering Item 2, let us first note that the values of pairs (V, P) must be consistent between the tuples obtained from Item 1 and those obtained from Item 2; this ensured by the IA. It is then easy to see that a grounding for the tuples obtained from Item 2 entails s is a satisfying assignment. In particular, for each clause C_i, having one tuple of the form $(*, +, i)$ in r ensures that for at least one literal l there is a tuple of the form $(l, +, i)$ in the grounding. This concludes the proof. □

Table 8. The relation r obtained via the reduction from an example SAT instance $\phi = C_1 \wedge C_2 \wedge C_3$, where $C_1 = p_2 \vee p_3$, $C_2 = p_1 \vee \overline{p_2} \vee p_3$, and $C_3 = \overline{p_3}$.

V	P	C		V	P	C
$*$	+	p_1		p_1	$*$	1
$*$	-	p_1		$\overline{p_1}$	$*$	1
p_2	$*$	p_1		$\overline{p_2}$	$*$	1
$\overline{p_2}$	$*$	p_1		$\overline{p_3}$	$*$	1
p_3	$*$	p_1		$*$	$*$	1
$\overline{p_3}$	$*$	p_1		$*$	+	1
p_1	$*$	p_2		$\overline{p_1}$	$*$	2
$\overline{p_1}$	$*$	p_2		p_2	$*$	2
$*$	+	p_2	$\cup$	$\overline{p_3}$	$*$	2
$*$	-	p_2		$*$	$*$	2
p_3	$*$	p_2		$*$	$*$	2
$\overline{p_3}$	$*$	p_2		$*$	+	2
p_1	$*$	p_3		p_1	$*$	3
$\overline{p_1}$	$*$	p_3		$\overline{p_1}$	$*$	3
p_2	$*$	p_3		p_2	$*$	3
$\overline{p_2}$	$*$	p_3		$\overline{p_2}$	$*$	3
$*$	+	p_3		p_3	$*$	3
$*$	-	p_3		$*$	+	3

Table 9. One possibility for the relation E is to connect tuples on the same row from both tables.

$r =$ A	B		$r_\times =$ A	B
0	$*$		0	0
1	$*$		1	0
$*$	2		1	2
0	$*$		0	1
$*$	1		1	1
$*$	$*$		0	2
$*$	0			

Although the data complexity and model checking problems are generally NP-complete, it can be shown that for *unary* PIAs (i.e., PIAs $X \perp_p Y$ where $|X| = |Y| = 1$) model checking lies in polynomial time. As shown next, this is achieved by representing the question as a maximum flow problem. Let us start by introducing few necessary definitions. A *network* is a directed graph $G = (V, E)$, where each edge $(u, v) \in E$ is associated with a *capacity* $c(u, v) \geq 0$. The network is called a *flow network* if it is furthermore associated with a source node $s \in V$ and a sink node $t \in V$. A *flow* is a mapping $f : E \to \mathbb{R}_{\geq 0}$ that satisfies:

1. *capacity constraint*: $f(u, v) \leq c(u, v)$ for all $(u, v) \in E$,
2. *flow conservation*: $\sum_{(v,u) \in E} f(v, u) = \sum_{(u,v) \in E} f(u, v)$ for all $u \in V \setminus \{s, t\}$.

The *total flow* of a flow f is defined as $|f| := \sum_{(s,v) \in E} f(s, v)$. The *maximal flow problem* is to determine the maximum total flow over all flows in a given flow network. In what follows we use the well-known integral flow theorem, which states that maximum total flow is integral if all the edge capacities are integral (see, e.g., [1]).

Theorem 10. *The data complexity and combined complexity problems for unary possible independence are in polynomial time.*

Proof. Let $r = (r', g)$ be a relation and $A \perp_p B$ a PIA over single attributes A and B. We write $r_\times$ for the Cartesian product of the non-null (set) projections of r on A and B; that is, $r_\times$ is the set of tuples t over $\{A, B\}$ such that $t(A) \in r'(A) \setminus \{*\}$ and $t(B) \in r'(B) \setminus \{*\}$. The flow network is then constructed in the following way. The nodes consist of the tuples in r' and $r_\times$, as well as fresh values s_0 and s_1 denoting the source and the sink, respectively. The edges and capacity constraints are built as follows:

1. For each $t \in r'$ there is an edge (s_0, t) with a capacity $c(s_0, t) = g(t)$
2. For each $t \in r'$ and $t' \in r_\times$ such that t' is a grounding of t, there is an edge (t, t') with a capacity $c(t, t') = 1$.
3. For each $t \in r_\times$ there is an edge (t, s_1) with a capacity $c(t, s_1) = 1$.

We claim that the maximum total flow is $|r_\times|$ if and only if $r \models A \perp_p B$.

Suppose first the maximum total flow $\sum_{v \in V} f(s, v)$ is $|r_\times|$. Consequently, f assigns each incoming edge (t, s_1) of the sink the maximum capacity: $f(t, s_1) = 1$. Due to flow conservation and the integral flow theorem, for each tuple $t' \in r_\times$ we find exactly one tuple $t \in r'$ such that $f(t, t') = 1$. Conversely, due to Item 1 and flow conservation, a tuple $t \in r'$ is associated with no more than $g(t)$ many tuples $t' \in r_\times$ such that $f(t, t') = 1$. Informally, t can distribute its incoming flow into at most $g(t)$ many tuples t' because the flow is integral. Since $f(t, t') = 1$ implies t' is a grounding of t, we obtain $r \models A \perp_p B$.

For the converse direction, assume $r \models A \perp_p B$. Then we find a grounding r' of r satisfying $A \perp B$. Consequently, the set $r_\times$, defined from r as above, is a subset of r'. It suffices to define a flow function f which has a total flow $|r_\times|$. Note that the maximum total flow cannot be greater than $|r_\times|$ due to the capacities in Item 3. Now, it is possible to choose a binary relation $E \subseteq r' \times r_\times$ (see Table 9) such that (1) for each $t \in r'$ there are at most $g(t)$ distinct $t' \in r_\times$ such that $(t, t') \in E$; and (2) for each $t \in r$ there is exactly one $t' \in r'$ such that $(t', t) \in E$. We let $f(t, t') = 1$ if $(t, t') \in E$, and $f(t, t') = 0$ if $(t, t') \in r' \times r_\times \setminus E$. The remaining values of f, for the edges outgoing the source and the edges incoming the sink, are uniquely determined by flow conservation. It follows by construction that f satisfies all the capacity constraints. We conclude that the total flow of f is $|r_\times|$, as required. □

We have now shown that the data complexity of model checking is NP-complete for the class of PIAs $X \perp Y$ where X or Y contains at least two attributes. When both X and Y are single attributes, we established that the problem is in polynomial time. We conclude this section by showing that for CIAs data complexity is in FO. For the next proposition, recall that the domain of each attribute has at least two elements.

Proposition 1. *$r \models X \perp_c X$ if and only if $r(X)$ is complete and satisfies $X \perp X$.*

Theorem 11. *The data complexity problem for IAs and CIAs is in* FO. *The combined complexity problem for CIAs is in polynomial time.*

Proof. Clearly it suffices to show the claim for CIAs. We claim that $r \models X \perp_c Y$ iff one of the following three properties hold:

(i) $r \models X \perp_c X$, (ii) $r \models Y \perp_c Y$, (iii) both of the following hold:

1. for all complete $t \in r(X)$ and $t' \in r(Y)$, there is $t'' \in r$ such that $t''(X) = t$ and $t''(Y) = t'$; and
2. any grounding of $r(XY)$ is included in $r(XY)$.

We show first that, assuming $r \not\models X \perp_c X$ and $r \not\models Y \perp_c Y$, the failure of either Item 1 or Item 2 leads to $r \not\models X \perp_c Y$. Suppose Item 1 is not true. Let $t \in r(X)$ and $t' \in r(Y)$ be two complete tuples such that $t''(X) \neq t$ or $t''(Y) \neq t'$ for any $t'' \in r$. Clearly, for each $t'' \in r$ we can then define a grounding s such that $s(X) \neq t$ or $s(Y) \neq t'$. For this, note that the domain of each attribute is at least of size 2. The obtained grounding of r then does not satisfy $X \perp Y$, which means that r does not satisfy $X \perp_c Y$.

Suppose then Item 1 holds but Item 2 does not hold. Let $s \notin r(XY)$ be a grounding of a tuple $t \in r(XY)$. Item 1 entails that $s(X) \notin r(X)$ or $s(Y) \notin r(Y)$. By symmetry, we may assume that $s(X) \notin r(X)$. Since $r \not\models Y \perp_c Y$, either $r \not\models Y \cap X \perp_c Y \cap X$ or $r \not\models Y \setminus X \perp_c Y \setminus X$. Since $r \not\models Y \cap X \perp_c Y \cap X$ entails $r \not\models X \perp_c Y$ by the decomposition and symmetry rules of certain independence, we may assume that $r \not\models Y \setminus X \perp_c Y \setminus X$. We then construct a grounding r' of r with the following properties:

- Some extension of t in r is grounded to s' such that $s'(X) = s(X)$.
- The remaining tuples in r are grounded to tuples s'' such that $s''(X) \neq s(X)$.
- The grounding with respect to $Y \setminus X$ is such that $r' \not\models Y \setminus X \perp Y \setminus X$.

The second item is possible since the domain of each attribute has at least 2 elements. As a result, r' contains only one tuple mapping X to $s(X)$, and $|r'(Y)| \geq 2$. It follows that $r' \not\models X \perp Y$, as required.

For the converse direction, suppose one of the three listed properties hold. In the case of $r \models X \perp_c X$ or $r \models Y \perp_c Y$, we obtain $r \models X \perp_c Y$ by the constancy, symmetry, and trivial independence rules of certain independence. Furthermore, $r \models X \perp_c Y$ is a straightforward consequence of Items 1 and 2. This concludes the proof of the claim.

A relation r over an ordered list of n attributes can be interpreted as a first-order structure $\mathfrak{A}_r = (U, f, D_1, \ldots, D_n, 0)$, where $U := D_1 \cup \cdots \cup D_n \cup \{0, \ldots, m\}$, $f : U^n \to \{0, \ldots, m\}$ is a function representing r, and D_i, for $i \in [n]$, is the domain of the ith attribute in r. The attributes of XY furthermore are assumed to occupy fixed positions in the ordered list of attributes. Then, using Proposition 1 and the claim proven above, it is straightforward to write a first-order formula ϕ such that $\mathfrak{A}_r \models \phi$ iff $r \models X \perp_c Y$. We conclude that the data complexity problem for CIAs is in FO. Regarding combined complexity, the items of the claim can be checked in polynomial time in the combined size of the relation and the CIA. □

From the results of Sect. 3, we immediately obtain the following theorem concerning the complexity of implication problems, where the problem is to decide, given a finite set $\Sigma \cup \{\tau\}$ of atoms, whether $\Sigma \models \tau$.

Theorem 12. *The implication problems of Theorems 3, 6, and 7 are in polynomial time.*

5 Conclusion and Future Work

We have initiated work on the general concept of independence in the presence of incomplete information. We have shown that results on the implications problem well-known from the idealised special case of complete relations are captured by the concept of certain independence in the general realistic case of incomplete relations. In addition, we have shown that the concept of possible independence is challenging in the sense of establishing general results on their implication problem, and intractable in terms of their model checking problem. Directions for future work include the axiomatisability and computational complexity for more general fragments of possible (and certain) independence, the discovery of PIAs and CIAs from given incomplete relations, and the existence/construction of Armstrong relations. More generally, it is interesting to look at alternative approaches to capturing incomplete information and probabilistic variants of PIAs and CIAs.

Acknowledgments. The authors thank the anonymous referees for their valuable comments and suggestions. M. Hannula: Partially supported by the European Research Council (ERC) under the European Union's Horizon 2020 research and innovation programme (grant agreement No 101020762). M. Hirvonen: Received funding from the European Research Council (ERC) under the European Union's Horizon 2020 research and innovation programme (grant agreement No 101020762) and from the Magnus Ehrnrooth foundation.

Disclosure of Interests. The authors have no competing interests to declare that are relevant to the content of this article.

References

1. Ahuja, R.K., Magnanti, T.L., Orlin, J.B.: Network Flows - Theory, Algorithms and Applications. Prentice Hall (1993)
2. Codd, E.F.: Extending the database relational model to capture more meaning. ACM Trans. Database Syst. **4**(4), 397–434 (1979)
3. Codd, E.F.: Missing information (applicable and inapplicable) in relational databases. SIGMOD Rec. **15**(4), 53–78 (1986)
4. Date, C.J.: Null values in database management. In: Proceedings of the Second British National Conference on Databases (BNCOD-2), University of Bristol, UK, 7–9 July 1982, pp. 147–166 (1982)
5. Elmasri, R., Navathe, S.B.: Fundamentals of Database Systems, 3rd edn. Addison-Wesley-Longman (2000)
6. Fagin, R.: Horn clauses and database dependencies. J. ACM **29**(4), 952–985 (1982). https://doi.org/10.1145/322344.322347
7. Geiger, D., Paz, A., Pearl, J.: Axioms and algorithms for inferences involving probabilistic independence. Inf. Comput. **91**(1), 128–141 (1991)

8. Grant, J.: Null values in SQL. SIGMOD Rec. **37**(3), 23–25 (2008)
9. Hannula, M., Hirvonen, M., Kontinen, J., Link, S.: Independence under incomplete information (2025). https://arxiv.org/abs/2505.05866
10. Herrmann, C.: On the undecidability of implications between embedded multivalued database dependencies. Inf. Comput. **122**(2), 221–235 (1995)
11. Imielinski, T., Lipski, Jr. W.: Incomplete information in relational databases. J. ACM **31**(4), 761–791 (1984)
12. Köhler, H., Leck, U., Link, S., Zhou, X.: Possible and certain keys for SQL. VLDB J. **25**(4), 571–596 (2016). https://doi.org/10.1007/s00778-016-0430-9
13. Kontinen, J., Link, S., Väänänen, J.: Independence in database relations. In: Libkin, L., Kohlenbach, U., de Queiroz, R. (eds.) WoLLIC 2013. LNCS, vol. 8071, pp. 179–193. Springer, Heidelberg (2013). https://doi.org/10.1007/978-3-642-39992-3_17
14. Leinders, D., den Bussche, J.V.: On the complexity of division and set joins in the relational algebra. J. Comput. Syst. Sci. **73**(4), 538–549 (2007)
15. Li, C.T.: Undecidability of network coding, conditional information inequalities, and conditional independence implication. IEEE Trans. Inf. Theory **69**(6), 3493–3510 (2023)
16. Libkin, L.: Certain answers as objects and knowledge. In: Principles of Knowledge Representation and Reasoning: Proceedings of the Fourteenth International Conference, KR 2014, Vienna, Austria, 20–24 July 2014 (2014)
17. Libkin, L.: SQL's three-valued logic and certain answers. ACM Trans. Database Syst. **41**(1), 1:1–1:28 (2016)
18. Lien, Y.E.: On the equivalence of database models. J. ACM **29**(2), 333–362 (1982)
19. Little, R., Rubin, D.: Statistical Analysis with Missing Data. Wiley Series in Probability and Mathematical Statistics. Probability and Mathematical Statistics. Wiley (2002)
20. Paredaens, J.: The interaction of integrity constraints in an information system. J. Comput. Syst. Sci. **20**(3), 310–329 (1980)
21. Ramakrishnan, R., Gehrke, J.: Database Management Systems, 3 edn. McGraw-Hill (2003)
22. Toussaint, E., Guagliardo, P., Libkin, L., Sequeda, J.: Troubles with nulls, views from the users. Proc. VLDB Endow. **15**(11), 2613–2625 (2022)
23. Zaniolo, C.: Database relations with null values. J. Comput. Syst. Sci. **28**(1), 142–166 (1984)

Extending Similarity Measures for Incomplete Database Instances with Locality-Sensitive Hashing

Tim Wolfgang Helmut Schwabe and Lena Wiese(✉)

Institute of Computer Science, Goethe-Universität Frankfurt, 60325 Frankfurt a. M., Germany
lwiese@cs.uni-frankfurt.de
https://www.dbda.cs.uni-frankfurt.de/

Abstract. Recent research has provided a framework for measuring similarity of incomplete database instances without considering the presence of complete key information; the aim is to identify similar tuples across database instances by purely relying on the tuples themselves. The framework proposes a straight forward approach for an approximate algorithm to reach sufficiently good results with computational efficiency. Introducing more advanced methods for nearest neighbour searches, such as locality sensitive hashing (LSH), is an opportunity to build on top of the original framework and further enhance the already achieved results. Hence, this paper introduces the appropriate definitions and proves the performance of an LSH integrated framework based on extensive experiments. Further, using an LSH integrated approach broadens the application space of the framework for more types of data as well as detecting partial instance matches, which highlights how promising this approach is for future work.

Keywords: locality sensitive hashing · nearest neighbour search · incomplete databases

1 Introduction

In today's data-driven landscape, organizations increasingly rely on large, heterogeneous data collections – commonly known as data lakes – to support decision-making or operational processes [10]. Such datasets, however, are often incomplete; in particular due to missing values but also due to evolving data curation practices, or intrinsic uncertainty associated with integrating data from diverse sources [10]. Additionally, incomplete database instances pose significant challenges when comparing datasets, because the potential absence of complete key information and the presence of labelled nulls complicate traditional matching techniques. Similarity measures that account for these imperfections are essential, not only for tasks such as data cleaning, version control, and integration,

A.-Y. Turhan and J. Virtema (Eds.): FoIKS 2026, LNCS 16475, pp. 176–194, 2026.
https://doi.org/10.1007/978-3-032-21540-6_11

but also for assessing the quality of data repair algorithms and tracking the evolution of datasets over time.

Related work [12] laid the foundation for comparing incomplete database instances by introducing a robust framework that formalises the notion of similarity in the presence of labelled nulls without complete key information. This framework employs a signature-based approach to derive approximate similarity scores, which effectively balances computational efficiency with the need to capture subtle differences between datasets. Despite the considerable advances achieved through these methods, the inherent NP-hardness of the instance comparison problem means that even approximate algorithms can struggle to scale when confronted with increasingly large and complex datasets. In this paper we address a critical scalability bottleneck in the comparison of incomplete database instances, and also offer a practical solution for enhancing data-driven applications in environments characterised by uncertainty and partial information.

Contributions. This paper extends prior work by integrating the principles of Locality Sensitive Hashing (LSH) into the signature algorithm. The primary contributions of the work presented in this paper are threefold.

- First, the theoretical framework for similarity measures in incomplete database instances is extended to accommodate the use of LSH, providing a formal justification for its integration.
- Second, an adjusted signature algorithm that leverages LSH is implemented to achieve significant improvements in computational efficiency while maintaining, or even enhancing, the quality of the similarity scores.
- Finally, the presented approach is validated through experimental evaluations, demonstrating that the LSH-enhanced algorithm can achieve faster processing times with at least a similar level of quality in matching results.

Outline. In the remainder of the paper, the challenges associated with comparing incomplete database instances are reviewed first (Sect. 2), while also reintroducing the fundamentals of the initial framework that was presented in prior work (Sect. 3). In addition, related work regarding LSH will be shown and discussed in Sect. 3. Afterwards, in Sect. 4 the methodologies of this paper will be explained in detail to introduce the design and implementation of the LSH-integrated signature algorithm as well as further techniques that are necessary for integrating the original framework and executing experiments. Subsequent Sect. 5 presents the experimental setup and results, which highlight the performance gains and improvements in quality over traditional methods. Finally, the broader implications of the presented approach and potential avenues for future research are discussed at the end in Sect. 6.

2 Related Work

2.1 Data Incompleteness

The problem of data incompleteness arises for example from the pervasive use of null values in relational databases; and it was argued that SQL handles them inadequately in [22]. Although nulls are essential in real-life scenarios, managing them creates multiple, foundational research problems with context-dependent theoretical backgrounds. Prior work [12] proposes a framework for computing similarity of instances with labelled nulls without requiring complete primary key information for identifying pairs of tuples across instances. As a side-effect, the proposed algorithms additionally return a mapping between instances' tuples, explaining the similarity score and providing information for further processing of the instances. In particular [12] highlights the following use cases:

- *Data versioning* tracks how one dataset evolves into another [4]; this process may be modeled by using similarity measures to map tuples. It handles tuple insertions, deletions, and merges (with injective or left-injective mappings), adapts to schema differences by filling missing attributes with nulls, and primarily focuses on complete matches.
- *Data exchange* transforms a source instance into a target instance that satisfies schema mapping constraints [9]. Since many target solutions may exist, systems often generate universal solutions guaranteeing correct query answering via homomorphisms, or core solutions, which are unique up to isomorphism. Comparing solutions requires tuple mappings that handle redundancy and merging: mappings must be left and right total, left-injective when comparing a universal to a core solution, and total (but not left-injective) when comparing two universal solutions.
- *Database repairs* [3] address instances that violate integrity constraints [14] by updating cell values or introducing variables to resolve conflicts. To evaluate or compare repairs across systems or against a gold standard, complete and fully injective tuple mappings are required. Instance similarity not only measures repair quality but also explains repairs by highlighting mismatched tuples and showing how they were corrected.

We will expand on [12] in our work to account for partial matches.

2.2 LSH Research and Applications

Locality Sensitive Hashing for approximate nearest neighbour search is a very well-known topic and there have been several publications proposing a refined and improved version of its original algorithm. Most recent work has shown implementations of LSH for video anomaly detection [15], differential privacy [11], cryptographic security [23], or high-energy physics [17]. While these are fairly specific implementations for certain use cases, there is also various work that focuses on introducing theoretically proven frameworks to implement LSH for improved results regarding both efficiency and quality [6,7,20,21]. [21] is the most recent one and even presents a small comparison of selected LSH implementations. However, the focus is strictly on query cost improvement and while the authors achieve this improvement with their implementation, they also increase the overhead of the indexing phase in LSH massively by using R*-tree structures [2] that are being updated dynamically and continuously at immense costs.

Hence, for the purposes of this paper we focus on the classic approach as well as too more memory-efficient implementations (ILSS and DHHash) for which more details are provided in Sect. 5.

3 Background

3.1 Databases

A database instance $I = (I_1, ..., I_k)$ consists of finite relations $I_i \subset (\text{Consts} \cup \text{Vars})^{n_i}$ with $n_i \geq 0$ and $i \in [1, k]$ where Consts(I) is the set of all constants in an instance and Vars(I) is the set of all labelled nulls (variables) in an instance; the active domain of an instance I is defined as $\text{adom}(I) = \text{Consts}(I) \cup \text{Vars}(I)$. According to [12] a value mapping $h : \text{adom}(I) \rightarrow \text{adom}(I')$ has to be such that $\forall c \in \text{Consts} : h(c) = c$. A tuple $t \in I$ is a set of constants and variables with k elements – according to attributes A defined in a relational schema R; each tuple has its own unique ID (t_{id}). A labelled null N_j is a traditional null with additional information about its value being shared with other nulls.

Similarity between two instances can be measured by searching for a mapping that connects tuples from one instance with tuples from another instance, so that after applying the mapping (used to merge information between the two instances) the number of missing values and tuples without a pairing with the other instance is as low as possible.

Example 1. Table 1 shows an example for two different instances with labelled nulls N_1, N_2, N_3 with information about vehicles; the instances I and I' are being referred to as the *left* and *right* instance respectively. We can create tuple pairs for matching tuples of the two instances, such as: $t_1 \rightarrow t_4, t_2 \rightarrow t_5, t_3 \rightarrow t_6$. If instance I had another tuple $t_7 = \langle 2016, \text{Audi}, \mathit{Gray} \rangle$, then it would ambiguous whether N_3 should be mapped to 2021 or 2016, because of an additionally possible tuple pair $t_7 \rightarrow t_6$.

Table 1. Exemplary instances I, I'

Instance I

	Year	Manufacturer	Colour
t_1	2016	N_2	Red
t_2	2014	N_2	Black
t_3	2021	Audi	Gray

Instance I'

	Year	Manufacturer	Colour
t_4	N_1	Ford	Red
t_5	2014	Ford	Black
t_6	N_3	Audi	Gray

Assuming that I is the main (left) database instance, for which the data quality should be enhanced by taking information from another instance I' into account, we can define two types of mappings, namely *functional* and *non-functional*. Functional mappings are either left or fully injective, and non-functional mappings are either right injective (only) or right (left) total. Thus according to [12], relationships between two instances have different properties:

- *left injective:* for all $t \in I$, there is only one tuple in I' being paired with t.
- *right injective:* for all $t \in I'$, there is only one tuple in I being paired with t.
- *fully injective:* a mapping m between I, I' being both left and right injective.
- *right (left) total:* a mapping m between I, I' being right (left) surjective.

3.2 Instance Comparison

As proposed in [12], similarity of two instances should result in a normalised score so that $0 \leq \text{similarity}(I, I') \leq 1$ and the measure should be symmetric, so that $\text{similarity}(I, I') = \text{similarity}(I', I)$, but for left injective, right injective, or right (left) total instance relationships, the similarity should result in a value less than 1. Thus, an *instance match* $M = (h_l, h_r, m)$ is defined, consisting of

- *value mappings* as defined above with the special cases h_l (mapping the left instance I) and h_r (mapping the right instance I')
- *tuple mappings* m that specify the pairs of tuples from I, I' that should be matched with each other as a subset $m \subset I \times I'$, but only if I, I' share the same relational schema R.

Building such instance matches is actually based on a *compatibility checking* phase [12]. First, compatible tuple pairs are formed, i.e., pairs for which matching value mappings can be constructed. These pairs are then combined in all possible combinations to form *candidates* for instance mappings. A score is calculated for each combination, and the best instance assignment is selected. Finally, a check is performed to determine whether one of these candidate assignments actually represents a complete and consistent mapping by extending the value mappings step by step such that $h_r(t) = h_r(t')$ for every $(t, t') \in m$.

Based on an instance match $M = (h_l, h_r, m)$, [12] propose a scoring mechanism for the similarity of two instances that calculates an average score for all cells in I, I'. The size of an instance $size(I)$ is defined by the total number of cells in an instance, given by $|I| \cdot arity(R)$. Respectively, $size(m(t))$ is the number of pairings in which a tuple t occurs for a given tuple mapping m, given by $|\{t_m \mid (t, t_m) \in m\}|$. The score of a single cell $score(M, t, t', A)$ is calculated for an attribute A (from relation schema R and hence shared by I and I') based on a tuple pair and the corresponding value mappings of the instance match; there are different scenarios for comparing specific cell values of two tuples. For example, the value mappings of the two values could be conflicting, which should result in the lowest possible score (0). This ensures that, among other things, tuples with conflicting constants are decreasing similarity as much as possible. Another example would be two constants that have the same value, which should result in the highest possible score (1), since they are a perfect match; more precisely, [12] introduces four distinct cases for which the scoring has to be calculated differently each time, namely

$$score(M,t,t',A) = \begin{cases} 0 & \text{if } \; h_l(t.A) \neq h_r(t'.A) \\ 1 & \text{if } \; t.A, t'.A \in \text{Consts} \wedge t.A = t'.A \\ \frac{2}{\sqcap(t.A,t'.A)} & \text{if } \; t.A, t'.A \in \text{Vars} \wedge h_l(t.A) = h_r(t'.A) \\ \frac{2\times\lambda}{\sqcap(t.A,t'.A)} & \text{otherwise, with } \; h_l(t.A) = h_r(t'.A) \end{cases} \tag{1}$$

λ is a penalty parameter for mapping a variable to a constant and should be chosen as $0 \leq \lambda < 1$, and the function $\sqcap$ penalises non-injectivity, by counting the number of variables that are mapped to the same value. More specifically, for any value, the degree of non-injectivity can be calculated by

$$\sqcap(v) = \begin{cases} 1 & \text{if } \; v \in \text{Consts} \\ |\{v' \mid h_l(v') = h_l(v)\}| & \text{if } \; v \in \text{Vars}(I) \\ |\{v' \mid h_r(v') = h_r(v)\}| & \text{if } \; v \in \text{Vars}(I') \end{cases} \tag{2}$$

In sum, the score for an instance match M is then defined as

$$\begin{aligned} score(M) &= \frac{\sum_{t\in I} score(M,t) + \sum_{t'\in I'} score(M,t')}{size(I) + size(I')} \\ \text{with} \quad score(M,t) &= \frac{\sum_{(t,t')\in m(t)} score(M,t,t')}{size(m(t))} \\ \text{and} \quad score(M,t,t') &= \sum_{A\in R} score(M,t,t',A) \end{aligned} \tag{3}$$

The so-called exact algorithm is essentially a brute force method to identify a set $\mathcal{M}$ of all possible instance matches and returning only the best instance match out of the set, which is given by $\max_{M\in\mathcal{M}}(score(M))$. The so-called signature algorithm is a scalable approximation algorithm that delivers reasonably good results with a much better performance than the exact algorithm. The main idea is to reduce the search space for any tuple by building a hash table that can be indexed with the signature of a tuple and returns a set of tuple IDs for tuples in another instance with the same signature.

Definition 1. *The signature $\mathcal{S}[t,A]$ of a tuple, with A being a set of attributes, is defined by $[A_1 : v_1, ..., A_i : v_i]$ where $i \in \{1,...,k\}$, $t.A_i \in$ Consts, and all attributes $A_i, ..., A_k$ appear in lexicographic order. Further, $\mathcal{S}_{max}[t]$ is the signature of a tuple that contains all constants given by $A_{max,t} = \{A \mid t[A] \in Consts\}$.*

For example, $\mathcal{S}_{max}[t_1]$ of tuple t_1 in Table 1 is [Colour : *Red*, Year : 2016].

3.3 Locality-Sensitive Hashing

Locality sensitive hashing (LSH) is a probabilistic technique designed to speed up similarity searches in high-dimensional spaces, known as approximate nearest neighbour search (ANN), by mapping similar data points to the same "buckets" with high probability [13]. Hence, LSH is a powerful methodology that probabilistically groups similar items into the same buckets, thereby reducing the computational overhead associated with exhaustive pairwise comparisons.

Definition. As defined per [7], a common LSH implementation based on p-stable distributions and Euclidean norms uses a family of hash functions that ensure similar items are more likely to collide in the same hash bucket by using random projections. Formally, an LSH family $H = \{hash : S \rightarrow U\}$ is said to be (r_1, r_2, p_1, p_2)-sensitive with respect to a distance metric D if it satisfies the following conditions for any two points $v, q \in S$ (where $B(q, r)$ denotes the set of points within r from q):

$$\begin{array}{llll} \text{if} & v \in B(q, r_1) & \text{then} & Pr[hash(q) = hash(v)] \geq p_1 \\ \text{if} & v \notin B(q, r_2) & \text{then} & Pr[hash(q) = hash(v)] \leq p_2 \end{array} \tag{4}$$

and it is required that $p_1 > p_2$ and $r_1 < r_2$ to ensure that the hashing mechanism effectively separates similar and dissimilar points. H can be used to solve the (r, c')-NN problem where $r_1 = r$ and $r_2 = c'r$ so that data-points with distances less than r_1 collide with probability of at least p_1 and data-points with distances greater than r_2 collide with probability of at most p_2. When a is a d-dimensional random vector that can be derived from the p-stable distribution, b is a random real number chosen uniformly from $[0, w]$, and w is a specified value, then the hash functions themselves can be of the form

$$hash_{a,b}(v) = \left\lfloor \frac{a \cdot v + b}{w} \right\rfloor \tag{5}$$

The LSH approach constructs multiple hash functions and combines them into a composite hash function (bucket) $g(v) = (hash_1(v), hash_2(v), ..., hash_k(v))$, which reduces the probability of collisions among dissimilar data points while ensuring that similar points remain in the same buckets. The hashed value of each source record v, $hash_i(v)$ with $1 \leq i \leq k$, is stored in a bucket $g_j(v)$ with $1 \leq j \leq L$. The result of this in practice are L hash tables that are indexed by the set of unique combined hash values $g(v)$, which are each pointing at a bucket that stores a set of indices for tuples in an instance, proposing that those tuples are similar to each other. However, in a refining final phase of the algorithm, distance metrics are used to identify false positives in a bucket, meaning that the tuples returned from the querying phase are being validated against the tuple that was used for querying by measuring the distance between them and sorting those out that are too far away from the querying tuple.

Parameters. The parameters k and L properly determine how much noise will be in the buckets created by LSH: k determines the length of the hashed value (i.e. uniqueness), and L as the number of hash tables determines the granularity (i.e. level of randomness) in hash buckets. Thus, lower values for k and higher values of L increase the probability to match objects that are further away from each other [16]. Formally, assume a user-defined recall δ, a maximum allowed distance R, and the collision probability p in dependence of c and w by

$$p(c) = \int_0^w \frac{1}{c} f(\frac{t}{c})(1 - \frac{t}{w})\, dt \tag{6}$$

where c is the distance between two vectors defined as $c = \| v_1 - v_2 \|_p$, e.g. the Euclidean distance, and $f(\cdot)$ is the probability density function for $N(\mu = 0, \sigma = 1)$ – then the values for k and L can be estimated as the smallest possible values so that the following condition holds:

$$1 - (1 - p^k(R))^L \geq 1 - \delta \tag{7}$$

Moreover, [7] has experimentally shown with synthetic data, that a value of $w = 4$ is usually good enough for most cases. More specifically, it is known that w should be chosen so that the ratio $\rho = \frac{\ln 1/p_1}{\ln 1/p_2}$ is as small as possible. Semantically, w is very important for the uniqueness of the created hash values and it depends on various circumstances, such as the hash function or dimension and complexity of the data. The effect of the hash function depends on both the input vectors and the function itself, and for the purpose of this paper, there are two different selected hash functions depending on the algorithm, namely for the DHHash Algorithm the one proposed in the corresponding paper [6] that builds on top of the fast Johnson-Lindenstrauss transform (FJLT) [1] and otherwise the on in Eq. 5. Suppose there is a vector $v = [1, 0, 0, 1, 0, 1]$ and w is set to 4 as it was recommend in [7]. Following Eq. 5 and setting $k = 5$ for showcase purposes, the result could be the following composite hash value $g(v) = (0, 0, -1, 0, 1)$. It is clearly visible, that this value for w always creates low hash values $hash(v)$ close to zero, which not only reduces individuality of $hash(v)$, but also of composite hash values $g(v)$, making it necessary to increase k in order to not match dissimilar tuples. Since w is the divisor in the hash function, it is known that larger values for w result in lower values for $hash(v)$, which is why if w is reduced to 1 for example, the resulting composite hash value $g(v)$ could look like this: $(2, 1, 3, -3, 2)$. It is clearly visible that now both $hash(v)$ and $g(v)$ are much more individual, which is why lower values for k are possible. This shows that sometimes it might also be useful to adjust w to be greater or smaller than 4, because there is no one-size-fits-all solution. This is especially true if no reasonably low values for k and L can be found. Nevertheless, the processing time of LSH, or rather the compatibility checks based on the set of similar tuples that are calculated for a querying tuple, highly depends on the values of k and L. For smaller k's and larger L's, the set of similar tuples grows large enough to make the approximate nearest neighbour search computationally expensive, similar to a linear search. Usually, it is reasonable to calculate k and L using Eq. 7 with a high recall. Setting parameters k and L will be illustrated with the following small example with a recall value delta specified as $\delta \geq 0.95$ and then adjusting k if the sets of similar tuples is too small or large. Table 2 shows the results of Eq. 7 for various pairs of k and L where the maximum allowed distance R is set to 2 and w is set to 4 as it is proposed by [7]. It is visible that a reasonable value pair considering a recall of 0.95 is found for $k = 4$ and $L = 3$.

Table 2. Exemplary results of Eq. 7 for maximum allowed distance $R = 2$, $w = 4$, and various value pairs of k, L.

L	2			3				4		
k	2	3	4	3	4	5	6	3	4	5
Eq. 7	0.34	0.11	0.03	0.16	0.05	0.02	0.01	0.21	0.07	0.02

4 Methodology

The existing framework from [12] is not suitable for partial instance matches, because all value mappings are defined to leave constants unchanged. We provide in the following the definition of a partial match that is defined by two tuples where at least one of the attributes has two conflicting (different) constants that have a certain similarity; that is their distance is larger than a specified distance threshold D_{max} according to some distance function $Dist$.

Definition 2 (Partial Match). *Let $R_{partial}$ be a subset of schema R that defines all attributes in I where a partial match is tolerable. Two tuples t, t' from I, I' are partially matching, written as $t \sim t'$ iff there is no attribute $A \in R \wedge A \notin R_{partial}$ for which $t.A, t'.A \in Consts$ and $t.A \neq t'.A$, and there is no attribute $A \in R_{partial}$ for which $t.A, t'.A \in Consts$ and $Dist(t.A, t'.A) > D_{max}$.*

For simplicity, any values that fulfil the maximum allowed distance constraint $Dist(v, v') \leq D_{max}$ will be referred to as $v \sim v'$ for the remainder of this paper. Instance matches from Sect. 3.2 are extended to be a sextuple of the form $M = (h_l, h_r, m, cc, im, pm)$ as follows:

Definition 3 (Extended Instance Match). *Let I and I' be two instances over schema R. An instance match is a sextuple $M = (h_l, h_r, m, cc, im, pm)$ where h_l is a value mapping for Vars(I), h_r is a value mapping for Vars(I'), and m, cc, im and pm are tuple mappings (as subsets of $I \times I'$) that are pairwise disjoint (e.g. with $m \cap cc = \emptyset$ etc.) such that*

- *m denotes the tuple pairs for which either one of the tuples or both are incomplete and need to be updated with information from the other tuple.*
- *tuple pairs in cc represent matchings with conflicting constants from $R \setminus R_{partial}$.*
- *tuple pairs in im represent identical matches, where each attribute is a constant and they all equal the respective counterpart in the other tuple.*
- *pm denotes the set of tuples that are only partially matching wrt. $R_{partial}$.*

An instance match M is a complete match iff $\forall(t_1, t_2) \in m : h_l(t_1) = h_r(t_2)$, $\forall(t_1, t_2) \in im : t_1 = t_2$, *and* $\forall(t_1, t_2) \in pm : t_1 \sim t_2$.

Next, the scoring of tuple pairs respective to a specific attribute (Eq. 1) can be adjusted as follows where $d(t.A, t'.A)$ returns a penalty based on a distance *Dist* between $t.A$ and $t'.A$ (potentially after normalization):

Definition 4 (Partial Tuple Pair Cell Score). *Given a distance Dist, the cell score of a partially matching tuple pair is calculated by*

$$score(M, t, t', A) = \begin{cases} 0 & \text{if} \quad h_l(t.A) \nsim h_r(t.A) \\ 1 \times d(t.A, t'.A) & \text{if} \quad t.A, t'.A \in Consts \wedge t.A \sim t'.A \\ \frac{2 \times d(t.A, t'.A)}{\sqcap(t.A, t'.A)} & \text{if} \quad t.A, t'.A \in Vars \wedge h_l(t.A) \sim h_r(t'.A) \\ \frac{2 \times \lambda \times d(t.A, t'.A)}{\sqcap(t.A, t'.A)} & \text{otherwise, with} \quad h_l(t.A) \sim h_r(t'.A) \end{cases} \tag{8}$$

The application of LSH proposes an interesting opportunity, namely the efficient identification of partial instance matches. By adapting the signature algorithm of [12] to incorporate LSH, our approach aims to enhance both the performance and quality of similarity computations, with performance relying on two dimensions, namely memory usage and processing time.

Definition 5 (LSH-Signature of a Tuple). *Given a tuple t over R, the signature of t is the composite hash value of a vector that is derived from a string of the form $[A_{i_1} : v_{i_1}, ..., A_{i_k} : v_{i_k}]$, where for each $j \in 1, ..., k$, A_{i_j} is an attribute of R such that $t[A_{i_j}] \in Consts(I)$. $g(\mathcal{S}^V[t, A_{max}])$ is used to denote the LSH-signature of a tuple t on the set of all attributes, given by $A_{max,t} = \{A \mid t[A] \in Consts(I)\}$.*

In particular, the integration of LSH enables a more efficient retrieval of candidate tuple pairs that are likely to be similar, which accelerates the matching process and improves the overall accuracy of the similarity score estimation.

Since the LSH integrated modification of the signature algorithm is also based on a signature representation of the tuples, the procedure from the original signature algorithm [12] can be adapted as it is seen in Algorithm 1. A single instance match is constructed greedily by starting off with an empty instance match that is iteratively updated as soon as another tuple pair is identified, meaning that the compatibility of later identified tuple pairs highly depends on those that were found earlier in the process. The compatibility checking step (as mentioned in Sect. 3.2) with the function COMPATIBLETUPLES has to be applied as well, because the problem of missing out on those kinds of matches remains, even when LSH is used. For example, tuples $t_1 = \langle N_1, N_2, Red\rangle$ and $t_2 = \langle N_1', Ford, N_2'\rangle$ are compatible (mergeable), but it is not guaranteed that they will end up in the same bucket based on hash similarity obtained by LSH.

Algorithm 3 shows the application of LSH, which is denoted by calculating signatures $g(\mathcal{S}^V[t, A_{max}])$. During the indexing phase, instead of building a SIGMAP out of the n signatures from the left instance, L different hash tables

Algorithm 1: SIGNATURELSH(I, I')

```
   input : Two instances I and I' for the same schema R
   output: An instance match M = (h_l, h_r, m)
1  T_l = I, T_r = I'
2  M ← (h_l, h_r, m) ← ∅
3  FINDSIGMATCHESLSH(T_l, T_r, M)
4  FINDSIGMATCHESLSH(T_r, T_l, M)
5  compatible ← COMPATIBLETUPLES(T_l, T_r)
6  foreach t ∈ T_l do
7      foreach t' ∈ compatible[t] do
8          if ISCOMPATIBLE(t, t', M) then
9              UPDATEINSTANCEMATCH(t, t', M)
10             if right injective then
11                 REMOVE(t', compatible)
12             if left injective then
13                 goto 6
14 return M
```

are constructed using the respective composite hash values $g(\mathcal{S}^V[t, A_{max}])$ for the selected LSH methodology. Afterwards, these L hash tables are queried only once by each tuple of the right instance, which returns a set of potentially similar tuples based on their composite hash values (line 8). Before checking the compatibility of these potential tuple pairs with respect to the instance match, the set of similar tuples is refined by filtering out all tuples that are farther away from the querying tuple than a prior specified distance threshold D_{max} (line 9).

For comparison, Algorithm 2 shows the original version of [12] displayed side-by-side here to illustrate the differences to our LSH-integrated approach. In particular, the querying phase of the original algorithm is more exhaustive, because it creates the power-set of all possible attribute combinations to get an extensive set of potentially similar tuples. In contrast to the signature-based identification approach from the original paper, the LSH integrated approach does not require to construct all signatures based on the power-set of the attributes in a tuple when querying the L hash tables (Algorithm 2, lines 7+8), because the LSH preserved locality does not require exact signature matches between tuples. Due to the (r_1, r_2, p_1, p_2)-sensitivity in Eq. 4, it is known that tuples that do not have the same set of attributes filled with constants will still be matched with high probability, if their signatures are only a distance of r_1 apart. Instead of multiple lookups for a single tuple, only one lookup is performed for which a small set of tuples within r_1 is returned and each has to be validated for compatibility. Additionally, Table 3 is a step-by-step comparison of the different steps in both algorithms and outlines the specific differences including an evaluation of the time complexity for each step.

Table 3. Step-by-step comparison of algorithms including time complexity. ($x \leq arity(R)$, $m \ll n$, $l \ll m$) *Not an independent step, sub-step of Querying

Step	Signature Alg.	LSH integrated Alg.
Indexing	$O(n)$: Populate a single hash table with $\mathcal{S}_{max}$ for all t in T_l	$O(nkL)$: Populate L hash tables with $g(\mathcal{S}^V[t, A_{max}])$ for all t in T_l
Querying	$O(n2^x)$: Generate a power-set of signatures for all t' in T_r and use them to derive a set of similar tuples from the hash table	$O(n)$: Derive a set of similar tuples from L hash tables with $g(\mathcal{S}^V[t', A_{max}])$ for all t' in T_r
Refining*	–	$O(m)$: Refine *similar* by filtering out all tuples that are farther than a maximum distance D_{max} away from t'
Compatibility*	$O(l)$: Validate the compatibility of all similar tuples	$O(l)$: Validate the compatibility of all similar tuples

Algorithm 2: FindMatches(T_l, T_r, M)

```
input : Sets of tuples T_l and T_r and an
        instance match M = (h_l, h_r, m)
// Indexing Phase
SIGMAP ← ∅
foreach t ∈ T_l do
    SIGMAP[S_max[t]] ←
      SIGMAP[S_max[t]] ∪ {t}

// Querying Phase
foreach t' ∈ T_r do
    A_ground = {A|t'[A] ∈ Consts}
    foreach A ∈ P(A_ground) do

        // Compatibility Phase
        foreach t ∈ SIGMAP[S[t, A]] do
            if IsCompatible(t, t', M)
              then
                UpdateInstMatch(t, t', M)
                if left injective then
                    Remove(t, SIGMAP)
                    Remove(t, T_l)
                if right injective then
                    Remove(t', T_r)
                    goto 6
```

Algorithm 3: FindMatchesLsh(T_l, T_r, M)

```
input : Sets of tuples T_l and T_r and an
        instance match M = (h_l, h_r, m)
// Indexing Phase
HASHTABLE_1..L ← ∅
foreach t ∈ T_l do
    foreach l ∈ [1, L] do
        HASHTABLE_l[g(S^V_max[t])] ←
          HASHTABLE_l[g(S^V_max[t])] ∪ {t}
// Querying Phase
foreach t' ∈ T_r do
    similar ← ∅
    foreach l ∈ [1, L] do
        similar ← similar ∪
          HASHTABLE_l[g(S^V_max[t'])]
    // Refinement Phase
    similar ← {t | Dist(t, t') ≤ D_max}
    // Compatibility Phase
    foreach t ∈ similar do
        if IsCompatible(t, t', M) then
            UpdateInstMatch(t, t', M)
            if left injective then
                Remove(t, HASHTABLE_1..L)
                Remove(t, T_l)
            if right injective then
                Remove(t', T_r)
                goto 5
```

5 Experimental Comparison

5.1 Data Sets

To answer the question if an LSH integrated approach for the signature algorithm is feasible, the algorithms and various configurations are tested on datasets that differ in complexity. Three of them are split into smaller sets of 1k, 10k, and 25k tuples to further vary the dimensionality and get extensive insights. The vehicle dataset (denoted D1) is the one with the least complexity, because it has highly categorical variables with only few value expressions for each, such as vehicle colour or fuel type for example. The job descriptions dataset (denoted as D2) is of medium complexity in comparison to the other two and can thus be seen as a hybrid version of the two extremer use cases. The supply chain dataset (denoted as D3) however is much more complex, because it has double the attributes and the range of value expressions for some of them is quite large as well. For example, it includes first and last names of customers that have placed an order, but there are only a few customers and each of them appear multiple times.

The datasets that the algorithms are being tested on are all derived from the openly available data science platform kaggle.com and selected so that a rather high variety of data complexity is covered by the experiments. Table 4 shows the three datasets as well as the three subsets and additional information about each of them. The complexity of a dataset is calculated by $\frac{1}{col}\sum_{i=1}^{col}\frac{U_i}{row}$ where col is the number of attributes/ columns, row is the number of tuples/ rows, and U_i is the number of unique values for the i-th attribute. Essentially, this returns the average uniqueness of attribute spaces in a dataset.

Table 4. List of datasets and their dimensionality/complexity.

	Dataset	#Rows	#Cols	Complexity
D1	Vehicles	1k	10	0.043
	Vehicles	10k	10	0.006
	Vehicles	25k	10	0.002
D2	Job Descriptions	1k	12	0.216
	Job Descriptions	10k	12	0.027
	Job Descriptions	25k	12	0.011
D3	Supply Chain	1k	20	0.149
	Supply Chain	10k	20	0.047
	Supply Chain	25k	20	0.023

5.2 Implementation

All implementations are done using Python[1]. The purpose of approximation algorithms such as the signature algorithm from [12] is to maintain quality of results while also significantly enhancing computational efficiency, which can be measured using both memory usage and processing time. As our baseline functions like SIGNATURE, FINDSIGMATCHES, and COMPATIBLETUPLES were implemented in conformity with algorithm 2, 3, and 4 as shown in [12]. The ground truth for validating results is calculated by starting off with complete datasets that are then randomly manipulated to create incomplete database information. To achieve this, the same methodology from the original paper is being used. Given a complete dataset, an incomplete left and right instance are created by randomly modifying a defined percentage of cells, e.g. 5%, where the probability of changing a constant to another constant or replacing it with a labelled null is 50% for each.

We introduce three LSH modified versions of the signature algorithm. The first version will be the classical implementation of LSH for p-stable distributions as it is outlined in [7], which can be seen as a baseline of what LSH theoretically can achieve. The second version will be a modification of the classic LSH methodology, namely ILSS [20], to specifically account for reduced memory usage, which is done by compressing the input vectors using a grouping technique so that the algorithm is able to store only smaller sized vectors. In addition, this also comes with a more efficient processing time. The third version will leverage the DHHash algorithm presented in [6]. This method is interesting because the authors present a provable and practical alternative that is able to improve processing time by significant amounts: in practice there is an average improvement of 20% experimentally achieved. Furthermore, the classic and DHHash approach allow the use of dense vectors for which it is interesting to see if there is a notable difference of results in comparison to the usage of sparse vector presentations.

To allow for a versatile application of Eq. 5, LSH requires numerical vector data on which the hash functions can be applied. When working with textual data, this arises some challenges, especially if it is non-categorical. In the field of Natural Language Processing (NLP), there are many known techniques for vectorization of textual data such as One-Hot encoding [18] or Term Frequency-Inverse Document Frequency (TF-IDF) [5]. Since these techniques produce vectors that are often sparse and grow with the dimensionality of the data and value space, they might not be feasible enough to capture the true nature of tuples' signatures that is given by the semantic context. Recent progress in NLP with the availability of pre-trained deep learning language models such as the BERT language model [8] propose opportunities for creating dense vectors out of textual data that also capture the semantics of the content. We applied these three options to identifying similar tuples in incomplete database instances when working with textual signature representations of tuples.

---

[1] The implemented code can be found on GitHub: https://github.com/Tim-Schwabe/lsh-master.

5.3 Results

For each experiment there are three different metrics that are being measured; all experiments are executed on a computer with an Intel i7-6700@3.40GHz and 16GB RAM. The first and most important one is the similarity score (maximal $score(M)$) from the original paper (see Table 5). Well performing algorithm configurations should achieve similarity scores that are close to or even better than the one from the signature algorithm. The second metric is the processing time for which the most significant differences and advancements are expected (see Table 6). Lastly, the memory usage will be captured to address potential problems for scalability (Table 7). The results shown in this section show the superiority of the LSH integrated approach over the signature algorithm from the original paper since the same or even better quality levels are often reached in much less time, though this is usually only possible at cost of memory usage.

Most importantly, experiments with the DHHash algorithm could not be executed for the supply chain dataset (D3) using the One-Hot or TF-IDF encoding technique due to its high inefficiency that caused to reach timeouts of over five hours. Similarly, the signature algorithm reached timeouts as well and could not be executed for the supply chain dataset of sizes 10k and 25k, probably because of an exhaustive power-set search that is caused by the high dimension and complexity of the dataset.

Table 5. Experimental results for the similarity scores of all algorithm configurations. C= Classic LSH, I = ILSS, D = DHHash, OH = One-Hot, TF = TF-IDF, BE = BERT model, GT= ground truth, Sig=signature

Dataset	GT	Sig.	C OH	C TF	C BE	I OH	D OH	D TF	D BE
D1, 1k	0.718	0.718	0.717	0.718	0.718	0.717	0.718	0.718	0.717
D1, 10k	0.714	0.711	0.706	0.712	0.711	0.708	0.707	0.707	0.710
D1, 25k	0.714	0.697	0.703	0.705	0.703	0.674	0.677	0.701	0.703
D2, 1k	0.576	0.576	0.576	0.576	0.576	0.576	0.576	0.576	0.576
D2, 10k	0.575	0.575	0.575	0.575	0.575	0.575	0.575	0.575	0.575
D2, 25k	0.580	0.580	0.580	0.580	0.580	0.580	0.580	0.580	0.580
D3, 1k	0.442	0.442	0.442	0.442	0.442	0.442	–	–	0.442
D3, 10k	0.480	–	0.480	0.480	0.480	0.480	–	–	0.480
D3, 25k	0.464	–	0.464	0.464	0.464	0.464	–	–	0.464

The most noticeable result in Table 5 is that for the more complex datasets, namely job descriptions (D2) and supply chain (D3), all of the algorithms, regardless of leveraging the LSH methodology or not, achieve to reach the same similarity score as the ground truth. Only for the less complex vehicle dataset (D1) there are a few variations for the similarity score, which could be a result of a higher level of tuple uniqueness for more complex datasets and vice versa.

Table 6. Experimental results for the processing times of all algorithm configuration. The time is measured in seconds.

Dataset	Sig.	C OH	C TF	C BE	I OH	D OH	D TF	D BE
D1, 1k	18	7	8	27	11	10	10	32
D1, 10k	916	528	542	778	609	664	596	870
D1, 25k	5735	4314	3746	4522	4501	3963	3905	5710
D2, 1k	44	7	8	41	21	120	115	43
D2, 10k	1067	443	493	844	602	1789	1916	901
D2, 25k	5521	2800	3118	3883	3170	5118	5423	4462
D3, 1k	17581	8	9	69	31	–	–	71
D3, 10k	–	553	681	2609	1282	–	–	3444
D3, 25k	–	3459	3892	5110	5914	–	–	5343

The processing times in Table 6 show a clear superiority of almost all LSH integrations over the signature algorithm. The signature algorithm usually takes twice the processing time of the best performing LSH integration and especially for the more complex datasets, the differences in processing times of the signature algorithms grow even further to six or even more than 1,000 times as much in case of the smaller datasets with 1k tuples. Notably, DHHash, even though promising theoretical improvements in efficiency, usually has one of the longest processing times across all algorithms and matches or even exceeds the processing time of the signature algorithm for D2, though the relative time difference between the LSH algorithms decreases as the data size increases. ILSS is mostly not more efficient than the classic LSH approach, even though some improvements in efficiency were theoretically expected due to smaller vector sizes.

Table 7. Experimental results for the memory usage of all algorithm configuration. The used memory is measured in MB.

Dataset	Sig.	C OH	C TF	C BE	I OH	D OH	D TF	D BE
D1, 1k	2	10	10	12	3	20	20	23
D1, 10k	13	119	119	53	32	159	159	60
D1, 25k	31	304	304	120	78	340	340	123
D2, 1k	3	30	30	13	6	205	205	23
D2, 10k	15	345	345	55	62	1045	1045	62
D2, 25k	36	861	861	126	155	1556	1556	129
D3, 1k	281	49	49	13	9	–	–	24
D3, 10k	–	1371	1372	61	198	–	–	68
D3, 25k	–	4152	4154	141	585	–	–	144

Finally, Table 7 shows the results for the maximum required memory usage during runtime of the experiments in MB. Against the expectations, the ILSS algorithm does not always use significantly less memory in comparison to the other LSH integrated approaches. For larger and more complex datasets such as D2 and D3, the algorithms that use the BERT model for vectorization require less memory than ILSS. This is because the BERT model returns vectors of fixed sizes that are often only a few hundred entries long, and the ILSS algorithm uses the One-Hot encoded vectors as a baseline. Consequently, algorithm configurations that are using the One-Hot or TF-IDF vectorization technique are by far the worst algorithms when it comes to memory usage; however, those are the ones that perform best from a processing time perspective. Lastly, it should be mentioned that the signature algorithm almost always is the most efficient algorithm in terms of memory usage, except for the most complex dataset D3.

6 Conclusion

The existing framework [12] is targeted at categorical data and does not allow partial mappings with conflicting constants, because the search space would drastically increase considering the approach of the signature algorithm that uses power-sets of all constants in a tuple. In constrast, in our approach the hashing nature of LSH combined with distance measurements enables partial instance matches based on near-duplicates where textual data, such as e-mail addresses for example, differs slightly due to human error or other reasons.

Our approach showed that there is a significant advantage of using an LSH-integrated method for similarity measures of incomplete database instances as opposed to the signature algorithm of [12], because not only was the same level of similarity score quality reached with significant gains in computational efficiency, but also the applicability for identifying partial instance matches has been experimentally confirmed. More specifically, it was shown that the classical implementation of LSH is the most appropriate one among the three selected for this paper and while the BERT model for vectorization might help with the quality of results, the One-Hot or TF-IDF vectorization techniques are significantly better overall due to the extended computational efforts of the BERT model. Consequently and due to minor successes of TF-IDF over One-Hot, the algorithm configuration Classic TF-IDF is determined to be the overall best for measuring similarity of incomplete database instances.

Assigning unique labels to nulls makes the framework applicable to the usage of standard nulls in SQL (without label-wise equality conditions) but could reduce matching quality by removing equality dependencies among tuples; the experimental validation regarding the quality loss in realistic use cases will be one topic of future work. Another extension can be the analysis of taxonomy-based similarity [19] in combination with the similarity matching framework. Furthermore, the difficulty of setting parameters k, L, and w in terms of computational efforts raises the question whether there are different approximate nearest neighbour algorithms that are simpler to configure and still improve the results just like LSH. This might be useful for practical day-to-day applications of the framework of this paper.

Disclosure of Interests. The authors have no competing interests to declare that are relevant to the content of this article.

References

1. Ailon, N., Chazelle, B.: The fast johnson–lindenstrauss transform and approximate nearest neighbors. SIAM J. Comput. **39**(1), 302–322 (2009). https://doi.org/10.1137/060673096
2. Beckmann, N., Kriegel, H.P., Schneider, R., Seeger, B.: The r*-tree: an efficient and robust access method for points and rectangles. SIGMOD Rec. **19**(2), 322–331 (1990). https://doi.org/10.1145/93605.98741
3. Bertossi, L.: Specifying and computing causes for query answers in databases via database repairs and repair-programs. Knowl. Inf. Syst. **63**(1), 199–231 (2021)
4. Bhattacherjee, S., Chavan, A., Huang, S., Deshpande, A., Parameswaran, A.: Principles of dataset versioning: exploring the recreation/storage tradeoff. In: Proceedings of the VLDB Endowment. International Conference on Very Large Data Bases, vol. 8, p. 1346 (2015)
5. Dalavi, S., Nivelkar, T., Patil, S., Sawant, A., Aylani, A.: Comparative analysis of vectorization techniques and machine learning models for hate speech detection. In: 2023 Global Conference on Information Technologies and Communications (GCITC), pp. 1–5 (2023). https://doi.org/10.1109/GCITC60406.2023.10426214
6. Dasgupta, A., Kumar, R., Sarlos, T.: Fast locality-sensitive hashing. In: Proceedings of the 17th ACM SIGKDD International Conference on Knowledge Discovery and Data Mining, KDD 2011, pp. 1073–1081. ACM, New York, NY, USA (2011). https://doi.org/10.1145/2020408.2020578
7. Datar, M., Immorlica, N., Indyk, P., Mirrokni, V.S.: Locality-sensitive hashing scheme based on p-stable distributions. In: Proceedings of the Twentieth Annual Symposium on Computational Geometry, SCG 2004, pp. 253–262. ACM, New York, NY, USA (2004). https://doi.org/10.1145/997817.997857
8. Devlin, J., Chang, M.W., Lee, K., Toutanova, K.: BERT: pre-training of deep bidirectional transformers for language understanding. In: Burstein, J., Doran, C., Solorio, T. (eds.) Proceedings of the 2019 Conference of the North American Chapter of the Association for Computational Linguistics: Human Language Technologies, Volume 1 (Long and Short Papers), pp. 4171–4186. Association for Computational Linguistics, Minneapolis, Minnesota, June 2019. https://doi.org/10.18653/v1/N19-1423, https://aclanthology.org/N19-1423/
9. Fagin, R., Kolaitis, P.G., Miller, R.J., Popa, L.: Data exchange: semantics and query answering. Theoret. Comput. Sci. **336**(1), 89–124 (2005)
10. Farid, M., Roatis, A., Ilyas, I.F., Hoffmann, H.F., Chu, X.: Clams: bringing quality to data lakes. In: Proceedings of the 2016 International Conference on Management of Data, SIGMOD 2016, pp. 2089–2092. ACM, New York, NY, USA (2016). https://doi.org/10.1145/2882903.2899391
11. Fernandes, N., Kawamoto, Y., Murakami, T.: Locality sensitive hashing with extended differential privacy. In: Bertino, E., Shulman, H., Waidner, M. (eds.) ESORICS 2021. LNCS, vol. 12973, pp. 563–583. Springer, Cham (2021). https://doi.org/10.1007/978-3-030-88428-4_28

12. Glavic, B., Mecca, G., Miller, R.J., Papotti, P., Santoro, D., Veltri, E.: Similarity measures for incomplete database instances. In: CEUR (ed.) EDBT 2024, 27th International Conference on Extending Database Technology, 25–28 March 2024, Paestum, Italy. Paestum (2024), cEUR
13. Leskovec, J., Rajaraman, A., Ullman, J.: Mining of massive datasets, 01 2020. https://doi.org/10.1017/9781108684163
14. Livshits, E., Kochirgan, R., Tsur, S., Ilyas, I.F., Kimelfeld, B., Roy, S.: Properties of inconsistency measures for databases. In: Proceedings of the 2021 International Conference on Management of Data, pp. 1182–1194 (2021)
15. Lu, Y., Cao, C., Zhang, Y., Zhang, Y.: Learnable locality-sensitive hashing for video anomaly detection. IEEE Trans. Circuits Syst. Video Technol. **33**(2), 963–976 (2023). https://doi.org/10.1109/TCSVT.2022.3205348
16. Matei, B., et al.: Rapid object indexing using locality sensitive hashing and joint 3d-signature space estimation. IEEE Trans. Pattern Anal. Mach. Intell. **28**, 1111–26 (2006). https://doi.org/10.1109/TPAMI.2006.148
17. Miao, S., Lu, Z., Liu, M., Duarte, J., Li, P.: Locality-sensitive hashing-based efficient point transformer with applications in high-energy physics (2024), https://arxiv.org/abs/2402.12535
18. Poslavskaya, E., Korolev, A.: Encoding categorical data: is there yet anything 'hotter' than one-hot encoding? (2023), https://arxiv.org/abs/2312.16930
19. Schäfer, J.M., Wiese, L.: A comparison of two database partitioning approaches that support taxonomy-based query answering. In: Proceedings of the 22nd International Conference on Information Integration and Web-based Applications & Services, pp. 426–435 (2020)
20. Shen, H., Li, T., Li, Z., Ching, F.: Locality sensitive hashing based searching scheme for a massive database. In: IEEE SoutheastCon 2008, pp. 123–128 (2008). https://doi.org/10.1109/SECON.2008.4494271
21. Tian, Y., Zhao, X., Zhou, X.: Db-lsh 2.0: locality-sensitive hashing with query-based dynamic bucketing. IEEE Trans. Knowl. Data Eng. **36**(3), 1000–1015 (2024). https://doi.org/10.1109/TKDE.2023.3295831
22. Toussaint, E., Guagliardo, P., Libkin, L., Sequeda, J.: Troubles with nulls, views from the users. Proc. VLDB Endowment **15**(11), 2613–2625 (2022)
23. Wei, R., Kerschbaum, F.: Cryptographically secure private record linkage using locality-sensitive hashing. Proc. VLDB Endow. **17**(2), 79–91 (2023). https://doi.org/10.14778/3626292.3626293

Analyzing the Behavior of Database Applications Through Size Descriptions

Jan Van den Bussche[1] and Emmanuel Waller[2(✉)]

[1] Data Science Institute, Hasselt University, Hasselt, Belgium
jan.vandenbussche@uhasselt.be

[2] LISN, Paris-Saclay University, Gif-sur-Yvette, France
waller@lisn.fr

Abstract. We propose a description language capturing a simple but central aspect of the possible "lives" (the behavior) of a database application, namely the ability for the relations to grow, shrink, or keep the same size. We first consider arbitrary behaviors and investigate the basic properties of such descriptions. We characterize consistency, redundancy, and subsumption, and show that every behavior has a unique minimal complete description. We then consider the problem of computing the minimal complete description of a given database application. We model such applications as collections of procedures, specified by update programs based on relational algebra. The general problem is undecidable, even for an application consisting of a single procedure with a single update language statement. We also identify decidable cases and provide partial complexity characterisations.

Keywords: Dynamics of information · Static analysis of update programs

1 Introduction

The analysis of database evolution is an important area of research [6]. Since the database reflects the relevant processes that take place in a business or enterprise, a good description of how the database evolves provides valuable information to the business analyst. Standard approaches use various forms of temporal logic to express properties of database evolutions, e.g., [1,7,8,11]. In the present paper, we explore an alternative approach, which is more coarse-grained and is focused on the size changes of the tables in the database.

Indeed, our hypothesis is that information about which tables grow, shrink, or keep the same size already provides useful information on the behavior of various business processes. An information system is typically organized as a collection of related entities; data about the entities and their relationships is stored in various tables [10]. Each entity has a lifecycle. When the entity is created, this is reflected in the growth of one or more entity tables. Relationships between entities will be created, which is again reflected in the growth of the

A.-Y. Turhan and J. Virtema (Eds.): FoIKS 2026, LNCS 16475, pp. 195–210, 2026.
https://doi.org/10.1007/978-3-032-21540-6_12

corresponding tables. Similarly, relationships that end cause certain tables to shrink. For example, on booking.com, customers and properties are entities, and customers booking certain properties are relationships. When detailed attributes of entities or relationships are updated, this typically only modifies the entries of a table row and will reflect as the table keeping its size. Finally, entities may be withdrawn, again reflected as a shrink in a table.

In this paper, we begin by developing a general theory of size descriptions. We consider arbitrary evolutions of database states, which we call database lives. We introduce a description language where formulas express how the sizes of tables change in the transitions between successive states in a life. We investigate the basic properties of descriptions, providing characterizations of consistency, redundancy, and subsumption. We introduce the general notion of *behavior* as a (possibly infinite) set of lives. In our framework, every behavior will turn out to have a unique minimal complete description.

In the second part of this paper, we investigate the problem of automatically deriving the minimal complete description of the behavior of database applications. We introduce a formal model of real-life database applications, where database queries and updates are embedded in imperative code. We formalize queries using relational algebra, and model SQL updates (insert, delete, update) using the formalism of update programs already proposed in our earlier work with Ameloot [4].[1] The novel feature of our model is that it has explicit notions of *procedures*, written in the language of update programs, and *procedure calls* with parameters. A similar model of embedded SQL was proposed by Itzhaky et al. [9], not with our focus on analyzing the lives of an application, but rather for the purpose of verifying individual programs by inferring weakest preconditions.

Since our model allows arbitrary relational algebra expressions as queries, it is not unexpected that the general problem of inferring the minimal complete description of a given application is undecidable. Still, our description language is novel, and we aim to delinate the boundary of undecidability. Thereto we need to develop original proof techniques that establish connections between various forms of satisfiability, various update operations, and various size-change primitives. Moreover, we will also identify cases where the problem is decidable.

To our knowledge, this work is the first to analyze database evolutions through the lens of size changes. Hence, this paper opens many directions for further research. These are discussed in the conclusion.

This paper is organized as follows. Section 2 establishes some basic terminology and notation. Section 3 introduces our description language and develops the general theory. Section 4 introduces the formal model of database applications. Section 5 presents decidability and undecidability results on inferring minimal complete descriptions of applications. Section 6 concludes. Proofs are omitted due to space limitations.

[1] Seminal work on update and transaction languages was done by Abiteboul and Vianu [3].

2 Preliminaries

We recall some basic notions and terminology from the theory of relational databases [2]. From the outset we assume a countably infinite universe **dom** of data elements. For a natural number k, a k-ary *relation* is a finite subset of $\mathbf{dom} \times \cdots \times \mathbf{dom}$ (k times), or, in other words, a finite set of k-tuples of data elements.

A *database schema* is a nonempty finite set $\mathbf{S}$ of *relation names* where every relation name has an associated arity (a natural number). An *instance* I of $\mathbf{S}$ is an assignment of a relation $I(R)$ to every relation name $R \in \mathbf{S}$, so that if R has arity k then $I(R)$ is k-ary. The set of all elements from **dom** occurring in I is called the *active domain* of I and denoted by $adom(I)$.

Remark 1. In the general framework, arities will not play a role, but they will play a role in our investigation of database applications.

3 General Theory of Size Descriptions

3.1 Database Lives

Let $\mathbf{S}$ be a schema. A *database life* over $\mathbf{S}$ (or *life* for short) is a finite sequence of at least two instances of $\mathbf{S}$, starting with the empty instance (i.e., the instance where all relations are empty).

An ordered pair (I, I') of instances (of the same schema), also written simply as I, I', is called a *transition*. If I and I' occur consecutively in a life l, we say that the transition *occurs in* l.

Remark 2. One may wonder why we insist that a life starts with the empty instance. Our goal is to model database evolutions which are typically governed by an application. (We will formalize applications later in this paper.) Every such application will start with a "filling" stage providing an initial operational state of the database. Our assumption that a life starts with the empty instance is equivalent to assuming that the filling process is part of the application. Even when the initial state is imported from somewhere else, it is reasonable to assume that it is semantically coherent, i.e., it could have been generated by the filling process.

3.2 Descriptions

Let $\mathbf{S}$ be a schema. A *size primitive* over $\mathbf{S}$ (or *primitive* for short) is a term of the form $R^{\nearrow}$, $R^{\searrow}$, or $R^{=}$, with R a relation name in $\mathbf{S}$. These primitives are referred to as *grow*, *shrink*, and *same-size*, respectively. A transition I, I' *satisfies* a primitive p, denoted by $I, I' \models p$, in the following cases:

- $p = R^{\nearrow}$ and $|I(R)| < |I'(R)|$;
- $p = R^{\searrow}$ and $|I(R)| > |I'(R)|$;
- $p = R^{=}$ and $|I(R)| = |I'(R)|$.

Here, given any set X, we denote by $|X|$ the *size* of X, i.e., the number of its elements.

A *formula* over $\mathbf{S}$ is a set of primitives over $\mathbf{S}$ containing, for every relation name R in $\mathbf{S}$, exactly one primitive.

Example 1. Over a schema consisting of two relation names R and S, all possible formulas are $\{R^{\nearrow}, S^{\nearrow}\}$; $\{R^{\nearrow}, S^{\searrow}\}$; $\{R^{\nearrow}, S^{=}\}$; $\{R^{\searrow}, S^{\nearrow}\}$; $\{R^{\searrow}, S^{\searrow}\}$; $\{R^{\searrow}, S^{=}\}$; $\{R^{=}, S^{\nearrow}\}$; $\{R^{=}, S^{\searrow}\}$; and $\{R^{=}, S^{=}\}$. □

A transition I, I' *satisfies* a formula F, denoted by $I, I' \models F$, if I, I' satisfies all primitives in F.

Two remarks are in order:

Remark 3. 1. From the above definition, we see that a formula is interpreted as a *conjunction* of primitives.
2. Clearly, every transition satisfies exactly one formula.

Definition 1. *A* description *over* $\mathbf{S}$ *is a set of formulas over* $\mathbf{S}$.

A life l satisfies a description D, denoted by $l \models D$, if every transition in l satisfies some formula in D.

Remark 4. By the above definition, a description is interpreted as a *disjunction* of formulas. For clarity, in examples we will often write descriptions as disjunctions. For example, over a single relation name R, we may write the "tautological" description $\{\{R^{\nearrow}\}, \{R^{\searrow}\}, \{R^{=}\}\}$ as $\{R^{\nearrow}\} \vee \{R^{\searrow}\} \vee \{R^{=}\}$. We can then also write $\{\{R^{=}\}\}$ simply as $\{R^{=}\}$.

Definition 2. *The set of all lives satisfying a given description D is denoted by $lives(D)$.*

3.3 Fundamental Properties of Descriptions

In the following we assume some fixed arbitrary schema $\mathbf{S}$ is given.

Consistency

Definition 3. *A description D is called* consistent *if $lives(D)$ is not empty.*

Example 2. A simple example of an inconsistent description, over a single relation name R, has only the formula $\{R^{\searrow}\}$. Indeed, any life starts with the empty instance, and no transition can start from the empty instance and satisfy $R^{\searrow}$. A simple example of a consistent description is $\{R^{\nearrow}\}$. The tautological description $\{R^{\nearrow}\} \vee \{R^{\searrow}\} \vee \{R^{=}\}$ is also consistent (every possible life satisfies it). Finally, note that $\{R^{=}\}$ is also consistent, but the only lives that satisfy it are sequences of the empty instance. □

The above example suggests the following characterization. We say that a formula is *grow only* if it does not contain any shrink primitive.

Proposition 1. *A description is consistent if and only if it contains a grow-only formula.*

Realizable Formulas and Reduced Descriptions. Let us say that a formula F is *realized* in a life l if some transition in l satisfies F. Now a formula F in a description D is said to be *realizable with respect to* D if there exists a life that satisfies D and that realizes F. Intuitively, a formula in D that is unrealizable with respect to D serves no purpose in D and can be removed from D.

Example 3. Over two relation names R and S, consider the description $D = F_1 \vee F_2$ with $F_1 = \{R^{\nearrow}, S^{=}\}$ and $F_2 = \{R^{=}, S^{\searrow}\}$. Clearly, F_1 is realizable with respect to D as shown by any life I_0, I_1 where I_0 is empty, R is nonempty in I_1, and S is empty in I_1. In contrast, F_2 is unrealizable with respect to D. Indeed, since D contains no formula where S grows, and every life starts with the empty instance, S will be empty in every instance of every life that satisfies D. Hence, no transition in such a life can shrink S. □

The above example suggests that a formula F is unrealizable with respect to D if F contains a shrink primitive for a relation that cannot be made nonempty. We formalize this by the following syntactic notion of "fillable". The link with realizability will be established by Theorem 1.

Definition 4. *Let D be a description. The set $\mathcal{F}$ of* fillable *relation names with respect to D is the smallest set of relation names from* $\mathbf{S}$ *with the following property. If there exists a formula $F \in D$ such that $R^{\nearrow} \in F$ and for every $S^{\searrow} \in F$ we have $S \in \mathcal{F}$, then $R \in \mathcal{F}$.*

Remark 5. The set of fillable relation names can be constructed inductively. We initialize $\mathcal{F}_0 = \emptyset$. For any natural number k, we define $\mathcal{F}_{k+1}$ as the set of relation names that occur growing in some formula that only contains shrink primitives for relations in $\mathcal{F}_k$. For example, to build $\mathcal{F}_1$, we can only use grow-only formulas. We obtain $\mathcal{F}_0 \subseteq \mathcal{F}_1 \subseteq \cdots \subseteq \mathcal{F}_k$ until some k such that $\mathcal{F}_k = \mathcal{F}_{k+1}$, which exists since the number of relation names is finite. This $\mathcal{F}_k$ equals the set of fillable relation names.

Example 4. Consider the description

$$\{R_1^{\nearrow}, R_2^{\nearrow}, R_3^{\searrow}, R_4^{\nearrow}\} \vee \{R_1^{\searrow}, R_2^{\nearrow}, R_3^{=}, R_4^{=}\} \vee \{R_1^{\nearrow}, R_2^{=}, R_3^{=}, R_4^{=}\}.$$

The fillable relations are R_1 and R_2. □

We arrive at the following characterization:

Theorem 1. *F is realizable with respect to D if and only if D is consistent and for every $S^{\searrow}$ in F we have that S is fillable with respect to D.*

The theorem can be proven from the two following lemmas. (Lemma 1 for the only-if direction, and Lemma 2 for the if-direction.)

Lemma 1. *Assume R is nonempty in an instance in a life that satisfies some description D. Then R is fillable with respect to D.*

Lemma 2. *Let D be a consistent description. For every natural number n there exists a life satisfying D and containing an instance where all relations that are fillable with respect to D have size at least n.*

The above Lemma is stated stronger than needed for the if-direction of Theorem 1, which needs only a life satisfying D and ending in an instance where all fillable relations are nonempty. The stronger form is needed to allow an inductive proof that follows the inductive construction from Remark 5 and that correctly deals with formulas involving shrinks. Moreover, the stronger form will also be needed in the proof of Lemma 3.

We say that a description D is *reduced* if all formulas in D are realizable with respect to D. Theorem 1 implies the following characterization:

Proposition 2. *D is reduced if and only if every relation name that is mentioned as growing or shrinking in D is fillable.*

The reduced descriptions are the ones that are "minimal" in the following sense:

Proposition 3. *D is reduced if and only if $lives(D') \subsetneq lives(D)$ for every $D' \subsetneq D$.*

Subsumption. For descriptions D_1 and D_2 it is natural to say that D_2 *subsumes* D_1, denoted by $D_1 \preceq D_2$, if $lives(D_1) \subseteq lives(D_2)$. Clearly, if $D_1 \subseteq D_2$ then $D_1 \preceq D_2$. The converse does not hold in general but it holds when D_1 is reduced:

Theorem 2. *If $D_1 \preceq D_2$ and D_1 is reduced, then $D_1 \subseteq D_2$.*

This theorem is proven using the following useful property of reduced descriptions:

Lemma 3. *Let D be a consistent, reduced description. Then there exists a life satisfying D in which every formula of D is realized.*

3.4 Describing Behaviors

We define the following general notion:

Definition 5. *A* behavior *over a schema* $\mathbf{S}$ *is a set of lives over* $\mathbf{S}$.

One should generally think of a behavior as the set of lives that can be generated through some database application. We will soon define a language for specifying such applications. Here, we already introduce some language-independent notions.

We have already studied lots of behaviors, since, for any description D, the set $lives(D)$ is a behavior. The goal is to describe some given behavior B using the behavior of a description D. We can use the standard terminology to compare the behavior of D to B:

- D is *sound* for B if $lives(D) \subseteq B$.
- D is *complete* for B if $B \subseteq lives(D)$.

The descriptions studied in this paper are somehow coarse-grained, as they describe only the growth or shrinking of relations, and thus allow quite arbitrary transitions. Hence, a given behavior will typically not have nontrivial sound descriptions. In this paper we will mainly be interested in obtaining a complete description instead. Moreover, we would like it to be as tight as possible. Formally, we say that D is a *minimal* complete description for B if D is complete for B and no strict subset of D is complete for B.

We can see that the object of our quest always exists and is unique:

Proposition 4. *Every behavior B has a unique minimal complete description; this description is reduced.*

In Sect. 5 we will investigate the effective computability of minimal complete descriptions for the behaviors of database applications, introduced next.

4 A Formal Model of Database Applications

In this section we define *database applications*, which are finite collections of *procedures*. Each procedure will consist of a parameter declaration and an update program. We will use the formal model of update programs proposed in our earlier work with Ameloot [4]. In that proposal, update programs are built from an arbitrary query language. In the present work, we will use relational algebra as the query language.

4.1 Relational Algebra Expressions and Update Programs

To fix notation, we recall the relational algebra as we will use it in this paper. We then recall the formal model of update programs.

Let $\mathbf{S}$ be a database schema. The relational algebra expressions over $\mathbf{S}$ (abbreviated rae) are inductively built as follows.

- Every relation name $R \in \mathbf{S}$ is an rae with the arity given by the schema.
- For any constant $c \in \mathbf{dom}$, we allow $\{c\}$ as an rae of arity one.
- If e is an rae of arity m, and $i, j \in \{1, \dots, m\}$, then $\sigma_{i=j}(e)$ is an rae of arity m.
- If e is an rae of arity m, and $i_1, \dots, i_k \in \{1, \dots, m\}$, then $\pi_{i_1,\dots,i_k}(e)$ is an rae of arity k.
- If e_1 and e_2 are raes of the same arity m, then $e_1 \cup e_2$, as well as $e_1 \cap e_2$ and $e_1 - e_2$ are raes of arity m.
- If e_1 and e_2 are raes of arities m and k respectively, then $e_1 \times e_2$ is an rae of arity $m + k$.

Given an instance I of $\mathbf{S}$, an rae e of arity m evaluates to an m-ary relation $e(I)$ as follows. The semantics of a relation name R is given by the instance. The semantics of $\cup$, $\cap$ and $-$ is given by the corresponding set operations. The semantics of $\times$ is Cartesian product. The semantics of $\{c\}$ is the singleton unary relation $\{(c)\}$. For a relation r of the appropriate arity, the projection $\pi_{i_1,\dots,i_k}(r)$ equals $\{(a_{i_1},\dots,a_{i_k}) \mid \bar{a} \in r\}$ and the selection $\sigma_{i=j}(r)$ equals $\{\bar{a} \in r \mid a_i = a_j\}$.

Remark 6. We will feel free to use abbreviations that are definable by raes, for example, $\emptyset$, inclusions, boolean connectives, if-then-else, quantifiers, relational calculus formulas, etc. [2]. □

We define three update operations:

Insert For a relation name R and an rae e of the same arity as R, the operation $\mathsf{insert}_R(e)$, applied to an instance I, results in the instance J that is the same as I except that $J(R) = I(R) \cup e(I)$.

Delete For a relation name R and an rae e of the same arity as R, the operation $\mathsf{delete}_R(e)$, applied to an instance I, results in the instance J that is the same as I except that $J(R) = I(R) - e(I)$.

Modify For a relation name R of arity k and an rae e of arity $2k$, the operation $\mathsf{modify}_R(e)$, applied to an instance I, is defined as follows. A $2k$-ary relation can be used as a function from k-tuples to k-tuples, on condition that it does not contain two tuples of the form (t, t') and (t, t'') where t, t' and t'' are k-tuples and $t' \neq t''$. If $e(I)$ is not a function in this way, the operation is undefined. Otherwise, it results in the instance J that is the same as I except that

$$J(R) = \{t \in I(R) \mid \neg\exists t' : (t, t') \in e(I)\} \cup \{t' \mid \exists t \in I(R) : (t, t') \in e(I)\}.$$

The modify operation formalizes the update statement in SQL, which requires that only scalar subqueries (i.e., functions) can be used in the assignment clauses. We say that a modify operation as above is *always defined* if $e(I)$ is a function on every instance I.

We next define *update programs* as follows.

- Every update operation (insert, delete, modify) is a program.
- If Π_1 and Π_2 are programs, then $\Pi_1; \Pi_2$ (sequential composition) is also a program.
- If e is an rae and Π_1 and Π_2 are programs, then '$\mathsf{if}\ e\ \mathsf{then}\ \Pi_1\ \mathsf{else}\ \Pi_2\ \mathsf{endif}$' is a program.
- If e is an rae and Π is a program, then '$\mathsf{while}\ e\ \mathsf{do}\ \Pi\ \mathsf{enddo}$' is a program.

The result of executing a program Π on an instance I results in an instance $\Pi(I)$ defined in the obvious way. The meaning of $\mathsf{if}\ e$ is $\mathsf{if}\ e \neq \emptyset$ and similarly for while. If a modify operation has an undefined result, or a while loop does not terminate, the result of the program is not defined.

Remark 7. A no-op can be simulated by $\mathsf{insert}_R(\emptyset)$, so $\mathsf{if}\ e \neq \emptyset\ \mathsf{then}\ \Pi\ \mathsf{endif}$ without else can be simulated by $\mathsf{if}\ e \neq \emptyset\ \mathsf{then}\ \Pi\ \mathsf{else}$ no-op endif.

4.2 Database Applications

We are now ready to define procedures, applications, and their behavior.

A *procedure* over a schema $\mathbf{S}$ is a triple $(Param, k, \Pi)$, where *Param* is a relation name not in $\mathbf{S}$ and Π is an update program over $\mathbf{S}$ extended with relation name *Param* of arity k. We refer to k as the *parameter arity* of the procedure. A *procedure call* is of the form $P(\bar{a})$, where P is a procedure and $\bar{a}$ is a k-tuple of values in **dom**, with k the parameter arity of P. The result of $P(\bar{a})$ in an instance I of $\mathbf{S}$ is defined to be the result of executing Π on I', where I' is the expansion of I by setting relation *Param* to the singleton $\{\bar{a}\}$.

A *database application* (or *application* for short) over $\mathbf{S}$ is a finite nonempty set A of procedures over $\mathbf{S}$. A life l over $\mathbf{S}$ is said to be a life *of application* A if for every transition (I, J) in l, we have that J is the result of a procedure call $P(\bar{a})$ applied to I, where $P \in A$. We refer to the set of all lives of A as the *behavior* of A, denoted by $lives(A)$.

Remark 8. Since the result of a program may be undefined because of ill-defined modify operations or infinite while-loops, it is possible in extreme cases that an application does not have any life. An example is the application with a single procedure with the following program:

```
while true do
  if R = ∅ then insert_R({c}) else delete_R({c}) endif
enddo.
```

Another example uses as program instead the operation $\mathsf{modify}_R(\{c\}\times\{c,d\})$, for different constants c and d, as this operation is always undefined.

Less extremely, it is possible that a life in the behavior of an application A ends in an instance on which all procedure calls are undefined. Then this life is not continued in any other life in the behavior of A.

Example 5. Consider a vacation house reservation application over a schema with relations House(hid, location, price); Customer(cid, name); Voucher(vid, cid, amount); and Stay(cid, hid, week). We have the following procedures. For the sake of readability, we take some liberty with the formalism.

Procedure *newCustomer* with Param(cid, name, vid, amount):

```
if π_1(Param) ⊈ π_1(Customer) ∧ π_3(Param) ⊈ π_1(Voucher)
then insert_Customer(π_{1,2}(Param));
     insert_Voucher(π_{3,1,4}(Param))
endif
```

Procedure *buyVoucher* with Param(vid, cid, amount) inserts a new voucher for an existing customer. Procedure *newHouse* with Param(hid, location, price) inserts a new house. The programs are similar to the one above.

Procedure *reserve* with Param(cid, hid, week, vid):

if $\pi_{1,4}(\text{Param}) \subseteq \pi_{2,1}(\text{Voucher})$
$\quad \wedge\, \pi_{2,7}\, \sigma_{4=5}(\text{Param} \times \text{Voucher}) \subseteq \pi_{1,3}(\text{House})$
$\quad \wedge\, \pi_{2,3}(\text{Param}) \not\subseteq \pi_{2,3}(\text{Stay})$
then $\text{insert}_{\text{Stay}}(\pi_{1,2,3}(\text{Param}))$;
$\qquad \text{delete}_{\text{Voucher}}(\pi_{2,3,4}\, \sigma_{1=2}(\pi_4(\text{Param}) \times \text{Voucher}))$
endif

Our final two procedures have an update program consisting of a single operation. Procedure *changePrice* with Param(hid, price):

$\text{modify}_{\text{House}}(\pi_{1,2,3,1,2,5}\, \sigma_{1=4}(\text{House} \times \text{Param}))$.

Procedure *reset*, without a parameter:

$\text{delete}_{\text{Stay}}(\text{Stay})$.

5 Descriptions of Applications

As seen in Proposition 4, every behavior has a minimal complete description. In this section we investigate whether the minimal complete description of the behavior of a given application is effectively computable.

Table 1. Minimal complete description of the behavior of the vacation house reservation application.

House	Customer	Voucher	Stay	procedure
=	=	=	=	*newCustomer*
=	↗	↗	=	*newCustomer*
=	=	=	=	*buyVoucher*
=	=	↗	=	*buyVoucher*
=	=	=	=	*newHouse*
↗	=	=	=	*newHouse*
=	=	=	=	*reserve*
=	=	↘	↗	*reserve*
=	=	=	=	*changePrice*
=	=	=	=	*reset*
=	=	=	↘	*reset*

Example 6. Recall the application from Example 5. The minimal complete description of its behavior is shown, in tabular form, in Table 1. The table also shows which procedures can give rise to which formulas. The first line of the table, which represents the formula $\{\text{House}^=, \text{Customer}^=, \text{Voucher}^=, \text{Stay}^=\}$, reflects the possibility that none of the relations change size. This happens, for example,

when *newCustomer* is called with an existing cid, due to the if-condition in the program. It happens also each time we call *changePrice*. Indeed, the expression in the modify operation always returns a function, because relation Param is always a singleton and attribute hid is always a key for relation House in every instance of every life. This key constraint holds because procedure *newHouse* will only insert when given a new hid. □

Below we will show undecidability results, but we will also identify decidable cases. First, we investigate the inference of individual size primitives. In Sect. 5.2 we turn to the inference of formulas. We will also consider an extension of our formal model with value invention.

5.1 Inferring Size Primitives

Recall that a life l is said to realize a formula F if some transition in l satisfies F. Similarly, we say that l realizes a size primitive p if some transition in l satisfies p. We now formally define the following decision problem:

Problem: GROW.
Input: An application A over a database schema $\mathbf{S}$, and a relation name R in $\mathbf{S}$.
Decide: There exists a life of A that realizes $R^{\nearrow}$.

Similarly we can define the problems SHRINK and SAMESIZE which are about realizing $R^{\searrow}$ and $R^{=}$, respectively.

Deciding GROW

Example 7. Consider an application A consisting of a single procedure P over two binary relations R_1, R_2, with parameter arity two, with e an rae over R_2 alone:

if e then insert$_{R_1}(Param)$ else insert$_{R_2}(Param)$ endif

We see that there exists a life of A where R_1 grows if and only if e is satisfiable, i.e., nonempty on some instance. Indeed, if e is satisfiable, let I be a minimal instance on which e is nonempty. Let $I(R_2) = \{t_1, \ldots, t_n\}$. We can make n calls $P(t_1)$, ..., $P(t_n)$, which generates a life ending in the instance J where $J(R_1)$ is empty and $J(R_2) = \{t_1, \ldots, t_n\}$. Making one more call $P(t)$ will insert t into R_1, causing R_1 to grow. □

Since satisfiability of relational algebra expressions over a binary relation is undecidable [2,5], the above example shows:

Theorem 3. *Problem* GROW *is undecidable, even in restriction to applications with a single procedure that does not use while-loops.*

Remark 9. Some variations of the application A seen in Example 7 are possible. We can avoid if-then-else in the update program but use two statements instead:

$\mathsf{insert}_{R_1}(\text{if } e \text{ then } \mathit{Param} \text{ else } \emptyset)$;
$\mathsf{insert}_{R_2}(\text{if } e = \emptyset \text{ then } \mathit{Param} \text{ else } \emptyset)$.

Here the if-then-else constructs are not those of the update language, but are expressed in relational algebra.

We can also use two procedures, with a single operation each:

Procedure P_1: $\mathsf{insert}_{R_1}(\text{if } e \text{ then } \mathit{Param} \text{ else } \emptyset)$.
Procedure P_2: $\mathsf{insert}_{R_2}(\mathit{Param})$.

We see in both of these variations that there exists a life of the application where R_1 grows, if and only if e is satisfiable. □

In contrast, we can identify the following decidable case:

Theorem 4. *Problem* GROW *is decidable for applications over a single relation.*

The proof exploits the C-genericity of relational algebra expressions to test the procedure from the empty instance using only a finite set of parameter tuples.

We can determine the precise complexity of the problem identified in the above theorem for a class of applications that we call *single-statement.* Let us define single-statement programs as those built from update operations using only the if-then-else construction. So, sequential composition and while-loops are not allowed. An application is called single-statement if every procedure has a single-statement program.

Proposition 5. *Problem* GROW *for single-statement applications over a single relation name is PSPACE-complete.*

The proof leverages the PSPACE combined complexity of relational algebra evaluation for the upper bound, and leverages the PSPACE-hard expression complexity of relational algebra evaluation for the lower bound.

Remark 10. Determining the complexity of executing general update programs is an interesting topic for further research. In the above we restrict to single-statement programs so that we can rely on known results on the complexity of evaluating relational algebra. Note that, using sequential composition, an update program can encode a relational algebra expression of exponential size. For example, consider the following program over a binary relation name R:

$\mathsf{insert}_T(\pi_{1,4}\,\sigma_{2=3}(R \times R))$;
$\mathsf{insert}_T(\pi_{1,4}\,\sigma_{2=3}(T \times T))$;
$\vdots$
$\mathsf{insert}_T(\pi_{1,4}\,\sigma_{2=3}(T \times T)$.

Let n be the number of operations. Thinking of relation R as a directed graph, this program computes in T all pairs (a, b) such that there is a walk from a to b of length 2^i for some $i \in \{1, \ldots, n\}$.

Deciding SHRINK. Call an application A *insert-only* if for every relation name R, if an operation delete_R or modify_R appears anywhere in the application, then the application does not contain any operation insert_R. Of course this means that for each operation delete_R or modify_R in the program, relation R will remain empty since it is never inserted into. As a consequence, no R can ever shrink. We conclude that Problem SHRINK is trivially decidable for insert-only applications.

Outside of insert-only applications, Problem SHRINK is typically undecidable, as shown by the following Theorem. The proof requires some ingenuity in constructing detailed programs that, despite the imposed syntactical limitations, can exactly simulate undecidable problems about relational algebra expressions.

Theorem 5. *Problem* SHRINK *is undecidable, even in restriction to applications over a single binary relation name, in the following classes:*

1. *A single procedure consisting of a single if-then-else statement, with a single insert operation as the then-case, and a single delete operation as the else-case.*
2. *A single procedure consisting of a single if-then-else statement, with a single insert operation as the then-case, and a single, always-defined, modify operation as the else-case.*
3. *Two procedures, one consisting of a single insert statement, and one consisting of a single delete statement.*
4. *Two procedures, one consisting of a single insert statement, and one consisting of a single, always-defined, modify statement.*

Deciding SAMESIZE. Recall the class of insert-only applications defined in the previous subsection. We saw there that such applications can never realize a shrink primitive. We can also define the notion of insert-only for individual programs, in a similar way. Naturally, a procedure is then called insert-only if its program is. For the same-size primitive, we now observe the following behavior. We omit while-loops and modify operations as these may have undefined results (compare Remark 8).

Proposition 6. *Let A be an application with at least one insert-only procedure without while-loops and without modify operations, and let R be a relation name from the database schema. Then there always exists a life of A that realizes $R^=$.*

The idea behind the proof is that calling the insert-only procedure repeatedly with the same parameter must necessarily converge.

As soon as we deviate even slightly from the case described in the above proposition, the problem becomes undecidable, as shown next. The first two cases of the following theorem are the same as in Theorem 5, but quite different reductions had to be invented to prove them.

Theorem 6. *Problem* SAMESIZE *is undecidable, even in restriction to applications over a single binary relation name, with a single procedure, in the following classes:*

1. *A single if-then-else statement, with a single insert operation as the then-case, and a single delete operation as the else-case.*
2. *A single if-then-else statement, with a single insert operation as the then-case, and a single, always-defined, modify operation as the else-case.*
3. *A single if-then-else statement, with a single insert operation as the then-case, and a while-loop with a no-op body as the else-case.*[2]

5.2 Computing the Minimal Complete Description

Ideally we would like to be able to compute the minimal complete description of a given application. Since, over any given database schema, the number of possible formulas is finite, this amounts to solving the following problem.

Problem: FORMULA
Input: An application A over a database schema $\mathbf{S}$, and a formula F over $\mathbf{S}$.
Decide: There exists a life of A that realizes F.

Problem FORMULA is a more general problem than the problems GROW, SHRINK and SAMESIZE. Thus, FORMULA is undecidable and can only be decidable for classes of inputs where the three more specific problems are decidable. Given the results of the previous subsection, this results in the class of insert-only applications over a single relation name, without while-loops. When there is only one relation name, there is no difference between inferring formulas and inferring size primitives. We conclude:

Theorem 7. *For insert-only applications over a single relation name, without while-loops, the minimal complete description is effectively computable.*

Remark 11. We can extend the above result to "partitioned" applications, where the procedures can be partitioned into groups so that all procedures in each group work on a single relation name, and these relation names are different for different groups. For example, assume application A is partitioned into A_1 and A_2, on relation names R_1 and R_2 respectively. If D_1 (D_2) is the minimal complete description of A_1 (A_2), then the minimal complete description of A equals

$$\{F \cup \{R_2^=\} \mid F \in D_1\} \cup \{F \cup \{R_1^=\} \mid F \in D_2\}.$$

5.3 Programs with Value Invention

In practice, procedures often use an auto-increment feature that generates fresh identifiers. Relational algebra programs with value invention are known to be highly expressive [2]. Indeed, we next show that Proposition 6 no longer holds if this feature is introduced.

We formalize auto-increment by extending the notion of procedure from a triple $(Param, k, \Pi)$ to a 4-tuple $P = (Param, k, v, \Pi)$, with $v \in \{0, \ldots, k\}$. The

[2] For no-op, see Remark 7.

idea is that in a call, the last v parameters will be invented values. Formally, the parameter tuple $\bar{a}$ given in the call now has arity $k-v$ instead of k. When calling $P(\bar{a})$ on instance I, the program is executed on the expansion of I where relation *Param* is now instantiated with $\{(\bar{a}, \bar{z})\}$, with $\bar{z}$ a v-tuple of domain elements outside the active domain of I. Accordingly, we say that P is auto-incrementing if $v \neq 0$.

We show:

Proposition 7. *Problem* SAMESIZE *is undecidable for applications over a single ternary relation name R, with a single auto-incrementing procedure, having a single insert operation as its program.*

In this proof, although all other hypotheses of Proposition 6 hold, the auto-increment can introduce new elements in the active domain, which allows us to simulate arbitrary computations by insertions only.

Remark 12. Theorem 4 continues to hold in the presence of auto-increment; the proof remains exactly the same. Indeed, the proof focuses on the very first transition, which starts from the empty instance, so the auto-incrementing is irrelevant.

6 Conclusion

We have proposed the novel perspective of analyzing the database evolution through the lens of size changes. We see many directions for further research.

One natural direction is to revisit the decidability and undecidability results (Sect. 5) when we restrict the language used to express the queries embedded in the update language. In this work, we have used relational algebra, which has an undecidable satisfiability problem. Omitting the difference operator leads to the class of unions of conjunctive queries, which have a decidable implication problem [2].

In our current analysis of database applications, we do not consider any constraints on the order in which procedures can be called. In practice such constraints will often be naturally governed by a given workflow or process model.

Also, in our current approach, descriptions only look at what can happen in individual transitions of a life. A more fine-grained approach could be to label every transition of a life with its proper size formula. This yields a view of lives as strings of size formulas. Since the set of possible size formulas over a given database schema forms a finite alphabet, this allows us to combine our size-change perspective with standard temporal logics for expressing properties of strings and traces.

Finally, in Example 6, we saw that the analysis of behaviors can hinge on constraints (e.g., keys) on reachable database states that are implied by the application. Seminal work in this direction was done by Abiteboul and Vianu [3]. We feel this line of research still has a lot of promise and potential.

References

1. Abdulla, P., Aiswarya, C., Atig, M., Montali, M., Rezine, O.: Recency-bounded verification of dynamic database-driven systems. In: Proceedings 35th ACM Symposium on Principles of Database Systems, pp. 195–210 (2016)
2. Abiteboul, S., Hull, R., Vianu, V.: Foundations of Databases. Addison-Wesley (1995)
3. Abiteboul, S., Vianu, V.: A transaction-based approach to relational database specification. J. ACM **36**(4), 758–789 (1989)
4. Ameloot, T., Van den Bussche, J., Waller, E.: On the expressive power of update primitives. In: Proceedings 32nd ACM Symposium on Principles of Database Systems, pp. 139–150 (2013)
5. Börger, E., Grädel, E., Gurevich, Y.: The Classical Decision Problem. Springer (1997)
6. Calvanese, D., De Giacomo, G., Montali, M.: Foundations of data-aware process analysis: a database theory perspective. In: Proceedings 32nd ACM Symposium on Principles of Database Systems, pp. 1–12 (2013)
7. Deutsch, A., Hull, R., Li, Y., Vianu, V.: Automatic verification of database-centric systems. ACM SIGLOG News **5**(2), 37–56 (2018)
8. Deutsch, A., Sui, L., Vianu, V.: Specification and verification of data-driven Web applications. J. Comput. Syst. Sci. **73**(3), 442–474 (2007)
9. Itzhaky, S., et al.: On the automated verification of web applications with embedded SQL. In: Benedikt, M., Orsi, G. (eds.) Proceedings 20th International Conference on Database Theory. LIPIcs, vol. 68, pp. 16:1–16:18. Schloss Dagstuhl–Leibniz Center for Informatics (2017)
10. Silberschatz, A., Korth, H., Sudarshan, S.: Database System Concepts. Mc Graw-Hill, 7th edn. (2019)
11. Spielmann, M.: Verification of relational transducers for electronic commerce. J. Comput. Syst. Sci. **66**(1), 40–65 (2003)

Foundations

From FPT Decision to FPT Enumeration

Nadia Creignou[1], Timo Camillo Merkl[2], Reinhard Pichler[2](✉), and Daniel Unterberger[2]

[1] Aix Marseille Univ, CNRS, LIS, Marseille, France
nadia.creignou@univ-amu.fr
[2] TU Wien, Vienna, Austria
{timo.merkl,reinhard.pichler,daniel.unterberger}@tuwien.ac.at

Abstract. Fixed-parameter tractable (FPT) algorithms have been successfully applied to many intractable problems – with a focus on decision and optimization problems. Their aim is to confine the exponential explosion to some parameter, while the time complexity only depends polynomially on the instance size. In contrast, intractable enumeration problems have received comparatively little attention so far. The goal of this work is to study how FPT decision algorithms could be turned into FPT enumeration algorithms. We thus inspect several fundamental approaches for designing FPT decision or optimization algorithms and we present ideas how they can be extended to FPT enumeration algorithms.

1 Introduction

Many practically relevant computational problems in a wide range of applications are intractable. A meanwhile well-established approach of dealing with intractable problems is to aim at fixed-parameter tractable (FPT) algorithms (see [12,26] for comprehensive collections of FPT-results). That is, the exponential explosion can be confined to some parameter (typically some structural property of the problem instances or of the desired solution) while the time complexity only depends polynomially on the size of the problem instance.

FPT-algorithms have been mainly developed for *decision problems* (e.g., does there exist a solution?) or *optimization problems* (e.g., what is the max/min value attainable by all solutions?). However, in many settings, the user might be interested in *all* (or at least a significant portion) of the solutions or optimal solutions to a problem. This is particularly the case when querying data or knowledge base systems, where the user is usually interested in retrieving all (or at least a significant portion) of the answers rather than just a simple "yes". We are thus faced with an *enumeration problem*, whose task is to output the entire solution set without duplicates (i.e., outputting the same solution twice). Note that even seemingly simple problems may have a huge (potentially exponential) number of solutions. Hence, as was shown in the foundational paper by Johnson et al. [18], even the notion of tractability has to be redefined. The enumeration complexity class that is often considered as an analog of the decision complexity

A.-Y. Turhan and J. Virtema (Eds.): FoIKS 2026, LNCS 16475, pp. 213–231, 2026.
https://doi.org/10.1007/978-3-032-21540-6_13

class P is DelayP, i.e., "polynomial delay". It consists of those problems which have an algorithm that requires polynomial time in the size of the instance to output the first solution, to output any further solution, and to terminate after the last solution. The study of enumeration problems and the development of DelayP-algorithms has received a lot of attention, especially in the areas of graph theory and databases, see e.g., [3,5,7,19,21].

But what happens if the task of finding the first or a further solution is intractable? A natural approach is to borrow ideas from decision and optimization problems and to aim for FPT-delay, i.e., algorithms that find the first or next solution in FPT-time. Surprisingly, this line of research has received little attention so far; notable exceptions are [9,10,13,15,17,23]. The aim of our work is to shed some light on this under-researched area and to provide assistance to algorithm developers in designing FPT-delay enumeration algorithms. To this end, we revisit the most common techniques in the design of FPT decision and optimization algorithms and look for their extension to FPT-delay enumeration algorithms. For the basic FPT approaches considered here, we will mainly follow the presentation in [12]. Apart from kernelization [4,10,17] and tree decompositions (in particular, enumeration algorithms via Courcelle's Theorem [8]), these techniques have not yet made their way into enumeration. Another FPT approach, that has already been extended to enumeration [10] but is not mentioned in [12], are backdoors. In particular, for various variants of the SAT-problem, they have received quite some attention [14,16,24].

Among the enumeration methods that we apply are adaptations and extensions of typical enumeration approaches [22] such as "flashlight algorithms" (which search for solutions in a top-down traversal of some tree structure and repeatedly use a decision algorithm as a "flashlight" to see if a certain branch contains solutions before expanding it) or exploiting the closure under union of DelayP [27]. A particular challenge of enumeration problems comes from the requirement that duplicates have to be avoided. Here, we strongly draw inspiration from the landmark paper of Lawler [20], where a basic technique for avoiding duplicates by appropriate partitioning of the solution space was presented.

The paper is organized as follows: in Sect. 2, we recall some fundamental definitions of parameterized enumeration. The main part of the paper is devoted to the design of DelayFPT algorithms by carrying over basic FPT-methods from decision algorithms, namely partition algorithms as an extension of bounded search trees (in Sect. 3), enumeration algorithms for a union of (not disjoint!) "FPT-many" subsets of solutions (in Sect. 4), iterative compression-based enumeration algorithms (in Sect. 5) and dynamic programming algorithms (in Sect. 6). The design of enumeration algorithms via these FPT-methods is illustrated by instructive examples, and we propose formalizations to generalize these ideas. We conclude with Sect. 7. Further details are provided in [11].

2 Parameterized Complexity and Enumeration

We assume familiarity with basic notions of complexity and graph theory. A *parameterized problem* is defined by a ternary predicate $Q \subset \Sigma^* \times \mathbb{N} \times \Sigma^*$ for some alphabet Σ. A tuple $(I, k) \in \Sigma^* \times \mathbb{N}$ is an instance, k is its parameter, and $Q(I, k) := \{S \in \Sigma^* \mid (I, k, S) \in Q\}$ is its solution set. The task of deciding whether $Q(I, k) \neq \emptyset$ is the *decision problem* Q, while the task of enumerating $Q(I, k)$ without duplicates is the *enumeration problem* Q. An instance $(I, k) \in \Sigma^* \times \mathbb{N}$ with $Q(I, k) \neq \emptyset$ is a *yes-instance*, otherwise a *no-instance*. We will denote the size of an instance (I, k) by $|(I, k)|$.

Definition 1. *Let Q be a decision problem. We say Q can be decided in* FPT*-time if there exists an algorithm $\mathcal{A}$ that, for any instance $(I, k) \in \Sigma^* \times \mathbb{N}$, decides if $Q(I, k) \neq \emptyset$ with a runtime bounded by $h(k)p(|(I, k)|)$ for some computable function $h\colon \mathbb{N} \to \mathbb{N}$ and polynomial p. We call the class of all problems admitting* FPT*-time algorithms* FPT.

An *enumeration algorithm* $\mathcal{A}$ for an enumeration problem Q is an algorithm which, when given an instance (I, k) of Q as input, outputs the elements of $Q(I, k)$ without duplicates. An enumeration problem is in the class DelayP, if it has an algorithm with a polynomial bound on its *delay*. By "delay" we mean the maximum time between two consecutive solutions, including the time until the first solution is output and the time after the last solution is output. The natural parameterized analog is DelayFPT, which we define next.

Definition 2. *Let Q be an enumeration problem. We say Q can be enumerated with* FPT*-delay if there exists an algorithm $\mathcal{A}$ which, for any instance $(I, k) \in \Sigma^* \times \mathbb{N}$, enumerates all solutions in $Q(I, k)$ with a delay bounded by $h(k)p(|(I, k)|)$ for some computable function $h : \mathbb{N} \to \mathbb{N}$ and polynomial p. We call the class of all problems Q admitting such an* FPT*-delay enumeration algorithm* DelayFPT.

3 Partition Algorithms

Search tree algorithms, which work by iteratively splitting a given problem instance into sub-instances, are among the most commonly used techniques in FPT algorithms for decision problems. The correctness of such algorithms hinges on the fact that, in case of a yes-instance, at least one of the sub-instances resulting from a splitting step leads to a feasible solution. In case of enumeration, we have to be careful that the splitting step *partitions* the set of solutions, so as to preserve all solutions and avoid duplicates. We therefore start our discussion of DelayFPT enumeration algorithms by studying various forms of *partition algorithms*.

3.1 Bounded Search Tree Partition Algorithms

We know from decision algorithms that, if the total size of the search tree is bounded by a function of the parameter only and every step takes FPT-time, then such an algorithm runs in FPT-time. To carry these ideas over to enumeration algorithms, several extensions are required. On one hand, we still need bounds (that only depend on the parameter k) on the breadth and depth of the search tree. In addition, following the philosophy of [20], we now have to make sure that, with every splitting step, (i) *every* solution is contained in some branch, (ii) *no* solution is contained in *more than one branch*, and (iii) the solutions of the *instances at the leaf nodes* of the search tree can be enumerated with DelayFPT.

We illustrate these ideas on the FEEDBACK VERTEX SET IN TOURNAMENTS (FVST, for short) problem. For a directed graph $G = (V, A)$, we call $S \subseteq V$ a *feedback vertex set*, if $G[V \setminus S]$ (that is the subgraph of G induced by the vertex set $V \setminus S$) is acyclic. A *Tournament* $T = (V, A)$ is a directed graph such that, for any u and v in V, exactly one of (u, v) and (v, u) is in A. In the FVST enumeration problem, we are given a tournament $T = (V, A)$ and a parameter $k \in \mathbb{N}$, and we want to enumerate all feedback vertex sets of size at most k.

The FVST decision problem can be shown to be in FPT via bounded search trees (see [12, Section 4.2]). Below we show how we can get an enumeration algorithms satisfying the above requirements (i) – (iii) by maintaining additional information.

Proposition 1. *The* FEEDBACK VERTEX SET IN TOURNAMENTS *problem is in* DelayFPT *using polynomial space.*

Proof. Our algorithm for enumerating the feedback vertex sets of a tournament T maintains the problem instance (T, k) together with two vertex sets $C, F \subseteq V(T)$ as additional information. The intended meaning of these vertex sets is as follows: We store in C vertices of T that we definitely want to delete and in F the vertices that we definitely want to retain. Hence, our enumeration algorithm recursively searches for feedback vertex sets U in the tournament $T[V \setminus C]$ having $U \cap F = \emptyset$. Initially, we set $F = C = \emptyset$.

A tournament has a directed cycle if and only if it has a directed triangle (see [12, Lemma 4.3]). We can find such a triangle (or confirm that none exists) in time $O(|V|^3)$. If none exists, then we can output all feedback vertex sets S of size $\leq k$ with $C \subseteq S$ and $S \cap F = \emptyset$ with polynomial delay. Otherwise, since each feedback vertex set must have non-empty intersection with this triangle, we branch by adding any non-empty subset of the triangle vertices disjoint from F to C (≤ 7 possibilities), reduce k accordingly, and add the remaining triangle vertices to F. We recursively apply these steps, i.e., finding a directed triangle and branching over non-empty intersections. As we only need to store the path of the currently examined recursion tree (in addition to the children with possibly some arbitrary ordering of them for all nodes on the path) and the depth is at most k, we only need polynomial space.

We verify that the requirements on a bounded search tree partition algorithm are fulfilled: the breadth of the search tree is bounded by 7 and the depth is bounded by k (since the parameter is strictly decreased in each sub-instance). Clearly, the splitting preserves all solutions and the additional information in the sets F, C excludes duplicates. Finally, for a sub-instance with $k = 0$, we know that the solution set is empty if the subgraph of T induced by $V \setminus C$ contains a cycle; otherwise we output the solution $S \supseteq C$ as described above.

Generalization and Formalization. Intuitively, we need a method f to create child instances of a given instance such that the solution space is partitioned by the solution space of the child instances. We recursively apply f until the instances are fully processed, i.e., until all solutions can be easily enumerated with a method f_0. To limit the size of the possible search tree and to formalize when instances are fully processed, we need a function γ, which assigns each instance (I, k) a natural number m such that the tree rooted at (I, k) has a height of at most m (where m can, in turn, only depend on the parameter k), and $m = 0$ if and only if the instance is fully processed. The following definition is intended to capture these requirements.

Definition 3. *For an enumeration problem Q, we call a tuple of functions (f, γ) a* bounded search tree partition algorithm *if, for some computable functions $b, h \colon \mathbb{N} \to \mathbb{N}$ (for breadth and height, respectively), the following conditions hold:*

- $f \colon \Sigma^* \times \mathbb{N} \to \mathcal{P}(\Sigma^* \times \mathbb{N})$ *is an* FPT*-time function such that for all $(I, k) \in \Sigma^* \times \mathbb{N}$:*
  - $|f(I, k)| \leq b(k)$,
  - *for all* $(I', k') \in f(I, k)$, $|(I', k')| \leq |(I, k)|$ *and* $k' \leq k$,
  - $Q(I, k) = \biguplus_{(I',k') \in f(I,k)} Q(I', k')$, *where* $\biguplus$ *denotes the disjoint union,*
- $\gamma \colon \Sigma^* \times \mathbb{N} \to \mathbb{N}$ *is an* FPT*-time function such that for all $(I, k) \in \Sigma^* \times \mathbb{N}$:*
  - $\gamma(I, k) \leq h(k)$,
  - *if* $\gamma(I, k) \neq 0$, *then for all* $(I', k') \in f(I, k)$, $\gamma(I', k') < \gamma(I, k)$.

Additionally, we require that there must exist a function f_0, which enumerates $Q(I, k)$ with FPT*-delay when $\gamma(I, k) = 0$.*

As we will see in the rest of this section, the condition that both breadth and height are bounded by a function of the parameter only, can be quite restrictive.

In the definition above, the first condition on f controls the breadth of the search tree, while the function γ is a measure that decreases at each step, and thus bounds the depth of the search tree. Both are bounded by a function of k, which thus also applies to the size of the search tree. The two last conditions on f ensure that traversing the search tree will provide all solutions with no repetitions. Therefore, we get the following result.

Proposition 2. *Let Q be a parameterized enumeration problem. If Q has a bounded search tree partition algorithm (f, γ), then Q is in* DelayFPT.

To fit our FVST algorithm from the proof of Proposition 1 into this general framework, we consider a generalized version of FVST (we will call it GFVST) where instances are extended by sets C and F. Then the FVST problem corresponds to the special case of GFVST with $C = F = \emptyset$. Function f defines one splitting step, where an instance of GFVST gives rise to up to $b(k) = 7$ new instances. The function γ is initially set to k and decreased by the number of vertices added to C in each splitting step. To trigger the application of function f_0 for outputting all solutions of a given instance, we set γ to 0 if no more directed triangle exists in the graph. Of course, γ also becomes 0 when the "budget" of allowed vertex deletions has been exhausted. For further details, see [11].

3.2 Flashlight Partition Algorithms

Next, we aim at relaxing the bound on the size of the search tree. More specifically, we bound both the breadth and the depth by an FPT-function rather than by a function of the parameter k alone. To guarantee that we find a new solution after FPT-time, we are only allowed to explore a branch in the search tree if it leads to a feasible solution and we have to go through the tree in a depth-first manner. This can be guaranteed by using a "flashlight" algorithm, i.e., a decision algorithm that decides in FPT-time whether an instance has a solution or not. Again, we need to ensure that the branching properly partitions the solution space and that solutions of instances at leaf nodes can be enumerated with DelayFPT.

We illustrate the idea of flashlight partition algorithms by considering the enumeration variant of the CLOSEST STRING problem, which is defined as follows: we are given a set of strings $X = \{x_1, \ldots, x_n\}$ of length L over an alphabet Σ and a parameter $k \in \mathbb{N}$. The task is to find all strings s of length L such that $d_H(s, x_j) \leq k$ for each $1 \leq j \leq n$, where $d_H(x, y)$ is the Hamming distance between strings x and y. We call such a string s a *center string*.

FPT-membership of the decision variant of CLOSEST STRING (i.e., does there exist a center string?) can be shown by a bounded search tree algorithm (see [12, Section 3.5]). However, for an enumeration algorithm, we again need to maintain more information to make sure that every splitting of a problem instance *partitions* the solution set.

Proposition 3. *The* CLOSEST STRING *problem is in* DelayFPT *using* FPT *space.*

Proof. Our algorithm for enumerating the center strings of a given instance (X, k) maintains, in addition to the instance, a string $\omega \in \Sigma^*$. The idea of ω is that we only search for center strings with prefix ω. Initially, we set ω to the empty string. As flashlight, we use an FPT-algorithm for the CLOSEST STRING decision problem, checking if there exists a center string with prefix ω. Such an FPT-algorithm is easily obtained by adapting the bounded search tree algorithm from Sect. 3.5 in [12].

Now let X be an instance of the CLOSEST STRING enumeration problem together with a prefix ω as additional information. We split this problem instance into sub-instances by iterating through all possible characters $\sigma \in \Sigma$ and tentatively generating all possible prefixes $\omega \cdot \sigma$. However, from these, we only keep the yes-instances (which can be determined in FPT-time by the flashlight).

The depth of the search tree at an instance (X, k) with additional information ω is therefore $|\omega| \leq L$, where L the length of the strings in X. The breadth is bounded by the size of the alphabet Σ. Clearly, fixing the prefix of solutions partitions the solution space. Moreover, no solution gets lost if we only keep those sub-instances that contain a solution according to the flashlight. Thus, in total, by traversing this search tree in a depth-first fashion and outputting the solutions at the leaves, we get an FPT-delay using FPT space.

Generalization and Formalization. As with bounded search tree partition, we need to make sure that each step can be done in FPT-time and partitions the solution space, and that the solutions at the leaf nodes can be enumerated with FPT-delay. The maximal depth γ may now also depend on $|I|$, with the dependence being polynomial. An FPT-decision "flashlight" algorithm is thus needed to check the existence of solutions. We formalize these requirements in the following definition.

Definition 4. *For an enumeration problem Q, we call a tuple of functions (f, γ) a* flashlight partition algorithm *if, for some computable function $h\colon \mathbb{N} \to \mathbb{N}$ and polynomial p, the following conditions hold:*

- $f\colon \Sigma^* \times \mathbb{N} \to \mathcal{P}(\Sigma^* \times \mathbb{N})$ *is an* FPT*-time function such that for all* $(I, k) \in \Sigma^* \times \mathbb{N}$*:*
  - *for all* $(I', k') \in f(I, k)$, $|(I', k')| \leq |(I, k)|$ *and* $k' \leq k$,
  - *for all* $(I', k') \in f(I, k)$, $Q(I', k') \neq \emptyset$,
  - $Q(I, k) = \biguplus_{(I',k') \in f(I,k)} Q(I', k')$,
- $\gamma\colon \Sigma^* \times \mathbb{N} \to \mathbb{N}$ *is an* FPT*-time function such that for all* $(I, k) \in \Sigma^* \times \mathbb{N}$*:*
  - $\gamma(I, k) \leq h(k)p(|(I, k)|)$,
  - *if* $\gamma(I, k) \neq 0$, *then for all* $(I', k') \in f(I, k)$, $\gamma(I', k') < \gamma(I, k)$.

Additionally, we require that there must exist a function f_0, which enumerates $Q(I, k)$ with FPT*-delay when* $\gamma(I, k) = 0$.

The "flashlight" is implicit in the function f, which (in FPT-time) only generates subproblems (I', k') with non-empty solution set (by the second condition on f in Definition 4). The depth of the search tree is bounded by an FPT-function because of the measure γ that decreases at each step along a branch. Together with the "flashlight", which guarantees that no branch of the search tree is explored in vain, we thus get FPT-delay. We note that this method is related to the algorithmic paradigm of self-reducibility studied in [10].

Proposition 4. *Let Q be a parameterized enumeration problem. If Q has a flashlight partition algorithm (f, γ), then Q is in* DelayFPT*.*

Again, to fit our Closest String algorithm from the proof of Proposition 3 into this framework, we consider a generalized version of this problem where instances are extended by a prefix ω. The Closest String problem then corresponds to the special case with an empty prefix ω. Crucially, the function f now serves two purposes: on one hand, it splits the current instance into new instances by appending one more character to ω; on the other hand, it serves as "flashlight" and only retains those new instances which have a solution that extends the current prefix. Initially, γ is set to L. It is then decremented in every splitting step, when we extend the prefix by one character. The function f_0 for enumerating all solutions of an instance when γ reaches the value 0 is particularly simple in this case: we just need to output the prefix ω (which now has length L) of the current instance. For further details, see [11].

3.3 Solution Search Partition Algorithms

We now want to remove the restriction on the depth of the search tree altogether. The idea is to alternately perform two steps, namely (1) find a solution and (2) split the remaining search space. Intuitively, we thus try to find a spanning tree of the solution space. As before, the algorithm consists in traversing a tree. However, unlike the two previous methods, this tree is not implicitly made up of sub-instances and partial solutions, with final solutions only at the leaves or computable from the leaves. Now, each node of the tree constitutes an instance from which a solution S of the original instance can be produced in FPT-time. Clearly, in the splitting step, we need to create sub-instances that partition the solutions of (I, k) *excluding the solution* S. We repeat this branching, exploring the search tree depth-first, until we arrive at a no-instance, at which point we consider the remaining branches.

To maintain FPT-delay between the output of two successive solutions, we can use the "alternative output" technique (see [22,28]), which prevents the backtracking through long paths without outputting any solution: it outputs the solutions *before* the recursive call when the current depth-first search level is even, and *after* the recursive call when it is odd.

We now construct a solution search partition algorithm for INTEGER LINEAR PROGRAMMING WITH K VARIABLES parameterized by the number of variables: let k and m be positive integers, let A be an $m \times k$ matrix with integer coefficients and $b \in \mathbb{Z}^m$, and let k be the parameter. The task is to enumerate all vectors $x \in \mathbb{Z}^k$ satisfying the system of inequalities $Ax \leq b$. Note that the number of solutions is potentially infinite. To ensure that we can output each solution in FPT-time (and implicitly eliminate the problem of an infinite solution space), we assume that the absolute values of the components of a solution vector are bounded by some function $2^{h(k)p(L)}$, where L is the instance-size, h is a computable function, and p is a polynomial. Otherwise, it could happen that simply outputting a single solution cannot be done in FPT-time due to its size. This can be easily enforced by adding appropriate entries to A and b. Crucially, one can find in FPT-time (w.r.t. k) one solution vector where all components have an FPT-bounded binary representation (see [12, Theorem 6.5]). We denote this algorithm by $\mathcal{A}$.

Proposition 5. INTEGER LINEAR PROGRAMMING WITH K VARIABLES *is in* DelayFPT.

Proof. We utilize the FPT-time algorithm $\mathcal{A}$, which either finds a solution vector where all components have FPT-bounded size (in binary representation) or detects that no such solution exists. If a solution has been found, say

$(s_1, \ldots, s_k)$, then we create new instances by adding (in)equalities of the form $(x_1 = s_1) \wedge \cdots \wedge (x_i = s_i) \wedge (x_{i+1} > s_{i+1})$ or $(x_1 = s_1) \wedge \cdots \wedge (x_i = s_i) \wedge (x_{i+1} < s_{i+1})$ for some $0 \leq i < k$. This produces $2k$ sub-instances for any given instance. Moreover, these sub-instances clearly partition the solution space of a given problem instance while excluding the current solution $(s_1, \ldots, s_k)$. For each variable, we only need to keep up to two (in)equalities of this form (i.e., the most restrictive ones). Actually, we can ensure that the size of the considered instance never increases by initially adding the two inequalities $-2^{h(k)p(L)} < x_i < 2^{h(k)p(L)}$ for each i. Hence, the number of (in)equalities in any given instance explored through our algorithm is at most $2k$ more than in the original instance. In other words, the size of all sub-instances thus produced is polynomially bounded in the size of the input problem instance. Hence, by applying the "alternative output" technique (see [22,28]) recalled above, we thus achieve FPT delay, even without a bound on the depth of the search tree.

Generalization and formalization. We now remove the depth bound γ entirely, and thus the focus is on finding a method by which, for any given solution S, we can find (and calculate in FPT-time) child instances for which the solution spaces are disjoint and exclude precisely S. We need a method f to generate these child instances, but also a method g to find a solution to any given instance. Also, if no solution exists, we want f to return the empty set. The following definition captures these requirements.

Definition 5. *For an enumeration problem Q, we call a tuple of functions (f, g) a* solution search partition algorithm*, if the following conditions hold:*

- $g\colon \Sigma^* \times \mathbb{N} \to \Sigma^*$ *is an* FPT*-time function such that for all* $(I, k) \in \Sigma^* \times \mathbb{N}$*:*
  - $g(I, k)$ *computes a solution* $S \in Q(I, k)$*, if it exists.*
- $f\colon \Sigma^* \times \mathbb{N} \times \Sigma^* \to \mathcal{P}(\Sigma^* \times \mathbb{N})$ *is an* FPT*-time function such that for all* $(I, k, S) \in \Sigma^* \times \mathbb{N} \times \Sigma^*$*:*
  - *if* $Q(I, k) = \emptyset$*, then* $f(I, k, S) = \emptyset$*,*
  - $Q(I, k) \setminus \{S\} = \biguplus_{(I', k') \in f(I,k,S)} Q(I', k')$*,*
  - *for all* $(I', k') \in f(I, k, S)$*,* $|(I', k')| \leq |(I, k)|$ *and* $k' \leq k$*,*

Note that, due to the need to store the path we are exploring, which is unbounded in size, there is also no bound on the space requirement of such an algorithm.

Proposition 6. *Let Q be a parameterized enumeration problem. If Q has a solution search partition algorithm (f, g), then Q is in* DelayFPT.

For Integer Linear Programming with k Variables, g is the original FPT algorithm, which we can apply directly as we do not need to generalize the problem setting for our enumeration. Function f is used to create the $2k$ sub-instances with added inequalities. It is also responsible for eliminating redundant (in)equalities to make sure that we never get an instance with more than two additional (in)equalities per variable (compared with the original system of inequalities). The condition $k' \leq k$ on instances produced by function f is trivially satisfied since we never add a variable.

4 Union Enumeration

In Sect. 3, we discussed FPT-delay algorithms that partition the solution space into parts that can be efficiently enumerated individually. As we have outlined, for some problems, this can be naturally achieved. However, for other problems and other classical techniques to design FPT decision algorithms, preventing this overlap is less natural (e.g., in the problem considered below). Thus, we next discuss a method for dealing with non-empty intersections of some parts.

More concretely, suppose that the solution space $\mathcal{S} = \bigcup_i \mathcal{S}_i$ is given as a union, such that the $\mathcal{S}_i$'s are not pairwise disjoint. It would be tempting to enumerate one subset $\mathcal{S}_i$ after the other and, before outputting the next solution $S \in \mathcal{S}_i$, check if it was already output when processing $\mathcal{S}_1, \dots, \mathcal{S}_{i-1}$. However, it may happen that we encounter a long sequence of already output solutions and, therefore, FPT-delay is no longer guaranteed. Instead, we use a technique developed in [27, Section 2.5] for enumerating elements of a union of sets without duplicates. Besides the efficient enumerability of each set in the union (in our case with FPT-delay), this technique requires membership checks to be efficiently doable (in our case in FPT). Thus, intuitively, we seek to first split the solution space into FPT-many subsets of solutions such that, (i) *every* solution is part of some subset, (ii) every subset can be *enumerated* with FPT-delay, and (iii) *checking* whether a solution is part of a subset can be done in FPT-time.

A clear application of this method is for derandomized color coding algorithms. Thus, we will illustrate the method by considering the LONGEST PATH problem, which asks for *simple paths*, i.e., paths that contain every vertex at most once, of length k in a given graph G, where k is the parameter. We here consider the length of a simple path to be the number of vertices it contains instead of the number of edges.

Proposition 7. LONGEST PATH *is in* DelayFPT.

Proof. We are given a graph $G = (V, E)$ and an integer k. The idea of color coding introduced in [1] applied to LONGEST PATH is the following:

1. Introduce k colors and color each vertex $v \in V$ in one color $\gamma(v) \in \{1, \dots, k\}$.
2. For $C = \{1, \dots, k\}$, find a C-*colorful* path in G for γ, i.e., a path where every color $i \in C$ appears exactly once on the path.

We first discuss how to find all colorful paths in G under a given coloring $\gamma\colon V \to \{1, \dots, k\}$. For that, we follow a dynamic programming approach and compute, for every $C \subseteq \{1, \dots, k\}$ and $u \in V$, the following set $P(C, u)$:

$$P(C,u) := \{v \in V \mid \text{there exists a } C\text{-colorful path } (v_1, \dots, v_{|C|}) \text{ in } G \text{ such that } v_{|C|-1} = v, v_{|C|} = u, \text{ and } C = \{\gamma(v_1), \dots, \gamma(v_{|C|})\}\}.$$

That is, for a vertex u and subset of colors $C \subseteq \{1, \dots, k\}$, we keep track of those vertices v that are the predecessors of u on C-colorful paths that end in u. Then, clearly, $P(\{1, \dots, k\}, u) \neq \emptyset$ if and only if there is a colorful path (of length k) that ends in u.

To compute all sets $P(C, u)$, we start by iterating through the edges $vw \in E, \gamma(w) \neq \gamma(v)$ and add v to $P(\{\gamma(w), \gamma(v)\}, w)$ (symmetrically for w as well). Then, for $|C| > 2$ and $\gamma(u) \in C$, we compute $P(C, u)$, using the equality

$$P(C, u) = \{v \in V \mid vu \in E \text{ and } P(C \setminus \{\gamma(u)\}, v) \neq \emptyset\}.$$

Thus, in total, we can compute all $P(C, u)$ in FPT-time. Moreover, we can enumerate all $\{1, \ldots, k\}$-colorful paths in G for γ with FPT-delay by using these sets. Concretely, we can simply use k nested loops: The first loop iterates through all $v_1 \in V$ such that $P(\{1, \ldots, k\}, v_1) \neq \emptyset$. The second loop iterates through all $v_2 \in P(\{1, \ldots, k\}, v_1)$. The i-th loop iterates through all $v_i \in P(\{1, \ldots, k\} \setminus \{\gamma(v_1), \ldots, \gamma(v_{i-2})\}, v_{i-1})$. By construction, none of the considered sets can be empty and each $(v_1, \ldots, v_k)$ considered is a unique $\{1, \ldots, k\}$-colorful path because it neither shares a color with $v_1, \cdots, v_{i-2}$ nor with v_{i-1}.

Note that for a given coloring γ and path π, it is easy to decide if the algorithm described above will output π. To do this, simply check whether π is $\{1, \ldots, k\}$-colorful for γ.

Next we will discuss the colorings we use in more detail. For this, we make use of *perfect hash families.* A perfect hash family is a set of colorings Γ (using k colors) such that for any subset $\pi \subseteq V$ of size k there exists a coloring $\gamma \in \Gamma$ that colors the vertices $v \in \pi$ with unique colors, i.e., if $u, v \in \pi, u \neq v$, then $\gamma(u) \neq \gamma(v)$. According to [25], we can find such a family of colorings Γ of size $e^k k^{O(logk)} \log n$ in time $e^k k^{O(logk)} n \log n$, i.e., in FPT-time. Let Π_γ be the $\{1, \ldots, k\}$-colorful paths for $\gamma \in \Gamma$. Note that every path in G of length k is $\{1, \ldots, k\}$-colorful for some $\gamma \in \Gamma$.

In total, we have that the set of all paths of length k is $\bigcup_{\gamma \in \Gamma} \Pi_\gamma$, we can enumerate each Π_γ in DelayFPT, and we can check membership of Π_γ in FPT (actually also polynomial time). Now let us apply the technique developed in [27] for avoiding duplicates. To that end, we do the following: We take an arbitrary order of the colorings $\{\gamma_1, \ldots, \gamma_{|\Gamma|}\} = \Gamma$. Then, we start enumerating Π_{γ_1} until the algorithm described above finds its first solution π_1. At that point, we pause the enumeration of Π_{γ_1} and check whether one of $\Pi_{\gamma_2}, \ldots, \Pi_{\gamma_{|\Gamma|}}$ contains π_1. If this is the case, we discard π_1 and simply start enumerating Π_{γ_2} up to the first solution π_2. At that point, we also pause the enumeration of Π_{γ_2} and check whether one of $\Pi_{\gamma_3}, \ldots, \Pi_{\gamma_{|\Gamma|}}$ contains π_3. We continue this process recursively. That is, we are searching for the first Π_{γ_i} whose next solution is π_i but which is not part of any $\Pi_{\gamma_{i+1}}, \ldots, \Pi_{\gamma_{|\Gamma|}}$. Now we can output π_i and *not* output $\pi_1, \ldots, \pi_{i-1}$ (they are discarded from $\Pi_{\gamma_1}, \ldots, \Pi_{\gamma_{i-1}}$). Note that the solutions $\pi_1, \ldots, \pi_{i-1}$ will be output later using a different coloring $\gamma \in \Gamma$. We apply this recursive procedure until for every Π_{γ_i} every $\pi_i \in \Pi_{\gamma_i}$ was either output or discarded.

Each recursive procedure call requires at most $|\Gamma|$-many calls to a DelayFPT enumeration procedure and $|\Gamma|$-many FPT membership calls. Thus, in total, Longest Path is in DelayFPT.

Generalization and Formalization. Intuitively, our union enumeration method seeks to first split the solution space into subsets of solutions such that these subsets cover the entire solution space but they are, in general, not disjoint. To combine the enumeration algorithms of these subsets into an enumeration of the entire solution space while avoiding duplicates, we assign an instance (I, k) a finite number of identifiers (e.g. certain colorings on a graph) $c(I, k) = \{\gamma_1, \cdots \gamma_l\}$, and we need a function f that enumerates a subset of solutions $P_i \subseteq Q(I, k)$ for each identifier γ_i without taking too long between consecutive solutions. While we require that these P_i cover the entire set $Q(I, k)$, there may be pairwise overlaps. As has been discussed above, in order to guarantee FPT-delay, we use a technique developed in [27] for enumerating elements of a union of sets without duplicates. Besides the efficient enumerability of each set in the union (in our case FPT-delay), this technique requires an (in our case FPT) function g to decide whether a solution S belongs to the solution set P_i of a given identifier γ_i in order to quickly check if there is any overlap between solution sets. We formalize this idea in the following definition.

Definition 6. *For an enumeration problem Q, we call a tuple of functions (c, f, g) a* union enumeration algorithm *if, for some computable function $h\colon \mathbb{N} \to \mathbb{N}$ and polynomial p, the following conditions hold:*

- $c\colon \Sigma^* \times \mathbb{N} \to \mathcal{P}(\Sigma^*)$ *and $c(I, k)$ can be computed in time $O(h(k)p(|(I, k)|))$,*
- $f\colon \Sigma^* \times \mathbb{N} \times \Sigma^* \to \mathcal{P}(\Sigma^*)$ *is such that for all $(I, k, \gamma) \in \Sigma^* \times \mathbb{N} \times \Sigma^*$:*
  - $\bigcup_{\gamma \in c(I,k)} f(I, k, \gamma) = Q(I, k)$,
  - *for every $\gamma \in c(I, k)$, the delay of $f(I, k, \gamma)$ is $O(h(k)p(|(I, k)|))$,*
- $g\colon \Sigma^* \times \mathbb{N} \times \Sigma^* \times \Sigma^* \to \{0, 1\}$ *is such that for all $(I, k, \gamma, S) \in \Sigma^* \times \mathbb{N} \times \Sigma^* \times \Sigma^*$:*
  - $g(I, k, \gamma, S) = 1$ *if and only if $S \in f(I, k, \gamma)$,*
  - $g(I, k, \gamma, S)$ *can be computed in time $O(h(k)p(|(I, k)|))$.*

It remains to make explicit how to efficiently enumerate a union of non-necessarily disjoint sets. This is done in the proof of the following proposition (for details, see [11]).

Proposition 8. *Let Q be a parameterized enumeration problem. If Q has a union enumeration algorithm (f, g, c), then Q is in* DelayFPT.

To fit our Longest Path algorithm from the proof of Proposition 7 into this framework, we would first compute a perfect hash family Γ and, for given instance $I = G = (V, E)$, set $c(G, k) = \Gamma$. Moreover, we define $f(G, k, \gamma)$ as the set of $\{1, \ldots, k\}$-colorful paths, and $g(G, k, \gamma, \pi)$ to indicate if π is a $\{1, \ldots, k\}$-colorful path. As discussed above, all of these steps can be done in FPT-delay, resp. FPT-time.

5 Iterative Compression

Iterative compression is another classic method to develop FPT decision algorithms. Intuitively, the basic idea is to start with a solution S_{sub} of a small sub-instance (I_{sub}, k), and to gradually increase the size of the sub-instance while maintaining a solution until we arrive back at the original instance (I, k). Maintaining the solution S_{sub} and growing the instance (I_{sub}, k) is done in two steps: (1) We start by growing I_{sub} to I_{next} while, at the same time, we increase the parameter k to k'. Here, the increase in the parameter and the access to a solution of the smaller instance should help us to efficiently find a solution S'_{next} of (I_{next}, k'). (2) Then, we *compress* S'_{next} down to a solution S_{next} of (I_{next}, k).

We thus naturally arrive at a solution of (I, k) if it exists. To transform a decision iterative compression algorithm into an enumeration one, it seems natural to simply transform the compression step into an enumeration algorithm. That is, instead of compressing S'_{next} down to a single solution of (I_{next}, k), we should aim at an algorithm that manages to enumerate *all* solutions of (I_{next}, k) with the help of S'_{next}. In fact, the adaptation is only necessary in the very last compression step, i.e., where (I_{next}, k) is our original instance.

We will illustrate how an iterative compression decision algorithm can be transformed into an enumeration algorithm with the well-known VERTEX COVER, i.e., given a graph $G = (V, E)$, we are looking for vertex covers of size $\leq k$ where k is the parameter. Recall, that a set $S \subseteq V$ is a vertex cover if $G[V \setminus S]$ only contains isolated vertices.

Proposition 9. VERTEX COVER *is in* DelayFPT.

Proof. Let (G, k) be an instance of VERTEX COVER. For the graph $G = (V, E)$ with $V = \{v_1, \cdots, v_n\}$, let G_i denote the subgraph induced by the vertex set $\{v_1, \ldots, v_i\}$. These graphs G_i will be the sub-instances considered by the iterative compression algorithm. We can do the following:

First, note that, trivially, $\emptyset$ is a vertex cover of $G_0 = (\emptyset, \emptyset)$ and, hence, (G_0, k) can be our starting instance and $\emptyset$ our initial solution S_0. Then, inductively, for a vertex cover S_i of G_i of size $\leq k$, the set $S'_{i+1} = S_i \cup \{v_{i+1}\}$ is a vertex cover of G_{i+1} of size $\leq k+1$. To compress S'_{i+1} to a vertex cover of size k of G_{i+1}, we observe that we can partition the set of all vertex covers of G_{i+1} according to their intersection with S'_{i+1}. Conversely, given a vertex cover S of G_{i+1}, we can split S'_{i+1} into subsets $C, F \subseteq S'_{i+1}$ with $S'_{i+1} \cap S = C$ and $S'_{i+1} \setminus S = F$. Let $N_{G_{i+1}}(F)$ be the union of the neighbors of the vertices F in G_{i+1}, excluding F itself. Clearly, if a vertex cover S of G_{i+1} does not contain any of the vertices in F, then it must contain all of $N_{G_{i+1}}(F)$. In fact, there exists a vertex cover S having $S \cap S_{i+1} = C$ if and only if $C \cup N_{G_{i+1}}(F)$ is a vertex cover. Hence, to compress S'_{i+1}, it suffices to iterate over all partitionings $S'_{i+1} = C \cup F$. Note that there are only up to FPT-many partitions. For each partition, we simply have to check whether $S_{i+1} = C \cup N_{G_{i+1}}(F)$ is a vertex cover of size at most k.

As long as $i + 1 < n$, we can use *the first* vertex cover S_{i+1} of size $\leq k$ of G_{i+1} as the compressed solution. (The decision procedure would also do this at $i + 1 = n$.) Thus, we proceed with S_{i+1} to G_{i+2}. In contrast, at $i + 1 = n$, we now have to output *all* vertex covers of $G_{i+1} = G$ of size $\leq k$. The good thing is that the compression procedure nicely allows for that. To do so, we simply go over all $S_n = S_{i+1} = C \cup N_G(F)$ that are vertex covers of size $\leq k$.

Then, for each such S_n, we output every $\hat{S}_n \supseteq S_n$ where $\hat{S}_n \setminus S_n \subseteq V \setminus S'_n$ and $|\hat{S}_n| \leq k$. That is, we output S_n and all supersets of S_n with $\leq k$ elements, obtained by only adding vertices from $V \setminus S'_n$. This guarantees that we will never produce duplicates. Moreover, it is easy to see that this enumeration can be done with FPT-delay. Thus, in total, this enumeration version of iterative compression solves Vertex Cover with FPT-delay.

Generalization and Formalization. To transform decision algorithms based on iterative compression into enumeration algorithms, we describe the *growing* and *compression* steps very abstractly. Concretely, we *grow* the instances I one character $\sigma \in \Sigma$ at a time. Thus, from a solution S_{sub} of (I_{sub}, k) we want to be able to determine a solution S'_{next} of $(I_{\text{sub}} \cdot \sigma, k+1)$ in the growing step, and then compress it down to a solution S_{next} of $(I_{\text{sub}} \cdot \sigma, k)$. These two steps are performed by the functions g and c, respectively, in the definition below. Note that for the iterative compression method to work, we need solvability to be preserved when taking sub-instances. Hence, we restrict ourselves here to enumeration problems Q which are such that for any character $\sigma \in \Sigma$, if $Q(I \cdot \sigma, k) \neq \emptyset$, then $Q(I, k) \neq \emptyset$. Note that, while we formalize these steps as growing and compressing k by 1 and I by a single character, these steps obviously also work for other ways of growing and compressing instances and solutions.

Definition 7. *Let Q be an enumeration problem such that for any character $\sigma \in \Sigma$, if $Q(I \cdot \sigma, k) \neq \emptyset$, then $Q(I, k) \neq \emptyset$. We call a tuple of functions (g, c) an* iterative compression algorithm *for Q, if the following conditions hold:*

- *$g\colon \Sigma^* \times \Sigma \times \mathbb{N} \times \Sigma^* \to \Sigma^*$ is an* FPT*-time function such that, for $(I, k, S) \in Q$, we have $g(I, \sigma, k, S) \in Q(I \cdot \sigma, k+1)$ for any $\sigma \in \Sigma$,*
- *$c\colon \Sigma^* \times \mathbb{N} \times \Sigma^* \to \mathcal{P}(\Sigma^*)$ is a function which, for any $(I, k+1, S) \in Q$, enumerates all $S' \in Q(I, k)$ with* FPT*-delay.*

An FPT-delay algorithm based on this definition works as follows. We first restrict our problem to a small part, where finding a solution is trivial (e.g., a small or empty subgraph for graph problems or a constant sized I in general). Then we apply two steps repeatedly: The first step, corresponding to the function g, is the growing step, in which we take our reduced instance and solution and reintroduce deleted information one step at a time, increasing both instance and parameter such that we can easily find a new solution S to this new instance $(I', k+1)$. The second step, corresponding to the function c, is the compression step, where we use S to find all solutions in $Q(I', k)$ (and stop if none are found). We continue rebuilding and then compressing (until the first solution is found) until we arrive at our initial instance and can now output all solutions in $Q(I, k)$. Note that we could actually allow the parameter in each iteration of g to grow by a function $b(k)$, provided that c can compress the solution down to size k.

Proposition 10. *Let Q be a parameterized problem. If Q has an iterative compression algorithm (g, c), then Q is in* DelayFPT.

To relate our algorithm from the proof of Proposition 9 to this framework, we have used a slightly more general growing function g, which allowed us to extend a solution by yet another vertex (and not just a single character). The function c takes a vertex cover S of size $k+1$ as input and enumerates all vertex covers of size $\leq k$ of the same graph. This enumeration is done by partitioning the resulting vertex covers according to their intersection with S.

6 Dynamic Programming

Dynamic programming (DP) is a widely used method for solving problems by splitting instances recursively into ever smaller sub-instances, and ultimately inductively combining the solutions of smaller sub-instances to solutions of bigger ones. DP also has many applications in the area of fixed-parameter algorithms, see, e.g., the LONGEST PATH problem revisited in Sect. 4. Above all, DP algorithms use a table T, whose size is bounded by $O(f(k)n^{O(1)})$, to represent the sub-instances of interest. Then the minimum machinery needed are methods for initializing T and for propagating entries of T from smaller sub-instances to bigger ones, "backlinks" (from a bigger sub-instance to smaller ones) to keep track of the "provenance" of each entry in T, and another method for propagating partial solutions from smaller sub-instances to bigger ones. The DP-based enumeration algorithm discussed in Sect. 4 was rather straightforward, as every sub-instance had a unique backlink. However, in general, quite some additional care is required to avoid duplicates.

To illustrate the additional measures often needed to get a proper FPT-enumeration algorithm via DP, we consider the STEINER TREE problem. That is, we are given an undirected graph $G = (V, E)$ with an edge weight function assigning positive weights to each edge and a subset $K \subseteq V$ of "terminal nodes". A *Steiner tree* for K in a graph G is a connected subgraph H of G that contains K. The weight of a subgraph H is the sum of its edge weights. Then the enumeration problem consists of enumerating all Steiner trees with minimum weight. The decision problem (i.e., does there exist a Steiner tree of weight $\leq B$ for some bound B) is known to be FPT w.r.t. $k = |K|$. It has an elegant FPT-algorithm (see [12, Section 6.1.2]), which works as follows:

W.l.o.g., we may assume that $|K| > 1$ and that each terminal has degree 1 in G and its neighbor is a non-terminal. The first assumption is justified as otherwise $(K, \emptyset)$ is the only minimal weight Steiner tree and the second assumption is justified as otherwise we can simply modify G to have this property. That is, for each $k \in K$ a new neighbor $v_k \notin V$ to v_k with an arbitrarily weighted edge. Then, $K' := \{v_k \mid k \in K\}$ are the new terminal nodes for $G' = (V \cup K', E \cup \{kv_k \mid k \in K\})$. Note that (G, K) and (G', K') admit the same minimal weight Steiner tree (modulo adding/removing K').

The data structure to be propagated by the DP algorithm consists of entries $T[D, v]$ with $D \subseteq K$ and $v \in V \setminus K$. Then $T[D, v] = w$ means that the minimum weight of a Steiner tree of $D \cup \{v\}$ in G is w. The idea of the vertex v (which of course does not necessarily have degree 1 in G) is that we combine Steiner trees of "sub-instances" (i.e., two disjoint subsets $D_1, D_2 \subseteq K$) by merging them at vertex v to get a Steiner tree of $D_1 \cup D_2$. In the sequel, we will refer to Steiner trees with minimal weight simply as "Steiner trees" (omitting the minimality). Moreover, we will denote the set of Steiner trees of $D \cup \{v\}$ in G as $\mathcal{S}(D, v)$ and call them the "solutions" of $T[D, v]$. The set of Steiner trees of G is obtained as the union of those $\mathcal{S}(K, v)$, such that $T[K, v]$ is minimum over all v.

The data structure T is filled in as follows: as initialization step of T, we compute all entries of the form $T[\{t\}, v] = \text{dist}(t, v)$, where $t \in K$, $v \in V \setminus K$, and $\text{dist}(t, v)$ denotes the distance (i.e., the minimal weight of a connecting path) from t to v. Then, existing entries of T are combined recursively via the formula

$$T[D, v] = \min_{\substack{u \in V \setminus K \\ \emptyset \neq D' \subsetneq D}} \{T[D', u] + T[D \setminus D', u] + \text{dist}(u, v)\} \tag{1}$$

Intuitively, a Steiner tree for $D \cup \{v\}$ is obtained by merging Steiner trees for $D' \cup \{u\}$ and $(D \setminus D') \cup \{u\}$ at vertex u and then adding a minimal weight connecting path from u to v. This includes the special case that $u = v$. It is shown in [12, Lemma 6.2] that one thus gets all entries $T[D, v]$ with $\emptyset \neq D \subseteq K$ and $v \in V \setminus K$. Hence, deciding if a Steiner tree of weight $\leq B$ exists comes down to checking if an entry $T[K, v] \leq B$ exists. To also output a solution in case of a yes-instance, one has to maintain backlinks for each application of the above recursion and assemble a Steiner tree of $D \cup \{v\}$ by merging two subtrees and adding a shortest path as described above. Maintaining such backlinks and combining solutions from smaller sub-instances to solutions of bigger ones is routine in the area of DP algorithms.

However, if we want to enumerate *all* Steiner trees, we are immediately faced with the challenge of avoiding *duplicates*. Indeed, an entry $T[D, v]$ can possibly be obtained by combining entries $T[D', u_1]$ and $T[D \setminus D', u_1]$ but also by combining entries $T[D'', u_2]$ and $T[D \setminus D'', u_2]$ with $D' \neq D''$ and/or $u_1 \neq u_2$. Likewise, the solutions of $\mathcal{S}[D, v]$ (i.e., Steiner trees of $D \cup \{v\}$]) obtained by combining solutions of $\mathcal{S}[D', u_1]$ and $\mathcal{S}[D \setminus D', u_1]$ and the solutions of $\mathcal{S}[D, v]$ obtained by combining solutions of $\mathcal{S}[D'', u_2]$ and $\mathcal{S}[D \setminus D'', u_2]$ are not necessarily disjoint. Hence, recursively iterating through all possible backlinks, starting from the entries $\mathcal{S}[K, v]$ with minimal weight, would inevitably produce duplicates.

To achieve unique provenance, intuitively, we have to make sure that for each Steiner tree $S \in \mathcal{S}[D, v]$ there is a unique partitioning $D = D' \cup D \setminus D'$ and a unique merge node $u \in V \setminus K$. This requires several modifications compared with the decision algorithm, namely: (1) we (arbitrarily) fix a strict order on the terminals in K, (2) we extend entries in table T to $T[D, v, b]$, where b is a bit indicating if, in the Steiner trees of $D \cup \{v\}$ represented by $T[D, v, b]$, v has degree 1 (indicated by $b = 1$) or degree > 1 (indicated by $b = 0$), and (3) we impose the restriction that the recursion in Equation (1) may only be applied if D' contains the smallest terminal in D (according to the chosen order) and the left operand is of the form $T[D', u, 1]$, i.e., u has degree 1 in all Steiner trees thus represented. Analogously, we adapt the definition of $\mathcal{S}[D, v, b]$.

We claim that, with these modifications, we indeed achieve a unique provenance of each entry $\mathcal{S}[D, v, b]$ and that we can recurse through the backlinks of these entries so as to output all Steiner trees of a given problem instance with FPT-delay. The formal proof of this claim is given in [11]. We thus get:

Proposition 11. Steiner Tree *is in* DelayFPT.

7 Conclusion

We have revisited several well-established methods for designing FPT decision algorithms in order to transform them into FPT-delay enumeration algorithms. We have illustrated by various examples the subtle differences and the special care required for enumeration algorithms – in particular, the need to obtain all solutions and to avoid duplicates.

While we have explored the design of FPT-delay enumeration algorithms starting from FPT-time techniques, one could also proceed in the other direction and adapt enumeration techniques to the parameterized setting. For instance, the well-known reverse-search method [2], as well as the new and very promising proximity search method [6] would probably be worth a systematic investigation from the FPT point of view.

Acknowledgements. The work of N. Creignou has been supported by the Agence Nationale de la Recherche (ANR) project PARADUAL [ANR-24-CE48-0610-01]. The work of T. Merkl, R. Pichler, and D. Unterberger has been supported by the Vienna Science and Technology Fund (WWTF) [10.47379/ICT2201].

References

1. Alon, N., Yuster, R., Zwick, U.: Color-coding. J. ACM **42**(4), 844–856 (1995)
2. Avis, D., Fukuda, K.: Reverse search for enumeration. Discret. Appl. Math. **65**(1–3), 21–46 (1996)
3. Berlowitz, D., Cohen, S., Kimelfeld, B.: Efficient enumeration of maximal k-plexes. In: Proc. SIGMOD 2015. pp. 431–444. ACM (2015)
4. Bougeret, M., Gomes, G.C.M., dos Santos, V.F., Sau, I.: Enumeration kernels for vertex cover and feedback vertex set. In: Agrawal, A., van Leeuwen, E.J. (eds.) 20th International Symposium on Parameterized and Exact Computation, IPEC 2025, Warsaw, Poland, September 17–19, 2025. LIPIcs, vol. 358, pp. 23:1–23:18. Schloss Dagstuhl - Leibniz-Zentrum für Informatik (2025). https://doi.org/10.4230/LIPICS.IPEC.2025.23, https://doi.org/10.4230/LIPIcs.IPEC.2025.23
5. Conte, A., Grossi, R., Marino, A., Rizzi, R.: Efficient enumeration of graph orientations with sources. Discret. Appl. Math. **246**, 22–37 (2018)
6. Conte, A., Grossi, R., Marino, A., Uno, T., Versari, L.: Proximity search for maximal subgraph enumeration. SIAM J. Comput. **51**(5), 1580–1625 (2022)
7. Conte, A., Uno, T.: New polynomial delay bounds for maximal subgraph enumeration by proximity search. In: Proc. STOC 2019. pp. 1179–1190. ACM (2019)

8. Courcelle, B., Mosbah, M.: Monadic second-order evaluations on tree-decomposable graphs. Theor. Comput. Sci. **109**(1&2), 49–82 (1993)
9. Creignou, N., Ktari, R., Meier, A., Müller, J., Olive, F., Vollmer, H.: Parameterised enumeration for modification problems. Algorithms **12**(9), 189 (2019)
10. Creignou, N., Meier, A., Müller, J., Schmidt, J., Vollmer, H.: Paradigms for parameterized enumeration. Theory Comput. Syst. **60**(4), 737–758 (2017)
11. Creignou, N., Merkl, T.C., Pichler, R., Unterberger, D.: From fpt decision to fpt enumeration. CoRR abs/2512.24137 (2025), https://doi.org/10.48550/arXiv.2512.24137
12. Cygan, M., Fomin, F.V., Kowalik, L., Lokshtanov, D., Marx, D., Pilipczuk, M., Pilipczuk, M., Saurabh, S.: Parameterized Algorithms. Springer (2015)
13. Damaschke, P.: Parameterized enumeration, transversals, and imperfect phylogeny reconstruction. Theor. Comput. Sci. **351**(3), 337–350 (2006)
14. Dreier, J., Ordyniak, S., Szeider, S.: SAT backdoors: Depth beats size. J. Comput. Syst. Sci. **142**, 103520 (2024). https://doi.org/10.1016/J.JCSS.2024.103520, https://doi.org/10.1016/j.jcss.2024.103520
15. Fernau, H.: On parameterized enumeration. Computing and Combinatorics (2002)
16. Gaspers, S., Szeider, S.: Strong backdoors to bounded treewidth SAT. In: 54th Annual IEEE Symposium on Foundations of Computer Science, FOCS 2013, Berkeley, CA, USA, October, 26–29, 2013. pp. 489–498. IEEE Computer Society (2013) https://doi.org/10.1109/FOCS.2013.59, https://doi.org/10.1109/FOCS.2013.59
17. Golovach, P.A., Komusiewicz, C., Kratsch, D., Le, V.B.: Refined notions of parameterized enumeration kernels with applications to matching cut enumeration. J. Comput. Syst. Sci. **123**, 76–102 (2022)
18. Johnson, D.S., Papadimitriou, C.H., Yannakakis, M.: On generating all maximal independent sets. Inf. Process. Lett. **27**(3), 119–123 (1988)
19. Kanté, M.M., Limouzy, V., Mary, A., Nourine, L.: On the enumeration of minimal dominating sets and related notions. SIAM J. Discret. Math. **28**(4), 1916–1929 (2014)
20. Lawler, E.L.: A solution to computing the k best solutions to discrete optimization problems and its application to the shortest path. Manage. Sci. **18**(7), 401–405 (1972)
21. Livshits, E., Kimelfeld, B.: Counting and enumerating (preferred) database repairs. In: Proc. PODS 2017, pp. 289–301. ACM (2017)
22. Marino, A.: Algorithms for biological graphs. Ph.D. thesis, University of Florence, Italy (2012)
23. Meier, A.: Parametrised enumeration. Leibniz Universität Hannover, Habilitationsschrift (2020)
24. Misra, N., Ordyniak, S., Raman, V., Szeider, S.: Upper and lower bounds for weak backdoor set detection. In: Järvisalo, M., Gelder, A.V. (eds.) Theory and Applications of Satisfiability Testing - SAT 2013–16th International Conference, Helsinki, Finland, July 8–12, 2013. Proceedings. Lecture Notes in Computer Science, vol. 7962, pp. 394–402. Springer (2013). https://doi.org/10.1007/978-3-642-39071-5_29, https://doi.org/10.1007/978-3-642-39071-5_29
25. Naor, M., Schulman, L.J., Srinivasan, A.: Splitters and near-optimal derandomization. In: Proc. FOCS 1995, pp. 182–191. IEEE Computer Society (1995)

26. Niedermeier, R.: Invitation to Fixed-Parameter Algorithms. Oxford University Press (2006)
27. Strozecki, Y.: Enumeration complexity and matroid decomposition. Ph.D. thesis, Université Paris Diderot, Paris, France (2010)
28. Uno, T.: Two general methods to reduce delay and change of enumeration algorithms. Tech. rep, NII (2003)

When Symmetry Yields NP-Hardness: Affine ML-SAT on S5 Frames

Andreas Krebs[1] and Arne Meier[2(✉)]

[1] Universität Tübingen, Hannover, Germany
mail@krebs-net.de
[2] Leibniz Universität Hannover, Hannover, Germany
meier@thi.uni-hannover.de

Abstract. Hemaspaandra et al. [JCSS 2010] conjectured that satisfiability for multi-modal logic restricted to the connectives XOR and 1, over frame classes T, S4, and S5, is solvable in polynomial time. We refute this for S5 frames, by proving NP-hardness.

Keywords: Modal Logic · Satisfiability · Complexity · Exclusive-or · Transitivity · Reflexivity · Symmetry

1 Introduction

Modal logic is an established formal concept that traces its roots back to the work of C. I. Lewis [22] in the late 1920s. It garnered significant attention in the 1960s, notably due to contributions from Kripke and Hughes [20,21]. Since then, research in this domain has continued to flourish [7,17]. Modal logic has inspired numerous extensions such as temporal logics [11,15,27,29,31,34], hybrid logics [1,2,32], and description logics [3,8,9]. Additionally, modal logics have found widespread applications within information and knowledge systems [4,10, 14,16,18,23,25].

The core concept of modal logic is the extension of classical propositional logic through the introduction of two *modalities*: $\Box$ (box) and $\Diamond$ (diamond). These modalities facilitate reasoning about necessity (all accessible worlds) and possibility (some accessible worlds). Kripke semantics then interpret formulas over frames—labelled states with transition relations—enabling reasoning over sets of worlds rather than single assignments, as in propositional logic.

This extension results in increased computational complexity, with the satisfiability problem being PSPACE-complete. Recognising the inherent difficulty, Hemaspaandra et al. [19] examined the satisfiability problem for modal logic through the lens of Post's lattice [28], in 2010. Informally, their focus was on restricting all possible sets of Boolean functions, in combination with possible subsets of modalities $\{\Box, \Diamond\}$, and classifying these *fragments* of the modal satisfiability problem with respect to different frame classes that stem from the well-known modal logic systems **K** (all frames), **KD** (total preorder frames), **K4**

A.-Y. Turhan and J. Virtema (Eds.): FoIKS 2026, LNCS 16475, pp. 232–242, 2026.
https://doi.org/10.1007/978-3-032-21540-6_14

(transitive frames), **S4** (reflexive and transitive frames), **S5** (equivalence relation frames, i.e., reflexive, transitive, and symmetric), and **T** (reflexive frames). To streamline notation, we employ the names of the logics to denote their corresponding frame classes. Now, Hemaspaandra et al. [19] classified the computational complexity for almost every fragment, except those restricted to the Boolean connectives $\oplus, \top$—exclusive-or combined with the constant true—over the frame classes **T**, **S4**, and **S5**. They conjectured that these cases could be solvable in polynomial time, akin to their results for **K** and **KD**.

Interestingly, previous research indicates that problems involving the affine function $\oplus$ presents significant challenges. Despite several attempts to classify problems related to extensions of Boolean propositional logic using Post's lattice, these fragments have often eluded complete classification (i.e., matching upper and lower complexity bounds) [5,6,12,13,24,30,33]. Hence, it appears prudent to further examine the impact of $\oplus$ on the tractability of such problems.

Therefore, one of our main motivations is to address the counterintuitive nature of the exclusive-or function and the prevailing perplexity it evokes. The main result of this paper demonstrates that the satisfiability problem for affine multi-modal logic with exclusive-or is NP-hard on S5 frames. This result refutes the conjecture of Hemaspaandra et al. [19] for S5 frames.

The paper is organized as follows. First, we introduce the notions of multi-modal logic, Kripke structures, and frame classes. Section 3 presents the NP lower bound proof for the frame class **S5**, and we conclude thereafter.

2 Preliminaries

Complexity. In this paper, we use the complexity classes P and NP. The reduction used is a polynomial-time many-one reduction, computable by a deterministic Turing machine running in polynomial time. Further background information can be found in the standard textbook by Papadimitriou [26].

Modal Logic. We provide a brief introduction to modal logic; for a more comprehensive treatment, see Blackburn et al. [7]. Let ϕ be a propositional formula and A be a set of variables. We write $A \models \phi$ if and only if the assignment $\theta(a) = 1$ for all $a \in A$ satisfies ϕ.

In this paper, we consider k-multi-modal formulas over a countably infinite set of propositions PROP, the connective $\oplus$, as well as the unary operators $\Diamond_i$ for $i \in \{1, \ldots, k\}$. Formally, the set of all *affine k-multi-modal formulas* $\oplus\mathcal{ML}^k$ is defined by the following grammar:

$$\varphi ::= \top \mid \bot \mid p \mid \varphi \oplus \varphi \mid \Diamond_i \varphi,$$

where $p \in$ PROP. As usual, the $\Box$ operator can be defined using negation and $\Diamond$ as follows: $\Box_i \varphi \equiv (\Diamond_i(\varphi \oplus \top)) \oplus \top$, where $\varphi \oplus \top \equiv \neg\varphi$ is realised. We further use $\oplus\mathcal{ML}^k_M$ to denote the set of affine k-multi-modal formulas over the modalities in $M \subseteq \{\Box, \Diamond\}$.

From a semantic perspective, we use Kripke structures to define the satisfaction relation $\models$.

Definition 1. *Let* $M = (W, \mathbf{R}, \xi)$ *be a Kripke structure, i.e.,* W *be a set of worlds,* $\mathbf{R} = \{R_1, \ldots, R_n\}$ *be a set of transition relations* $R_i \colon W \to W$ *for* $i \in [n]$*, and* $\xi \colon \mathrm{PROP} \to 2^W$ *be a labeling function. Furthermore, let* $\varphi, \psi \in \oplus\mathcal{ML}^k_{\{\Box,\Diamond\}}$*. Then we define for* $w \in W$ *that*

$M, w \models \top$ *always,*
$M, w \models \bot$ *never,*
$M, w \models p$ *if and only if* $w \in \xi(p)$*,*
$M, w \models \varphi \oplus \psi$ *if and only if either* $M, w \models \varphi$ *or* $M, w \models \psi$*,*
$M, w \models \Diamond_i \varphi$ *if and only if there is a* w' *such that* (wR_iw' *and* $M, w' \models \varphi$)*.*

For formulas in $\oplus\mathcal{ML}^1_{\{\Box,\Diamond\}}$*, we simply write* $M = (W, R, \xi)$ *and omit the bold font* $\mathbf{R}$ *to indicate that we consider only a single transition relation. We say that a formula* φ *is* satisfiable *if and only if there exists a Kripke structure* $M = (W, \mathbf{R}, \xi)$ *and a world* $w \in W$ *such that* $M, w \models \varphi$ *is true. Furthermore, we call* $(W, \mathbf{R})$*—that is, a model without a labeling function* ξ*—a* frame.

In this paper, we consider frames that satisfy specific properties, such as transitivity or reflexivity. In particular, we work with the frame classes shown in Fig. 1. If a given Kripke structure M, or a frame $(W, \mathbf{R})$, satisfies the properties of some frame class $\mathbf{F}$, then we say M is an $\mathbf{F}$-structure, or $(W, \mathbf{R})$ is an $\mathbf{F}$-frame.

Frame class	**Description**
T	the set of reflexive frames
S4	the set of reflexive, transitive frames
S5	the set of reflexive, transitive, symmetric frames

Frame property	**FO definition**
reflexive frames	$\forall w \in W : wRw$
transitive frames	$\forall u, v, w \in W : (uRv \land vRw) \to uRw$
symmetric frames	$\forall u, v \in W : uRv \to vRu$

Fig. 1. Frame classes and First-Order definitions of frame properties.

The decision problem of interest is the satisfiability problem for affine k-multi-modal logic. The general definition of this problem is as follows.

Problem: $\mathbf{F}$-$\oplus\mathrm{MSAT}^k_{\{M\}}$
Input: A formula $\varphi \in \oplus\mathcal{ML}^k_M$.
Question: Does there exist an $\mathbf{F}$-structure $M = (W, \mathbf{R}, \xi)$, and a world $w \in W$ such that $M, w \models \varphi$?

In the case we investigate, we have $M = \{\Box, \Diamond\}$. Given a Kripke structure $M = (W, \mathbf{R}, \xi)$, we define a *substructure* $S \subseteq M$ to be of the form $S = (W', \mathbf{R}|_{W'}, \xi|_{W'})$, where $W' \subseteq W$, $\mathbf{R}|_{W'}$ is the restriction of each relation $R \in \mathbf{R}$ to $R \cap (W' \times W')$, and $\xi|_{W'}$ is the restriction of ξ to worlds in W'.

3 Affine ML-SAT on S5 Frames Is NP-Hard

In this section, we are going to prove the NP-hardness result of our problem with respect to the frame class **S5**.

Consider a 3CNF formula $f = \bigwedge_{i=1}^{l} C_i$, where C_i is a clause with 3 literals, i.e., $C_i = l_{i1} \vee l_{i2} \vee l_{i3}$. The literals are either a or $\neg a$ for variables $a \in A$, and A is the set of variables.

Remark 1. We assume that the parentheses are inserted such that the connective $\wedge$ only appears as a binary connective and the depth of the formula is logarithmic in the number of clauses. So every subformula of f is either of the form $(l_{i1} \vee l_{i2} \vee l_{i3})$ or is a conjunction $(g \wedge h)$, where g and h are subformulas of f. This will be a crucial point in the course of the proof.

Let us now define the property of independent subformulas, which will be used later in the proof of Theorem 1.

Definition 2. *Let g, h be subformulas of f. We say that g is* independent *from h if there exists a clause in g consisting of variables which all are not present in h. If g is independent from h and h is independent from g then we say g and h are* strongly independent.

Example 1. Let $f = (a \vee b \vee c) \wedge (\overline{d} \vee f \vee e) \wedge (\overline{e} \vee f \vee g)$, and the subformulas $g = (a \vee b \vee c)$, $h = (\overline{d} \vee f \vee e) \wedge (\overline{e} \vee f \vee g)$. Then g and h are strongly independent, but $g' = g \vee (\overline{d} \vee f \vee e)$ is not strongly independent of h.

This property will ensure that in our upcoming construction we never have a subformula $(g \wedge h)$ where $g \equiv h$.

Theorem 1. **S5**-$\oplus$MSAT$^2_{\{\Box,\Diamond\}}$ *is* NP-*hard.*

Proof of Theorem 1. The main idea is a reduction from 3SAT to **S5**-$\oplus$MSAT$^2_{\{\Box,\Diamond\}}$. Given a 3CNF formula, we transform it into another 3CNF formula such that, for every subformula $g \wedge h$, g and h are independent, while preserving the satisfiability of the original formula.

Lemma 1. *Let A and B be two disjunct sets of variables. Given a formula $f = \bigwedge_{i=1}^{l} C_i$ over the variables A then the formula $f' = \bigwedge_{i=1}^{l} (C_i \wedge (b_i \vee b_i \vee b_i))$ over the variables $B = \{b_1, \ldots, b_l\}$ is satisfiable iff f is satisfiable. Moreover for any subformula $(g \wedge h)$ of f', we have that g and h are strongly independent.*

Proof of Lemma 1. It is clear that f is satisfiable iff f' is satisfiable, since when all variables of B are assigned to true f and f' are syntactically the same formula.

Also given any subformula $(g \wedge h)$ of f', then either $h = (b_i \vee b_i \vee b_i)$ for some i or both g and h contain a clause consisting of a different variable of B. (Lemma 1)□

Using the previous lemma, we will assume from now on that for every subformula $g \wedge h$ of f, g and h are independent.

We are now able to define the inductive translation $\phi_{(\cdot)}$ from propositional 3CNF formulas to formulas in $\oplus\mathcal{ML}^2_{\{\Box,\Diamond\}}$ as follows:

$$\begin{aligned} \phi_a &= (\Box_1 a) \oplus (\Box_2\Box_1 a) && \text{, if } a \text{ is a positive literal} \\ \phi_{\neg a} &= (\Box_1 \neg a) \oplus (\Box_2\Box_1 \neg a) && \text{, if } \neg a \text{ is a negative literal,} \\ \phi_C &= \Diamond_1(\phi_{l_1} \oplus \phi_{l_2} \oplus \phi_{l_3}) && \text{, if } C = l_1 \vee l_2 \vee l_3 \text{ is a clause,} \end{aligned}$$

and given a subformula $(g \wedge h)$ we define

$$\psi_g = \phi_g \oplus \Box_2\phi_g, \quad \text{and} \quad \psi_h = \phi_h \oplus \Box_2\phi_h,$$
$$\phi_{g\wedge h} = (\Diamond_1(\psi_g \oplus \psi_h)) \oplus (\Diamond_1\psi_g) \oplus (\Diamond_1\psi_h).$$

With an appropriate bracketing of f (see Remark 1), the formula ϕ_f will have polynomial size in the size of f. Note that ψ_g and ψ_h are satisfied in subparts of any model, whereas $\psi_{g\wedge h}$ is either true or false in the complete model.

We now claim that f is satisfiable if and only if ϕ_f is satisfiable. We will prove this claim in two separate statements. First, consider the easy direction "$\Rightarrow$".

Proposition 1. *If ϕ_f is satisfiable, then f is satisfiable.*

Proof of Proposition 1. Assume that ϕ_f is satisfiable, i.e., there exists M, w such that $M, w \models \phi_f$. Consider the set $A = \{\, a_i \mid M, w \models a_i \,\}$. We show that $A \models f$ by induction on the structure of f. Let $W = \{\, w' \mid w \sim_1 w' \,\}$. Our inductive hypothesis is if there exists a state $w' \in W$ such that $W, w' \models \phi_f$ then $A \models f$.

Let f' be an arbitrary subformula of f.

Case $f' = a$:
Let $w' \in W$ such that $w' \models \phi_a$. Then $M, w' \models (\Box_1 a)\oplus(\Box_2\Box_1 a)$ (by definition of ϕ_a), which implies that $M, w' \models (\Box_1 a)$ (by reflexivity of M), and hence for every $w'' \in W$ we have that $M, w'' \models a$ (as all worlds in W are $\sim_1$-reachable) and therefore $a \in A$.
By a symmetric argument $M, w'' \models \phi_{\neg a}$ implies for every $w''' \in W$ we have that $M, w''' \models \neg a$. Hence, if there exist $w' \in W$ such that $w' \models \phi_{\neg a}$ then $a \notin A$.

Case $f' = l_1 \vee l_2 \vee l_3$:
Firstly, note that if there exists a $w' \in W$ such that $M, w' \models \phi_{l_1 \vee l_2 \vee l_3}$, then there exists $w'' \in W$ such that $M, w'' \models \phi_{l_i}$ for some $i = 1, 2, 3$. Then, by induction hypothesis, we know that $A \models l_i$. Therefore, we have that $A \models l_1 \vee l_2 \vee l_3$.

Case $f' = g \wedge h$**:**
We show that if there exists a $w' \in W$ such that $M, w' \models \phi_{g \wedge h}$, then there exists $w'', w''' \in W$ such that $M, w'' \models \phi_g$ and $M, w''' \models \phi_h$. Assume, w.l.o.g. that for all w'', $M, w'' \not\models \phi_g$. Therefore for all w'', we have $M, w'' \not\models \psi_g$ and hence $M, w'' \not\models \phi_{g \wedge h}$.
So we assume that there exists $w'', w''' \in M$, such that $M, w'' \models \phi_g$ and $M, w''' \models \phi_h$. By induction hypothesis, this implies $A \models g$ and $A \models h$. Therefore, we have that $A \models g \wedge h$.

Hence, we have that $A \models f$ and the proposition holds. (Proposition 1)□

Now consider the more difficult part to prove, i.e., the direction "$\Leftarrow$".

Proposition 2. *If f is satisfiable then ϕ_f is satisfiable.*

Proof of Proposition 2. Fix a formula f, and a satisfying assignment A. For a model M and an assignment A, we define the *A-core* of M to be a nonempty set $S \subseteq M$ which satisfies the following properties:

- S is an equivalence class under $\sim_1$, and
- for all $w \in S$ we have that $M, w \models a_i$ if and only if $A \models a_i$.

Let g be a subformula of f. We say that a model M is a *nice* model for g if M has a non-empty core S in which all worlds satisfy g. Looking back at the proof of Proposition 1, one will notice that we actually proved that every satisfying model for ϕ_f is, in fact, a nice model for f. For this direction, we will construct nice models by induction over the structure of the formula, starting with single clauses and providing a construction for $(g \wedge h)$.

Lemma 2. *For every clause C, we have a nice model for the formula ϕ_C.*

Proof of Lemma 2. Let $C = l_1 \vee l_2 \vee l_3$ be some clause and A be a valid assignment for f. Therefore, we know that $A \models C$, that is, one of the literals, say l_j, for a $j \in [3]$ is satisfied by A. Consider an assignment A' such that $A' \models l_{j'}$ for all $j' \neq j$ and $A' \not\models l_j$. Of course, such an assignment exists.

Now define the nice model as depicted in Fig. 2. The model M for ϕ_C consists of states w and v, where the propositions in w is A and the propositions in v is A'. We have the following relations among the states: $(w \sim_{\{1,2\}} w), (v \sim_{\{1,2\}} v), (w \sim_2 v)$.

Then it is clear that $M, w \models \phi_{l_{j'}}$ and for all $j' \neq j$, we have that $M, w \not\models l_j$. Therefore, we have that $M, w \models \phi_{C_i}$.

Note that the core of this model consists of just the single state w. Also observe that all the properties required for a nice model are satisfied. (Lemma 2)□

For the subsequent construction, we need to find a model for $(g \wedge h)$ given models for g and h. The following result shows that the nice property of models is preserved under arbitrary extensions.

Lemma 3. *Let g be a formula and let M be a nice model for g with core S. Let M' be an arbitrary model with (a possibly empty) core S'. Then there exists a nice model $\hat{M}$ which satisfies g.*

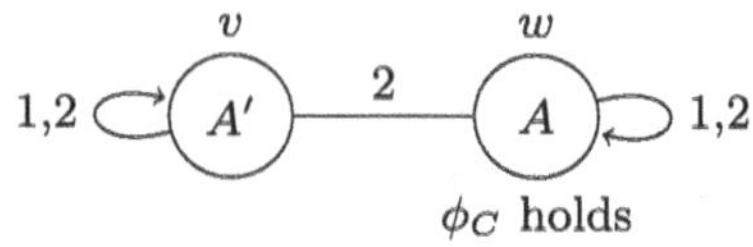

Fig. 2. Satisfying nice model for Lemma 2.

Proof of Lemma 3. Consider the new model $\hat{M} = M \cup M'$, where $S \cup S'$ are pairwise connected by $\sim_1$. Then $\hat{M}$ is a nice model with core $S \cup S'$. In particular, for all $m \in S \cup S'$, we have that

$$\hat{M}, m \models \phi_g.$$

Due to the form of ϕ_g, which begins with a $\Diamond_1$ operator, this property holds immediately. (Lemma 3)□

The next lemma demonstrates an interesting property of *independent* formulas (see Definition 2). Recall that we assume for any subformula $(g \wedge h)$ of f, the formulas g and h are independent.

Lemma 4. *Let g, h be independent subformulas of f, and let M be model and world $m \in M$ such that $M, m \models \phi_g \wedge \phi_h$. Then there exists a model N and world $n \in N$ such that $N, n \models \phi_g \wedge \neg\phi_h$.*

Proof of Lemma 4. This follows directly from the definition of independence: since we can find a clause in h whose variables do not appear in g, we can falsify this clause and thereby falsify h, while the satisfiability of g remains unaffected. (Lemma 4)□

We now claim that for any formula $\phi_{h \wedge g}$, where h and g are independent and both are conjunctions of clauses, we can construct a nice model.

Lemma 5. *Let g and h be independent subformulas of f that correspond to sets of clauses. If there are nice models for ϕ_h, ϕ_g, then there exists a nice model for $\phi_{h \wedge g}$.*

Proof of Lemma 5. Let M_g, M_h be nice models of ϕ_g, ϕ_h with cores S_g, S_h, respectively. Furthermore, let w_g, w_h be two additional worlds with propositions A (recall that A is the satisfying assignment of f). We connect all worlds of $S = \{w_g, w_h\} \cup S_g \cup S_h$ pairwise via $\sim_1$ giving the set S.

Applying Lemma 4 on copies of M_g and M_h then constructs models $\bar{M}_g$, $\bar{M}_h$, and worlds v_g and v_h such that $\bar{M}_g, v_g \models \phi_g \wedge \neg\phi_h$ and $\bar{M}_h, v_h \models \phi_h \wedge \neg\phi_g$. We now make a $\sim_2$-edge between w_g and v_h and a $\sim_2$-edge between w_h and v_g as shown in Fig. 3.

Now we claim that the resulting model M is a nice model with core S.

Due to Lemma 3 the following is true: For all $w \in S$, we have that $M, w \models \phi_g$, and for all $w \in S$, we have that $M, w \models \phi_h$.

By the additional $\sim_2$-edges at w_g, w_h which are the only (!) $\sim_2$-edges at these states we have that $M, w_g \models \psi_g$ and $M, w_h \models \psi_h$. Then also $M, w_h \models \neg\psi_g$ and $M, w_g \models \neg\psi_h$, as in v_g and in w_h the formula ϕ_g is true.

The last fact immediately gives the following. For all $w \in S$, we have that $M, w \models \Diamond_1\psi_g$. For all $w \in S$, we have that $M, w \models \Diamond_1\psi_h$. For all $w \in S$, we have that $M, w \models \Diamond_1(\psi_g \oplus \psi_h)$, due to w_g (resp., w_h).

Hence, for all $w \in S$, we have that $M, w \models \phi_{g\wedge h}$. (Lemma 5)□

Finally, we can complete the proof of Proposition 2, showing that if f is satisfiable, then ϕ_f is satisfiable.

Assume that f is satisfiable. We now show, by induction on the depth of the formula, that there exists a model M_f and a state m_f such that $M_f, m_f \models \phi_f$.

The base case is given by Lemma 2. Every clause C_i is now a conjunction with the B_i propositional clause. The clauses C_i and B_i satisfy the condition for independent subformulas and therefore we can apply Lemma 5 and get a nice model which satisfies $\phi_{C_i \wedge b_i}$. We can continue applying Lemma 5, since there will always be a literal different in the combining subformulas. (Proposition 2)□

Since Propositions 1 and 2 have been proven and the reduction can be computed in polynomial time, the theorem follows. (Theorem 1)□

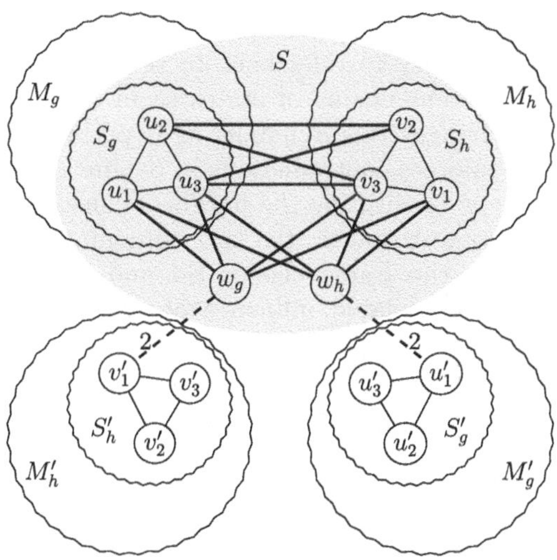

Fig. 3. A nice model for conjunction used in the proof of Lemma 5. Thick lines are $\sim_1$ transitions, wherease thick dashed lines are $\sim_2$ transitions.

A few insights into the two left open cases

As noted in the introduction, two cases from Hemaspaandra et al. [19] remain open: **S4**-$\oplus$MSAT$^1_{\{\Box,\Diamond\}}$ and **T**-$\oplus$MSAT$^2_{\{\Box\}}$.

We are still investigating these cases but want to offer preliminary insights here. The NP-hardness proof above relied crucially on frame symmetry to construct nice models, a property absent in **S4** and **T**. This precludes reusing cores as before, rendering such constructions inapplicable.

Now consider $\phi \oplus \psi$ where ϕ and ψ have unequal modal depths. For satisfiability, a model of sufficient depth can falsify the deeper formula outside the submodel evaluating the shallower one. This observation could help in adapting the polynomial-time algorithm of Hemaspaandra et al. [19] to these cases, supporting their conjecture. Yet, we have not fully formalised this intuition into a complete and rigorous proof.

4 Conclusion

In this paper, we have resolved one of the open cases identified by Hemaspaandra et al. [19]. Specifically, our result demonstrates that, for the frame class **S5**, their conjecture does not hold under the widely accepted complexity assumption that $\mathrm{P} \neq \mathrm{NP}$. In particular, we have established the NP-hardness of the satisfiability problem in this setting.

An intriguing observation emerges regarding the role of symmetry in **S5**, which appears to be the pivotal factor enabling this NP-hardness. In reflexive and transitive frames, the modalities allow movement only forward through the model, without the ability to refer back to previous states. Consequently, interactions between different chains of states seem impossible. However, the presence of symmetry changes this dynamic, as it permits returning to earlier states. This capability enforces contradictions in regions of the model that were visited previously, thereby facilitating the hardness construction.

As future work, we plan to tackle the two remaining open cases from [19], namely those concerning the frame classes **S4** and **T**. Additionally, further research could explore the isolated influence of symmetry by examining the complexity of the modal satisfiability problem in purely reflexive and symmetric frames. The other open cases for different logics mentioned in the introduction also present promising avenues for investigation.

Acknowledgments. The second author appreciates funding by the German Research Foundation (DFG) under the grant ME 4279/3-1.

Disclosure of Interests. The authors have no competing interests to declare that are relevant to the content of this article.

References

1. Areces, C., Blackburn, P., Marx, M.: Hybrid logic is the bounded fragment of first-order logic. In: Proceedings of the WOLLIC-99, pp. 35–50 (1999)
2. Areces, C., Blackburn, P., Marx, M.: A road-map on complexity for hybrid logics. In: Flum, J., Rodriguez-Artalejo, M. (eds.) CSL 1999. LNCS, vol. 1683, pp. 307–321. Springer, Heidelberg (1999). https://doi.org/10.1007/3-540-48168-0_22

3. Baader, F., Calvanese, D., McGuinness, D.L., Nardi, D., Patel-Schneider, P.F. (eds.): The Description Logic Handbook: Theory, Implementation, and Applications, 2nd edn., vol. 1. Cambridge University Press (2003)
4. Baader, F., Laux, A.: Terminological logics with modal operators. In: Proceedings of the 14th International Joint Conference on Artificial Intelligence (IJCAI 1995). pp. 808–814. Montreal, Canada (1995). https://www.ijcai.org/Proceedings/95-1/Papers/104.pdf
5. Bauland, M., Mundhenk, M., Schneider, T., Schnoor, H., Schnoor, I., Vollmer, H.: The tractability of model checking for LTL: the good, the bad, and the ugly fragments. ACM Trans. Comput. Logic (TOCL) **12**(2), 13:1-13:28 (2011)
6. Bauland, M., Schneider, T., Schnoor, H., Schnoor, I., Vollmer, H.: The complexity of generalized satisfiability for Linear Temporal Logic. LMCS **5**(1), 1–21 (2009)
7. Blackburn, P., van Bentham, J., Wolter, F.: Handbook of Modal Logic. Nort Holland, Amsterdam (2006)
8. Brachman, R.J., Levesque, H.J.: The tractability of subsumption in frame-based description languages. In: AAAI, pp. 34–37 (1984)
9. Brachman, R.J., Schmolze, J.G.: An overview of the KL-ONE knowledge representation system. Cognit. Sci. **9**(2), 171–216 (1985). https://doi.org/10.1207/s15516709cog0902_1
10. Brewka, G., Dix, J., Konolige, K.: Nonmonotonic Reasoning: An Overview, vol. 73. CSLI Publications, Stanford (1997)
11. Clarke, E., Emerson, E.A., Sistla, A.: Automatic verification of finite-state concurrent systems using temporal logic specifications. ACM Trans. Program. Lang. Syst. **8**(2), 244–263 (1986)
12. Creignou, N., Schmidt, J., Thomas, M.: Complexity of propositional abduction for restricted sets of Boolean functions. In: Proceeding of the 12th International Conference on the Principles of Knowledge Representation and Reasoning, pp. 8–16. AAAI Press (2010)
13. Creignou, N., Schmidt, J., Thomas, M., Woltran, S.: Sets of Boolean connectives that make argumentation easier. In: Janhunen, T., Niemelä, I. (eds.) JELIA 2010. LNCS (LNAI), vol. 6341, pp. 117–129. Springer, Heidelberg (2010). https://doi.org/10.1007/978-3-642-15675-5_12
14. Egenhofer, M.J., Golledge, R.G. (eds.): Spatial and Temporal Reasoning in Geographic Information Systems. Oxford University Press (1998)
15. Emerson, E.A., Jutla, C.S.: The complexity of tree automata and logics of programs. SIAM J. Comput. **29**(1), 132–158 (2000)
16. Engelfriet, J., Venema, Y.: A modal logic of information change. In: TARK, pp. 125–131. Morgan Kaufmann (1998)
17. Goldblatt, R.: Mathematical modal logic: a view of its evolution. In: Gabbay, D., Woods, J. (eds.) Logic and the Modalities in the Twentieth Century, Handbook of the History of Logic, vol. 7, pp. 1–98. North-Holland, Amsterdam (2006)
18. Guarino, N.: Formal Ontology in Information Systems: Proceedings of the First International Conference (FOIS'98), June 6–8, Trento, Italy. Frontiers in artificial intelligence and applications, IOS Press (1998). https://books.google.de/books?id=Wf5p3_fUxacC
19. Hemaspaandra, E., Schnoor, H., Schnoor, I.: Generalized modal satisfiability. J. Comput. Syst. Sci. **76**(7), 561–578 (2010)
20. Hughes, G., Cresswell, M.: An Introduction to Modal Logic. Methuen, London (1968)
21. Kripke, S.: Semantical considerations on modal logic. In: Acta Philosophica Fennica. vol. 16, pp. 84–94 (1963)

22. Lewis, C.I.: A Survey of Symbolic Logic. University of California Press, Berkley (1918)
23. Longley, P.A., Goodchild, M.F., Maguire, D.J., Rhind, D.W.: Geographic Information Science and Systems, 4th edn. Wiley, Chichester (2015)
24. Meier, A., Mundhenk, M., Schneider, T., Thomas, M., Weber, V., Weiss, F.: The complexity of satisfiability for fragments of hybrid logic—Part I. In: Královič, R., Niwiński, D. (eds.) MFCS 2009. LNCS, vol. 5734, pp. 587–599. Springer, Heidelberg (2009). https://doi.org/10.1007/978-3-642-03816-7_50
25. Misiuna, K.: A modal logic of information. Logic Logical Philos. **21**(1), 33–51 (2012). https://doi.org/10.12775/LLP.2012.003
26. Papadimitriou, C.H.: Computational Complexity. Addison-Wesley (1994)
27. Pnueli, A.: The temporal logic of programs. In: Proceedings of the 18th Symposium on Foundations of Computer Science, pp. 46–57. IEEE Computer Society Press (1977)
28. Post, E.: The two-valued iterative systems of mathematical logic. Ann. Math. Stud. **5**, 1–122 (1941)
29. Prior, A.N.: Past, Present, and Future. Clarendon Press, Oxford (1967)
30. Reith, S.: Generalized Satisfiability Problems. Ph.D. thesis, Fachbereich Mathematik und Informatik, Universität Würzburg (2001)
31. Schnoebelen, P.: The complexity of temporal logic model checking. In: Advances in Modal Logic. vol. 4, pp. 393–436 (2002)
32. Schwentick, T., Weber, V.: Bounded-variable fragments of hybrid logics. In: Thomas, W., Weil, P. (eds.) STACS 2007. LNCS, vol. 4393, pp. 561–572. Springer, Heidelberg (2007). https://doi.org/10.1007/978-3-540-70918-3_48
33. Thomas, M.: The complexity of circumscriptive inference in post's lattice. In: Erdem, E., Lin, F., Schaub, T. (eds.) LPNMR 2009. LNCS (LNAI), vol. 5753, pp. 290–302. Springer, Heidelberg (2009). https://doi.org/10.1007/978-3-642-04238-6_25
34. Vardi, M.Y., Stockmeyer, L.: Improved upper and lower bounds for modal logics of programs: preliminary report. In: STOC '85: Proceedings of the seventeenth annual ACM Symposium on Theory of computing. LNCS, pp. 240–251 (1985)

Revisiting the Fluted and Forward Fragments with Guards

Hongkai Yin(✉)

Central European University, Quellenstraße 51, 1100 Wien, Austria
yin_hongkai@phd.ceu.edu

Abstract. The guarded fluted (forward) fragment is the intersection of the guarded fragment and the fluted (forward) fragment of first-order logic. In this paper we showcase a simple and special model construction technique which turns each first-order structure into a modal structure and back. Based on that, we devise a translation of the two guarded fragments to the basic modal logic extended with the universal modality, providing a simulation of the guarded fluted fragment as well as a new proof of the ExpTime-completeness of the satisfiability problem. Moreover, our technique induces a variant of the unraveling construction. As an application of the unraveling, we prove the Łoś-Tarski Preservation Theorem in the two fragments.

Keywords: First-order logic · Modal logic · Computational complexity · Model theory · Łoś-Tarski Preservation Theorem

1 Introduction

The fluted and the forward fragments of first-order logic result from very similar syntactic restrictions on the first-order language. In formulas of these fragments, variables always occur in atoms in a fixed order, which is also the order in which they are to be quantified. Such formulas arise naturally as formalizations of quantified sentences in natural languages. For example,

Every student likes some philosophers
$\forall x_1(\mathsf{stud}(x_1) \rightarrow \exists x_2(\mathsf{phil}(x_2) \wedge \mathsf{like}(x_1, x_2)))$

Every professor introduces some Greeks to some students
$\forall x_1(\mathsf{prof}(x_1) \rightarrow \exists x_2(\mathsf{greek}(x_2) \wedge \exists x_3(\mathsf{stud}(x_3) \wedge \mathsf{intro}(x_1, x_2, x_3))))$.

The origin of the fluted fragment can be traced back to W. V. Quine's work on predicate functor logic [15], while the formal definition and the term 'fluted formula' were fixed by W. Purdy [13] (see the bibliographic notes in [11, Ch. 6]). It is proved by Pratt-Hartmann et al. [12] that the satisfiability problem for the fluted fragment is decidable but non-elementary, refuting a result in [14]. The forward fragment is proposed recently by B. Bednarczyk [2]. It syntactically

A.-Y. Turhan and J. Virtema (Eds.): FoIKS 2026, LNCS 16475, pp. 243–260, 2026.
https://doi.org/10.1007/978-3-032-21540-6_15

subsumes the fluted fragment, but the two fragments are shown in [3] to have the same expressive power (if we consider only sentences).

The guarded fragment of first-order logic, originally introduced by Andréka et al. [1], is a well known fragment with nice computational and model-theoretic properties. It is obtained by relativizing quantification in a specific way, which we have been used to in the relational semantics for modal logic. The satisfiability problem for the guarded fragment is shown by E. Grädel [6] to be 2-ExpTime-complete if there is no bound on the number of variables in use, and ExpTime-complete otherwise.

The guarded fluted (forward) fragment, as the name suggests, is the intersection of the guarded and the fluted (forward) fragments. Specifically, the guarded fluted fragment is subsumed by the guarded forward fragment and is strictly less expressive than the latter [3, Thm. 4]. The satisfiability problem for the guarded forward fragment is ExpTime-complete [2, Thm. 4]. Also, the Craig Interpolation Property holds in both fragments [3, Thm. 13].

In this paper we showcase a simple and special model construction technique which turns each first-order structure into a modal structure and back. With that in hand, we devise a translation of the guarded fluted (forward) fragment to $\mathbf{K_U}$, the basic modal logic extended with the universal modality [5], providing a simulation of the guarded fluted fragment by $\mathbf{K_U}$ as well as an alternative (and perhaps simpler) proof of the ExpTime-completeness of the satisfiability problems for the two guarded fragments. (Satisfiability in $\mathbf{K_U}$ is shown to be ExpTime-complete by E. Spaan [16].) The translation is in the style of A. Herzig's translation of the ordered fragment to **KD** [7]. (The ordered fragment is another sub-fragment of the fluted (forward) fragment; a comparison of the ordered and the fluted fragments can be found in [8, Sec. 3.4].)

The technique has also a close connection to the model theory of the two guarded fragments. While the method of unraveling is already given in [1] for the full guarded fragment, Bednarczyk and Jaakkola [4] have a more specific approach in the guarded fluted (forward) fragment. We show that our technique is closely related to the latter. Further, using the unraveling, we establish the Łoś-Tarski Preservation Theorem in the two fragments.

The rest of the article is arranged as follows. In Sect. 2 we review the two guarded fragments and $\mathbf{K_U}$, and present the technique for turning first-order structures into modal structures and back. In Sect. 3 we define the translation, and prove that satisfiability is preserved in both directions. In Sect. 4 we review the bisimulations of the two fragments and the unraveling construction. In Sect. 5 we prove the Łoś-Tarski Preservation Theorem.

2 Languages and Structures

In the present work we consider the equality-free first-order language and the basic modal language extended by the universal modality. The first-order language is purely relational, i.e., it involves no function symbols or constants, and does not contain nullary predicates. The first-order and the modal languages are correlated in the sense that each predicate in the first-order language, regardless of its arity, is used as a proposition letter in the modal language. A structure interpreting the first-order language is called an FO-structure, and a (relational) structure interpreting the modal language is called an ML-structure.

We now review the syntax of the guarded forward and fluted fragments. Given a tuple $s = (s_1, \ldots, s_n)$, an *infix* of s is a continuous subsequence of it; by a *suffix* of s we understand an infix of the form $(s_\ell, \ldots, s_n)$. An infix (suffix) of length k is called a k-infix (k-suffix). The empty tuple is denoted by ε and is considered an infix and suffix of any finite tuple. The length of a tuple s is denoted by $|s|$. For any first-order formula φ, we denote by $var(\varphi)$ the set of *free* variables of φ.

Definition 1 (Guarded forward formulas). *For $m \geq 0$, we define the sets of* guarded forward m-formulas, GFF_m, *by simultaneous structural induction as follows.*

- *If p is of arity $k \leq m$ and $(x_i, \ldots, x_j)$ is a k-infix of $(x_1, \ldots, x_m)$, then $p(x_i, \ldots, x_j) \in \mathrm{GFF}_m$.*
- *GFF_m is closed under boolean combinations.*
- *If $r(x_\ell, \ldots, x_n) \in \mathrm{GFF}_n$, $\varphi \in \mathrm{GFF}_n$, and $var(\varphi) \subseteq \{x_\ell, \ldots, x_n\}$, then $\forall x_{m+1} \cdots x_n(r(x_\ell, \ldots, x_n) \rightarrow \varphi)$ and $\exists x_{m+1} \cdots x_n(r(x_\ell, \ldots, x_n) \wedge \varphi)$, where $\ell \leq m+1 \leq n$, are in $\mathrm{GFF}_{m'}$ for any $m' \geq m$.*

The set of guarded forward formulas *is* $\mathrm{GFF} = \bigcup_{m \geq 0} \mathrm{GFF}_m$.

Formulas in GFF_m and GFF are also referred to as GFF_m- and GFF-formulas respectively. The atomic formulas $r(x_\ell, \ldots, x_n)$ mentioned in the third clause of the definition are called *guards*. We observe that the free variables of each GFF_m-formula are *among* $x_1, \ldots, x_m$, and, in particular, every GFF_0-formula is a sentence.

The guarded fluted fragment GFL is essentially the result of confining each GFF_m to those formulas whose free variables form a suffix of $(x_1, \ldots, x_m)$, and is thus a subfragment of GFF.

Definition 2 (Guarded fluted formulas). *For $m \geq 0$, we define the sets of* guarded fluted m-formulas, GFL_m, *by simultaneous structural induction as follows.*

- *If p is of arity $k \leq m$, then $p(x_{m-k+1}, \ldots, x_m) \in \mathrm{GFL}_m$, where $(x_{m-k+1}, \ldots, x_m)$ is the k-suffix of $(x_1, \ldots, x_m)$.*
- *GFL_m is closed under boolean combinations.*
- *If $r(x_\ell, \ldots, x_n) \in \mathrm{GFL}_n$, $\varphi \in \mathrm{GFL}_n$, and $var(\varphi) \subseteq \{x_\ell, \ldots, x_n\}$, then $\forall x_{m+1} \cdots x_n(r(x_\ell, \ldots, x_n) \rightarrow \varphi)$ and $\exists x_{m+1} \cdots x_n(r(x_\ell, \ldots, x_n) \wedge \varphi)$ are in GFL_m, where $\ell \leq m+1 \leq n$.*

The set of guarded fluted formulas *is* $\mathrm{GFL} = \bigcup_{m \geq 0} \mathrm{GFL}_m$.

Formulas in GFL_m and GFL are also referred to as GFL_m- and GFL-formulas respectively. Again, the atomic formulas $r(x_\ell, \dots, x_n)$ mentioned in the third clause of the definition are called *guards*. We can easily verify that the free variables of any GFL_m-formula form a (possibly empty) suffix of $(x_1, \dots, x_m)$, and in particular, every GFL_0-formula is a sentence. In the following formulas,

$$\exists x_1 x_2 (r(x_1, x_2) \wedge (\neg p(x_1) \vee q(x_2)))$$
$$\forall x_1 (p(x_1) \rightarrow \exists x_2 (r(x_1, x_2) \wedge p(x_2)))$$
$$\forall x_1 (p(x_1) \rightarrow \forall x_2 (\neg q(x_2) \rightarrow r(x_1, x_2))),$$

the first one is a GFF_0-formula but not in GFL; the second is both a GFL_0-formula and GFF_0-formula; the third one is neither in GFL nor in GFF because there is no guard for the quantifier $\forall x_2$, but it is included the (full) fluted and also forward fragments.

Although the full fluted fragment is not the focus of this paper, it plays a role in some intermediate results. For $m \geq 0$, the sets of *fluted m-formulas*, FL_m, are defined by simultaneous structural induction as follows.

- If p is of arity $k \leq m$, then $p(x_{m-k+1}, \dots, x_m) \in FL_m$, where $(x_{m-k+1}, \dots, x_m)$ is the k-suffix of $(x_1, \dots, x_m)$.
- FL_m is closed under Boolean combinations.
- If $\varphi \in FL_{m+1}$, then $\forall x_{m+1} \varphi \in FL_m$ and $\exists x_{m+1} \varphi \in FL_m$.

The set of *fluted formulas* is $FL = \bigcup_{m \geq 0} FL_m$. Formulas in FL_m and FL are also referred to as FL_m- and FL-formulas. As in GFL, the free variables of any FL_m-formula form a (possibly empty) suffix of $(x_1, \dots, x_m)$. We can easily verify that $GFL_m \subseteq FL_m$ and $GFL \subseteq FL$.

Notation: If a formula φ has exactly k free variables, and $\bar{a} = (a_1, \dots, a_n)$ $(n \geq k)$ is an n-tuple of elements of some FO-structure $\mathfrak{A}$, we write $\mathfrak{A} \models \varphi[\bar{a}]$ to indicate that $(a_{n-k+1}, \dots, a_n)$, the k-suffix of $\bar{a}$, satisfies φ in $\mathfrak{A}$, assuming that the i-th item of $(a_{n-k+1}, \dots, a_n)$ is assigned to the free variable with the i-th least index. For example, if $\varphi(x_2, x_3)$ is a formula with exactly x_2, x_3 free, and $\bar{a} = (a_1, a_2, a_3, a_4)$, then $\mathfrak{A} \models \varphi(x_2, x_3)[\bar{a}]$ means that (a_3, a_4) satisfies $\varphi(x_2, x_3)$ in $\mathfrak{A}$, with $a_3 \mapsto x_2$ and $a_4 \mapsto x_3$. This convention is maintained until the end of Sect. 3.

We use U for the universal modality and E to abbreviate $\neg U \neg$. The basic modal language with the universal modality is defined as usual. Let $\mathfrak{M} = (W, R, V)$ be an ML-structure. Recall the truth conditions for modalities:

- $\mathfrak{M}, w \models \Box \varphi$ iff $\mathfrak{M}, v \models \varphi$ for all $v \in W$ such that $(w, v) \in R$;
- $\mathfrak{M}, w \models \Diamond \varphi$ iff $\mathfrak{M}, v \models \varphi$ for some $v \in W$ such that $(w, v) \in R$;
- $\mathfrak{M}, w \models U \varphi$ iff $\mathfrak{M}, v \models \varphi$ for all $v \in W$;
- $\mathfrak{M}, w \models E \varphi$ iff $\mathfrak{M}, v \models \varphi$ for some $v \in W$.

We denote by $\mathbf{K_U}$ the modal logic $\mathbf{K}$ extended with the universal modality.

Given tuples $s = (s_1, \dots, s_m)$ and $t = (t_1, \dots, t_n)$, by $s \cdot t$ we denote the concatenation of them, i.e., $s \cdot t = (s_1, \dots, s_m, t_1, \dots, t_n)$. For any non-empty finite tuple s, we denote by $\mathsf{last}(s)$ the last item of s.

Recall that each predicate of the first-order language is regarded as a proposition letter in the modal language. We associate with each FO-structure an ML-structure as below.

Definition 3. *Let $\mathfrak{A}$ be an FO-structure over a domain A. The ML-structure associated with $\mathfrak{A}$ is $\mathfrak{A}^* = (W, R, V)$, where:*

- $W = \bigcup_{n>0} A^n$, *i.e., the set of* non-empty *finite tuples of elements of A;*
- *for any $w, v \in W$, we have $(w, v) \in R$ iff $v = w{\cdot}a$ for some $a \in A$ (note that each $a \in A$ is also considered a 1-tuple);*
- *for any proposition letter (predicate) p,*

$$V(p) = \{w \in W \mid \text{ there exists } v \in p^{\mathfrak{A}} \text{ such that } v \text{ is a suffix of } w\}.$$

Given any ML-structure $\mathfrak{M} = (W, R, V)$, a *path* in $\mathfrak{M}$ is a non-empty tuple $\bar{w} = (w_1, \ldots, w_n)$ of elements of W such that $(w_i, w_{i+1}) \in R$ for all $i \in \{1, \ldots, n-1\}$. The length of the path $\bar{w} = (w_1, \ldots, w_n)$ is n, and we call it an n-path. In particular, each $w \in W$ is a 1-path. For $n > 0$, we write $\vec{W}_n$ for the set of n-paths in $\mathfrak{M}$. Since each n-path is an n-tuple of elements of W, we have $\vec{W}_n \subseteq W^n$. We also write $\vec{W}$ for the set of all paths in $\mathfrak{M}$, i.e., $\vec{W} = \bigcup_{n>0} \vec{W}_n$.

Definition 4. *For any ML-structure $\mathfrak{M} = (W, R, V)$, the FO-structure $\mathfrak{M}^{\#}$ associated with $\mathfrak{M}$ is defined as follows.*

- *The domain of $\mathfrak{M}^{\#}$ is W.*
- *For each k-ary predicate p, $p^{\mathfrak{M}^{\#}} = \{\bar{w} \in \vec{W}_k \mid \mathsf{last}(\bar{w}) \in V(p)\}$.*

In other words, $\mathfrak{M}^{\#}$ shares the same domain with $\mathfrak{M}$, and for each proposition letter p, if it is a k-ary predicate in the first-order language, its interpretation in $\mathfrak{M}^{\#}$ is the set of all k-paths in which the last item satisfies p in $\mathfrak{M}$.

3 Translation

We now present a mapping from FL-formulas to modal formulas, which resembles the translation of the ordered fragment due to A. Herzig [7].

Definition 5. *The translation, f, is a mapping from* FL*-formulas to modal formulas and it is defined recursively as follows ($\bullet$ stands for a binary boolean connective).*

$$f(p(x_{m-k+1}, \ldots, x_m)) = p$$

$$f(\neg\varphi) = \neg f(\varphi)$$

$$f(\varphi \bullet \psi) = f(\varphi) \bullet f(\psi)$$

$$f(\forall x_{m+1}\varphi) = \begin{cases} \Box f(\varphi), & \text{if } \forall x_{m+1}\varphi \text{ is open;} \\ U f(\varphi), & \text{otherwise.} \end{cases}$$

$$f(\exists x_{m+1}\varphi) = \begin{cases} \Diamond f(\varphi), & \text{if } \exists x_{m+1}\varphi \text{ is open;} \\ E f(\varphi), & \text{otherwise.} \end{cases}$$

The mapping does essentially the following: ignore the argument sequence of each predicate, and replace each universal (existential) quantifier by $\Box$ ($\Diamond$) if the quantified formula is open, otherwise by U (E). For example,

$$f[\forall x_1(p(x_1) \rightarrow \exists x_2(q(x_2) \wedge \neg r(x_1, x_2)))] = U(p \rightarrow \Diamond(q \wedge \neg r)).$$

Proposition 1. *Let $\mathfrak{A}$ be an FO-structure over A and $\mathfrak{A}^* = (W, R, V)$ the associated ML-structure. Then: for any $\varphi \in \mathrm{FL}$ and $w \in W$ with $|w| \geq |var(\varphi)|$, we have that $\mathfrak{A} \models \varphi[w]$ iff $\mathfrak{A}^*, w \models f(\varphi)$. (Recall that each $w \in W$ is a non-empty tuple of elements of A, and $|w|$ stands for the length of w.)*

Proof. This is an induction on the structure of FL-formulas. Recall that if φ is an FL-formula with exactly k free variables and $|w| \geq k$, by $\mathfrak{A} \models \varphi[w]$ we mean the k-suffix of w satisfies φ in $\mathfrak{A}$. The atomic case is immediate by the definition of V in $\mathfrak{A}^*$. The boolean cases are also straightforward. Now we deal with the cases of universally quantified formulas. The cases of existentially quantified formulas can be treated similarly.

Suppose $\varphi = \forall x_{m+1}\psi$ is open. Then $f(\varphi) = \Box f(\psi)$, and we have:

$$\begin{aligned}
\mathfrak{A} \models \forall x_{m+1}\psi[w] &\iff \mathfrak{A} \models \psi[w{\cdot}a] \text{ for any } a \in A \\
&\iff \mathfrak{A}^*, w{\cdot}a \models f(\psi) \text{ for any } a \in A \\
&\iff \mathfrak{A}^*, w \models \Box f(\psi).
\end{aligned}$$

The first step is by the syntax of FL; the second is by the induction hypothesis; the third is by the definition of R in $\mathfrak{A}^*$.

Suppose $\varphi = \forall x_{m+1}\psi$ is closed. Then $f(\varphi) = Uf(\psi)$, and we have:

$$\begin{aligned}
\mathfrak{A} \models \forall x_{m+1}\psi[w] &\iff \mathfrak{A} \models \psi[a] \text{ for any } a \in A \\
&\iff \mathfrak{A} \models \psi[u] \text{ for any } u \in W \\
&\iff \mathfrak{A}^*, u \models f(\psi) \text{ for any } u \in W \\
&\iff \mathfrak{A}^*, w \models Uf(\psi).
\end{aligned}$$

The first step holds because ψ has at most one free variable. Also, for any $u \in W$, we have that $\mathfrak{A} \models \psi[u]$ iff $\mathfrak{A} \models \psi[\mathsf{last}(u)]$, and since $\{\mathsf{last}(u) \mid u \in W\} = A$, the second step holds. The third step is by the induction hypothesis. The final step holds by the truth condition for U. $\Box$

By Proposition 1, if an FL-formula is satisfiable then its translation is satisfiable in $\mathbf{K_U}$. The other direction does not hold for FL-formulas in general, but we have the following result for GFL-formulas.

Proposition 2. *Let $\mathfrak{M} = (W, R, V)$ be an ML-structure and $\mathfrak{M}^{\#}$ its associated FO-structure. For any $\varphi \in \mathrm{GFL}$ and $\bar{w} \in \vec{W}$ with $|\bar{w}| \geq |var(\varphi)|$, we have that $\mathfrak{M}, \mathsf{last}(\bar{w}) \models f(\varphi)$ iff $\mathfrak{M}^{\#} \models \varphi[\bar{w}]$. (Note that each $\bar{w} \in \vec{W}$ is a non-empty tuple of elements of W, and $|\bar{w}|$ denotes its length.)*

Proof. We prove the claim by a structural induction on GFL-formulas. The atomic case is immediate by Definition 4, and the boolean cases are straightforward. We work on the cases of universally quantified formulas below. The cases of existentially quantified formulas are relatively easy and omitted.

Suppose $\varphi = \forall x_{m+1} \dots x_n(r(x_\ell, \dots, x_n) \rightarrow \psi)$, where $\psi \in \mathrm{GFL}_n$ and $\ell < m+1 \leq n$. Note that φ is open and hence $f(\varphi) = \Box^{n-m}(r \rightarrow f(\psi))$. The following statements are equivalent, with the justifications listed below.

$$\mathfrak{M}, \mathsf{last}(\bar{w}) \vDash \Box^{n-m}(r \rightarrow f(\psi)). \tag{1}$$

$$\mathfrak{M}, \mathsf{last}(\bar{v}) \vDash r \rightarrow f(\psi) \text{ for any } \bar{v} \in \vec{W}_{n-m} \text{ with } \bar{w}\cdot\bar{v} \in \vec{W}. \tag{2}$$

$$\mathfrak{M}^{\#} \vDash r(x_\ell, \dots, x_n) \rightarrow \psi[\bar{w}\cdot\bar{v}] \text{ for any } \bar{v} \in \vec{W}_{n-m} \text{ with } \bar{w}\cdot\bar{v} \in \vec{W}. \tag{3}$$

$$\mathfrak{M}^{\#} \vDash r(x_\ell, \dots, x_n) \rightarrow \psi[\bar{w}\cdot\bar{u}] \text{ for any } \bar{u} \in W^{n-m}. \tag{4}$$

$$\mathfrak{M}^{\#} \vDash \forall x_{m+1} \dots x_n(r(x_\ell, \dots, x_n) \rightarrow \psi)[\bar{w}]. \tag{5}$$

(1) $\Leftrightarrow$ (2): by the definition of paths. (2) $\Leftrightarrow$ (3): by the induction hypothesis. (3) $\Rightarrow$ (4): let $\bar{u} \in W^{n-m}$ and $\mathfrak{M}^{\#} \vDash r(x_\ell, \dots, x_n)[\bar{w}\cdot\bar{u}]$; then, by the definition of $\mathfrak{M}^{\#}$, the $(n-\ell+1)$-suffix of $\bar{w}\cdot\bar{u}$ is a path in $\mathfrak{M}$; also, note that $\mathsf{last}(\bar{w})$ is contained in the $(n-\ell+1)$-suffix of $\bar{w}\cdot\bar{u}$, hence $\bar{u} \in \vec{W}_{n-m}$ and $\bar{w}\cdot\bar{u} \in \vec{W}$, and by (3) we have $\mathfrak{M}^{\#} \vDash \psi[\bar{w}\cdot\bar{u}]$. (3) $\Leftarrow$ (4): $\vec{W}_{n-m} \subseteq W^{n-m}$. (4) $\Leftrightarrow$ (5): by the truth condition for $\forall$.

Suppose $\varphi = \forall x_{m+1}\psi$ is a closed GFL_m-formula. We can easily check, by Definition 2, that ψ is a GFL_{m+1}-formula with one free variable. Then $f(\varphi) = Uf(\psi)$, and we have:

$$\begin{aligned} \mathfrak{M}, \mathsf{last}(\bar{w}) \vDash Uf(\psi) &\iff \mathfrak{M}, v \vDash f(\psi) \text{ for any } v \in W \\ &\iff \mathfrak{M}^{\#} \vDash \psi[v] \text{ for any } v \in W \\ &\iff \mathfrak{M}^{\#} \vDash \forall x_{m+1}\psi \\ &\iff \mathfrak{M}^{\#} \vDash \forall x_{m+1}\psi[\bar{w}]. \end{aligned}$$

The first step is by the truth condition for U; the second is by the induction hypothesis (note that each $v \in W$ is a 1-path); the third is by the truth condition for $\forall$; the last step holds because the formula is closed. □

Recall that for any ML-structure $\mathfrak{M} = (W, R, V)$, any $w \in W$, and any modal formula ψ whose main operator is U or E, we have $\mathfrak{M}, w \vDash \psi$ iff $\mathfrak{M} \vDash \psi$ ($\mathfrak{M} \vDash \psi$ means ψ is globally true in $\mathfrak{M}$). Thus, given any $\varphi \in \mathrm{GFL}_0$, observing that $f(\varphi)$ is a boolean combination of formulas with main operator U or E, we do not need to distinguish between local and global satisfaction for $f(\varphi)$.

Proposition 3. *A* GFL_0*-formula* φ *is satisfiable iff* $f(\varphi)$ *is satisfiable in* $\mathbf{K_U}$.

Proof. Immediate by Propositions 1 and 2. □

Given any set Γ of GFL_0-formulas and GFL_0-formula φ, writing $f(\Gamma)$ for the f-image of Γ, we have, by Proposition 3 (and compactness), that

$$\Gamma \vDash \varphi \iff f(\Gamma) \vDash_{\mathbf{K_U}} f(\varphi).$$

In words: logical consequences in sentences of GFL are reflected under the translation by logical consequences in $\mathbf{K_U}$. Thus, the translation f serves as a *simulation* [9] of GFL by $\mathbf{K_U}$.

Things are a bit more complicated when it comes to the translation of GFF. We start by converting each GFF_0-formula into an equisatisfiable FL_0-formula in a specific form.

Proposition 4. *Let $\varphi \in \text{GFF}_0$. We can construct, in time bounded by a polynomial function of $\|\varphi\|$ (the length of φ), an equisatisfiable FL_0-formula $\tilde{\varphi} = \varphi' \wedge \bigwedge\Theta$ such that φ' is a GFL_0-formula and Θ is a finite set of FL_0-formulas of the following two forms:*

$$\begin{aligned}\gamma &= \forall x_1 \ldots x_m(\exists x_{m+1} \ldots x_n(r(x_1, \ldots, x_n) \wedge q(x_1, \ldots, x_n)) \rightarrow \psi)\\ \delta &= \forall x_1 \ldots x_m(\psi \rightarrow \forall x_{m+1} \ldots x_n(r(x_1, \ldots, x_n) \rightarrow q(x_1, \ldots, x_n))),\end{aligned}$$

where ψ is a GFL_m-formula and $1 \leq m$.

Proof. Given a GFF_0-formula φ, we construct a sequence of GFF_0-formulas $\varphi_0, \varphi_1, \ldots$ together with a sequence of sets of FL_0-formulas $\Theta_0, \Theta_1, \ldots$ We start by putting $\varphi_0 = \varphi$ and $\Theta_0 = \emptyset$, and for $k \geq 0$, φ_{k+1} and Θ_{k+1} are constructed from φ_k and Θ_k as follows.

First, take a maximally nested subformula χ of φ_k in the form below (the n, r, ψ here are unrelated to those appearing in the statement of the proposition):

$$\chi = \mathrm{Q}x_n(r(x_\ell, \ldots, x_n) \bullet \psi), \text{ where: } (\mathrm{Q}, \bullet) \in \{(\forall, \rightarrow), (\exists, \wedge)\} \text{ and } \psi \notin \text{GFL}_n.$$

Note that $\chi \notin$ GFL. The goal here is to convert ψ into a GFL_n-formula, so that χ is turned into a GFL-formula. Suppose that ψ is a boolean combination of formulas $\psi_1, \ldots, \psi_j$, each of which is either atomic or quantified. Note that each atomic GFF-formula is by definition also a GFL-formula, and, by saying that χ is a 'maximally nested' subformula of that kind, we assume that each quantified formula among $\psi_1, \ldots, \psi_j$ is a GFL-formula. If any one of $\psi_1, \ldots, \psi_j$ is a closed GFL-formula but not in GFL_n, we can turn it into a closed GFL_n-formula by renaming its (bound) variables, so in the following we assume that $\psi_1, \ldots, \psi_j$ are open GFL-formulas.

For each $i \in \{1, \ldots, j\}$, let q_i be a fresh predicate of arity $n - \ell + 1$. Then let

$$\psi' = \psi[\psi_i / q_i(x_\ell, \ldots, x_n)].$$

Notice that $q_i(x_\ell, \ldots, x_n) \in \text{GFL}_n$ and thus $\psi' \in \text{GFL}_n$. Also, for each $i \in \{1, \ldots, j\}$, if $\psi_i \in \text{GFL}_p$ $(\ell \leq p \leq n)$, let

$$\begin{aligned}\gamma_i &= \forall x_\ell \ldots x_p(\exists x_{p+1} \ldots x_n(r(x_\ell, \ldots, x_n) \wedge q_i(x_\ell, \ldots, x_n)) \rightarrow \psi_i)\\ \delta_i &= \forall x_\ell \ldots x_p(\psi_i \rightarrow \forall x_{p+1} \ldots x_n(r(x_\ell, \ldots, x_n) \rightarrow q_i(x_\ell, \ldots, x_n))).\end{aligned}$$

Note that γ_i is equivalent to

$$\forall x_\ell \ldots x_n(r(x_\ell, \ldots, x_n) \rightarrow (q_i(x_\ell, \ldots, x_n) \rightarrow \psi_i)),$$

and δ_i is equivalent to

$$\forall x_\ell \ldots x_n(r(x_\ell, \ldots, x_n) \to (\psi_i \to q_i(x_\ell, \ldots, x_n))).$$

In other words, $\gamma_i \wedge \delta_i$ is a definition of q_i (by ψ_i) within the interpretation of r. Also, note that γ_i and δ_i are closed, and they can be turned into FL_0-formulas by renaming bound variables. Then, treating γ_i and δ_i as FL_0-formulas, let

$$\begin{aligned}\varphi_{k+1} &= \varphi_k[\psi/\psi'] \\ \Theta_{k+1} &= \Theta_k \cup \{\gamma_1, \ldots, \gamma_j\} \cup \{\delta_1, \ldots, \delta_j\}.\end{aligned}$$

We can easily verify that $\varphi_{k+1} \wedge \bigwedge \Theta_{k+1}$ is equisatisfiable to $\varphi_k \wedge \bigwedge \Theta_k$. Also, assuming that $\varphi_k \in \mathrm{GFF}_0$, we have $\varphi_{k+1} \in \mathrm{GFF}_0$.

Obviously, in the end we will arrive at a formula φ_s free from subformulas in violation of the formation rules of GFL. Let $\tilde{\varphi} = \varphi_s \wedge \bigwedge \Theta_s$, and we are done. It is also easy to see that the construction runs in polynomial time. □

Proposition 5. *Let $\mathfrak{M} = (W, R, V)$ be an ML-structure and $\mathfrak{M}^\#$ the associated FO-structure. Let γ, δ be given as in Proposition 4. Then: (i) $\mathfrak{M} \models f(\gamma)$ iff $\mathfrak{M}^\# \models \gamma$; (ii) $\mathfrak{M} \models f(\delta)$ iff $\mathfrak{M}^\# \models \delta$.*

Proof. We prove (i); the proof of (ii) is essentially the same. Since f is defined for FL and $\gamma \in \mathrm{FL}_0$,

$$f(\gamma) = U\Box^{m-1}(\Diamond^{n-m}(r \wedge q) \to f(\psi)), \text{ where } \psi \text{ is a } \mathrm{GFL}_m\text{-formula.}$$

The following statements are equivalent:

$$\mathfrak{M} \models U\Box^{m-1}(\Diamond^{n-m}(r \wedge q) \to f(\psi)). \tag{1}$$

$$\mathfrak{M}, \mathsf{last}(\bar{w}) \models \Diamond^{n-m}(r \wedge q) \to f(\psi), \text{ for any } \bar{w} \in \vec{W}_m. \tag{2}$$

$$\mathfrak{M}^\# \models \exists x_{m+1} \ldots x_n(r(x_1, \ldots, x_n) \wedge q(x_1, \ldots, x_n)) \to \psi[\bar{w}] \text{ for any } \bar{w} \in \vec{W}_m. \tag{3}$$

$$\mathfrak{M}^\# \models \exists x_{m+1} \ldots x_n(r(x_1, \ldots, x_n) \wedge q(x_1, \ldots, x_n)) \to \psi[\bar{u}] \text{ for any } \bar{u} \in W^m. \tag{4}$$

$$\mathfrak{M}^\# \models \forall x_1 \ldots x_m(\exists x_{m+1} \ldots x_n(r(x_1, \ldots, x_n) \wedge q(x_1, \ldots, x_n)) \to \psi). \tag{5}$$

(1) ⇔ (2): by the truth conditions for U and $\Box$. (2) ⇔ (3): by Proposition 2 (note that the formula in (3) is a GFL_m-formula). (3) ⇒ (4): suppose $\bar{u} \in W^m$ and $\mathfrak{M}^\# \models \exists x_{m+1} \ldots x_n(r(x_1, \ldots, x_n) \wedge q(x_1, \ldots, x_n))[\bar{u}]$; then there is $\bar{v} \in W^{n-m}$ such that $\mathfrak{M}^\# \models r(x_1, \ldots, x_n)[\bar{u}\cdot\bar{v}]$; then, by the definition of $\mathfrak{M}^\#$, we have $\bar{u}\cdot\bar{v} \in \vec{W}_n$, whence $\bar{u} \in \vec{W}_m$, and then by (3) we get $\mathfrak{M}^\# \models \psi[\bar{u}]$. (3) ⇐ (4): $\vec{W}_m \subseteq W^m$. (4) ⇔ (5): by the truth condition for $\forall$. □

For any FL_0 formula φ, since $f(\varphi)$ is a boolean combination of modal formulas with main operator U or E, we do not distinguish between local and global satisfaction in the following proposition.

Proposition 6. *Let $\tilde{\varphi} = \varphi' \wedge \bigwedge \Theta$ be an* FL_0*-formula specified in Proposition 4. Let $\mathfrak{A}$ be an FO-structure, and $\mathfrak{M}$ an ML-structure. Then: (i) $\mathfrak{A} \vDash \tilde{\varphi}$ iff $\mathfrak{A}^* \vDash f(\tilde{\varphi})$; (ii) $\mathfrak{M} \vDash f(\tilde{\varphi})$ iff $\mathfrak{M}^\# \vDash \tilde{\varphi}$. Thus, $\tilde{\varphi}$ is satisfiable iff $f(\tilde{\varphi})$ is satisfiable in* $\mathbf{K_U}$.

Proof. Since $\tilde{\varphi} \in \mathrm{FL}_0$, (i) follows from Proposition 1. For (ii), observe that $f(\tilde{\varphi}) = f(\varphi') \wedge \bigwedge\{f(\theta) \mid \theta \in \Theta\}$, where $\varphi' \in \mathrm{GFL}_0$ and each $\theta \in \Theta$ is in the form of γ or δ, then the result is immediate by Propositions 2 and 5. □

The following result on complexity is mostly not new (cf. [2]) but now we have a different (and perhaps simpler) proof.

Proposition 7. *The satisfiability problems for* GFF *and* GFL *are* ExpTime-*complete.*

Proof. Given any sentence φ in GFF, we assume that $\varphi \in \mathrm{GFF}_0$ by variable renaming. We first convert φ to $\tilde{\varphi}$ by Proposition 4, compute $f(\tilde{\varphi})$, and then test it for satisfiability in $\mathbf{K_U}$. The correctness of this sketched algorithm is guaranteed by Proposition 6. Since $\mathbf{K_U}$-satisfiability is in ExpTime [16], so is GFF-satisfiability.

We are left to show that GFL-satisfiability has the matching lower bound. We make use of the following result [11, Lemma 2.20].[1] Let $\mathrm{L_{alt}}$ be the fragment of first-order logic consisting of formulas of the following form:

$$\begin{aligned}&\exists x_1 \alpha(x_1) \wedge \forall x_1 \gamma(x_1)\\ &\qquad \wedge \forall x_1(\alpha(x_1) \rightarrow \exists x_2(r(x_1, x_2) \wedge \beta(x_2)))\\ &\qquad\qquad \wedge \forall x_1(\alpha(x_1) \rightarrow \forall x_2(r(x_1, x_2) \rightarrow \gamma(x_2))),\end{aligned}$$

where α and β are conjunctions of unary literals, γ is a disjunction of unary literals, and r is a binary predicate. The satisfiability problem for $\mathrm{L_{alt}}$ is ExpTime-hard because it is sufficient to encode any alternating Turing machine running in polynomial space.

Notice that $\mathrm{L_{alt}}$ is *not* included in GFL. However, each $\mathrm{L_{alt}}$-formula can be converted into an equisatisfiable GFL-formula using the following trick [11, Lem. 4.1]. Let q be a fresh unary predicate, and we rewrite each $\mathrm{L_{alt}}$-formula by the following schema:

$$\begin{aligned}&\exists x_1(q(x_1) \wedge \alpha(x_1)) \wedge \forall x_1(q(x_1) \rightarrow \gamma(x_1))\\ &\quad \wedge \forall x_1(q(x_1) \rightarrow (\alpha(x_1) \rightarrow \exists x_2(r(x_1, x_2) \wedge q(x_2) \wedge \beta(x_2))))\\ &\qquad \wedge \forall x_1(q(x_1) \rightarrow (\alpha(x_1) \rightarrow \forall x_2(r(x_1, x_2) \rightarrow (q(x_2) \rightarrow \gamma(x_2))))).\end{aligned}$$

Given any $\mathrm{L_{alt}}$-formula φ, let φ' be the formula resulting from the rewriting, and let $\varphi'' = \varphi' \wedge \exists x_1(q(x_1) \wedge q(x_1))$. It is easy to check that φ'' is a GFL_0-formula. Intuitively, φ' is the result of restricting quantification in φ to the interpretation of q, which is guaranteed to be non-empty by $\exists x_1(q(x_1) \wedge q(x_1))$. Thus, if $\mathfrak{A} \vDash \varphi$,

[1] This was suggested by an anonymous reviewer of an earlier version of this paper.

then, taking $\mathfrak{A}^+$ to be the expansion of $\mathfrak{A}$ such that $q^{\mathfrak{A}^+} = A$, we have $\mathfrak{A}^+ \models \varphi''$; conversely, if $\mathfrak{B} \models \varphi''$, we can easily verify that $\mathfrak{B}\restriction q^{\mathfrak{B}} \models \varphi$. Hence, the mapping $\varphi \mapsto \varphi''$ is a (log-space) reduction of $\mathrm{L}_{\mathrm{alt}}$-satisfiability to GFL-satisfiability, and we may conclude that GFL-satisfiability is also ExpTime-hard. Observe also that φ'' uses only two variables, so even the two-variable subfragment of GFL is ExpTime-hard. □

4 Bisimulation and Unraveling

In the following we use 'X' as a place holder for either 'GFF' or 'GFL', and '*affix*' as a place holder for either 'infix' or 'suffix'. The idea of using these placeholders is borrowed from [3].

From now on each X_n-formula is always evaluated with an n-tuple in a structure, and we adopt this new convention: for any FO-structure $\mathfrak{A}$, any $\bar{a} = (a_1, \ldots, a_n) \in A^n$, and any X_n-formula φ, we write $\mathfrak{A} \models \varphi[\bar{a}]$ to indicate that φ is satisfied by $\bar{a}$ in $\mathfrak{A}$, assuming that a_i is assigned to x_i for each $i \in \{1, \ldots, n\}$.

Given a structure $\mathfrak{A}$ and a tuple $\bar{a}$ of elements of A, the pair $(\mathfrak{A}, \bar{a})$ is called a pointed structure. (Note that we do not require elements of $\bar{a}$ be distinct.) We say that $(\mathfrak{A}, \bar{a})$ satisfies φ if $\mathfrak{A} \models \varphi[\bar{a}]$. An X_n-type is a maximal consistent set of atomic X_n-formulas and their negations. We say that $(\mathfrak{A}, \bar{a})$ satisfies an X_n-type if it satisfies every formula in the type.

Given tuples $(s_1, \ldots, s_\ell)$ and $(t_1, \ldots, t_n)$, we say that the latter *extends* the former if $\ell < n$ and $s_i = t_i$ for all $i \in \{1, \ldots, \ell\}$. In particular, we stipulate that any non-empty tuple extends the empty tuple ε.

For any FO-structure $\mathfrak{A}$ and any tuple $\bar{a}$ of elements of A, we say that $\bar{a}$ is *guarded* (in $\mathfrak{A}$) if there is a predicate r such that $\bar{a} \in r^{\mathfrak{A}}$. In the following definition, *when* X *is read as* GFF *(*GFL*), affix should be read as infix (suffix).*

Definition 6 (Bisimulations [3, Def. 2]). *An* X*-bisimulation between FO-structures $\mathfrak{A}$ and $\mathfrak{B}$ is a non-empty relation $Z \subseteq \bigcup_{n \geq 0}(A^n \times B^n)$ such that for any $\bar{a} = (a_1, \ldots, a_n)$ and $\bar{b} = (b_1, \ldots, b_n)$ with $(\bar{a}, \bar{b}) \in Z$, the following conditions hold:*

- ***(atomic harmony)*** *$(\mathfrak{A}, \bar{a})$ and $(\mathfrak{B}, \bar{b})$ satisfy the same X_n-type, with $n = |\bar{a}| = |\bar{b}|$;*
- ***(forth)*** *for any guarded tuple $\bar{a}'$ in $\mathfrak{A}$ that extends a (possibly empty) affix $(a_i, \ldots, a_j)$ of $\bar{a}$, there is a tuple $\bar{b}'$ in $\mathfrak{B}$ such that $\bar{b}'$ extends the affix $(b_i, \ldots, b_j)$ of $\bar{b}$ and $(\bar{a}', \bar{b}') \in Z$;*
- ***(back)*** *for any guarded tuple $\bar{b}'$ in $\mathfrak{B}$ that extends a (possibly empty) affix $(b_i, \ldots, b_j)$ of $\bar{b}$, there is a tuple $\bar{a}'$ in $\mathfrak{A}$ such that $\bar{a}'$ extends the affix $(a_i, \ldots, a_j)$ of $\bar{a}$ and $(\bar{a}', \bar{b}') \in Z$.*

An X-bisimulation between pointed structures $(\mathfrak{A}, \bar{a})$ and $(\mathfrak{B}, \bar{b})$ is an X-bisimulation Z between $\mathfrak{A}$ and $\mathfrak{B}$ with $(\bar{a}, \bar{b}) \in Z$. We write $(\mathfrak{A}, \bar{a}) \sim_{\mathrm{X}} (\mathfrak{B}, \bar{b})$ if there is an X-bisimulation between $(\mathfrak{A}, \bar{a})$ and $(\mathfrak{B}, \bar{b})$. We write $(\mathfrak{A}, \bar{a}) \equiv_{\mathrm{X}} (\mathfrak{B}, \bar{b})$ if $|\bar{a}| = |\bar{b}| = n$ and $(\mathfrak{A}, \bar{a})$ and $(\mathfrak{B}, \bar{b})$ satisfy the same X_n-formulas.

Proposition 8 ([3, Lemma 3]). *Let $\mathfrak{A}$ and $\mathfrak{B}$ be FO-structures. If $(\mathfrak{A}, \bar{a}) \sim_{\mathrm{X}} (\mathfrak{B}, \bar{b})$ then $(\mathfrak{A}, \bar{a}) \equiv_{\mathrm{X}} (\mathfrak{B}, \bar{b})$. The other direction holds if $\mathfrak{A}$ and $\mathfrak{B}$ are ω-saturated.*

Now we present a construction of unravelings with respect to the two guarded fragments. *Given any FO-structure $\mathfrak{A}$, its unraveling is the FO-structure associated with the ML-structure associated with $\mathfrak{A}$.* For simplicity, we introduce the construction directly below, without the mention of the correspondences between FO- and ML-structures.

For now on, given any non-empty set A and $W = \bigcup_{n>0} A^n$, we use $\vec{W}_k$ for the set of elements of W^k $(k > 0)$ such that

$$(w_1, \dots, w_k) \in \vec{W}_k \text{ iff for any } i \in \{1, \dots, k-1\}, w_{i+1} = w_i{\cdot}a \text{ for some } a \in A.$$

Also, let $\vec{W} = \bigcup_{k>0} \vec{W}_k$.

Definition 7 (Unraveling). *Let $\mathfrak{A}$ be an FO-structure over the domain A. The unraveling $\mathfrak{A}'$ of $\mathfrak{A}$ is the FO-structure with domain $W = \bigcup_{n>0} A^n$ and, for any k-ary predicate p:*

$$p^{\mathfrak{A}'} = \{(w_1, \dots, w_k) \in \vec{W}_k \mid (\mathsf{last}(w_1), \dots, \mathsf{last}(w_k)) \in p^{\mathfrak{A}}\}.$$

For $k > 0$, we call $\vec{W}_k$ the set of k-paths in $\mathfrak{A}'$, and $\vec{W}$ the set of paths in $\mathfrak{A}'$. Moreover, let F be a function with domain $\vec{W} \cup \{\varepsilon\}$ such that: $F(\varepsilon) = \varepsilon$, and for any $(w_1, \dots, w_k) \in \vec{W}_k$ $(k > 0)$,

$$F(w_1, \dots, w_k) = (\mathsf{last}(w_1), \dots, \mathsf{last}(w_k)).$$

We call F the canonical mapping *for $\mathfrak{A}'$. Note that $F \subseteq \bigcup_{n \geq 0}(W^n \times A^n)$.*

The unraveling defined here is a variation of the one proposed by Bednarczyk and Jaakkola [4, Def. 20]. The only significant difference between the two versions is that, in our definition, the construction of path does not depend on the interpretation of predicates of the original structure.

We stress that the unraveling $\mathfrak{A}'$ may be regarded as a tree-like structure, and relations hold only on paths. The following proposition shows why this notion of unraveling makes sense.

Proposition 9. *F is an X-bisimulation between $\mathfrak{A}'$ and $\mathfrak{A}$.*

Proof. Let $(w_1, \dots, w_n) \in \vec{W}$. Then $F(w_1, \dots, w_n) = (\mathsf{last}(w_1), \dots, \mathsf{last}(w_n))$, and for any k-infix $(x_i, \dots, x_j)$ of $(x_1, \dots, x_n)$ and k-ary predicate p we have

$$\begin{aligned} \mathfrak{A}' \vDash p(x_i, \dots, x_j)[w_1, \dots, w_n] &\iff (w_i, \dots, w_j) \in p^{\mathfrak{A}'} \\ &\iff (\mathsf{last}(w_i), \dots, \mathsf{last}(w_j)) \in p^{\mathfrak{A}} \\ &\iff \mathfrak{A} \vDash p(x_i, \dots, x_j)[\mathsf{last}(w_1), \dots, \mathsf{last}(w_n)]. \end{aligned}$$

Thus, atomic harmony holds between $(w_1, \dots, w_n)$ and $F(w_1, \dots, w_n)$. In the following we check the forth and back conditions.

Let $(w_i, \ldots, w_j)$ be a k-affix of $(w_1, \ldots, w_n)$, and $\bar{v} = (w_i, \ldots, w_j, v_{k+1}, \ldots, v_m)$ be a guarded m-tuple in $\mathfrak{A}'$. Since $\bar{v}$ satisfies some m-ary predicate in $\mathfrak{A}'$, it is a path. Then $F(\bar{v})$ is defined, and, obviously, $F(\bar{v})$ extends $F(w_i, \ldots, w_j)$.

Let $(\mathsf{last}(w_i), \ldots, \mathsf{last}(w_j))$ be a k-affix of $F(w_1, \ldots, w_n)$, and $(\mathsf{last}(w_i), \ldots, \mathsf{last}(w_j), a_{k+1}, \ldots, a_m)$ a guarded m-tuple in $\mathfrak{A}$. For $\ell \in \{k+1, \ldots, m\}$, let

$$v_\ell = w_j \cdot a_{k+1} \cdot \ldots \cdot a_\ell.$$

We can easily verify that $(w_i, \ldots, w_j, v_{k+1}, \ldots, v_m)$ is a path in $\mathfrak{A}'$ and

$$\begin{aligned} & F(w_i, \ldots, w_j, v_{k+1}, \ldots, v_m) \\ = & (\mathsf{last}(w_i), \ldots, \mathsf{last}(w_j), \mathsf{last}(v_{k+1}), \ldots, \mathsf{last}(v_m)) \\ = & (\mathsf{last}(w_i), \ldots, \mathsf{last}(w_j), a_{k+1}, \ldots, a_m). \end{aligned}$$

Finally, since there is no nullary predicates, atomic harmony trivially holds for $(\varepsilon, \varepsilon)$; also, the forth and back conditions for $(\varepsilon, \varepsilon)$ are the special cases where the affix mentioned above is empty. □

The notion of generated substructures in modal logic carries over into the current context, as formulated below.

Definition 8 (Generated sub-trees). *Let $\mathfrak{A}'$ be the unraveling of $\mathfrak{A}$, and $\bar{w} = (w_1, \ldots, w_n)$ a path in $\mathfrak{A}'$. Then the sub* GFF*-tree of $\mathfrak{A}'$ generated by $\bar{w}$ is the restriction of $\mathfrak{A}'$ to $\{w_1 \cdot \bar{v} \mid \bar{v} \in \bigcup_{n \geq 0} A^n\}$, and is written $\mathfrak{A}'_{\text{GFF}}(\bar{w})$; the sub* GFL*-tree of $\mathfrak{A}'$ generated by $\bar{w}$ is the restriction of $\mathfrak{A}'$ to $\{w_n \cdot \bar{v} \mid \bar{v} \in \bigcup_{n \geq 0} A^n\} \cup \{w_1, \ldots, w_{n-1}\}$, and is written $\mathfrak{A}'_{\text{GFL}}(\bar{w})$.*

We will see the use of generated sub-trees in the next section.

5 Łoś-Tarski Preservation Theorem

We adopt the following definition of existential formulas: a first-order formula is *existential* if its negation normal form does not contain any universal quantifier.

For any FO-structures $\mathfrak{A}$ and $\mathfrak{B}$, we say that $\mathfrak{A}$ is a *substructure* of $\mathfrak{B}$ and $\mathfrak{B}$ is an *extension* of $\mathfrak{A}$, in notation: $\mathfrak{A} \subseteq \mathfrak{B}$, if $A \subseteq B$ and the interpretation of any predicate in $\mathfrak{A}$ is the result of restricting that in $\mathfrak{B}$ to A. A first-order formula is preserved under extensions iff it is logically equivalent to an existential formula. This is known as the Łoś-Tarski Preservation Theorem.

In what follows we prove the analogs of the theorem in the two guarded fragments. The exact formulation of the result will be given in due course.

Given FO-structures $\mathfrak{A}$ and $\mathfrak{B}$, an X-*embedding from* $\mathfrak{A}$ *to* $\mathfrak{B}$ is a non-empty relation $H \subseteq \bigcup_{n \geq 0}(A^n \times B^n)$ satisfying the **atomic harmony** and the **forth** condition for X-bisimulations (the **back** condition is not required). An X-embedding from $(\mathfrak{A}, \bar{a})$ to $(\mathfrak{B}, \bar{b})$ is an X-embedding H from $\mathfrak{A}$ to $\mathfrak{B}$ with $(\bar{a}, \bar{b}) \in H$.

We write $(\mathfrak{A}, \bar{a}) \to_{\mathrm{X}} (\mathfrak{B}, \bar{b})$ if $|\bar{a}| = |\bar{b}| = n$ and for any *existential* X_n-formula φ the following implication holds:

$$\mathfrak{A} \models \varphi[\bar{a}] \Longrightarrow \mathfrak{B} \models \varphi[\bar{b}].$$

In other words, $(\mathfrak{A}, \bar{a}) \to_{\mathrm{X}} (\mathfrak{B}, \bar{b})$ means $(\mathfrak{B}, \bar{b})$ satisfies all existential X_n-formulas satisfied by $(\mathfrak{A}, \bar{a})$.

Proposition 10. *If* $(\mathfrak{A}, \bar{a}) \to_{\mathrm{X}} (\mathfrak{B}, \bar{b})$ *and* $\mathfrak{B}$ *is* ω*-saturated, then there exists an* X*-embedding from* $(\mathfrak{A}, \bar{a})$ *to* $(\mathfrak{B}, \bar{b})$*.*

Proof. Let $(\mathfrak{A}, \bar{a}) \to_{\mathrm{X}} (\mathfrak{B}, \bar{b})$ with $\mathfrak{B}$ ω-saturated, and let

$$H = \{(\bar{c}, \bar{d}) \in \textstyle\bigcup_{n \geq 0}(A^n \times B^n) \mid (\mathfrak{A}, \bar{c}) \to_{\mathrm{X}} (\mathfrak{B}, \bar{d})\}.$$

Our goal is to show that H is an X-embedding from $(\mathfrak{A}, \bar{a})$ to $(\mathfrak{B}, \bar{b})$. We clearly have $(\bar{a}, \bar{b}) \in H$. The two conditions are discussed below.

Let $\bar{c} = (c_1, \ldots, c_n), \bar{d} = (d_1, \ldots, d_n)$, and $(\bar{c}, \bar{d}) \in H$. Note that atomic X_n-formulas and their negations are existential. Since $(\mathfrak{A}, \bar{c}) \to_{\mathrm{X}} (\mathfrak{B}, \bar{d})$, they satisfy the same X_n-type.

Now we consider the forth condition. The following reasoning is an adaptation of the standard proof (see e.g. [11, Lem. 4.23]). Let $\bar{c}'$ be a guarded m-tuple in $\mathfrak{A}$ such that $\mathfrak{A} \models r(x_1, \ldots, x_m)[\bar{c}']$ and $\bar{c}'$ extends a k-affix $\bar{c}_k = (c_i, \ldots, c_j)$ of $\bar{c}$. We need to show that there exists an m-tuple $\bar{d}'$ in $\mathfrak{B}$ such that $\bar{d}'$ extends the k-affix $\bar{d}_k = (d_i, \ldots, d_j)$ of $\bar{d}$ and $(\mathfrak{A}, \bar{c}') \to_{\mathrm{X}} (\mathfrak{B}, \bar{d}')$. Now, taking $d_i, \ldots, d_j$ as constants, let

$$\Delta = \{\psi(d_i, \ldots, d_j, x_{k+1}, \ldots, x_m) \mid \psi \in \mathrm{X}_m \text{ is existential and } \mathfrak{A} \models \psi[\bar{c}']\}.$$

Here, $\psi(d_i, \ldots, d_j, x_{k+1}, \ldots, x_m)$ stands for the result of substituting $d_i, \ldots, d_j$ for $x_1, \ldots, x_k$ respectively in ψ. (Recall that the free variables of each X_m-formula are among $x_1, \ldots, x_m$.)

Now we write $(\mathfrak{B}, d_i, \ldots, d_j)$ for the simple expansion of $\mathfrak{B}$ in which each of $d_i, \ldots, d_j$ is used as a constant denoting itself. We next show that Δ is consistent with $\mathrm{Th}(\mathfrak{B}, d_i, \ldots, d_j)$, the set of true sentences in $(\mathfrak{B}, d_i, \ldots, d_j)$. Suppose to the contrary that Δ is inconsistent with $\mathrm{Th}(\mathfrak{B}, d_i, \ldots, d_j)$. By compactness, there exists a finite subset $\Delta' \subseteq \Delta$ which is not consistent with $\mathrm{Th}(\mathfrak{B}, d_i, \ldots, d_j)$. Let $\delta(d_i, \ldots, d_j, x_{k+1}, \ldots, x_m) = \bigwedge \Delta'$. Then:

$$(\mathfrak{B}, d_i, \ldots, d_j) \models \neg\exists x_{k+1} \ldots x_m \delta(d_i, \ldots, d_j, x_{k+1}, \ldots, x_m).$$

Writing $\delta(x_1, \ldots, x_m)$ for the result of substituting $x_1, \ldots, x_k$ for $d_i, \ldots, d_j$ respectively in $\delta(d_i, \ldots, d_j, x_{k+1}, \ldots, x_m)$, we have

$$\mathfrak{B} \models \neg\exists x_{k+1} \ldots x_m \delta(x_1, \ldots, x_m)[d_i, \ldots, d_j],$$

and then

$$\mathfrak{B} \models \neg\exists x_{k+1} \ldots x_m (r(x_1, \ldots, x_m) \wedge \delta(x_1, \ldots, x_m))[d_i, \ldots, d_j]. \qquad (\beta)$$

By the definition of Δ, we have $\mathfrak{A} \models \delta(x_1, \ldots, x_m)[\bar{c}']$; also, recall that $\mathfrak{A} \models r(x_1, \ldots, x_m)[\bar{c}']$. Then:

$$\mathfrak{A} \models r(x_1, \ldots, x_m) \wedge \delta(x_1, \ldots, x_m)[\bar{c}'].$$

Since $\bar{c}'$ extends $\bar{c}_k = (c_i, \ldots, c_j)$, the k-affix of $\bar{c}$, we have

$$\mathfrak{A} \models \exists x_{k+1} \ldots x_m (r(x_1, \ldots, x_m) \wedge \delta(x_1, \ldots, x_m))[c_i, \ldots, c_j]. \qquad (\alpha)$$

Notice that $\exists x_{k+1} \ldots x_m (r(x_1, \ldots, x_m) \wedge \delta(x_1, \ldots, x_m))$ is an existential X_k-formula. Thus, by (α) and (β), it is *not* the case that $(\mathfrak{A}, \bar{c}_k) \rightarrow_{\mathrm{X}} (\mathfrak{B}, \bar{d}_k)$. On the other hand, we can easily check that $(\mathfrak{A}, \bar{c}_k) \rightarrow_{\mathrm{X}} (\mathfrak{B}, \bar{d}_k)$ follows from $(\mathfrak{A}, \bar{c}) \rightarrow_{\mathrm{X}} (\mathfrak{B}, \bar{d})$, hence a contradiction.

Since Δ is consistent with $\mathrm{Th}(\mathfrak{B}, d_i, \ldots, d_j)$ and $\mathfrak{B}$ is ω-saturated, Δ is satisfied by some $(m-k)$-tuple in $(\mathfrak{B}, d_i, \ldots, d_j)$. As a result, there exists $\bar{d}' \in B^m$ such that $\bar{d}'$ extends $\bar{d}_k$ and $(\mathfrak{B}, \bar{d}')$ satisfies all existential X_m-formulas satisfied by $(\mathfrak{A}, \bar{c}')$. Thus, we have $(\mathfrak{A}, \bar{c}') \rightarrow_{\mathrm{X}} (\mathfrak{B}, \bar{d}')$ as required. □

We say that an X_n-formula φ is *preserved under extensions* if for any FO-structures $\mathfrak{A}$, $\mathfrak{B}$ such that $\mathfrak{A} \subseteq \mathfrak{B}$, and any $\bar{a} \in A^n$, the following implication holds:

$$\mathfrak{A} \models \varphi[\bar{a}] \Longrightarrow \mathfrak{B} \models \varphi[\bar{a}].$$

The proof of the following result is inspired by that of [1, Thm. 4.4.1].

Proposition 11 (Łoś-Tarski). *An* X_n*-formula is preserved under extensions iff it is logically equivalent to an existential* X_n*-formula. Thus, the Łoś-Tarski preservation theorem holds in* X.

Proof. The 'if' (right-to-left) direction is a trivial result in first-order model theory, and can be proved by a routine induction. For the 'only-if' (left-to-right) direction, let φ be an X_n-formula that is preserved under extensions. Let $\mathbf{exist}(\varphi)$ be the set of existential consequences of φ in X_n:

$$\mathbf{exist}(\varphi) = \{\psi \in \mathrm{X}_n \mid \varphi \models \psi \text{ and } \psi \text{ is existential}\}.$$

With compactness, we are left to show that $\mathbf{exist}(\varphi) \models \varphi$. Let $\mathfrak{B}$ be an FO-structure and $\bar{b} \in B^n$, and suppose $\mathfrak{B} \models \mathbf{exist}(\varphi)[\bar{b}]$. Recall that every structure has an ω-saturated elementary extension (see e.g. [10, Thm. 5.1]). If $\mathbf{exist}(\varphi) \models \varphi$ is established among ω-saturated structures, then it holds among all structures. Thus, we assume, without loss of generality, that $\mathfrak{B}$ is ω-saturated.

Let $\Theta = \{\neg\psi \mid \psi \in \mathrm{X}_n \text{ is existential and } \mathfrak{B} \not\models \psi[\bar{b}]\}$. We claim that Θ is consistent with φ. Suppose to the contrary that it is not. Then, by compactness, there exist $\neg\psi_1, \ldots, \neg\psi_m \in \Theta$ such that $\varphi \models \neg(\neg\psi_1 \wedge \cdots \wedge \neg\psi_m)$, and thus $\varphi \models \psi_1 \vee \cdots \vee \psi_m$. Note that $\psi_1 \vee \cdots \vee \psi_m$ is an existential X_n-formula. Then, by the definition of $\mathbf{exist}(\varphi)$, we have $\psi_1 \vee \cdots \vee \psi_m \in \mathbf{exist}(\varphi)$, whence $\mathfrak{B} \models \psi_1 \vee \cdots \vee \psi_m[\bar{b}]$. On the other hand, by the definition of Θ, $\mathfrak{B} \not\models \psi_i[\bar{b}]$ for all $i \in \{1, \ldots, m\}$, and then $\mathfrak{B} \not\models \psi_1 \vee \cdots \vee \psi_m[\bar{b}]$, hence a contradiction.

Since Θ is consistent with φ, there exists a structure $\mathfrak{A}$ and $\bar{a} \in A^n$ such that $\mathfrak{A} \models \Theta[\bar{a}]$ and $\mathfrak{A} \models \varphi[\bar{a}]$. Observe that for any existential X_n-formula ψ:

$$\mathfrak{B} \not\models \psi[\bar{b}] \Longrightarrow \neg\psi \in \Theta \Longrightarrow \mathfrak{A} \models \neg\psi[\bar{a}] \Longrightarrow \mathfrak{A} \not\models \psi[\bar{a}].$$

By contraposition, $\mathfrak{A} \models \psi[\bar{a}] \Longrightarrow \mathfrak{B} \models \psi[\bar{b}]$, hence $(\mathfrak{A}, \bar{a}) \rightarrow_X (\mathfrak{B}, \bar{b})$. Then, by Proposition 10, there exists an X-embedding H from $(\mathfrak{A}, \bar{a})$ to $(\mathfrak{B}, \bar{b})$.

Let $\mathfrak{A}', \mathfrak{B}'$ be the unravelings of $\mathfrak{A}, \mathfrak{B}$ respectively. We write W_A for the domain of $\mathfrak{A}'$ and W_B for the domain of $\mathfrak{B}'$, i.e., $W_A = \bigcup_{n>0} A^n$ and $W_B = \bigcup_{n>0} B^n$. Also, we write $\vec{W}_A, \vec{W}_B$ for the set of paths in $\mathfrak{A}', \mathfrak{B}'$ respectively.

Let F_A be the canonical mapping for $\mathfrak{A}'$, and F_B the canonical mapping for $\mathfrak{B}'$. By Proposition 9, F_A is an X-bisimulation between $\mathfrak{A}'$ and $\mathfrak{A}$, and F_B is an X-bisimulation between $\mathfrak{B}'$ and $\mathfrak{B}$.

Let $(F_B)^{-1}$ be the inverse of F_B, i.e., for any $\bar{d} \in \bigcup_{n\geq 0} B^n$ and $\bar{v} \in \vec{W}_B \cup \{\varepsilon\}$, we put $(\bar{d}, \bar{v}) \in (F_B)^{-1}$ iff $F_B(\bar{v}) = \bar{d}$.

Recall that H is an X-embedding from $(\mathfrak{A}, \bar{a})$ to $(\mathfrak{B}, \bar{b})$. Let G be the composition of F_A, H, and $(F_B)^{-1}$:

$$G = (F_B)^{-1} \circ H \circ F_A.$$

In other words, for any $\bar{w} \in \vec{W}_A \cup \{\varepsilon\}$ and $\bar{v} \in \vec{W}_B \cup \{\varepsilon\}$, we put $(\bar{w}, \bar{v}) \in G$ iff there exists $(\bar{c}, \bar{d}) \in H$ such that $(\bar{w}, \bar{c}) \in F_A$ and $(\bar{d}, \bar{v}) \in (F_B)^{-1}$. We can easily verify that $G \subseteq \bigcup_{n\geq 0}({W_A}^n \times {W_B}^n)$ and is an X-embedding from $\mathfrak{A}'$ to $\mathfrak{B}'$. Also, there are $\bar{w}_{\bar{a}} \in \vec{W}_A \cup \{\varepsilon\}$ and $\bar{v}_{\bar{b}} \in \vec{W}_B \cup \{\varepsilon\}$ such that $F_A(\bar{w}_{\bar{a}}) = \bar{a}$, $F_B(\bar{v}_{\bar{b}}) = \bar{b}$ and $(\bar{w}_{\bar{a}}, \bar{v}_{\bar{b}}) \in G$.

Since an X-embedding only needs to satisfy atomic harmony and the forth condition, it is not hard to see that there exists $\hat{G} \subseteq G$ such that:

- $\hat{G}$ is functional, i.e., if $(\bar{w}, \bar{v}) \in \hat{G}$ and $(\bar{w}, \bar{v}') \in \hat{G}$ then $\bar{v} = \bar{v}'$;
- $\hat{G}$ is an X-embedding from $\mathfrak{A}'$ to $\mathfrak{B}'$;
- $(\bar{w}_{\bar{a}}, \bar{v}_{\bar{b}}) \in \hat{G}$.

In what follows we treat $\hat{G}$ as a (partial) function from $\vec{W}_A \cup \{\varepsilon\}$ to $\vec{W}_B \cup \{\varepsilon\}$.

Now we set out to construct an extension of $\mathfrak{A}'$ that is X-bisimilar to $\mathfrak{B}'$. We assume that A is countable and disjoint from B. Then W_A is countable and disjoint from W_B, and $\vec{W}_A$ is also countable. Fixing an enumeration of elements of $\vec{W}_A$, we construct a chain of structures and a chain of relations:

$$\mathfrak{A}_0 \subseteq \mathfrak{A}_1 \subseteq \cdots \subseteq \mathfrak{A}_n \subseteq \ldots \qquad\qquad Z_0 \subseteq Z_1 \subseteq \cdots \subseteq Z_n \subseteq \ldots$$

First, let $\mathfrak{A}_0 = \mathfrak{A}'$ and $Z_0 = \hat{G}$. For each $n \geq 0$, $\mathfrak{A}_{n+1}$ and Z_{n+1} are constructed based on $\mathfrak{A}_n$ and Z_n as follows.

We write A_n for the domain of $\mathfrak{A}_n$. Let $\bar{w} = (w_1, \ldots, w_\ell)$ be the first fresh element of $\vec{W}_A$ such that $\hat{G}(\bar{w})$ is defined. Then take a set D disjoint from A_n and W_B. Writing $D \cup \bar{w}$ for $D \cup \{w_1, \ldots, w_\ell\}$, and assuming that D has a suitable cardinality, let $\mathfrak{A}_{n+1}$ be *the extension of* $\mathfrak{A}_n$ *over* $A_n \cup D$ satisfying the following conditions:

1. There is a bijection h from $\mathfrak{A}_{n+1}\restriction(D \cup \bar{w})$ to $\mathfrak{B}'_{\mathrm{X}}(\hat{G}(\bar{w}))$, the sub X-tree of $\mathfrak{B}'$ generated by $\hat{G}(\bar{w})$, such that

$$(h(w_1), \ldots, h(w_\ell)) = \hat{G}(\bar{w});$$

and for any tuple $\bar{v} = (v_1, \ldots, v_k)$ of elements of $D \cup \bar{w}$ and any k-ary predicate p, if $v_i \in D$ for some $i \in \{1, \ldots, k\}$, then

$$\bar{v} \in p^{\mathfrak{A}_{n+1}} \iff (h(v_1), \ldots, h(v_k)) \in p^{\mathfrak{B}'}.$$

2. For any tuple $\bar{u}$ of elements of $A_n \cup D$ and any predicate p, if $\bar{u} \in p^{\mathfrak{A}_{n+1}}$ then $\bar{u}$ consists only of elements of A_n or elements of $D \cup \bar{w}$.

We may easily check that $\mathfrak{A}_{n+1}$ is well-defined. Intuitively, $\mathfrak{A}_{n+1}$ is the result of attaching a unique 'copy' of $\mathfrak{B}'_{\mathrm{X}}(\hat{G}(\bar{w}))$ to $\mathfrak{A}_n$, where the 'copy' of $\hat{G}(\bar{w})$ is 'merged' with $\bar{w}$. Further, observe that there is an X-bisimulation between $\mathfrak{A}_{n+1}\restriction(D \cup \bar{w})$ and $\mathfrak{B}'_{\mathrm{X}}(\hat{G}(\bar{w}))$ connecting $\bar{w}$ and $\hat{G}(\bar{w})$. Writing $Z_{\bar{w}}$ for this X-bisimulation, let $Z_{n+1} = Z_n \cup Z_{\bar{w}}$, and thus we have defined the two chains.

Finally, let $\mathfrak{C} = \bigcup_{n \geq 0} \mathfrak{A}_n$. The domain of $\mathfrak{C}$ is $C = \bigcup_{n \geq 0} A_n$; and for each predicate p, $p^{\mathfrak{C}} = \bigcup_{n \geq 0} p^{\mathfrak{A}_n}$. Let $\mathfrak{C}+\mathfrak{B}'$ be the disjoint union of $\mathfrak{C}$ and $\mathfrak{B}'$, I the identity function on $\vec{W}_B$. We obviously have $\mathfrak{A}' \subseteq \mathfrak{C}+\mathfrak{B}'$. Moreover, let $Z = I \cup \bigcup_{n \geq 0} Z_n$. Then it is routine to check that Z is an X-bisimulation between $\mathfrak{C}+\mathfrak{B}'$ and $\mathfrak{B}'$.

Recall that F_A is a bisimulation between $\mathfrak{A}'$ and $\mathfrak{A}$, F_B is a bisimulation between $\mathfrak{B}'$ and $\mathfrak{B}$, $F_A(\bar{w}_{\bar{a}}) = \bar{a}$, and $F_B(\bar{v}_{\bar{b}}) = \bar{b}$. We also have $(\bar{w}_{\bar{a}}, \bar{v}_{\bar{b}}) \in Z$ from $(\bar{w}_{\bar{a}}, \bar{v}_{\bar{b}}) \in \hat{G}$. Recall also that $\mathfrak{A} \models \varphi[\bar{a}]$. By the invariance under bisimulations, we have $\mathfrak{A}' \models \varphi[\bar{w}_{\bar{a}}]$. Then, since φ is preserved under extensions, we have $\mathfrak{C}+\mathfrak{B}' \models \varphi[\bar{w}_{\bar{a}}]$, and then $\mathfrak{B}' \models \varphi[\bar{v}_{\bar{b}}]$ and $\mathfrak{B} \models \varphi[\bar{b}]$ by the invariance under bisimulations. Since we started from $\mathfrak{B} \models \mathbf{exist}(\varphi)[\bar{b}]$ and now get $\mathfrak{B} \models \varphi[\bar{b}]$, we may conclude that $\mathbf{exist}(\varphi) \models \varphi$. □

6 Conclusion

We have presented a simple technique for deriving ML-structures from FO-structures and back. The correspondence between the two semantics indicated by the technique allows for a translation of GFL and GFF to $\mathbf{K_U}$. The translation serves perfectly as a simulation of GFL by $\mathbf{K_U}$. While additional predicates are needed for a polynomial-time translation of GFF, we still got a reduction of GFF-satisfiability to $\mathbf{K_U}$-satisfiability, and hence a new proof of the ExpTime upper bound. This part of the work can be seen as a follow-up to Herzig's translation, which provides a simulation of the ordered fragment by **KD**.

We have also touched on the model theory of the two guarded fragments. In particular, our technique induces a construction of unravelings which is essentially the same as the one proposed by Bednarczyk and Jaakkola. In addition, following the proof idea of Andréka et al., we have proved the Łoś-Tarski theorem, an important property that a nice logic is expected to have.

Acknowledgments. Many thanks to Bartosz Bednarczyk and the anonymous reviewers for their valuable suggestions.

Disclosure of Interests. The author has no competing interests to declare that are relevant to the content of this article.

References

1. Andréka, H., Németi, I., van Benthem, J.: Modal languages and bounded fragments of predicate logic. J. Philos. Log. **27**(3), 217–274 (1998). https://doi.org/10.1023/A:1004275029985
2. Bednarczyk, B.: Exploiting forwardness: satisfiability and query-entailment in forward guarded fragment. In: Faber, W., Friedrich, G., Gebser, M., Morak, M. (eds.) JELIA 2021. LNCS (LNAI), vol. 12678, pp. 179–193. Springer, Cham (2021). https://doi.org/10.1007/978-3-030-75775-5_13
3. Bednarczyk, B., Jaakkola, R.: Towards a model theory of ordered logics: expressivity and interpolation. In: Szeider, S., Ganian, R., Silva, A. (eds.) 47th International Symposium on Mathematical Foundations of Computer Science, MFCS 2022. Leibniz International Proceedings in Informatics (LIPIcs), vol. 241, pp. 15:1–15:14. Schloss Dagstuhl - Leibniz-Zentrum für Informatik, Dagstuhl, Germany (2022). https://doi.org/10.4230/LIPIcs.MFCS.2022.15
4. Bednarczyk, B., Jaakkola, R.: Towards a model theory of ordered logics: expressivity and interpolation (extended version) (2022). https://doi.org/10.48550/arXiv.2206.11751
5. Goranko, V., Passy, S.: Using the universal modality: gains and questions. J. Log. Comput. **2**(1), 5–30 (1992). https://doi.org/10.1093/logcom/2.1.5
6. Grädel, E.: On the restraining power of guards. J. Symb. Log. **64**(4), 1719–1742 (1999). https://doi.org/10.2307/2586808
7. Herzig, A.: A new decidable fragment of first-order logic. In: Abstracts of the 3rd Logical Biennial Summer School and Conference in Honour of S. C. Kleene (1990)
8. Hustadt, U., Schmidt, R.A., Georgieva, L.: A survey of decidable first-order fragments and description logics. J. Relat. Meth. Comput. Sci. **1**, 251–276 (2004)
9. Kracht, M., Wolter, F.: Normal monomodal logics can simulate all others. J. Symb. Log. **64**(1), 99–138 (1999). https://doi.org/10.2307/2586754
10. Poizat, B.: A Course in Model Theory. Springer, New York (2000). https://doi.org/10.1007/978-1-4419-8622-1
11. Pratt-Hartmann, I.: Fragments of First-Order Logic. Oxford University Press (2023)
12. Pratt-Hartmann, I., Szwast, W., Tendera, L.: The fluted fragment revisited. J. Symb. Log. **84**(3), 1020–1048 (2019). https://doi.org/10.1017/jsl.2019.33
13. Purdy, W.C.: Fluted formulas and the limits of decidability. J. Symb. Log. **61**(2), 608–620 (1996). https://doi.org/10.2307/2275678
14. Purdy, W.C.: Complexity and nicety of fluted logic. Stud. Logica. **71**(2), 177–198 (2002). https://doi.org/10.1023/A:1016596721799
15. Quine, W.V.: The Ways of Paradox, and Other Essays. Harvard University Press (1976)
16. Spaan, E.: Complexity of Modal Logics. Ph.D. thesis, University of Amsterdam (1993)

Explanations

Causality-Based Scores Alignment in Explainable Data Management

Felipe Azúa[1] and Leopoldo Bertossi[2,3](✉)

[1] University of Edinburgh, Edinburgh, UK
f.r.i.azua@sms.ed.ac.uk
[2] Carleton University, Ottawa, Canada
bertossi@scs.carleton.ca
[3] IMFD, Santiago, Chile

Abstract. Different attribution scores have been proposed to quantify the relevance of database tuples for query answering in databases; e.g. Causal Responsibility, the Shapley Value, the Banzhaf Power-Index, and the Causal Effect. They have been analyzed in isolation. This work is a first investigation of score alignment depending on the query and the database; i.e. on whether they induce compatible rankings of tuples. We concentrate mostly on causality-based scores; and provide a syntactic dichotomy result for queries: on one side, pairs of scores are always aligned, on the other, they are not always aligned. It turns out that the presence of exogenous tuples makes a crucial difference in this regard.

1 Introduction

Explanations for query answers in databases (DBs) can be provided in terms of *attribution scores*. By assigning numbers to DB tuples, they quantify their relevance or importance for a query answer at hand. Among those scores, we find *Causal Responsibility* [9,30], *Resilience* [28] (closely related to the former), the *Shapley Value* [10,26,27], the *Banzhaf Power-Index* [27] (related to the Shapley value), and the *Causal Effect* [36]. These are all *local scores*, i.e. for a single query answer obtained from a relational DB [7]. Although some of these scores have been extended to probabilistic databases (PDBs) [3,25], in this work we consider only non-probabilistic relational DBs.

The above mentioned scores have been investigated in isolation from each other, in terms of their algorithmic, complexity-related, and general mathematical properties. However, comparisons among them in terms of the results they return have received little attention. There is no reason to expect that those scores return the same *numbers*. However, we might be interested in knowing whether they *rank* the DB tuples in the same order. This is important in that we may want to identify the most relevant tuples for the query answer, but not necessarily in their specific numeric scores. If this is the case, it is useful to know in advance that for a certain classes of queries, this form of relevance is invariant under different scores.

In this work, we address the problem of identifying conditions on queries and DBs under which attribution scores are aligned or not (more details below

A.-Y. Turhan and J. Virtema (Eds.): FoIKS 2026, LNCS 16475, pp. 263–282, 2026.
https://doi.org/10.1007/978-3-032-21540-6_16

in this section). We concentrate mainly in two of those scores, as previously defined and applied to DBs: Responsibility and the Causal Effect, denoted with Resp and CES, resp. We unveil conditions on queries and DBs that lead to the alignment of these scores or the lack of it. We also obtain a few results on the alignment of those scores with the Shapley value, denoted with Shapley.

Resp is based on *responsibility* [12] as introduced in the context of *actual causality* and *counterfactual interventions* [20–22]. The latter can be seen as hypothetical changes performed on a causal model, to identify other changes. By doing so, one can detect cause-effect relationships. CES has its origin in the *causal effect* measure of *statistical causality and observational studies* [23,34], where one usually cannot predefine and build control groups, but they have to be recovered from the available data [19,31,33].

CES was first and successfully applied as an explanation score in data management in [36], as an alternative to Resp, when the latter did not provide intuitive results. However, there are cases of queries and DBs for which Resp returns more intuitive results than CES [35, chap. 7]. Accordingly, an analysis of their alignment is a relevant and interesting problem. In this work, CES takes a prominent role. It has been less investigated by the data management community than the other scores.[1]

The Shapley Value is well-known in *Coalition Game Theory* as a measure of the contribution of individual players to a shared *game (or wealth) function* [32,37]. In [27], it was applied with the query (Boolean or aggregate) as the game function, to quantify the contribution of tuples to the answer. The same was done with the Banzhaf Power-Index [5]. Actually, in [27], it was established that CES coincides with the Banzhaf Power-Index as applied to DBs. We denote this particular case of the latter with BPI. The "ordinal equivalence", i.e. induction of the same order, of general game-theoretic scores, e.g. of the Shapley Value and the Banzhaf Power-Index, has been investigated in game-theory [17,18]. However, those results do not provide useful information in our setting.[2]

In actual causality, counterfactual interventions affect *endogenous variables*, but not *exogenous variables*. In our case, this amounts to having a partition of the DB into *endogenous and exogenous tuples*. Interventions affecting the former can be thought as tuple insertions and deletions. When the query is monotone, only deletions matter. This kind of partition of the DB has also been considered with Resp [30], with both Shapley and BPI [27], and CES [3,36]. It turns out that exogenous tuples have an effect on the values taken by the scores, and their computational properties. Actually, as we show in this work, the possible presence of exogenous tuples may also have an impact on score alignment.

In this work, our main contribution is a full syntactic characterization of Boolean conjunctive queries (BCQs) for which CES and Resp are aligned for every DB that may contain exogenous tuples, as is commonly the case. Furthermore,

---

[1] CES was extended in [3] to arbitrary PDBs, as the *Generalized Causal-Effect Score*, and its general axiomatic properties and complexity were investigated.

[2] Those results basically reduce the problem of score alignment to that of alignment of the integrals defining them.

we exhibit syntactic classes of queries for which these two scores are always aligned for every DB without exogenous tuples. Finally, we compare CES and Resp with Shapley, exhibiting syntactic classes of BCQs for which the scores are not aligned. These results open the ground for a more thorough analysis. To the best of our knowledge, this work is the first theoretical investigation of the alignment of attribution scores in data management. Beyond the interest in the particular scores we consider, this work also offers a sort of general template and methodology for analyzing the alignment of other possible scores in the context of DBs (that possibly contain exogenous tuples).

This paper is structured as follows. In Sect. 2, we provide necessary background, including Resp, Shapley and BPI; and related work. In Sect. 3, we present CES. In Sect. 4, we show motivating examples of (non-)alignment, and define alignment. In Sect. 5, the main section, we investigate the alignment of CES and Resp. In Sect. 6, we bring Shapley into the alignment analysis. In Sect. 7, we draw some conclusions and point to future work. Proofs of results can be found in an extended version of this paper [4].

2 Background

1. Databases. A relational schema $\mathcal{S}$ contains a domain of constants, $\mathcal{C}$, and a set of predicate symbols of finite arities, $\mathcal{P}$. An *atom* is of the form $P(t_1, \ldots, t_n)$, with n-ary $P \in \mathcal{P}$ and $t_1, \ldots, t_n$ are constants or variables. A *tuple* is a *ground* atom, i.e. without variables. A database (instance), D, for $\mathcal{S}$ is a finite set of ground atoms. A *conjunctive query* (CQ), $\mathcal{Q}(\bar{x})$, is a formula of the form: $\exists \bar{y}\, (P_1(\bar{x}_1) \wedge \cdots \wedge P_m(\bar{x}_m))$, whose free variables are $\bar{x} := (\bigcup \bar{x}_i) \smallsetminus \bar{y}$. If $\mathcal{Q}$ has n free variables, $\bar{c} \in \mathcal{C}^n$ is an *answer* to $\mathcal{Q}$ from D if $D \models \mathcal{Q}[\bar{c}]$, i.e. $Q[\bar{c}]$ is true in D when the variables in $\bar{x}$ are componentwise replaced by the values in $\bar{c}$. $\mathcal{Q}[D]$ denotes the set of answers to $\mathcal{Q}$ from D. $\mathcal{Q}$ is a *Boolean CQ* when $\bar{x}$ is empty. For a Boolean query (BQ), when it is *true* in D, $\mathcal{Q}[D] := \{1\}$. Otherwise, if it is *false*, $\mathcal{Q}[D] := \{0\}$. However, we write $\mathcal{Q}[D] = 1$ and $\mathcal{Q}[D] = 0$, resp. This paper concentrates on *Monotone BQs* (MBQs), in particular, BCQs. For MBQs it holds, by definition, $\mathcal{Q}[D] \leq \mathcal{Q}[D']$ when $D \subseteq D'$. For a BCQ $\mathcal{Q}$, $\mathit{Var}(\mathcal{Q})$ denotes the set of its variables. For $v \in \mathit{Var}(\mathcal{Q})$, $\mathit{Atoms}(v)$ denotes the set of atoms in $\mathcal{Q}$ where v appears; and $\mathit{Atoms}(\mathcal{Q})$ denotes the set of all atoms in $\mathcal{Q}$. A CQ is *self-join-free* (SJF) if no predicate symbol appears more than once.

2. Actual Causality and Responsibility in DBs. For causality purposes, some of the tuples in a DB D are *endogenous*, and can be subject to *counterfactual interventions*, in this case, deletions, insertions, or value updates. The other tuples are *exogenous*, and are taken as a given, leaving them outside a specific kind of analysis, but they participate in query answering. The partition $D = D^{en} \cup D^{ex}$ is application dependent. A tuple $\tau \in D^{en}$ is a *counterfactual cause* for a BQ $\mathcal{Q}$ if: $D \models \mathcal{Q}$, and $(D \smallsetminus \{\tau\}) \not\models \mathcal{Q}$. A tuple $\tau \in D^{en}$ is an *actual cause* for $\mathcal{Q}$ if there is $\Gamma \subseteq D^{en}$, such that: $D \models \mathcal{Q}$, $(D \smallsetminus \Gamma) \models \mathcal{Q}$, and $(D \smallsetminus (\Gamma \cup \{\tau\})) \not\models \mathcal{Q}$ [30]. The set Γ is called a *contingency set* for τ. $\mathit{Cont}(D, \mathcal{Q}, \tau)$, or simply, $\mathit{Cont}(D, \tau)$, denotes the set of contingency sets for τ.

The *responsibility* of τ as an actual cause for $\mathcal{Q}$ is defined by $\rho(D,\mathcal{Q},\tau) := \frac{1}{1+|\Gamma|}$, where $|\Gamma|$ is the cardinality of a minimum-size contingency set for τ [12,30]. (We sometimes write $\rho(D,\tau)$ or $\rho(\tau)$.) A counterfactual cause is an actual cause with maximum responsibility, 1. If τ is not an actual cause, its responsibility is defined as 0. Responsibility as used in DBs will be denoted with Resp. It quantifies the causal contribution of a tuple to a query answer [8,9,30].

3. Shapley Value and Banzhaf Power-Index. For their application in DBs, a BQ $\mathcal{Q}$ becomes the game function [10,26,27]:

$$Shapley(D,\mathcal{Q},\tau) \;=\; \sum_{S\subseteq(D^{en}\smallsetminus\{\tau\})} \frac{|S|!\cdot(|D^{en}|-|S|-1)!}{|D^{en}|!} \times \Delta(\mathcal{Q},S,\tau), \quad (1)$$

$$BPI(D,\mathcal{Q},\tau) \;:=\; \sum_{S\subseteq D^{en}\smallsetminus\{\tau\}} \frac{1}{2^{|D^{en}|-1}} \times \Delta(\mathcal{Q},S,\tau), \quad \text{with} \quad (2)$$

$$\Delta(\mathcal{Q},S,\tau) \;:=\; \mathcal{Q}[S\cup D^{ex}\cup\{\tau\}] \;-\; \mathcal{Q}[S\cup D^{ex}]. \quad (3)$$

Since $\mathcal{Q}$ is Boolean, $\mathcal{Q}[S] \in \{0,1\}$. The definition of the Shapley value guarantees that *it is the only measure* of players' contributions to the coalition game's shared wealth function that satisfies certain desirable properties [32,37]. Those properties provide a categorical axiomatization for the Shapley value. There is also a categorical axiomatization for the BPI [16]. In the following we will denote these attribution scores in DBs with Shapley and BPI, resp.

4. Probabilistic Databases. Given a relational DB, D, a PDB, D^p associated to D can be conceived as the *collection* $\mathcal{W}$ *of possible worlds*, i.e. of all subinstances W of D; where each $W \in \mathcal{W}$ has an associated probability $p(W)$. It holds $\sum_{W\in\mathcal{W}} p(W) = 1$ [38]. Accordingly, D^p can be identified with a discrete *probability space* $\langle\mathcal{W},p\rangle$, with p probability distribution on $\mathcal{W}$. The probability of tuple τ being in D (as seen through D^p) is $P(\tau) := \sum_{\tau\in W\in\mathcal{W}} p(W)$. Since, D is finite, $\mathcal{W}$ and the W are all finite. A numeric query $\mathcal{Q}$ on D becomes a random variable on $\mathcal{W}$; with Bernoulli distribution if it is a BQ, in which case the probability of $\mathcal{Q}$ (being true) is $P(\mathcal{Q}) := P(\mathcal{Q}=1) := \sum_{W\in\mathcal{W}:\ W\models\mathcal{Q}} p(W)$.

The particular case of a *tuple-independent PDB* (TID) is a regular relational DB whose relations have an extra attribute with probabilities for the tuples. Tuples are stochastically independent from each other. Example 1 shows a TID. The first tuple, τ_1, is in the DB with probability p_1. For a possible world $W \in \mathcal{W}$, the corresponding (non-probabilistic) relation R_W will contain only some of the tuples in R, and has the probability: $p(R_W) := \Pi_{\tau_i\in R_W} p_i \times \Pi_{\tau_j\in(R\smallsetminus R_W)}(1-p_j)$.

In general, for a TID and a possible world W:

$$p(W) \;:=\; \Pi_{R_W}\, p(R_W).$$

Table 1. A TID.

R	A	B	C	p
τ_1	a_1	b_1	c_1	0.8
τ_2	a_2	b_2	c_2	0.3
τ_3	a_3	b_3	c_3	0.2
τ_4	a_4	b_4	c_4	0.6
τ_5	a_5	b_5	c_5	1

Example 1. For the TID in Table 1, the possible world $R_W = \{\tau_1,\tau_3,\tau_5\}$, has the probability:

$$p(R_W) = 0.8 \times (1 - 0.3) \times 0.2 \times (1 - 0.6) \times 1.$$

■

For a TID D^p and $W \in \mathcal{W}$, W^p denotes the TID that contains only the tuples in W with their probabilities in D^p. For example, W^p could contain only tuples τ_2, τ_4 with probabilities 0.6 and 0.3, resp. We use the notations $P_D(\mathcal{Q})$ and $P_W(\mathcal{Q})$. When clear from context, we simply use $P(\mathcal{Q})$. For a TID D^p associated to D, exogenous tuples have probability 1. Then, for every $W \in \mathcal{W}$ with $D^{ex} \not\subseteq W$, $p(W) = 0$. When all the (endogenous) tuples' probabilities are the same, we have a *uniform TID*. If this probability is $\frac{1}{2}$, it is a $U(\frac{1}{2})$-TID.

5. Related Work. The Shapley Value and the BPI have been first used in [26,27], to quantify the contribution of tuples to answers for BCQs and aggregate queries. The authors of [15] concentrate on computational aspects of the Shapley value applied to query answering. See [10] for a recent review. In [11], the Shapley value in DBs is connected with the Generalized Model Counting Problem -in this case, the number of subinstances of a given size that satisfy the query- to obtain computational and complexity results for new classes of queries, including some unions of CQs. In [24], the problem of computing the Shapley value of variables in Boolean circuits is connected with query evaluation in PDBs, obtaining dichotomy results (similar to those in [13]) for the complexity of Shapley value computation for query answering in DBs. In [25], the expected value of the Shapley value on TIDs is investigated.

In [2], *rankings* induced by the Shapley values are investigated, rather than the values themselves. In [14], the interest is in the combination of *data provenance* and the Shapley values, for the computation of the latter. In [1], research delves more deeply into experimental results around the BPI for query answering. The computational aspects and the complexity of Responsibility in data management were first investigated in [9,29,30]. In [8], Responsibility under integrity constraints was formalized and investigated. Close to Responsibility in DBs, we find the notion of *resilience* [28]. The use of the *causal effect* in data management was proposed in [36]. Its connection with the BPI was first established in [27], from which first results about its complexity were obtained.

3 The Causal-Effect Score in Databases

The definition of the *Causal Effect Score* (CES) in DBs that we give is different from -but equivalent to- that in [36].[3] In the following, D is an instance, $\mathcal{W}$ is

[3] The new one becomes a particular case of the *Generalized Causal-Effect Score* [3], that is defined for arbitrary PDBs. In [36] (see also [7]), for the case of DBs with associated TIDs, interventions are applied on the *lineage of the query*, which can be seen as a causal model. It is common to apply interventions on variables of a causal model [31]. Those interventions on the lineage act on the random propositional variables X_τ associated to tuples τ, which are made *true* (inserted) or *false* (deleted) via $do(X_\tau = 1)$ or $do(X_\tau = 0)$.

the class of all subinstances of D, D^p is a PDB assigning a distribution to $\mathcal{W}$. Each tuple $\tau \in D$ has a probability of being true in D (but 1 if exogenous).

CES is defined through *interventions* on the distribution of D^p. They are of the forms $do(\tau \text{ in})$ and $do(\tau \text{ out})$, with the intuitive meaning that τ is *made true* in D. Similarly, $do(\tau \text{ out})$ indicates that τ is *made false* in D.

We use expressions of the form $P(\mathcal{Q} = 1 \mid do(\tau \text{ in}))$, where P is the distribution induced by p on the BQ $\mathcal{Q}$ treated as a random variable on $\mathcal{W}$. Intuitively, it means "the probability of the query being true given that tuple τ is made true". This seeming conditionalizations on $do(\tau \text{ in})$ and $do(\tau \text{ out})$ should be seen as perturbations of the original distribution p on $\mathcal{W}$, as we now define.

Definition 1. [3] Consider an instance $D = D^{en} \cup D^{ex}$, an associated PDB $D^p = \langle \mathcal{W}, p \rangle$, and $\tau \in D^{en}$. The interventions on D^p create the new PDBs:

(a) $D^p(do(\tau \text{ in})) := \langle \mathcal{W}, p^{+\tau} \rangle$, such that, for $W \in \mathcal{W}$:
$$p^{+\tau}(W) := \sum_{W' \in \mathcal{W} \,:\, W' \cup \{\tau\} = W} p(W').$$
(b) $D^p(do(\tau \text{ out})) := \langle \mathcal{W}, p^{-\tau} \rangle$, such that, for $W \in \mathcal{W}$:
$$p^{-\tau}(W) := \sum_{W' \in \mathcal{W} \,:\, W' \smallsetminus \{\tau\} = W} p(W').$$
(c) For a BQ $\mathcal{Q}$, and $v \in \{0, 1\}$:
$$P(\mathcal{Q} = v \mid do(\tau \text{ in})) := p^{+\tau}(\{W \in \mathcal{W} \mid \mathcal{Q}[W] = v\}), \text{ and}$$
$$P(\mathcal{Q} = v \mid do(\tau \text{ out})) := p^{-\tau}(\{W \in \mathcal{W} \mid \mathcal{Q}[W] = v\}).$$

■

Remark 1. (a) In Definition 1, the PDB may be any TID. In Definition 1(c): $P(\mathcal{Q} = 1 \mid do(\tau \text{ in})) = \sum_{W \in \mathcal{W},\ W \cup \{\tau\} \models \mathcal{Q}} p(W)$. Similarly for the other cases. (b) For τ as a ground query: $P(\tau \mid do(\tau \text{ in})) := P(\tau = 1 \mid do(\tau \text{ in})) = \sum_{W \in \mathcal{W},\ \tau \in W \cup \{\tau\}} p(W) = 1$; and $P(\tau \mid do(\tau \text{ out})) = 0$, as intuitively expected. (c) When $\tau \notin W \in \mathcal{W}$, $p^{+\tau}(W) = 0$; and, when $\tau \in W \in \mathcal{W}$, $p^{-\tau}(W) = 0$. (d) For a TID D and different $\tau, \tau' \in D^{en}$: $P^{+\tau}(\tau') = P^{-\tau}(\tau') = P(\tau')$, where $P^{+\tau}(\tau') := \sum_{W : \tau' \in W} p^{+\tau}(W)$ and $P^{-\tau}(\tau') := \sum_{W : \tau' \in W} p^{-\tau}(W)$. That is, an intervention $do(\tau \text{ in})$ ($do(\tau \text{ out})$, resp.) on a TID changes the probability of τ to 1 (0, resp.), leaving the other probabilities unchanged. ■

Example 2. (Ex. 1 cont.) Assume all tuples in the TID D are endogenous. $\mathcal{W}$ contains all the subsets of R; one of them is $W = \{\tau_1, \tau_3, \tau_5\}$, for which:

$$p^{+\tau_3}(W) := \sum_{W' \in \mathcal{W} \,:\, W' \cup \{\tau_3\} = W} p(W') = p(W) + p(\{\tau_1, \tau_5\})$$
$$= p(W) + 0.8 \times (1 - 0.3) \times (1 - 0.2) \times (1 - 0.6) \times 1.$$
$$p^{-\tau_3}(W) := \sum_{W' \in \mathcal{W} \,:\, W' \smallsetminus \{\tau_3\} = W} p(W') = \sum_{\emptyset} p(W') = 0.$$

■

Definition 2. Let D be a relational instance with an associated $U(\frac{1}{2})$-TID $D^p = \langle \mathcal{W}, p \rangle$, and $\mathcal{Q}$ a BQ. The *causal-effect score*, denoted CES, of $\tau \in D^{en}$ on $\mathcal{Q}$ is:

$$CE(D, \mathcal{Q}, \tau) \;:=\; \mathbb{E}(\mathcal{Q} \mid do(\tau \text{ in})) - \mathbb{E}(\mathcal{Q} \mid do(\tau \text{ out})).$$

■

CES captures the expected difference in query value between having and not having the tuple in the DB. Recall that every BQ becomes a random variable over the intervened possible worlds. For a BQ, it holds:

$$\begin{aligned} CE(D, \mathcal{Q}, \tau) &= \sum_{v \in \{0,1\}} v \times P(\mathcal{Q} = v \mid do(\tau \text{ in})) - \sum_{v \in \{0,1\}} v \times P(\mathcal{Q} = v \mid do(\tau \text{ out})) \\ &= P(\mathcal{Q} = 1 \mid do(\tau \text{ in})) - P(\mathcal{Q} = 1 \mid do(\tau \text{ out})). \end{aligned}$$

Example 3. [36] Given instance D, we are interested in computing causal attributions of the tuples to making true the query that asks if there is a path from a to b, on the basis of relation E showing direct connections between nodes. This BQ $\mathcal{Q}$ can be expressed in Datalog (or a union of CQs for a fixed instance).

In order to use CES, we build a $U(\frac{1}{2})$-TID, as here below. It holds:

E^p	A	B	p
τ_1	a	b	1/2
τ_2	a	c	1/2
τ_3	c	b	1/2
τ_4	a	d	1/2
τ_5	d	e	1/2
τ_6	e	b	1/2

$CE(D, \mathcal{Q}, \tau_1) = 0.65625$, $CE(D, \mathcal{Q}, \tau_2) = CE(D, \mathcal{Q}, \tau_3) = 0.21875$, and $CE(D, \mathcal{Q}, \tau_4) = CE(D, \mathcal{Q}, \tau_5) = CE(D, \mathcal{Q}, \tau_6) = 0.09375$.

As noticed in [36], the responsibilities are all 1/3, despite the fact that they make the query true through paths of different lengths. ■

In [36] its was established that, for a MBQ $\mathcal{Q}$, a database D, and $\tau \in D^{en}$, τ is an *actual cause* of $\mathcal{Q}$ in D iff $CE(D, \mathcal{Q}, \tau) > 0$. In [27], it was shown that the CES coincides with BPI: $CE(D, \mathcal{Q}, \tau) = BPI(D, \mathcal{Q}, \tau)$.

Notice that CES uses an auxiliary PDB, but the original DB is not probabilistic, and CES is not a probabilistic score in that the value is not a probability. The score in Definition 2 coincides with that defined in [36] via the query lineage. Resp, Shapley and BPI of Sect. 2 are not probabilistic scores, and they do not use an intermediate PDB. *From now on, we will consider only* $U(\frac{1}{2})$*-TIDs.*

4 Score Alignment

In this section, we define score alignment, and provide motivating examples.

Example 4. (Ex. 3 cont.) CES, Resp and Shapley are shown in Table 2.

Here, the less informative score is Resp, which assigns $\frac{1}{3}$ to all the tuples in D, despite the fact that the numbers of tuples in each path are different. CES and Shapley return different scores, but produce the same qualitative *rankings* for the tuples, i.e. they are equally ordered according to their scores. ■

Table 2. CES, Resp and Shapley for each tuple in D.

Tuples	CES (and BPI)	Resp	Shapley
τ_1	0.65625	1/3	0.5833
τ_2, τ_3	0.21875	1/3	0.1333
τ_4, τ_5, τ_6	0.09375	1/3	0.05

Intuitively, two scores are aligned if the induced orders are compatible.

Definition 3. (score alignment) Let D be a DB, $\tau, \tau' \in D^{en}$, and $\mathcal{Q}$ a BQ.
(a) For a score $\mathsf{sc}(D, \mathcal{Q}, \cdot)$ as a real-valued function on D^{en}, its associated *ranking* is the total preorder relation on D^{en} defined by: $\tau \preceq^{\mathsf{sc}} \tau'$ iff $\mathsf{sc}(D, \mathcal{Q}, \tau) \leq \mathsf{sc}(D, \mathcal{Q}, \tau')$, with the strict associated relation: $\tau \prec^{\mathsf{sc}} \tau'$ iff $\mathsf{sc}(D, \mathcal{Q}, \tau) < \mathsf{sc}(D, \mathcal{Q}, \tau')$, for which it holds: If $\tau \prec^{\mathsf{sc}} \tau'$, then $\tau \preceq^{\mathsf{sc}} \tau'$, but not $\tau' \preceq^{\mathsf{sc}} \tau$.
(b) Score sc' is *aligned* with score sc for $(\mathcal{Q}, D)$ if, for every $\tau, \tau' \in D^{en}$: when $\mathsf{sc}(\tau) \leq \mathsf{sc}(\tau')$ holds, then also $\mathsf{sc}'(\tau) \leq \mathsf{sc}'(\tau')$ holds.
(c) Scores sc, sc' are *aligned* for $(\mathcal{Q}, D)$ when at least one of them is aligned with the other. Scores sc, sc' are *aligned* for $\mathcal{Q}$ when, for every instance D compatible with $\mathcal{Q}$, they are aligned for $(\mathcal{Q}, D)$.
(d) $\preceq^{CE}$, $\preceq^{\rho}$, and $\preceq^{Sh}$ denote the preorders for CES, Resp and Shapley, resp. ■

Notice from (b) that if sc' is constant, then it is aligned with any other score. Table 2 in Example 4 shows that all pairs of scores are aligned. The counterexamples right below show that there are pairs $(\mathcal{Q}, D)$ for which rankings are not aligned.

Table 3. (a) Instance $D^\star$. (b) CES and Resp for $(D^\star, \mathcal{Q}_{\mathsf{RST}})$.

R	X
τ_1	a
τ_2	b
τ_3	e

S	X	Y
τ_4	a	b
τ_5	a	c
τ_6	a	d
τ_7	b	b
τ_8	b	c
τ_9	b	d
τ_{10}	e	f

T	Y
τ_{11}	b
τ_{12}	c
τ_{13}	d
τ_{14}	f

τ	CES	Resp
τ_3	0.1292	1/3
τ_4	0.0829	1/5
τ_{11}	0.1868	1/4

Example 5. (CES vs Resp) Consider instance $D^\star$ in Table 3(a), with only endogenous tuples, and $\mathcal{Q}_{\mathsf{RST}}\colon \exists x \exists y (R(x) \wedge S(x, y) \wedge T(y))$. CES and Resp for τ_3, τ_4 and τ_{11} are shown in Table 3(b). The induced orders are: $\tau_4 \prec^{CE} \tau_3 \prec^{CE} \tau_{11}$ and $\tau_4 \prec^{\rho} \tau_{11} \prec^{\rho} \tau_3$. Then, Resp and CES are not aligned for $(\mathcal{Q}_{\mathsf{RST}}, D^\star)$. ■

Table 4. (a) Instance $D^\star$. (b) CES, Resp and Shapley for $(\mathcal{Q}_{\mathsf{RS}}, D^\star)$.

R	X	Y
τ_1	a	c_1
τ_2	b	c_2
τ_3	b	c_3

S	X	Z
τ_4	a	c_4
τ_5	a	c_5
τ_6	b	c_6
τ_7	b	c_7
τ_8	b	c_8
τ_9	b	c_9

τ	CES	Resp	Shapley
τ_1	57/256	1/3	400/2520
τ_4	19/256	1/4	151/2520
τ_6	15/256	1/5	169/2520

Example 6. (CES and Resp vs Shapley) Consider instance $D^\star$ in Table 4(a), with only endogenous tuples, and $\mathcal{Q}_{\mathsf{RS}}\colon \exists x \exists y \exists z(R(x,y) \wedge S(x,z))$. CES, Resp and Shapley for τ_1,τ_4, τ_6 are shown in Table 4(b): $\tau_6 \prec^{CE} \tau_4 \prec^{CE} \tau_1$ and $\tau_6 \prec^{\rho} \tau_4 \prec^{\rho} \tau_1$. CES and Resp are aligned (for these tuples). However, $\tau_4 \prec^{Sh} \tau_6 \prec^{Sh} \tau_1$. Then, Shapley is not aligned with CES or Resp for $(\mathcal{Q}_{\mathsf{RS}}, D^\star)$. ■

5 CES and Resp Alignment

Here, we investigate the alignment of CES and Resp, with a BCQ $\mathcal{Q}$ as our main parameter. That is, under what conditions on $\mathcal{Q}$, the scores are aligned for $\mathcal{Q}$ *for every instance*; and whether there is an instance D for which they are not aligned. We will consider the presence and absence of exogenous tuples. In Sect. 5.4, we investigate alignment in the absence of exogenous tuples. Until then, we allow instances to have them. We need first some definitions.

Definition 4. (query components and coincident variables) Let $\mathcal{Q}$ be a BCQ.
(a) The undirected graph G associated to $\mathcal{Q}$ has $\mathcal{Q}$'s atoms as nodes; and as edges, the pairs of atoms, (A_i, A_j), that have at least one variable in common.
(b) The *components* of $\mathcal{Q}$ are the connected components of G, usually denoted with $C_1, \ldots, C_n$; and $\mathcal{Q}_i$ denotes the existential closure of the conjunction of atoms in C_i (we call it a subquery of $\mathcal{Q}$).
(c) $\emptyset \neq V \subseteq \mathit{Var}(\mathcal{Q})$ is a *coincident set of variables* if all $\mathit{Atoms}(v)$, with $v \in V$, coincide. $\mathit{Coin}(\mathcal{Q})$ denotes the set of all (maximal) coincident sets; and its elements are called *coincidences.* Singleton coincidences are said to be *trivial.* ■

To simplify the presentation, we will assume that queries do not have constants. Our results still hold if they have them (see Appendix B in [4]).

Example 7. The graph G associated to query $\mathcal{Q}\colon \exists x \exists y \exists z \exists w(R(x,y) \wedge S(x) \wedge T(z,w) \wedge U(z))$ has the set of nodes $\mathit{Atoms}(\mathcal{Q}) = \{R(x,y), S(x), T(z,w), U(z)\}$. The edges are $\{R(x,y), S(x)\}$ and $\{T(z,w), U(w)\}$. The components are: $C_1 = \{R(x,y), S(x)\}$ and $C_2 = \{T(z,w), U(w)\}$, with associated subqueries $\mathcal{Q}_1 : \exists x \exists y(R(x,y) \wedge S(x))$ and $\mathcal{Q}_2 \colon \exists z \exists w(T(z,w) \wedge U(z))$. $\mathit{Atom}(x) = \{R(x,y), S(x)\}$, and $Atom(y) = \{R(x,y)\}$. Since these two sets are different, $\{x,y\}$ is not a coincidence. Actually, $Coin(\mathcal{Q}) = \{\{x\},\{y\},\{z\},\{w\}\}$, containing only trivial coincidences. $\mathcal{Q}'$: $\exists x \exists y \exists z(R(x,y) \wedge T(x,y,z) \wedge U(z))$ has a single component, and $Coin(\mathcal{Q}') = \{\{x,y\}, \{z\}\}$ contains the non-trivial coincidence $\{x,y\}$. ■

Notice that: (a) $Coin(\mathcal{Q})$ is a partition of $Var(\mathcal{Q})$. (b) If $\mathcal{Q}$ contains only trivial coincidences, $|Coin(\mathcal{Q})| = |Var(\mathcal{Q})|$, as in Example 7. (c) Any two components of a query do not share variables. For $v \in Var(\mathcal{Q})$, $\{v\}$ is a coincidence.

Components can be identified with "independent" subqueries. Conversely, variables in a same coincidence can be treated as if they were only one and the same (see Proposition 3 in Sect. 5.3). We will take advantage of this when dealing with queries with multiple components. We concentrate next on queries with a single component and only trivial coincidences. In Sect. 5.3, results for them will be used for general BCQs.

5.1 Single-Component BCQs and Trivial Coincidences

The two propositions in this section will give us particular alignment and non-alignment results. We will use them later on to obtain more general results.

Proposition 1. Consider a query of the form $\mathcal{Q}_{R_n}$: $\exists x(R_1(x) \wedge R_2(x) \wedge \cdots \wedge R_n(x))$, with $n \geq 1$. For every instance D with or without exogenous tuples, CES and Resp are aligned for $(\mathcal{Q}_{R_n}, D)$. ■

Remark 2. The particular query $\mathcal{Q}_{R_n}$ has a single component, and only the trivial coincidence $\{x\}$. To use it and other queries to obtain non-alignment results for a given class, $\mathcal{C}$, of queries, we will use the following idea and technique:
(a) Start with a counterexample, i.e. a particular query $\mathcal{Q}$ and a particular instance D_0, for which the non-alignment result holds. $\mathcal{Q}$ belongs to $\mathcal{C}$, and is, in some sense, "contained" in the other queries in $\mathcal{C}$.
(b) Given an arbitrary query $\mathcal{Q}'$ in $\mathcal{C}$, query $\mathcal{Q}$ is reconstructed as a part of $\mathcal{Q}'$.
(c) In order to obtain an instance D for $\mathcal{Q}'$ (where there is no alignment), make D an extension of D_0 by adding exogenous tuples to the latter. In this way, every tuple in D_0 has a corresponding tuple in D, and tuples in D will be endogenous iff the original tuples in D_0 are endogenous.
(d) Tuples in D corresponding to tuples in D_0, have the same CES and Resp scores as in D_0.

This technique will be used for Proposition 2, with (counter)Example 8. ■

Example 8. Consider the query $\mathcal{Q}_2: \exists x \exists y(R(x,y) \wedge S(x))$, and D_2 the instance in Table 5, with $D_2^{ex} = \{\tau_4\}$ (underlined). It holds: $\tau_3 \prec^{CE} \tau_1$ and $\tau_1 \prec^{\rho} \tau_3$. CES and Resp are not aligned for $(\mathcal{Q}_2, D_2)$. $\mathcal{Q}_2$ has a single component, and only trivial coincidences: $\{x\}$ and $\{y\}$. ■

Proposition 2. Let $\mathcal{Q}$ be a BCQ with a single component, without non-trivial coincidences, and $|Var(\mathcal{Q})| \geq 2$. There is an instance D with exogenous tuples, such that CES and Resp are not aligned for $(\mathcal{Q}, D)$. ■

Table 5. (a) Instance D_2. (b) CES and Resp for τ_1 and τ_3.

R	X	Y
τ_1	a	a
τ_2	a	b
τ_3	b	a

S	X
τ_4	a
τ_5	b

τ	CES	Resp
τ_1	0.375	1/3
τ_3	0.125	1/2

Table 6. (a) Instance D built from D_2 (in Ex. 8). (b) CES and Resp.

R_1	X	Y	Z
$\underline{\tau_1}$	c'	a	a
$\underline{\tau_2}$	c'	a	b
$\underline{\tau_3}$	c'	b	a

R_2	Y	W
$\underline{\tau_4}$	a	c'
τ_5	b	c'

R_3	Y	Z	W
τ_6	a	a	c'
τ_7	a	b	c'
τ_8	b	a	c'

R_4	W
$\underline{\tau_9}$	c'

τ	CES	Resp
τ_6	0.375	1/3
τ_8	0.125	1/2

The following example illustrates the proof of Proposition 2, showing the construction of DB D.

Example 9. Consider $\mathcal{Q}$: $\exists x \exists y \exists z \exists w (R_1(x,y,z) \wedge R_2(y,w) \wedge R_3(y,z,w) \wedge R_4(w))$ that satisfies the hypothesis of Proposition 2. Consider variables y and z, for which $Atoms(z) \subsetneqq Atoms(y)$, and atoms $R_2(y,w)$ and $R_3(y,z,w)$.[4] Next, build D (following the general proof in [4]) with the relations in Table 6(a), and exogenous tuples in $D^{ex} = \{\tau_1, \tau_2, \tau_3, \tau_4, \tau_9\}$ (underlined).

It turns out that CES and Resp are not aligned for $(\mathcal{Q}, D)$: $\tau_8 \prec^{CE} \tau_6$ and $\tau_6 \prec^{CE} \tau_8$. Notice that D is built from D_2 in Example 8: Tuples R_2 and R_3 in D are in 1-to-1 correspondence with those in S and R in D_2; the rest are exogenous. ■

5.2 Non-Trivial Coincidences

We now deal with BCQs that can be multi-component and have non-trivial coincidences. Proposition 4, the main result of this section, will help us extend results of Sect. 5.1 to sef-join-free BCQs (SJF-BCQs), in Sect. 5.3.

Proposition 3. (mapping coincident variables) Let $\mathcal{Q}$ be a SJF-BCQ for schema $\mathcal{S}$; $x, y \in Var(\mathcal{Q})$ with $Atoms(x) = Atoms(y)$. Let $\mathcal{Q}'$ be the BCQ for schema $\mathcal{S}'$ obtained by decreasing the arity of predicates of atoms in $Atoms(x)$ by 1, and replacing the joint occurrences of x, y by a fresh variable v. Then, for every instance D for $\mathcal{S}$, there is an efficiently computable f on D, such that $D' := f(D)$ is an instance for $\mathcal{S}'$, and for every $S \subseteq D$: $\mathcal{Q}[S] = \mathcal{Q}'[f(S)]$. ■

We illustrate the proposition and its proof by means of an example.

[4] The selected variables and atoms are similar to variables x, y and atoms R_x and R_y in the proof of Proposition 2 in [4].

Table 7. (a) Instance D.

R	X	Y
$\underline{\tau_1}$	a	b
$\underline{\tau_2}$	a	c
τ_3	a	d
τ_4	b	b

S	Y	Z	X
τ_5	b	a	a
τ_6	b	b	a
τ_7	c	a	a
τ_8	d	a	a
τ_9	b	a	b
τ_{10}	c	a	c

T	Z
τ_{11}	a
τ_{12}	b

(b) Instance D'.

R'	V
$\underline{\tau_1'}$	c_1
$\underline{\tau_2'}$	c_2
τ_3'	c_3
τ_4'	c_4

S'	V	Z
τ_5'	c_1	a
τ_6'	c_1	b
τ_7'	c_2	a
τ_8'	c_3	a
τ_9'	c_4	a
τ_{10}'	c_5	a

U	Z
τ_{11}'	a
τ_{12}'	b

Example 10. Consider $\mathcal{Q}: \exists x \exists y \exists x (R(x,y) \wedge S(y,z,x) \wedge T(z))$, and D in Table 7(a), with $D^{ex} = \{\tau_1, \tau_2\}$. It holds $Atoms(x) = Atoms(y)$. Accordingly, we make the pair formed by x and y collapse into a single variable v, with corresponding attribute V. The new schema is $\mathcal{S}' = \{R'(V), S'(V,Z), U(Z)\}$, and the new query is $\mathcal{Q}'$: $\exists v \exists z (R'(v) \wedge S'(v,z) \wedge U(z))$. With this query, we decrease the cardinality of the two-element coincidence, from 2 for $\{x,y\}$, to 1 for $\{v\}$.

Instance D' in Table 7(b) is compliant with $\mathcal{S}'$. It is obtained via $f: D \to D'$, sending $f(\tau_i)$ to τ_i', defined, for constants e, f, by: $f(R(e,f)) := R'(c(e,f))$, $f(S(e,f,g)) := S'(c(e,g),f)$, and $f(T(e)) := T(e)$, where $c(e,f)$ is a unique fresh constant for the combination (e,f), which may appear in more that one relation for $\mathcal{S}$, (similarly for the other new constants). Moreover, the set of exogenous tuples of D' is $D'^{ex} = \{\tau_1', \tau_2'\}$.

The position of the new variable v in relation T' does not change the outcome of the transformation. Whether we use $T'(v,z)$ of $T'(z,v)$, the new tuples assign the fresh constants to the intended position for v, and maintain the original constants in the position of z. In either case, the new query $\mathcal{Q}'$ produces the same result as that of $\mathcal{Q}$ on any $S \subseteq D$ mapped to D'. ■

For a SJF-BCQ, with each relation appearing only once, the variable ordering is irrelevant. If a relation appears more than once, with different variable orders, collapsing variables can lead to inconsistent mappings.

Example 11. Consider $\mathcal{Q}_{\mathsf{sj}} : \exists x \exists y (R(x,y) \wedge R(y,x))$, with a self-join, and $D = \{R(a,b), R(c,c)\}$. Since $Atoms(x) = Atoms(y)$, we collapse x, y into a single new variable v. With a new relation $R'(\cdot)$ and $f: D \to D'$ defined by $f(R(a,b)) = R'(c_1)$ and $f(R(c,c)) = R'(c_2)$, we obtain $\mathcal{Q}_{\mathsf{sj}}'$: $\exists v (R'(v) \wedge R'(v))$, and $D' = \{R'(c_1), R'(c_2)\}$. It holds: $\mathcal{Q}_{\mathsf{sj}}[\{R(a,b)\}] = 0 \neq \mathcal{Q}_{\mathsf{sj}}'[\{f(R(a,b))\}] = \mathcal{Q}_{\mathsf{sj}}'[\{R'(c_1)\}] = 1$. The mapping fails to preserve query answering. ■

Remark 3. (a) *From now on, we will consider only SJF-BCQs.*
(b) For simplicity, Proposition 3 presents the case of two variables in a coincidence. However, the result can be generalized to all the variables in a coincidence by iteratively decreasing the coincidence until its size becomes 1.

(c) For a BCQ $\mathcal{Q}$ with a non-trivial coincidence, the *reduced form* of $\mathcal{Q}$, denoted by $\mathcal{Q}^{red}$, is the result of iteratively decreasing the number of coincident variables, until making each $V \in \mathit{Coin}(\mathcal{Q})$ collapse into a singleton. In Example 10, $\mathcal{Q}^{red}$ is $\mathcal{Q}'$. $\mathcal{Q}^{red}$ has no non-trivial coincidence; then $\mathit{Coin}(\mathcal{Q}^{red})$ and $\mathit{Var}(\mathcal{Q}^{red})$ are in 1-to-1 correspondence, and $\bigcup \mathit{Coin}(\mathcal{Q}^{red}) = \mathit{Var}(\mathcal{Q}^{red})$. A query with only trivial coincidences is its own reduced version.
(d) f (in Proposition 3) assigns, to each combination of constants that occurs in the input instance, in positions of the coincident variables, a fresh constant in a target instance. The resulting schema and data transformation depend on the query. D^{red} denotes the *reduced form* of D, obtained by applying the one-step reduction f^{red}, which is the iterative and terminating application of f to D.
(e) The set of exogenous tuples is preserved, that is, a tuple in the target instance is exogenous iff its corresponding tuple in the original instance is exogenous. ■

Proposition 4. Let $\mathcal{Q}$ be a SJF-BCQ, possibly with non-trivial coincidences.
(a) For every instance D for (the schema of) $\mathcal{Q}$, CES and Resp are aligned for $(\mathcal{Q}, D)$ iff they are aligned for $(\mathcal{Q}^{red}, D^{red})$.
(b) For every instance $D^\star$ for $\mathcal{Q}^{red}$, there is an instance D for $\mathcal{Q}$, such that CES and Resp are aligned for $(\mathcal{Q}^{red}, D^\star)$ iff they are aligned for $(\mathcal{Q}, D)$. ■

We illustrate Proposition 4 to obtain alignment and non-alignment results.

Example 12. Consider BCQs $\mathcal{Q}_1, \mathcal{Q}_2$, with their *reduced versions*, $\mathcal{Q}_1^{red}, \mathcal{Q}_2^{red}$:
$\mathcal{Q}_1\!: \exists x \exists y \exists z(R(x,y,z) \wedge S(x,y,z) \wedge T(x,y,z))$, $\mathcal{Q}_1^{red}\!: \exists v(R'(v) \wedge S'(v) \wedge T'(v))$,
$\mathcal{Q}_2\!: \exists x \exists y \exists w(R(x,y,w) \wedge S(x,y) \wedge T(x,y))$, $\mathcal{Q}_2^{red}$: $\exists v' \exists w(R'(v',w) \wedge S'(v') \wedge T'(v'))$.

From Proposition 4(a), for any D for $\mathcal{Q}_1$, the scores are aligned for $(\mathcal{Q}_1, D)$ iff they are aligned for (Q_1^{red}, D^{red}). By Proposition 1, CES and Resp are aligned for $(\mathcal{Q}_1^{red}, D^{red})$. It follows that the scores are always aligned for $(\mathcal{Q}_1, D)$.

Since $\mathcal{Q}_2^{red}$ satisfies the conditions of Proposition 2, there is a D' with CES, Resp not aligned for $(\mathcal{Q}_2^{red}, D')$. By Proposition 4(b), there is an instance D for $\mathcal{Q}$, with CES and Resp not aligned for $(\mathcal{Q}_2, D)$.

To obtain D from D' (illustrating the proof of Proposition 4(b) in [4]), it is easy to define and apply an inverse f^{-1} of f (giving rise to an inverse of f^{red}) in Remark 3(d), which replaces each constant introduced by f by a pair of identical constants that originally occupied the positions of two coincident variables. ■

5.3 General SJF-BCQs

Now we address the general case where queries may have multiple components and any kind of coincidences. We start by stating the main result of this section.

Theorem 1. Let $\mathcal{Q}$ be an SJF-BCQ, with components $C_1, \ldots, C_n$, and their associated subqueries $\mathcal{Q}_1, \ldots, \mathcal{Q}_n$, as in Definition 4. It holds:
(a) When $n = 1$ and $|\mathit{Coin}(\mathcal{Q})| = 1$; and also when $n \geq 2$ and, for every $i = 1, \ldots, n$, $|\mathit{Atoms}(\mathcal{Q}_i)| = 1$, it holds that CES and Resp are aligned for $(\mathcal{Q}, D)$ for every instance D with or without exogenous tuples.

(b) In any other case, there is an instance D with exogenous tuples for which CES and Resp are not aligned.[5] ■

This is a *dichotomy result* that fully and syntactically classifies SJF-BCQs, with the caveat that case (b) requires exogenous tuples (see Sect. 5.4).

Table 8. (a) Instance D. (b) CES and Resp.

R_1	X	Z
$\underline{\tau_1}$	a	a
τ_2	b	b

R_2	X	Y	Z
τ_3	a	a	a
τ_4	a	b	a
τ_5	b	a	b

R_3	X	Z
$\underline{\tau_6}$	a	a
$\underline{\tau_7}$	b	b

τ	CES	Resp
τ_3	0.09375	1/3
τ_5	0.03125	1/2

Example 13. The BCQ $\mathcal{Q}: \exists x \exists y \exists z(R_1(x,z) \wedge R_2(x,y,z) \wedge R_3(x,z))$ has one component. Furthermore, $|Coin(\mathcal{Q})| = |\{\{x,z\},\{y\}\}| = 2$. By Theorem 1(b), there is an instance D for which CES and Resp are not aligned for $(\mathcal{Q}, D)$. The proof of Proposition 2 provides an algorithm to build D (as illustrated in Example 9), that in Table 8(a), with underlined exogenous tuples. Table 8(b) shows the non-alignment of CES and Resp for $(\mathcal{Q}, D)$: $\tau_5 \prec^{CE} \tau_3$ and $\tau_3 \prec^{\rho} \tau_5$.

For $\mathcal{Q}'$: $\exists x \exists y \exists z \exists v \exists w(R_1(x,y) \wedge R_2(z) \wedge R_3(w,v))$, for which $C_1' = \{R_1(x,y)\}$, $C_2' = \{R_2(z)\}$ and $C_3' = \{R_3(w,v)\}$, Theorem 1(a) tells us that, for every instance D, possibly with exogenous tuples, CES and Resp are aligned for D. ■

Theorem 1(a) follows from the results in Sect. 5.1 and Proposition 4. Part (b) follows from Propositions 5 and 6 right below.

Proposition 5. Let $\mathcal{Q}$ be a SJF-BCQ with components $C_1, \ldots, C_n$, and associated queries $\mathcal{Q}_i$, with $n \geq 2$. If, for $i = 1, \ldots, n$, $|Atoms(\mathcal{Q}_i)| = 1$, CES and Resp are aligned for $(\mathcal{Q}, D)$, for every instance D, with or without exogenous tuples. ■

Proposition 6 right below implies Theorem 1(b), specifically to queries with more than one component, and appeals to the technique described in Remark 2, with which we will use the following counterexample.

Example 14. For $\mathcal{Q}$: $\exists x \exists y(R(x) \wedge S(y) \wedge T(y))$, and $D^\star$ in Table 9(a) without exogenous tuples, CES and Resp are not aligned for $(\mathcal{Q}, D^\star)$ (see Table 9(b)). ■

Proposition 6. Let $\mathcal{Q}$ be a SJF-BCQ with at least two components, of which at least one has two or more atoms. There is an instance D with exogenous tuples where CES and Resp are not aligned. ■

[5] This does not prevent the existence, for some queries in this class, of an instance without exogenous tuples where the scores are not aligned.

Table 9. (a) Instance $D^\star$. (b) CES and Resp.

R	X
τ_1	a
τ_2	b
τ_3	c

S	Y
τ_4	a
τ_5	b

T	Y
τ_6	a
τ_7	b

τ	CES	Resp
τ_1	0.28125	1/3
τ_4	0.125	1/2

Example 15. We illustrate Proposition 6 with $\mathcal{Q}: \exists x \exists y \exists z \exists v \exists w (R_1(x,y) \wedge R_2(z) \wedge R_3(z) \wedge R_4(z) \wedge R_5(w,v))$ that has components: $C_1 = \{R_1(x,y)\}$, $C_2 = \{R_2(z), R_3(z), R_4(z)\}$, $C_3 = \{R_5(w,v)\}$. Since C_2 has three atoms, by Proposition 6, an instance D can be built where the scores are not aligned, as follows: Select components C_2 and C_3. From C_2 select atoms $R_2(z), R_3(z)$; and from C_3, atom $R_5(w,v)$. Tuples from R_2, R_3, R_5 are endogenous; and the rest, exogenous (underlined). Table 10(a) shows instance D. Table 10(b) shows that CES and Resp are not aligned for $(\mathcal{Q}, D)$.

In relation to the scores for subqueries $\mathcal{Q}_1, \mathcal{Q}_2, \mathcal{Q}_3$ corresponding to C_1, C_2, C_3, Proposition 1 tells us they are are always aligned for $\mathcal{Q}_2$. By Proposition 4 and Remark 3, the scores are always aligned for $\mathcal{Q}_1$ and $\mathcal{Q}_3$ iff they are aligned for their reduced forms, which in both cases is of the form $\mathcal{Q}^{red}: \exists v(R(v))$. By Proposition 1, the scores are aligned for $\mathcal{Q}^{red}$. We can see that alignment for the subqueries does not entail alignment for original query. However, Corollary 1 below tells us that the inverse does hold. ■

Table 10. (a) Instance D. (b) CES and Resp.

R_1	A	B
$\underline{\tau_1}$	c'	c'

R_2	A
τ_2	a
τ_3	b

R_3	A
τ_4	a
τ_5	b

R_4	A
$\underline{\tau_6}$	a
$\underline{\tau_7}$	b

R_5	A	B
τ_8	a	c'
τ_9	b	c'
τ_{10}	c	c'

τ	CES	Resp
τ_2	0.125	1/2
τ_8	0.28125	1/3

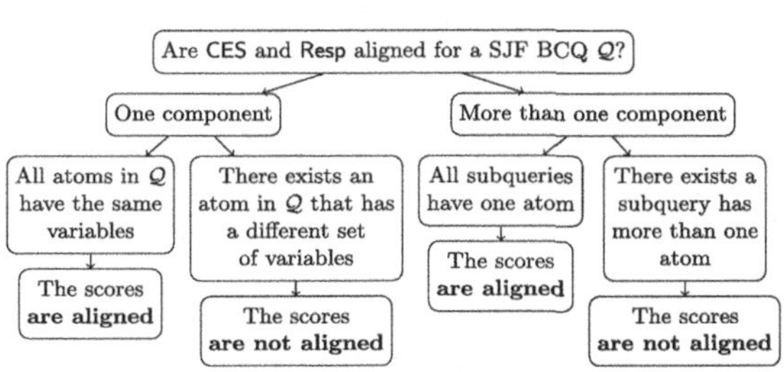

Fig. 1. Query Classification (Theorem 1).

With Theorem 1 we have a full characterization of the space of SJF-BCQs, as shown in Fig. 1. The next result follows from Propositions 1, 3 and 5.

Corollary 1. *Let $\mathcal{Q}$ be a SJF-BCQ with at least two components. If* CES *and* Resp *are aligned for $(D, \mathcal{Q})$, D any instance, they are aligned for D and the subqueries built from its components.* ■

5.4 Alignment in the Absence of Exogenous Tuples

Notice that the non-alignment result in Theorem 1(b) holds for instances with exogenous tuples. Until now, we do not know what happens in that case when instances do not have them. This is what we investigate now. Actually, we will show that exogenous tuples are required for non-alignment for two classes of queries that fall under Theorem 1(b), those in Propositions 7 and 8 below: For them, CES and Resp are always aligned. *In this section, we assume that instances do not have exogenous tuples.*

Proposition 7. For a single-component BCQ $\mathcal{Q}$ with $|Atoms(\mathcal{Q})| \leq 2$, $|Coin(\mathcal{Q})| \leq 3$, CES and Resp are aligned for every D (w/o exogenous tuples). ■

Table 11. (a) Instance D. (b) Scores in D. (c) Scores in D'.

(a)

R	X	Y
τ_1	a	a
τ_2	a	b
τ_3	b	a

S	X	Z
$\underline{\tau_4}$	a	c_1
τ_5	b	c_2

(b)

τ	CES	Resp
τ_1	0.375	1/3
τ_3	0.125	1/2

(c)

τ	CES	Resp
τ_1	0.1875	1/3
τ_3	0.3125	1/2

Example 16. Consider $\mathcal{Q}_{\mathsf{RS}}$: $\exists x \exists y \exists z(R(x, y) \wedge S(x, z))$ of Example 6. By Proposition 7, CES and Resp are aligned for every instance without exogenous tuples. In contrast, if exogenous tuples are allowed, Proposition 2 allows us to build an instance D, that in Table 11(a), with exogenous τ_4, where these scores are not aligned (as shown in Table 11(b)). However, for $D' = D$, with $(D')^{ex} = \emptyset$, the scores are now aligned (see Table 11(c)). ■

Proposition 8. For the query $\mathcal{Q}_{R_1,S_m}$: $\exists \bar{x} \exists \bar{y}(R_1(\bar{x}, \bar{y}) \wedge S_1(\bar{x}) \wedge \ldots \wedge S_m(\bar{x}))$, with $\bar{x}$ and $\bar{y}$ are non-empty, mutually exclusive strings of variables, CES and Resp are aligned for every instance without exogenous tuples. ■

Example 15 showed that the inverse of Corollary 1 does not hold for a particular instance with exogenous tuples. The following example shows that the inverse still does not hold without exogenous tuples.

Table 12. .

R	τ_1	τ_2	τ_3	τ_4	τ_5	τ_6	τ_7	τ_8	τ_9	τ_{10}	τ_{11}	τ_{12}	τ_{13}
X	a	b	b	b	b	b	c	c	c	c	c	c	c
Y	a	a	b	c	d	e	a	b	c	d	e	f	g

S	X
τ_{14}	a
τ_{15}	b
τ_{16}	c

T	Z	W
τ_{17}	a	a
τ_{18}	a	b
τ_{19}	a	c
τ_{20}	b	a

U	Z
τ_{21}	a
τ_{22}	b

τ	CES	Resp
τ_1	0.0751	1/3
τ_{17}	0.0754	1/4
τ_{21}	0.5284	1/2

Example 17. For $\mathcal{Q}: \exists x \exists y \exists z \exists w(R(x,y) \wedge S(x) \wedge T(z,w) \wedge U(z))$, and the instance (without exogenous tuples) in Table 12, CES and Resp are not aligned for $(D, \mathcal{Q})$. $\mathcal{Q}$ has the subqueries $\mathcal{Q}_a: \exists x \exists y(R(x,y) \wedge S(x))$ and $\mathcal{Q}_b: \exists z \exists w(T(z,w) \wedge U(z))$, associated to its components. By Proposition 8, CES and Resp are aligned for $(\mathcal{Q}_a, D')$ and $(\mathcal{Q}_b, D')$, for every D' without exogenous tuples. ■

6 Alignment of Shapley with CES and Resp

Until now we haven't consider the alignment of Shapley with other scores. Example 6 showed that it is not aligned with CES or Resp for the particular combination $(\mathcal{Q}_{\mathsf{RS}}, D^\star)$, with $\mathcal{Q}_{\mathsf{RS}}: \exists x \exists y \exists z(R(x,y) \wedge S(x,z))$. Using $(\mathcal{Q}_{\mathsf{RS}}, D^\star)$ for the technique in Remark 2, we can generalize this non-alignment result to a broader class of BCQs. In this section, we require instances to have exogenous tuples.

Proposition 9. Let $\mathcal{Q}$ be a BCQ containing at least two atoms A_R and A_S, with predicates R, S, resp., such that: (a) $\mathit{Var}(A_R) \cap \mathit{Var}(A_S) \neq \emptyset$, (b) $\mathit{Var}(A_R) \not\subseteq \mathit{Var}(A_S)$, and (c) $\mathit{Var}(A_S) \not\subseteq \mathit{Var}(A_R)$.[6] There is D with exogenous tuples for which Shapley is not aligned with any of CES or Resp on $(\mathcal{Q}, D)$. ■

Query $\mathcal{Q}_{\mathsf{RS}}$ belongs to the class in Proposition 9. The next example illustrates Proposition 9; the instance is built according to the proof of the proposition (in [4]).

Example 18. $\mathcal{Q}: \exists x \exists y \exists z \exists v \exists w(R_1(x,y,z) \wedge R_2(y,z) \wedge R_3(y,z,w,v) \wedge R_4(v))$ belongs to the class in Proposition 9. Table 13(a) shows instance D where neither CES nor Resp are aligned with Shapley. Underlined tuples are exogenous. ■

[6] These conditions tell us that the BCQ is *non-hierarchical* [38].

Table 13. (a) Instance D. (b) Scores.

R_1	X	Y	Z
τ_1	c_1	a	a
τ_2	c_2	b	b
τ_3	c_3	b	b

R_2	Y	Z
$\underline{\tau_4}$	a	a
$\underline{\tau_5}$	b	b

R_3	Y	Z	W	V
τ_6	a	a	c_4	c'
τ_7	a	a	c_5	c'
τ_8	b	b	c_6	c'
τ_9	b	b	c_7	c'
τ_{10}	b	b	c_8	c'
τ_{11}	b	b	c_9	c'

R_4	V
$\underline{\tau_{12}}$	c'

τ	CES	Resp	Shapley
τ_1	57/256	1/3	400/2520
τ_6	19/256	1/4	151/2520
τ_8	15/256	1/5	169/2520

7 Conclusions

The comparison of attribution scores for tuples participating in query answering in DBs, such Resp, Shapley, BPI, CES, has not received much attention. We have provided a first analysis of their alignment, i.e. of wether they induce compatible rankings of tuples. We have identified classes of self-join-free BCQs for which Resp and CES are aligned, and others for which they are not. Our syntactic test is applicable to any SJF-BCQ, obtaining a dichotomy result. Exogenous tuples becomes crucial. An analysis of queries with self-joins is still open.

We have exhibited a broad class of queries for which CES (and also Resp) and Shap are not aligned. Our results require the presence of exogenous tuples. We do not know what happens in their absence.

Questions about the alignment of Shapley and BPI (and indirectly, CES in our case) are still open in Game Theory [17], where commonly no distinction between exogenous and endogenous players is made.

Aligned scores may have very *different score distributions* on the tuples. Obtaining results about the *comparison of score distributions* is an open problem.

It is not obvious how to address this important and practical question about which score to use. Appealing to the characterizing properties of the scores seems to be unavoidable. Both Shapley and BPI have them, and those of BPI is inherited by CES. There is also an axiomatization for the *generalized* CES score [3]. In [6], there is a recent axiomatization of Responsibility for explainable machine learning. These general properties should shed some light on the score distribution problem as well. Properties of these scores by themselves will not solve the problem of applicability in databases. We need, an agreement on what is a good score-based explanation for query answering, which is still open.

Acknowledgements. Felipe Azúa has been supported by the Millennium Institute for Foundational Research on Data (IMFD, Chile). Leopoldo Bertossi has been financially supported by the IMFD, and NSERC-DG 2023-04650. Part of this work was done while Felipe Azúa was visiting the "Laboratory of Informatics, Modelling and Optimization of the Systems" (LIMOS), at U. Clermont-Ferrand, France. He appreciates their support and hospitality.

References

1. Abramovich, O., Deutch, D., Frost, N., Kara, A., Olteanu, D.: Banzhaf values for facts in query answering. In: Proceedings of the SIGMOD 2024 (2024)
2. Arad, D., Deutch, D., Frost, N.: LearnShapley: learning to predict rankings of facts contribution based on query logs. In: Proceedings of the CIKM, pp. 4788–4792 (2022)
3. Azúa, F., Bertossi, L.: The causal-effect score in data management. In: Proceedings of the 4th Conference on Causal Learning and Reasoning, CLeaR 2025, vol. 275, pp. 874–893. PMLR (2025). arXiv arXiv:2502.02495
4. Azúa, F., Bertossi, L.: Causality-Based Scores Alignment in Explainable Data Management. arXiv Paper arXiv:2503.14469 (2025)
5. Banzhaf III, J.: Weighted Voting Doesn't Work: A Mathematical Analysis. Rutgers L. Rev. **19**(31) (1964)
6. Biradar, G., Izza, Y., Lobo, E., Viswanathan, V., Zick, Y.: Axiomatic aggregations of abductive explanations. In: Proceedings of the AAAI (2024)
7. Bertossi, L.: From database repairs to causality in databases and beyond. Trans. Large Scale Data Knowl. Centered Syst. LIV **14160**, 119–131 (2023)
8. Bertossi, L., Salimi, B.: Causes for query answers from databases: datalog abduction, view-updates, and integrity constraints. Int. J. Approx. Reason. **90**, 226–252 (2017)
9. Bertossi, L., Salimi, B.: From causes for database queries to repairs and model-based diagnosis and back. Theor. Comput. Syst. **61**(1), 191–232 (2017)
10. Bertossi, L., Livshits, E., Kimelfeld, B., Monet, M.: The Shapley value in database management. ACM SIGMOD Rec. **52**(3), 6–17 (2023)
11. Bienvenu, M., Figueira, D., Lafourcade, P.: When is Shapley value computation a matter of counting? Proc. ACM Manag. Data (PODS) **2**, 105 (2024)
12. Chockler, H., Halpern, J.: Responsibility and blame: a structural-model approach. J. Artif. Intell. Res. **22**, 93–115 (2004)
13. Dalvi, N., Suciu, D.: The dichotomy of probabilistic inference for unions of conjunctive queries. J. ACM **59**(6), 30:1–30:87 (2012)
14. Davidson, S., Deutch, D., Frost, N., Kimelfeld, B., Koren, O., Monet, M.: ShapGraph: an holistic view of explanations through provenance graphs and Shapley values. In: Proceedings of the SIGMOD (2022)
15. Deutch, D., Frost, N., Kimelfeld, B., Monet, M.: Computing the Shapley value of facts in query answering. In: Proceedings of the SIGMOD, pp. 1570–1583 (2022)
16. Dubey, P., Shapley, L.S.: Mathematical properties of the Banzhaf power index. Math. Oper. Res. **4**(2), 99–131 (1979)
17. Freixas, J.: On ordinal equivalence of the Shapley and Banzhaf values for cooperative games. Int. J. Game Theor. **39**, 513–527 (2010)
18. Freixas, J., Marciniak, D., Pons, M.: On the ordinal equivalence of the Johnston, Banzhaf and Shapley power indices. Eur. J. Oper. Res. **216**, 367–375 (2012)
19. Gelman, A., Hill, J.: Data Analysis Using Regression and Multilevel/Hierarchical Models. Cambridge University Press (2007)
20. Halpern, J.: A modification of the Halpern-Pearl definition of causality. In: Proceedings of the IJCAI, pp. 3022–3033 (2015)
21. Halpern, J.: Actual Causality. MIT Press (2016)
22. Halpern, J.Y., Pearl, J.: Causes and explanations: a structural-model approach. part i: causes. Br. J. Philos. Sci. **56**(4), 843–887 (2005)

23. Holland, P.W.: Statistics and causal inference. J. Am. Stat. Assoc. **81**(396), 945–960 (1986)
24. Kara, A., Olteanu, D., Suciu, D.: From Shapley Value to Model Counting and Back. In: Proceedings of the ACM on Management of Data (2024)
25. Karmarkar, P., Monet, M., Senellart, P., Bressan, S.: Expected Shapley-like scores of Boolean functions: complexity and applications to probabilistic databases. In Proc. ACM Manag. Data (PODS) **2**, 92 (2024)
26. Livshits, E., Bertossi, L., Kimelfeld, B., Sebag, M.: Query games in databases. ACM SIGMOD Rec. **50**(1), 78–85 (2021)
27. Livshits, E., Bertossi, L., Kimelfeld, B., Sebag, M.: The shapley value of tuples in query answering. Log. Meth. Comput. Sci. **17**(3) (2021)
28. Makhija, N., Gatterbauer, W.: A unified approach for resilience and causal responsibility with integer linear programming and LP relaxations. In: Proceedings of the SIGMOD (2023)
29. Meliou, A., Gatterbauer, W., Halpern, J., Koch, Ch., Moore, K.E., Suciu, D.: Causality in Databases. IEEE Data Eng. Bull. **33**(3), 59–67 (2010)
30. Meliou, A., Gatterbauer, W., Moore, K.F., Suciu, D.: The complexity of causality and responsibility for query answers and non-answers. Proc. VLDB Endow. **4**(1), 34–45 (2010)
31. Pearl, J.: Causality: Models, Reasoning and Inference, 2nd edn. Cambridge University Press, USA (2009)
32. Roth, A.E. (ed.): The Shapley Value: Essays in Honor of Lloyd S. Cambridge University Press, Shapley (1988)
33. Roy, S., Salimi, B.: Causal inference in data analysis with applications to fairness and explanations. In: Reasoning Web. Causality, Explanations and Declarative Knowledge. LNCS, vol. 13759, pp. 105–131. Springer, Heidelberg (2023). https://doi.org/10.1007/978-3-031-31414-8_3
34. Rubin, D.B.: Estimating causal effects of treatments in randomized and nonrandomized studies. J. Educ. Psychol. **66**, 688–701 (1974)
35. Salimi, B.: Query-answer causality in databases and its connections with reverse reasoning tasks in data and knowledge management. Ph.D. Thesis, Carleton University, Canada (2016)
36. Salimi, B., Bertossi, L., Suciu, D., Van den Broeck, G.: Quantifying causal effects on query answering in databases. In: Proceedings of the TaPP. USENIX Association (2016)
37. Shapley, L.: A value for an n-person game. In: Contributions to the Theory of Games II, pp. 307–331. Princeton University Press (1953)
38. Suciu, D., Olteanu, D., Ré, Ch., Koch, Ch.: Probabilistic Databases. Synthesis Lectures on Data Management. Morgan & Claypool Publishers (2011)

An Order-Theoretic View on Optimal Repairs and Complete Sets of Unifiers

Franz Baader[1,2](✉)

[1] Institute of Theoretical Computer Science, TU Dresden, Dresden, Germany
[2] Center for Scalable Data Analytics and AI Dresden/Leipzig (ScaDS.AI), Dresden, Germany
franz.baader@tu-dresden.de

Abstract. The optimal repair property, which says that there is a finite set of optimal (i.e., entailment-maximal) repairs that covers all repairs, has turned out to be useful both in the context of ontology engineering and in belief change. We provide abstract order-theoretic conditions that guarantee the existence of finite sets of optimal repairs covering all repairs, and illustrate their use with abstract examples as well as with more practical examples from the realm of Description Logic (DL). The order-theoretic view on optimal repairs also reveals that there is a strong similarity between the optimal repair property and the existence of a finite complete set of unifiers for unification modulo equational theories. Applying Siekmann's proposal to divide unification problems into the unification types unitary, finitary, infinitary, and zero to repair problems, we obtain a more fine-grained classification of repair problems. For the DL examples introduced in this paper, we observe that types unitary, finitary and zero can occur, but none of these examples provides us with an infinitary repair problem. However, we also show that unification problems can actually be viewed as repair problems in the abstract framework introduced in our previous work on contractions based on optimal repairs. Thus, within this framework, known results on unification types of certain equational theories provide us with examples of repair problems of these types.

1 Introduction

Representing knowledge in a logic-based knowledge representation language allows one to derive implicit consequences from a given knowledge base (KB). Prominent examples of logic-based KR languages are description logics (DLs) [10]. Modifying a KB such that a certain unwanted consequence no longer follows has been investigated in the area of belief change under the name of contraction [2,22] and in ontology engineering under the name of repair [15,25,36,39]. Belief base contractions [22,29] and classical repair approaches for DL-based knowledge bases [25,36] compute subsets of the given KB. These approaches have been criticised for being syntax-dependent and removing too many consequences [5,15,23,28,35].

A.-Y. Turhan and J. Virtema (Eds.): FoIKS 2026, LNCS 16475, pp. 283–303, 2026.
https://doi.org/10.1007/978-3-032-21540-6_17

On the DL side, optimal repairs have been proposed as a solution to this problem [12]. Optimal repairs maximize the set of consequences of the knowledge base rather than the set of its explicit statements, while still being representable by a finite KB. In general, such optimal repairs need not exist even in cases where there is a repair (see Proposition 2 in [15] and Example 4 in this paper). Even if optimal repairs exist, they may not cover all repairs in the sense that every repair is an instance of an optimal one. If in this case one considers only optimal repairs, then one may lose certain repair options. In the context of repairing DL-based KBs, we were able to determine application-relevant settings were this cannot happen, i.e., where every repair problem has a finite set of optimal repairs that covers all repairs, and where this set of optimal repairs can effectively be computed [11–14,26].

On the belief change side, we have developed in [20] a new approach for constructing contraction operations, called partial product contractions, which uses optimal repairs in place of classical repairs (called remainders in the belief change literature [24]). However, instead of introducing this approach for a specific instance, we defined a very general framework within which partial product contractions can be constructed. Basically, this framework considers a reflexive and transitive entailment relation between KBs, without making explicit assumptions on the structure of the KBs and their semantics. The repair goal is formulated using repair requests and a repair function that determines which KBs are considered to be repairs of a given KB w.r.t. such a repair request. The framework makes several other assumptions, but for the purpose of this paper, only the *optimal repair property* is relevant, which says that every repair problem has a finite set of optimal repairs that covers all repairs in the sense that every repair is entailed by an optimal repair (see Definition 1).

In the *first part of this paper* (Sects. 3 and 4), we will investigate the optimal repair property from an order-theoretic point of view, which is possible since the entailment relation can be seen as a quasi-order. We will employ this view to characterize the optimal repair property using well-quasi-orders (wqos) in Sect. 3. Then we consider several instances of the general framework where KBs are concepts of the DL $\mathcal{EL}$ and show in Sect. 4 that they satisfy the optimal repair property, though there are also variants that do not.

In the *second part of this paper* (Sect. 5), we go beyond the optimal repair property by investigating the possible reasons for the optimal repair property to fail. This is inspired by the use of the order-theoretic view in [4] to characterize unification type zero. In fact, if one replaces repair problems with unification problems and entailment between KBs with the instantiation quasi-order between substitutions, then one sees that there is a close relationship between repair problems satisfying the optimal repair property and unification problems that are unitary or finitary. This allows us to transfer the unification hierarchy [19,31] consisting of unification types unitary, finitary, infinitary, and zero to repair problems. Analyzing the repair problems from Sect. 4 in a more fine-grained way, we see that repair types unitary, finitary, and zero can occur, but type infinitary is not possible in these examples. Whether this has deeper reasons or is just an artefact of the chosen instances is not clear at the moment.

In the *third part of this paper* (Sect. 6), we show that (a generalization of) unification modulo equational theories can be seen as an instance of the general repair framework introduced in [20]. We then analyze under what conditions the unification type of the equational theory transfers to the corresponding repair problems.

Not all proofs of the results presented in this paper can be given here. They can be found in the technical report [6].

2 Preliminaries

We start with describing the DL $\mathcal{EL}$ [8,10] since it will later be used in the instances of the general repair framework presented in the second part of this section.

The Description Logic $\mathcal{EL}$. $\mathcal{EL}$ concepts are built inductively, starting with concept names A from a set N_C of such names, and using the concept constructors $\top$ (top concept), $C \sqcap D$ (conjunction), and $\exists r.C$ (existential restriction), where C, D are $\mathcal{EL}$ concepts and r belongs to a set N_R of role names. A general concept inclusion (GCI) of $\mathcal{EL}$ is of the form $C \sqsubseteq D$ for $\mathcal{EL}$ concepts C, D, and an $\mathcal{EL}$ TBox is a finite set of such GCIs.

The semantics of $\mathcal{EL}$ is defined in a model-theoretic way, using the notion of an *interpretation* $\mathcal{I}$, which is a pair $\mathcal{I} = (\Delta^\mathcal{I}, \cdot^\mathcal{I})$, where the domain $\Delta^\mathcal{I}$ is a non-empty set and the interpretation function $\cdot^\mathcal{I}$ maps each concept name $A \in N_C$ to $A^\mathcal{I} \subseteq \Delta^\mathcal{I}$ and each role name $r \in N_R$ to a binary relation $r^\mathcal{I} \subseteq \Delta^\mathcal{I} \times \Delta^\mathcal{I}$. The interpretation of an $\mathcal{EL}$ concept is defined inductively as follows: $\top^\mathcal{I} := \Delta^\mathcal{I}$, $(C \sqcap D)^\mathcal{I} := C^\mathcal{I} \cap D^\mathcal{I}$, and $(\exists r.C)^\mathcal{I} := \{d \in \Delta^\mathcal{I} \mid \exists e \in \Delta^\mathcal{I}$ such that $(d, e) \in r^\mathcal{I}$ and $e \in C^\mathcal{I}\}$. A model $\mathcal{I}$of the $\mathcal{EL}$ TBox $\mathcal{T}$is an interpretation that satisfies all its GCIs, i.e., $C^\mathcal{I} \subseteq D^\mathcal{I}$ holds for all $C \sqsubseteq D \in \mathcal{T}$. Given $\mathcal{EL}$ concepts C, D and an $\mathcal{EL}$ TBox $\mathcal{T}$, we say that C is *subsumed by D w.r.t. $\mathcal{T}$*$(C \sqsubseteq^\mathcal{T} D)$ if $C^\mathcal{I} \subseteq D^\mathcal{I}$ in all models $\mathcal{I}$of $\mathcal{T}$. The $\mathcal{EL}$ concepts C, D are equivalent (written $C \equiv^\mathcal{T} D$) if $C \sqsubseteq^\mathcal{T} D$ and $D \sqsubseteq^\mathcal{T} C$.

We will see in Sect. 4 that we must restrict the TBox to being cycle-restricted for the optimal repair property to hold, where an $\mathcal{EL}$ TBox $\mathcal{T}$is *cycle-restricted* if there is no $\mathcal{EL}$ concept C and $m \geq 1$ (not necessarily distinct) role names $r_1, \ldots, r_m$ such that $C \sqsubseteq^\mathcal{T} \exists r_1. \cdots \exists r_m.C$. As pointed out in [7], it can be decided in polynomial time whether a given $\mathcal{EL}$ TBox is cycle-restricted.

The Optimal Repair Property. Following [20], we assume that we are given a set of *knowledge bases* (KBs) and an *entailment relation* between knowledge bases. We usually write KBs as $\mathcal{K}$, possibly primed ($\mathcal{K}'$) or with an index ($\mathcal{K}_i$), and entailment as $\models$, i.e., $\mathcal{K} \models \mathcal{K}'$ means that $\mathcal{K}$ *entails* $\mathcal{K}'$, or equivalently that $\mathcal{K}'$ is *entailed by* $\mathcal{K}$. We assume that entailment satisfies the following properties:

- $\mathcal{K} \models \mathcal{K}$ (reflexivity),
- $\mathcal{K} \models \mathcal{K}'$ and $\mathcal{K}' \models \mathcal{K}''$ implies $\mathcal{K} \models \mathcal{K}''$ (transitivity).

From an order-theoretic point of view, this means that entailment (viewed as a $\geq$ relation) is a quasi-order. We call two knowledge bases $\mathcal{K}$ and $\mathcal{K}'$ *equivalent* (and write $\mathcal{K} \equiv \mathcal{K}'$) if $\mathcal{K} \models \mathcal{K}'$ and $\mathcal{K}' \models \mathcal{K}$. We say that $\mathcal{K}$ *strictly entails* $\mathcal{K}'$ if $\mathcal{K} \models \mathcal{K}'$, but $\mathcal{K}' \not\models \mathcal{K}$. In this case we write $\mathcal{K} \models_s \mathcal{K}'$. Note that $\models_s$ is the $>$ relation corresponding to the $\geq$ relation $\models$. The relation $\equiv$ on KBs is indeed an equivalence relation, and we write the equivalence class of a KB $\mathcal{K}$as $[\mathcal{K}]$, i.e., $[\mathcal{K}] := \{\mathcal{K}' \mid \mathcal{K} \equiv \mathcal{K}'\}$.

When defining repairs, we assume that we have additional syntactic entities called repair requests. Given a KB $\mathcal{K}$, a *repair request* α determines a set of KBs $\text{Rep}(\mathcal{K}, \alpha)$ such that

(a) $\mathcal{K} \models \mathcal{K}'$ holds for every element $\mathcal{K}' \in \text{Rep}(\mathcal{K}, \alpha)$, and
(b) $\mathcal{K}' \in \text{Rep}(\mathcal{K}, \alpha)$ and $\mathcal{K}' \models \mathcal{K}''$ imply $\mathcal{K}'' \in \text{Rep}(\mathcal{K}, \alpha)$.

We call the elements of $\text{Rep}(\mathcal{K}, \alpha)$ *repairs* of $\mathcal{K}$for α.

Example 1. In this example, knowledge bases are concepts of the DL $\mathcal{EL}$, and entailment is subsumption w.r.t. the empty TBox, i.e., $C \models D$ iff $C \sqsubseteq^{\emptyset} D$. On the one hand, we use $\mathcal{EL}$ concepts also as repair requests and define $\text{Rep}_{\text{ent}}(C, D) := \{C' \mid C \models C', C' \not\models D\}$. This means that we are looking for a subsumer of C that is not subsumed by D. It is easy to see that the function Rep_{ent} satisfies conditions (a) and (b). Such repair problems were considered in [5,20,32].

On the other hand, let $\text{Sig}(C)$ be the set of concept and role names occurring in the concept C. We use finite sets of concept and role names as repair requests, and define $\text{Rep}_{\text{for}}(C, \alpha) := \{C' \mid C \models C', \text{Sig}(C') \cap \alpha = \emptyset\}$. The goal is here to forget the names from α, i.e., to find a concept that subsumes C and does not contain any of the names in α. Again, condition (a) is satisfied by definition, and (b) holds since it is easy to see that $C' \sqsubseteq^{\emptyset} C''$ implies $\text{Sig}(C') \supseteq \text{Sig}(C'')$ (see Lemma 3 below). Such repair problems were considered in [20].

Our second example is more abstract.

Example 2. Assume that KBs are pairs of natural numbers, i.e., elements of $\mathbb{N} \times \mathbb{N}$, and let $\models$ be the lexicographic product order $\geq^{lex}$ induced by the usual order $\geq$ on natural numbers, i.e. $(k, \ell) \geq^{lex} (k', \ell')$ if $k > k'$, or $k = k'$ and $\ell \geq \ell'$. We use natural numbers as repair requests and set $\text{Rep}((k, \ell), r) := \{(k', \ell') \mid (k, \ell) \geq^{lex} (k', \ell'), k' \leq r\}$. Condition (a) is again satisfied by definition, and (b) holds since it is easy to see that $(k', \ell') \geq^{lex} (k'', \ell'')$ implies $k' \geq k''$.

We are interested in repair settings that satisfy the optimal repair property.

Definition 1. *The repair function* Rep *satisfies the* optimal repair property *if, for every pair* $\mathcal{K}, \alpha$ *consisting of a KB and a repair request (called a* repair problem*), there exists a finite set of KBs* $\text{Orep}(\mathcal{K}, \alpha)$ *satisfying*

- *every element* $\mathcal{K}'$ *of* $\text{Orep}(\mathcal{K}, \alpha)$ *is a* repair *of* $\mathcal{K}$ *for* α *(repair property),*

- *every element* $\mathcal{K}'$ *of* $\mathrm{Orep}(\mathcal{K},\alpha)$ *is* optimal*, i.e., there is no repair of* $\mathcal{K}$ *for* α *that strictly entails* $\mathcal{K}'$ *(optimality),*
- $\mathrm{Orep}(\mathcal{K},\alpha)$ covers *all repairs, i.e., for every repair* $\mathcal{K}''$ *of* $\mathcal{K}$ *for* α*, there is an element* $\mathcal{K}'$ *of* $\mathrm{Orep}(\mathcal{K},\alpha)$ *such that* $\mathcal{K}'$ *entails* $\mathcal{K}''$ *(coverage).*

In our first example, the optimal repair property is satisfied for both types of repairs, basically because the set of subsumer of a given $\mathcal{EL}$ concept, i.e., $\mathrm{Subs}(C) := \{D \mid C \sqsubseteq^{\emptyset} D\}$, is finite up to equivalence (see Sect. 4).

In the second example, optimal repairs need not exist although there are repairs, and thus the optimal repair property is not satisfied. For example, $\mathrm{Rep}((1,0),0) = \{(0,\ell) \mid \ell \in \mathbb{N}\}$. Clearly, this set is non-empty, but it does not contain an optimal repair. In fact, for every $(0,\ell) \in \mathrm{Rep}((1,0),0)$, we have $(0,\ell+1) \in \mathrm{Rep}((1,0),0)$ and $(0,\ell+1) \models_s (0,\ell)$.

3 An Order-Theoretic View

Here we use $\geq$ to denote entailment and $>$ to denote strict entailment. Our requirement that entailment be reflexive and transitive then means that $\geq$ is a quasi-order on the set of all knowledge bases. We use A to denote the set of all knowledge bases and write a, b (possibly primed or with index) for its elements. With $\equiv$ we denote the equivalence relation induced by the quasi-order $\geq$, i.e., $a \equiv b$ iff $a \geq b$ and $b \geq a$. We write $[a]$ for the equivalence class of $a \in A$ and $[A]$ for the set of all these equivalence classes. The quasi-order $\geq$ on A induces a partial order on $[A]$, which we write (by a slight abuse of notation) again as $\geq$, i.e., we defined $[a] \geq [b]$ if $a \geq b$.

Optimal Repairs. In our definition of repairs, we require that all repairs are entailed by the original KB. From the order-theoretic point of view, this means that we consider the cone induced by the given KB. For $a \in A$, we define $\mathrm{Cone}(a) := \{b \in A \mid a \geq b\}$. Repairs for a given repair request α are required to be downward-closed subsets of $\mathrm{Cone}(a)$, i.e., the sets $\mathrm{Rep}(a,\alpha)$ must satisfy the following two properties:

1. $\mathrm{Rep}(a,\alpha) \subseteq \mathrm{Cone}(a)$, and
2. if $b \in \mathrm{Rep}(a,\alpha)$, then $b' \in \mathrm{Rep}(a,\alpha)$ for all b' with $b \geq b'$.

Optimal repairs are the maximal elements of $\mathrm{Rep}(a,\alpha)$.

Definition 2. *Let* $\geq$ *be a quasi-order on the set* A*, and* B *a downward-closed subset of* A*. The subset* O *of* B *is* complete *for* B *if it covers all elements of* B*, i.e., if for every* $b' \in B$ *there is* $b \in O$ *such that* $b \geq b'$*.*

We can now characterize the optimal repair property as follows (see [6] for the proof).

Theorem 1. *Let A be a set of KBs, $\geq$ the quasi-order on A corresponding to the entailment relation between KBs, and* Rep *a repair function that assigns to every tuple (a, α) consisting of an element $a \in A$ and a repair requests α a downward-closed subset* $\text{Rep}(a, \alpha)$ *of* $\text{Cone}(a)$*. Then the following are equivalent:*

1. Rep *satisfies the optimal repair property.*
2. *For every input tuple (a, α), the set* $\text{Rep}(a, \alpha)$ *contains a finite complete set.*
3. *For every input tuple (a, α), the set of all maximal elements of* $[\text{Rep}(a, \alpha)] := \{[b] \mid b \in \text{Rep}(a, \alpha)\}$ *is finite and complete for* $[\text{Rep}(a, \alpha)]$.

Note that there are two possible reasons that may be responsible for the third condition of this theorem to fail. On the one hand, the set of maximal elements of $[\text{Rep}(a, \alpha)]$ may be complete, but not finite. On the other hand, the set of maximal elements may not be complete. The repair set $\text{Rep}((1, 0), 0)$ in Example 2 provides us with an example for this second case.

If the repair sets are always finite up to equivalence, then the second condition of this theorem is always satisfied since we can take a set of representatives for $[\text{Rep}(a, \alpha)]$ as finite complete set.

Corollary 1. *If* $\text{Rep}(a, \alpha)$ *is finite up to equivalence for every input tuple (a, α), then* Rep *satisfies the optimal repair property. This is in particular the case if* $\text{Cone}(a)$ *is finite up to equivalence for every element a of A.*

Well-Quasi-Orders. Well-quasi-orders [27,34] can be used both to characterize the optimal repair property and finiteness of cones. We write $a \mid b$ if the elements a, b are incomparable w.r.t. $\geq$, i.e., if neither $a \geq b$ nor $b \geq a$ holds. An infinite sequence of elements $a_0, a_1, a_2, \ldots$ is an *infinite descending chain* if $a_i > a_{i+1}$ for all $i \geq 0$, and it is an *infinite anti-chain* if $a_i \mid a_j$ for all distinct $i, j \geq 0$.

Definition 3. *The quasi-order $\geq$ is a well-quasi-order (wqo) if there are neither infinite descending chains nor infinite anti-chains w.r.t. $\geq$.*

Obviously, any quasi-order on a finite set is a wqo. The following alternative characterizations of wqos is proved in [6].

Lemma 1. *Let $\geq$ be a quasi-order on A. Then the following are equivalent:*

1. *The quasi-order $\geq$ is a wqo.*
2. *For every subset $[B]$ of $[A]$, the set of its minimal elements is finite and* co-complete, *i.e., for every $[b'] \in [B]$ there is a minimal element $[b]$ of $[B]$ such that $[b'] \geq [b]$.*

Comparing the second condition in Lemma 1 with the third condition of Theorem 1, we note that the latter requires the set of maximal elements to be finite and complete, whereas the former requires the set of minimal elements to be finite and co-complete. If we turn around the order, then these two conditions coincide. Given a quasi-order $\geq$, we denote the corresponding inverse quasi-order by $\geq^-$, i.e., $a \geq^- b$ iff $b \geq a$. Theorem 1 together with Lemma 1 thus yields the following sufficient condition for the optimal repair property.

Theorem 2. *Let A be a set of KBs, $\geq$ the quasi-order on A corresponding to the entailment relation between KBs, and* Rep *a repair function that assigns to every tuple (a, α) consisting of an element $a \in A$ and a repair requests α a downward-closed subset* $\mathrm{Rep}(a, \alpha)$ *of* $\mathrm{Cone}(a)$*. If the inverse quasi-order $\geq^-$ is a wqo on* $\mathrm{Rep}(a, \alpha)$ *for every input tuple (a, α), then* Rep *satisfies the optimal repair property. The converse implication need not hold.*

Proof. The implication stated in this theorem is an immediate consequence of Theorem 1 and Lemma 1.

The repair problem considered in Example 3 below yields a counterexample to the converse implication. In fact, this repair problem satisfies the optimal repair property, but the concepts $C_0, C_1, C_2, \ldots$ satisfy $C_0 \sqsubset^{\mathcal{T}} C_1 \sqsubset^{\mathcal{T}} C_2 \sqsubset^{\mathcal{T}} \cdots$. Thus, these concepts constitute an infinite descending chain for the inverse of the subsumption quasi-order $\sqsubseteq^{\mathcal{T}}$. □

Since the restriction of a wqo to a subset of its domain is again a wqo, requiring that $\geq^-$ is a wqo on $\mathrm{Cone}(a)$ for every $a \in A$ is also a sufficient condition for the optimal repair property to be satisfied.

Requiring that $\geq$ itself is a wqo (on $\mathrm{Rep}(a, \alpha)$ or $\mathrm{Cone}(a)$) does not guarantee the optimal repair property, as demonstrated by Example 2. In fact, it is easy to see that the order $\geq^{lex}$ used there is a wqo since it is linear (and thus excluding anti-chains of size more than 1) and well-founded (and thus excluding infinite descending chains). Nevertheless, showing that $\geq$ is a wqo may be a useful step towards proving that $\mathrm{Cone}(a)$ is finite, which then yields the optimal repair property by Corollary 1. For this, we consider the one-step relation induced by $\geq$, as introduced in [15].

Definition 4. *The* one-step relation[1] *induced by the quasi-order $\geq$ is defined as*

$$>_1 := \{(a, b) \in > \mid \textit{ there is no } c \textit{ such that } a > c > b\}.$$

We say that $>_1$ generates *$\geq$ if its reflexive-transitive closure is again $\geq$. In this case we also say that $\geq$ is* one-step generated.

If $\geq$ is one-step generated, then every smaller element can be reached by a finite one-step sequence, i.e., if $a > b$, then there are finitely many elements $c_0, \ldots, c_n$ $(n \geq 1)$ such that $a = c_0 >_1 c_1 >_1 \ldots >_1 c_n = b$. This yields the following characterization of quasi-orders that are *not* one-step generated stated in [15].

Lemma 2 ([15]). *The quasi-order $\geq$ is* not *one-step generated iff there is a pair of strictly comparable elements $a > b$ such that every finite chain $a = c_0 > c_1 > \ldots > c_n = b$ can be* refined *in the sense that there is an $i, 0 \leq i < n$, and an element c such that $c_i > c > c_{i+1}$.*

[1] This is sometimes also called the transitive reduction of $\geq$ [1].

Note that satisfaction of this condition does not imply that there is an infinite descending sequence starting with a. It only implies that there are descending sequences of arbitrary length between a and b. For example, the partial order $\geq^{lex}$ of Example 2 satisfies this condition. In fact, $(1,0) >^{lex} (0,0)$ and any finite $>^{lex}$-sequence between these two tuples is of the form $(1,0) >^{lex} (0,k_1) >^{lex} \ldots (0,k_{n-1}) >^{lex} (0,0)$ with $k_1 > \ldots > k_{n-1} > 0$. Choosing $c := (0, k_1+1)$, we obtain $(1,0) >^{lex} c >^{lex} (0,k_1)$.

Following [15], we say that the one-step generated quasi-order $\geq$ is *finitely branching* if for every element a the cardinality of the set $\{b \mid a >_1 b\}$ is finite up to equivalence. We are now ready to characterize quasi-orders for which all cones are finite up to equivalence.

Proposition 1. *The quasi-order $\geq$ is one-step generated, finitely branching, and well-founded iff* Cone(a) *is finite up to equivalence for every element a.*

Proof. "$\Leftarrow$" First, assume that $\geq$ is not one-step generated. By Lemma 2, this implies that there are elements $a > b$ such that there are descending sequences $a = c_0 > c_1 > \ldots > c_n = b$ of arbitrary length between a and b. However, since all the elements of such a sequence belong to Cone(a), the maximal length of such a sequence is bounded by the cardinality of a set of representatives for the equivalence classes in Cone(a), which is finite. Thus, $\geq$ is one-step generated. For every element a, the set $\{b \mid a >_1 b\}$ is a subset of Cone(a), and thus finite up to equivalence, which shows that $\geq$ is finitely branching. Similarly, any descending chain issuing from a is contained in Cone(a), and thus cannot be infinite.

"$\Rightarrow$" If $\geq$ is one-step generated, then every element of Cone(a) can be reached by a finite $>_1$-sequence from a. Thus, Cone(a) can be seen as a tree with root a and edges corresponding to $>_1$-relationships, where we merge equivalent elements into a single node. By König's lemma, finitely branching and well-founded imply that this tree is finite. □

Obviously, if $\geq$ is a wqo, then it is also well-founded. In addition, since the representatives of the equivalence classes in the sets $\{b \mid a >_1 b\}$ are $>$-incomparable, these sets must be finite up to equivalence. Together with Corollary 1, the above proposition thus yields the following result.

Corollary 2. *Let A be a set of KBs, $\geq$ the quasi-order on A corresponding to the entailment relation between KBs, and* Rep *a repair function that assigns to every tuple (a, α) consisting of an element $a \in A$ and a repair requests α a downward-closed subset* Rep(a, α) *of* Cone(a)*. Then* Rep *satisfies the optimal repair property if $\geq$ is a one-step generated wqo.*

4 Instances Satisfying the Optimal Repair Property

As instances that satisfy the optimal repair property, we consider concepts of the DL $\mathcal{EL}$ as KBs and the subsumption relation (both without TBox and w.r.t. a cycle-restricted TBox) as entailment. In both cases, we will see that the optimal repair property holds since the cone of a given KB is finite up to equivalence. Since, for an $\mathcal{EL}$ concept C, its cone consist of the subsumers of C, we will denote it as Subs(C) (or $\text{Subs}^{\mathcal{T}}(C)$ in the presence of a TBox $\mathcal{T}$). In these two cases, it turns out that proving finiteness of these subsumer sets directly is easier than resorting to Proposition 1. We will also see that, for non-cycle-restricted TBoxes, the optimal repair property need not hold.

Concepts of the DL $\mathcal{EL}$. When using subsumption $\sqsubseteq^{\emptyset}$ between concepts of the description logic $\mathcal{EL}$ as entailment relation, then we must consider the order-theoretic properties of the sets Subs(C) for $\mathcal{EL}$ concepts C. As already mentioned, $C \sqsubseteq^{\emptyset} D$ implies $\text{Sig}(C) \supseteq \text{Sig}(D)$, and thus all elements of Subs(C) are built over a fixed finite signature. In addition, the role depth $\text{rd}(D)$ of the elements $D \in \text{Subs}(C)$ is bounded by the role depth of C, where the role depth $\text{rd}(C)$ of an $\mathcal{EL}$ concept C is the maximal nesting of existential restrictions in C. The following lemma, whose proof can be found in [6], states these results formally.

Lemma 3. *If C, D are $\mathcal{EL}$ concepts such that $C \sqsubseteq^{\emptyset} D$, then* $\text{Sig}(C) \supseteq \text{Sig}(D)$ *and* $\text{rd}(C) \geq \text{rd}(D)$.

It is well-known that, for a finite signature and variable set, there are up to equivalence only finitely many first-order formulas of a given fixed bound on the quantifier depth. In the context of DLs, this results was, e.g., formulated in [17] for the DL $\mathcal{ALE}$, which contains $\mathcal{EL}$: for given finite sets of concept and role names, there are up to equivalence only finitely many concepts for a given fixed upper-bound on the role depth of the concepts. Lemma 3 thus provides us with the following result.

Proposition 2. *If C is an $\mathcal{EL}$ concept, then* Subs(C) *is finite up to equivalence.*

By Corollary 1, this implies that the optimal repair property is satisfied both for Rep_{ent} and Rep_{for}. However, since these results are special cases of the results shown in the next subsection (see Corollaries 3 and 4, and note that the empty TBox is cycle-restricted), we do not formulate them as separate corollaries here.

Concepts of the DL $\mathcal{EL}$ w.r.t. a cycle-restricted TBox. Given an $\mathcal{EL}$ TBox $\mathcal{T}$, we define $\text{Subs}^{\mathcal{T}}(C) := \{D \mid C \sqsubseteq^{\mathcal{T}} D\}$, and extend the notion of entailment repairs to $\text{Rep}^{\mathcal{T}}_{\text{ent}}(C, D) := \{C' \mid C \sqsubseteq^{\mathcal{T}} C', C' \not\sqsubseteq^{\mathcal{T}} D\}$. For arbitrary TBoxes, finiteness up to equivalence of the set $\text{Subs}^{\mathcal{T}}(C)$ cannot be guaranteed.

Example 3. For the TBox $\mathcal{T} := \{A \sqsubseteq \exists r.A\}$, the concepts $C_n := \exists r. \cdots \exists r.\top$, which are nestings of $n \geq 0$ existential restrictions with the top concept $\top$ at the end, are infinitely many $\mathcal{EL}$ concepts in $\text{Subs}^{\mathcal{T}}(A)$ that are pairwise non-equivalent w.r.t. $\mathcal{T}$. In fact, we have $C_{n+1} \sqsubseteq^{\mathcal{T}} C_n$, but $C_n \not\sqsubseteq^{\mathcal{T}} C_{n+1}$.

If we consider the repair set $\text{Rep}^{\mathcal{T}}_{\text{ent}}(A, A)$, then we see that all the concepts C_n are contained in this set. Thus, we have a situation that is similar to the one encountered in Example 2. Nevertheless, the optimal repair property is still satisfied since the set of repairs also contains $D := \exists r.A$, which satisfies $D \sqsubseteq^{\mathcal{T}} C_n$ for all $n \geq 0$. In fact, $\{D\}$ is a set of repairs that covers all repairs. To show this, it is enough to prove that $D \sqsubseteq^{\mathcal{T}} E$ holds for every element E of $\mathrm{Rep}^{\mathcal{T}}_{\mathrm{ent}}(A, A)$. This proof can be found in [6].

This example shows that repair sets that contain infinite increasing[2] chains may nevertheless satisfy the optimal repair property. However, in general this property may be violated in the presence of general $\mathcal{EL}$ TBoxes, as illustrated by the following variant of Example 3, which is similar to the example used in the proof of Proposition 1 in [15].

Example 4. Let $\mathcal{T} := \{A \sqsubseteq \exists r.A, \exists r.A \sqsubseteq A\}$ and consider $\mathrm{Rep}^{\mathcal{T}}_{\mathrm{ent}}(A, A)$. We claim that this repair set is non-empty, but does not contain an optimal repair. Obviously, all the concepts C_n introduced in Example 3 belong to $\mathrm{Rep}^{\mathcal{T}}_{\mathrm{ent}}(A, A)$. In addition, it is easy to see that no concept in $\mathrm{Rep}^{\mathcal{T}}_{\mathrm{ent}}(A, A)$ can contain the concept name A. In fact, concepts subsuming A w.r.t. $\mathcal{T}$ must be built using only A, r, and $\top$, and if such a concept contains A then it is also subsumed by A w.r.t. $\mathcal{T}$. Thus, the concepts in $\mathrm{Rep}^{\mathcal{T}}_{\mathrm{ent}}(A, A)$ must be built using only $\top$ and r. For this reason, $\sqsubseteq^{\mathcal{T}}$ coincides with $\sqsubseteq^{\emptyset}$ on $\mathrm{Rep}^{\mathcal{T}}_{\mathrm{ent}}(A, A)$. Now assume that C is an optimal repair in $\mathrm{Rep}^{\mathcal{T}}_{\mathrm{ent}}(A, A)$, and let m be its role depth. It is easy to see that the concept $C \sqcap C_{m+1}$ satisfies $A \sqsubseteq^{\mathcal{T}} C \sqcap C_{m+1} \sqsubseteq^{\mathcal{T}} C$ and $C \sqcap C_{m+1} \not\sqsubseteq^{\mathcal{T}} A$. The latter non-subsumption follows from the fact that neither C nor C_{m+1} contains A. Consequently, $C \sqcap C_{m+1} \in \mathrm{Rep}^{\mathcal{T}}_{\mathrm{ent}}(A, A)$, and thus optimality of C yields $C \sqcap C_{m+1} \equiv^{\mathcal{T}} C$, which implies $C \sqsubseteq^{\mathcal{T}} C_{m+1}$ and thus $C \sqsubseteq^{\emptyset} C_{m+1}$. Lemma 3 shows that the latter subsumption is not possible since the role depth of C_{m+1} is larger than that of C. Thus, our assumption that $\mathrm{Rep}^{\mathcal{T}}_{\mathrm{ent}}(A, A)$ contains an optimal repair has been refuted.

Finiteness of $\mathrm{Subs}^{\mathcal{T}}(C)$ holds, however, if we restrict the attention to cycle-restricted TBoxes. The following lemma can easily be shown by adapting results for entailment between qABoxes from [12].

Lemma 4. *Let $\mathcal{T}$ be a cycle-restricted $\mathcal{EL}$ TBox and C an $\mathcal{EL}$ concept. Then one can compute in at most exponential time an $\mathcal{EL}$ concept $\mathrm{sat}^{\mathcal{T}}(C)$ such that $C \sqsubseteq^{\mathcal{T}} D$ iff $\mathrm{sat}^{\mathcal{T}}(C) \sqsubseteq^{\emptyset} D$ holds for all $\mathcal{EL}$ concepts D.*

This lemma implies that $\mathrm{Subs}^{\mathcal{T}}(C) = \mathrm{Subs}(\mathrm{sat}^{\mathcal{T}}(C))$. By Proposition 2, $\mathrm{Subs}(\mathrm{sat}^{\mathcal{T}}(C))$ is finite even up to equivalence w.r.t. the empty TBox, and thus all the more up to equivalence w.r.t. $\mathcal{T}$.

Proposition 3. *If $\mathcal{T}$ is a cycle-restricted $\mathcal{EL}$ TBox and C an $\mathcal{EL}$ concept, then $\mathrm{Subs}^{\mathcal{T}}(C)$ is finite up to equivalence.*

As an immediate consequence of Corollary 1 we thus obtain that $\mathrm{Rep}^{\mathcal{T}}_{\mathrm{ent}}$ has the optimal repair property.

[2] Recall that in this setting the quasi-order $\geq$ induced by the entailment relation corresponds to $\sqsubseteq^{\mathcal{T}}$, and thus a chain that is decreasing w.r.t. subsumption is increasing w.r.t. this quasi-order.

Corollary 3. *Let $\mathcal{T}$ be a cycle-restricted $\mathcal{EL}$ TBox and $\mathrm{Rep}^{\mathcal{T}}_{ent}$ the repair function that is defined as $\mathrm{Rep}^{\mathcal{T}}_{ent}(C,D) := \{C' \mid C \sqsubseteq^{\mathcal{T}} C', C' \not\sqsubseteq^{\mathcal{T}} D\}$. Then $\mathrm{Rep}^{\mathcal{T}}_{ent}$ satisfies the optimal repair property.*

When trying to extend the definition of $\mathrm{Rep}_{\mathrm{for}}$ to the setting with a TBox $\mathcal{T}$, one must be careful since, in contrast to the case of $\sqsubseteq^{\emptyset}$, subsumption w.r.t. $\mathcal{T}$ may not preserve the signature, i.e., the signature part of Lemma 3 does no hold if we replace $\sqsubseteq^{\emptyset}$ with $\sqsubseteq^{\mathcal{T}}$. Thus, the condition that repair sets must be closed under entailment would not be satisfied if we used a straightforward extension of $\mathrm{Rep}_{\mathrm{for}}$ to $\mathrm{Rep}^{\mathcal{T}}_{\mathrm{for}}$ in which $\sqsubseteq^{\mathcal{T}}$ replaces $\sqsubseteq^{\emptyset}$.

In [20], this problem is addressed by imposing a compatibility condition on the TBox and the signature used as repair request, which ensures that the signature part of Lemma 3 holds also w.r.t. $\sqsubseteq^{\mathcal{T}}$. Here, we restrict the entailment relation instead, i.e., we define $C \sqsubseteq^{\mathcal{T}}_{\supseteq} D$ if $C \sqsubseteq^{\mathcal{T}} D$ and $\mathrm{Sig}(C) \supseteq \mathrm{Sig}(D)$, set $\mathrm{Rep}^{\mathcal{T}}_{\mathrm{for}}(C,\alpha) := \{C' \mid C \sqsubseteq^{\mathcal{T}}_{\supseteq} C', \mathrm{Sig}(C') \cap \alpha = \emptyset\}$, and use $\sqsubseteq^{\mathcal{T}}_{\supseteq}$ rather than $\sqsubseteq^{\mathcal{T}}$ when comparing repairs in the definition of the optimal repair property. Since the set $\mathrm{Subs}^{\mathcal{T}}(C)_{\supseteq} := \{D \mid C \sqsubseteq^{\mathcal{T}}_{\supseteq} D\}$ is a subset of $\mathrm{Subs}^{\mathcal{T}}(C)$, it is clearly also finite up to equivalence.[3] Thus, Corollary 1 yields the following result.

Corollary 4. *Let $\mathcal{T}$ be a cycle-restricted $\mathcal{EL}$ TBox and $\mathrm{Rep}^{\mathcal{T}}_{for}$ the repair function that is defined as $\mathrm{Rep}^{\mathcal{T}}_{for}(C,\alpha) := \{C' \mid C \sqsubseteq^{\mathcal{T}}_{\supseteq} C', \mathrm{Sig}(C') \cap \alpha = \emptyset\}$. Then $\mathrm{Rep}^{\mathcal{T}}_{for}$ satisfies the optimal repair property.*

5 Beyond the Optimal Repair Property

Considering Item 3 of Theorem 1, we see that there are two possible reasons for the optimal repair property to fail: the set of all maximal elements of $[\mathrm{Rep}(a,\alpha)]$ may still be complete, but not finite, or this set may not even be complete. In case the optimal repair property holds, we can also distinguish two cases, depending on whether $[\mathrm{Rep}(a,\alpha)]$ has a unique greatest element or more than one maximal element.

Following the terminology employed in unification theory [19], we distinguish between the following types of repair problems.

Definition 5. *Let A be a set of KBs, $\geq$ the quasi-order on A corresponding to the entailment relation between KBs, and* Rep *a repair function that assigns to every repair problem (a,α) consisting of an element $a \in A$ and a repair requests α a downward-closed subset* $\mathrm{Rep}(a,\alpha)$ *of* $\mathrm{Cone}(a)$. *The repair problem (a,α) is*

- unitary *if $[\mathrm{Rep}(a,\alpha)]$ has a greatest element (i.e., the set of its maximal elements has cardinality 1), and this greatest element covers $[\mathrm{Rep}(a,\alpha)]$,*
- finitary *if the set of maximal elements of $[\mathrm{Rep}(a,\alpha)]$ is finite, but not a singleton set, and this set covers $[\mathrm{Rep}(a,\alpha)]$,*

[3] Note that, due to Corollary 3, equivalence w.r.t. the empty TBox is contained in the equivalence relation induced by $\sqsubseteq^{\mathcal{T}}_{\supseteq}$.

- infinitary *if the set of maximal elements of* $[\mathrm{Rep}(a,\alpha)]$ *is infinite, and this set covers* $[\mathrm{Rep}(a,\alpha)]$,
- of type zero *if the set of maximal elements of* $[\mathrm{Rep}(a,\alpha)]$ *does not cover* $[\mathrm{Rep}(a,\alpha)]$.

Unitary and finitary repair problems satisfy the optimal repair property, whereas infinitary and type zero repair problems do not.

We call a repair problem *solvable* if it has at least one repair, and *unsolvable* otherwise. Obviously, unsolvable repair problems satisfy the optimal repair property since the empty set of maximal repairs covers the empty set of repairs. However, such problems do not have any of the types introduced in the above definition. For solvable repair problems, it is easy to see that they must have exactly one of the four types introduced in Definition 5.

Using the distinction between unitary and finitary repair problems, we can now give a more fine-grained version of Corollary 3.

Proposition 4. *Let $\mathcal{T}$ be a cycle-restricted $\mathcal{EL}$ TBox and $\mathrm{Rep}^{\mathcal{T}}_{ent}$ the repair function that is defined as $\mathrm{Rep}^{\mathcal{T}}_{ent}(C,D) := \{C' \mid C \sqsubseteq^{\mathcal{T}} C', C' \not\sqsubseteq^{\mathcal{T}} D\}$. Then every solvable repair problem for $\mathrm{Rep}^{\mathcal{T}}_{ent}$ is either unitary or finitary, and both types can occur. The latter is already true for the empty TBox.*

Proof. The first part of the proposition is an immediate consequence of Corollary 3. To show the second part, we present both a unitary and a finitary repair problem for $\mathcal{T} = \emptyset$. First, consider $C = A \sqcap B = D$. It is easy to see that, up to equivalence, $\mathrm{Rep}^{\mathcal{T}}_{\mathrm{ent}}(C,D)$ consists of A, B, and $\top$, where A and B are maximal. Thus, this repair problem is finitary. Second, consider $C = A = D$. It is easy to see that, up to equivalence, $\mathrm{Rep}^{\mathcal{T}}_{\mathrm{ent}}(C,D)$ consists of $\top$, and thus this repair problem is unitary. □

For $\mathrm{Rep}^{\mathcal{T}}_{\mathrm{for}}$, we can strengthen Corollary 4 by showing that all solvable repair problems are unitary if $\mathcal{T}$ is cycle-restricted.

Proposition 5. *Let $\mathcal{T}$ be a cycle-restricted $\mathcal{EL}$ TBox and $\mathrm{Rep}^{\mathcal{T}}_{for}$ the repair function that is defined as $\mathrm{Rep}^{\mathcal{T}}_{for}(C,\alpha) := \{C' \mid C \sqsubseteq^{\mathcal{T}}_{\supseteq} C', \mathrm{Sig}(C') \cap \alpha = \emptyset\}$. Then every solvable repair problem for $\mathrm{Rep}^{\mathcal{T}}_{for}$ is unitary.*

Proof. Let (C,α) by a solvable repair problem for $\mathrm{Rep}^{\mathcal{T}}_{\mathrm{for}}$, i.e., $\mathrm{Rep}^{\mathcal{T}}_{\mathrm{for}}(C,\alpha) \neq \emptyset$. By Corollary 4, we know that this repair problem is unitary or finitary. Assume that it is finitary. Then there are two elements C_1, C_2 in $\mathrm{Rep}^{\mathcal{T}}_{\mathrm{for}}(C,\alpha)$ that are maximal w.r.t. $\sqsubseteq^{\mathcal{T}}_{\supseteq}$ and incomparable w.r.t. $\sqsubseteq^{\mathcal{T}}_{\supseteq}$. Since both C_1 and C_2 subsume C w.r.t. $\mathcal{T}$, we know that $C \sqsubseteq^{\mathcal{T}} C_1 \sqcap C_2$. In addition, $\mathrm{Sig}(C) \supseteq \mathrm{Sig}(C_i)$ for $i = 1,2$ yields $\mathrm{Sig}(C) \supseteq \mathrm{Sig}(C_1) \cup \mathrm{Sig}(C_2) = \mathrm{Sig}(C_1 \sqcap C_2)$. Thus, we have shown that $C \sqsubseteq^{\mathcal{T}}_{\supseteq} C_1 \sqcap C_2$. Finally, since neither C_1 nor C_2 contains an element of α, $C_1 \sqcap C_2$ also does not. This shows that $C_1 \sqcap C_2 \in \mathrm{Rep}^{\mathcal{T}}_{\mathrm{for}}(C,\alpha)$.

It is also easy to see that $C_1 \sqcap C_2 \sqsubseteq^{\mathcal{T}}_{\supseteq} C_i$ for $i = 1,2$. Maximality of C_1 and C_2 implies that these entailments cannot be strict. Thus, C_1, $C_1 \sqcap C_2$, and C_2

must be equivalent w.r.t. $\sqsubseteq_{\supseteq}^{\mathcal{T}}$, which contradicts our assumption that C_1 and C_2 are incomparable. Thus, two such incomparable maximal elements cannot exist in $\mathrm{Rep}_{\mathrm{for}}^{\mathcal{T}}(C, \alpha)$, which shows that the repair problem (C, α) is unitary. □

For a non-cycle-restricted TBox, repair problems may also be of type unitary or finitary. In fact, Example 3 provides us with a repair problem (A, A) for the non-cycle-restricted TBox $\mathcal{T} = \{A \sqsubseteq \exists r.A\}$ that is unitary, although $\mathrm{Rep}_{\mathrm{ent}}^{\mathcal{T}}(A, A)$ is not finite. However, we have shown in Example 4 that the same repair problem has type zero if one uses the non-cycle-restricted TBox $\{A \sqsubseteq \exists r.A, \exists r.A \sqsubseteq A\}$ instead. We can show that in this setting (i.e., $\mathcal{EL}$ concepts w.r.t. an arbitrary TBox and $\mathrm{Rep}_{\mathrm{ent}}$) type infinitary cannot occur.

Proposition 6. *Let $\mathcal{T}$ be a non-cycle-restricted $\mathcal{EL}$ TBox and $\mathrm{Rep}_{ent}^{\mathcal{T}}$ the repair function that is defined as $\mathrm{Rep}_{ent}^{\mathcal{T}}(C, D) := \{C' \mid C \sqsubseteq^{\mathcal{T}} C', C' \not\sqsubseteq^{\mathcal{T}} D\}$. Then every solvable repair problem for $\mathrm{Rep}_{ent}^{\mathcal{T}}$ is unitary, finitary, or of type zero, and all three types can occur.*

Proof. We have already seen in Example 3 and Example 4, respectively, that type unitary and type zero may occur for non-cycle-restricted TBoxes. It is easy to adapt the example of a finitary repair problem from the proof of Proposition 4 to work also w.r.t. a non-cycle-restricted TBox by replacing the empty TBox with $\mathcal{T} = \{A' \sqsubseteq \exists r.A'\}$, which does not influence the repair problem $\mathrm{Rep}_{\mathrm{ent}}^{\mathcal{T}}(A \sqcap B, A \sqcap B)$.

It remains to show that type infinitary cannot occur. Thus, assume to the contrary that $\mathcal{T}$ is a non-cycle-restricted $\mathcal{EL}$ TBox and (C, D) an infinitary repair problem for $\mathrm{Rep}_{\mathrm{ent}}^{\mathcal{T}}$. One can view this repair problem as a repair problem for quantified ABoxes (qABoxes) [12], where the input qABox is the qABox representation of the $\mathcal{EL}$ ABox $\{C(a)\}$ and the repair request is $D(a)$. If repairs are required to be finite qABoxes, then the optimal repair property need not be satisfied. However, if one allows for rational qABoxes (which is a restricted class of infinite qABoxes), then it is satisfied again [11]. Thus, there is a finite set of rational qABoxes $\{\exists X_1.\mathcal{A}_1, \ldots, \exists X_n.\mathcal{A}_n\}$ that are entailed by (the qABox representation of) $\{C(a)\}$, do not entail $D(a)$, and cover all repairs. Since the repair problem (C, D) is infinitary, there are two $\sqsubseteq^{\mathcal{T}}$-incomparable maximal elements C_1, C_2 of $\mathrm{Rep}_{\mathrm{ent}}^{\mathcal{T}}(C, D)$ such that $\{C_1(a)\}$ and $\{C_2(a)\}$ are entailed by the same rational qABox $\exists X_i.\mathcal{A}_i$. Consequently, $\exists X_i.\mathcal{A}_i$ also entails $\{(C_1 \sqcap C_2)(a)\}$. Since $\exists X_i.\mathcal{A}_i$ does not entail $D(a)$, neither can $\{(C_1 \sqcap C_2)(a)\}$, which shows that $C_1 \sqcap C_2 \in \mathrm{Rep}_{\mathrm{ent}}^{\mathcal{T}}(C, D)$. Maximality of C_1 and C_2 implies that C_1, $C_1 \sqcap C_2$, and C_2 must be equivalent w.r.t. $\sqsubseteq^{\mathcal{T}}$, which contradicts our assumption that C_1 and C_2 are incomparable. □

For $\mathrm{Rep}_{\mathrm{for}}^{\mathcal{T}}$, neither type finitary nor type infinitary is possible since these repair sets are always closed under conjunction.

Proposition 7. *Let $\mathcal{T}$ be a non-cycle-restricted $\mathcal{EL}$ TBox and $\mathrm{Rep}_{for}^{\mathcal{T}}$ the repair function that is defined as $\mathrm{Rep}_{for}^{\mathcal{T}}(C, \alpha) := \{C' \mid C \sqsubseteq_{\supseteq}^{\mathcal{T}} C', \mathrm{Sig}(C') \cap \alpha = \emptyset\}$. Then every solvable repair problem for $\mathrm{Rep}_{for}^{\mathcal{T}}$ is either unitary or of type zero, and both types can occur.*

Proof. To obtain an example of a unitary repair problem, one just takes one for the empty TBox, and adds a cyclic GCI that does not influence the repair problem. For type zero, one can re-use Example 4, but now employ $\alpha := \{A\}$ as repair request. The proof that neither type finitary nor type infinitary is possible is identical to the one of Proposition 5. □

6 Unification as an Instance

Given a *signature* Σ consisting of a finite set of function symbols (with associated arities) and a countably infinite set of *variables* V, the set $T(\Sigma, V)$ of *terms* over Σ with variables in V is defined in the usual way [19]. An equational theory E is given by a finite set of identities $s \approx t$ between terms, which are (implicitly) assumed to be universally quantified. Such a set of identities E induces the congruence relation $\approx_E$ on terms, which can either be defined syntactically through rewriting or semantically through first-order interpretations of Σ, with $\approx$ as identity relation [16].

A *substitution* σ is a mapping from V to $T(\Sigma, V)$ that has a finite *domain* $\mathrm{Dom}(\sigma) := \{x \in V \mid \sigma(x) \neq x\}$. It can be homomorphically extended to a mapping from $T(\Sigma, V)$ to $T(\Sigma, V)$ by defining $\sigma(f(t_1, \ldots, t_n)) := f(\sigma(t_1), \ldots, \sigma(t_n))$. The *variable range* $\mathrm{VRan}(\sigma)$ of σ consists of the set of variables occurring in the terms $\sigma(x)$ for $x \in \mathrm{Dom}(\sigma)$. Substitutions can be compared using the instantiation quasi-order: given an equational theory E, a finite set of variables $X \subseteq V$, and two substitutions σ, τ, we say that σ is *more general* than τ (or τ is an *instance* of σ) w.r.t. E and X (written $\sigma \geq_E^X \tau$)[4] if there is a substitution λ such that $\lambda(\sigma(x)) \approx_E \tau(x)$ holds for all $x \in X$.

We use substitutions as knowledge bases and the instantiation quasi-order as entailment. Repair requests are unification problems. Let E be an equational theory and $X \subseteq V$ a finite set of variables. A *unification problem* for E and X is a finite set of equations $\Gamma = \{s_1 \approx_E^? t_1, \ldots, s_n \approx_E^? t_n\}$ such that $s_1, t_1, \ldots, s_n, t_n$ are terms containing only variables from X. An *E-unifier* of Γ is a substitution θ that solves all the equations in Γ, i.e., satisfies $\theta(s_i) \approx_E \theta(t_i)$ for all $i, 1 \leq i \leq n$. The unification problem Γ is *solvable* if it has an E-unifier. Given a substitution σ with $\mathrm{Dom}(\sigma) \cup \mathrm{VRan}(\sigma) \subseteq X$ and a unification problem Γ for E and X, we define

$$\mathrm{Rep}_{\mathrm{uni}}^E(\sigma, \Gamma) := \{\theta \mid \sigma \geq_E^X \theta \text{ and } \theta \text{ is an } E\text{-unifier of } \Gamma\}.$$

In unification theory, one usually considers only a unification problem Γ (without an additional substitution σ), and looks for E-unifiers of Γ. This is the special case of the repair problem defined above where σ is the identity substitution σ_{id} with empty domain. The following lemma is an immediate consequence of the fact that every substitution is an instance of the identity substitution.

---

[4] In unification theory [19], the order is usually written the other way round, i.e., more general substitutions are the smaller ones, but here it is more convenient to consider instances to be the smaller substitutions since this is more in line with our representation of entailment as a quasi-order $\geq$ in Sect. 3.

Lemma 5. $\mathrm{Rep}^E_{uni}(\sigma_{id}, \Gamma) = \{\theta \mid \theta \textit{ is an } E\textit{-unifier of } \Gamma\}$.

In the case of a substitution σ with non-empty domain, we can find elements of $\mathrm{Rep}^E_{\mathrm{uni}}(\sigma, \Gamma)$ by considering the unification problem

$$\sigma(\Gamma) := \{\sigma(s_1) \approx^?_E \sigma(t_1), \ldots, \sigma(s_n) \approx^?_E \sigma(t_n)\}$$

and then use the E-unifiers of this problem to construct the instances of σ that are unifiers of Γ. Before we can make this idea more formal, we need to introduce some notation. Given two substitutions σ and λ, their *composition* $\lambda\sigma$ is the substitution obtained by first applying σ and then λ. We write $\sigma \approx^X_E \theta$ if $\sigma(x) \approx_E \theta(x)$ for all $x \in X$. The relation $\approx^X_E$ can be extended to sets of substitutions $\mathcal{S}_1$ and $\mathcal{S}_2$ by setting $\mathcal{S}_1 \approx^X_E \mathcal{S}_2$ if these sets yield the same $\approx^X_E$ equivalence classes, i.e., for every element of $\mathcal{S}_1$ there is an $\approx^X_E$-equivalent element in $\mathcal{S}_2$ and vice versa.

Lemma 6. $\mathrm{Rep}^E_{uni}(\sigma, \Gamma) \approx^X_E \{\lambda\sigma \mid \lambda \textit{ is an } E\textit{-unifier of } \sigma(\Gamma)\}$.

Proof. First, assume that θ is an element of $\mathrm{Rep}^E_{\mathrm{uni}}(\sigma, \Gamma)$. Then θ is an E-unifier of Γ and there exists a substitution λ such that $\theta(x) \approx_E \lambda(\sigma(x))$ holds for all $x \in X$. Note that this means that $\theta \approx^X_E \lambda\sigma$. Thus, to show that the right-hand side of the identity in the formulation of the lemma contains a substitution that is $\approx^X_E$-equivalent to θ, it is sufficient to prove that λ is an E-unifier of $\sigma(\Gamma)$. Assume that $\Gamma = \{s_1 \approx^?_E t_1, \ldots, s_n \approx^?_E t_n\}$. Since the terms in Γ contain only variables from X, we thus have $\lambda(\sigma(s_i)) \approx_E \theta(s_i) \approx_E \theta(t_i) \approx_E \lambda(\sigma(t_i))$ for all $i, 1 \leq i \leq n$, which shows that λ is an E-unifier of $\sigma(\Gamma)$.

Second, assume that λ is an E-unifier of $\sigma(\Gamma)$. Then $\lambda(\sigma(s_i)) \approx_E \lambda(\sigma(t_i))$ holds for all $i, 1 \leq i \leq n$, which shows that $\lambda\sigma$ is an E-unifier of Γ. Since $\sigma \geq^X_E \lambda\sigma$ obviously holds, we thus obtain that $\lambda\sigma$ is an element of $\mathrm{Rep}^E_{\mathrm{uni}}(\sigma, \Gamma)$. □

Unification types are defined analogously to repair types using $\geq^X_E$ as entailment relation (see the standard definition of the type of a unification problem in [18,19] and the order-theoretic characterization of unification types given in Sect. 3.3.1 of [19]).

Proposition 8. *Let Γ be a unification problem for the equational theory E and X a finite set of variables containing all the variables in Γ. Then the repair type of (σ_{id}, Γ) for Rep^E_{uni} coincides with the unification type of Γ if this unification problem is solvable. Otherwise, both the repair problem and the unification problem Γ are unsolvable.*

In the general case with arbitrary substitution σ, we must consider the unification type of $\sigma(\Gamma)$, but the correspondence need not be exact and does not hold for all types. We order unification types w.r.t. how "bad" they are (larger is worse) by setting type zero > infinitary > finitary > unitary.

Theorem 3. *Let σ be a substitution with* $\mathrm{Dom}(\sigma) \cup \mathrm{VRan}(\sigma) \subseteq X$ *and Γ a unification problem for the equational theory E and the finite set of variables X. Then the repair type of (σ, Γ) for Rep^E_{uni} is not worse than the unification type of $\sigma(\Gamma)$ if this unification problem is solvable and of type unitary or finitary. Unsolvability of the repair problem (σ, Γ) implies unsolvability of the unification problem $\sigma(\Gamma)$ and vice versa.*

Proof. The main observation on which this result is based is the following: if λ_1, λ_2 are substitutions such that $\lambda_1 \geq^X_E \lambda_2$, then $\lambda_1\sigma \geq^X_E \lambda_2\sigma$. To see this assume that $x \in X$ and that $\lambda_2 \approx^X_E \lambda\lambda_1$. Since $\mathrm{VRan}(\sigma) \subseteq X$, this implies $\lambda_2(\sigma(x)) \approx_E \lambda(\lambda_1(\sigma(x)))$, and since this holds for all $x \in X$, we obtain $\lambda_2\sigma \approx^X_E \lambda(\lambda_1\sigma)$ as required.

Now, assume that $\sigma(\Gamma)$ is solvable and unitary. Then there is a complete set $\{\theta\}$ of E-unifiers of $\sigma(\Gamma)$. We claim that $\theta\sigma$ is an optimal repair for $\mathrm{Rep}^E_{\mathrm{uni}}(\sigma, \Gamma)$ and it covers all repairs. It is sufficient to show the latter since optimality of $\theta\sigma$ is an immediate consequence of this. Thus, assume that $\tau \in \mathrm{Rep}^E_{\mathrm{uni}}(\sigma, \Gamma)$. Then there exists a substitution λ such that $\lambda\sigma \approx^X_E \tau$ and τ is an E-unifier of Γ. It is easy to see that this implies that λ is an E-unifier of $\sigma(\Gamma)$ (see the proof of Lemma 6), and thus $\theta \geq^X_E \lambda$. By the observation made above, this yields $\theta\sigma \geq^X_E \lambda\sigma \approx^X_E \tau$, and thus τ is an instance of $\theta\sigma$. This shows that the repair type of (σ, Γ) is unitary, and thus not worse than the unification type of $\sigma(\Gamma)$.

If $\sigma(\Gamma)$ is solvable and finitary, then there is a finite complete set $\{\theta_1, \ldots, \theta_n\}$ of E-unifiers of $\sigma(\Gamma)$. As in the unitary case, we can show that $\{\theta_1\sigma, \ldots, \theta_n\sigma\}$ is a set of repairs of $\mathrm{Rep}^E_{\mathrm{uni}}(\sigma, \Gamma)$ that covers all repairs. By removing repairs that are not optimal from this set, we obtain a finite set of optimal repairs that covers all repairs, and thus the repair type of (σ, Γ) is unitary or finitary.

Finally, we have observed above that an element τ of $\mathrm{Rep}^E_{\mathrm{uni}}(\sigma, \Gamma)$ yields an E-unifier λ of $\sigma(\Gamma)$. Consequently, if $\sigma(\Gamma)$ is not solvable, then there cannot be a solution of the repair problem, i.e., $\mathrm{Rep}^E_{\mathrm{uni}}(\sigma, \Gamma)$ must be empty. Conversely, any solution λ of $\sigma(\Gamma)$ clearly yields a repair $\lambda\sigma$ in $\mathrm{Rep}^E_{\mathrm{uni}}(\sigma, \Gamma)$. Thus, if $\mathrm{Rep}^E_{\mathrm{uni}}(\sigma, \Gamma) = \emptyset$, then $\sigma(\Gamma)$ cannot be solvable. □

Research in unification theory has produced many results on the unification types of specific equational theories, where the *unification type of an equational theory* is the worst type of a unification problem for this theory (see [19] for an overview). For example, the empty theory is unitary [33], commutativity of a binary function symbol is finitary [38], associativity of a binary function symbol is infinitary [30], and associativity and idempotency of a binary function symbol is of type zero [3, 37]. In particular, associativity yields an example of a repair problem whose type is infinitary.

Example 5. Let f be a binary function symbol and a a constant symbol, define $A := \{f(x, f(y, z)) \approx f(f(x, y), z)\}$, and consider the unification problem $\Gamma := \{f(x, a) \approx^?_A f(a, x)\}$ for A and $X := \{x\}$. Then all unifiers of Γ map x to a term built from f and a only. Let θ_n be the unifier with domain $\{x\}$ that maps x to the term $f(a, f(a, \ldots, f(a, a)\ldots))$ with n occurrences of a. Then it is easy to see that the set $\{\theta_1, \theta_2, \theta_3, \ldots\}$ is an infinite minimal complete set of A-unifiers of Γ.

Consequently, by Proposition 8, the repair problem (σ_{id}, Γ) is infinitary, which is a repair type that we did not encounter in the context of $\mathcal{EL}$ concepts.

The results on the unification type of equational theories in the literature are shown under the assumption that the instantiation quasi-order on substitutions is defined w.r.t. the finite set of variables occurring in the unification problem (restricted instantiation quasi-order). If one were to compare unifiers w.r.t. the set V of all variables (unrestricted instantiation quasi-order), then a different unification type would be obtained in some cases. In fact, in [9] it is shown that the unification type for the equational theories ACUI, ACU, and AC switches from respectively unitary, unitary, and finitary for the restricted instantiation quasi-order to infinitary in all three cases for the unrestricted instantiation quasi-order. For the equational theory axiomatizing equivalence of $\mathcal{EL}$ concepts, the unification type improves from type zero to infinitary when replacing the restricted instantiation quasi-order with the unrestricted one [9].

In the present paper, we use comparison w.r.t. a finite set of variables X that contains the set of variables occurring in the unification problem, but may be larger than this set. However, as shown in Lemma 4 of [9], this difference does not impact the unification type. Consequently, the unification types shown in unification theory for the setting where unifiers are compared w.r.t. the variable occurring in the unification problem also apply to the setting introduced in this paper, where unifiers are compared w.r.t. a finite set of variables X that contains all the variables occurring in the unification problem. The following is now an immediate consequence of Theorem 3.

Corollary 5. *Let E be an equational theory whose unification type is unitary or finitary. Then every repair problem (σ, Γ) for Rep^E_{uni} satisfies the optimal repair property.*

7 Conclusion

We have used the order-theoretic view on optimal repairs to find sufficient criteria for the optimal repair property to hold. When considering the instantiation quasi-order between substitutions rather than a reflexive and transitive entailment relation, these results can also be used to show that a unification problem or equational theory has unification type unary or finitary. In practice, one then still needs to develop appropriate algorithms for computing optimal repairs or complete sets of unifiers. In fact, the optimal repair property and unification types unitary/finitary were until now often shown by exhibiting algorithm for computing the appropriate finite sets of repairs or unifiers. On the repair side, this was, e.g., done in [11–14,26] (for equational unification, see [19] for references to algorithms computing minimal complete sets of unifiers). Also note that, in [20], we have shown the optimal repair property for $\mathrm{Rep}_{\mathrm{ent}}$ and $\mathrm{Rep}_{\mathrm{for}}$ by describing algorithms for computing sets of optimal repairs, and then showing that these sets cover all repairs. Nevertheless, we believe that applying such abstract criteria may turn out to be useful as a first step when investigating a new kind of repair or unification problem. The characterizations and necessary/sufficient conditions for unification type zero presented in [4] were recently employed in [9,21] to prove unification type zero for equational theories induced by certain modal and description logics. They may also turn out to be useful for showing that a given repair problem has type zero.

The fact that unification problems can be seen as repair problems in the repair framework of [20] shows how general this framework is. It also provides us with examples of repair problems that have type infinitary. It is currently unclear whether this type can also occur in the more traditional repair setting where entailment is the entailment relation of some logic and the repair goal is non-entailment of an unwanted consequence.

Acknowledgements. Partially supported by DFG, Grant 389792660, within TRR 248 "Center for Perspicuous Computing", and by the German Federal Ministry of Education and Research (BMBF, SCADS22B) and the Saxon State Ministry for Science, Culture and Tourism (SMWK) by funding the competence center for Big Data and AI "ScaDS.AI Dresden/Leipzig".

References

1. Aho, A.V., Garey, M.R., Ullman, J.D.: The transitive reduction of a directed graph. SIAM J. Comput. **1**(2), 131–137 (1972). https://doi.org/10.1137/0201008
2. Alchourrón, C.E., Gärdenfors, P., Makinson, D.: On the logic of theory change: partial meet contraction and revision functions. J. Symb. Log. **50**(2), 510–530 (1985). https://doi.org/10.2307/2274239
3. Baader, F.: The theory of idempotent semigroups is of unification type zero. J. Autom. Reason. **2**(3), 283–286 (1986). https://doi.org/10.1007/BF02328451
4. Baader, F.: Characterizations of unification type zero. In: Dershowitz, N. (ed.) RTA 1989. LNCS, vol. 355, pp. 2–14. Springer, Heidelberg (1989). https://doi.org/10.1007/3-540-51081-8_96
5. Baader, F.: Relating optimal repairs in ontology engineering with contraction operations in belief change. ACM SIGAPP Appl. Comput. Rev. **23**(3), 5–18 (2023). https://doi.org/10.1145/3626307.3626308
6. Baader, F.: An order-theoretic view on optimal repairs and complete sets of unifiers. LTCS-Report 25-02, Chair of Automata Theory, Institute of Theoretical Computer Science, Technische Universität Dresden, Dresden, Germany (2025). https://lat.inf.tu-dresden.de/research/reports.html
7. Baader, F., Borgwardt, S., Morawska, B.: Extending unification in $\mathcal{EL}$ towards general TBoxes. In: Brewka, G., Eiter, T., McIlraith, S.A. (eds.) Proceedings of the Thirteenth International Conference on Principles of Knowledge Representation and Reasoning, KR 2012. AAAI Press (2012). http://www.aaai.org/ocs/index.php/KR/KR12/paper/view/4491
8. Baader, F., Brandt, S., Lutz, C.: Pushing the $\mathcal{EL}$ envelope. In: Kaelbling, L.P., Saffiotti, A. (eds.) Proceedings of the Nineteenth International Joint Conference on Artificial Intelligence, IJCAI-05, pp. 364–369. Professional Book Center (2005). http://ijcai.org/Proceedings/05/Papers/0372.pdf

9. Baader, F., Fernández Gil, O.: The unification type of an equational theory may depend on the instantiation preorder. In: Fernandez, M. (ed.) Proceedings of the 9th International Conference on Formal Structures for Computation and Deduction, FSCD 2024. Leibniz International Proceedings in Informatics (LIPIcs), vol. 337, pp. 8:1–8:24 (2025). https://doi.org/10.4230/LIPICS.FSCD.2025.8
10. Baader, F., Horrocks, I., Lutz, C., Sattler, U.: An Introduction to Description Logic. Cambridge University Press (2017)
11. Baader, F., Koopmann, P., Kriegel, F.: Optimal repairs in the description logic $\mathcal{EL}$ revisited. In: Gaggl, S.A., Martinez, M.V., Ortiz, M. (eds.) Proceedings of the 18th European Conference on Logics in Artificial Intelligence, JELIA 2023. LNCS, vol. 14281, pp. 11–34. Springer, Heidelberg (2023). https://doi.org/10.1007/978-3-031-43619-2_2
12. Baader, F., Koopmann, P., Kriegel, F., Nuradiansyah, A.: Computing optimal repairs of quantified ABoxes w.r.t. static $\mathcal{EL}$ TBoxes. In: Platzer, A., Sutcliffe, G. (eds.) 28th International Conference on Automated Deduction, Proceedings, Automated Deduction - CADE 28. LNCS, vol. 12699. Springer, Heidelberg (2021). https://doi.org/10.1007/978-3-030-79876-5_18
13. Baader, F., Koopmann, P., Kriegel, F., Nuradiansyah, A.: Optimal ABox repair w.r.t. static $\mathcal{EL}$ TBoxes: from quantified ABoxes back to ABoxes. In: The Semantic Web - 19th International Conference, ESWC 2022, Proceedings. LNCS, vol. 13261, pp. 130–146. Springer, Heidelberg (2022). https://doi.org/10.1007/978-3-031-06981-9_8
14. Baader, F., Kriegel, F.: Pushing optimal ABox repair from $\mathcal{EL}$ towards more expressive Horn-DLs. In: Kern-Isberner, G., Lakemeyer, G., Meyer, T. (eds.) Proceedings of the 19th International Conference on Principles of Knowledge Representation and Reasoning, KR 2022 (2022). https://proceedings.kr.org/2022/3/
15. Baader, F., Kriegel, F., Nuradiansyah, A., Peñaloza, R.: Making repairs in description logics more gentle. In: Thielscher, M., Toni, F., Wolter, F. (eds.) Proceedings of the Sixteenth International Conference on Principles of Knowledge Representation and Reasoning, KR 2018, pp. 319–328. AAAI Press (2018). https://aaai.org/ocs/index.php/KR/KR18/paper/view/18056
16. Baader, F., Nipkow, T.: Term Rewriting and All That. Cambridge University Press (1998)
17. Baader, F., Sertkaya, B., Turhan, A.: Computing the least common subsumer w.r.t. a background terminology. J. Appl. Log. **5**(3), 392–420 (2007). https://doi.org/10.1016/J.JAL.2006.03.002
18. Baader, F., Siekmann, J.H.: Unification theory. In: Gabbay, D.M., Hogger, C.J., Robinson, J.A., Siekmann, J.H. (eds.) Handbook of Logic in Artificial Intelligence and Logic Programming, volume 2, Deduction Methodologies, pp. 41–126. Oxford University Press (1994)
19. Baader, F., Snyder, W.: Unification theory. In: Robinson, J.A., Voronkov, A. (eds.) Handbook of Automated Reasoning, vol. 1, pp. 445–532. Elsevier and MIT Press (2001). https://doi.org/10.1016/B978-044450813-3/50010-2
20. Baader, F., Wassermann, R.: Contractions based on optimal repairs. In: Marquis, P., Ortiz, M., Pagnucco, M. (eds.) Proceedings of the 21st International Conference on Principles of Knowledge Representation and Reasoning, KR 2024 (2024). https://doi.org/10.24963/KR.2024/9
21. Cabrer, L.: Unification on subvarieties of pseudocomplemented distributive lattices. Notre Dame J. Formal Logic **57**(4), 477–502 (2016). https://doi.org/10.1215/00294527-3659307

22. Hansson, S.O.: A dyadic representation of belief. In: Gärdenfors, P. (ed.) Belief Revision, Cambridge Tracts in Theoretical Computer Science, vol. 29, pp. 89–121. Cambridge University Press (1992)
23. Hansson, S.O.: Changes of disjunctively closed bases. J. Logic Lang. Inf. **2**(4), 255–284 (1993). http://www.jstor.org/stable/40180034
24. Hansson, S.O.: A Textbook of Belief Dynamics - Theory Change and Database Updating. Applied Logic Series, vol. 11. Kluwer (1999)
25. Kalyanpur, A., Parsia, B., Sirin, E., Cuenca-Grau, B.: Repairing unsatisfiable concepts in OWL ontologies. In: Sure, Y., Domingue, J. (eds.) ESWC 2006. LNCS, vol. 4011, pp. 170–184. Springer, Heidelberg (2006). https://doi.org/10.1007/11762256_15
26. Kriegel, F.: Optimal fixed-premise repairs of $\mathcal{EL}$ TBoxes. In: Bergmann, R., Malburg, L., Rodermund, S.C., Timm, I.J. (eds.) Advances in Artificial Intelligence – 45th German Conference on AI, Proceedings. LNCS, KI 2022, vol. 13404, pp. 115–130. Springer, Heidelberg (2022). https://doi.org/10.1007/978-3-031-15791-2_11
27. Kruskal, J.B.: The theory of well-quasi-ordering: a frequently discovered concept. J. Comb. Theor. A **13**(3), 297–305 (1972). https://doi.org/10.1016/0097-3165(72)90063-5
28. Matos, V.B., Guimarães, R., Santos, Y.D., Wassermann, R.: Pseudo-contractions as gentle repairs. In: Lutz, C., Sattler, U., Tinelli, C., Turhan, A.-Y., Wolter, F. (eds.) Description Logic, Theory Combination, and All That. LNCS, vol. 11560, pp. 385–403. Springer, Cham (2019). https://doi.org/10.1007/978-3-030-22102-7_18
29. Nebel, B.: A knowledge level analysis of belief revision. In: Brachman, R., Levesque, H., Reiter, R. (eds.) First International Conference on Principles of Knowledge Representation and Reasoning, KR'89, pp. 301–311. Morgan Kaufmann (1989)
30. Plotkin, G.: Building in equational theories. Mach. Intell. **7**, 73–90 (1972)
31. Raulefs, P., Siekmann, J.H., Szabó, P., Unvericht, E.: A short survey on the state of the art in matching and unification problems. SIGSAM Bull. **13**(2), 14–20 (1979). https://doi.org/10.1145/1089208.1089210
32. Rienstra, T., Schon, C., Staab, S.: Concept contraction in the description logic $\mathcal{EL}$. In: Calvanese, D., Erdem, E., Thielscher, M. (eds.) Proceedings of the 17th International Conference on Principles of Knowledge Representation and Reasoning, KR 2020, pp. 723–732 (2020).https://doi.org/10.24963/kr.2020/74
33. Robinson, J.A.: A machine oriented logic based on the resolution principle. J. ACM **12**(1), 23–41 (1965). https://doi.org/10.1145/321250.321253
34. Rosenstein, J.G.: Linear Orderings. Academic Press (1982)
35. Santos, Y.D., Matos, V.B., Ribeiro, M.M., Wassermann, R.: Partial meet pseudo-contractions. Int. J. Approx. Reason. **103**, 11–27 (2018). https://doi.org/10.1016/j.ijar.2018.08.006
36. Schlobach, S., Huang, Z., Cornet, R., Harmelen, F.: Debugging incoherent terminologies. J. Autom. Reason. **39**(3), 317–349 (2007). https://doi.org/10.1007/s10817-007-9076-z
37. Schmidt-Schauß, M.: Unification under associativity and idempotence is of type nullary. J. Autom. Reason. **2**(3), 277–281 (1986). https://doi.org/10.1007/BF02328450

38. Siekmann, J.: Unification of commutative terms. In: Ng, E.W. (ed.) Symbolic and Algebraic Computation. LNCS, vol. 72, pp. 22–22. Springer, Heidelberg (1979). https://doi.org/10.1007/3-540-09519-5_53
39. Troquard, N., Confalonieri, R., Galliani, P., Peñaloza, R., Porello, D., Kutz, O.: Repairing ontologies via axiom weakening. In: McIlraith, S.A., Weinberger, K.Q. (eds.) Proceedings of the Thirty-Second AAAI Conference on Artificial Intelligence, (AAAI-18), pp. 1981–1988. AAAI Press (2018). https://www.aaai.org/ocs/index.php/AAAI/AAAI18/paper/view/17189

Short and Simple Explanations for Datalog Derivations

Jelle Hellings(✉) and Yuchen You

McMaster University, 1280 Main Street W., Hamilton, ON L8S 4L7, Canada
{jhellings,youy10}@mcmaster.ca

Abstract. Simple and short query explanations that detail how a query result is obtained from an input dataset are a powerful way to gain insight into the results of queries. Unfortunately, simple and short explanations for recursive queries are non-trivial: query results of recursive queries typically have a huge set of equally-valid explanations. Toward providing simple and short query explanations, we believe that there is a strong need for an improved understanding of *explanations* of recursive queries.

In this paper, we present such a framework by studying explanations of facts derived using Datalog derivation rules. To enable *simple* explanations, we present a standard tree-based formal representation of explanations and we formalize four *conceptually distinct* types of simple explanations based on their tree structure. Next, we show how to *effectively compute* two types of simple explanations, which opens the door for practical algorithms to explain Datalog query results. Finally, we prove that computing the other two types of simple explanations involves solving NP-complete decision problems and, hence, is inherently hard.

Keywords: Datalog · Query Explanation · Evaluation Algorithm

1 Introduction

Understanding why a given tuple is in the output of a simple join-select-project query (e.g., elementary SQL queries) is typically straightforward: one can easily trace the tuples in the output to corresponding tuples in the input tables. Unfortunately, this simplicity disappears quickly when trying to explain the results of more complex queries.

As an important example of complex queries, we can consider queries whose definition and evaluation involves *recursion*. Such recursive queries are central in relational and graph querying and have applications in data integration, automated reasoning, AI, computational linguistics, information retrieval, logic programming, and descriptive logic [2,3,5,10,12,16,18,23,24,29]. Due to the presence of recursion in queries, individual values in the output of recursive query results can have a *large* or even *unbounded* number of valid distinct explanations [7,24]. Hence, understanding or explaining query results of recursive queries remains a challenge.

A.-Y. Turhan and J. Virtema (Eds.): FoIKS 2026, LNCS 16475, pp. 304–323, 2026.
https://doi.org/10.1007/978-3-032-21540-6_18

In this paper, we make the next step toward formal *explanations* of recursive queries by studying the explanation of queries expressed in Datalog [1,20], a powerful logic-based recursive query formalism for relational and graph data. One can *explain* a derived Datalog fact via the individual derivation steps used to derive the fact. Typically, these derivation steps can be represented via a tree-based format. To obtain such *tree-based explanations*, one can use variants of standard Datalog evaluation algorithms that keep track of the derivation steps made during evaluation. The explanations obtained in this way are not guaranteed to be easy to understand, however. Hence, for *practical* explanations, we need a way to find *short and simple* explanations.

We note that obtaining explanation is closely related to the general question of *why*-provenance for Datalog [6–8,15,17,30], the main difference being that *why*-provenance focuses on explaining from which parts of the underlying data a fact can be derived, this *without providing an explicit explanation* of the derivation steps that can derive the fact.

Toward *short and simple* Datalog explanations, we formalize simple explanations and study the complexity of computing these explanations. In specific:

1. First, in Sect. 3, we show how we will use *derivation trees* as the formal tree-based representation of Datalog derivations (and, hence, explanations).
2. Second, in Sect. 4, we formalize four complexity metrics based on the *structure* of these derivation trees: base fact complexity, derivation complexity, unique derivation complexity, and derivation depth complexity.
3. Third, in Theorem 1, we prove that these four types of complexity metrics are distinct: an explanation that minimizes one of these metrics does not necessarily minimize the other three. Hence, this gives rise to four distinct types of *simple* explanations
4. Then, in Sect. 5, we show that simple explanations based on *derivation complexity* and *derivation depth complexity* can be practically computed by annotating standard Datalog evaluation algorithms. This opens the door for practical derivation engines to integrate explanations in their evaluation algorithms.
5. Next, in Sect. 6, we show that simple explanations based on *base fact complexity* and *unique derivation complexity* cannot be practically computed under the common assumption that $\mathsf{P} \neq \mathsf{NP}$: the *data complexity* of the decision problem determining whether a simple explanation exists under these complexity measures is NP-complete.
6. Finally, in Sect. 7, we discuss the practicality of simple explanations.

Furthermore, in Sect. 2, we introduce the notation and terminology used in this paper; in Sect. 8, we discuss the related work; and in Sect. 9 we conclude on our findings.

2 Preliminaries

We assume a universe of constants $\mathbb{U}$. In this paper, we study Datalog programs [1,20] with recursion, with inequalities, but without negation.

Definition 1. *A Datalog program is a pair $\langle B, D\rangle$ in which B is a set of Datalog rules defining* base facts *and D is a set of Datalog rules defining* derived facts. *An n-ary Datalog rule in B (a base rule) is of the form "head $\leftarrow \bullet$" in which the* head *is of the form $R(\mathcal{U})$ with R the name of the rule and $\mathcal{U}$ a list of n constants. An n-ary Datalog rule in D (a derivation rule) is of the form "head $\leftarrow$ body" in which*

1. *the* head *is of the form $R(\mathcal{V})$ with R the name of the rule and $\mathcal{V}$ a list of n free variables of the rule; and*
2. *the* body *consists of a non-empty conjunction of terms of the form $S(\mathcal{W})$, with S the name of an m-ary Datalog rule and $\mathcal{W}$ a list of m variables, or of the form $V \neq W$ with V, W variables.*

The arity *of a rule with a head of the form $R(\mathcal{V})$, with $\mathcal{V}$ a list of n free variables, is $|\mathcal{V}| = n$. We require that the body of a derivation rule $R(\mathcal{V})$ must use all variables in $\mathcal{V}$.*

To simplify presentation, we assume that all Datalog rules in a program $\langle B, D\rangle$ for a given rule name R have the same arity and are of the same type (either all rules are base rules or all rules are derivation rules).

Example 1. Consider the graph of Fig. 1, *left.* This graph represents the following base facts:

$$\begin{aligned} &\mathsf{ParentOf}(\texttt{Alicia}, \texttt{Dafni}) \leftarrow \bullet, && \mathsf{ParentOf}(\texttt{Alicia}, \texttt{Ivan}) \leftarrow \bullet,\\ &\mathsf{ParentOf}(\texttt{Bo}, \texttt{Eva}) \leftarrow \bullet, && \mathsf{ParentOf}(\texttt{Celeste}, \texttt{Dafni}) \leftarrow \bullet,\\ &\mathsf{ParentOf}(\texttt{Dafni}, \texttt{Eva}) \leftarrow \bullet, && \mathsf{ParentOf}(\texttt{Gale}, \texttt{Frieda}) \leftarrow \bullet,\\ &\mathsf{ParentOf}(\texttt{Eva}, \texttt{Harry}) \leftarrow \bullet; && \\ &\mathsf{FriendOf}(\texttt{Celeste}, \texttt{Gale}) \leftarrow \bullet, && \mathsf{FriendOf}(\texttt{Gale}, \texttt{Celeste}) \leftarrow \bullet,\\ &\mathsf{FriendOf}(\texttt{Frieda}, \texttt{Eva}) \leftarrow \bullet, && \mathsf{FriendOf}(\texttt{Eva}, \texttt{Frieda}) \leftarrow \bullet. \end{aligned}$$

This dataset conveys many additional relationships between people that can be derived using derivation rules. Consider the 2-ary derivation rules

$$\begin{aligned} \mathsf{GrandparentOf}(v, w) &\leftarrow \mathsf{ParentOf}(v, u) \land \mathsf{ParentOf}(u, w);\\ \mathsf{SiblingOf}(v, w) &\leftarrow \mathsf{ParentOf}(u, v) \land \mathsf{ParentOf}(u, w) \land v \neq w. \end{aligned}$$

On the above dataset, these Datalog rules evaluate to the derived facts in Fig. 1, *right.* Datalog rules can utilize recursion to derive even more complex relationships. For example,

$$\begin{aligned} \mathsf{AncestorOf}(v, w) &\leftarrow \mathsf{ParentOf}(v, w);\\ \mathsf{AncestorOf}(v, w) &\leftarrow \mathsf{ParentOf}(v, u) \land \mathsf{AncestorOf}(u, w). \end{aligned}$$

On the above dataset, this Datalog rule evaluates to the derived facts that include all ParentOf pairs, all GrandparentOf pairs, and the pairs $(\texttt{Alicia}, \texttt{Harry})$ and $(\texttt{Celeste}, \texttt{Harry})$.

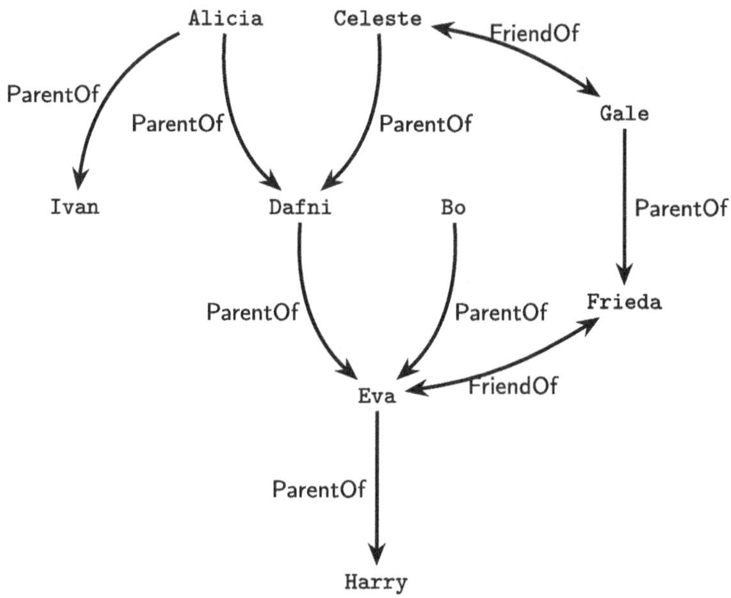

GrandparentOf	
Alicia	Eva
Celeste	Eva
Dafni	Harry
Bo	Harry

SiblingOf	
Dafni	Ivan
Ivan	Dafni

Fig. 1. A simple social network illustrating the relationships between people.

There are often many ways to derive the same facts. For example, the above AncestorOf rules derive the same relationship between people as the following alternative rules:

$$\mathsf{AltAncestorOf}(v, w) \leftarrow \mathsf{ParentOf}(v, w);$$
$$\mathsf{AltAncestorOf}(v, w) \leftarrow \mathsf{AltAncestorOf}(v, u) \wedge \mathsf{AltAncestorOf}(u, w).$$

The semantics for the above Datalog rules are self-explanatory. Next, we formalize the proof-theoretic semantics for Datalog programs that we use in this paper [1,20].

Definition 2. *Let R be the name of an n-ary rule in Datalog program $\langle B, D\rangle$. The tuple $(c_1, \dots, c_n)$ is in the evaluation of R if either*

1. *R is the name of a base rule and the rule "$R(c_1, \dots, c_n) \leftarrow \bullet$" $\in B$ exists; or*
2. *R is the name of a derivation rule, the rule*

$$\text{“}R(v_1, \dots, v_n) \leftarrow S_1(w_{1,1}, \dots, w_{1,m_1}) \wedge \dots \wedge S_j(w_{j,1}, \dots, w_{j,m_j})\text{”} \in D$$

exists, and a variable assignment $\mu : \{w_{1,1}, \dots, w_{j,m_j}\} \to \mathbb{U}$ exists such that $\mu(v_1) = c_1, \dots, \mu(v_n) = c_n$ and, for all $i, 1 \le i \le j$, the tuple $(\mu(w_{i,1}), \dots, \mu(w_{i,m_i}))$ is in the evaluation of rule S_i.

Example 2. Consider the example Datalog rules of Example 1 as visualized in Fig. 1. The tuple (`Celeste`, `Harry`) is in the evaluation of rule AncestorOf because

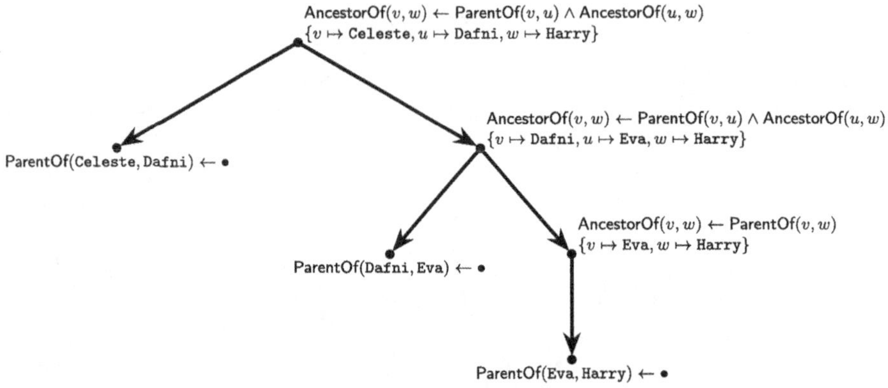

Fig. 2. The derivation tree of the fact AncestorOf(Celeste, Harry).

1. The tuples (Celeste, Dafni), (Dafni, Eva), and (Eva, Harry) are in the evaluation of ParentOf because the base rules ParentOf(Celeste, Dafni) $\leftarrow \bullet$, ParentOf(Dafni, Eva) $\leftarrow \bullet$, and ParentOf(Eva, Harry) $\leftarrow \bullet$ exist.
2. The tuple (Eva, Harry) is in the evaluation of AncestorOf because the derivation rule AncestorOf$(v, w) \leftarrow$ ParentOf(v, w) and variable assignment $\{v \mapsto \texttt{Eva}, w \mapsto \texttt{Harry}\}$ exists such that (Eva, Harry) is in the evaluation of ParentOf.
3. The tuple (Dafni, Harry) is in the evaluation of AncestorOf because the derivation rule AncestorOf$(v, w) \leftarrow$ ParentOf$(v, u) \wedge$ AncestorOf(u, w) and variable assignment $\{v \mapsto \texttt{Dafni}, u \mapsto \texttt{Eva}, w \mapsto \texttt{Harry}\}$ exists such that (Dafni, Eva) is in the evaluation of ParentOf and (Eva, Harry) is in the evaluation of AncestorOf.
4. Finally, the tuple (Celeste, Harry) is in the evaluation of AncestorOf because the derivation rule AncestorOf$(v, w) \leftarrow$ ParentOf$(v, u) \wedge$ AncestorOf(u, w) and variable assignment $\{v \mapsto \texttt{Celeste}, u \mapsto \texttt{Dafni}, w \mapsto \texttt{Harry}\}$ exists such that (Celeste, Dafni) is in the evaluation of ParentOf and (Dafni, Harry) is in the evaluation of AncestorOf.

3 Explaining Datalog

Example 2 *explains* why a tuple is in the evaluation of a Datalog rule by providing a *step-by-step proof* of the derivation of the tuple. Such proofs are typically represented by a *derivation tree*. Next, we formalize these derivation trees, which we will then use to represent explanations and to reason about the complexity of explanations.

Definition 3. *Consider a derivation for the tuple $(c_1, \dots, c_n)$ in the evaluation of the rule named R. The* derivation tree *for fact $R(c_1, \dots, c_n)$ is defined recursively as follows:*

1. *if R is the name of a base rule and the rule $r =$ "$R(c_1, \dots, c_n) \leftarrow \bullet$" $\in B$ exists, then this derivation step is represented by a* leaf node *labeled r; and*
2. *if R is the name of a derivation rule and the explanation of fact $R(c_1, \dots, c_n)$ uses the rule*

$$r = \text{“}R(v_1, \dots, v_n) \leftarrow S_1(w_{1,1}, \dots, w_{1,m_1}) \wedge \dots \wedge S_j(w_{j,1}, \dots, w_{j,m_j})\text{”} \in D$$

and variable assignment $\mu : \{w_{1,1}, \dots, w_{j,m_j}\} \rightarrow \mathbb{U}$, then this derivation step is represented by an internal node *labeled r, μ with, for all $i, 1 \leq i \leq j$, a child representing the derivation of the fact $S_i(\mu(w_{i,1}), \dots, \mu(w_{i,m_i}))$.*

Example 3. Consider
the derivation in Example 2 of fact $\mathsf{AncestorOf}(\texttt{Celeste}, \texttt{Harry})$. In Fig. 2, we visualized the derivation tree for this fact. The derivation visualized in Fig. 2 is the *only* possible derivation of fact $\mathsf{AncestorOf}(\texttt{Celeste}, \texttt{Harry})$. In many practical cases, such a unique derivation does not exist, however. Consider the rule name Edge representing the graph with edges $(n_1, n_2), (n_2, n_3), (n_3, n_1)$ (a cycle with three nodes) and consider the derivation rules

$$\mathsf{TC}(v, w) \leftarrow \mathsf{Edge}(v, w);$$
$$\mathsf{TC}(v, w) \leftarrow \mathsf{TC}(v, u) \wedge \mathsf{TC}(u, w).$$

In Fig. 3, we visualized the derivation tree for the tuple (n_1, n_3) in the evaluation of TC. This explanation is not the simplest, however: the green-colored subtree in the left bottom is itself a much simpler derivation of the same fact $\mathsf{TC}(n_1, n_3)$.

Most Datalog evaluation algorithms can be annotated to not only determine all tuples in the evaluation of a rule name, but also to provide an explanation of each such tuple (by keeping track of the derivation steps made during evaluation). We refer to Fig. 4 for an illustration on how a standard *semi-naive* evaluation algorithm for Datalog [1,20,21,28] can be annotated for this purpose.

4 Short and Simple Datalog Explanations

As illustrated in Example 3 and Fig. 3, not all explanations are equal. Furthermore, the derivation of $\mathsf{TC}(n_1, n_3)$ illustrated in Fig. 3 can easily be bootstrapped into an infinite number of distinct explanations of $\mathsf{TC}(n_1, n_3)$. Hence, to maximize the *readability* and *understandability* of an explanation, we need to obtain *short and simple* explanations. Before we can reason about whether an explanation is short and simple, we first need to determine what the *complexity* of an explanation is. Next, we define four alternative *cost measures* for the complexity of an explanation based on structural properties on their derivation trees.

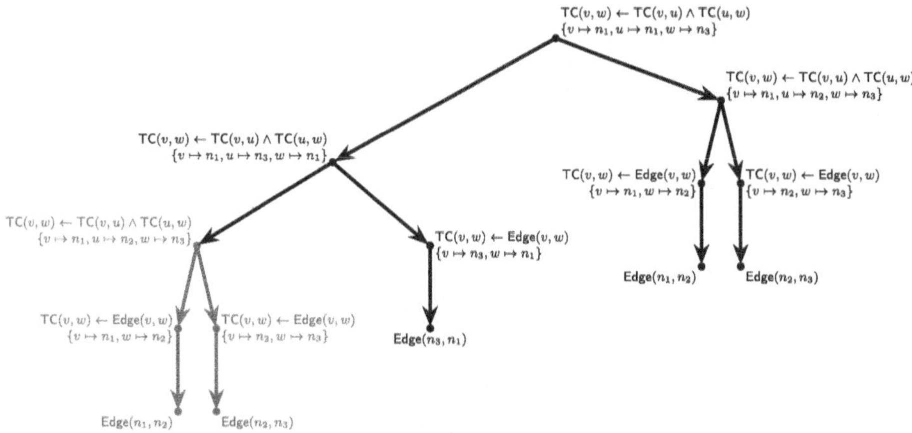

Fig. 3. The derivation tree of the tuple (n_1, n_3) in the evaluation of the rule named TC on the three-node cycle graph with nodes $\{n_1, n_2, n_3\}$. Note that the green-colored subtree in the left bottom is itself a simpler derivation of the same fact $\mathsf{TC}(n_1, n_3)$.

Definition 4. *Consider a derivation for the fact f in the evaluation of the Datalog rule named R and consider a derivation tree $\mathcal{T}$ explaining this fact.*

1. *The* base-fact complexity *$\mathcal{C}$-base($\mathcal{T}$) is defined by the number of distinct leaf node labels used in $\mathcal{T}$ (hence, the number of distinct base rules used in the explanation).*
2. *The* derivation complexity *$\mathcal{C}$-deriv($\mathcal{T}$) is defined by the number of internal nodes used in $\mathcal{T}$ (hence, the total number of derivation steps used in the explanation).*
3. *The* unique derivation complexity *$\mathcal{C}$-uderiv($\mathcal{T}$) is defined by the number of distinct internal node labels used in $\mathcal{T}$ (hence, the total number of unique derivation steps used in the explanation, in which the repeated use of a derivation of a fact only counts once).*
4. *The* derivation depth complexity *$\mathcal{C}$-ddepth($\mathcal{T}$) is defined by the length of the longest path in $\mathcal{T}$ from the root of the tree to a leaf (hence, the depth of the derivation steps used in the explanation).*

Example 4. Let $\mathcal{T}$ be the derivation tree visualized in Fig. 3 and let $\mathcal{T}'$ be the green-colored subtree in the left bottom of $\mathcal{T}$. Both $\mathcal{T}$ and $\mathcal{T}'$ explain the derivation of fact $\mathsf{TC}(n_1, n_3)$. We have

$$
\begin{aligned}
\mathcal{C}\text{-base}(\mathcal{T}) &= 3, & \mathcal{C}\text{-base}(\mathcal{T}') &= 2;\\
\mathcal{C}\text{-deriv}(\mathcal{T}) &= 9, & \mathcal{C}\text{-deriv}(\mathcal{T}') &= 3;\\
\mathcal{C}\text{-uderiv}(\mathcal{T}) &= 6, & \mathcal{C}\text{-uderiv}(\mathcal{T}') &= 3;\\
\mathcal{C}\text{-ddepth}(\mathcal{T}) &= 4, & \mathcal{C}\text{-ddepth}(\mathcal{T}') &= 2.
\end{aligned}
$$

According to all four complexity measures we introduced, the tree $\mathcal{T}'$ has lower complexity than tree $\mathcal{T}$. Hence, the explanation provided by tree $\mathcal{T}'$ is simpler

---

Algorithm SEMINAIVE-ANNOTATED($\langle B, D\rangle$):

We write leaf-node(r) to denote the leaf node with label r.
result := a dictionary with $\{h \mapsto \text{leaf-node}(\text{“}h \leftarrow \bullet\text{”}) \mid \text{“}h \leftarrow \bullet\text{”} \in B\}$.
new := a queue initialized with facts $\{h \mid \text{“}h \leftarrow \bullet\text{”} \in B\}$.
done := $\emptyset$.
while *new* $\neq \emptyset$ **do**
  Remove fact $S(d_1, \ldots, d_n)$ from the bottom of *new* and add it to *done*
  while there exists a derivation rule

$$\text{r} = \text{“}R(v_1, \ldots, v_m) \leftarrow S_1(w_{1,1}, \ldots, w_{1,m_1}) \wedge \cdots \wedge S_j(w_{j,1}, \ldots, w_{j,m_j})\text{”} \in D$$

  and variable assignment $\mu : \{w_{1,1}, \ldots, w_{j,m_j}\} \rightarrow \mathbb{U}$ such that

  i. there exists an i with $S(d_1, \ldots, d_n) = S_i(\mu(w_{i,1}), \ldots, \mu(w_{i,m_i}))$, $1 \leq i \leq j$;
  ii. for each $i, 1 \leq i \leq j$, we have $S_i(\mu(w_{i,1}), \ldots, \mu(w_{i,m_i})) \in$ *done*; and
  iii. $R(\mu(v_1), \ldots, \mu(v_m)) \notin$ (*done* $\cup$ *new*)

  do
    Add $R(\mu(v_1), \ldots, \mu(v_m))$ to the top of *new*.
    n := an internal node with label r, μ and j children *result*$(S_i(\mu(w_{i,1}), \ldots, \mu(w_{i,m_i})))$, $1 \leq i \leq j$.
    Add $R(\mu(v_1), \ldots, \mu(v_m)) \mapsto n$ to *result*.
  end while
end while
return *result*.

Fig. 4. A variant of the standard semi-naive Datalog evaluation algorithm that is annotated toward constructing derivation trees for each fact. In this algorithm, the colored parts indicate the annotations that construct derivation trees.

than the one provided by $\mathcal{T}$. Furthermore, the derivation tree $\mathcal{T}'$ is the smallest-possible tree of the fact $\mathsf{TC}(n_1, n_3)$. Hence, we are justified to say that the derivation tree $\mathcal{T}'$ provides a *simple* explanation.

Example 4 illustrates an explanation of a derived fact that minimizes all four cost metrics we introduced. Furthermore, this explanation is *unique*: all other possible explanations have higher costs. Unfortunately, such a unique explanation that minimizes all four cost metrics is not guaranteed to exist, as we shall prove next:

Theorem 1. *Let $\mathcal{C}_1, \mathcal{C}_2 \in \{\mathcal{C}\text{-base}, \mathcal{C}\text{-deriv}, \mathcal{C}\text{-uderiv}, \mathcal{C}\text{-ddepth}\}$, $\mathcal{C}_1 \neq \mathcal{C}_2$, be two distinct cost measures. There exist a Datalog program with rule name R and with tuple t in the evaluation of R such that any derivation of fact $R(t)$ with minimal $\mathcal{C}_1$ complexity does not have minimal $\mathcal{C}_2$ complexity.*

Proof. We can prove each of the twelve cases $\mathcal{C}_1, \mathcal{C}_2 \in \{\mathcal{C}\text{-base}, \mathcal{C}\text{-deriv}, \mathcal{C}\text{-uderiv}, \mathcal{C}\text{-ddepth}\}$, $\mathcal{C}_1 \neq \mathcal{C}_2$ by providing an explanation that is minimal with respect to $\mathcal{C}_1$, but not with respect to $\mathcal{C}_2$. In each case, we can use base facts that we specify in the form of the edge-labeled graph of Fig. 5.

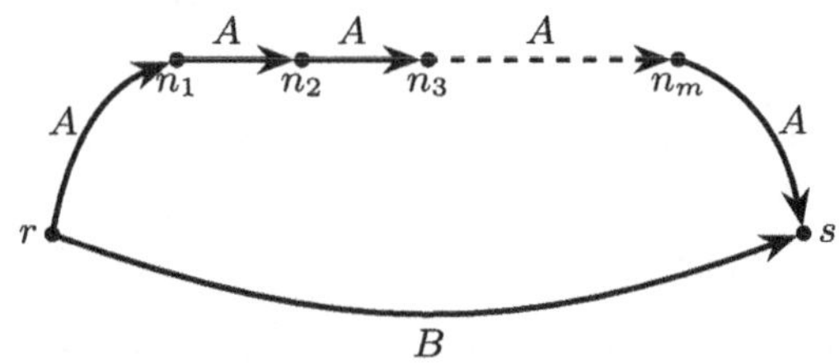

Fig. 5. A graph with two paths connecting nodes r and s: one A-labeled path of $m+1$ edges and one B-labeled path of one edge.

This graph represents $m+2$ base facts: $m+1$ edges labeled A, and one edge labeled B. In each case, we use the following derivation rules:

$$\begin{aligned}\mathsf{Path}\text{-}A(v,w) &\leftarrow A(v,w),\\ \mathsf{Path}\text{-}A(v,w) &\leftarrow A(v,u) \land \mathsf{Path}\text{-}A(u,w)\end{aligned}$$

There is only one way to explain $\mathsf{Path}\text{-}A(r,s)$: this explanation uses all $m+1$ edges labeled A and uses $m+1$ internal nodes. Next, we illustrate the proof for the case $\mathcal{C}_1 = \mathcal{C}$-base. All other cases are analogous.

Let $\mathcal{C}_1 =$ **$\mathcal{C}$-base and** $\mathcal{C}_2 \in \{$**$\mathcal{C}$-deriv**, **$\mathcal{C}$-uderiv**, **$\mathcal{C}$-ddepth**$\}$. Consider the following derivation rules:

$$\begin{aligned}\mathsf{Path}\text{-}A'(v,w) &\leftarrow A(v,w),\\ \mathsf{Path}\text{-}A'(v,w) &\leftarrow A(v,u) \land \mathsf{Path}\text{-}A'(u,w);\\ \mathsf{Path}\text{-}A''(v,w) &\leftarrow \mathsf{Path}\text{-}A'(u,w);\\ \mathsf{Ans}(v,w) &\leftarrow \mathsf{Path}\text{-}A(v,w) \land \mathsf{Path}\text{-}A''(v,w),\\ \mathsf{Ans}(v,w) &\leftarrow \mathsf{Path}\text{-}A(v,w) \land B(v,w).\end{aligned}$$

There are two possible explanations for the fact $\mathsf{Ans}(r,s)$: one that uses the rule $\mathsf{Ans}(v,w) \leftarrow \mathsf{Path}\text{-}A(v,w) \land \mathsf{Path}\text{-}A'(v,w)$, and another that uses the rule $\mathsf{Ans}(v,w) \leftarrow \mathsf{Path}\text{-}A(v,w) \land \mathsf{Path}\text{-}B(v,w)$. Let $\mathcal{T}$ and $\mathcal{T}'$ be the derivation trees for the first and second explanation, respectively.

The tree $\mathcal{T}$ uses only all $m+1$ A-labeled edges as base facts, $m+1$ internal nodes for explaining $\mathsf{Path}\text{-}A(r,s)$, $m+1$ internal nodes for explaining $\mathsf{Path}\text{-}A'(r,s)$, one additional internal node for explaining $\mathsf{Path}\text{-}A''(r,s)$, and one additional internal node for explaining $\mathsf{Ans}(r,s)$. The longest path from the root of $\mathcal{T}$ to a leaf is $m+3$: the path goes via the internal node explaining $\mathsf{Path}\text{-}A''(r,s)$ to the node explaining $\mathsf{Path}\text{-}A'(r,s)$, and the depth of the tree rooted at $\mathsf{Path}\text{-}A'(r,s)$ is $m+1$.

The tree $\mathcal{T}'$ uses all $m+2$ edges as base facts, $m+1$ internal nodes for explaining $\mathsf{Path}\text{-}A(r,s)$, and one additional internal node for explaining $\mathsf{Ans}(r,s)$.

The longest path from the root of $\mathcal{T}'$ to a leaf is $m + 2$: the path goes from the root to the node explaining Path-$A(r, s)$, and the depth of the tree rooted at Path-$A(r, s)$ is $m + 1$.

We conclude

$$\begin{aligned} \mathcal{C}\text{-base}(\mathcal{T}) &= m + 1, & \mathcal{C}\text{-base}(\mathcal{T}') &= m + 2; \\ \mathcal{C}\text{-deriv}(\mathcal{T}) &= 2(m + 1) + 2, & \mathcal{C}\text{-deriv}(\mathcal{T}') &= m + 2; \\ \mathcal{C}\text{-uderiv}(\mathcal{T}) &= 2(m + 1) + 2, & \mathcal{C}\text{-uderiv}(\mathcal{T}') &= m + 2; \\ \mathcal{C}\text{-ddepth}(\mathcal{T}) &= m + 3, & \mathcal{C}\text{-ddepth}(\mathcal{T}') &= m + 2. \end{aligned}$$

Hence, $\mathcal{T}$ is the only explanation with minimal $\mathcal{C}$-base complexity and does not have minimal $\mathcal{C}$-deriv, $\mathcal{C}$-uderiv, and $\mathcal{C}$-ddepth complexity.

Due to Theorem 1, it is justifiable to consider explanations with low complexity according to only one of the four cost measurements we introduced.

Definition 5. *Consider a derivation for the tuple t in the evaluation of the Datalog rule named R and consider a derivation tree $\mathcal{T}$ explaining fact $R(t)$. We say that tree $\mathcal{T}$ is* $\mathcal{C}$-simple, *$\mathcal{C} \in \{\mathcal{C}\text{-base}, \mathcal{C}\text{-deriv}, \mathcal{C}\text{-uderiv}, \mathcal{C}\text{-ddepth}\}$ if, for every derivation tree $\mathcal{T}'$ explaining fact $R(t)$, we have $\mathcal{C}(\mathcal{T}) \leq \mathcal{C}(\mathcal{T}')$.*

5 Computing Simple Explanations

We have established *four* types of simple explanations based on four distinct complexity measures for the derivation trees representing explanations. Next, we will provide algorithms to compute $\mathcal{C}$-deriv-simple and $\mathcal{C}$-ddepth-simple explanations.

First, we consider the computation of $\mathcal{C}$-deriv-simple explanations. For this task, we introduce the SNA-PQ algorithm of Fig. 6. This algorithm derives new facts in a similar way as the standard semi-naive Datalog evaluation algorithm [1, 20, 21, 28], except that SNA-PQ will explore derivation steps involving newly derived facts in *derivation complexity* order. To do so, the algorithm uses a priority queue to store newly derived facts ordered on their derivation complexity cost and process them based on this order, this in a similar way as the usage of a priority queue to process nodes based on their distance to a source node in Dijkstra's algorithm [11, Section 22.3]. We note that the SNA-PQ algorithm is a generalization of the MINIMIZESETGG [24] algorithm from context-free path queries to general Datalog rules and is similar to the *Dijkstra-like algorithm* of Alrabbaa et al. [2] that can be used to find optimal proofs for entailment in descriptive logic.

Theorem 2. *Let R be the name of an n-ary rule in Datalog program $\langle B, D\rangle$. The pair $R(c_1, \ldots, c_n) \mapsto z$ is in the result of* SNA-PQ*($\langle B, D\rangle$) if and only if tuple $(c_1, \ldots, c_n)$ is in the evaluation of R. Furthermore, z is the root of a derivation tree that is a $\mathcal{C}$-deriv-simple explanation of fact $R(c_1, \ldots, c_n)$.*

Algorithm SNA-PQ($\langle B, D\rangle$):

We write leaf-node(r) to denote the leaf node with label r.
result := a dictionary with $\{h \mapsto \text{leaf-node}(\text{“}h \leftarrow \bullet\text{”}) \mid \text{“}h \leftarrow \bullet\text{”} \in B\}$.
new := a priority queue initialized with facts $\{h \mid \text{“}h \leftarrow \bullet\text{”} \in B\}$.
/* This priority queue is ordered on the *derivation complexity* of facts. */
done := $\emptyset$.
while *new* $\neq \emptyset$ **do**
  Remove fact $S(d_1, \dots, d_n)$ with lowest priority from *new* and add it to *done*.
  while there exists a derivation rule

$$r = \text{“}R(v_1, \dots, v_m) \leftarrow S_1(w_{1,1}, \dots, w_{1,m_1}) \wedge \dots \wedge S_j(w_{j,1}, \dots, w_{j,m_j})\text{”} \in D$$

  and variable assignment $\mu : \{w_{1,1}, \dots, w_{j,m_j}\} \rightarrow \mathbb{U}$ such that

  i. there exists an i with $S(d_1, \dots, d_n) = S_i(\mu(w_{i,1}), \dots, \mu(w_{i,m_i}))$, $1 \leq i \leq j$;
  ii. for each $i, 1 \leq i \leq j$, we have $S_i(\mu(w_{i,1}), \dots, \mu(w_{i,m_i})) \in$ *done*; and
  iii. $R(\mu(v_1), \dots, \mu(v_m)) \notin$ *done*

  do
    if $R(\mu(v_1), \dots, \mu(v_m))$ is already in *new* **then**
      Compare this new derivation for $R(\mu(v_1), \dots, \mu(v_m))$ with the one already stored in *result* and determine which derivation has the lowest *derivation complexity*. Update the priority for $R(\mu(v_1), \dots, \mu(v_m))$ in *new* and update the derivation in *result* to represent the derivation with the lowest *derivation complexity*.
    else
      Add $R(\mu(v_1), \dots, \mu(v_m))$ to the top of *new*.
      n := an internal node with label r, μ and j children
        result$(S_i(\mu(w_{i,1}), \dots, \mu(w_{1,m_i})))$, $1 \leq i \leq j$.
      Add $R(\mu(v_1), \dots, \mu(v_m)) \mapsto n$ to *result*.
    end if
  end while
end while
return *result*.

Fig. 6. A variant of the standard semi-naive Datalog evaluation algorithm that is annotated toward constructing $\mathcal{C}$-deriv-simple derivation trees for each fact. To ensure derivation trees are constructed with *increasing* derivation complexity, the order in which facts are constructed is managed by the priority queue *new* (that holds each newly-created fact ordered on the derivation complexity of their derivation).

Proof. To simplify notation, we use the shorthand $\mathsf{cost}(f)$ to denote the $\mathcal{C}$-deriv-complexity of the derivation in *result* for fact f and we use the shorthand $\mathsf{optimal}(f)$ to denote the $\mathcal{C}$-deriv-complexity of any $\mathcal{C}$-deriv-simple explanation of fact f. We assume $\mathsf{cost}(f) = \infty$ for facts $f \notin$ *result*.

Let x be the cost of the first fact in *new*, starting at $x = 0$ when initially entering the loop at Line 5 . One can prove this proposition by proving that the following invariants hold on the loop at Line 5:

(i) The facts $g \in new$ are ordered on increasing $\mathsf{cost}(g)$.
(ii) For all facts g, we either have:
  (a) fact g is in *done* with $\mathsf{cost}(g) = \mathsf{optimal}(g) \leq x$; or
  (b) fact g is in *new* with $x \leq \mathsf{cost}(g) = \mathsf{optimal}(g)$; or
  (c) $\mathsf{cost}(g) > \mathsf{optimal}(g) > x$ and, for every tree $\mathcal{T}$ representing a $\mathcal{C}$-deriv-simple explanation of fact g and every fact $g' \in \mathcal{T}$ with $\mathsf{cost}(g') > \mathsf{optimal}(g')$, every path from g' to a leaf in $\mathcal{T}$ will reach a fact g'' such that $g'' \in (new \cup done)$ and $\mathsf{cost}(g'') = \mathsf{optimal}(g'')$, and at least one of these reachable facts g'' is in *new*.

After Lines 2–4 , *result* and *new* hold all base facts, no facts are in *done*, and all facts $g \in new$ are base facts with $\mathsf{cost}(g) = \mathsf{optimal}(g) = 0$. As all derived facts g have $\mathsf{optimal}(g) \geq 1$, no derived facts are included in $done \cup new$, and all explanations end in base facts, the Invariants (i)–(ii) initially hold.

Now assume the Invariants (i)–(ii) hold for the first i iterations of the loop at Line 5 . Next, we consider the $i+1$-th iteration of the loop at Line 5 . As *new* is a priority queue (Line 3), Invariant (i) always holds. Hence, we only have to prove that Invariant (ii) is maintained during the loop and, hence, holds again at Line 16.

Let $f = S(d_1, \dots, d_n)$ be the fact removed from *new* at Line 6. As $f \in new$ at the start of the round and $\mathsf{cost}(f) = x$, we can apply Invariant (ii)b to conclude $\mathsf{cost}(f) = \mathsf{optimal}(f)$. Hence, after adding f to *done* at Line 6 , Invariant (ii)a applies to f.

Now consider any other fact $g \neq f$. We distinguish three cases:

1. $\mathsf{cost}(g) = \mathsf{optimal}(g)$ at the start of the loop. By either Invariant (ii)a or Invariant (ii)b , we have $g \in (new \cup done)$. Due to Condition iii (Line 7), no facts $g \in done$ will be inspected during the $i + 1$-th loop. Likewise, due to the conditions on Line 9, no facts $g \in new$ with $\mathsf{cost}(g) = \mathsf{optimal}(g)$ will be updated during the $i + 1$-th loop. Hence, at the end of the loop, either Invariant (ii)a or Invariant (ii)b still applies to g.
2. $\mathsf{cost}(g) > \mathsf{optimal}(g)$ at the start of the loop and for all trees $\mathcal{T}$ representing a $\mathcal{C}$-deriv-simple explanation of fact g we either have $f \notin \mathcal{T}$ or there exist facts $g'' \in \mathcal{T}$ with $g'' \in new$, $\mathsf{cost}(g'') = \mathsf{optimal}(g'')$, and $g'' \neq f$. Consider any tree $\mathcal{T}$ representing a $\mathcal{C}$-deriv-simple explanation of fact g and any fact $g'' \in \mathcal{T}$ with $\mathsf{cost}(g'') = \mathsf{optimal}(g'')$ with $g'' \neq f$. By Invariant (ii) , $g'' \in (new \cup done)$ at the start of the loop. As $g'' \neq f$, $g'' \in (new \cup done)$ at the end of the loop and all conditions put on $\mathcal{T}$ and g'' by Invariant (ii)c are maintained. Now choose such a $g'' \in \mathcal{T}$ with $\mathsf{cost}(g'') = \mathsf{optimal}(g'')$, $g'' \neq f$, and $g'' \in new$ at the start of the loop. At the end of the loop, we still have $g'' \in new$. By Invariant (i) , $\mathsf{cost}(g'') \geq \mathsf{cost}(f) = x$. Hence, $\mathsf{cost}(g) > \mathsf{cost}(g'')$ and Invariant (ii)c still applies to g at the end of the $i + 1$-th loop.

3. $\mathsf{cost}(g) > \mathsf{optimal}(g)$ at the start of the loop and there exists a tree $\mathcal{T}$ representing a $\mathcal{C}$-deriv-simple explanation of fact g with, for all facts $g'' \in \mathcal{T}$, either $g'' \in \mathit{done}$ or $g'' = f$ or $g'' = g$. In this case, f is a child of the root of tree $\mathcal{T}$ (the fact g) and during execution of the $i+1$-th loop, the loop at Line 7 will consider the derivation represented by $\mathcal{T}$ (or any other $\mathcal{C}$-deriv-simple explanation involving f) and either adds g to *new* and *result* such that $\mathsf{cost}(g) = \mathsf{optimal}(g)$ (Lines 11–13) or updates the existing derivation for g in *new* and *result* such that $\mathsf{cost}(g) = \mathsf{optimal}(g)$ (Line 9). In both cases, Invariant (ii)b applies to g at the end of the $i+1$-th loop. □

Next, we consider the computation of $\mathcal{C}$-ddepth-simple explanations. It turns out that we can use the SemiNaive-Annotated algorithm of Fig. 4 for this task: if we process newly-created facts via a normal *queue* (instead of a priority queue ordered on derivation complexity as SNA-PQ does), then we process newly-created facts in order of the depth of derivations used to create these facts (instead of the derivation complexity). We conclude the following:

Proposition 1. *Let R be the name of an n-ary rule in Datalog program $\langle B, D\rangle$. The pair $R(c_1, \dots, c_n) \mapsto z$ is in the result of* SemiNaive-Annotated*$(\langle B, D\rangle)$ if and only if $R(c_1, \dots, c_n)$ is in the evaluation of R. Furthermore, z is the root of a derivation tree that is a $\mathcal{C}$-ddepth-simple explanation of fact $R(c_1, \dots, c_n)$.*

As Datalog queries are monotone, the base-fact complexity of any $\mathcal{C}$-base-simple explanation of a fact f in the evaluation of rule named R can be computed in a brute-force manner. Consider a Datalog program $\langle B, D\rangle$ such that f is in the evaluation of rule named R. Now let $B' \subseteq B$ be a minimum-sized subset of the base facts B such that fact f is in the evaluation of R with respect to the Datalog program $\langle B', D\rangle$. For any $\mathcal{C}$-base-simple explanation represented by tree $\mathcal{T}$ of fact f, we must have $\mathcal{C}\text{-base}(\mathcal{T}) = |B'|$. Furthermore, after finding base facts B', it is straightforward to find a $\mathcal{C}$-base-simple explanation for fact f, e.g., by using Algorithm SemiNaive-Annotated$(\langle B', D\rangle)$ to derive an explanation for f.

Likewise, we can compute any $\mathcal{C}$-uderiv-simple explanation of fact f by finding a minimum-sized subset of those derived facts D that appear in a derivation tree explaining f. To build an explanation out of D, we can use a variant of Algorithm SemiNaive-Annotated$(\langle B', D\rangle)$ that is restricted to only produce the derived facts in D.

6 The Complexity of Some Simple Explanations

In the previous section, we introduced brute-force methods to compute $\mathcal{C}$-base-simple and $\mathcal{C}$-uderiv-simple explanations. These methods are impractically slow for larger datasets. In the following, we will prove that it is unlikely that substantially faster algorithms exist. We do so by showing that a suitable *decision-version* of the problem of computing $\mathcal{C}$-base-simple and $\mathcal{C}$-uderiv-simple explanations is NP-hard by a reduction from the *vertex-cover problem*.

Definition 6. *Let $G = (V, E)$ be a graph with nodes V and undirected edges E (hence, $(m, n) \in E$ if and only if $(n, m) \in E$). A* vertex cover *of G is a subset $V' \subset V$ such that if $(m, n) \in E$ then either $m \in V'$ or $n \in V'$ (or both). Hence, V' contains at least one end point of every edge in the graph.*

The decision-version of the vertex-cover problem *is as follows: given a graph G and integer k, is there a vertex-cover of size k (or less).*

Lemma 1 ([27]). *The vertex-cover problem is NP-complete.*

Next, we formalize a suitable decision-version of finding a simple explanation.

Definition 7. *Let $\mathcal{C} \in \{\mathcal{C}\text{-base}, \mathcal{C}\text{-deriv}, \mathcal{C}\text{-uderiv}, \mathcal{C}\text{-ddepth}\}$. The* $\mathcal{C}$-simple explanation problem *is as follows: given a Datalog program, fact f, and integer k, is there an explanation $\mathcal{T}$ for the derivation of fact f with $\mathcal{C}(\mathcal{T}) \leq k$.*

To show that both the $\mathcal{C}$-base-simple explanation problem and the $\mathcal{C}$-uderiv-simple explanation problem are NP-hard, we will next construct a reduction of the vertex-cover problem to both the $\mathcal{C}$-base-simple explanation problem and the $\mathcal{C}$-uderiv-simple explanation problem.

Consider a graph $G = (V, E)$ with N undirected edges. Assume there is a minimal-sized vertex cover of G of size k. In our Datalog program, we represent each node $v \in V$ by the base fact $Node(v) \leftarrow \bullet$.

To simplify presentation, we choose a subset $U \subset E$ such that every edge in E has a single representation in U: for every undirected edge $(m, n) \in E$, either $(m, n) \in U$ or $(n, m) \in U$, but not both.

Let $\mathbb{I} = \{1, \dots, N\}$ be the set of $|U|$ consecutive integers. We shall use $\mathbb{I}$ as *edge symbols* to identify edges and let $b : U \rightarrow \mathbb{I}$ be a bijection mapping each edge to a unique integer in $\mathbb{I}$. Let $(m, n) \in U$ be an edge and let $i = b((m, n)) \in \mathbb{I}$ be the integer representing (m, n). In our Datalog program, we represent this edge by two base facts $EndPoint(i, m) \leftarrow \bullet$ and $EndPoint(i, n) \leftarrow \bullet$.

Next, let $i, 1 \leq i < N$, be a non-last integer in $\mathbb{I}$ and let $j = i + 1$. Our Datalog program introduces the base fact $SymbolOrder(i, j) \leftarrow \bullet$ to establish this order on edge symbols.

Hence, there exists a unique *SymbolOrder*-labeled path from 1 to N that visits every edge symbol in $\mathbb{I}$. Now consider the Datalog derivation rules:

$$\begin{aligned}
IndirectNode(v) &\leftarrow Node(v);\\
CoveringNode(v) &\leftarrow EndPoint(v, m) \wedge IndirectNode(m);\\
OrderStep(v, w) &\leftarrow SymbolOrder(v, w) \wedge CoveringNode(v);\\
OrderVisit(v, w) &\leftarrow OrderStep(v, w);\\
OrderVisit(v, w) &\leftarrow OrderVisit(v, u) \wedge OrderStep(u, w);\\
OrderPath(v, w) &\leftarrow OrderVisit(v, w) \wedge CoveringNode(w).
\end{aligned}$$

We note that the fact $OrderPath(1, \mathrm{N})$ represents a unique *SymbolOrder*-labeled path from 1 to N that visits every edge symbol in $i \in \mathbb{I}$. Furthermore, the explanation for fact $CoveringNode(i)$ associates each edge symbol i on this path with one of its end points (which is a node part of the vertex cover represented by the explanation).

Now consider a derivation tree $\mathcal{T}$ explaining the derivation of fact *OrderPath*$(1, N)$. This tree will consist of the following:

1. The derived fact *OrderPath*$(1, N)$.
2. The derived facts *OrderVisit*$(1, N)$ and *CoveringNode*(N).
3. The derived facts *OrderVisit*$(1, i)$ and *OrderStep*$(i, i+1)$, for all $i, 3 \leq i < N$.
4. The derived facts *OrderVisit*$(1, 2)$ and *OrderStep*$(1, 2)$.
5. The base facts *SymbolOrder*$(i, i+1)$ and the derived facts *CoveringNode*(i), for all $i, 1 \leq i < N$.
6. The base facts *EndPoint*(i, n) for all $i, 1 \leq i \leq N$ with $n \in V$.
7. For each of these *EndPoint*(i, n), a derived fact *IndirectNode*(n) and base fact *Node*(n).

Let V' be the set of nodes used in the facts *EndPoint*(i, n), $i, 1 \leq i \leq N$, used in $\mathcal{T}$. By construction, V' is a vertex cover. Note that $\mathcal{T}$ includes derived facts *IndirectNode*(n) and base fact *Node*(n) if and only if $n \in V'$. Hence, the size $k = |V'|$ of vertex cover V' is equivalent to the number of derived facts with head *IndirectNode* in $\mathcal{T}$ and is also equivalent to the number of base facts with head *Node* in $\mathcal{T}$.

Due to the above breakdown of explanation $\mathcal{T}$, we can conclude that $\mathcal{T}$ includes $(3N - 1) + k$ derived facts (one with head *OrderPath*, $N - 1$ with head *OrderVisit*, $N - 1$ with head *OrderStep*, N with head *CoveringNode*, and k with head *IndirectNode*), and that $\mathcal{T}$ includes $2(N - 1) + k$ base facts ($N - 1$ with head *SymbolOrder*, $N - 1$ with head *EndPoint*, and k with head *Node*).

Theorem 3. *The $\mathcal{C}$-base-simple explanation problem and the $\mathcal{C}$-uderiv-simple explanation problem are* NP*-complete, even for Datalog programs in which all heads have at-most two symbols and all bodies of derivation rules have at-most two terms.*[1]

Proof. First, we prove that both problems are NP-hard. Consider the vertex-cover problem for undirected graph $G = (V, E)$ and integer k. Using the above Datalog construction, there exists a vertex-cover of size k if and only if there exists an explanation $\mathcal{T}$ for fact *EdgePath*$(1, N)$ with $\mathcal{C}$-base$(\mathcal{T}) = 2(N - 1) + k$ or with $\mathcal{C}$-uderiv$(\mathcal{T}) = (3N - 1) + k$.

Next, we prove both problems are in NP. To do so, we adapt the brute-force methods for computing $\mathcal{C}$-base-simple explanations and $\mathcal{C}$-uderiv-simple explanations outlined at the end of Sect. 5 to show how, for any integer k, one can represent solutions to the $\mathcal{C}$-base-simple explanation problem and the $\mathcal{C}$-uderiv-simple explanation problem using sets of at-most k base facts ($\mathcal{C}$-base-simple

[1] Hence, the *data complexity* (the complexity in terms of only the number of base facts) [33] for both the $\mathcal{C}$-base-simple explanation problem and the $\mathcal{C}$-uderiv-simple explanation problem is already NP-hard, even though the data complexity of normal Datalog query evaluation, for Algorithm SEMINAIVE-ANNOTATED, and for Algorithm SNA-PQ is polynomial.

explanation problem) or at-most k derived facts ($\mathcal{C}$-uderiv-simple explanation problem) and how one can certify such a representation efficiently using the SEMINAIVE-ANNOTATED algorithm.

7 Discussion

In this paper, we have established *four* types of simple explanations, two of which ($\mathcal{C}$-deriv-simple and $\mathcal{C}$-ddepth-simple explanations) can be computed efficiently in practice. The ability to efficiently compute a simple explanation does *not* guarantee that the resulting explanations are practically usable, however: even simple explanations can become very large.

The *size* of simple explanations for Datalog programs depends on the complexity of the derivation rules and the patterns present in the base facts. For many common types of Datalog queries, reasonable upper bounds on the size of simple explanations exist, however:

1. all non-recursive programs will have simple explanations whose size is upper bounded by the number of derivation rules; and
2. all simple recursive programs (e.g., transitive closures, reachability, and other constructions typically used in navigational graph queries [3,10,12,23,24]) will have simple explanations whose size is upper bounded by the number of base facts.

Due to results on simple explanations for context-free path queries [23,24], no guarantees for small simple explanations can be provided for Datalog programs with more complex forms of recursion, however.

8 Related Work

There is an abundant literature on data provenance [9], provenance for Datalog [7,8,15,17,30], explaining graph queries [24], explaining SHACL [14], and the concept of short explanations [24,26]. There is only limited work toward explaining Datalog queries, however. We provide a brief overview.

Explaining Graph Queries. Several recent works have focused on explaining navigation-based graph queries using either paths in the graph or subgraphs of the graph, e.g., explanations for regular path queries or context-free path queries [4,13,19,22,24,25,31,32]. These types of graph queries are a fragment of the type of queries that can be expressed via Datalog, e.g., the explanations of context-free path queries [24] are a very restricted example of explanations with low derivation complexity. We vastly generalize the limited results of these works by considering explanations in Datalog, a much more expressive query language. Furthermore, we look at multiple fundamental types of *short and simple* explanations instead of focusing on a single path-based or subgraph-based semantics for explanations.

Why-Provenance for Datalog. Typical works on provenance for Datalog focus on providing thorough explanation of facts f by explaining all the different ways in which one can derive f [6–8,15,17,30]. For example, the explanation of a fact f is its support [7]: all different subsets of the set of base facts that can be used to derive f. As such a thorough explanation is too large for practical use, the focus of several works [15,17,30] is on finding a practically-computable and representative small-enough sample of this thorough explanation. We take a different approach by only looking for a *single* explanation that is short and simple (according to fundamental notions of complexity of explanations).

Of these recent works on Datalog provenance, the work by Calautti et al. [7] is closest to our approach: in their work, the provenance of a fact f consist of the set $S(f)$ of all supports for f. The smallest support in $S(f)$ corresponds to the notion of a $\mathcal{C}$-base-simple explanation that we study. They show that obtaining the provenance of fact f involves solving NP-complete decision problems. Our results on the complexity of $\mathcal{C}$-base-simple explanations (Theorem 3) are more general, however: $\mathcal{C}$-base-simple explanations for fact f are simpler than the provenance for f and our results already hold for simple derivations involving only Datalog rules with at-most two terms and an arity at-most-2. Furthermore, our work considers not only $\mathcal{C}$-base-simple explanations, but also other fundamental notions of short and simple explanations.

9 Conclusions and Future Work

Toward improving *explanations* for the results of complex recursive queries, we formally studied short and simple explanations of Datalog derivations. We introduced four distinct notions to measure the complexity of explanations (base fact, derivation, unique derivation, and derivation depth complexity) and introduce four corresponding types of *simple* explanations that minimize one of these complexity measures. In addition, we provided efficient evaluation algorithms to compute explanations with minimal derivation or derivation depth complexity. Finally, we showed that computing explanations with minimal base fact complexity or unique derivation complexity involves solving NP-complete decision problems and, hence, is inherently hard.

We are encouraged by our results: they indicate that *simple explanations* are practically possible with respect to derivation and derivation depth complexity. Hence, the next step is to engineer practically-efficient algorithms to produce such explanations. The algorithms in our paper are only suitable for select use-cases, however: they are *bottom-up algorithms* that are notoriously costly when one is only interested in a subset of the data (e.g., only facts for a few rule names or only facts matching a given selection). To provide practical evaluation algorithms for such applications, we are interested in the development of *top-down* and *goal-oriented* algorithms, e.g., based on magic set evaluation. Based on the results in this paper, we believe adaptations of existing efficient Datalog evaluation techniques are achievable.

References

1. Abiteboul, S., Hull, R., Vianu, V.: Foundations of Databases: The Logical Level, 1st edn. Addison-Wesley (1995)
2. Alrabbaa, C., Baader, F., Borgwardt, S., Koopmann, P., Kovtunova, A.: Finding good proofs for description logic entailments using recursive quality measures. In: Platzer, A., Sutcliffe, G. (eds.) CADE 2021. LNCS (LNAI), vol. 12699, pp. 291–308. Springer, Cham (2021). https://doi.org/10.1007/978-3-030-79876-5_17
3. Barceló, P.: Querying graph databases. In: Proceedings of the 32nd Symposium on Principles of Database Systems, pp. 175–188. ACM (2013)
4. Barrett, C., Jacob, R., Marathe, M.: Formal-language-constrained path problems. SIAM J. Comput. **30**(3), 809–837 (2000)
5. Bellomarini, L., Benedetto, D., Gottlob, G., Sallinger, E.: Vadalog: a modern architecture for automated reasoning with large knowledge graphs. Inf. Syst. **105**(C) (2020). https://doi.org/10.1016/j.is.2020.101528
6. Bourgaux, C., Bourhis, P., Peterfreund, L., Thomazo, M.: Revisiting semiring provenance for datalog. In: Proceedings of the 19th International Conference on Principles of Knowledge Representation and Reasoning, pp. 91–101 (2022). https://doi.org/10.24963/kr.2022/10
7. Calautti, M., Livshits, E., Pieris, A., Schneider, M.: The complexity of why-provenance for datalog queries (2023). https://arxiv.org/abs/2303.12773
8. Calautti, M., Livshits, E., Pieris, A., Schneider, M.: Computing the why-provenance for datalog queries via SAT solvers. In: Proceedings of the AAAI Conference on Artificial Intelligence, pp. 10459–10466 (2024). https://doi.org/10.1609/aaai.v38i9.28914
9. Cheney, J., Chiticariu, L., Tan, W.C.: Provenance in databases: why, how, and where. Found. Trends Databases **1**(4), 379–474 (2009)
10. Consens, M.P., Mendelzon, A.O.: GraphLog: a visual formalism for real life recursion. In: Proceedings of the Ninth ACM SIGACT-SIGMOD-SIGART Symposium on Principles of Database Systems, pp. 404–416. ACM (1990)
11. Cormen, T.H., Leiserson, C.E., Rivest, R.L., Stein, C.: Introduction to Algorithms, 4th edn. The MIT Press (2022)
12. Cruz, I.F., Mendelzon, A.O., Wood, P.T.: A graphical query language supporting recursion. In: Proceedings of the 1987 ACM SIGMOD International Conference on Management of Data, pp. 323–330. ACM (1987)
13. Cucumides, T., Reutter, J., Vrgoč, D.: Size bounds and algorithms for conjunctive regular path queries. In: 26th International Conference on Database Theory (ICDT 2023). Leibniz International Proceedings in Informatics (LIPIcs), vol. 255, pp. 13:1–13:17. Schloss Dagstuhl (2023). https://doi.org/10.4230/LIPIcs.ICDT.2023.13
14. Delva, T., Dimou, A., Jakubowski, M., den Bussche, J.V.: Data provenance for SHACL. In: Proceedings 26th International Conference on Extending Database Technology, pp. 285–297. OpenProceedings.org (2023). https://doi.org/10.48786/EDBT.2023.23
15. Deutch, D., Gilad, A., Moskovitch, Y.: Selective provenance for datalog programs using top-k queries. Proc. VLDB Endow. **8**(12), 1394–1405 (2015). https://doi.org/10.14778/2824032.2824039
16. Dowling, W.F., Gallier, J.H.: Linear-time algorithms for testing the satisfiability of propositional horn formulae. J. Logic Program. **1**(3), 267–284 (1984). https://doi.org/10.1016/0743-1066(84)90014-1

17. Elhalawati, A., Krötzsch, M., Mennicke, S.: An existential rule framework for computing why-provenance on-demand for datalog. In: Rules and Reasoning: 6th International Joint Conference on Rules and Reasoning, RuleML+RR 2022, pp. 146–163. Springer (2022). https://doi.org/10.1007/978-3-031-21541-4_10
18. Fuhr, N.: Probabilistic datalog–a logic for powerful retrieval methods. In: Proceedings of the 18th Annual International ACM SIGIR Conference on Research and Development in Information Retrieval, pp. 282–290. ACM (1995). https://doi.org/10.1145/215206.215372
19. García, R., Angles, R.: An algebra for path manipulation in graph databases. In: Advances in Databases and Information Systems, pp. 61–74. Springer (2022)
20. Greco, S., Molinaro, C.: Datalog and Logic Databases. Springer (2016). https://doi.org/10.1007/978-3-031-01854-1
21. Green, T.J., Huang, S.S., Loo, B.T., Zhou, W.: Datalog and recursive query processing. Found. Trends Databases **5**(2), 105–195 (2013). https://doi.org/10.1561/1900000017
22. Grigorev, S., Ragozina, A.: Context-free path querying with structural representation of result. In: Proceedings of the 13th Central & Eastern European Software Engineering Conference in Russia. ACM (2017). https://doi.org/10.1145/3166094.3166104
23. Hellings, J.: Conjunctive context-free path queries. In: Proceedings of the 17th International Conference on Database Theory (ICDT), pp. 119–130. OpenProceedings.org (2014). https://doi.org/10.5441/002/icdt.2014.15
24. Hellings, J.: Explaining results of path queries on graphs: Single-path results for context-free path queries. Inf. Syst. **128**, 102475 (2025). https://doi.org/10.1016/j.is.2024.102475
25. Hofman, P., Martens, W.: Separability by short subsequences and subwords. In: 18th International Conference on Database Theory. Leibniz International Proceedings in Informatics (LIPIcs), vol. 31, pp. 230–246. Schloss Dagstuhl–Leibniz-Zentrum fuer Informatik (2015)
26. Jaakkola, R., Janhunen, T., Kuusisto, A., Rankooh, M.F., Vilander, M.: Short boolean formulas as explanations in practice. In: Logics in Artificial Intelligence, pp. 90–105. Springer (2023). https://doi.org/10.1007/978-3-031-43619-2_7
27. Karp, R.M.: Reducibility among Combinatorial Problems, pp. 85–103. Springer (1972). https://doi.org/10.1007/978-1-4684-2001-2_9
28. Ketsman, B., Koutris, P.: Modern datalog engines. Found. Trends Databases **12**(1), 1–68 (2022). https://doi.org/10.1561/1900000073
29. Lanzinger, M., Sferrazza, S., Gottlob, G.: MV-Datalog+/-: effective rule-based reasoning with uncertain observations (extended abstract). In: Proceedings of the Thirty-Second International Joint Conference on Artificial Intelligence, pp. 6447–6451. International Joint Conferences on Artificial Intelligence Organization (2023). https://doi.org/10.24963/ijcai.2023/718
30. Lee, S., Ludäscher, B., Glavic, B.: Approximate summaries for why and why-not provenance. Proc. VLDB Endow. **13**(6), 912–924 (2020). https://doi.org/10.14778/3380750.3380760

31. Martens, W., Niewerth, M., Popp, T., Rojas, C., Vansummeren, S., Vrgoč, D.: Representing paths in graph database pattern matching. Proc. VLDB Endow. **16**(7) (2023). https://doi.org/10.14778/3587136.3587151
32. Terekhov, A., Khoroshev, A., Azimov, R., Grigorev, S.: Context-free path querying with single-path semantics by matrix multiplication. In: Proceedings of the 3rd Joint International Workshop on Graph Data Management Experiences & Systems (GRADES) and Network Data Analytics (NDA). ACM (2020). https://doi.org/10.1145/3398682.3399163
33. Vardi, M.Y.: The complexity of relational query languages (extended abstract). In: Proceedings of the Fourteenth Annual ACM Symposium on Theory of Computing, pp. 137–146. ACM (1982). https://doi.org/10.1145/800070.802186

Poster Papers

Towards Neuro-symbolic Classification of Abrasive Wear in Scanning Electron Microscopy

Andreas Brännström[1], Esteban Guerrero[1], Maria Wojtowicz[2], Jonna Hasselaar[2], Staffan Jacobson[2], Urban Wiklund[2], and Juan Carlos Nieves[1](✉)

[1] Department of Computing Science, Umeå University, Umeå, Sweden
{andreasb,esteban,jcnieves}@cs.umu.se

[2] Ångström Laboratory, Department of Materials Science and Engineering, Uppsala University, Uppsala, Sweden
{maria.wojtowicz,jonna.hasselaar,staffan.jacobson,urban.wiklund}@angstrom.uu.se

Abstract. The analysis of abrasive wear is central to sustainable material design and tool development, yet current practice relies on manual inspection of scanning electron microscopy (SEM) images, limiting scalability and reproducibility. We propose early work towards a neuro-symbolic approach that integrates convolutional neural networks for SEM image segmentation with an expert-elicited taxonomy of wear features encoded in Answer Set Programming. A curated dataset of 400 laboratory and field SEM images with expert-labeled annotations supports interpretable detection of wear mechanisms. This approach aims to reduce the dependency on large datasets, increase interpretability, in automated abrasive wear analysis. The contribution opens the way for scalable and transparent decision processes in tribology, with implications for efficient materials development and extended service life of industrial tools.

Keywords: Neuro-symbolic AI · Semantic segmentation · Knowledge representation · Abrasive wear analysis

1 Introduction

Abrasive wear is a major cause of material degradation in industrial tools and components [10,11,17,21,28]. In agricultural applications, soil particles interacting with tillage tools rapidly reduce tool functionality [9,15,16,20], leading to increased energy consumption, higher fuel use, and frequent tool replacement, with significant economic and environmental consequences [7]. Improving tool lifespan therefore depends on understanding the mechanisms underlying abrasive wear. When examined using scanning electron microscopy (SEM) [25], worn surfaces exhibit complex and highly irregular morphologies, where overlapping scratches, debris, and transferred material obscure key features, making reliable

A.-Y. Turhan and J. Virtema (Eds.): FoIKS 2026, LNCS 16475, pp. 327–333, 2026.
https://doi.org/10.1007/978-3-032-21540-6_19

interpretation time-consuming and expert-dependent. To address these limitations, automated abrasive wear analysis has been widely studied [5,18,19,22,26], including CNN-based image analysis [26], multisensor fusion for predictive monitoring [12], and machine learning approaches for wear characterization and prediction [1]. However, progress is hindered by the absence of a shared, formal vocabulary for describing abrasion mechanisms and observable surface features, as well as by the lack of standardized reference datasets [13]. As a result, existing approaches remain largely data-driven, rely on dataset-specific labels, and offer limited alignment with expert tribological reasoning. Neuro-symbolic approaches address this gap by integrating learning-based perception with explicit knowledge representation [3,23]. In particular, Answer Set Programming (ASP) [8] provides a declarative framework for representing expert knowledge and reasoning under incomplete information, and has been applied in hybrid systems that combine symbolic reasoning with data-driven perception across a range of domains [2,24,27].

In this paper, we present initial steps toward a neuro-symbolic framework for abrasive wear analysis. We elicit and formalize expert tribological knowledge as a vocabulary of abrasion mechanisms and observable surface features, together with evidential rules encoded in ASP. The proposed framework combines an Encoder–Decoder neural network for SEM image segmentation with this symbolic knowledge base, where neural outputs are abstracted into neural encoder–decoder atoms (ned-atoms) that associate segmented image evidence with symbolic feature predicates. These ned-atoms provide probabilistic facts to the ASP layer, which performs rule-based inference over abrasion mechanisms, enabling interpretable and reproducible wear classification.

2 Knowledge Elicitation

A knowledge elicitation study was conducted to elicit tribology expert knowledge. Two tribology experts (20+ years of experience) were interviewed, after which the material was analyzed using established knowledge elicitation methodology [4,6]. In this process, expert statements were coded into a vocabulary of abrasion mechanisms and observable surface features. For example, experts described a type of mechanism where surface material is laterally displaced without removal of the original surface, referred to as "*ploughing*". This was described as: "[...] the original surface is visible in the scratch bottom [...]" and "[...] scratch walls are well defined [...]". In contrast, scratches showing material removal were associated with "*cutting*". This was described as: "[...] no defined scratch walls are present [...]" and "[...] scratch walls exhibit overhang or chipping [...]" (see Table 1 for a selected part of the qualitative analysis).

This vocabulary provides the conceptual basis for the evidential rules over scratches. We encode the rules in Answer Set Programming (ASP) [8] using definite clauses of the form $h \leftarrow b_1, \ldots, b_m$, where h and b_i $(1 \leq i \leq m)$ are propositional atoms. A program P^{exp}, capturing expert tribology knowledge, includes the following rules, where *scratch(S)*:

Table 1. Extracted codes from interview transcript (selected excerpt).

No.	Coded definitions
1	"Ploughing is dominating when the original surface is visible in the bottom of the scratch." [PLOUGHING-DOMINATING][ORIGINAL-SURFACE-VISIBLE]
2	"Ploughing is dominating when the scratch walls are well defined and otherwise featureless." [PLOUGHING-DOMINATING][DEFINED-WALLS][FEATURELESS-BOTTOM][UNDEFINED]
3	"A small depth-to-width ratio reinforces the impression of ploughing." [PLOUGHING-REINFORCED][DEPTH-WIDTH-RATIO-LOW]
4	"Cutting is dominating when no defined scratch walls are present." [CUTTING-DOMINATING][NO-DEFINED-WALLS]
5	"Cutting is indicated when the scratch walls exhibit overhang." [CUTTING-WEAK-SIGN][WALL-OVERHANG][WALL-OVERHANG-PRESENT]
6	"Cutting is dominating when scratch wall overhang is large relative to the scratch width." [CUTTING-DOMINATING][WALL-OVERHANG-HIGH]
7	"A clear sign of cutting is present when scratch wall overhang is of medium extent." [CUTTING-CLEAR-SIGN][WALL-OVERHANG-MEDIUM]
8	"A weak sign of cutting is present when scratch wall overhang is small." [CUTTING-WEAK-SIGN][WALL-OVERHANG-LOW]

$$ploughing\_dominating(S) \leftarrow original\_surface\_visible(S, \text{yes}).$$
$$ploughing\_dominating(S) \leftarrow wall\_definition(S, \text{defined}),\ bottom(S, \text{featureless}).$$
$$ploughing\_reinforced(S) \leftarrow depth\_width\_ratio(S, \text{low}).$$
$$ploughing\_reinforced(S) \leftarrow contrast(S, \text{low}).$$
$$cutting\_dominating(S) \leftarrow wall\_definition(S, \text{undefined}).$$
$$cutting\_weak\_sign(S) \leftarrow wall\_definition(S, \text{defined}),\ wall\_overhang(S, \text{present}).$$
$$cutting\_dominating(S) \leftarrow wall\_definition(S, \text{defined}),\ wall\_overhang(S, \text{high}).$$
$$cutting\_clear\_sign(S) \leftarrow wall\_definition(S, \text{defined}),\ wall\_overhang(S, \text{medium}).$$
$$cutting\_weak\_sign(S) \leftarrow wall\_definition(S, \text{defined}),\ wall\_overhang(S, \text{low}).$$

Here, *dominating*, *clear sign*, *weak sign*, and *reinforced* denote different evidence categories for an abrasion mechanism. Each rule links a small set of observable feature atoms (e.g., wall definition, surface visibility, overhang, chipping) to higher-level abrasion predicates, thereby operationalizing the expert vocabulary for this domain. For instance, rules deriving *ploughing_ dominating* are triggered by features indicating plastic deformation without material removal, while rules deriving *cutting_ ** predicates capture progressively stronger evidence of material removal at scratch walls. Together, the elicited concepts and rules provide a formal vocabulary for meta-reasoning about low-level abrasive wear observations. In the next section, these rules will be extended with probabilistic facts, which are produced by Encoder-Decoder neural networks (NED). Then, the set of rules and probabilistic facts will define NED programs.

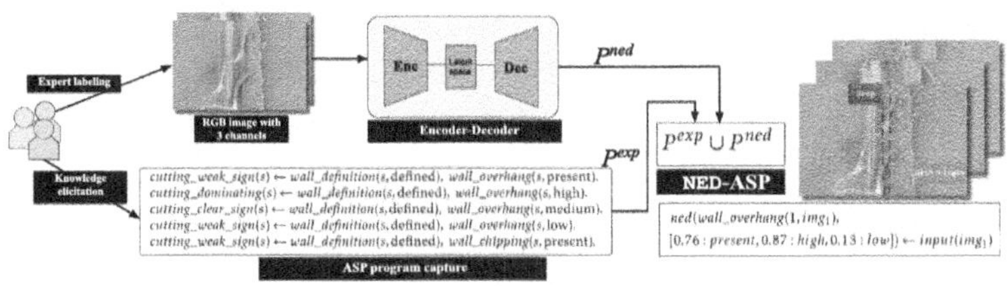

Fig. 1. Expert tribologist define the scratches (knowledge elicitation) and labeled part of the images set. The `NED` program provide a description of a metal scratch.

3 `NED`-Programs

We extend NeurASP [27] by introducing *neural encoder-decoder atoms* (`ned-atoms`) based on an Encoder-Decoder neural network architecture (see Fig. 1) that we call $\texttt{NED} : \mathcal{I} \rightarrow \mathcal{Z} \times \mathcal{O}$. Here, the latent representation $\mathbf{z}$ facilitates both *prediction* (logits) and *reconstruction* (synthesis).

Definition 1 (*ned-atom*). *Let $t \in T$ be an input tensor term (where T is a set of input tensors) and $\mathbf{V} = \{v_i\}_{i=1}^{n}$ be random variables over domains D_i. A **ned-atom** is defined as: $\mathbf{c} \triangleq ned\left(\varphi(e,t), [v_1 \dots v_m]^{d_1}, \dots, [v_1 \dots v_n]^{d_k}\right)$ where φ is the `NED` operation. $\Sigma^{ned}_{(T,\mathbf{V})}$ is akk the possible ned-atoms built from T and $\mathbf{V}$.*

Definition 2 (*ned-rule*). *A **ned-rule** is a rule of the form $a^{\mathbf{ned}} \leftarrow a_1, \dots, a_n$, where $a^{\mathbf{ned}} \in \Sigma^{ned}_{(\mathcal{I},\mathcal{V})}$ is a **ned-atom** and each a_i ($1 \leq i \leq n$) is an atom. A **ned-rule** is* safe *if all input-tensor variables that appear in $a^{\mathbf{ned}}$ also appear in an atom a_i.*

An instance of a `ned-rule` of the above form associates a perceptual predicate with an input SEM image.

$$ned(wall\_overhang(1, img), [present, high, low]) \leftarrow input(img). \tag{1}$$

Given a ned-rule, we get probabilistic facts of the form $\pi : a$, where a is a ground atom and $\pi \in [0, 1]$. For instance, grounding Rule (1) yields the following set of probabilistic facts.

$$\mathcal{F}_{img} = \begin{Bmatrix} 0.76 : wall\_overhang(present), \\ 0.87 : wall\_overhang(high), \\ 0.13 : wall\_overhang(low) \end{Bmatrix}.$$

Informally speaking, the semantics of ned-programs is characterized as follows: Given a set of ned-rules, we get a set of probabilistic facts $\mathcal{F}_{img}$. These facts are treated as observations and added to the symbolic program, yielding the grounded program $P_{img} = P^{exp} \cup \mathcal{F}_{img}$. The semantic of this program is handled by the probabilistic ASP semantics in [14].

4 Discussion and Future Work

This work introduces a novel neuro-symbolic framework for the characterization of abrasive wear, representing a significant departure from traditional data-driven models [26]. To our knowledge, the integration of expert-captured knowledge within an Encoder-Decoder neural-symbolic architecture is a novel contribution to the field of tribology. A key technical contribution is the introduction of `ned`-atoms, which extend from a previous neuro-symbolic approach [27] that is primarily constrained to discriminative classification, our `ned`-atom formulation allows for a multi-feature mapping of latent variables to multiple symbolic predicates. Furthermore, the underlying NED-architecture is dual-purpose; it supports both discriminative tasks (identifying wear mechanisms) and generative processes (reconstructing surface morphologies), thus unifying perception and reconstruction within a single symbolic framework. Future work will scale the vocabulary through broader expert consensus. We will explore the NED architecture's generative capabilities. Moreover, we will fully formalize the logical and operational semantics of NED programs.

Acknowledgments. This work was partially supported by the Wallenberg AI, Autonomous Systems and Software Program (WASP) and the Wallenberg Initiative Materials Science for Sustainability (WISE) funded by the Knut and Alice Wallenberg Foundation.

References

1. Angermann, C., et al.: Surface topography characterization using a simple optical device and artificial neural networks. Eng. Appl. Artif. Intell. **123**, 106337 (2023)
2. Berglund, W., Brännström, A.: Heuristic search and constraint verification for value-centric electrification planning. In: Hagedorn, L., Schmid, U., Winter, S., Woltran, S. (eds.) Interdisciplinary Science and Research Conference on Digital Humanism, pp. 3–18. Springer, Cham (2025). https://doi.org/10.1007/978-3-032-11108-1_1
3. Bhuyan, B.P., Ramdane-Cherif, A., Tomar, R., Singh, T.: Neuro-symbolic artificial intelligence: a survey. Neural Comput. Appl. **36**(21), 12809–12844 (2024)
4. Brännström, A., Wester, J., Nieves, J.C.: A formal understanding of computational empathy in interactive agents. Cogn. Syst. Res. **85**, 101203 (2024)
5. Chang, H., Borghesani, P., Peng, Z.: Automated assessment of gear wear mechanism and severity using mould images and convolutional neural networks. Tribol. Int. **147**, 106280 (2020)
6. Chun Tie, Y., Birks, M., Francis, K.: Grounded theory research: a design framework for novice researchers. SAGE Open Med. **7**, 2050312118822927 (2019)
7. Ferguson, S., Fielke, J., Riley, T.: Wear of cultivator shares in abrasive South Australian soils. J. Agric. Eng. Res. **69**(2), 99–105 (1998)
8. Gebser, M., Kaminski, R., Kaufmann, B., Schaub, T.: Answer Set Solving in Practice. Morgan and Claypool Publishers (2012)
9. Goel, G.S.: A numerical study of tillage tool wear during plowing of sandy soil. Ph.D. thesis. The University of North Carolina at Charlotte (2013)
10. Hokkirigawa, K., Kato, K.: An experimental and theoretical investigation of ploughing, cutting and wedge formation during abrasive wear. Tribol. Int. **21**(1), 51–57 (1988)
11. Hutchings, I.: Tribology: friction and wear of engineering materials (1992). Edward Arnold (fax:+ 44 (0) 732 461321) 1992, 352pp, ε19. 95 paperback, ISBN 0 340 56184
12. Jones, T., Cao, Y.: Tool wear prediction based on multisensor data fusion and machine learning. Int. J. Adv. Manuf. Technol., 1–13 (2025)
13. Lim, S.C., Ashby, M.: Overview no. 55 wear-mechanism maps. Acta metallurgica **35**(1), 1–24 (1987)
14. Mauá, D.D., Cozman, F.G.: Complexity results for probabilistic answer set programming. Int. J. Approx. Reason. **118**, 133–154 (2020)
15. Owsiak, Z.: Wear of spring tine cultivator points in sandy loam and light clay soils in Southern Poland. Soil Tillage Res. **50**(3–4), 333–340 (1999)
16. Quirke, S., Scheffler, O., Allen, C.: An evaluation of the wear behaviour of metallic materials subjected to soil abrasion. Soil Tillage Res. **11**(1), 27–42 (1988)
17. Rabinowicz, E., Dunn, L., Russell, P.: A study of abrasive wear under three-body conditions. Wear **4**(5), 345–355 (1961)
18. Sieberg, P.M., Hanke, S.: Challenges and potentials in the classification of wear mechanisms by artificial intelligence. Wear **522**, 204725 (2023)
19. Sieberg, P.M., Kurtulan, D., Hanke, S.: Wear mechanism classification using artificial intelligence. Materials **15**(7), 2358 (2022)
20. Singh, J., Chatha, S.S., Sidhu, B.S.: Abrasive wear characteristics and microstructure of fe-based overlaid ploughshares in different field conditions. Soil Tillage Res. **205**, 104771 (2021)
21. Stachowiak, G., Stachowiak, G.: The effects of particle characteristics on three-body abrasive wear. Wear **249**(3–4), 201–207 (2001)

22. Valenzuela, B., Viáfara, C., Penagos, J., Martínez, F.: Wear mechanisms and severity level classification in iron ore transfer chute linings by propagating regional labels coded as embedding deep learning vectors. Mater. Today Commun. **38**, 107952 (2024)
23. Wang, S., Han, Z., Wei, H., Wu, T., Zhou, J.: An integrated knowledge and data model for adaptive diagnosis of lubricant conditions. Tribol. Int. **199**, 109914 (2024)
24. Wielinga, S., Heyninck, J.: Interpretable hybrid machine learning models using FOLD-R++ and answer set programming. arXiv preprint arXiv:2506.19573 (2025)
25. Wojtowicz, M., Elo, R., Heinrichs Lindgren, J., Wiklund, U., Bäckström, A., Jacobson, S.: Influence of soil type on initial wear mechanisms of tillage tools when studied in a new mobile pendulum test. In: Proceedings of the Leeds–Lyon Symposium on Tribology (2025)
26. Wu, X., Liu, Y., Zhou, X., Mou, A.: Automatic identification of tool wear based on convolutional neural network in face milling process. Sensors **19**(18), 3817 (2019)
27. Yang, Z., Ishay, A., Lee, J.: NeurASP: embracing neural networks into answer set programming. In: International Joint Conference on Artificial Intelligence (2020). https://api.semanticscholar.org/CorpusID:262500883
28. Zum Gahr, K.H.: Wear by hard particles. Tribol. Int. **31**(10), 587–596 (1998)

The Intermediate Knowledge Problem

Mattias Brännström[(✉)], Themis Dimitra Xanthopoulou, and Andreas Brännström

Department of Computing Science, Umeå University, Umeå, Sweden
{mattias.brannstrom,themis.xanthopoulou,andreas.brannstrom}@umu.se

Abstract. We examine the Intermediate Knowledge Problem (IKP): the challenge of maintaining coherent, goal-aligned intermediate representations during multi-step reasoning. The issue is particularly acute in automated knowledge elicitation and engineering, where analysis relies on provisional and revisable artifacts. Using Grounded Theory as a running example, we illustrate why existing symbolic systems and large language model based pipelines provide limited support for such intermediate knowledge, identifying a central obstacle to automating knowledge elicitation and engineering methods.

Keywords: Knowledge engineering · Intermediate knowledge

1 Introduction

Knowledge Elicitation and Engineering (KEE) [17,18] is the systematic activity of constructing an explicit and structured representation of domain knowledge for use in computational systems. KEE is not merely an extraction of pre-existing facts, but a teleological (purposeful, goal directed) modeling process in which relevant concepts, relations, and assumptions are identified, organized, and refined with respect to a given task or application [18]. As such, KEE supports the development of artifacts such as ontologies [19], conceptual models [11], and task-oriented knowledge structures that underpin knowledge-based and decision-support systems [2,8], drawing on sources including expert interaction, documents, and empirical or observational data.

Elicitation is not a linear transformation from data to theory, but an incremental, task-oriented, and highly perspective-dependent analytic activity, in which even neutral representations are necessarily partial [7,13]. In qualitative research, the move from data to theories, characterized as the conceptual leap, is considered a mysterious and highly individualistic process that resists simple methodological prescription [10]. Grounded Theory (GT) [14], a qualitative research method, exemplifies this incremental character by relying on intermediate artifacts such as annotations, memos, and emerging conceptual distinctions, such as codes and categories, to structure analysis as understanding develops.

This incremental and essentially teleological character poses challenges for automated reasoning and elicitation systems. Contemporary artificial reasoning

A.-Y. Turhan and J. Virtema (Eds.): FoIKS 2026, LNCS 16475, pp. 334–340, 2026.
https://doi.org/10.1007/978-3-032-21540-6_20

systems, from rule-based frameworks [12,20] to large language models [1,4], excel at deriving outputs from inputs but struggle to maintain continuity of understanding across the multiple steps that link the two. Between initial data and a final conclusion lies a sequence of intermediate representations, partial results, evolving hypotheses, and contextual reframings, through which a system must preserve what it has already learned while adapting to what it newly infers. We refer to this requirement as the *Intermediate Knowledge Problem* (IKP).

Definition 1 (Intermediate Knowledge Problem). *The* Intermediate Knowledge Problem (IKP) *is the problem of sustaining a coherent, causally and semantically grounded body of intermediate knowledge (IK) within a multi-step process of reasoning, learning, or analysis. It concerns how meaning, evidential grounding, and interpretive commitments are preserved and transformed across material representations (M) that are derived from, or evolve out of, raw or evidential material (R) toward a goal (Q).*

The IKP arises whenever reasoning is extended over time or distributed across modules, prompts, or agents. Each reasoning step may alter not only what is known, but also the interpretive frame within which earlier knowledge is understood. If this evolving body of intermediate knowledge is not explicitly represented, systems risk semantic drift, loss of contextual relevance, and incoherent integration of results. Addressing the IKP therefore requires representational structures that can preserve, revise, and reinterpret IK in a manner aligned with the overall purpose of reasoning, rather than merely accumulating textual traces of prior outputs. The remainder of this paper explores the IKP, where GT is used as a running example.

2 Characterizing the Intermediate Knowledge Problem

Table 1. Summary of naïve approaches without explicit intermediate knowledge (IK).

	IK	Key limitations
A	$\varnothing$	Context-free acts; no interpretive commitments.
B	$\bigcup_0^t M_t$	*IK* merely becomes new material for interpretation.
C	M_t (formalized)	Premature formalization; loses evidential grounding.
D	Embedding(R)	Collapse of perspective; loss of goal-directedness.

We illustrate the IKP by considering the modeling steps of GT (see Fig. 1). In GT, codes are not fixed in advance but emerge through iterative comparison between data segments, prior coding decisions, and the analyst's sensitizing concepts, remaining provisional and subject to revision throughout the process [14].

We will call accumulating prior outputs the *material trace* M suffixed by t if referring to a particular timestep $0 \leq t \leq n$. During coding, segments of the raw data R are examined and interpreted by assigning codes. We can consider four *'naive'* approaches to automating this, where IK is not explicitly represented (summarized in Table 1.

A: *IK* is $\varnothing$ and not Represented Beyond M. Here IK is not involved at all. This fails because individual coding acts in GT are not self-sufficient: the appropriateness of a code depends on prior distinctions, and interpretive commitments not contained in the codes M_t themselves.

B: *IK* $= \bigcup_0^t M_t$. If IK is seen just as the accumulation of prior material it becomes more material requiring reinterpretation rather than a stable interpretive frame. New coding collapses into reinterpretation of prior material where new coding decisions are only weakly constrained by earlier ones.

C: *IK* is a Formalization of M_t, e.g. Ontologies or Graphs. At the coding stage, this fixes interpretive distinctions too early, turning provisional sense-making into detached formal symbols and thereby breaking their evidential grounding while crystallizing early assumptions.

D: *IK* is Implicit in Latent Representations. Learned parameters or embeddings may capture statistical regularities of the source material but collapse perspective: they encode correlations without preserving the purposive, question-dependent reasoning that motivates the analysis.

Hence, IK cannot be reduced to merely M—the resulting codes or their accumulation (cases **A, B**)—nor to neutral descriptions or implicit statistical encodings over R (case **D**). Instead, it must function as a *teleologically constrained epistemic structure* that is both *persistent* (addressing the deficiencies in cases **A** and **B**) and *commitment-preserving* (addressing those in **B** and **C**), constraining interpretation relative to prior commitments and the goal Q.

In the following section, we illustrate these requirements through the successive steps of Grounded Theory, using it as a concrete example of how intermediate knowledge supports continuity between raw data, interpretive acts, and emerging theory.

3 Intermediate Knowledge in Grounded Theory

Given that IK cannot be left unaddressed, we take a step toward exploring the IKP by making explicit the epistemic continuity required for automation and multi-step reasoning, using the steps of GT as a concrete illustration (Fig. 1). We tentatively illustrate IK as an action guiding dual-relational **epistemic graph** defined as the tuple (and graphically illustrated):

$$IK = \langle V, E_S, E_H, \gamma, \Sigma \rangle$$

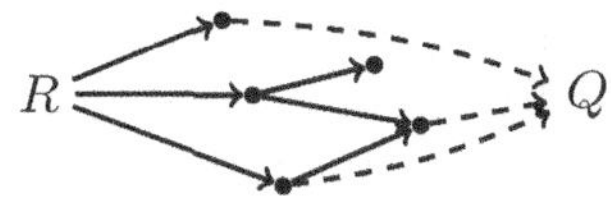

where V are epistemic nodes including evidence $R \subseteq V$ and goal $Q \in V$, E_S denoted by $v_i \rightarrow v_j, (v_i, v_j) \in V$ are grounded relations (data-derived or entailed), E_H denoted by $v_i \dashrightarrow v_j, (v_i, v_j) \in V$ are hypothetical relations (goal-directed expectations) which capture teleological commitments. The partial grounding map $\gamma : V \rightharpoonup \Sigma$ associates epistemic nodes with elements of an evidential or theoretical substrate from which they are derived. The graph suggests epistemic actions guided by hypothetical relations. Updates are additive and either introduce new nodes, relations, or internal structure.

Teleological coherence requires that IK initially contains at least one hypothetical path from R to Q, expressing the assumption that analysis of R can address the guiding question Q. In GT, such hypothetical structure reflects the theoretical frame with which analysis begins. Memos and early interpretations explicitly contribute to building IK from the outset.

We can see the process of GT from raw data to theory as a stepwise attempt to *ground* hypothetical relations E_H into data-derived relations E_S. When a path $R \rightarrow ... \rightarrow Q$ is established, this path is a grounded theory answering Q. While analogous to chunking in automated pipelines, in GT, **Segmentation** explicitly semantically relates segments. Segments each relate to R with solid E_S arrows but additional nodes and relations may be introduced. M_1 consist of the segments.

In GT, **Open coding** is the descriptive and interpretative process of assigning codes to segments. M_2 is the resulting segment, code pairs. Without IK, coding loses coherence and teleology. Every decision of introducing a new code can be seen as a change in E_H, supposing new paths to Q. Codes added to segments contribute to grounding E_S.

In the **Categorization** step, identified codes are grouped together forming a hierarchical taxonomy over the source material and consolidate similar codes. M_3 is the resulting taxonomy. Without IK, this categorization is difficult as codes on their own are semantically light, expressed with labels or short sequences. Taking IK into account, however, codes have additional semantics and categorization can be reduced to grouping over E_S by shared paths and possibly consolidating over shared γ.

In **Axial Coding** new E_S connections between nodes represent causal or processual understanding suggested by data E_S and E_H, something difficult to achieve without IK. M_4 is or is approaching an ontology structure. **Theory**

formation is a teleological selection over themes: solidly related categories and paths bridging R and Q. Here M_5 is the theory and converge with IK.

In GT, data collection and coding are iterated until theoretical saturation, making M non-monotonic and open to revision. For IK to provide stability towards grounding $R \rightarrow \ldots \dashrightarrow Q$, IK must grow preserving commitments, possibly analogous to an epistemic search guided by a heuristic on E_H.

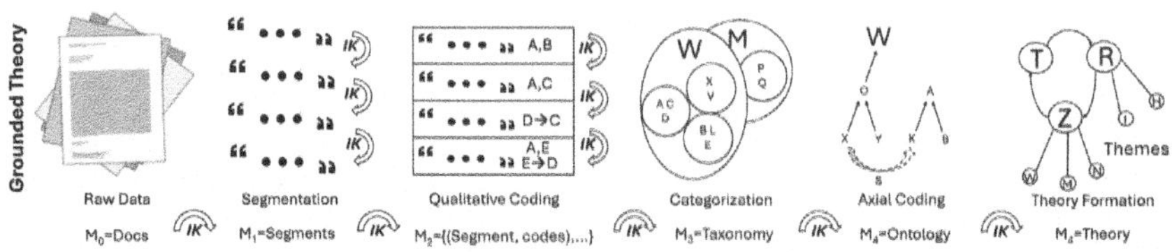

Fig. 1. Steps of Grounded Theory; Intermediate knowledge (IK).

4 Discussion and Future Work

Most existing automated knowledge elicitation approaches focus primarily on the resulting knowledge artifacts rather than on the dynamics of the elicitation process itself. Sabou, et al. (2024) [16] surveys a body of work on knowledge engineering systems that combine machine learning and Semantic Web technologies for tasks such as knowledge graph creation, extension, and completion, covering embedding-based approaches [9,21], data-driven knowledge graph construction systems [3], and rule-based or hybrid neurosymbolic methods [5,6,12,20]. Within this literature, representation learning over symbolic structures is commonly used to support knowledge base completion [9], or through pipelines that incorporate entity attributes for relation prediction [21]. Other systems construct knowledge graphs directly from data sources [3]. In addition, symbolic knowledge is derived through rule induction over existing graphs [5,6,15].

Throughout these approaches, intermediate representations serve the production of final artifacts rather than sustaining goal-directed reasoning. Without such direction, elicitation lacks a stable epistemic standpoint, reflecting the limits of perspective-free representations [7,13]. Recent LLM-based elicitation pipelines exhibit incomplete coverage, misclassifications, and hallucinations [1,4], widely attributed to limitations in control and grounding during multi-step generation.

Taken together, this indicates a structural lack of persistent intermediate representations during elicitation, particularly with respect to their goal alignment. This paper deliberately stops at examining the problem. A necessary next step is a formal characterization of the IKP, enabling rigorous evaluation, followed by implementations that make IK explicit. Grounded Theory provides a natural test case, with hybrid human-machine workflows as a realistic near-term direction and automated pipelines as a longer-term benchmark for evaluating IKP solutions in agentic systems.

Acknowledgments. This work was partially supported by the Wallenberg AI, Autonomous Systems and Software Program (WASP) funded by the Knut and Alice Wallenberg Foundation.

References

1. Van den Bent, S., Pernisch, R., Schlobach, S.: Investigating knowledge elicitation automation with large language models. Semantic Web J. (2025)
2. Berglund, W., Brännström, A.: Heuristic search and constraint verification for value-centric electrification planning. In: Interdisciplinary Science and Research Conference on Digital Humanism, pp. 3–18. Springer (2025)
3. Buscaldi, D., Dessì, D., Motta, E., Osborne, F., Reforgiato Recupero, D.: Mining scholarly data for fine-grained knowledge graph construction. In: CEUR Workshop Proceedings, vol. 2377, pp. 21–30 (2019)
4. Dong, S.: Leveraging llms for unstructured direct elicitation of decision rules. Cust. Needs Solut. **11**(1), 10 (2024)
5. Gad-Elrab, M.H., Stepanova, D., Urbani, J., Weikum, G.: Exception-enriched rule learning from knowledge graphs. In: International Semantic Web Conference, pp. 234–251. Springer (2016)
6. Galárraga, L., Teflioudi, C., Hose, K., Suchanek, F.M.: Fast rule mining in ontological knowledge bases with amie+. VLDB J. **24**(6), 707–730 (2015)
7. Giere, R.N.: Scientific perspectivism. University of Chicago press (2019)
8. Granström, J., Brännström, A.: Ontology-based risk assessment in smelting plant logistics. In: The 4th International Conference on Hybrid Human-Artificial Intelligence, Pisa, Italy, June 9–13, 2025, pp. 24–24 (2025)
9. Hao, J., Chen, M., Yu, W., Sun, Y., Wang, W.: Universal representation learning of knowledge bases by jointly embedding instances and ontological concepts. In: Proceedings of the 25th ACM SIGKDD International Conference on Knowledge Discovery & Data Mining, pp. 1709–1719 (2019)
10. Klag, M., Langley, A.: Approaching the conceptual leap in qualitative research. Int. J. Manage. Rev. **15**(2), 149–166 (2013). https://doi.org/10.1111/j.1468-2370.2012.00349.x, https://doi.org/10.1111/j.1468-2370.2012.00349.x
11. Krogstie, J., Lindland, O.I., Sindre, G.: Defining quality aspects for conceptual models. In: Information System Concepts: Towards a consolidation of views, pp. 216–231. Springer (1995)
12. Minervini, P., Costabello, L., Muñoz, E., Nováček, V., Vandenbussche, P.Y.: Regularizing knowledge graph embeddings via equivalence and inversion axioms. In: Joint European Conference on Machine Learning and Knowledge Discovery in Databases, pp. 668–683. Springer (2017)
13. Nagel, T.: The view from nowhere. oxford University Press (1989)
14. Oktay, J.S.: Grounded theory. Oxford University Press (2012)
15. Roy, A., et al.: Diag2graph: Representing deep learning diagrams in research papers as knowledge graphs. In: 2020 IEEE international conference on image processing (ICIP), pp. 2581–2585. IEEE (2020)
16. Sabou, M., Llugiqi, M., Ekaputra, F.J., Waltersdorfer, L., Tsaneva, S.: Knowledge engineering in the age of neurosymbolic systems. Neurosymbolic Artif. Intell. **1**, 29498732251320080 (2025)
17. Schreiber, G.: Knowledge engineering. Foundations of artificial intelligence **3**, 929–946 (2008)

18. Studer, R., Benjamins, V.R., Fensel, D.: Knowledge engineering: principles and methods. Data Knowl. Eng. **25**(1–2), 161–197 (1998)
19. Uschold, M., Gruninger, M.: Ontologies: principles, methods and applications. Knowl. Eng. Rev. **11**(2), 93–136 (1996)
20. Wang, M., Rong, E., Zhuo, H., Zhu, H.: Embedding knowledge graphs based on transitivity and asymmetry of rules. In: Pacific-Asia Conference on Knowledge Discovery and Data Mining, pp. 141–153. Springer (2018)
21. Zhang, Z., Cao, L., Chen, X., Tang, W., Xu, Z., Meng, Y.: Representation learning of knowledge graphs with entity attributes. IEEE Access **8**, 7435–7441 (2020)

Axiomatizing Variants of Approximate Inclusion

Matilda Häggblom(✉)

University of Helsinki, Helsinki, Finland
matilda.haggblom@helsinki.fi

Abstract. We study two approximate variants of inclusion atoms and examine the axiomatization and computational complexity of their implication problems. The approximate variants allow for some imperfection in a team (corresponding to a unirelational database), and differ in how this degree is measured. One considers the error relative to the size of the team, while the other applies a fixed threshold independent of size. We obtain complete axiomatizations for both under some arity restrictions. In particular, restricted to unary atoms, the implication problem for each approximate variant is decidable in polynomial time.

Keywords: Inclusion dependency · Uncertainty · Team semantics · Implication problem · Axiomatization

1 Introduction

A collection of data can be represented by a team [10], i.e., a set of assignments. Evaluating team atoms that describe relationships between variables is often more fruitful when done in a team as opposed to a single assignment. For instance, evaluating whether the value of a variable y is functionally dependent on the value of a variable x is trivial in a single assignment, while a team can contain two assignments that assign the same value to x but different values to y. Since teams correspond to unirelational databases, variables to attributes, and team atoms to dependencies, the results of this paper are transferable from the team semantic setting to the database setting.

To reason meaningfully about team atoms that capture dependency relations between variables in a team that contains errors, we permit these atoms to *approximately* hold. For team atoms that capture dependency relations—such as functional and inclusion dependencies—the approximations may permit moving to a similar subteam or superteam before verifying the satisfaction of the atom. This approach connects naturally to subset and superset repairs studied in the literature on consistent query answering (see, e.g., [2]).

Two fundamental team atoms, dependence and exclusion atoms, are downward-closed: if a team satisfies the atom, then so do all its subteams. Naturally, their approximate variants allow moving to a sufficiently large subteam before checking the satisfaction of the original atom. Each of their implication

A.-Y. Turhan and J. Virtema (Eds.): FoIKS 2026, LNCS 16475, pp. 341–346, 2026.
https://doi.org/10.1007/978-3-032-21540-6_21

problems has been studied in [7,11]. The implication problem asks whether a given set of atoms entails another, and its axiomatization provides a system of axioms and rules to resolve this question. These axiomatizations thus offer a logical account of entailments between atoms, with potential applications in improving algorithms related to the discovery of such dependency relations.

Another widely studied team atom is the *inclusion atom* [4], which is not downward-closed but union-closed: if any nonempty number of teams satisfies the inclusion atom, then so does their union. An inclusion atom has the form $x \subseteq y$ and is satisfied in a team if all values of x are among the values of y. For instance, an inclusion atom `MANAGER` $\subseteq$ `EMPLOYEE` expresses that all managers are employees. If a team does not satisfy such an inclusion atom—due to some minor issue like a spelling mistake—it may still be warranted to evaluate if it *approximately* holds, up to some degree of error.

We investigate two approximate variants of the inclusion atom $x \subseteq y$, one in which the number of values of x allowed to be absent from y is fixed, and one where this number is relative to the size of the team. Approximate inclusion atoms/dependencies are also motivated in the database setting. In a flawed database, the discovery of an approximate inclusion atom can help with data management tasks such as schema enforcement and data cleaning (see, e.g., [9]).

Our main result is obtained by adapting the system for inclusion dependencies [1] and completeness proofs from the literature [5,11] to axiomatize the implication problems for two approximate inclusion atoms under certain arity restrictions. Furthermore, we determine the computational complexity of their corresponding decision problems. This paper takes initial steps toward axiomatizing approximate variants of union-closed team atoms and identifies multiple directions for future work.

2 Approximate Inclusion Atoms

Let us first recall basic definitions related to teams and inclusion atoms. A team T is a finite set of assignments $s : \mathcal{V} \longrightarrow M$, where $\mathcal{V}$ is a set of variables and M is a set of values. We write $x, y, \ldots$ for finite (possibly empty) sequences of variables, with $|x|, |y|, \ldots$ denoting the lengths of the sequences. For $x = x_1 \ldots x_n$ and $y = y_1 \ldots y_m$, xy denotes the sequence $x_1 \ldots x_n y_1 \ldots y_m$. We write $s(x)$ as shorthand for the tuple $s(x_1) \ldots s(x_n)$, and $T[x]$ to denote the set of values x is assigned to by the assignments in T, i.e., $\{s(x) \mid s \in T\}$.

Inclusion atoms are of the form $x \subseteq y$, where $|x| = |y|$ is the arity of the atom. We assume that no variable is repeated within the respective sequences x and y. The semantics clause for inclusion atoms is as follows.

$$T \models x \subseteq y \text{ iff } T[x] \subseteq T[y].$$

For a set of atoms Σ, we write $\Sigma \models x \subseteq y$ if for all teams T, $T \models x \subseteq y$ whenever $T \models u \subseteq v$ for all $u \subseteq v \in \Sigma$.

We define *quantity approximate inclusion* (Q-INC) atoms $x \subseteq_n y$ that allow at most n values of $T[x]$ to be absent from $T[y]$, independent of the size of the team. We also define *ratio approximate inclusion* (R-INC) atoms $x \subseteq_p y$, where the permissible number of missing values depends on the size of the team.

Definition 1. *Let $n \in \mathbb{N}$ and $p \in [0,1] \cap \mathbb{Q}$.*

(Q-INC) $T \models x \subseteq_n y$ iff $|T[x] \setminus T[y]| \leq n$.
(R-INC) $T \models x \subseteq_p y$ iff $|T[x] \setminus T[y]| \leq p|T|$.

For both variants, $x \subseteq_0 y$ coincides with the standard inclusion atom.

Next, we adapt the system for inclusion dependencies from [1] to the approximate variants.

Definition 2. *We obtain rules Q1-Q5 for Q-INC atoms by letting $a, b \in \mathbb{N}$, and similarly, rules R1-R6 for R-INC atoms by letting $a, b \in [0,1] \cap \mathbb{Q}$.*

$(Q1/R1)$ $x \subseteq_0 x$.
$(Q2/R2)$ *If* $x \subseteq_a z$ *and* $z \subseteq_b y$, *then* $x \subseteq_{a+b} y$.
$(Q3/R3)$ *If* $xyz \subseteq_a uvw$, *then* $xzy \subseteq_a uwv$, *provided that* $|x| = |u|$, $|y| = |v|$.
$(Q4/R4)$ *If* $xy \subseteq_a uv$, *then* $x \subseteq_a u$.
$(Q5/R5)$ *If* $x \subseteq_a y$, *then* $x \subseteq_b y$, *provided that* $b \geq a$.
$(-/R6)$ $x \subseteq_1 y$.

To be precise, rule R2 only includes the instances when $a + b \leq 1$. Note that by the syntax of the atoms, rules Q4 and R4 demand that $|x| = |u|$ and $|y| = |v|$.

Proving that the rules are sound is straightforward. Furthermore, we obtain completeness results for Q-INC and R-INC atoms under certain arity restrictions, thereby allowing us to omit some of the rules.

Theorem 1. *(i) Let $\Sigma \cup \{x \subseteq_n y\}$ be a finite set of Q-INC atoms with the arities of the atoms in Σ being at most that of $l = |x|$. If $\Sigma \models x \subseteq_n y$, then $\Sigma \vdash x \subseteq_n y$ using rules from $\{Q1, Q2, Q3, Q5\}$.*
(ii) Let $\Sigma \cup \{x \subseteq_p y\}$ be a finite set of unary R-INC atoms. If $\Sigma \models x \subseteq_p y$, then $\Sigma \vdash x \subseteq_p y$ using rules from $\{R1, R2, R5, R6\}$.

Proof sketch. In both cases, we assume that we do not have the stated derivation, and construct counterexample teams T that satisfy all atoms in the assumption set Σ, but not the atom in the conclusion. Let i^l be the tuple $i \dots i$ of length l.

(i) Suppose that $\Sigma \not\vdash x \subseteq_n y$. We construct T by taking the disjoint union of counterexample teams T_i, $i \in \{1, \dots, n+1\}$, for standard inclusion atoms as in [5], each using two values $\{i, i^*\}$. Importantly, in each T_i, all tuples over $\{i, i^*\}$ are in $T_i[v]$ for variable sequences v shorter than $|x| = l$, and at most one tuple is missing from $T_i[v']$ if $|v'| = l$. Define $T = T_1 \cup \dots \cup T_{n+1}$ by letting $s \in T_i$ if and only if:
(1) $s : \mathcal{V} \longrightarrow \{i, i^*\}$, and
(2) for every sequence w such that $|w| = l$ and $\Sigma \vdash x \subseteq_m w$, where m is the smallest such integer, we require $s(w) \neq i^l$ for each $1 \leq i \leq m$.
We see an example of such a counterexample team in Table 1.

(ii) We construct a counterexample team inspired by the one for approximate dependence atoms in [11]. Suppose that $\Sigma \not\vdash x \subseteq_p y$ and let $n-1$ be the least common denominator for the approximations in $\Sigma \cup \{x \subseteq_p y\}$. For each approximation q, let q' be such that $q = \frac{q'}{n-1}$. Let $w \in \mathcal{V}$, and let $T = \{s_1, \dots, s_n\}$ be built according to the smallest q for which $\Sigma \vdash x \subseteq_q w$, by defining

$$s_i(w) = \begin{cases} 1 & \text{if } i \leq q' + 1, \\ i & \text{otherwise.} \end{cases}$$

An example of this construction appears in Table 2.

□

Table 1. If $\Sigma \not\vdash x_1x_2 \subseteq_2 y_1y_2$ and $\Sigma = \{x_1x_2 \subseteq_2 w_1w_2,\ w_1w_2 \subseteq_1 y_1y_2\}$, then the counterexample team $T = T_1 \cup T_2 \cup T_3$ according to the proof of Theorem 1 item (i) is as illustrated, where any assignment that includes the listed tuple in a dashed row is not in T_i, while all remaining assignments to the values $\{i, i^*\}$ are in T_i, where $i \in \{1, 2, 3\}$.

T_1:	x_1	x_2	w_1	w_2	y_1	y_2
	-	-	~~1~~	~~1~~	-	-
	-	-	-	-	~~1~~	~~1~~
	1	1				

T_2:	x_1	x_2	w_1	w_2	y_1	y_2
	-	-	~~2~~	~~2~~	-	-
	-	-	-	-	~~2~~	~~2~~
	2	2				

T_3:	x_1	x_2	w_1	w_2	y_1	y_2
			3	3		
	-	-	-	-	~~3~~	~~3~~
	3	3				

Table 2. If $\Sigma \not\vdash x \subseteq_{\frac{1}{2}} y$ and $\Sigma = \{x \subseteq_{\frac{1}{4}} w,\ w \subseteq_{\frac{1}{2}} y\}$, then the counterexample team T built according to the proof of Theorem 1 item (ii) is as depicted.

T:	x	w	y
s_1	1	1	1
s_2	2	1	1
s_3	3	3	1
s_4	4	4	1
s_5	5	5	5

We end by stating the computational complexity results for the atoms' decision problems. Notably, the decision problem for unary Q-INC/R-INC atoms can be solved in polynomial time.

Theorem 2. *(i) Deciding whether* $\Sigma \models x \subseteq_n y$ *is PSPACE-complete, given that* $\Sigma \cup \{x \subseteq_n y\}$ *is a finite set of Q-INC atoms with the atoms in* Σ *having arity at most* $|x|$.
(ii) Deciding whether $\Sigma \models x \subseteq_a y$ *is in PTIME, given that* $\Sigma \cup \{x \subseteq_a y\}$ *is a finite set of either unary Q-INC atoms or unary R-INC atoms.*

Proof sketch. For item (i), modify the proof for inclusion dependencies in [1] by taking the approximations into account. For item (ii), use Dijkstra's algorithm.

3 Conclusion and Future Work

The completeness results in Theorem 1 provide initial steps toward axiomatizing approximate union-closed atoms by considering Q-INC and R-INC atoms, with related complexity results presented in Theorem 2.

Removing the arity restriction in Theorem 1 for Q-INC atoms is future work, and might require extending the current system with more rules. Given the semantic simplicity of Q-INC atoms, exploring them in poly-teams [6], which correspond to multirelational databases, offers a promising direction for extending the current completeness result with more potential for practical implementations in data management tasks.

Similarly, introducing a complete axiomatization for R-INC atoms without restricting to unary ones is a natural pursuit, though likely accompanied by an increase in computational complexity. One approach is to construct new counterexample teams for inclusion atoms beyond those found in the literature [1,5]. Another is to consider other 'ratio-approximate' variants, such as ones with *insertion semantics* $T \models x \subseteq_p^i y$ iff $|T[x] \setminus T[y]| \leq p|T[x]|$ (see, e.g., [9]). However, transitivity is then not sound: $\{x \subseteq_p^i z, z \subseteq_q^i y\} \not\models x \subseteq_r^i y$ for $p, q > 0$ and $r < 1$. On the other hand, since transitivity is not sound, we could expect better complexity results.

Other union-closed atoms can be considered, such as the *k-anonymity atom* $x\Upsilon^k y$, which asserts that each value of x appears with at least k different values of y. A quantity approximate version could allow n-many values of x to violate this condition. The standard rules for k-anonymity atoms in [12] with the approximations, remain sound. Completeness results and connections to the practical k-anonymity algorithms for databases (see, e.g., [8]) are left to be explored.

Lastly, to utilize the team-semantic setting, the languages of Q-INC and R-INC atoms could be enriched by connectives and quantifiers to study approximate variants of the union-closed *inclusion logic* from [4]. Approximation operators could also be applied to first-order formulae, as done in [3] for the downward-closed dependence logic, with connections to *multiteams* that model databases with duplicate rows.

Acknowledgments. The author wants to thank Åsa Hirvonen, Fan Yang, and the anonymous reviewers for their helpful suggestions regarding the paper.

Disclosure of Interests. The author has no competing interests to declare that are relevant to the content of this article.

References

1. Casanova, M.A., Fagin, R., Papadimitriou, C.H.: Inclusion dependencies and their interaction with functional dependencies. J. Comput. Syst. Sci. **28**(1), 29–59 (1984). https://doi.org/10.1016/0022-0000(84)90075-8
2. ten Cate, B., Fontaine, G., Kolaitis, P.G.: On the data complexity of consistent query answering. In: Proceedings of the 15th International Conference on Database Theory. ICDT '12, New York, NY, USA, pp. 22–33. Association for Computing Machinery (2012). https://doi.org/10.1145/2274576.2274580
3. Durand, A., Hannula, M., Kontinen, J., Meier, A., Virtema, J.: Approximation and dependence via multiteam semantics. In: Gyssens, M., Simari, G. (eds.) FoIKS 2016. LNCS, vol. 9616, pp. 271–291. Springer, Cham (2016). https://doi.org/10.1007/978-3-319-30024-5_15
4. Galliani, P.: Inclusion and exclusion dependencies in team semantics – on some logics of imperfect information. Ann. Pure Appl. Logic **163**(1), 68–84 (2012). https://doi.org/10.1016/j.apal.2011.08.005
5. Häggblom, M.: Inclusion with repetitions and boolean constants - implication problems revisited. In: Casini, G., Dundua, B., Kutsia, T. (eds.) JELIA 2025. LNCS, vol. 16094, pp. 109–124. Springer, Cham (2025). https://doi.org/10.1007/978-3-032-04590-4_8
6. Hannula, M., Kontinen, J., Virtema, J.: Polyteam semantics. In: Artemov, S., Nerode, A. (eds.) LFCS 2018. LNCS, vol. 10703, pp. 190–210. Springer, Cham (2018). https://doi.org/10.1007/978-3-319-72056-2_12
7. Häggblom, M.: Axiomatization of approximate exclusion. In: Proceedings of the 21st International Conference on Principles of Knowledge Representation and Reasoning, pp. 405–409 (2024). https://doi.org/10.24963/kr.2024/38
8. Kenig, B., Tassa, T.: A practical approximation algorithm for optimal k-anonymity. Data Min. Knowl. Disc. **25**, 134–168 (2012). https://doi.org/10.1007/s10618-011-0235-9
9. Su, Q., Wang, Z., Tan, Z., Ma, S.: Discovering approximate inclusion dependencies. Proc. VLDB Endow. **18**(4), 1210–1222 (2024). https://doi.org/10.14778/3717755.3717777
10. Väänänen, J.: Dependence logic: a new approach to independence friendly logic. London Mathematical Society Student Texts, Cambridge University Press, Cambridge (2007). https://doi.org/10.1017/CBO9780511611193
11. Väänänen, J.: The logic of approximate dependence. In: Başkent, C., Moss, L.S., Ramanujam, R. (eds.) Rohit Parikh on Logic, Language and Society. OCL, vol. 11, pp. 227–234. Springer, Cham (2017). https://doi.org/10.1007/978-3-319-47843-2_12
12. Väänänen, J.: An atom's worth of anonymity. Logic J. IGPL (2022). https://doi.org/10.1093/jigpal/jzac074

On Translating Epistemic Operators in a Logic of Awareness

Yudai Kubono(✉)

Graduate School of Science and Technology, Shizuoka University, Ohya, Shizuoka 422-8529, Japan
kubono.yudai.23@shizuoka.ac.jp

Abstract. Awareness-Based Indistinguishability Logic (henceforth, AIL) is an extension of Epistemic Logic by introducing the notion of awareness, distinguishing explicit knowledge from implicit knowledge. In this framework, each of these notions is represented by a modal operator. On the other hand, HMS models, developed in the economics literature, also provide a formalization of those notions. Nevertheless, the behavior of the epistemic operators in AIL within HMS models has yet to be explored. In this paper, we define a transformation of an AIL model into an HMS model and prove that a translation between the fragments of the language of AIL preserves truth under this transformation. As a result, we clarify the semantic role of an epistemic operator in AIL, which is essential to define explicit knowledge, within HMS models. Furthermore, we demonstrate the differences in the implicit knowledge captured by AIL and HMS models. This work lays the groundwork for a comparative analysis between the model classes.

Keywords: Awareness logic · Epistemic logic · Multi-agent systems

1 Introduction

Awareness-Based Indistinguishability Logic [5] (henceforth, AIL) is an extension of Epistemic Logic (henceforth, EL), a variant of modal logic, by introducing the notion of *awareness*, distinguishing *explicit knowledge* from *implicit knowledge*. In this framework, each of these notions, along with other epistemic notions to define explicit knowledge, is represented by a modal operator. AIL excludes specific undesirable formulae that are valid in the previous study [2]. On the other hand, HMS models, first proposed in [4], also provide a formalization of awareness and explicit knowledge. Following the economic tradition, this structure belongs to the event-based approach [3], which employs operators on events represented as subsets of states (or worlds), unlike EL and AIL.

Nevertheless, the behavior of epistemic operators in AIL within HMS models has yet to be explored. In this paper, we define a transformation of an AIL model into an HMS model and then prove that a translation between the fragments of

A.-Y. Turhan and J. Virtema (Eds.): FoIKS 2026, LNCS 16475, pp. 347–352, 2026.
https://doi.org/10.1007/978-3-032-21540-6_22

the language of AIL preserves truth under this transformation. Via the translation, we clarify the semantic role of an epistemic operator in AIL, which is induced by awareness and is essential to define explicit knowledge, within HMS models. Furthermore, we demonstrate the differences in the implicit knowledge captured by AIL and HMS models.

2 Preliminaries

We introduce two languages that are fragments of the AIL language [5]. We focus only on these fragments in this paper.

Let $\mathcal{P}$ be a countable set of atomic propositions and $\mathcal{G}$ a finite set of agents. The base language $\mathcal{L}_{PL}(\mathcal{P})$ is the set of formulae generated by the following grammar:

$$\mathcal{L}_{PL}(\mathcal{P}) \ni \varphi ::= p \mid \neg\varphi \mid \varphi \wedge \varphi,$$

where $p \in \mathcal{P}$. Other logical connectives $\vee$, $\rightarrow$, and $\leftrightarrow$ are defined in the usual manner. Furthermore, the languages $\mathcal{L}^*_{HMS}(\mathcal{P}, \mathcal{G})$ and $\mathcal{L}^*_{AIL}(\mathcal{P}, \mathcal{G})$ are the sets of formulae generated by the following grammars:

$$\mathcal{L}^*_{HMS}(\mathcal{P}, \mathcal{G}) \ni \psi ::= \varphi \mid A_i\varphi \mid I_i\varphi;$$
$$\mathcal{L}^*_{AIL}(\mathcal{P}, \mathcal{G}) \ni \psi ::= \varphi \mid A_i\varphi \mid [\approx]_i I_i [\approx]_i \varphi,$$

where $\varphi \in \mathcal{L}_{PL}(\mathcal{P})$ and $i \in \mathcal{G}$. We call the formulae in $\mathcal{L}^*_{AIL}$ AIL formulae. Furthermore, to avoid confusion, we sometimes attach superscripts indicating the languages to operators, such as A_i^{HMS} and A_i^{AIL}. The operators A and I represent awareness and implicit knowledge, respectively. The other operator $[\approx]_i$ is a technical background one used to define explicit knowledge in [5].

The Models in AIL. A Model of AIL is presented in Kripke-style. We often call it an AIL model.

Definition 1 ([5]). *An epistemic model with awareness M is a tuple $\langle W, \{\sim_i, \mathscr{A}_i\}_{i\in\mathcal{G}}, V\rangle$, where:*

- *W is a non-empty set of possible worlds;*
- *$\sim_i$ is an equivalence relation on W;*
- *$\mathscr{A}_i : W \rightarrow 2^{\mathcal{P}}$ is an awareness function satisfying that if $(w, v) \in \sim_i$, then $\mathscr{A}_i(w) = \mathscr{A}_i(v)$;*
- *$V : \mathcal{P} \rightarrow 2^W$ is a valuation.*

Furthermore, for each $i \in \mathcal{G}$, A-equivalence relation $\approx_i$ on W is defined by $(w, v) \in \approx_i$ iff, $\mathscr{A}_i(w) = \mathscr{A}_i(v)$ and $w \in V(p)$ iff $v \in V(p)$ for every $p \in \mathscr{A}_i(w)$.

A subset $\mathscr{A}_i(w)$ is called an *awareness set* for agent i at w. The equivalence classes under $\approx_i$ collect worlds regarded as 'the same' for i's current aware atomic propositions.

For instance, let p, q be atomic propositions. For brevity, let us represent each world as a tuple of the literals; e.g., (p, q) represents the world in which both p and q are true. An AIL model, in which four agents have awareness sets $\{p, q\}$, $\{p\}$, $\{q\}$, and $\emptyset$, respectively, at every world, has four types of partitions: $\{[(p,q)],[(p,\neg q)],[(\neg p,q)],[(\neg p,\neg q)]\}$; $\{[(p,q)],[(\neg p,q)]\}$; $\{[(p,q)],[(p,\neg q)]\}$; $\{[(p,q)]\}$, where $[(p,q)]$ denotes the equivalence class of (p,q) under the relevant A-equivalence relation.

We provide the satisfaction relation in our language $\mathcal{L}^*_{AIL}$. The clauses for atomic propositions and connectives are defined similarly to those in the standard Kripke model; hence, we omit them here. Let $At(\varphi)$ denote the set of atomic propositions occurring in φ.

Definition 2 ([5], restricted to $\mathcal{L}^*_{AIL}$). *For each epistemic model with awareness M and possible world $w \in W$, the satisfaction relation $\vDash_{AIL^*}$ is given as follows:*

$$\begin{aligned} M, w \vDash_{AIL^*} A_i\varphi \quad &\textit{iff} \quad At(\varphi) \subseteq \mathscr{A}_i(w); \\ M, w \vDash_{AIL^*} I_i\varphi \quad &\textit{iff} \quad M, v \vDash_{AIL^*} \varphi \textit{ for all } v \textit{ such that } (w,v) \in \sim_i; \\ M, w \vDash_{AIL^*} [\approx]_i I_i [\approx]_i\varphi \quad &\textit{iff} \quad M, v \vDash_{AIL^*} \varphi \textit{ for all } v \textit{ such that} \\ &\qquad (w,v) \in \approx_i \circ \sim_i \circ \approx_i, \end{aligned}$$

where $\sim_i \circ \approx_i$ is the sequential composition of $\approx_i$ and $\sim_i$.

In the original paper, explicit knowledge is defined in terms of awareness and the transitive closure of the sequential composition of $\approx_i$ and $\sim_i$; hence, $[\approx]_i I_i [\approx]_i$ corresponds to a subset of this closure.

Implicit Knowledge-Based HMS Models. In [1], the authors defined *implicit knowledge-based HMS models* (henceforth, iHMS models) based on the original HMS models [4]. Since the models are structurally closer to AIL models, which makes them easier to compare, we employ iHMS models as the target models into which $\mathcal{L}^*_{AIL}$ is translated.

An iHMS model is a tuple $\langle \{S_\Phi\}_{\Phi\subseteq\mathcal{P}}, (r^\Phi_\Psi)_{\Psi\subseteq\Phi\subseteq\mathcal{P}}, (\Lambda_i, \alpha_i)_{i\in\mathcal{G}}, v\rangle$ consisting of a non-empty collection of non-empty disjoint state-spaces; a family of projections between states; implicit possibility correspondences; awareness functions; and a valuation. Each space serves as a restriction on vocabulary instead of an awareness set. The states in a space associated with an agent's awareness (and spaces associated with other agents' awareness from the agent's viewpoint, for multi-agent cases) can be interpreted as a subjective description of an epistemic situation in the agent's mind. For instance, let p, q be atomic propositions and let us represent each state as a tuple of the literals. An iHMS model comprises four state-spaces: $\{(p,q),(p,\neg q),(\neg p,q),(\neg p,\neg q)\}$; $\{(p),(\neg p)\}$; $\{(q),(\neg q)\}$; $\emptyset$.

We do not reproduce the formal definition of the models here; for the detailed definition, along with the eight assumptions required for these models and the definition of operators on events, see [1]. Note that in this paper, we focus only on the models that satisfy the assumptions and omit this restriction from the terminology. Furthermore, we use our own notations such as $e_{A_i}(E)$ and $e_{I_i}(E)$ for the awareness and implicit knowledge operators, where E is an event.

3 Interpreting AIL Formulae in HMS Models via a Translation

We define the HMS-transform of an AIL model. In this transform, partitions by A-equivalence relations and mappings between them serve as state-spaces and projections in iHMS models.

Definition 3. *Let M be an epistemic model with awareness such that $\mathscr{A}_i(w) = \mathscr{A}_i(v)$ for every $i \in \mathcal{G}$ and for all $w, v \in W$. The HMS-transform of M is a tuple $t^{M\rightarrow}(M) = \langle \{W_\Phi\}_{\Phi \subseteq \mathcal{P}}, (m^\Phi_\Psi)_{\Psi \subseteq \Phi \subseteq \mathcal{P}}, (\Lambda^*_i, \alpha^*_i)_{i \in \mathcal{G}}, v^* \rangle$, where:*

- *$W_\Phi := W/\approx_\Phi$, where $\approx_\Phi$ is defined by $(w, v) \in \approx_\Phi$ iff, $w \in V(p)$ iff $v \in V(p)$ for every $p \in \Phi$. We denote $\bigcup_{\Phi \subseteq \mathcal{P}} W_\Phi$ as W^*, an element of W^* as w^*, and an equivalence class including w in W_Φ as $[w]_\Phi$.*
- *$m^\Phi_\Psi : W_\Phi \rightarrow W_\Psi$ is defined by $m^\Phi_\Psi([w]_\Phi) = [w]_\Psi$.*
- *$\Lambda^*_i : W^* \rightarrow 2^{W^*} \setminus \{\emptyset\}$ is defined by $[v]_\Phi \in \Lambda_i([w]_\Phi)$ iff $(w', v') \in \sim_i$ for some $w' \in [w]_\Phi$ and $v' \in [v]_\Phi$, if $\Phi = \mathcal{P}$; and by $\Lambda_i([w]_\Phi) = \{m^{\mathcal{P}}_\Phi(w^*) \mid w^* \in \Lambda_i([w]_{\mathcal{P}})\}$ otherwise.*
- *$\alpha^*_i : W^* \rightarrow \{W_\Phi\}_{\Phi \subseteq \mathcal{P}}$ is defined by $W_\Psi = \alpha^*_i([w]_\Upsilon)$ iff $\Psi = \mathscr{A}_i(w) \cap \Upsilon$.*
- *$v^* : \mathcal{P} \rightarrow 2^{W^*}$ is defined by $v^*(p) = \bigcup_{\{p\} \subseteq \Phi \subseteq \mathcal{P}} \{[w]_\Phi \mid w \in V(p)\}$.*

An iHMS model has a space associated with a set of atomic propositions that does not correspond to any agent's awareness set, unlike a partition by an A-equivalence relation. Hence, we define each space by partitioning W with $\approx_\Phi$ for each $\Phi \subseteq \mathcal{P}$.

Lemma 1. *For any AIL model M, the HMS-transform $t^{M\rightarrow}(M)$ is an implicit knowledge-based HMS model.*

Proof. The proof follows from the construction of the HMS-transform. It relies, for Λ^*_i, on the fact that $\sim_i$ is an equivalence relation, and, for α^*_i, on the fact that $\alpha^*_i([w]_\Phi)$ specifies a space whose associated vocabulary is a subset of Φ.

HMS models, including iHMS models, are structures that belong to the event-based approach [3], which focuses on events and dispenses with formulae. To define a truth-preserving translation of the formulae, we need to introduce the satisfaction relation for HMS-transforms.

Definition 4. *For any HMS-transforms $t^{M\rightarrow}(M)$ and $w^* \in W^*$, the satisfaction relation $\vDash_{HMS}$ is given as follows:*

$$
\begin{aligned}
t^{M\rightarrow}(M), w^* \vDash_{HMS} p &\text{ iff } w^* \in v(p);\\
t^{M\rightarrow}(M), w^* \vDash_{HMS} \neg\varphi &\text{ iff } w^* \in \neg||\varphi||;\\
t^{M\rightarrow}(M), w^* \vDash_{HMS} \varphi \wedge \psi &\text{ iff } w^* \in ||\varphi|| \cap ||\psi||;\\
t^{M\rightarrow}(M), w^* \vDash_{HMS} A_i\varphi &\text{ iff } w^* \in e_{A_i}(||\varphi||);\\
t^{M\rightarrow}(M), w^* \vDash_{HMS} I_i\varphi &\text{ iff } w^* \in e_{I_i}(||\varphi||).
\end{aligned}
$$

where $||\varphi|| := \{w^* \mid t^{M\rightarrow}(M), w^* \vDash_{HMS} \varphi\}$ for all $\varphi \in \mathcal{L}^*_{HMS}$.

In order for the satisfaction relation to be well-defined, we must prove that the truth set $||\varphi||$ of every formula is an event in HMS-transforms.

Lemma 2. *For every $\varphi \in \mathcal{L}^*_{HMS}$ and HMS-transform $t^{M\rightarrow}(M)$, $||\varphi||$ is a $W_{At(\varphi)}$-based event.*

Proof. The proof is by induction on the structures of φ. It is sufficient to show that there exists $B \subseteq W_{At(\varphi)}$ such that $||\varphi|| = \bigcup_{At(\varphi)\subseteq\Phi\subseteq\mathcal{P}}(m^{\Phi}_{At(\varphi)})^{-1}(B)$ for each case, where $m^{\Phi}_{\Psi}(B) := \{m^{\Phi}_{\Psi}([w]_{\Phi}) \mid [w]_{\Phi} \in B\}$ for $B \subseteq W_{\Phi}$. Such B is obtained by taking $\{w^* \in W_{At(\psi)} \mid W_{At(\psi)} \leq \alpha^*_i(w^*)\}$ for $A_i\psi$, and by taking $\bigcup_{w^*\in W^*}\{\Lambda^*_i(w^*) \mid \Lambda^*_i(w^*) \subseteq ||\psi|| \cap W_{At(\psi)}\}$ for $I_i\psi$.

Definition 5. *The translation $t : \mathcal{L}^*_{AIL} \rightarrow \mathcal{L}^*_{HMS}$ is defined as follows:*

$$t(p) = p; \qquad t(\neg\varphi) = \neg t(\varphi);$$
$$t(\varphi \wedge \psi) = t(\varphi) \wedge t(\psi); \qquad t(A^{AIL}_i\varphi) = A^{HMS}_i t(\varphi);$$
$$t([\approx]_i I^{AIL}_i [\approx]_i\varphi) = I^{HMS}_i(t(\varphi)).$$

The translation replaces each occurrence of the $[\approx]_i I_i [\approx]_i$ with the I_i operator.

Finally, we prove that the translation is truth-preserving between an AIL model and its HMS-transform. For every $\varphi \in \mathcal{L}^*_{AIL}$, we say that φ satisfies *A-condition* at $w \in W$ precisely when, if φ is of the form $A_i\psi$ or $[\approx]_i I_i [\approx]_i\psi$ then $At(\psi) = \mathscr{A}_i(w)$.

Theorem 1. *Let M be an epistemic model with awareness such that $\mathscr{A}_i(w) = \mathscr{A}_i(v)$ for every i and for all $w, v \in W$, $t^{M\rightarrow}(M)$ be its HMS-transform, and $w \in W$. For every $\varphi \in \mathcal{L}^*_{AIL}$, if φ satisfies A-condition at w, then $M, w \vDash_{AIL^*} \varphi$ iff $t^{M\rightarrow}(M), [w]_{At(\varphi)} \vDash_{HMS} t(\varphi)$.*

Proof. The proof is by induction on the structure of φ, using Lemma 2. For the case of $A_i\psi$, this immediately follows from A-condition. For the case of $[\approx]_i I_i [\approx]_i\psi$, the proof follows from that $[w]_{At([\approx]_i I_i [\approx]_i\psi)}$ is defined by $\approx_i$ and that Λ^*_i is defined by $\sim_i$.

The result implies that the $[\approx]_i I_i [\approx]_i$ operator in an AIL model is reduced to the I_i operator at i's subjective state in the corresponding iHMS model, under some assumptions. This is ascribed to the structure of iHMS models, in which the implicit knowledge is evaluated within states that appear under a vocabulary restriction imposed by an agent's awareness. In AIL, in contrast, the knowledge is defined independently of an agent's awareness, with each agent's subjective states expressed through $\approx_i$. In other words, while iHMS models internalize an agent's viewpoint into a state (or an evaluation point), AIL models externalize it by $\approx_i$. Hence, the $[\approx]_i$ operator serves as an indicator of an agent's viewpoint within iHMS models, which means from whose viewpoint a formula is evaluated.

4 Conclusion

In this paper, we defined the transformation from an AIL model to an HMS model and then proved that the translation between the fragments of the AIL language preserves truth under this transformation. Thus, we demonstrated that the $[\approx]_i I_i [\approx]_i$ operator in an AIL model is reduced to the I_i operator at the subjective state of i in the corresponding iHMS model, under some assumptions. This work lays the groundwork for a comparative analysis of these model classes.

Our result implies that information about whose viewpoint a state is from, which an evaluation point itself has in iHMS models, is externalized by the $[\approx]_i$ operator in AIL; the $[\approx]_i$ operator serves as an indicator of an agent's viewpoint within iHMS models. Furthermore, our truth-preserving translation shows that iHMS models capture a different notion of implicit knowledge than AIL does. In iHMS models, explicit knowledge coincides with the intersection of implicit knowledge and awareness [1]. It is left for future work to explore the formal comparison between explicit knowledge in iHMS models and that in AIL.

Acknowledgements. We thank the anonymous reviewers, Satoshi Tojo, and Nobu-Yuki Suzuki for their helpful comments. This work was financially supported by 23K21869.

References

1. Belardinelli, G., Schipper, B.C.: Implicit knowledge in unawareness structures. Synthese **204**(5), 141 (2024)
2. Fagin, R., Halpern, J.Y.: Belief, awareness, and limited reasoning. Artif. Intell. **34**, 39–76 (1988)
3. Fagin, R., Halpern, J.Y., Moses, Y., Vardi, M.Y.: Reasoning About Knowledge. MIT Press (1995)
4. Heifetz, A., Meier, M., Schipper, B.C.: Interactive unawareness. J. Econ. Theory **130**(1), 78–94 (2006)
5. Kubono, Y., Tojo, S.: A representation of explicit knowledge and epistemic indistinguishability in a logic of awareness. J. Appl. Log. (in press). arXiv:2512.22477

Learning SMT Algorithm Selection with High-Level Natural-Language Descriptions

Zhengyang Lu[1](✉), Paul Sarnighausen-Cahn[2], Jiahao Chen[3], Arie Gurfinkel[1](✉), Florin Manea[2](✉), and Vijay Ganesh[3](✉)

[1] University of Waterloo, Waterloo, Canada
john.lu2@uwaterloo.ca

[2] University of Göttingen and CIDAS, Göttingen, Germany
florin.manea@goettingen.de

[3] Georgia Institute of Technology, Atlanta, USA
vijay.ganesh@gatech.edu

Abstract. Machine-learning-based algorithm selection has demonstrated improvements in SMT solving by exploiting solver complementarity across diverse problem families. Existing SMT algorithm selectors primarily rely on handcrafted syntactic features to represent problem instances for machine-learning models. In this work, we explore whether high-level natural-language descriptions of SMT instances can provide additional useful information. We present `SMT-Select`, an SMT algorithm selection framework that combines traditional syntactic features with semantic embeddings derived from natural-language descriptions using pretrained transformer models. It further improves upon the algorithm selection pipeline of the state-of-the-art selector `MachSMT`. Evaluated on SMT-COMP 2024 benchmarks across 9 logics, `SMT-Select` achieves improved performance in 7 logics when description-based features are added, while performance degrades in the remaining two logics, where the SMT-LIB descriptions exhibit very limited variability. To address this limitation, we outline future work on LLM-based agents for generating higher-quality SMT instance descriptions, supported by preliminary demos.

Keywords: Algorithm Selection · SMT · Representation Learning · Natural Language Processing

1 Introduction

Satisfiability Modulo Theories (SMT) solvers decide the satisfiability of first-order logic formulas and are a core reasoning tool in formal verification and

Z. Lu, A. Gurfinkel, F. Manea and V. Ganesh—Corresponding authors.

A.-Y. Turhan and J. Virtema (Eds.): FoIKS 2026, LNCS 16475, pp. 353–358, 2026.
https://doi.org/10.1007/978-3-032-21540-6_23

program analysis [2]. Due to the inherent difficulty and diversity of SMT problems, no single algorithm performs best across all SMT instances; instead, different solvers exhibit complementary strengths across different problem families. This motivates algorithm selection, which seeks to exploit solver complementarity by selecting the most suitable solver for each problem instance. Machine-learning (ML) based methods have emerged as an effective data-driven approach for this problem: `SATzilla` [14] pioneered ML-based algorithm selection in the SAT domain, and `MachSMT` [10] later extended the idea to SMT solving.

As in many ML applications, the effectiveness of algorithm selection critically depends on how problem instances are represented. Most algorithm selectors rely on handcrafted, domain-specific features intended to capture properties of problem instances relevant to solver performance. For example, in the SMT domain, `MachSMT` used a set of 189 syntactic features, primarily based on symbol counts, to characterize problem instances. Subsequent systems, such as `MedleySolver` [8] and `Z3alpha` [6], adopt similar syntactic features to guide solvers or heuristic selection. Beyond handcrafted features, there has been a growing interest in leveraging advances in ML-based feature learning. Loreggia et al. [4] proposed learning instance representations by converting instance texts into grayscale images and applying convolutional neural networks, while `GraSS` [15] leveraged graph neural networks over abstract syntax trees of problem instances.

More recently, advances in transformer-based models for text representation have enabled feature learning directly from textual inputs [13]. In this direction, Pellegrino et al. [7] proposed using a transformer encoder to learn features for algorithm selection from high-level problem descriptions written in ESSENCE [3], a domain-specific language for modeling combinatorial optimization problems.

For SMT, raw SMT-LIB instances are typically too long to be used directly as transformer inputs. We therefore focus on high-level natural-language descriptions associated with SMT instances. These descriptions, often provided by instance creators, capture information such as instance origin, intended semantics, key constraints, and application context, but are inherently coarse and usually omit instance-specific details. We therefore explore using such descriptions in conjunction with syntactic features that capture instance-specific information.

Our Contributions

1. We develop `SMT-Select`, an SMT algorithm selection framework that augments syntactic features with embeddings learned from natural-language descriptions. Across 9 evaluated SMT logics, this augmentation improves performance in 7 cases compared to using syntactic features alone.
2. `SMT-Select` implements an improved algorithm selection pipeline over the state-of-the-art `MachSMT`, yielding better performance with syntactic features alone in all evaluated logics.

2 Algorithm Selection with Natural-Language Descriptions

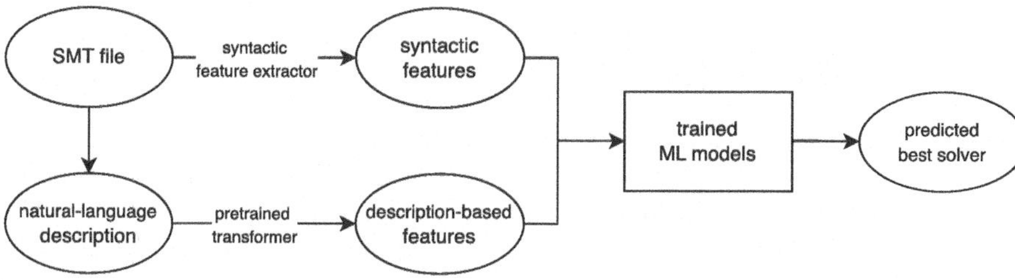

Fig. 1. Workflow of `SMT-Select` during inference for algorithm selection.

Given an SMT instance, an algorithm selector chooses the solver expected to perform best from a portfolio of candidate solvers. Figure 1 illustrates the inference-time workflow of `SMT-Select`. The selector first extracts feature representations from two sources: syntactic features are obtained using a dedicated feature extractor, while description-based features are derived from the corresponding natural-language description of the instance. These features are then combined into a unified feature representation of the SMT instance, which is used by the trained machine-learning model to predict the most suitable solver. The selected solver is subsequently executed on the instance.

Description-Based Feature Learning. Transformer-based language models enable learning semantic representations from natural-language text by encoding inputs into fixed-dimensional vectors [13]. Recent pretrained models produce high-quality text embeddings without task-specific training and transfer effectively across downstream tasks. In this work, we use the pretrained sentence embedding model `all-mpnet-base-v2` [11] from the Sentence-Transformers library, which is based on the MPNet architecture [12]. The model encodes each natural-language description into a fixed-length 768-dimensional embedding, which is then used as input features for the algorithm selection model. Descriptions exceeding 384 subword tokens are truncated. We currently do not fine-tune the embedding language model, leaving task-specific adaptation to future work.

Algorithm Selection Paradigm. Given a feature representation of an SMT instance, `SMT-Select` adopts a cost-sensitive pairwise classification (PWC) approach [14] for algorithm selection. The selector is trained on performance data from all solvers over a set of training benchmarks, constructing a binary classifier for each solver pair to predict which solver performs better on a given instance. Training is cost-sensitive, assigning higher weights to training samples with larger performance differences. At inference time, the pairwise classifiers vote for their preferred solvers, and the solver with the most votes is selected and executed.

3 Experiments

3.1 Experimental Setup

Following standard practice in ML-based algorithm selection, we train algorithm selectors using solver performance data on training benchmarks and evaluate them on held-out test benchmarks. Our experiments are based on the SMT-COMP 2024 [1] non-incremental benchmarks and performance data, focusing on 9 selected SMT-COMP logics based on three criteria: (1) benchmark size of at least 500, (2) a performance gap of at least 1% and 25 instances between the competition winner and the virtual best solver, and (3) natural-language description coverage of at least 75%. Our goal is to learn selectors over the portfolio of competition solver participants.

For each logic, benchmarks are randomly partitioned into four folds, and experiments are conducted using 4-fold cross-validation, with three folds for training and one for testing in each run, in order to obtain more robust and reliable performance estimates by reducing the variance induced by a particular train-test split. Performance data from all participating solvers are used for both training and evaluation. The performance data are obtained from the SMT-LIB Catalog 2025 [9].

In our experiments, we evaluate `SMT-Select` under three feature configurations: syntactic features alone, description-based features alone, and their combination. Syntactic features consist of logic-specific symbol counts, while description-based features are embeddings of natural-language descriptions generated using the pretrained `all-mpnet-base-v2` model, which imposes a maximum sequence length of 384 tokens. In 7 of the 9 logics, no or negligible truncation occurs. In BV, 6.8% of benchmarks are truncated, with an average of 3.5 tokens removed per truncated benchmark. In QF_NRA, 13.8% of benchmarks are truncated, with an average of 99.5 tokens removed per truncated benchmark.

The implementation of our algorithm selection framework is adapted from Btor2-Select [5]. In contrast to the recommended settings in `MachSMT`, which employs a regression-based empirical-hardness-model approach, our implementation uses PWC instead, relying on simpler SVM models rather than AdaBoost. Our implementation achieves an improved performance over `MachSMT` when using syntactic features alone, as demonstrated by our experimental results in Table 1. The results of `MachSMT` for QF_SLIA are not included because `MachSMT` encountered parsing errors on a subset of benchmarks in QF_SLIA.

3.2 Experimental Results

Table 1 reports the cross-validation results, averaged over four folds, for each logic. The results are measured as the fraction of the PAR-2 performance gap

Table 1. 4-fold cross-validation results. Metric: PAR-2 VBS–SBS gap closed (%) for `MachSMT` and `SMT-Select`. Values are mean ± std over folds, evaluated on each fold's held-out validation split.

Logic	MachSMT (Synt.)	SMT-Select		
		Synt.	Desc.	Synt.+Desc.
ABV	-8.7 ± 46.7	**79.2** $\pm$ 9.3	-0.7 ± 1.2	71.2 ± 8.9
ALIA	14.6 ± 14.8	**60.3** $\pm$ 6.7	6.9 ± 10.0	50.0 ± 7.1
BV	-1.0 ± 23.6	24.4 ± 7.3	31.0 ± 15.0	**44.6** $\pm$ 18.1
QF_IDL	-51.1 ± 47.4	59.6 ± 11.6	40.8 ± 29.2	**68.4** $\pm$ 10.1
QF_LIA	77.7 ± 4.7	87.9 ± 2.4	85.5 ± 2.9	**90.5** $\pm$ 2.2
QF_NRA	10.5 ± 25.6	35.1 ± 11.9	37.2 ± 16.6	**46.7** $\pm$ 12.6
QF_SLIA	–	91.1 ± 2.6	86.6 ± 2.9	**93.9** $\pm$ 1.6
UFLIA	-166.5 ± 86.4	10.0 ± 24.7	-19.8 ± 20.7	**18.2** $\pm$ 22.2
UFNIA	-53.0 ± 58.7	26.4 ± 11.4	0.0 ± 0.0	**32.7** $\pm$ 10.7

between the virtual best solver (VBS) and the single best solver (SBS) closed by the algorithm selector. The VBS represents an ideal oracle that always selects the best solver per instance, while the SBS denotes the best individual solver. A larger fraction of the SBS-VBS gap closed indicates better performance, with 100% matching the VBS and negative values performing worse than the SBS.

Across the 9 evaluated logics, `SMT-Select` benefits from augmenting syntactic features with description-based features in 7 cases, where the combined representation outperforms syntactic features alone. In particular, for the BV and QF_NRA logics, description-based features by themselves outperform purely syntactic features. The improved performance suggests that natural-language descriptions capture useful high-level information for these logics.

However, for ABV and ALIA, selector performance degrades when description embeddings are incorporated. A closer examination of the SMT-LIB descriptions for these two logics reveals very little variability: in both cases, more than 95% of benchmarks belong to a single family and share an identical description. Under such conditions, description embeddings are unlikely to provide meaningful discriminative information.

4 Conclusions and Next Steps

We investigate the use of natural-language description features for SMT algorithm selection and observe that, in most cases, they provide complementary information to traditional syntactic features, leading to improved selection performance, except in scenarios where the descriptions exhibit very limited variability.

Looking forward, we plan to investigate the use of LLM-based agents to improve the quality and individuality of existing descriptions, as well as to automatically generate descriptions for instances that lack them. We have built a prototype of such an agent, and interested readers may refer to an example of a generated description (example) and the agent implementation (repository).

Acknowledgment. The work of Zhengyang Lu is supported by the NSERC Canada Graduate Scholarship - Doctoral (CGS-D). The work of Florin Manea is supported by the German Research Foundation (DFG) - Heisenberg grant 466789228.

References

1. Bromberger, M., Bobot, F., Jonáš, M.: SMT-COMP 2024. https://smt-comp.github.io/2024/ (2024), Accessed 22 Dec 2025
2. De Moura, L., Bjørner, N.: Satisfiability modulo theories: introduction and applications. Commun. ACM (2011)
3. Frisch, A.M., Harvey, W., Jefferson, C., Hernández, B.M., Miguel, I.: Essence: a constraint language for specifying combinatorial problems. Constraints (2008)
4. Loreggia, A., Malitsky, Y., Samulowitz, H., Saraswat, V.A.: Deep learning for algorithm portfolios. In: AAAI (2016)
5. Lu, Z., Chien, P., Lee, N., Gurfinkel, A., Ganesh, V.: Btor2-Select: machine learning based algorithm selection for hardware model checking. In: CAV (2025)
6. Lu, Z., Siemer, S., Jha, P., Day, J., Manea, F., Ganesh, V.: Layered and staged monte carlo tree search for smt strategy synthesis. In: IJCAI (2024)
7. Pellegrino, A., Akgün, Ö., Dang, N., Kiziltan, Z., Miguel, I.: Transformer-based feature learning for algorithm selection in combinatorial optimisation. In: CP (2025)
8. Pimpalkhare, N., Mora, F., Polgreen, E., Seshia, S.A.: MedleySolver: online SMT algorithm selection. In: SAT, pp. 453–470. Springer (2021)
9. Schurr, H., Preiner, M., Niemetz, A., Barrett, C.W., Fontaine, P., Tinelli, C.: SMT-LIB catalog 2025 (version 1), July 2025, https://doi.org/10.5281/zenodo.16290040, Accessed 16 Dec 2025
10. Scott, J., Niemetz, A., Preiner, M., Nejati, S., Ganesh, V.: MachSMT: a machine learning-based algorithm selector for SMT solvers. In: TACAS (2021)
11. Sentence-Transformers: all-mpnet-base-v2. https://huggingface.co/sentence-transformers/all-mpnet-base-v2 (2021)
12. Song, K., Tan, X., Qin, T., Lu, J., Liu, T.: MPNet: masked and permuted pre-training for language understanding. In: NeurIPS 2020 (2020)
13. Vaswani, A., et al.: Attention is all you need. In: NIPS (2017)
14. Xu, L., Hutter, F., Hoos, H.H., Leyton-Brown, K.: Evaluating component solver contributions to portfolio-based algorithm selectors. In: SAT (2012)
15. Zhang, Z., et al.: GraSS: combining graph neural networks with expert knowledge for SAT solver selection. In: KDD (2024)

Towards a VLM-Based Foundation for Generalised Neurosymbolic Visual Commonsense

Jakob Suchan[1,3(✉)], Salim Baloch[1,3], and Mehul Bhatt[2,3]

[1] Constructor University, Bremen, Germany
[2] Örebro University, Örebro, Sweden
[3] CoDesign Lab EU – Cognitive Vision, Europe
cognitive-vision@codesign-lab.org
https://codesign-lab.org/cognitive-vision

Abstract. Commonsense visual sensemaking requires robust mechanisms to extract scene elements and other visual features from perceived imagery, as well as rich conceptual commonsense knowledge and reasoning to interpret the perceived interactive dynamic. In this context, we position ongoing work on using integrated Vision Language Models (VLM) and Answer Set Programming (ASP) based reasoning about (dynamic) spatial configurations using VLMs as a neural foundation for symbolic modeling of dynamic scene structures. We sketch preliminary results highlighting practical usability by application to the task of Visual Question Answering (VQA) with the STRIDE-QA driving dataset.

Keywords: Visual Commonsense · Declarative AI · Neurosymbolic AI

1 Introduction

High-level interleaved multimodal perception, interpretation and decision-making in everyday "in-the-wild" embodied systems settings requires the coordination of attention, integration of sensory inputs, and dynamic exploration of possible worlds and outcomes under tight temporal constraints [1,12]. For instance, consider a typical driving situation requiring navigating complex urban traffic together with other vehicles and vulnerable road users (e.g., pedestrians, cyclists). The driver's ability to maintain space-time situational awareness of the situation, for instance in an approximately 4-6 s interval comprising of the immediate past and future, constitutes the driver's **space-time mental model**, namely [1]:

- the ability to semantically interpret and explain the space-time sensory perception of the environment, conceptually making sense of the configuration and dynamics of mutually interacting people, objects, artefacts, and events and actions in space and time both in an active realtime as well as offline setting.

A.-Y. Turhan and J. Virtema (Eds.): FoIKS 2026, LNCS 16475, pp. 359–365, 2026.
https://doi.org/10.1007/978-3-032-21540-6_24

Computationally achieving this level of foundational commonsense visual sensemaking and real-time performance in a manner that is robust, explainable, verifiable, and context agnostic remains an open problem.

Neurosymbolic visual commonsense methods have recently gained traction as a promising line of research with the aim to achieve a general integration of state-of-the-art methods in knowledge representation and reasoning and (deep learning based) computer vision [3,8,11,13,15] (see review in [1]). In particular, the use of declarative techniques in logic and answer set programming (ASP) [2] standout as sustained lines of work from viewpoints such as (semantic) visual-question answering in logic and constraint logic settings [3,8,11], and non-monotonic visual abduction for (neurosymbolic) spatio-temporal belief maintenance in dynamic domains within ASP settings [12,13]. Differences in the technical framing and supported computational capabilities of these select exemplary works notwithstanding, the general motivation underlying remains unified: to integrate powerful low-level visual processing capabilities to extract (geometric) scene elements and visual features from the imagery with high-level, expressive conceptual commonsense knowledge with the aim to support neurosymbolic interpretation of either static and/or dynamic stimuli.

We emphasise that real-time interactive visual sensemaking requires a conceptual grounding of low–level visuospatial features in space and time, and supporting issues such as identity maintenance, inertia, high-level introspection & anticipation for counterfactual reasoning. The ongoing work positioned in this paper leverages upon the established strengths of VLMs for low-level visual computing in a manner that can (neurosymbolically) integrate with commonsense abstractions of spatio-temporal dynamics encompassing aspects such as space, time, events, actions and motion. We build upon and advance [12], a recently developed ASP-based visual commonsense foundation that already demonstrates the need and value of such a neurosymbolic integration from the viewpoints of explainability, dynamics, and real-time reasoning requirements.

2 Neurosymbolic Visual Commonsense in Dynamic Domains: A VLM-Based General Foundation

Contemporary VisionLanguage Models (VLMs) (e.g., [9,10,14]) enable general and scalable cross-modal feature analyses for the learning of compositional alignments between modalities from large-scale paired data. This form of learning is highly suited for zero-shot and few-shot generalisation facilitating transfer across tasks such as captioning and question answering with (static) image data. However, standard video based models typically require the whole video sequence at once thereby making them unsuitable for handling interactive dynamics (especially keeping in mind aspects such as explainability and verifiability). For online, real-time visual sensemaking, the visual input needs to be processed frame by frame, and the temporal dynamics are captured by explicit representations of the perceived motion. While VLMs typically utilise LSTM, GRU or temporal transformer architectures to handle such kinds of dynamic information, we argue

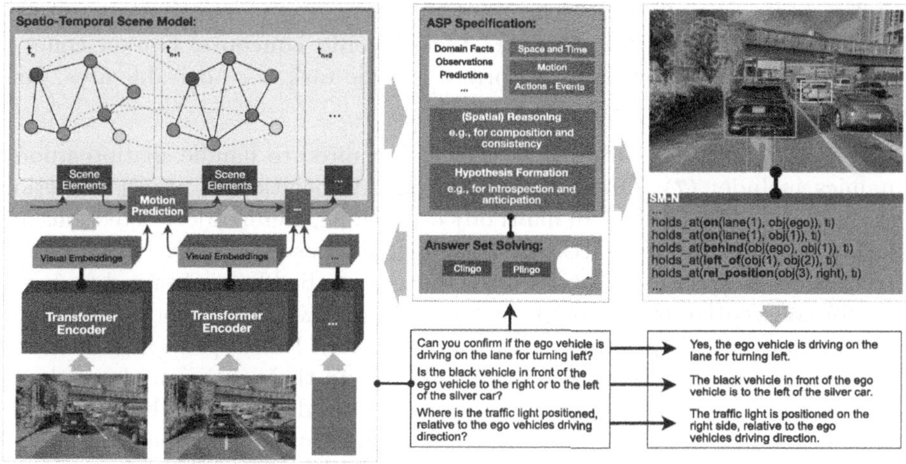

Fig. 1. VLM Foundations for Visual Commonsense: A general pipeline for integrating neural visuospatial features with high-level commonsense reasoning.

that systematic and general commonsense abstractions for declarative reasoning about spatio-temporal dynamics in interaction provides a much richer and more expressive methodology for visual sensemaking with dynamic imagery (and may also be used to augment the standard approaches alluded before). To this end, we propose a general pipeline, which is declaratively modelled within ASP such that a robust, elaboration tolerant, and domain-independent methodology may be realised for practical applications in real-time autonomous systems, such as autonomous driving or cognitive robotic.

Large scale vision foundation models facilitate the training of rather small scale heads for specific sub-tasks based on rich feature embeddings of the pre-trained VLM. Based on this principle, we posit that VLM-based low-level visual computing foundations are a strong foundation for visual commonsense reasoning if systematically integrated within an answer set programming driven neurosymbolic visual commonsense framework (Fig. 1). In present scope are the following static and dynamic visuospatial features:

A. STATIC FEATURES. To extract scene elements, their properties, and the relations between them specialized heads are trained on the feature embeddings extracted by the VLM. In particular, these include, among others, the following elements: **(1). Object detection.** Open vocabulary object detection, predicting geometric entities representing objects in the scene, e.g. regions, bounding-boxes, etc.; **(2). Segmentation.** Segmenting instances (i.e. masks for detected objects), and semantic region categories to obtain a pixel-wise segmentation of the scene; **(3). Properties.** Scene and object properties, capturing specifics of the setting (e.g. environment, setting, etc.), and individual properties of scene elements (e.g., color, texture, etc.); **(4). Relations.** Visuospatial relations holding between scene elements, such as spatial relations (e.g., behind, in front, overlapping, etc.), visibility (e.g., partially occluded, etc.), similarity (e.g., for ReID using object embeddings across frames) etc.; **(5). Task-specific concepts.** Obtain conceptual scene elements relevant to perform a specific task, e.g., drivable area, lane markings, stability, etc.

B. DYNAMIC FEATURES. Key elements required to handle spatiotemporal dynamics include: **(7). Object association.** Association of object detection over time as commonly done in multi object tracking. Here, object detections are associated to previous instances of the same object based on spatial features and appearance features; **(8). Motion cues.** Feature embeddings obtained from the VLM for consecutive frames used with an optical flow head to obtain scene and object motion; **(9). Expectation based detection.** Detect previously detected objects based on extracted feature embeddings and their anticipated position.

Static **(A)** and dynamic **(B)** features are integrated into the ASP based visual commonsense framework to provide a conceptual grounding for visuospatial reasoning. In particular, this supports reasoning about (spatial) composition and consistency, hypothetical reasoning aimed at introspection and anticipation for mental model simulation etc.

Ongoing Use-Case: Interactive Commonsense in Driving. As an example from work-in-progress, consider the scene in Fig. 1 from the STRIDE-QA [4] dataset. Here, VLM based visual processing facilitates the extraction of scene elements related to the spatial reasoning questions from the dataset, and ASP based reasoning provides a systematic way to obtain consistent and explainable answer sets for these questions, which can subsequently used to generate natural language answers. For instance, consider the question "Is the black vehicle in front of the ego vehicle to the right or to the left of the silver car?". In order to answer this question, we need to detect the two cars and obtain their restive colors. Furthermore, we need to reason about their spatial configuration: the black vehicle is to the front of the ego vehicle, and the black car is to the left of the silver car. Finally, we then need to generate a natural language answer from the fact that the black car is to the left of the silver car.

• **Object Detection and Property Extraction.** For object detection we utilize Grounding DINO [6], a transformer-based open-vocabulary object detector for scene element identification based on DINOv2 [7]. The model processes 1860×2880 resolution frames with text prompts specifying both object categories and properties (e.g., "silver car . white van . blue vehicle"). To facilitate property extraction, we train specialized classification heads on the DINOv2 object embeddings (768-dimensional features). We extract crops from detected bounding boxes and train multi-label classifiers for different properties (e.g., color, size, etc.). The color head consists of a 3-layer MLP (768→256→128→10) trained for 20 epochs using Adam optimizer with binary cross-entropy loss and class-weighted sampling to handle imbalanced distributions.

• **Segmentation.** For object segmentation, we integrate a Segment Anything Model (SAM) [5] using bounding boxes from Grounding DINO as prompts. SAM generates three candidate masks per object with predicted IoU scores; we select the mask with the highest IoU. This two-stage approach achieves valuable segmentation coverage of detected objects, combining Grounding DINO's semantic understanding with SAM's pixel-level precision.

- **Visual Similarity.** Visual similarity of detected objects, e.g., for maintaining identity in dynamic scenes, is based on the visual appearance of detected objects using DINOv2 feature embeddings. Towards this, we are extracting the embeddings representing the objects and applying a cosine similarity measure to obtain an account for the similarity of the feature embeddings.

- **Commonsense Reasoning.** Reasoning with extracted visual elements is based on the ASP-driven visual commonsense framework of [12]; the framework provides the foundational mechanisms for maintaining a space-time mental model of the perceived scene and also facilitates high-level reasoning about scene dynamics. For instance, in the example from Fig. 1, the detected objects, i.e., the vehicles, are represented by their geometric extents, and their dynamics are captured by association of detections to object tracks based on visual and spatial criteria using mechanisms such as abuctive inference. Spatial reasoning tasks such as question-answering, whether the black vehicle in front of the ego vehicle is to the right or to the left of the silver car, are then solved using qualitative spatial relations, e.g., *in front of, left of, right of*, together with the object properties such as the color of the vehicles within an ASP-based declarative problem specification. Resulting stable models may respectively be used to generate a natural language answer, or to guide learning of the VLM heads.

3 Discussion and Outlook

We position ongoing work at the intersection of "Vision and AI/KR" aimed at advancing a recently developed ASP-driven neurosymbolic visual commonsense framework [12] with VLMs in a manner such that a general, modular, extensible, domain-independent, and state-of-the-art neurosymbolic visual commonsense methodology is available for further technical advancements and application in diverse autonomous systems domains. Contemporary transformer architecture driven VLMs operate on static observations, therefore lacking mechanisms for perception-guided action. Particularly from the perspective of (inter)active sensemaking, which is the central concern of this work, VLMs by themselves remain inherently incapable of modelling dynamic perceptual uncertainty, spatio-temporal embodiment, causality, and counterfactual simulation thereby limiting their ability to plan informative actions or adapt perception based on goals. Interactive sensemaking settings –such as in cognitive robotics, autonomous driving– requiring closed-loop perception, long-horizon understanding, or learning from real-time experience generally still remain an open problem beyond the scope of such contemporary end-to-end architectures. By combining the power of deep learning based neural techniques for visual computing with robust declarative modelling of high-level spatio-temporal dynamics, diverse synergies may be exploited from viewpoints such as explainability, verification, and broader emerging considerations relevant to regulated/responsible AI.

References

1. Bhatt, M., Suchan, J.: Artificial visual intelligence - perceptual commonsense for human-centred cognitive technologies. In: Chetouani, M., Dignum, V., Lukowicz, P., Sierra, C. (eds.) Human-Centered Artificial Intelligence - Advanced Lectures, 18th European Advanced Course on AI, ACAI 2021, Berlin, Germany, 11–15 October 2021, extended and improved lecture notes. LNCS, vol. 13500, pp. 216–242. Springer (2021). https://doi.org/10.1007/978-3-031-24349-3_12
2. Brewka, G., Eiter, T., Truszczyński, M.: Answer set programming at a glance. Commun. ACM **54**(12), 92–103 (2011). https://doi.org/10.1145/2043174.2043195
3. Eiter, T., et al.: Explainable zero-shot visual question answering via logic-based reasoning. In: Gilpin, H.L., Giunchiglia, E., Hitzler, P., van Krieken, E. (eds.) Proceedings of The 19th International Conference on Neurosymbolic Learning and Reasoning. Proceedings of Machine Learning Research, PMLR 2025, vol. 284 (2025)
4. Ishihara, K., Sasaki, K., Takahashi, T., Shiono, D., Yamaguchi, Y.: Stride-QA: visual question answering dataset for spatiotemporal reasoning in urban driving scenes. In: AAAI-26 Conference of the Association for the Advancement of Artificial Intelligence, Singapore. AAAI Press (2026)
5. Kirillov, A., et al.: Segment anything. In: Proceedings of the IEEE/CVF International Conference on Computer Vision (ICCV 2023)
6. Liu, S., et al.: Grounding DINO: marrying DINO with grounded pre-training for open-set object detection. In: Computer Vision – ECCV 2024: 18th European Conference, Milan, Italy, September 29–October 4, 2024, Proceedings, Part XLVII, pp. 38–55. Springer, Heidelberg (2024). https://doi.org/10.1007/978-3-031-72970-6_3
7. Oquab, M., et al.: DINOv2: learning robust visual features without supervision. arXiv preprint arXiv:2304.07193 (2024)
8. Padalkar, P., Gupta, G.: Symbolic rule extraction from attention-guided sparse representations in vision transformers. Theory Pract. Logic Program. **25**(4), 722–738 (2025). https://doi.org/10.1017/S1471068425100318
9. Radford, A., et al.: Learning transferable visual models from natural language supervision. In: Meila, M., Zhang, T. (eds.) Proceedings of the 38th International Conference on Machine Learning. Proceedings of Machine Learning Research, vol. 139 (PMLR 2021)
10. Siméoni, O., et al.: DINOv3 (2025). https://arxiv.org/abs/2508.10104
11. Suchan, J., Bhatt, M.: Semantic question-answering with video and eye-tracking data: AI foundations for human visual perception driven cognitive film studies. In: Kambhampati, S. (ed.) Proceedings of the Twenty-Fifth International Joint Conference on Artificial Intelligence, IJCAI 2016, New York, USA. IJCAI/AAAI Press (2016)
12. Suchan, J., Bhatt, M., Monsen, J.: ASP-driven visual commonsense: a general framework for reasoning about embodied interaction in the wild. In: Proceedings of the 22nd International Conference on Principles of Knowledge Representation and Reasoning, KR 2025 (2025). https://doi.org/10.24963/kr.2025/61
13. Suchan, J., Bhatt, M., Varadarajan, S.: Commonsense visual sensemaking for autonomous driving - on generalised neurosymbolic online abduction integrating vision and semantics. Artif. Intell. **299**, 103522 (2021). https://doi.org/10.1016/J.ARTINT.2021.103522

14. Xiao, B., et al.: Florence-2: advancing a unified representation for a variety of vision tasks. In: Proceedings of the IEEE/CVF Conference on Computer Vision and Pattern Recognition (CVPR 2024)
15. Yang, Z., Ishay, A., Lee, J.: NeurASP: embracing neural networks into answer set programming. In: Bessiere, C. (ed.) Proceedings of the Twenty-Ninth International Joint Conference on Artificial Intelligence, IJCAI 2020, pp. 1755–1762. International Joint Conferences on Artificial Intelligence Organization (2020). https://doi.org/10.24963/ijcai.2020/243

Planning and Temporal Planning by Qualitative Temporal Reasoning

Diedrich Wolter(✉) and Tobias Schwartz

University of Lübeck, Lübeck, Germany
{diedrich.wolter,tobias.schwartz}@uni-luebeck.de

Abstract. In this paper we bring together qualitative temporal reasoning and planning in order to pave the way for a new approach to planning and temporal planning. Both fields are concerned with arrangement problems of temporal intervals. We present a method to construct qualitative temporal reasoning tasks from planning problems, effectively reducing a class of planning tasks to qualitative temporal reasoning. The construction proposed in this paper enables additional temporal planning constraints to be considered, thereby making the method applicable to both classical planning and temporal planning.

Keywords: Qualitative Temporal Reasoning · (Temporal) Planning

1 Introduction

Planning, sometimes called STRIPS planning, is the task of finding a sequence of actions that leads from an initial state to a goal state described by sets of atomic propositions. The paradigm introduced by Fikes and Nilsson is still central today and has been extended in the PDDL language to encompass, e.g., temporal constraints and timed effects [6,7,9]. Qualitative temporal reasoning, on the other hand, provides constraint languages over infinite domains of temporal entities. Allen's interval algebra [1] and its refinements allow us to describe order, overlap, and duration relations; qualitative calculi [5] support symbolic inference over such disjunctive relations. Although qualitative reasoning has long been argued to be relevant to planning [3], earlier integrations like the CHIMP planner [11] still kept the actual plan search outside the qualitative layer.

We constructively link both fields by showing how a grounded planning task with optional temporal constraints can be reduced to a qualitative constraint network (QCN) over the $\mathcal{INDU}$ calculus [10]. Similar to SAT-based planning [8], we bridge the complexity gap from PSPACE-hard planning to NP-complete $\mathcal{INDU}$ reasoning by fixing a maximum plan length. The resulting encoding mirrors the temporal structure of a plan, leverages qualitative solvers for planning, and supports duration constraints at the level of qualitative relations.

A.-Y. Turhan and J. Virtema (Eds.): FoIKS 2026, LNCS 16475, pp. 366–371, 2026.
https://doi.org/10.1007/978-3-032-21540-6_25

2 Preliminaries

STRIPS Planning defines a planning problem as tuple $\Pi = (F, A, s_I, G)$ where F is a finite set of facts (atomic propositions), A is a finite set of actions, $s_I \subseteq F$ is the initial state, and $G \subseteq F$ the goal. Each action $a \in A$ comes with positive preconditions $\mathcal{P}^+(a)$, negative preconditions $\mathcal{P}^-(a)$, add effects $\mathcal{E}^+(a)$, and delete effects $\mathcal{E}^-(a)$ with $\mathcal{E}^+(a) \cap \mathcal{E}^-(a) = \emptyset$. Action a is applicable in state s iff $\mathcal{P}^+(a) \subseteq s$ and $\mathcal{P}^-(a) \cap s = \emptyset$, and it produces $a[s] = (s \setminus \mathcal{E}^-(a)) \cup \mathcal{E}^+(a)$. A plan is a sequence $\pi = \langle a_1, \ldots, a_n \rangle$ applicable in s_I whose execution yields a state containing G. We employ a grounded setting, where all parameterized action schemas are instantiated up front.

Temporal Planning enriches STRIPS planning by associating actions with durations and temporal constraints. A problem $\Pi_T = (\Pi_s, \mathcal{C})$ pairs a grounded STRIPS problem Π_s with linear constraints $\mathcal{C}$ over start times, end times, and durations (e.g., $|a_i| = 2$). A temporal plan $\pi = \{(t_i, a_i, d_i)\}_{i=1}^n$ schedules actions with start times t_i and durations $d_i > 0$; we focus on sequential plans where $t_i + d_i = t_{i+1}$. A plan is valid if the action sequence solves Π_s and satisfies $\mathcal{C}$.

Qualitative Constraint Networks (QCNs) are tuples $\mathcal{N} = (V, \Gamma)$ with variables V over an infinite domain D and constraint mapping $\Gamma : V \times V \to 2^{\mathsf{B}}$, where B is a set of jointly exhaustive and pairwise disjoint base relations. $\Gamma(x, y)$ lists the possible qualitative relationships between x and y; a solution refines each constraint to a single base relation such that the network is consistent. The $\mathcal{INDU}$ calculus [10] extends Allen's 13 interval relations [1] (Fig. 1 left) with duration comparisons ($<$, $=$, $>$), yielding 25 base relations. For example, intervals $x = [1, 3]$ and $y = [3, 6]$ satisfy $x\ m^< \ y$: x meets y and $|x| < |y|$. We use wildcard notation $o^* = \{o^<, o^=, o^>\}$ and $*^=$ for the seven equal-duration relations. Deciding consistency of an $\mathcal{INDU}$ QCN is NP-complete [2].

3 Problem Setting and Construction Principle

Planning by qualitative temporal reasoning amounts to arranging interval variables so that their qualitative arrangement represents a valid plan. Given a temporal planning problem $\Pi_T = (\Pi_s, \mathcal{C})$ with $\Pi_s = (F, A, s_I, G)$ and a plan length bound n, we build a qualitative constraint network $\mathcal{N}_{\Pi_T, n}$ whose solutions correspond exactly to plans of length n that satisfy $\mathcal{C}$. The construction retains atomicity of STRIPS actions but supports additional duration constraints.

Running Example. Let $F = \{p, q\}$ and $A = \{a, b\}$ with $\mathcal{P}^+(a) = \{p\}$, $\mathcal{E}^-(a) = \{p\}$, $\mathcal{E}^+(a) = \{q\}$, and $\mathcal{P}^+(b) = \{q\}$, $\mathcal{E}^+(b) = \{p\}$. The initial state is $s_I = \{p\}$ and the goal is $G = \{p, q\}$. Duration constraints require $|a| = 2$ and $|b| = 1$. The unique linear plan is $\pi = \{(0, a, 2), (2, b, 1)\}$ with makespan 3.

To make the encoding independent of the yet-to-be-found plan, we introduce *action shells* $s^{[1]}, \ldots, s^{[n]}$ and *proposition shells* $s_p^{[i]}$ that form a temporal scaffold between two special intervals S (encoding the initial state) and E (encoding the goal). Real action intervals must either coincide with these shells (indicating that

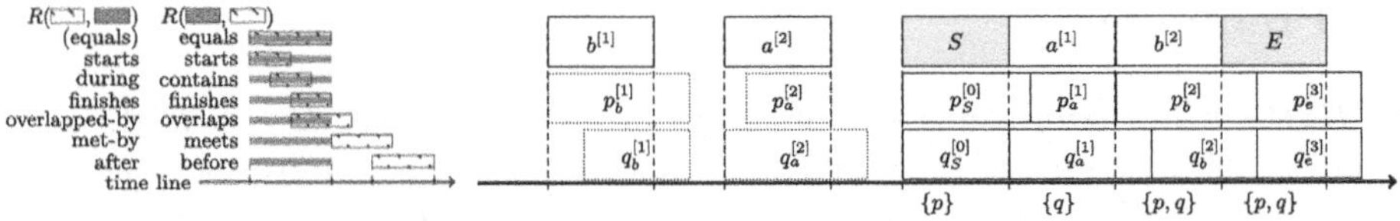

Fig. 1. Left: Temporal Allen relations. **Right:** Intervals representing running example plan $\langle a, b\rangle$. Selected actions $a^{[1]}, b^{[2]}$ between S and E; unselected actions $a^{[2]}, b^{[1]}$ before S. State annotations show valid propositions at each stage.

they occupy that position in the plan) or be forced outside the S–E window, effectively deselecting them. Proposition shells ensure that facts "flow" from one timestep to the next in accordance with preconditions and effects. Figure 1 right shows the resulting layout for the running example and highlights how valid propositions are reflected by the extent of their intervals.

4 Shell-Based Encoding Using $\mathcal{INDU}$ Constraints

Following SAT-based planning, we create timestamped copies of actions and propositions for plan length n. To enable selection, we introduce *action shells* $s^{[1]}, \ldots, s^{[n]}$ representing temporal slots, and *proposition shells* $s_p^{[i]}$ tracking validity. Shells are placeholders linked by *meets** relations between start S and end E. Action a is represented by n timestamped intervals $a^{[i]}$. Figure 1 shows this layout: plan $\langle a, b\rangle$ is represented by $a^{[1]}, b^{[2]}$ between S and E; unselected actions before S. Proposition validity is encoded by temporal arrangement: propositions meet at action boundaries (invalid) or extend beyond action start (valid).

Borrowing exclusive selection from a SAT encoding in Allen relations [12], we define $\mathrm{Sel}_S(X, A, B)$ that binds interval X to either A or B, using a container F that includes disjoint intervals A, B. By symmetry, exactly one of $X\ eq^{=}\ A$ or $X\ eq^{=}\ B$ holds; the non-selected interval is pushed before S. See Fig. 2 left for illustration. Formally, we have $\mathrm{Sel}_S(X, A, B) = \{X\ \{>^*, mi^*\}\ S,\ X\ \{f^<\}\ F,\ S\ \{d^<\}\ F, A\ \{s^<, f^<\}\ F, B\ \{s^<, f^<\}\ F, A\ \{<^*, >^*\}\ B,\ X\ \{>^*, eq^=\}\ A,\ X\ \{>^*, eq^=\}\ B\}$. $\mathrm{Sel}_S(X, \mathcal{I})$ generalizes selection to sets $\mathcal{I}$ recursively: $\mathrm{Sel}_S(X, A, Z_1) \cup \mathrm{Sel}_S(Z_1, \mathcal{I} \setminus \{A\})$ for $|\mathcal{I}| > 2$, ensuring $X = I$ for exactly one $I \in \mathcal{I}$. Action encoding $\mathrm{Act}(a, \mathcal{P}^+, \mathcal{P}^-, \mathcal{E}^+, \mathcal{E}^-, \mathcal{P}^0)$, where $\mathcal{P}^0$ denotes propositions occurring neither as precondition nor effect, ties proposition intervals to action a via $\mathcal{INDU}$ constraints, formally $\mathrm{Act}(a, \mathcal{P}^+, \mathcal{P}^-, \mathcal{E}^+, \mathcal{E}^-, \mathcal{P}^0) = \{a\ \{o^*\}\ p_1 \mid p_1 \in \mathcal{P}^+ \wedge p_1 \in \mathcal{E}^+\} \cup \{p_2\ \{f^<\}\ a \mid p_2 \in \mathcal{P}^+ \wedge p_2 \in \mathcal{E}^-\} \cup \{p_3\ \{eq^=\}\ a \mid p_3 \in \mathcal{P}^- \wedge p_3 \in \mathcal{E}^-\} \cup \{a\ \{s^<\}\ p_4 \mid p_4 \in \mathcal{P}^- \wedge p_4 \in \mathcal{E}^+\} \cup \{a\ \{o^*, s^*\}\ p_5 \mid p_5 \notin (\mathcal{P}^- \cup \mathcal{P}^+) \wedge p_5 \in \mathcal{E}^+\} \cup \{p_6\ \{f^<, eq^=\}\ a \mid p_6 \notin (\mathcal{P}^- \cup \mathcal{P}^+) \wedge p_6 \in \mathcal{E}^-\} \cup \{p_7\ \{eq^=, oi^=\}\ a \mid p_7 \in \mathcal{P}^0\}$, where $p_1, \ldots, p_7$ are fresh interval variables. We write $\mathrm{Enc}_a(p)$ for the interval representing proposition p in action a.

Duration constraints are encoded via $\mathcal{INDU}$ relations enforcing weighted sums of action durations. We construct an interval X with $|X| = \frac{k}{l} \cdot |Y|$ by

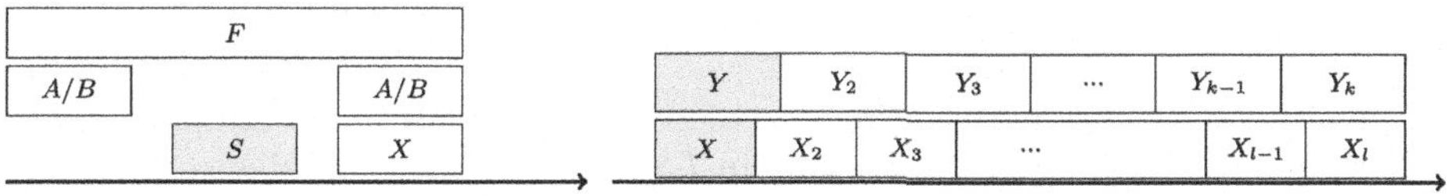

Fig. 2. Left: Illustration of exclusive selection constraint. **Right:** Duration constraint $|X| = \frac{k}{l} \cdot |Y|$ via interval subdivision using $\mathcal{INDU}$ relations.

Algorithm 1. Encode planning instance as concise $\mathcal{INDU}$ QCN

Require: Grounded planning problem $\Pi_T = (F, A, s_I, G, \mathcal{C})$, plan length bound n
create S, E with Act, add proposition encodings $\text{Enc}_S(p)$, $\text{Enc}_E(p)$
create action and proposition shells, connect them via *meets**
for $i = 1$ to n **do**
  for each $a \in A$ **do**
    instantiate $a^{[i]}$ and proposition intervals via Act constraint
    constrain $a^{[i]}$ to either equal $s^{[i]}$ or be disjoint from all shells and S, E
  end for
  add selection constraints $\text{Sel}_S(s^{[i]}, \{a^{[i]} \mid a \in A\})$
end for
add duration constraints $\text{Dur}(\mathcal{C})$
return QCN $\mathcal{N}_{\Pi_T,n}$

---

subdividing Y into k equal parts and X into l parts using $m^=$ relations (Fig. 2). $\text{Dur}(\mathcal{C})$ denotes the subdivision constraints realizing $\mathcal{C}$.

Algorithm 1 summarizes our construction of the encoding $\mathcal{N}_{\Pi_T,n}$.

Theorem 1 (Soundness). *If $\mathcal{N}_{\Pi_T,n}$ is consistent, any solution yields a valid plan of length n satisfying $\mathcal{C}$.*

Proof (Sketch). Let Φ be a solution. By Sel_S, exactly one $a^{[i]}$ equals $s^{[i]}$ per timestep; all others lie before S. The binding constraints force proposition intervals of selected actions to align with proposition shells, which chain via *meets**. Since Act encodes preconditions as overlaps (true) or boundary-meets (false), the proposition flow from S through shells to E ensures all preconditions hold and effects propagate correctly. By construction of $\text{Dur}(\mathcal{C})$, all duration constraints are satisfied. Thus $\langle a_1, \ldots, a_n \rangle$ is a valid plan satisfying $\mathcal{C}$.

Theorem 2 (Completeness). *If Π_T admits a plan of length n, then $\mathcal{N}_{\Pi_T,n}$ is consistent.*

Proof (sketch). Given valid temporal plan $\pi = \{(t_i, a_i, d_i)\}_{i=1}^n$ satisfying $\mathcal{C}$, construct a solution: set $a_i^{[i]}$ $eq^=$ $s^{[i]}$ and place all other action intervals before S. Since π is valid, preconditions hold at each step, so proposition intervals can be instantiated to satisfy all Act constraints. Since π satisfies $\mathcal{C}$, all duration constraints are also satisfied. The resulting assignment satisfies all QCN constraints.

The encoding uses $O((|A| + |F|) \cdot n)$ intervals, polynomial in input size, plus linear-size chains for duration constraints.

5 Conclusions

We give the first constructive reduction of grounded STRIPS and temporal planning to qualitative temporal reasoning in $\mathcal{INDU}$. The shell-based encoding mirrors planning structure, keeps temporal information explicit, and integrates additional duration constraints of temporal planning at the qualitative level. Earlier qualitative contributions, e.g., the Meta-CSP based CHIMP planner [11], still relied on external reasoning for plan synthesis, while CSP-based formulations such as based on Graphplan [4] lose the natural temporal interpretation.

Like SAT-based planning, we encode a grounded planning task and cap plan length to bridge the PSPACE/NP gap. "No-op" actions can be added to over-approximate the required length. We hope that this formulation stimulates development of qualitative solvers tailored to planning workloads. In future work we also aim to study how robust QCN solving [13] can be leveraged for planning so as to tolerate perturbations of start states or action outcomes.

References

1. Allen, J.F.: Maintaining knowledge about temporal intervals. Commun. ACM, 832–843 (1983). https://doi.org/10.1145/182.358434
2. Balbiani, P., Condotta, J., Ligozat, G.: On the consistency problem for the INDU calculus. J. Appl. Log. **4**(2), 119–140 (2006). https://doi.org/10.1016/j.jal.2005.06.002
3. Cohn, A.G., Hazarika, S.M.: Qualitative spatial representation and reasoning: an overview. Fund. Inform. **46**(1–2), 1–29 (2001). ISSN: 0169-2968
4. Do, M.B., Kambhampati, S.: Planning as constraint satisfaction: solving the planning graph by compiling it into CSP. Artif. Intell. **132**(2), 151–182 (2001). https://doi.org/10.1016/S0004-3702(01)00128-X
5. Dylla, F., Lee, J.H., Mossakowski, T., Schneider, T., van Delden, A., van de Ven, J., Wolter, D.: A survey of qualitative spatial and temporal calculi: algebraic and computational properties. ACM Comput. Surv. **50**(1), 7:1–7:39 (2017). https://doi.org/10.1145/3038927
6. Fikes, R., Nilsson, N.: STRIPS: a new approach to the application of theorem proving to problem solving. Artif. Intell. **2**, 189–208 (1971). https://doi.org/10.1016/0004-3702(71)90010-5
7. Fox, M., Long, D.: PDDL2.1: an extension to PDDL for expressing temporal planning domains. J. Artif. Intell. Res. **20**, 61–124 (2003). https://doi.org/10.1613/jair.1129
8. Kautz, H., Selman, B.: Planning as satisfiability. In: Proceedings of ECAI 1992, pp. 359–363 (1992). ISBN: 0471936081
9. McDermott, D.: Reasoning about autonomous processes in an estimated-regression planner. In: Proceedings of ICAPS-03 (2003). https://aaai.org/papers/icaps-03-015-reasoning-about-autonomous-processes-in-an-estimated-regression-planner/
10. Pujari, A.K., Vijaya Kumari, G., Sattar, A.: *INDu*: an interval & duration network. In: Foo, N. (ed.) AI 1999. LNCS (LNAI), vol. 1747, pp. 291–303. Springer, Heidelberg (1999). https://doi.org/10.1007/3-540-46695-9_25
11. Stock, S., Mansouri, M., Pecora, F., Hertzberg, J.: Hierarchical hybrid planning in a mobile service robot. In: Proceedings of KI 2015. LNCS, vol. 9324, pp. 309–315. Springer, Cham (2015). https://doi.org/10.1007/978-3-319-24489-1_28

12. Vilain, M., Kautz, H., van Beek, P.: Constraint propagation algorithms for temporal reasoning: a revised report. In: Readings in Qualitative Reasoning About Physical Systems, pp. 373–381. Morgan Kaufmann (1990). https://doi.org/10.1016/B978-1-4832-1447-4.50034-1
13. Wehner, J., Sioutis, M., Wolter, D.: On robust vs fast solving of qualitative constraints. J. Heuristics **29**(4–6), 461–485 (2023). https://doi.org/10.1007/s10732-023-09517-8

Author Index

A.-Y. Turhan and J. Virtema (Eds.): FoIKS 2026, LNCS 16475, pp. 373–374, 2026.
https://doi.org/10.1007/978-3-032-21540-6

The manufacturer's authorised representative in the EU is Springer Nature Customer Service Centre GmbH, Europaplatz 3, 69115 Heidelberg, Germany. If you have any concerns regarding our products, please contact ProductSafety@springernature.com

Printed and bound by CPI Group (UK) Ltd, Croydon, CR0 4YY
11/08/2026
02193495-0001